TO BE
DISPOSED
BY
AUTHORITY

D0267637

PUBLIC ENTERPRISE
IN PRACTICE

RICHARD PRYKE

Public Enterprise
in Practice

The British Experience of
Nationalization over Two Decades

MacGibbon & Kee   London

Granada Publishing Limited
First published in Great Britain 1971 by MacGibbon & Kee Ltd
3 Upper James Street London WIR 4BP

ISBN 0 261 63211 6
Printed in Great Britain by Cox & Wyman Ltd
Fakenham, Reading and London

For Jo

CONTENTS

LIST OF TABLES

List of Tables

PREFACE

THIS book began as a study of the nationalized industries' investment criteria for the Department of Applied Economics at Cambridge University under the general supervision of Mr Michael Posner. However as the project got under way it became evident that it was unrealistic to consider investment policy in isolation, and that most of the fundamental questions about the economics of the nationalized industries had never been answered. As a result the purpose of the study gradually changed and it was ultimately decided to make a general survey of the economic performance of the public enterprise sector. Nevertheless the original object has constantly been kept in mind and the whole of the third part of the book has been devoted to the way in which the nationalized industries have framed and evaluated their investment programmes. This section of the book also contains a case study of the West Midlands Gas Board which was undertaken before the purpose of the inquiry was redefined.

Because of the change in the purpose, and even more important the extension in the scope of the project, it has taken far longer to complete than was originally contemplated. From the autumn of 1964 until the autumn of 1967 I worked full time at the Department of Applied Economics in Cambridge assembling the information and developing the statistics on which it has been based. Since then I have been a lecturer in the Department of Economics at the University of Liverpool; and the writing of the book has had to be undertaken during leisure time and that part of the week which has not been absorbed by teaching. Although virtually all the text of the book has been written at Liverpool it rests upon the research which was undertaken at Cambridge, and I would like to acknowledge the debt which I owe to the Department of Applied Economics. In particular I would like to thank those in charge for being so tolerant of what must have seemed extremely slow progress. This book could not have been written without the generous support of the Department and I would like the fact to be placed squarely on record. However I should also have found it difficult or impossible to finish it but for the interest Professor Arthur Beacham has taken while I have been at Liverpool, and I would like to express my sincere gratitude to him for providing the opportunity for its completion. Last but not least I would like to thank Michael Posner for his help and in particular for the way in which he allowed the project to be reorientated.

In the writing of this book I have received an immense amount of help from others. I would like to thank the nationalized industries for providing so much information and for scarcely ever refusing to provide facts and figures. I would also, having acknowledged my general debt, like to thank the following individuals: Mr W. H. Oakland and his colleagues in the NCB Statistics Department; Mr F. J. Hannant and Mr A. M. Clarke also of the NCB; Mr R. G. Hancock and Mr T. A. Boley of the Electricity Council; Mr D. R. Berridge and Mr R. H. Burdett of the CEGB; Mr C. W. Smith of BOAC; Mr R. A. R. Wilson and Mr M. V. S. Court of BEA; Mr D. W. Glassborow of the National Bus Company; Mr K. V. Smith, Dr S. C. Joy, Mr W. I. Winchester, Mr A. W. Tait and Mr M. Connolly of British Rail; Mr T. C. B. Watson of the Gas Council; Mr P. Lewis, Mr I. J. Harthill and Mr G. E. Cooper of or formerly of West Midlands Gas Board; Mr V. Clements and Mr J. Worthington of the National Freight Corporation; and Mr G. Zeitlin of Freightliners. I am grateful to Sir Reginald Wilson, Sir Basil Smallpeice and Lord Hurcomb for reading through various chapters and giving me their comments. I would like to thank Lord Beeching and Mr Arthur Pearson for discussing the railways with me and Mr Gerald Fiennes for providing valuable information.

The CSO has been most helpful and I would like to thank Mr J. Hibbert, Mr R. A. Bowditch and Mr E. A. Woodruff. I have also received valuable assistance from abroad and would like to thank Dr R. Sander of Steinkohlenbergbauverein; Mr Delacarte of SCNF, Mr A. L. Litke of the Federal Power Commission; and Mr F. R. Forte of the Electricity Council of New England. Much valuable information on the nationalized industries was obtained from answers to questions put down in Parliament by a number of MPs, including Mr Ian Mikardo and Mr John Parker. I would like to thank my present colleagues at Liverpool and my former colleagues at Cambridge for their help and advice. In particular I would like to thank Mr Brian Deakin, Professor George Peters, Professor Beacham who kindly read through the first part of the book, Professor Reddaway who commented on an early draft of Chapter 6 and above all Mr Richard Lecomber who made the estimates of price elasticity which I have frequently drawn upon and quote. I should also like to thank the Department of Employment and Productivity for letting me extract information from their data on stoppages. For the errors and shortcomings which remain I must, however, bear responsibility. Finally I am extremely grateful to Mrs Barbara Leonard and Mrs Doreen Tellett for typing and retyping the manuscript.

It was originally intended that this book should contain a Statistical

Annex describing in detail both Mr Lecomber's elasticity calculations and the sources and methods used for Tables 3, 4, 9 and 19. As its publication has proved impossible these sources and methods have been briefly described at the foot of the Tables or in the notes at the end of the book. I expect that this will meet the needs of all save a handful of readers, but I shall be pleased to provide copies of the Annex material on request.

It is inevitable due to the time lag which occurs in the publication of statistics and the time which is absorbed in printing that books should be slightly out of date by the time they finally appear. Moreover, there comes a point when the author has to decide that if his book is ever to be published he must stop revising what he has written although it has already been overtaken by events. In the present case little or no attention has been paid to what has happened since the end of 1968, which is a convenient point at which to stop because it is the end of the second decade of public ownership. There is actually only one place where, if the text had been revised in the light of experience during 1960 and 1970, any modification of the argument would have been necessary. The section on the nationalized industries' strike record is the exception because in contrast to previous years there was a dramatic increase in the number of working days lost in the public enterprise sector. However, I have allowed what I have said on the basis of experience up to the end of 1968 to stand not only because of a general disinclination to revise it yet again but also because special factors have been at work.

I realize now, having completed this large volume, why even the driest and dullest of books contain one purple patch of eloquence, namely the place in the Preface where the author thanks his wife for her help. In the present case my debt to my wife is particularly great because of the long years which the book has taken to complete. At times it has seemed that it would trespass on eternity and destroy our family life and I would like with all the emphasis and sincerity I can command to thank Jo for her support and forbearance. It is therefore right that this book should be dedicated to the person who, although her name does not appear on the title page, has contributed so much and so generously to its completion.

R.W.S.P.

Liverpool July 1970 and May 1971

PART ONE

Technical Efficiency

CHAPTER 1

Introduction

ALTHOUGH the nationalized industries are a subject of perennial interest and have, with the exception of steel, been in public ownership for twenty years or more we know surprisingly little about their economic performance. This is remarkable in view of the millions of words which have been devoted to their problems and policies. However the great bulk of what has so far been written has been ephemeral, or has been concerned with some limited aspect of their affairs or with their organization.

For instance in the early years after their acquisition by the state scores of articles, pamphlets and books were written about their administrative structure. Yet the students of public administration who were mainly responsible contributed very little of permanent value. This was partly because they were writing before the nationalized industries had had time to settle down and sort out their difficulties; and partly because they jumped to the conclusion that large-scale organizations suffered from weaknesses which could only be cured by decentralization. The major weakness of what the public administrators had to say was that it ignored the fact that the nationalized industries are primarily economic institutions and must be judged accordingly. To what extent the organizational weaknesses which they diagnosed were affecting the nationalized industries' performance was a question which they scarcely posed and certainly made no attempt to answer.[1]

By the middle of the fifties the students of public administration had, with the exception of the indefatigable Professor W. A. Robson, lost interest in public enterprise. Unfortunately the ground they vacated was not taken over, as it should have been, by economists. The reasons why the latter have paid so little attention to the nationalized industries are far from clear, but one possible explanation is that they have accepted the conventional view that the ownership of an industry is irrelevant to its economic performance. If so there is obviously no case for studying the nationalized industries *en bloc* for they have little or nothing in common. Asked to defend his profession against the charge that it has ignored the nationalized industries the economist might reply that it is no more sensible to make a joint study of coal, gas, electricity, railways

3

and air transport than it is of, say, film production, cement, horticulture and bespoke tailoring. What is wanted, he might counter, are individual books and articles about each of the various industries which happen to be nationalized or about subjects like transport or fuel policy; and this is what economists have produced. The trouble with this argument is that it begs the question. How can it be known that ownership is irrelevant unless the nationalized industries are studied?

Whatever the explanation for the scant attention which the public enterprise sector has received, there can be no doubt that it has been ignored. This is shown not only by the lack of books or even articles assessing its performance but also by our almost total ignorance of even the most elementary facts. Has the production of the nationalized industries been increasing faster or slower than that of the private sector? If any economist or statistician knows the answer he has kept it to himself. How rapidly has output per man been rising in the nationalized industries? Information of a more or less dubious type is available for some, but only some, of the nationalized industries, and nothing is known about the performance of the sector as a whole. How much have the nationalized industries' prices increased? Here again the amount of information available is severely limited and what there is tends to be misleading. Even our knowledge of the industries' financial performance is woefully defective. Although figures for profits and losses are of course given in their accounts we do not for the most part know whether their depreciation provisions are sufficient to cover the cost of replacing the plant and equipment which is used up in the process of production. However there is no need to make a full inventory of our ignorance here as its extent will become obvious as the book proceeds.

As the economic spadework on the nationalized industries has not yet been undertaken it is hardly surprising to discover that no real attempt has ever been made to assess their general performance. For the yardstick by which the performance of public enterprise should be judged we can do no better than quote Professor R. H. Tawney's classic description of the objects of nationalization: 'The transfer of property in return for compensation, which nationalization involves, is a means, not an end. Its purpose is to ensure that services, on which the general welfare depends, shall be conducted with a single eye to that objective, under authorities accountable for their proceedings to the public. Its success depends, therefore, not on the mere change of ownership, but on the degree to which advantage is taken of the opportunity offered by it to secure first-class management, to carry through measures of re-organization which private enterprise was unable or unwilling to undertake, and to enlist the active co-operation of employees in increasing production. It is to be judged by its practical results on consumers, on workers, and on the national prosperity.'[2]

Technical Efficiency

Although Professor Tawney gives an excellent indication of the questions about the nationalized industries which need to be answered, and of the yardstick by which their performance is to be judged, his statement is too general to provide a useful framework for the investigation of their success or failure. It is therefore necessary to delineate more closely the topics which will need to be inquired into and the way in which success or failure can be judged. One essential requirement is that the nationalized industries should be technically efficient in the sense of using the smallest possible amount of resources to produce the goods and services which they have decided to provide. Other things being equal, it is evident that the welfare of the community will be higher where the most efficient methods of production are used than where, for instance, obsolete plant is employed or labour is used wastefully.

However obvious this may seem, it is a point which tends to be disregarded by economists, especially of the more theoretically minded type. Indeed one of the fundamental assumptions of economic theory is, to quote a well-known textbook by Professor A. W. Stonier and Professor D. C. Hague, that 'entrepreneurs always produce each output as cheaply as possible, given the technical production conditions. We assume that the entrepreneur always keeps money costs of production as low as he is able. This is an essential assumption, for . . . it would be impossible to point to an equilibrium position where the firm was at rest if one could not say whether costs had been kept to a minimum or not'.[3] Both the assumption of entrepreneurial infallibility and the argument which has been used to justify it are manifest nonsense. Even if businesses never produced where their costs were lowest we could still, in theory, say what their equilibrium position would be. All that would be necessary for the purpose of the model would be the selection of a notional cost somewhat below the cost at which it is assumed that the inefficient businessman actually produces.

The reasons why economists are so reluctant to assume that their 'entrepreneurs' are unenterprising need not detain us, except to observe that it probably has something to do with the fact that modern economics originated as an attack upon Government intervention in the economy, to which it is impossible to object if businesses are seriously inefficient. Whatever the explanation, it is certainly true that economists tend to ignore the question of technical efficiency and that the nationalized industries have been no exception to the rule. For instance Mr Ralph Turvey, in a recent collection of papers on public enterprise, excused the under-representation of discussions of technical efficiency with the curious argument that 'It may well be that competent administration, good labour relations, and technical brilliance on the part of public enterprise contribute more to economic growth than do the niceties of economic calculation. This book concentrates on the latter, however, an area in which economists have far more to say.'[4]

The present book will in contrast have a large amount to say about the technical efficiency of the nationalized industries, which surely cannot be taken for granted. Indeed, with the exception of the present chapter, the whole of the first part of the book will be devoted to the subject. The principal economic tool which will be used in these chapters will be productivity comparisons. As the productivity of any industry or undertaking is the quality of output it produces per unit of input, productivity and technical efficiency are practically the same thing. Or at least they would be if there were any satisfactory way of measuring the contribution which capital makes to production. As we shall see there are ways in which this can be done but, if only because of the lack of information about the quantity of capital which is being used, it is difficult to have any great confidence in the results which are obtained. It has therefore been necessary to rely in the main on calculations of labour productivity. An attempt has been made in Chapter 6, however, to see whether figures of output per man hour give a misleading impression of the relative speed at which output per unit of labour and capital has been increasing in the nationalized industries and in the private sector of the economy.

There are a number of angles from which labour productivity can be viewed and a variety of comparisons which can be undertaken. The most obvious starting point seems to be the question of how fast the productivity of the different nationalized industries has been increasing since they were brought into public ownership. The next step is then to explain and investigate the statistical pattern which emerges. For instance, we shall try to answer the question, which the public administrators ignored, of whether the early administrative difficulties which nationalization involved had any perceptible effect on the industries' productivity. The attempt to clothe the bare statistical bones with flesh will occupy Chapters 2, 3, 4 and 5.

Then in Chapter 6 we shall attempt to put the nationalized industries' performance in perspective by, among other things, comparing their rate of productivity growth with the rate in the private sector and examining factors, such as the use of capital, which may account for the nationalized industries' relative position in the productivity race. Finally in Chapters 7 and 8 the nationalized industries' productivity is compared with that of foreign undertakings in the same line of business. These like-with-like comparisons are of particular interest because it is possible not only to make comparisons over time but also to discover how the level of output per worker in Britain compares with that in foreign countries. Armed with this information the reader may find it possible at the end of Part 1 to reach some conclusions about the technical efficiency or inefficiency of the nationalized industries.

Allocative Efficiency

In the rest of the book we shall be concerned in the main with the problem of allocative efficiency, which is the degree to which resources are so allocated that no shift will bring about an increase in the national welfare. This is a complex and somewhat imprecise concept but one which is absolutely essential. Other things being equal the national welfare will be maximized when it is impossible, by reallocating the resources which have already been drawn into economic activity, to increase the national income. Again the national welfare will, other things being equal, tend to be increased if the distribution of income is made more equal and be reduced if it becomes less equal, because the poor have more need of extra goods and services than those who are already affluent. To say this begs a large number of questions and raises a host of moral and philosophic issues. However, this is not a treatise on welfare economics so these will be ignored except where they have some practical importance.

Although it is perfectly possible to question these two principles concerning the national income and its distribution, I suspect that they will be accepted by most of those who read this book although there will, for instance, be a large number of views as to what will and will not serve to increase the national income. However it is the basic principles which are important. It is the purpose of this book to inquire whether the nationalized industries have, through their allocative (and technical) efficiency, promoted the national welfare by raising the national income to a higher level than it might otherwise have reached or whether they have on the contrary reduced it through their inefficiency. But the working definition of the national welfare which has been adopted does mean that those who identify it with, say, workers' control or the maximization of consumers' choice by means of competition will find this book disappointing and must turn elsewhere.

The subject of allocative efficiency is introduced in Part 2 by an examination of the finances of the nationalized industries. Here we shall simply try to establish the facts about the profits and losses which they have earned without inquiring too closely what this proves about the allocation of resources. However one of the main reasons why we are interested in knowing whether an undertaking makes losses is obviously the probability that some resources will have been wasted if it does, and the national income will be lower than it could have been. Chapter 9 contains a general survey of the nationalized industries' financial position, including a discussion of the way in which their prices have changed, and the size of the profits and losses which they have earned. Then in Chapters 10, 11 and 12 a much closer look will be taken at the finances of British Rail and BOAC, the nationalized undertakings which have incurred large losses. The object will be to try to discover why their losses have occurred and what lessons can be learned.

In Part 3 of the book we shall examine the nationalized industries' investment. In Chapters 13, 14 and 15, having taken a brief look at the extent and development of their capital expenditure, the way in which the industries have framed their investment programmes will be considered. This involves inquiring into the accuracy of their demand forecasts and of their estimates of the cost of their projects. Then we shall examine the methods by which they have calculated the prospective rate of return on their investment and allowed, among other things, for the timing of the profits which they hoped to earn. In the main this survey is based on published sources but in the latter part of Chapter 15 a brief case study is made of the West Midlands Gas Board's methods of investment appraisal. Finally in Chapter 16 the discussion is rounded off with an examination of the minimum rate of return which the nationalized industries should and in practice have required before investing. Although it would be wrong to jump to the conclusion that resources have been wasted if, for instance, it is discovered that the nationalized industries have used the wrong methods of appraisal there is obviously less risk of misallocation when the right methods are employed. Evidence of a more direct type as to the quality of public enterprise investment is provided in Chapter 17 which discusses the extent to which the gas and electricity industries have secured the economies of scale which have been available.

In the last part of the book there is a full-dress discussion of the impact which the nationalized industries have had on the welfare of the community. This occupies Chapters 18 and 19. Here we shall try to assess the relative importance of technical and allocative efficiency and try to obtain some idea of the extent to which the national income may have been reduced by the deficits which they have incurred, the protection which they have received and the low rate of return which they may have earned on their capital.

To complete the discussion of the effect which the nationalized industries have on the national welfare it will be necessary to investigate the possible adverse effects which a shift towards what might appear to be more rational economic behaviour would have. We shall try to discover, for instance, whether a swifter rundown of the coal industry would harm the balance of payments or cause unemployment.

Finally in Chapter 20, which concludes the book, we shall try to reach a verdict about whether the public enterprise sector has had a favourable or unfavourable impact on the national welfare and to decide in what ways, if any, the transfer of an industry to public ownership affects its performance. These are ambitious aims and it may be found that only tentative answers can be made to some of the questions which have been posed. However, we now have more than twenty years' experience of nationalization on which to draw and a reassessment of public enterprise is long overdue.

The Public Enterprise Sector

In the remainder of this introductory chapter we shall identify the nationalized industries with which we shall be concerned and discover how important a part of the economy they form. This study covers the operations of the following industries and undertakings: coal, gas, electricity, railways, the air corporations, British Road Services, and the nationalized road passenger services. Collectively these undertakings should be known as the 'public enterprise sector', a term which will frequently be used. They are usually, however, referred to as the 'nationalized industries'. This is a loose way of describing them, but because of the term's common usage it would be pedantic to try to avoid it.

The public enterprise sector includes those publicly-owned trading concerns in Britain which are not under the direct control of a Government Minister and which are engaged in production as opposed to, say, finance or the provision of basic facilities for use by other firms. This rules out a certain amount of industrial activity undertaken by Government Departments; it excludes the BBC because it obtains most of its revenue from licences; and it rules out, for instance, the British Transport Docks Board since this is mainly engaged in the provision of port facilities and does not handle much cargo itself.

It has also been a condition for inclusion in the public enterprise sector that the industry or undertaking should have been a full member during most of the post-war period. We have therefore excluded the Post Office, which has only just ceased to be a Government Department, and the steel industry, which though nationalized in 1951 was afterwards largely denationalized, and was not renationalized until 1967. However London Transport has been treated as part of the sector because, although it has now been handed over to the Greater London Council, it was a nationalized undertaking for most of the period.

Although this is not a book about the organization and origin of the nationalized industries it may be helpful to present, in the form of a table, the dates at which the different nationalized undertakings came into public ownership and the main changes in their organization which have taken place as a result of subsequent legislation.

Table 1

ACQUISITION AND ORGANIZATION OF PUBLIC
ENTERPRISE

Body	Vesting or Commencing Date, etc.	Notes
Central Electricity Board	1927; absorbed by British Electricity Authority 1948	Aim: to construct and operate the electricity grid and to control but not own the major generating stations
London Passenger Transport Board	1933; absorbed by British Transport Commission 1948	Board members not appointed by Minister but by trustees
British Overseas Airways Corporation	1940; did not begin operating as a commercial enterprise until 1 April 1946	
North of Scotland Hydro-Electric Board	1943	
British South American Airways Corporation	1 August 1946; absorbed by BOAC 1 August 1949	
British European Airways Corporation	1 August 1946	

Body	Vesting or Commencing Date, etc.	Notes
National Coal Board	1 January 1947	Besides coal mines took over colliery coke ovens, brick works, etc.
British Transport Commission	1 January 1948; dissolved 1 January 1963	Aim: to control the railways and the railways' ships and docks, etc.; to nationalize long-distance road haulage; to acquire bus undertakings
British Electricity Authority and Area Electricity Boards	1 April 1948; British Electricity Authority dissolved 1 April 1955	British Electricity Authority to control grid and generation; Area Boards to distribute electricity under the Authority's supervision
Gas Council and Area Gas Boards	1 May 1949	Area Gas Boards to make and distribute gas; Gas Council to co-ordinate
British Electricity Authority divided into Central Electricity Authority and South of Scotland Electricity Board	1 April 1955; CEA dissolved 1 January 1958	Besides the Authority's two Scottish divisions the South of Scotland Electricity Board took over the two Scottish Area Boards
Central Electricity Authority divided into Electricity Council and Central Electricity Generating Board	1 January 1958	Electricity Council took over the duty of co-ordinating the industry in England and Wales
British Transport Commission divided into:	1 January 1963	
British Railways Board		Besides mainline railways took over shipping services and associated ports

Body	Vesting or Commencing Date, etc.	Notes
London Transport Board	Transferred to Greater London Council 1 January 1969	
British Transport Docks Board		Took over major BTC ports
British Waterways Board		
Transport Holding Company		Took over BRS and BTC buses, etc.
Transport Holding Company divided into:	1 January 1969	
National Bus Company		Took over Holding Co's English and Welsh Buses, etc., and on 1 January 1969 London Transport's country and Green Line Buses
Scottish Transport Group		Took over Holding Co's Scottish buses, etc.
National Freight Corporation		Took over BRS from Holding Co. and freight sundries and road collection and delivery services from British Rail; became joint owner on a 51/49 per cent basis of the BR Freightliners

Most of Table 1 is self-explanatory but the partial nationalization of road transport requires further explanation. When the British Transport Commission took over the railways it also acquired their extensive interests in road passenger transport. The Commission was given power under the Act which created it to acquire road passenger undertakings and, with effect from January 1948, it purchased Thomas Tillings, the large bus group in which it already had a sizeable stake. As from 31 March 1948 the Commission also purchased the Scottish Motor Traction Company in which it again had a large interest. A little later a number of other bus companies were taken over and integrated into the Tillings and Scottish bus groups.[5] The BTC also inherited from the railways an equal stake with the British Electric Traction Group in its bus empire. As British Electric Traction provided the management of these companies until 1968, when BET was bought out by the Transport Holding Company, they have not been treated as part of the public enterprise sector.[6]

The old railway companies, besides their extensive interests in buses, had a small stake in road haulage. This too passed into the ownership of the British Transport Commission when the railways were nationalized and provided the first step towards the formation of British Road Services. The BTC proceeded during the period 1948–51 to bring long-distance road haulage into public ownership as the Transport Act, 1947, had provided. BRS had hardly had time to settle down before this unfortunate undertaking, whose tribulations are examined later, began to be denationalized in accordance with the Transport Act, 1953.[7] However, a new Act was passed in 1956 which put a stop to denationalization.

Public Enterprise's Place in the Economy

The size and importance of the different nationalized industries is perhaps best shown by their contribution to domestic production. This is measured by their net output, or their receipts less the value of the goods and services which they buy. The net output of the public enterprise sector is shown in Table 2. As might be expected electricity, coal, railways and gas account for the bulk of the sector. Together these heavyweights produce almost 90 per cent of its net output. They deserve, and will receive, a correspondingly large share of our attention in this book.

The public sector heavyweights constitute 'industries' in themselves, but the smaller undertakings only form part of the industries to which they belong. The air corporations accounted in 1966 for 90 per cent of the revenue which UK airlines received from scheduled services, but if charter and trooping work are included their share dropped to 78 per cent.[8] In 1967 the nationalized buses collected 37 per cent of all public road passenger transport receipts and the Tillings and Scottish Bus Groups carried 45 per cent of the passengers who travelled on scheduled bus services outside London and the municipalities.[9] The stake which BRS possesses in road goods transport is much smaller. When denationalization came to an end BRS accounted for only about 15 per cent of all ton miles of freight carried by road haulage contractors and the proportion is probably slightly lower now. However, in certain fields such as long-distance work and parcels BRS has a much larger share of the market.[10] The public sector heavyweights engage in a number of activities outside their own industries. British Railways, for instance, run hotels and shipping services while the NCB owns chemical works and makes bricks. None of these activities, however, is important enough to be treated as a separate industry.

Britain, we are constantly told, has a mixed economy. Yet as measured by its contribution to the national income, or indeed any other yardstick, the public enterprise sector forms only a small part of the economy.[11] In 1967 the sector had a net output of £2,500 million which represented 7·3 per cent of the gross domestic product. Even if the Post Office, the other public corporations which have not been treated as part of the sector, and the recently nationalized steel companies are thrown in the picture does not change beyond recognition. In this case the proportion rises to about 11 per cent.[12] The further inclusion of local authority trading services and other odds and ends which are possible candidates for a broadly defined public industrial sector would scarcely alter the position.

It is interesting to compare the net output of public enterprise with that of private enterprise. In 1967 companies and un-incorporated businesses had a net output of £23,900 million, which means that private enterprise was nine and a half times as large as public enterprise. Even manufacturing industry, which may be regarded as the private sector *par excellence*, had a net output of £11,300 million, which means that it was four and a half times as large. Remarkable as it may seem, the net output of the whole public enterprise sector is less than that of the engineering industry alone.[13]

At this point it will be objected that the nationalized industries are obviously more important than these comparisons suggest because they are our basic industries and as such form the 'commanding heights' of the economy. It would take us too far afield to discuss these notions here, but why, it may be asked, is public enterprise, which in 1963 accounted for only about £145 million of our exports of goods and services, more basic than engineering which accounted for £3,300 million?[14] Moreover, if Britain can legitimately be described as a mixed economy so also can some Communist countries, because a number of the East European economies have statistical credentials which are as good or better than our own.[15]

The public enterprise sector not only forms a relatively small part of the economy but its share of domestic output has been declining and its production has been increasing less rapidly than that of the rest of the economy. In 1950 and 1958 the public enterprise sector accounted for

Table 2

PUBLIC ENTERPRISE'S SHARE OF DOMESTIC OUTPUT

	1950		1958		1967	
	Net Output[1] (£ million)	Per cent of Public Enterprise Total	Net Output[1] (£ million)	Per cent of Public Enterprise Total	Net Output[1] (£ million)	Per cent of Public Enterprise Total
Electricity	132	13·5	329	20·2	778	31·1
NCB[2]	384	39·2	656	40·3	609	24·3
British Rail[2]	263 }	28·0	333 }	21·5	541[3] }	23·0
London Transport Railways	11		17		34[3]	
Gas	79	8·1	135	8·3	237	9·5
BOAC	13 }	1·7	28 }	2·6	76 }	5·0
BEA	4		15		50	
Tillings and Scottish Buses	26 }	5·9	43 }	4·9	64 }	5·0
London Transport Road Services	32		37		60[3]	
BRS	36	3·7	35	2·1	55	2·2
Total Public Enterprise Sector	980	100·0	1,628	100·0	2,504	100·0
Gross Domestic Product (GDP)	11,971	1,222	19,795	1,216	34,438	1,375
of which						
Cos and unincorporated firms	8,794	897	14,176	871	23,896	954
Manufacturing	4,169	425	7,006	430	11,292[4]	451

[1] At factor cost before providing for stock appreciation.
[2] Including subsidiary activities.
[3] British Rail includes £153 million of Government subsidy, London Transport Railways includes £3 million and London Transport Road Services includes £8 million.
[4] Excludes State Steel.

Source: Information from CSO and British Rail; NIE 1969 Tables 11, 13 etc.; BTC 1949 p 44, 1950 p 73 etc.; H. E. Osborn *Journal of the Institute of Transport* 1958–60 p 144; THC 1967 pp 68, 69, 71, 72; Ministry of Transport *Passenger Transport in Great Britain* 1967 p 49; LTB 1967 p 9 etc.

8·2 per cent of the GDP, but by 1967 the proportion was down to 7·3 per cent and is likely to go on falling. The way in which its output, at constant prices, has been changing is shown in Table 3. Between 1948 and 1968 manufacturing production about doubled and GDP rose by around 70 per cent but the output of the nationalized industries increased by only 35 per cent.[16] After growing rapidly between 1948 and 1951 public enterprise production was more or less stagnant until 1959. Since then it has been increasing at a modest pace. As we shall see when we examine other aspects of the nationalized industries' development the late fifties form an important watershed.

Turning from the sector's output to that of the individual undertakings we find that they tend to be located at either end of the growth spectrum. Some have been expanding much faster than industry in general while others have been contracting. The first group contains the air corporations and electricity. During the period 1958–68 the airways traffic increased by 13·2 per cent per annum and the electricity industry's output increased by 7·8 per cent each year, which was a faster rate of growth than that of any other major industry.[17]

At the other end of the spectrum were the coal industry, the nationalized buses and the railways. In 1958 coal production was scarcely higher than it had been in 1948 and the output of the buses and the railways was significantly lower. Worse, however, was in store. Between 1958 and 1968 coal production declined by 3·3 per cent each year, bus traffic fell by 2·7 per cent per annum and rail output by 1·3 per cent. There were only two private industries whose output declined as fast as or faster than this. Between 1958 and 1966 shipbuilding experienced a fall of 3·7 per cent each year and the spinning and weaving of cotton, flax and man-made fibres fell by 2·1 per cent per annum.[18]

The gas industry and British Road Services were the odd men out within the public enterprise sector because they were located in the middle of the growth spectrum. However, neither has had a steady rate of growth. The gas industry's production, which was previously stagnant, has been growing rapidly since the early sixties and the output of BRS leapt up after 1963 largely because of its takeover activities. Prior to this its output had been more or less stable since the period of disposals came to an end. The catastrophic effect which denationalization had upon BRS is evident from the table. BRS must, due to nationalization and denationalization, have the dubious distinction of holding the British records for both expansion and contraction.

The reason why the output of the other nationalized concerns has changed in the way that it has is not as obvious as it is for BRS. To investigate, industry by industry, what forces of supply and demand

Table 3

INDEX NUMBERS OF PRODUCTION 1948–68 (1958 = 100)

	Electricity	Coal	Railways	Gas	BEA and BOAC	Nationalized Buses	BRS	Public Enterprise Sector	Manufacturing
1948	45·2	98·9	111·3	86·4	27·6	114·5	..	89·2	72·3
1949	47·9	102·0	111·9	89·6	30·1	115·4	..	91·5	76·9
1950	53·6	102·8	110·3	95·8	37·5	116·8	177·7	93·5	82·2
1951	59·5	105·9	112·9	98·6	49·5	119·2	201·8	97·7	85·7
1952	61·0	106·9	110·4	96·0	55·7	118·3	186·8	97·5	82·6
1953	65·4	106·1	111·6	98·3	62·2	118·8	186·8	98·8	87·7
1954	73·0	107·0	109·5	104·3	64·0	115·4	174·2	100·4	93·6
1955	80·2	105·1	106·3	103·6	74·1	113·7	126·3	99·7	99·6
1956	86·7	105·0	107·8	101·5	84·2	110·7	104·3	101·0	99·1
1957	91·2	104·5	108·3	98·4	95·2	104·5	93·7	101·5	101·3
1958	100·0	100·0	100·0	100·0	100·0	100·0	100·0	100·0	100·0
1959	109·2	95·9	98·5	98·9	118·3	98·5	102·7	100·3	106·0
1960	122·6	91·2	101·0	99·8	149·5	95·7	101·8	102·3	114·6
1961	132·4	88·5	97·2	101·3	169·3	92·8	100·6	102·9	114·8
1962	148·0	91·5	90·8	108·0	181·5	92·6	100·1	106·8	115·3
1963	162·7	90·9	90·5	111·1	203·9	91·7	103·5	110·3	120·0
1964	170·2	88·6	94·2	116·9	241·5	87·5	110·2	113·1	129·5
1965	182·9	84·8	90·3	125·2	281·4	81·0	127·6	115·2	133·8
1966	190·1	78·6	88·0	133·6	321·7	77·3	144·5	115·6	135·6
1967	197·2	76·7	83·4	145·1	339·4	76·2	147·4	116·8	134·2
1968	212·4	72·6	87·5	154·8	346·6	76·4	155·3	120·2	141·7
1969									

Source: Coal and railways from CSO; airways calculated using CSO method from *Economic Trends* 8/60 p xi, 2/66 p vii; AAS 1969 pp 223, 224 etc. The electricity and gas indices comprise respectively 14 and 25 indicators combined with 1954 revenue weights for 1948–58 and 1958 weights for 1958–68. Information mainly from MPSD e.g. 1968–69 pp 100, 124, 125, 160, 163. The nationalized bus index comprises passenger miles, or where not available journeys, on London Transport, on Tillings and on Scottish buses combined with 1954 and 1958 revenue weights (BTC 1949–61 Statement IX–2; LTB Statement S7; THC 1968 p 74 etc.). An allowance based on revenue lost was made for the 1958 London bus strike (BTC 1958 p 78). The BRS index is estimated capacity ton miles obtained by multiplying average capacity per vehicle by total miles for 1963–68 and loaded miles for 1950–62 (BTC 1962. 2 pp 129, 186 etc.; THC 1968 p 83 etc. and information from NFC on carrying capacity). The indices for the separate industries were combined with 1954 and 1958 net output weights which for electricity, coal, gas and airways were obtained from the CSO or calculated from CSO material (*The Index of Industrial Production* 1959 p 33; *Economic Trends* 8/60 p xi, 3/62 p v, 2/66 p vii). Net output for the remaining industries was calculated from information from BR, from BTC Annual Reports and from H. E. Osborn in *Journal of the Institute of Transport* 1958–60 p 144. Manufacturing production from NIE 1968 Table 15. For full description and sources see the Statistical Appendix.

have been responsible for the growth or contraction of their output would be an extremely laborious undertaking. However, a detailed study of the demand for the railways' passenger and freight services has been made in Chapter 10 where it forms part of the inquiry into British Rail's financial collapse.

Because the fortunes of the nationalized industries have differed so greatly, with some growing fast and others contracting, there have been marked changes in their relative importance during the past twenty years. This is readily apparent from Table 2. On the one hand there has been a large rise in the electricity industry's and the air corporations' share of the sector's net output. For electricity the proportion has increased from about 13 per cent in 1950 and 20 per cent in 1958 to over 30 per cent in 1967; while the air corporations' share, though still small, has shot up from less than 2 per cent at the beginning of the period to 5 per cent at the end. On the other hand the relative importance of coal and railways has declined. In 1950 and 1958 the NCB accounted for about 40 per cent of the sector's net output but by 1967 the proportion was less than a quarter. Between 1950 and 1958 the rail share slumped from 28 per cent to about 21 per cent. In 1967 it was 23 per cent but this increase was more apparent than real as it was due to the fact that the railways were by then in receipt of a large subsidy from the Government.

CHAPTER 2

Productivity: The Early Years

ALTHOUGH the performance of the nationalized industries is a national preoccupation second only to the balance of payments, there has been little serious discussion of their productivity. Indeed serious discussion has been virtually impossible due to the lack of any comprehensive or reliable statistics of the way in which their output per worker has been changing. In Table 4 the growth of productivity is shown both for the sector as a whole and for each of the industries and undertakings. Although they cannot be regarded as accurate to the last decimal place, which has only been included to facilitate further calculations, there is no reason to believe that they are less reliable than other indices of this type. What may be disputed is the significance of labour productivity gains, which may be due, for instance, to the substitution of capital for labour. This problem will be discussed later when the productivity performance of the public enterprise sector is compared with that of the private sector.[1] However in the present chapter and the following three attention will be largely confined to output per worker in the nationalized industries. There is plenty to be learnt from what has been happening to labour productivity within the public enterprise sector.

For instance one important point which emerges from Table 4 is that although most of the nationalized industries have made considerable progress since about 1958, the rate of advance during the first decade of public ownership was slow. Between 1948 and 1958 the sector's output per man hour increased by about 16 per cent, which represents only 1·5 per cent per annum. Moreover, more than half the rise took place between 1948 and 1951 after which the growth of productivity was very sluggish. The performance of the nationalized buses, of the railways, of coal and of BRS was particularly disappointing. In 1958 productivity on the buses was 6 per cent lower than it had been in 1948 and on the railways it was only 3 per cent higher having slumped disastrously during 1958. In the coal industry output per man hour increased by 9 per cent over the period but was scarcely higher than it had been in 1950. Similarly in BRS productivity was only 7 per cent greater than it had been in 1950 and no higher than it was in 1953. In the gas industry there was an 18 per cent rise in output per man hour between 1948 and 1958,

Table 4

INDEX NUMBERS OF LABOUR PRODUCTIVITY¹ 1948-68 (1958 = 100)

	Electricity	Coal	Railways	Gas	BEA and BOAC	Nationalized Buses	BRS	Public Enterprise Sector	Manu- facturing
1948	64·0	91·7	97·2	85·0	27·0	106·0	..	86·0	83·2
1949	60·9	96·6	98·8	86·5	33·7	106·2	..	88·0	86·8
1950	63·7	95·5	100·7	90·6	45·5	106·5	(93·7)	90·8	89·3
1951	67·9	99·6	105·2	90·1	58·7	106·9	98·8	93·2	90·1
1952	69·0	97·2	103·3	87·6	62·2	105·6	95·2	91·8	88·2
1953	72·5	99·1	105·0	91·8	67·3	107·4	100·3	94·3	91·7
1954	78·6	99·4	105·2	97·0	69·3	107·4	(104·6)	96·3	94·3
1955	82·8	98·6	104·8	96·6	76·3	109·0	(93·8)	96·6	97·0
1956	89·7	98·2	106·9	98·3	87·5	107·3	91·9	98·5	96·5
1957	92·9	96·8	106·5	97·4	97·0	101·6	89·4	98·3	98·9
1958	100·0	100·0	100·0	100·0	100·0	100·0	100·0	100·0	100·0
1959	107·0	105·3	103·4	103·4	115·9	103·0	105·9	105·3	104·8
1960	121·5	108·3	109·5	108·2	139·5	103·0	108·4	111·8	109·7
1961	126·0	112·9	107·3	113·0	146·7	100·2	110·4	114·6	109·3
1962	134·1	120·6	104·2	118·0	142·5	99·6	112·0	119·0	112·3
1963	141·5	126·4	110·8	120·0	163·9	99·5	117·1	125·0	118·4
1964	146·5	129·7	121·9	128·3	190·0	95·9	125·7	131·1	124·6
1965	167·5	134·4	125·1	138·3	224·0	89·7	138·1	139·6	128·6
1966	181·0	137·9	132·3	145·1	238·6	86·1	148·5	146·2	132·4
1967	189·6	143·1	136·7	158·6	238·2	84·7	155·4	152·1	135·5
1968	215·4	158·5	151·9	170·9	235·3	87·3	161·7	167·9	143·8

¹ Output per man hour, except for Nationalized Buses and prior to 1963 Railways where figures are for output per man year.

Source: Production from Table 3 and employment from Table 5. Hours worked from MLG/EPG (electricity, gas, air), BRS and for coal MPSD 1968-69 p 41 adjusted for the reduction in shift length during 1961 (UN/ECE *Concentration Indices in the European Coal Industry* 1967 p 4). Public enterprise productivity was obtained by combining the industry figures with 1954 and 1958 net output weights (for which see source to Table 3). Manufacturing productivity was calculated by the same method. Production and weights from *The Index of Industrial Production* 1959 pp 26-27; AAS 1967 p 136, 1968 p 137; and for 1968 from CSO. Employment from AAS 1959, 1960 p 104, 1967 p 109, 1969 p 120. Average hours from MLG/EPG.

Since 1958 the output of those nationalized industries where value added per worker is high (electricity, gas, airways) has risen rapidly while the output of those where it is low (coal, railways, buses) has contracted. A considerable rise in the sector's productivity would therefore have been shown, using the normal method of calculation, even if output per worker had remained the same in each industry; hence the alternative procedure described above.

which was more respectable, but even here productivity was stagnant during the mid-forties. The only nationalized industries which secured really large increases were airways and electricity. Electricity had an increase of 56 per cent and in the airways productivity shot up by well over three and a half times.

The slow increase in productivity within the public enterprise sector was not due to the growth of its labour force. As can be seen from Table 5 it was more or less stable during the first decade of nationalization. In 1948 the industries employed about 1,960,000; in 1952 their labour force reached a peak of about 2,010,000 and by 1957 had fallen back to 1,950,000. In 1958 it dropped to less than 1,920,000; the long and steep decline in the nationalized industries' work force had begun.[2] Because there was some rise in the general level of civil employment between 1948 and 1958 the sector's share of the total declined from 9·1 per cent to 8·3 per cent.[3] During this period the only nationalized industry to show a large and steady increase in its labour force was electricity. The effect of nationalization and denationalization on BRS is shown by the large swings in its employment.

The Problems of Take-over

One possible explanation for the disappointing productivity per-formance of the public enterprise sector during its first decade is the up-heaval which nationalization involved. That the transition from public to private ownership brought a host of problems can hardly be denied.

In most of the industries nationalization involved the take-over of a large number of concerns. There were 550 in electricity, 800 in coal, 1,000 in gas, and nearly 3,800 in road haulage.[4] The acquisition and merger of so many undertakings was obviously a formidable adminis-trative task. Only in railways and road passenger transport was the number of firms which were absorbed so small as to be easily manage-able.

Furthermore in a considerable part of the new public enterprise sector the largest concern accounted for such a small proportion of the output that an entirely new managerial structure had to be created. Even the leading private firms were not large enough to provide a con-venient administrative framework into which the industries' smaller concerns could be fitted. In road haulage Carter Paterson and Pickfords, the largest undertaking, only had about 3,000 vehicles and thus ac-counted for a mere 7 per cent of the 42,000 which BRS was to acquire.[5] Only a score or so of other concerns owned more than 100 vehicles and none operated as many as 1,000.[6] Moreover, the leading concerns mainly

Table 5

PUBLIC ENTERPRISE EMPLOYMENT[1] 1948-68 ('000)

	Electricity	Coal	Railways	Gas	BEA and BOAC	Nationalized Buses	BRS	All Public Enterprise[2]
1948	150	765	671	139	29	129	(17)	1,956
1949	165	756	663	141	26	130	44	1,981
1950	175	732	641	142	24	131	73	1,975
1951	180	739	629	145	24	133	79	1,982
1952	182	767	626	147	26	134	76	2,007
1953	185	762	623	144	27	132	70	2,000
1954	188	759	610	143	26	128	62	1,970
1955	193	757	594	142	27	124	50	1,941
1956	196	763	590	139	29	123	42	1,932
1957	198	775	596	136	30	123	40	1,949
1958	200	759	586	133	31	119	38	1,917
1959	203	716	558	128	31	114	37	1,850
1960	205	657	540	125	33	111	36	1,763
1961	211	632	531	123	36	111	36	1,731
1962	219	611	510	124	38	111	35	1,699
1963	227	582	478	125	38	110	35	1,654
1964	232	556	439	122	38	109	35	1,578
1965	244	520	402	121	38	108	36	1,518
1966	248	479	372	124	40	107	38	1,453
1967	246	454	349	123	43	107	38	1,407
1968	236	387	327	121	45	105	38	1,313

[1] The figures are as nearly as possible annual averages or for the middle of the year.

[2] Includes the subsidiary activities of British Rail and the NCB.

Source: For electricity MPSD 1955 p 129 etc. for 1948–53 and MPSD 1968–9 p 114 etc. for 1954–68. For coal MPSD 1968–9 p 39. For railways BTC.2. Statements VIII-1, VIII-5; BRB 1968 p 3 etc.; LTB Statement S4. For gas MPSD 1967 p 174; information from Ministry of Power. For Buses BTC.2 Statements VIII-4, VIII-5; LTB Statement S4; THC 1968 pp 74, 83. For BRS BTC *Transport Statistics*; BTC.2 Statement VIII-1; THC 1968 p 83. For airways BEA 1968–9. Appendix 8 etc.; BOAC 1968-9 pp 42, 43 etc. Allowance has been made for discontinuities, e.g. for the exclusion by BOAC of its engine overhaul and catering subsidiaries (1,750 workers in 1968).

specialized in parcels or in other special traffics. In coal the 25 largest undertakings, as late as the mid-thirties, only controlled about a third of the industry's production. In Northumberland, Lancashire and South Wales more than half the output was in the hands of two or three concerns but in the Yorkshire and East Midlands coalfield the largest firm only accounted for about 5 per cent.[7] The degree of concentration was, however, rather greater in gas and electricity. The top 25 electricity undertakings were in 1945 responsible for about 44 per cent of all sales, while in gas they had accounted for 58 per cent in 1937.[8]

When these industries were brought under unified control the new management structure almost inevitably took the form of a complex hierarchy of geographical areas and sub-areas. In BRS there were divisions, districts, and groups; in coal there were divisions, areas and sub-areas; and in each of the Area Electricity Boards there were sub-areas and districts.[9] In gas the pattern of organization was rather less uniform but, save for the North Thames Gas Board, which had inherited a functional organization from the Gas Light and Coke Company, each area was divided into divisions and sometimes there were sub-divisions.[10] Although the management structure adopted by the nationalized industries may now appear unnecessarily cumbersome there was probably little alternative. The Fleck Committee, when it studied the Coal Board's organization in 1954, came away convinced that divisions, areas, and sub-areas were all necessary, though it did take exception to the presence in some areas of both sub-areas and agents.[11]

Efficient management was made even more difficult by the frequent lack of suitable office accommodation. This again was largely due to the fact that the new public undertakings were almost always considerably larger than their predecessors. In gas and electricity there were difficulties in a considerable number of places.[12] The East Midlands Gas Board commenced operations with its head office organization split not only between different rooms in the same town but also between three different towns: Leicester, Northampton and Derby.[13] However, this was exceptional and in general the dearth of suitable office accommodation was less acute than in coal and road haulage.

According to the Coal Board:

> None of the colliery head offices proved adequate to house Divisional Boards and their staffs. At the vesting date no Divisional Board had been able to find permanent quarters which could house the Board and their staff under one roof. Most members of Divisional Boards were scattered in different buildings at considerable distances apart, and sometimes in different towns ... Difficulties were also experienced in getting accommodation

for the Area Headquarters. In hardly any case was it possible for the Area General Manager to begin operations with all his key staff under the same roof. Whole blocks of Area staff had to begin work in scattered offices often widely separated one from the other.[14]

These problems were difficult to overcome. Office building was then strictly controlled and when the Board purchased large old houses there was a barrage of protest. As late as 1952 the headquarters of the North Eastern Division were split between Sheffield and Doncaster and the Fleck Committee found that in several divisions and areas, offices were inadequate and staff were not yet housed under the same roof.[15]

British Road Services was in an even more difficult position than the NCB and its difficulties were by no means confined to office accommodation. According to Professor Gilbert Walker: 'An embarrassingly large number of hauliers, it appeared, did not own but leased their premises under surprisingly short tenancies, and the leasors (who might, of course, have been the hauliers under another title) were often unable or unwilling to make over the premises on acquisition. British Road Services, when such an undertaking was to be taken over, might find that they had acquired nothing but the vehicles.'[16] Where premises did exist they were sometimes like slums. The Acton Society described one depot, though this was no doubt an extreme case, as resembling a junk yard: 'An old railway carriage, dumped about fifty years before, was used as an office: close by was a bathing cabin which the old owners had made their private headquarters. No washing or lavatory amenities were available, and female clerks were given 2d. per day to use public facilities.'[17]

Even where the state of premises was satisfactory they were often too small to meet the needs of the new large-scale undertaking. Nearly one third of the properties which were taken over were unsuitable either as they stood, or for alteration or expansion.[18] Furthermore, it was difficult for BRS to put things right by building new premises. Until the process of acquisition had been completed BRS did not know exactly what premises it would possess or would require: a powerful argument for the policy of swift take-over which was adopted. But no sooner had acquisition been completed than the new Government decided to split the organization up and sell it off in small lots.

The difficulty which the new public undertakings faced over premises is but one example of the problems which arose in the process of nationalization. It has been described in some detail not because of its outstanding importance but because of its down-to-earth nature. Far more important, though far more difficult to quantify, was the problem of securing suitable managerial staff. One aspect was the volume of administrative work which the process of selection involved. However, the fundamental difficulty was the scarcity of men within the industries brought into public ownership who had any experience of the workings of large-scale organization and possessed the skills necessary for their successful operation. This was, of course, mainly due to the enormous difference in scale between the new public concerns and their private predecessors.[19] The situation was the more difficult because so few of those in managerial positions had any sympathy with the aims of nationalization and so many had just had their firms expropriated. This meant that they were less ready to adapt their ways and learn new skills than they might otherwise have been.

Managerial problems were less acute in gas and electricity than they were in coal and road haulage. The change in the scale of operations was less vast and a considerable part of the gas and electricity industries were already in municipal ownership. In electricity local authorities ac-counted for 60 per cent of all sales and in gas the proportion was 37 per cent.[20] Moreover, these industries had long operated within a frame-work of Government regulations. In both the amount of dividends which could be paid out was strictly controlled and in the electricity industry power stations were more or less under the direction of the Central Electricity Board. However, even in these industries, the dif-ficulties were real enough.[21] The same was true of the railways where, although there were only four large companies to take over, the transi-tion from private to public ownership was to prove exceptionally difficult. This was due to ingrained company loyalties which led to a cold war between the regions and the Railway Executive.[22]

Did Nationalization Harm Productivity?

It seems very doubtful whether the administrative and other dif-ficulties which nationalization involved had an adverse effect on pro-ductivity. Although the nationalized industries' performance was disappointing, if the first decade of public ownership is considered as a whole, it was satisfactory during the years immediately after they had been taken over. Between 1948 and 1951 the productivity of the public enterprise sector increased by about $8\frac{1}{2}$ per cent which was as large as the rise in manufacturing. It was not until after 1951 that the sector's rate of advance slowed down to a crawl. Yet it is obviously during the national-ized industries' earliest years, before they had time to settle down and sort out their administrative problems, that we should expect the dis-rupting effects of the transfer to public ownership to show up. That their productivity was not noticeably harmed does not prove by itself that the industries' take-over had no harmful effect. Output per man might have risen faster still but for the disruption which resulted from public acquisition; but the amount of harm cannot have been very great or it would be visible to the naked eye.

Nor does the picture change when the industries are put under the microscope. There is no sign, for instance, that nationalization was followed by a mushroom growth in the number of clerical and administrative workers. What does become apparent is the drive for greater efficiency which was launched after the industries had been taken over. In coal output per man shift (OMS) rose by 18 per cent during the period 1946–51 which was the first five years of public ownership.[23] The Coal Board's performance must be put into perspective. On the one hand OMS was, at the start of the period, considerably lower than it had been in 1936, which was the best pre-war year. To this extent the Board's record was less impressive than it appears. On the other hand Britain was the only country in Europe where by 1951 productivity had surpassed its peak pre-war level.[24] Although it is impossible to know how much this achievement owed to the industry's new management it is difficult to believe that the Coal Board's productivity campaign had no effect and it is hard to see what more could have been done. This campaign, which was launched immediately after vesting day, took the form of a large number of small reorganization and modernization schemes which could be completed quickly. 'The impression one gets,' reported an American economist, 'is one of initiative in attempting new methods; most managers agree that never before have so many new ideas been tried.'[25]

Nationalization might be expected to have led to a rapid increase in the number of white collar workers. It seems likely that the creation of a large and complex managerial structure in an industry like coal, where most of the undertakings had previously been small, would result in a large increase in the number of administrators and the volume of paper work. At the time it was widely supposed that nationalization led to bureaucracy and red tape. The growth in the number of white collar workers was, however, extremely modest. It increased from about 31,000 before nationalization to about 38,000 at the end of 1951, and part of the rise was due to the Board's policy of doing work for itself whenever practicable.[26] When the Fleck Committee examined the industry's organization in 1954 it dismissed the criticism that the number of staff was excessive and concluded that it should be higher.[27]

In the gas industry where, as in coal, nationalization revolutionized the administrative set-up there is no sign that productivity was impaired. During the period 1949–54, which was approximately the first five years of nationalization, output per man hour rose by 12 per cent. Productivity in gas tends to move in step with changes in production and during this period the industry had the advantage of a substantial increase in output. However, the increase in productivity was by no means confined to the distribution side of the industry where the benefits of rising sales would have made the chief impact. In fact the rise in output per man hour appears to have been almost as large on the production side between 1949 and 1954 as it was in the industry as a whole.[28] But the movement of production does account for the dip in gas productivity during 1952 when sales fell and for its stagnation after 1954.

At first sight there appears to have been a significant rise in the number of white collar workers in gas during the early years of nationalization.[29] This was due to the fact that local authority staff used to perform a considerable amount of administrative work on behalf of their gas undertakings. When the industry was nationalized it had, therefore, to take on extra administrative and clerical workers, although during the take-over period many local authorities went on providing services for the gas industry. It was estimated that the equivalent of 3,500 of their staff were engaged in this work.[30] If this is allowed for, as it has been in the productivity calculations, the industry's administrative and clerical staff rose by only 11 per cent between the autumn of 1948 and the autumn of 1953. Even this increase may be more apparent than real because the industry was now undertaking work for itself which it had previously paid others to provide.[31]

For the railways, unlike the coal, gas and electricity industries, the administrative upheaval which resulted from nationalization was relatively small and the immediate impact of public ownership appears to have been beneficial because it was followed by an economy campaign. During the five-year period 1948–53 output per man increased by 8 per cent. The increase in rail productivity was mainly due to a reduction in the numbers employed which was, in turn, largely due to a drive for greater efficiency and in particular of a decision in late 1948 to reduce rapidly the number of staff by 26,000. However, the reduction may have been partly involuntary as the railways had difficulty in recruiting and retaining workers.[32]

Although there is no reason to believe that nationalization had an immediate adverse effect on the efficiency of any of the industries which have so far been considered it has been strongly argued that in road haulage productivity was harmed. According to an article on BRS by Professor P.E. Hart, which appeared at the time, the tonnage hauled per vehicle and per employee fell each year since 1950, the first year of a roughly comparable series, and the corresponding figure per member of driving staff fell from 1950 to 1952 . . . Each particular measure has its own drawbacks, and its implications are correspondingly suspect, but each series acts as a check on every other series and they all indicate that under nationalization the road haulage industry has become less efficient each year since 1950, the year for which the first reliable measurements of output are possible. This conclusion does not mean that BRS has become less efficient simply because its scale of management has increased, for increases in size and in inefficiency may have gone together without there being any causal connection between them. However, the fact that the statistical tests of administrative efficiency did yield evidence consistent with managerial diseconomies suggests that increasing scale may be part of the explanation.[33]

Statistics of tons hauled per vehicle and per worker suffer from the obvious weakness that no account is taken of the distance which the tons are carried. What is wanted is a measure of work performed which allows both for quantity and for distance. In default of statistics of ton mileage, capacity ton mileage, excluding empty running, can be used. In terms of this yardstick labour productivity was $5\frac{1}{2}$ per cent higher in 1951 than it had been in 1950. During 1952, when traffic fell sharply, productivity declined but in 1953 it recovered and was 7 per cent higher than in 1950. During the second half of the year, which was the last period before disposals began, it was 10 per cent greater.

It would be wrong to attach too much weight to these figures. Although capacity ton miles is a more sophisticated measure of output than tonnage it is only a crude index. It does not allow for the substantial shifts in the pattern of traffic which took place during this period. For this reason the figure for 1950 is particularly suspect. Although the bulk of long distance road haulage had been nationalized by the end of 1949 a substantial number of vehicles were taken over by BRS during 1950 and their acquisition altered the balance of its business. Nevertheless productivity calculations based on capacity ton miles have at least some negative value. They lend no support to the idea that the nationalization of road haulage was followed by a decline in efficiency. To Professor Hart's charge the verdict must be 'not proven'.

There is reason to believe that during the early fifties BRS was operating at a high level of efficiency. In 1952 the Ministry of Transport carried out a survey of road goods transport for a sample week. It would be pointless to try to compare the performance of BRS and the private hauliers at that date because the latter were at the time restricted to journeys within 25 miles of their home base. However it is possible to make a comparison between BRS in 1952 and private hauliers in 1958 when the Ministry conducted a similar survey. For vehicles of over five tons unladen weight the ton mileage carried by BRS and the private hauliers was about the same allowing for the fact that the BRS lorries were somewhat smaller. The same was true of vehicles of between three and five tons except that this time it was the private vehicles which were slightly smaller. However for vehicles of less than three tons BRS produced more ton miles than could be explained by their advantage in terms of carrying capacity. The performance of BRS was not as good as this suggests because for every class of vehicle the tonnage carried over the period was less than that of the private hauliers. For instance in the case of vehicles of over five tons the BRS tonnage was 12 per cent less.[34] Nevertheless it is obviously a severe test to compare the operations of BRS in the early fifties with those of private hauliers in the late fifties, and the comparison therefore suggests that BRS was performing efficiently.

It can be argued that the appearance of efficiency and rising productivity was belied by the reduction in the quality of service which nationalization had involved.[35] That there was a short period of confusion and poor service while road haulage was being taken over and regrouped is generally agreed and seems likely enough. However the picture does not appear to have been as black as sometimes painted. In November 1950 the *Economist* paid BRS the following tribute: 'The wonder is not that mistakes and delays have occurred in the service which the public have come to expect from the road haulage industry, but that they have had a reasonable service at all. Indeed, given the fact that the speed at which they have had to work was not of their own choosing, the Road Haulage Executive have put up a very creditable performance.'[36] Moreover it seems clear that as BRS settled down there was a marked improvement in its service. This is shown by the testimony of those who, though well acquainted with the road haulage industry, were by no means over-sympathetic to BRS and public ownership.[37]

The most striking and conclusive evidence of the success of BRS in satisfying their major customers is the way in which the latter responded to denationalization. A survey of firms in the Birmingham area by Professor A. A. Walters and Mr Clifford Sharp, which was made at the time, disclosed that although the smaller traders welcomed the liquidation of BRS some of the larger firms

> expressed the fear that they would not be able to find a carrier sufficiently large and with a country-wide service to handle all their traffic. These firms recognized that they benefited considerably by having only one road

transport firm to deal with. In some cases BRS kept one of their officers permanently on the firm's premises, and records had been standardized. The transport manager no longer experienced the difficulty of finding a carrier to take small consignments to remote rural destinations at 'reasonable' rates – BRS performed all these services.[38]

What the large firms were afraid of was that the BRS's comprehensive network of regular trunk services would be disrupted. This had not existed prior to the creation of BRS because the road haulage industry was so fragmented and because, due to their intense individualism, the hauliers were unwilling to co-operate with each other through a clearing house system. The only real exception was in the parcels field but even here the unification of the industry led to a reduction in the amount of trans-shipment and the creation for the first time of a truly national service.[39] Close control of vehicles and the provision of information to customers were facilitated by the swift creation of a teleprinter network to which BRS depots were linked.[40]

Consequently when BRS was being broken up transport users, as represented by the Association of British Chambers of Commerce, brought pressure to bear on the Government to halt the process. This, together with the fact that denationalization was proving more difficult than had been expected, was why the Government passed the Disposal of Road Haulage Property Act, 1956, which brought disposals to an end.[41] Surprising as it may seem, capitalist interests intervened to preserve public ownership.

The absence of any sign, even in road haulage, that nationalization had a harmful effect on efficiency is truly remarkable. Whatever the wisdom of the undertaking, the smooth transition from private to public ownership must count among the great administrative achievements of our time. The success with which the take-over was handled has to some extent been recognized. For instance the Committee under Lord Fleck, the Chairman of ICI, which investigated the Coal Board made a number of detailed criticisms but concluded that

> the immense changes inherent in national ownership and single management, have created difficulties unparalleled in any other industry of which we have knowledge . . . We ourselves think that, on the whole, it is remarkable how much has been done since the Board was set up in 1946. In particular, the new organization for managing a thousand pits, previously run by 800 companies, was planned and brought into being in a matter of months. Those who performed this task did a remarkable job in the face of difficulties which could have been overwhelming.[42]

On the gas industry the all-party Select Committee on Nationalized Industries reported that '713 private companies, and 269 municipal undertakings, combined under nationalization to make up 12 Area Boards. The problems of organization which this entailed can be seen to be formidable, and one of the most impressive aspects of the integration of the industry has been the way in which these problems have been solved.'[43] Similar tributes have been paid to the electricity industry and, as we have seen, to BRS.[44]

The Morale of the Managers

Although the administrative achievements of the nationalized industries during their early years have been duly noted by a few observers, they have on the whole been ignored. At the time a barrage of criticism was directed against the nationalized industries' 'over-centralization', 'bureaucracy', 'waste', and 'general inefficiency'. Although the attack was led by the Press and the politicians a large number of academics joined in, until the disadvantages of nationalization soon became part of the conventional wisdom. The experts in public administration and the Acton Society Trust were particularly notable. In an influential series of pamphlets on the nationalized industries, for the most important of which Professor T. E. Chester was mainly responsible, the Trust left the impression that they were in urgent need of reorganization, that they were over-centralized, and that a much looser form of organization was desirable. These suggestions, as befitted an impartial body, were put in a tentative form but the logic of the argument was clear enough; and in a book, which he wrote with Professor Hugh Clegg, Chester went so far as to advocate the dissolution of the NCB and a sweeping programme of railway decentralization designed to return as nearly as possible to the situation which had existed prior to the railway amalgamation of 1923.[45]

The Trust's criticisms were not derived from an examination of the economic performance of the nationalized industries. They were based partly on the general assumption that in large-scale organizations workers lose their sense of belonging and middle managers lose their independence. In the Trust's *Management under Nationalization* it was asserted that this was an inherent defect of size and the argument that managerial dissatisfaction would diminish when things settled down, and a new generation of managers emerged, was curtly dismissed. It was not denied that they would fit in better and feel less frustrated but it was said that they ought not to, and a rhetorical reference was made to prisoners coming to love their chains.[46] Apart from this deep-rooted hostility to large-scale organization the other source of the Trust's criticisms was the field work which Professor Chester undertook among branch or district managers in several of the nationalized industries. This research suffered from the weakness that the investigators' only concern was management's views about the situation in which it was placed and the difficulties which it faced.[47] What they really wanted to know was whether management felt happy. Only if it is assumed that a contented management is also an efficient management would such an inquiry disclose how well the nationalized industries were running. The Acton Society not only made this assumption but almost seems to have believed that managerial contentment was the yardstick by which the success or failure of nationalization was to be judged.[48] The idea that tensions and frustration might arise from the drive for greater efficiency and the reluctance of managers to accept new and better techniques was only dimly perceived and grudgingly conceded.[49] The Acton research was also vitiated by the investigators' apparent desire to find evidence of managerial dissatisfaction. For instance they end their section on the Area General Manager of the NCB with the revealing statement that 'running through all his comments is the suggestion that *there are occasions* when his bonds prove irksome . . . this feeling is rarely made explicit.'[50]

It is therefore all the more significant that, with the partial exception of BRS, Professor Chester's inquiries revealed that branch and district managers were generally satisfied and that the new organizations appeared to be working reasonably well. Although managers had their grumbles the Trust did not find the evidence of serious dissatisfaction for which it was looking, though it went on talking as if it had. The situation in the coal industry shows just how well the new structure was working:

the formal authority of the Area General Manager is very considerable . . . Only rarely does he call on the Division for higher backing. In general, he feels that the scope of this authority compares favourably with that which he enjoyed before nationalization, when very few Agents could incur capital expenditure of the amounts now authorized. He agrees that in some cases his formal authority is restricted, but against this must be set the fact that what is left he now exercises on a considerably wider scale. Moreover, he is well aware that many things which today impinge on his freedom of action, especially in labour relations, are not so much the result of nationalization as the working out of long-term trends in the industry; of particular importance is the changed position of the miners since the war and the greatly increased power of the trade unions. The Area General Manager does not complain of delay in obtaining authorization from a higher level where decisions lie outside his formal authority. Minor matters of this type (he regards these as the majority) are usually decided by the Division within 48 hours; very often he receives an answer immediately by telephone from the Chairman himself. If the matter is particularly important, he himself visits Divisional headquarters, having previously notified them of the problem, and again he gets an immediate decision. Only in a few cases is a decision of the full Divisional Board necessary; then some delay is involved as the Board meets fortnightly. The biggest problems of authorization are reorganization projects, but even here the Area General Manager has no major complaint as far as the Division is concerned. Projects up to £250,000 take from six to twelve weeks to be approved: very often they have already been discussed at length by the Area staff and officers of the Divisional Production and Finance Departments. The Area General Manager thinks that the complaints frequently heard in other parts of the country arise more from the inefficiency on the part of Area staffs than from excessive interference by the Divisions. He has had a number of opportunities to examine schemes of other Areas and has found some of them badly prepared, with inadequate technical information. He admits that in the first year or two of nationalization the situation was far from satisfactory, and in many cases long delays were involved. He appreciates that, in particular, the Divisional Board needed time to set up the necessary machinery; however, this is now working smoothly and he himself is fairly satisfied. In matters which have to be approved by the National Coal Board, he still experiences delays – though he makes allowances for the fact that it takes time to scrutinize development schemes from all over the country.[51]

(The Fleck Committee, which heard similar complaints, found that the average time which the Board's headquarters took to approve major capital projects was only 7·1 weeks in 1953 and 8·7 in 1954.)[52]

The situation as described by the Acton investigators was less satisfactory in BRS than in coal but they found that in the electricity industry the power station manager was 'reasonably satisfied with the new framework of the industry; more so, in fact, than the Area General Manager'.[53] Not only did the Acton inquiries disclose that the new organizations were on the whole working well, but they also threw some light on why there was no collapse of management during the early years of nationalization, despite the formidable administrative difficulties with which it had to contend.

These difficulties represented an exciting challenge as well as a source of frustration. Although managers sometimes felt lost and helpless in the

large new organizations which were being created, their sense of alienation was tempered by the feeling they were participating in great events
and helping to create a unified and coherent structure in industries which
had previously been fragmented and chaotic. There was also a sense of
liberation from local authority control, from public utility regulation,
from lack of resources, and from the restrictions of an irrational pattern
of ownership. Even those who had opposed nationalization, and seen
their businesses expropriated, often had the satisfaction of swift promotion within the new organizations which were in the making to positions
more important than any which existed during the days of private
ownership.

This was not the conclusion which Professor Chester drew. He was
only interested in how the nationalized industries were failing, not why
they were working. Nevertheless it is the conclusion which his findings
suggest. Professor Chester reported that the Area General Manager in
coal welcomed the opportunities which nationalization brought for reorganization and modernization. He was for instance 'particularly proud
of the new functions which he is allowed to control in the new organization. He is very enthusiastic about the Area Scientific laboratory which
has been set up near his office . . . He is convinced that the lack of such
research facilities was one of the great drawbacks of the industry under
private enterprise.'[54] Again Professor Chester described the enthusiasm
of the BRS District Manager for the new organization and reported that
he was clearly enjoying the excitement of building a new enterprise from
scratch. He had 'openly opposed nationalization. Watching him at
work, however, it was clear that he is quite sincere in saying that, now
that he is a member of the organization, he will do everything in his
power to make it work.'[55] In electricity the power station manager
welcomed his release from local authority tutelage and was

quite firm about one major advantage which he feels nationalization has
brought. He calls this 'the wider view'. Before vesting day a Superintendent
was usually the employee of a small undertaking, and his horizon was
limited. Transfers from private firms to local authority undertakings were
rare, mainly because of the differences in superannuation schemes. The
industry was divided into two watertight compartments. Now he can see his
own position in the widest possible perspective: he receives regular information about the work within his Division and throughout the country, and
he is made conscious of the part his power station plays in the national
system.[56]

Obviously, as Professor Chester and others have reported, there was a considerable degree of managerial dissatisfaction during the early years of nationalization, but it would be wrong to overlook the compensating factors, as it was these which enabled managers to rise to the occasion and overcome the formidable difficulties with which they had to contend.

CHAPTER 3

Stagnation

The Impact of Denationalization

BEFORE the nationalized industries had time to settle down their operations were disrupted by further administrative upheavals. An attempt was now made to break them up either by denationalization, as in the case of BRS (and steel), or by decentralization as in railways. Although it was a new government which put these changes into effect, decentralization, at least, had a wide measure of support. As we have seen the Acton Society Trust was a conservative fellow traveller. In contrast to the period of nationalization the years of denationalization and decentralization had a severe impact on the productivity and efficiency of the undertakings which were involved.[1]

For BRS the denationalization episode was short but traumatic. The disposal of vehicles did not begin until January 1954, and was more or less complete by the end of 1955. During this period half of the BRS fleet was sold off.[2] This had a disastrous effect on the undertaking's productivity. Between the second half of 1953 and 1956 output per man hour appears to have declined by over 10 per cent. In 1957 it drifted still lower but this was due to fuel rationing during the Suez crisis and the sharp reduction in traffic to which this inevitably led.[3] However, in 1958 productivity recovered sharply and in 1959 appears to have been higher than ever before.

It has been suggested that the apparent reduction in the efficiency of BRS after 1953 was due to the change in the balance of the organization which denationalization produced.[4] The bulk of general haulage was sold off while the parcels service was retained virtually intact. When output is measured by capacity ton miles, as it has been, productivity will normally appear to be lower in parcels than in general haulage because of the large number of workers engaged in sorting. However, what information is available suggests that during the denationalization period capacity ton miles per employee moved in the same way in general haulage as they did in the undertaking as a whole.[5] The apparent decline in the efficiency of BRS between 1953 and 1958 seems therefore to have been more than a statistical illusion.

What is remarkable is not that productivity should have fallen when the enterprise was being sold up but that it recovered so rapidly when disposals ceased. It was almost inevitable that denationalization would, in the short run, lead to some reduction in productivity because of the form which it took. The bulk of the vehicles which were sold off were disposed of in small lots and purchasers were under no obligation to take on BRS staff. The undertaking was therefore faced with the virtually impossible task of reducing its labour force in line with the reduction in its vehicle fleet and work load. Although at least 7,000 workers were declared redundant BRS did not manage to prevent stagnation or contraction in the productivity of its drivers and maintenance staff between 1953 and 1955.[6] By 1958, the productivity of these workers, in terms of capacity ton miles, was considerably higher than ever before. But even here denationalization seems to have had an adverse effect. In 1958, vehicle miles per driver and per maintenance worker were both lower than they had been in 1953. The rise in capacity ton miles per worker would not have occurred but for the considerable increase in the average capacity of BRS lorries and the reduction in the proportion of empty running. As might have been expected BRS was not able to reduce its administrative, clerical and miscellaneous staff as fast as its drivers and maintenance workers. In 1958 the productivity of these overhead staff even in terms of capacity ton miles was much lower than it had been in 1953.[7] BRS was left with a somewhat top-heavy organization as a result of its forced contraction.

Although our primary concern in this Chapter is productivity it should also be observed that BRS's finances were seriously impaired. The reduction in productivity and the relative increase in the number of overhead workers were reflected financially by a slump in profits. During its early years BRS had had low profits and in 1950 there was even a small loss, the only deficit which the concern has ever made. The basic reason for its weak financial position was that the acquisition and re-grouping of private hauliers was in full swing. The administrative costs of this operation were considerable, some dislocation and loss of traffic resulted, and maintenance costs were high because of the poor state of so many of the vehicles taken over from the small firms which were acquired from late 1949 onwards. Furthermore, as the Transport Commission pointed out, when an undertaking is built up from scratch, like BRS, it must be endowed with many small items of working capital which are charged against revenue.[8] In view of the difficulties which beset British Road Services during the nationalization period what is surprising is not its low profitability but that any profits were earned at all. This was the financial reflection of the extraordinary administrative success with which, as we have seen, the operation was handled.[9]

Once acquisitions had been completed and the new undertaking had settled down large profits started to be earned. At their peak between mid-1953 and mid-1954 they totalled well over £10 million which represented a return of over 25 per cent on its net fixed assets.[10] However after this the denationalization of road haulage started to take its toll. By 1956 BRS profits had sunk to £1·8 million, or less than 6 per cent on net assets, and on the general haulage side of the business which had been most badly affected the surplus was very small.[11] In subsequent years profits slowly recovered but their growth was painfully slow.

The reduction in BRS's operating profits was by no means entirely due to the damage inflicted by compulsory contraction. It was, for instance, partly due to the intense competition within the road haulage industry which denationalization brought about.[12] However, there is no doubt that the slump in BRS's rate of return would have been much smaller had BRS's efficiency not been damaged and its costs distorted. This is shown by the way in which expenses fell when the undertaking was being sold off. Between 1953 and 1956 vehicle operating and maintenance expenses fell by 40 per cent, but overhead expenses were only cut by 18 per cent, and the cost of operating depots rose by 4 per cent. This increase was partly due to the fact that the parcels service, which was retained virtually intact, accounted for a high proportion of depot expenses. But the fact that overhead costs remained relatively stable was due to the difficulty which BRS had in reducing these costs in line with the reduction in traffic.[13] This, to the extent that staff costs were involved, was the financial counterpart of the decline in the productivity of administrative and clerical staff which we have observed.

Besides its direct and measurable impact on BRS's productivity (and finances) denationalization had at least two indirect effects. First it led to a halt in the construction of new depots and other buildings. Although, as we have seen, these were urgently required it was naturally decided not to start any new building work until disposals had been completed. Half-finished premises would not be readily saleable and small hauliers would not require large depots. The pitifully low level to which investment fell is shown by the fact that in 1954 expenditure on land and new buildings totalled less than £50,000. Yet when the parcels service was offered for sale it was estimated that, on this part of the business alone, expenditure of £4 million was necessary and that of this £1¼ million needed to be spent immediately.[14]

Second, denationalization weakened the management of BRS because it resulted in the loss of some of the organization's best personnel. As it initially appeared that BRS was going to be almost completely liquidated there was naturally a tendency for the most enterprising managers to leave and for the older and less enterprising to remain. The denationalization episode must also have tended to damp the spirits and blunt the initiative of those in charge. Having successfully accomplished the immense and exhilarating administrative task of taking over nearly 3,800 separate firms and 42,000 vehicles, and having welded them into a unified organization, they were now faced with the equally enormous, but this time heartbreaking task of destroying their handiwork. 'It is impossible,' wrote the Chairman of the Road Haulage Executive in 1951, 'to convey the atmosphere of thrill and adventure that pervades the activities of those who, starting with virtually nothing, have set about building the biggest road haulage undertaking in the world.'[15] But in 1956 after denationalization, Mr Quick Smith, a member of the BRS Board of Management, found it 'difficult to find words to describe the upheaval of these last few years without resorting to the vocabulary of film publicity . . . The administrative work involved provided a lifetime of experience with nightmarish qualities which will not soon be forgotten by those who took part in these exercises.'[16] Denationalization's adverse effect on the undertaking's management may well have been its most damaging consequence.

Coal: Productivity in the Pipeline

In coal productivity, after rising fairly rapidly during the early years of nationalization, became stagnant. Indeed in 1957 it was slightly lower than it had been during the early fifties. By then the most obvious short-term opportunities for increasing productivity had been taken but the Coal Board's reconstruction programme was at an early stage. *Plan for Coal* had only been published in 1950 and not until the year 1952 did capital expenditure on major colliery projects first exceed £10 million.[17] Because it takes so long to reconstruct a pit or sink a new one, schemes which had been completed by the end of 1958 represented under 30 per cent of the capital which the Board had already spent on major colliery projects. Even when projects had been completed there had seldom been time for the full benefits of modernization to be secured. Moreover power-loading, which has subsequently produced the most spectacular gains in productivity, had not yet been introduced on a wide scale. In 1958 it accounted for less than 30 per cent of deep-mined output and most power-loading machines had only been recently installed and were not yet being used to the best advantage.[18] The rise in output per man during 1958 marked the beginning of a new era of rapidly rising productivity.

The question naturally arises of whether the NCB could have done more to secure an increase in output per man between 1951 and 1958. The slow rise in the Coal Board's capital expenditure in the early years of nationalization appears to have been mainly due to shortage of staff with the necessary experience and qualifications. The Reid Committee had warned in 1945 that there was a 'serious dearth of mining engineers who possess the knowledge and experience necessary to undertake the far-reaching schemes of reorganization which are essential'. For this the Coal Board was obviously not to blame, although it may not have made the fullest use of the staff which it did possess.[19] The main criticism which can be made of the Board is that it was slow to take action to ensure that once projects were started they were completed as quickly as possible.

> Although [reported the Fleck Committee in 1955] there is generally adequate information at all levels about the amount of capital expenditure incurred against authorizations and budgets, not enough attention is given to ensuring that the work of capital construction and development is being done on time. In other words, we have not found a satisfactory system of 'progressing' capital expenditure being generally applied in the industry. There is evidence that a good deal of capital work is not up to schedule, and that the projects are completed late.[20]

This was a particular aspect of the general lack of central control during the period when the Board was under pressure to decentralize to the maximum and it illustrates the adverse effects which decentralization was having. After the publication of the Fleck Report had strengthened its position, however, the Board started to keep a close watch on the progress of the major capital schemes by means of its admirable reporting system. In 1956 the Board established a Reconstruction Department at Headquarters to ensure that these projects were executed with the greatest possible speed and efficiency.[21] One of the main requirements for faster completion was an increase in the rate at which new shafts were sunk and tunnels driven. The Coal Board had long been aware of the need to speed up tunnelling and had carried out a certain amount of research into the way in which this could be achieved. However one gains the impression from the Board's Annual Reports that it was restricted in scope and that too little was done to ensure that improved methods were put into practice. It was not until 1956, for instance, that a full investigation of foreign methods was completed or that national training courses in tunnelling were started. These efforts soon bore fruit and the speed at which tunnels were driven, which hitherto appears to have been lower than it had been in the Ruhr before the war, increased dramatically. The speed-up in shaft sinking, where there was much to be learned from foreign practice, was even more spectacular.[22]

No doubt if the Coal Board had taken action more quickly a somewhat higher proportion of its reconstruction schemes would have been completed by 1958. Nevertheless it seems most unlikely that the position would have been very different from what it was or whether the effect on productivity would have been more than marginal. Even if completion times had been cut they would have inevitably remained lengthy and a high proportion of the reconstruction projects which were in progress in 1958 had only been running for a few years.

Another possibility which seems worth investigating is whether the industry could by 1958 have made greater progress with the introduction of power-loading. From the first the Board grasped the importance of this new method of mining and was anxious to try out a wide variety of machines.[23] Yet until the invention of the Anderton Shearer in 1952 by one of the Board's Area General Managers, Mr J. Anderton, none of the available machines was suitable for operation under a wide range of conditions.[24] It was the Shearer which enabled the Board to launch its power-loading drive in July 1955 and which accounted for the main part of the additional tonnage of coal obtained by power-loading. The lead which was given from Headquarters played an important part in the introduction of power-loading for, as two of the Board's senior Area and Divisional officials commented, there was, except for the East Midlands, 'considerable suspicion if not actual opposition, towards power-loading.'[25] They claim that while the increase in production by power-loading 'coincided with, and can be related to, the extended use of a particular machine, the real urge arose from the meeting convened by the National Coal Board in 1955, when a clear statement on policy was given'. The introduction of power loading was certainly not hindered by the industry's over-centralization as Professor Duncan Burn alleged in the early fifties. Where local management was enthusiastic to introduce power-loading or to experiment with new types of machine, it was able to do so, as the story of the Shearer's development and of its swift introduction in Mr Anderton's Area indicates.[26]

Can the Board be criticized from the opposite direction for not having launched the power-loading campaign earlier? This does not seem a very plausible line of attack because, as we have seen, the Shearer, which formed its spearhead, was not invented until 1952, and obviously it took some time to develop the machine. What is evident is that if the Fleck Report had not been published when it was, the introduction of power-loading might have been delayed due to local hostility to new ideas and because the technical experts at Headquarters had ceased to expect their advice to be acted upon at lower levels. In the period from 1951 until the time of the Fleck Report the extent to which their advice was clothed in authority steadily declined. It therefore seems probable that, but for the Committee, the Board's senior officials would not have felt in a strong enough position to initiate the power-loading drive. However, the publication of the Report, which said that decentralization had been carried too far and criticized the Board for not insisting that its policies were carried out, enabled it to press ahead both here and with its campaign to reduce the excessive time which was being taken to complete its reconstruction projects. It is surely no accident that this, like the power-loading drive, was launched after the Fleck Committee had reported.[27]

The Capital-starved Railways

In 1957 rail output per worker was scarcely higher than it had been in 1951. Then in 1958, due to the collapse of rail traffic, productivity fell sharply and a large part of the progress which had been made during the early years of nationalization was wiped out. This progress had been largely due to a decision to reduce the rail labour force in the interests of greater efficiency. By the end of 1951, however, the most obvious economies in the use of labour had already been made and from then onwards there was only a small reduction in employment which was almost offset by the slow decline in rail output.

If the Government had made the necessary capital and steel available there would have been no difficulty in finding ways of improving efficiency and saving manpower. But due to the repeated imposition of capital cuts and the limited amount of steel which the railways were allowed it was impossible during the early years of nationalization for a modernization programme to be launched. Indeed the Transport Commission were unable even to maintain the level of investment at which they started in 1948. Early in 1949 the Commission had proposed that by 1952 rail investment should be 43 per cent higher than it had been in 1948. Due, however, to the restrictions which the Government imposed the volume of rail investment fell by about a fifth. As a result of these restrictions and also, perhaps, of the administrative upheaval caused by the Transport Act of 1953, it was not until 1954 that the rail Modernization Plan was prepared and not until early 1955 that it was published. Once the plan had been approved rail investment, which was already rising strongly, began to shoot up, although it was not until 1956 that its volume recovered to the pre-war level.[28] The late date at which modernization got under way meant that the Commission's investment programme was only just starting to bear fruit as the first decade of nationalization closed. For instance in 1958, diesels, which were subsequently to produce the most spectacular gains in productivity, still accounted for less than 10 per cent of train mileage.[29]

It is, of course, possible that the railways failed to make the most of the finance and the steel which they were permitted and conceivable that, if they had been better deployed, modernization could have been launched earlier. But an examination of British Rail's capital expenditure during the period before modernization commenced in earnest, suggests that there was little room for manœuvre and that the bulk of its investment was well directed. Between 1948 and 1954 a total of £284 million was invested. Of this £35 million was devoted to building and works, with the lion's share taken up by electrification schemes whose completion had been prevented by the war. A sum of £11 million was spent on cartage vehicles and related plant and equipment. As British Rail had not even managed to replace all its horse-drawn vehicles by the end of 1954 there can be little quarrel with this.[30] Apart from these relatively small items the rest of its capital expenditure was devoted to rolling stock.

On wagons a total of £128 million was spent. Although this sounds a considerable sum the modernization of the wagon fleet was a top priority. At nationalization the Transport Commission took over 544,000 old mineral wagons which had belonged to the NCB or other concerns. These were thoroughly uneconomic because of their excessive maintenance costs, low capacity, and erratic performance due to the obsolete system of lubrication on so many of them. It was discovered, for instance, that during 1949 each of the former privately-owned wagons had on average to be repaired five times whereas the wagons inherited from the railway companies only had to be repaired three times. The Railway Executive was naturally anxious to get rid of these wagons as quickly as possible, but despite the fact that old colliery wagons accounted for 70 per cent of the freight vehicles scrapped between 1948 and 1954, it still possessed 280,000 at the end of the period. Indeed it was not until the beginning of 1958 that the last of the grease-lubricated wagons were finally withdrawn.[31] It must therefore be concluded that, far from being excessive, expenditure on new wagons was inadequate. The same appears to have been true of the railways' investment in coaches. Despite the expenditure of £63 million it was necessary to continue using a substantial number of carriages which had come to the end of their normal lives. Not only was this uncomfortable for rail passengers but it also involved British Rail in a considerable amount of uneconomic repair work.[32]

Finally BR spent £36 million on new locomotives of which about £28 million was devoted to steam engines. This is the only part of the railways' capital expenditure which would clearly have been better devoted to some other use. It is important to recognize, however, that if the money had been used for electrification or dieselization, as it should have been, the modernization of the railways would not thereby have been greatly advanced. The reason is that although £28 million appears a formidable sum it represents only a small part of the cost of introducing new forms of traction. This is shown by the fact that about £400 million was included in the Modernization Plan for this purpose.[33]

The Steam Programme

Although there is little doubt that but for Government restrictions over capital expenditure and steel rail modernization would have been launched earlier, the question arises of whether ways could have been found of increasing productivity which did not involve large-scale investment and of whether, even if the capital had been available, the Commission would have used it to the best advantage. It does not follow (to take the second question first) that, because the Commission did not have the capital to begin introducing new forms of traction earlier, the railways would in fact have used it for this purpose, if the cash had been made available. Indeed the way in which British Rail not only went on building steam locomotives but actually started building an entirely new range of standard engines raises the serious doubt that it would not have done so.

The Railway Executive, who subject to the general direction of the Commission had charge of British Rail, began designing these engines immediately after nationalization. If the date had been 1918 rather than 1948 the idea would have been worth investigating; what Mr R. A. Riddles, the member of the Executive responsible for rolling stock, wanted to secure were the economies inherent in having a fleet composed of only a few types using, so far as possible, interchangeable parts. It was generally agreed that considerable savings could be achieved in this way, although this had never been shown in practice because no major railway had ever managed to achieve full standardization. The reason for this was that existing engines could only gradually be replaced as they came to the end of their lives. The economies of standardization were not sufficiently great to warrant the scrapping of otherwise serviceable locomotives, and steam engines have long lives; before replacement was complete some new type of locomotive would be introduced and this would prevent standardization. Although attractive in theory standardization was, therefore, almost impossible to bring about and would take a generation to complete. The Railway Executive when it began building its standard locomotives was adopting a policy which only made sense, if it made sense at all, if British Rail was to go on *building* steam engines for a long period. This, of course, was exactly what Mr Riddles had in mind. In the early fifties, as its evidence to the Ridley Committee shows, the Executive did not consider that new forms of traction would replace steam to any appreciable extent during the following decade.[34]

Yet it was already obvious to those with eyes to see that the future did not lie with steam. Strange to relate these included both the Chairman of the Transport Commission, Sir Cyril Hurcomb, and the Chairman of the Railway Executive, Sir Eustace Missenden. The latter told the Institute of Transport in November 1949 that 'The steam locomotive inherently is inefficient and an extravagant user of coal. It is expensive to operate, service and maintain. Its operating characteristics, and the dirt and smell, prevent it from providing the quality of service required and expected by the public and which the railways must give if they are to survive. What is there to replace steam traction?'[35] The opponents of steam were uncertain of the answer and Sir Cyril Hurcomb suggested to the Railway Executive that an impartial committee of non-engineers should be set up to investigate alternative forms of motive power. Although he made this proposal in the spring of 1948, and the committee started work by the end of the year, it was not until the autumn of 1951 that its report was received. The committee recognized the inherent limitations of steam and stated that it had been greatly impressed by the success of diesels in America and electrification in Europe. It recommended that large-scale experiments should be undertaken to determine the relative merits of electric and diesel traction for main-line work. As a result of a subsidiary recommendation, and after a working party had examined the problem, work was begun on the construction of diesel railcars for use on secondary services but no action was taken on the major proposal. This was partly because the abolition of the Railway Executive was in sight, which made it unwilling to sanction expensive long-term electrification schemes, and partly because Mr Riddles wanted electrification or nothing. He took the view that diesels were an unsatisfactory half-way house between steam and full electrification.[36]

What happened was that the railways continued building and designing steam engines because the steam enthusiasts knew what they wanted whereas those who saw that steam was doomed were uncertain as to whether British Rail should electrify or dieselize. According to Mr E. S. Cox, who was one of Mr Riddles' chief assistants, the decision to continue with steam traction was 'taken more or less by default . . . I say "by default" because the steam interests were all set to jump in with the utmost vigour, whereas a certain amount of fact finding was necessary for alternative forms of traction'.[37] However it seems possible that the decision only went by default because, due to the Government's restrictions over capital expenditure, so little was at stake and because neither electrification nor dieselization were available alternatives owing to their expense.

At that time a diesel engine cost two or three times as much as a steam locomotive with the same power and an electric engine was considerably more expensive, to say nothing of the heavy cost of fixed installations. If, therefore, the Railway Executive had decided to stop building steam engines it would have had to content itself with a small-scale experiment with diesels. This obviously is what it should have done because the experience would have been extremely valuable later when the restrictions on capital expenditure were lifted and it became possible to dieselize on a large scale. Instead, the Railway Executive, with incredible foolishness, cancelled some of the experimental diesels which the old railway companies had had on order and the Transport Commission found itself in the dark when it embarked on general dieselization at the time of the Modernization Plan.

The main point is that Mr Riddles and those who wanted to go on designing steam engines might not have had such an easy victory had capital not been rationed so severely. It cannot therefore be assumed that if more money had been available it would have been invested as inefficiently as the money which was available, or rather that part of it which was devoted to steam traction. The Government, by restricting the railways' capital expenditure, unwittingly played into the hands of the steam fanatics.[38] 'Had capital been available,' writes Lord Hurcomb, 'we should undoubtedly have started some main-line electrification . . . I should probably have advised starting on the east side of the country and electrifying at least to York, which would soon have meant Newcastle.'[39] Nevertheless the decision to construct the standard steam locomotives reflects no credit on the railways and was not the only example of a conservative approach to technical matters.

Productivity without Investment

Having examined, if not answered the question of whether, granted the necessary finance, British Rail would have begun introducing modern forms of traction earlier, we must try to discover whether productivity could have been raised by methods which did not require large-scale investment. In theory this was possible, because the railways were badly in need of rationalization when they were taken over and their operating methods were highly inefficient. A large number of branch-line services failed to pay their way and a substantial part of the route system was uneconomic. For instance, it seems doubtful whether, even as a group, the Scottish lines covered their costs. Certainly when these railways were compulsorily amalgamated under the Railways Act of 1921, they were divided between the LNER and the LMS because it was feared that if they were put under a separate company it would run at a loss. In 1948 it was estimated by a leading official of the Ministry of Transport and an outstanding authority on the economics of rail transport, that about one-third of the railways' route mileage could profitably be abandoned. The withdrawal of lightly-loaded stopping services and the closure of branch lines on which traffic was thin was therefore one obvious way in which productivity could be raised without investment.[40]

Even on those lines which it was worth retaining there must have been considerable scope for cutting out little-used stations. An investigation of 107 freight depots in North and West London and an adjacent country district showed that during a representative week half of the depots handled a mere 5 per cent of the wagons which were loaded or unloaded. As these lightly-used depots dealt with an average of only 3·3 wagons per day it is hardly surprising that it was discovered that their closure was highly desirable. This survey, it is true, was not made until some years after the railways had been nationalized but there is no reason to believe that the general position was any different in 1948 or that its findings were unrepresentative.[41] One disadvantage of keeping open so many under-used freight stations was that they involved the railways in an enormous amount of extra work at marshalling yards sorting out the wagons for each depot and, since nearly every depot had its daily call, in the running of a large number of lightly-loaded trains to pick up and deliver small batches of wagons. This failure to close unnecessary goods stations intensified the already considerable weaknesses of the traditional system of railway working, which was based on the movement of traffic in wagon rather than train loads.

What happened was that full wagons were collected from the stations and private sidings at which they originated and then marshalled into trains at a near-by marshalling yard for dispatch to different parts of the country. Sometimes they would be hauled by these trains straight to the marshalling yard at the other end of their journey, but often the wagons would move through intermediate yards at which they would be re-marshalled into other trains for the next stage of their journey. When they finally arrived at the local yard at the end of the journey they would then be dispatched to the sidings and stations for which they were bound. Thus a vast amount of time and energy were dissipated in shunting wagons about. It is a remarkable fact that in 1948 (and 1958) shunting occupied nearly half the time which freight engines spent at work. Besides the footplate staff whose time was spent in such an unproductive way a large body of workers was employed on coupling and uncoupling wagons.[42]

The trains which were so laboriously assembled and then broken up were incredibly short. In 1948 the average number of loaded wagons per train was only 24 (and by 1958 it was down to only 19). This was partly due to the fact that the great bulk of freight trains was composed of loose-coupled wagons because only a small part of the wagon fleet was fitted with power brakes. In the absence of a proper braking system, trains have to be short and light because of the difficulty of stopping if they are heavy.[43] The traditional system of railway working based on marshalling was not therefore the only reason why trains were so short, but it was almost certainly a contributory factor. Because marshalling was such a lengthy process, and because wagons stood idle for long periods waiting to be sorted and collected, transit times tended to be slow. This meant that the railways could not afford to delay trains once they had been assembled at marshalling yards until sufficient wagons had been gathered to build them up into long trains. If the railways were to have any hope of remaining competitive they had to be dispatched as quickly as possible even if this meant that they were very short. Yet this obviously had an adverse effect on productivity because the larger the number of trains the greater the number of train crews employed and the more track and engine maintenance which was necessary.

The railways did not manage to prevent journey times from being relatively long and, what was still worse from the customer's point of view, unpredictable. Although the staging of wagons was carried out in accordance with a set of rules it was impossible to keep any tight control over their movement. In December 1949 when a survey of general merchandise traffic was carried out it was found that 41 per cent of wagons received a one-day transit, that 45 per cent were delivered within two or three days, and that the remaining 14 per cent took more than three days.[44] At first sight the railways' performance does not appear too disastrous but it must be remembered that the average length of haul was only about 120 miles and that road transport was able, after BRS had got into its stride, to provide overnight delivery over the major part of the country. The continued use of the traditional methods of railway working, therefore, helps to explain why the railways became an unattractive mode of transport and partly accounts for the decline in their volume of traffic. This in turn had an adverse effect on British Rail's productivity, already at a low level due to the prodigal use of labour which shunting and short trains involved.

In theory what the railways should have done was to have switched over from wagon- to train-load operations. By the introduction of through-train working for the main flows of traffic, marshalling could have been confined to the beginning and end of every journey and, where it was possible to introduce company trains shuttling from one private siding to another, it could have been more or less eliminated. Moreover, by a drastic pruning of depots, the remaining marshalling could have been simplified and the number of lightly-loaded trains for the initial pick up and final delivery of wagons greatly reduced. This policy could not have been fully executed without a certain amount of capital expenditure. The marshalling yards which British Rail inherited had mainly been laid out in Victorian times for wagon-load operations and to suit the parochial needs of the old companies. As a result many of them were too small for through-train working which requires large yards where so much traffic is concentrated that block trains to each destination can be carved out.[45] Yet it seems likely that a considerable amount of progress in the right direction could have been made without large-scale investment. That the introduction of through-train working and company trains was the direction in which the railways should have been trying to move there can be no doubt. It is precisely what they have been doing during more recent years.

The Obstacle of Ignorance

There is no doubt that in theory British Rail could have secured a substantial increase in output per man through rationalization and better operating methods, and without the need for large-scale investment. In practice, however, there were a series of formidable obstacles which made it difficult or impossible for the railways to adopt this course of action. First there was the fact that until the Traffic Costing Service had been built up the railways were extraordinarily ignorant of where they were making profits and losses. The old companies had displayed virtually no interest in the subject but had been content to muddle on with the profits from one part of their business offsetting the losses which they made elsewhere. The Transport Commission from the beginning showed a much more lively interest in the structure of its costs than its predecessors had ever done, and after giving the problem some general consideration, and having made some preliminary studies, set up a Traffic Costing Service in 1951. It is no easy matter to distinguish the costs and revenues of particular services and routes, because of the difficulty of allocating joint costs and joint revenue. This not only raises a number of difficult theoretical issues but in many cases necessitates the collection of an enormous amount of detailed information which the railways' traditional accounting system was not designed to provide. Moreover it could not be assumed, once a limited inquiry had been completed, that what was true of one part of the system held good for other parts. The most striking conclusion to emerge from traffic costing was the immense variation which existed. In this situation it was unreasonable to expect that, with the best will in the world, British Rail would be able to make fast progress in determining which routes, depots and traffic should be abandoned and how its operating methods could be improved. Perhaps as Mr Christopher Foster has argued, traffic costing should have been accorded a higher priority; but even if progress had been somewhat faster it is inconceivable that it could have been so fast that those in charge of the railways could have had the necessary information available to draw up a detailed and comprehensive plan of action during the early years of nationalization.[46]

Nevertheless it was obviously possible to begin the work of rationalization and reorganization in a piecemeal fashion as local surveys were conducted and it became clear what immediate reforms could be made. To some extent this is what happened. For instance a detailed overhaul of freight working was begun and as a result traffic which had formerly passed through marshalling yards, or had been transferred from locomotive to locomotive at company boundaries, was either diverted to more direct routes or carried in through trains. This is shown by the increasing use of block trains for the movement of electricity coal. Between the spring of 1951 and the spring of 1952 the proportion of power station coal carried in this way increased from a fifth to a third and by early 1957 the figure was over 50 per cent. Unit trains were also introduced for the transport of raw materials to the steel industry and in a few cases British Rail took the further step of introducing circuit working with permanently coupled trains. These developments were reflected by a slight reduction in the proportion of freight engine hours which were absorbed in shunting. Between 1948 and 1954 it declined from 48 per cent to $45\frac{1}{2}$ per cent but by 1958 had started to creep up again due probably to the introduction of power brakes which made the coupling and uncoupling of wagons more laborious.[47] Again British Rail made a modest start during the early years of nationalization at eliminating its least-used passenger services. Thus in 1951, when its drive reached its peak, they were withdrawn from 640 miles of route and between 1950 and 1954 10 per cent of the route which had been open to passenger traffic was closed. After this the campaign seems to have lost impetus. During the period of 1955–8 passenger services were withdrawn from a further 5 per cent of the route but only a small part of the system was completely closed.[48]

Statutory Obligations

It seems likely that the Transport Commission would have moved faster during its early years had it not been for the obligations which had been imposed on it by the Transport Act, 1947. This charged the Commission with the duty of providing an 'adequate' system of public transport. The meaning of the word adequate was not defined but, as the Commission argued, the monopoly position which it was intended that the BTC should enjoy implied a general obligation to practise cross-subsidization and provide a comprehensive transport service in all areas of the country.[49] This obligation was recognized by the Commission whose first Chairman, Sir Cyril Hurcomb, stated in 1950 that

> any public service operating over a wide area is bound to conduct parts of its business at a lower level of profitability than it can secure from others, and on some parts perhaps to make a loss. That must ensue from any scheme which is by statute required to provide for the needs of the public, agriculture, commerce and industry in all parts of the country. The Transport Commission could not, and does not, say that it should not provide any service which is not fully remunerative. On the contrary, we recognize that there are many areas of the country and sections of the population which cannot be left unserved and from which we must be content to ask less than a full return; just as there are others able to yield a return above the average without hardship.

Hurcomb recognized that due to the growth of road competition, the scope for cross-subsidization on the railways had been greatly reduced but in view of the obligation which had been imposed on the Commission it was obviously impossible for it to embark upon a programme of extensive rationalization.[50]

In the long run the Commission would have greater freedom for manœuvre and could look forward to the withdrawal of rail services where its losses were high and its productivity was low. The Transport Act, 1947, not only saddled the Transport Commission with the burden of providing a comprehensive system of public transport but also enjoined it to pursue a policy of integration and, to that end, made provision for the nationalization of long-distance road haulage, and, where necessary, the acquisition of bus undertakings. The Commission would

c

therefore be able, where traffic was light and the rail service was unprofitable, to provide an alternative road service. Conversely, where freight traffic suitable for rail was passing by road it could be switched over. This was certainly the intention of the Commission which in 1950 laid down in a statement of its policy towards integration that

> The Road Haulage Executive will employ the Railway Executive's rail service for direct trunk haulage of long distance 'smalls' and wagon load traffic where the Railway Executive can make available suitable terminal accommodation, containers and train services. The Railway Executive will employ the Road Haulage Executive's road services for trunk haulage of cross-country traffic and wherever use of road services will reduce staging and transit time, and facilitate rail movements in direct train loads between main centres . . . Where branch lines are partly or wholly closed to freight traffic, the Road Haulage Executive will provide a substitute service where this can be justified.[51]

How fast and to what extent this policy would have been implemented it is impossible to tell. All that can be said is that the initial steps were about to be taken when in 1952 the Government announced that the policy of integration was at an end and that BRS was to be denationalized. This prevented the introduction of schemes from which substantial economies had been expected for the conveyance by rail of BRS traffic between such places as Glasgow and London, London and Cardiff, London and Exeter, and Leicester and Glasgow. Various plans for transferring 'smalls' on cross-country routes from rail to road had also to be put into cold storage, although some progress had already been made in the case of traffic passing between the Midlands and East Anglia.[52] Regardless, however, of the benefits which integration might have conferred from 1952 onwards, in the preceding years it had constituted a further obstacle to the rationalization of the railways. It meant that the Commission could not get down seriously to the job until road haulage had been nationalized and it had become clear which traffic it could take over and how the railways' operations could be dovetailed in with those of BRS. As the acquisition and regrouping of private road haulage concerns was in full swing up to the end of 1950 integration inevitably meant delay.

Pricing Policy and Poor Traffic

As the Commission was unable, due to its statutory obligations, to set about the job of eliminating unprofitable services with any real vigour it might have been expected that it would have at least started to adjust its charges in such a way that poor traffic was choked off and that profitable traffic was encouraged. However this, too, was prevented by the legislative restrictions with which the Transport Commission was hemmed about. This was little short of a disaster because a large part of the railways' traffic was of the type they were least fitted to carry, and had only been retained because their prices were a long way below their costs. On the other hand, a considerable tonnage of potentially good traffic was carried by road because the rail charge was excessively high. The study by Professor Walters and Mr Clifford Sharp to which reference has already been made suggests that in the early fifties British Rail had a disproportionate share of irregular traffic, of light traffic to out-of-the-way places, of traffic passing over relatively short distances, and of small consignments.

Regular traffic was defined as daily loads of about the same weight and of over one ton which were carried more than 25 miles. Walters and Sharp found, for firms in the Birmingham area, that regular traffic of this type accounted for about 40 per cent of the tonnage which they carried in their own vehicles, for about 30 per cent of the traffic which they gave BRS and private hauliers, but for only about 20 per cent of the goods which they dispatched by rail. In the autumn of 1953 22 major destinations accounted for 68 per cent of the tonnage which was dispatched by rail from the Birmingham area, but for BRS the corresponding proportion was as high as 82 per cent. Walters and Sharp comment that 'A much larger proportion of rail traffic was of comparatively small flows to relatively out-of-the-way or rural destinations. This is precisely the kind of traffic which the railways are least suited to carry, and for which the peaks of rail costs may generally be expected to be considerably higher than those of road hauliers.'[53]

While 24 per cent of the rail tonnage was hauled less than 75 miles, for the general haulage side of BRS the proportion was only 7 per cent. As the distance over which private hauliers could operate was still restricted in 1953, their figure was even higher than that of the railways (41 per cent). To this extent a comparison between British Rail and BRS gives a misleading impression of the proportions of rail and road haulage traffic which may be regarded as relatively short-distance work. Nevertheless the fact remains that only a comparatively small proportion of the railways' traffic was carried for long distances and that only where hauls exceeded 150 miles did BR succeed in obtaining a larger tonnage than BRS.[54] Perhaps the most striking finding by Walters and Sharp was that the average weight of BRS consignments was about double that of rail consignments. Twenty-eight per cent of the tonnage of general merchandise which passed by rail was accounted for by consignments of less than a ton as against only 11 per cent of the BRS total. Even relatively heavy consignments, which it might be expected would bulk large in rail traffic, formed a smaller proportion of the railways' traffic than of BRS's. For instance consignments of over six tons accounted for 56 per cent of BRS tonnage but only 43 per cent of rail carryings, though the inclusion of heavy minerals would have increased the figure to 64 per cent.[55]

That the railways' traffic was of such an unfavourable type appears to have been largely explained by the irrational structure of their charges. In their study Walters and Sharp worked out from the BRS rate schedule what it would have cost those firms which used rail to have sent their goods by road. They found that the cost by road was on average 14 per cent above the rail cost for short-distance traffic which was hauled less than 50 miles but that the rail charge was 5 per cent higher than the BRS charge for traffic hauled between 75 and 100 miles. Only where the goods were carried for over 150 miles was the cost by rail significantly lower than the cost by road.[56] Thus the railways' system of charges encouraged short-haul and high-cost traffic but discouraged traffic passing between 75 and 100 miles for which its costs must have been lower.

What was even more perverse was the way in which rail charges encouraged small consignments and in general failed to encourage large consignments. For all consignments up to one ton the cost by rail was lower than what it would have cost to send the goods by road. But for consignments of between one and six tons rail charges were either the same or greater than road charges. For consignments of over 10 tons rail and road costs were the same, excluding one exceptionally large consignment of steel.[57] These findings, it needs to be emphasized, were for traffic where, because it passed by rail, it was to be expected that average rail charges would be significantly lower than average road charges. The facts and figures which have been quoted are therefore even more striking than they may at first appear. Another point which should be stressed, if only to avoid confusion, is that what has been established is not that the railways charged less for carrying small consignments and short-distance traffic than for other more favourable traffic but that *relative to BRS* they charged least for the least favourable type of traffic.

Due to the railways' perverse pricing system and the unfavourable pattern of traffic to which it gave rise, British Rail obviously had less scope for introducing through-train working and making other necessary changes than it should have had. Perhaps the Railway Executive had opportunities to improve its system of working even within the existing pattern of traffic which it failed to exploit. But as we have seen, it was aware of the need to introduce through train working wherever possible and over the years made considerable progress in this direction for power station coal. It therefore seems likely that the principal reason why British Rail failed to introduce more block trains was that, until they could attract suitable traffic, the scope was limited.

Certainly this was what those in charge of the railways said at the time.

> On the freight side [Sir Cyril Hurcomb argued] the greatest economy in working, and the best use of the potentialities of locomotive power, could in theory be achieved by running fast, heavy trains over long distances without intermediate stops – trains composed of high-capacity wagons, fully loaded. This method of operation is possible in some countries. Traffic in Britain, on the average, does not move in bulk over long distances and between large centres. This applies with particular force to traffic other than minerals and coal and coke. For instance, in 1937 the average weight of consignments of general goods traffic loaded and unloaded in LMS goods depots and yards was only 4½ cwts . . . In the draft principles for a new Charges Scheme . . . we are seeking to relate the charges for transporting small consignments more closely to the costs of handling that type of traffic, but we do not imagine or expect that long-established methods of commercial and industrial operation can be altered in a short period.[58]

Unfortunately, however, the Charges Scheme to which Sir Cyril referred never came into force and, due to the legal restrictions and political difficulties with which the Transport Commission was confronted, it was not until 1957 that it was able to start relating its prices more closely to its costs. There is no need to go into detail, but briefly what happened was that the Commission had under the Transport Act, 1947, to submit a Charges Scheme to the Transport Tribunal which had final jurisdiction. In theory the Commission was given almost a free hand in the framing of its charges, provided of course that it could satisfy the Tribunal. However this was a vital qualification because the Tribunal and the Government, reflecting the views of rail users, proved almost unbelievably obscurantist. This was shown by the cavalier fashion in which they dealt with the Commission's proposals for relating passenger fares more closely to costs. The Commission, therefore, had no option but to adopt a cautious approach and to try to gain the approval of traders before submitting its new scheme for freight charges to the Tribunal. The preparation of the draft scheme and the negotiations with coastal shipping interests and the body which represented traders were inevitably time consuming and it was not until the end of 1951 that the Commission was ready to lay its proposals before the Tribunal.[59]

By this time a new Government was in office with a declared policy of introducing fresh legislation. It was therefore impossible for the Commission to submit its scheme and it was not until the Transport Act, 1953, was on the statute book that further action became possible. Since this provided for the denationalization of road haulage the Commission was freed from its duty of pursuing integration, and its obligation to provide an adequate system of public transport was also dropped, except for London passenger services. Where charges were concerned, a number of Victorian provisions which had made it difficult, though not impossible, for the railways to relate their prices to their costs were abolished; the publication of special rates agreed with traders was discontinued; and henceforth the Commission was only required to submit a scheme of maximum charges to the Transport Tribunal. This it did in the spring of 1955 but it was not until July 1957, after protracted hearings, that a modified version of the Commission's proposals finally came into effect. Because the maximum prices were based upon what it cost the railways to carry different types of traffic under adverse though not extreme conditions, British Rail was at long last relatively free to begin lowering its rates to attract traffic which it could carry cheaply and to raise its rates on high cost and low productivity traffic.[60]

Political Disturbance

The final obstacle to reorganization and rationalization which the railways faced was the disrupting effect of the Transport Act, 1953, and the decentralization to which it led. The decentralization of British Rail and the adverse effect which it had upon its management is a large subject which will be discussed later when we come to examine the reasons for the railways' financial collapse.[61] However what must be mentioned here is the way in which, during the early fifties, the new Transport Bill both deprived the railways of leadership and diverted attention from the urgent problem of how they could be modernized. The Railway Executive was condemned to death by the White Paper of May 1952 which foreshadowed the Bill. The prospect of extinction may, as Dr Johnson remarked, settle the mind wonderfully but it does not encourage planning for the future. Moreover, those who sit in the condemned cell are in no position to issue commands. Although the life of the Executive lingered on until October 1953, it had long before this lost its authority and power of initiative. In other circumstances this might have passed to the Commission but its Chairman, Lord Hurcomb, had come to the end of his term of office in August 1952 but was reappointed for a further year as a caretaker. His effective term of office, he writes, only lasted three years because 'the change of Government in 1951 meant two years of uncertainty amounting to inability to act'.[62] Moreover, the Commission's tiny staff was inevitably preoccupied by the immense administrative changes which were in progress. For instance, as the Commission explained, the pressure of work was such that even the BTC Annual Report appeared months late. It was not until the end of 1953, when the Commission's new Chairman, Sir Brian Robertson, was at last firmly in the saddle that planning and decision-taking could begin.[63] Even then time and energy which should have been devoted to the modernization and rationalization of the railway system were absorbed by the task of decentralizing its administrative structure because on this the Government of the day had set its heart.

Our survey of British Rail's productivity during the first decade of nationalization has of necessity been both wide-ranging and long. The conclusion to be drawn is that output per man rose so little partly because of the restrictions which the Government imposed on rail investment, and partly because of the formidable obstacles which stood in the way of raising productivity by means of rationalization and the adoption of improved operating methods. Although this would have been possible technically, and would not have required large-scale capital expenditure, progress was impeded by the Commission's ignorance – until the Costing Service had been built up – of the structure of its costs; by the Commission's duty to provide a comprehensive and integrated system of public transport; by the Transport Tribunal's control over rail charges which prevented pricing policy being used either to attract low-cost and high-productivity traffic or to discourage traffic which the railways were unfitted to carry; and by the hiatus and upheaval caused by the Transport Act of 1953.

CHAPTER 4

1958-68: The Productivity Decade

DURING the second decade of nationalization the productivity of the public enterprise sector increased at a rapid rate. After slowing down to a crawl during the period after 1951, the rate of productivity growth accelerated dramatically in the late fifties. In 1957 output per man hour appears to have been fractionally lower than it had been in the previous year, but in 1958 productivity rose by 1·7 per cent and then during 1959 shot up by 5·3 per cent. Since that time the annual growth in the nationalized industries' productivity has not fallen below 2·5 per cent (1961) and has been as high as 10·4 per cent (1968). Over the period 1958–68 there was an average rise of 5·3 per cent or 68 per cent in all. Nor is there any indication that the rate of advance is slowing down; if anything the reverse appears to be true. Between 1958 and 1963 productivity increased by 4·6 per cent per annum whereas between 1963 and 1968 there was an average increase of 6·1 per cent. Moreover, as we shall see, there are strong grounds for believing that output per man hour will continue to grow rapidly within the public enterprise sector.

When the nationalized industries are considered one by one, it becomes apparent that once again BEA and BOAC secured by far the largest increase. This is clear from Table 4, where the productivity indices are given, and from Table 7, where rates of increase are presented. Between 1958 and 1968 the air corporations' output per man hour increased by 135 per cent as against 68 per cent for the public enterprise sector as a whole. The performances of electricity and gas were also above average. Over the period their output per man hour rose by 115 per cent and 71 per cent respectively. BRS obtained a productivity increase of 62 per cent, though at the beginning of the period it was probably slightly lower than it had been before its operations were disrupted by denationalization.[1] Next came coal with a gain of 57 per cent and railways with an increase of 52 per cent. This means that their productivity increased by significantly less than that of the sector as a whole, although as we shall see their performance compared favourably with that of private industry.[2]

It should, however, be remembered that at the start of the period the coal industry's productivity was scarcely higher than it had been in the early fifties and that in railways it was considerably below its former peak level, having slumped disastrously during 1958. This was due to the sharp reduction in traffic and the sensitivity of rail productivity to changes in output. As traffic never recovered to its old level, but on the contrary went on declining, 1958 appears to be a better base line than 1957 or any previous year. By taking the period since 1958 we are able to see what progress the railways have been able to make when traffic has been falling rapidly but not so fast that they have had no chance to improve their productivity. Unlike the railways and coal, the performance of the nationalized buses was no better during the second decade of public ownership than it was during the first. Their productivity has continued to decline and by 1968 was 13 per cent lower than it had been in 1958.

The rise in the productivity of the public enterprise sector has taken the form of a relatively small increase in output combined with a large reduction in employment. Between 1958 and 1968, as can be seen from Table 5, its total labour force declined from about 1,920,000 to about 1,310,000, a reduction of about a third, whereas its production increased by only a fifth. As a result of the fall in employment the sector's share of all civil employment declined from 8·3 per cent in 1958 to only 5·4 per cent in 1968.[3] As might be expected, the coal industry and the railways lost the largest number of workers. In mining the labour force was cut from about 760,000 in 1958 to less than 390,000 in 1968, a reduction of almost 50 per cent, and the railways' work force was slashed from about 590,000 to about 330,000, a reduction of 46 per cent. Employment also fell on the nationalized buses and in gas, though by much smaller amounts, while in BRS it was no higher at the end of the period than it had been at the beginning. The only nationalized industries whose work force increased were electricity and the air corporations. The rise in electricity employment, however, was accompanied by a sharp reduction in average weekly hours so that in terms of man hours the industry's use of labour was slightly lower in 1968 than it had been in 1958.

The nationalized industries' productivity performance can be considered from a number of angles. The industries could, for example, be examined one by one to discover exactly how their gains have been secured. However, as a preliminary draft of this chapter showed, this is a boring and not particularly informative approach. It has, therefore, been decided to ask, and try to answer, a series of probing questions about their performance. First, we shall try to find out whether the sector's productivity is likely to go on rising at a rapid rate. Will their apparent success during the past decade turn out to be a flash in the pan? Second, there is the question of how much the increase in output per worker owes to the elimination of activities where productivity is below average. It is often argued that the gains which the NCB and BR appear to have made have been due to the simple process of closing pits and lines where output per man was lowest. Third, we shall want to know if the rise in productivity has been the automatic consequence of a few major technical developments. If it has, their gains are less surprising and less praiseworthy than they seem. This will be all the more true if the nationalized industries have not yet adopted up-to-date machinery and techniques which are in use abroad. On the other hand, it is possible that there have been innovators and the industries have rapidly adopted new processes and equipment which have become available. The fourth question which must, therefore, be asked is whether the nationalized industries have had a good record in the field of technical progress. Fifth, we shall in the following chapter try to discover how widely the available managerial techniques for increasing productivity have been used within the public enterprise sector. Have the nationalized industries, for instance, negotiated productivity agreements or introduced work study? Other questions, such as the extent to which the nationalized industries gains have been due to exceptionally heavy investment and the way in which they compare with those of other industries, readily spring to mind. These have not been ignored but will be considered in later chapters.

Will Productivity go on Rising Fast?

The question of whether the sector's productivity will go on rising fast can be quickly disposed of. It is highly probable that the rate of advance will be just as rapid during coming years as it has been in the past. Indeed it may well accelerate during the immediate future as a result of the exceptionally large productivity gains which are being secured in the gas industry. The Gas Council estimates that over the next few years net output per worker will increase by about 15 per cent per annum.[4] This is the result of North Sea gas but even in the rest of the public enterprise sector, which has not been blessed by progress to a similar degree, a rapid rate of productivity growth is likely. For instance, in electricity there is no reason to suppose that the growth in output per man hour will slow up. By the mid-seventies giant sets of 500 and 600 MW will account for nearly two-fifths of the CEGB's capacity compared with only a small part of the total in 1968.[5] Because this new capacity is very economical in the use of manpower there is likely to be a sharp rise in productivity on the generating side. When it becomes available, the Board will be able to close down some of its old and inefficient stations which, due to commissioning delays, have had to remain in operation. So far as the distribution of electricity is concerned, the scope which is known to exist for a more efficient use of labour, and the determined way in which this problem is now being tackled through the use of work study, almost guarantee that large gains in productivity will be secured.[6] It also seems likely that the coal industry's productivity will go on rising at a rapid rate. The Coal Board's estimates suggest that its OMS will increase by about 8½ per cent per annum between 1968–9 and 1975–6. This is almost certainly wishful thinking, but it does seem likely that productivity will go on rising at a rapid rate.

Turning to the nationalized transport industries, it appears from the air corporations' forecasts of traffic and staff that between 1958 and 1975 their productivity, as measured by passenger miles per worker, will increase by about 11 per cent per annum.[7] The railways will find it less easy to reduce their work force in the future than they have in the past, when there was ample scope for rationalization and they had the benefit of converting from steam to diesel traction. Nevertheless British Rail is well aware of the need to secure a productivity increase sufficient to off-set the rise in real wages and keep its charges competitive. The way this can be done is one of the main features of its new *Corporate Plan*. It seems likely that the railways will be assisted in their endeavours by a stabilization or even a slight increase in their traffic. Ministry of Transport estimates show an increase of 12 per cent in the ton mileage of freight traffic between 1958 and 1975. This was based upon the assumption that quantity licensing would be put into effect, but, even in its absence, it seems unlikely that there will be any substantial decline in the volume of freight traffic. This is because the reduction in coal and steel traffic which is in prospect will probably be offset by the increase in oil traffic and freightliner carryings. Between 1968 and 1975 the ton mileage of fuel and steel will, according to the Ministry's figures, decline by about 2½ billion ton miles, but freightliner traffic will increase from 0·6 to something like three billion ton miles. As for the railways' passenger traffic it seems unlikely that there will, in the face of improving standards and skilful promotion, be any marked decline.[8] Indeed there may well be some increase in the volume of passenger traffic. It seems probable, therefore, that rail productivity will go on rising at a rapid rate because, although savings in manpower will be less easy to secure than they have been in the past, the railways will no longer be working under the handicap of falling traffic and may even have the advantage of a slight increase. Even the nationalized buses, which in the field of productivity have been the black sheep of the public enterprise sector, are planning to make significant gains during the years to come. As we shall see,

London Transport is hoping that on its passenger side it will be able to reduce its labour force by about a quarter by 1975 largely due to the extension of one-man operation.[9]

Pit and Rail Closures and Productivity

It is sometimes suggested that in coal and railways at least there is a special explanation for the considerable growth in productivity. It is said that the rise which the NCB and British Rail have secured is less impressive than it appears because it has been largely due to the simple process of closing pits and branch lines where productivity is exceptionally low and heavy losses are being incurred. This type of argument has been used by the Prices and Incomes Board.[10] Both in coal and railways, however, closures explain a surprisingly small proportion of the rise in output per man. Between 1963 and 1967–8 OMS at the NCB's collieries rose by 3·8 per cent per annum and at those pits which remained open at the end of the period it increased by 2·8 per cent per year. This shows that during recent years only a quarter of the rise in the industry's productivity has been due to closures. Moreover, over the last decade the contribution made by closures has probably been less important than this suggests. In 1960, for instance, they accounted for only 12 per cent of the increase in OMS. It seems probable, therefore, that during the last decade the closure of unprofitable pits has only accounted for about 15–20 per cent of the rise in the coal industry's productivity.[11]

On the railways the contribution made by the closure of branch lines and the cutback in stopping services has been somewhat greater. It was stated in the Beeching Report that the number of staff who would be directly affected by the withdrawal of stopping services would be only about 16,200, though the subsequent closure of lines would add at least another 10,900. Even if a generous allowance is made for the indirect savings in manpower it appears from these figures that closures have only accounted for a small part of the reduction of 260,000 in British Rail's labour force which took place between 1958 and 1968.[12] However, as the impact of closures on employment seems surprisingly small, and as Dr Beeching was popularly supposed to have done his best to conceal the darker side of his plans, let us make a separate estimate.

It was estimated in the Reshaping Report that £33 million of expenses would be saved each year by the withdrawal of stopping services, although this excluded the cost of track and signalling and the saving in general administrative overheads which it was hoped eventually to secure. However, some of the services which it had been planned to withdraw are still in operation and it appears from the losses they incurred that there has been a direct saving of only about £25 million per annum. To this must be added an estimate of the saving which British Rail has achieved on track and signalling. If it is assumed that British Rail closed down that part of its route which was the least expensive to maintain it can be calculated from figures given in the Beeching Report and from the mileage of single track, double track and other route which disappeared between the beginning of 1963 and the end of 1968 that the railways saved about £19 million. These savings represented about 9 per cent of British Rail's total direct expenses and track costs. However, the withdrawal of these stopping services has probably involved a loss in revenue of about £11 million or just over 2 per cent of the total.[13] If it is assumed that British Rail secured the same saving in its employment as in its expenses this means that the withdrawal of stopping services and the closure of lines has increased productivity by about 7 per cent over the period 1962–8. This is obviously only a back-of-an-envelope calculation which could be either too high or too low. On the one hand the railways may not have been able to make the saving in administrative costs for which they were hoping and for which allowance has implicitly been made; on the other hand the reduction in costs (and revenue) from the withdrawal of freight services has been ignored. On balance it seems probable that closures may have made a somewhat greater contribution to productivity than our estimate suggests but it is doubtful whether over the period 1962–8 they have produced a rise of more than $1\frac{1}{2}$ per cent per year. As British Rail's productivity has increased by about $6\frac{1}{2}$ per cent per annum during this period, closures and the withdrawal of services appear to explain no more than a quarter of the railways' productivity rise.

Although closures seem to have made a more important contribution in railways than in coal they certainly do not account for the great bulk of the productivity gains which the railways have secured. Moreover, it would be quite wrong to assume that the progress which the NCB and British Rail have been able to make through closures has been easily won. The rundown of the coal industry has, in particular, been an extremely difficult undertaking. Not only has it required a great deal of careful planning but the Board has had the almost impossible task of steering the industry between the iceberg of insolvency and the submerged rock of labour unrest. If it moved too slowly with the closure of unprofitable pits there was the certain prospect of financial collapse. If it proceeded too fast the miners might become completely demoralized and decide to go slow, to abandon the sinking ship, or to mutiny. In this case also the industry would go bankrupt because its costs would get out of hand.[14]

Automatic Progress?

The next question which must be asked about the nationalized industries' productivity performance is whether the fast rate of progress has been due to a few major technical developments. Now it is clear that in most of the nationalized industries there have been major improvements in the type of equipment in use which have either directly or indirectly made an important contribution to productivity. The outstanding instance is perhaps the airways, where the dramatic increase in the size and speed of aircraft explains why their growth in productivity has been so enormous. Over the period 1958–68 the number of capacity ton miles (CTM) which their aircraft produced each hour they were in flight increased by 267 per cent, and the productivity of the corporations' flying staff, in terms of capacity ton miles, has increased by a similar amount. However, flying staff account for a surprisingly small proportion of the airways' employment and the indirect effect of the increase in the capacity and speed of airliners has been more important than its direct contribution. A large fast airliner does not require proportionately more maintenance than a small slow one. The increase in the size and speed of planes has therefore boosted the productivity of the air corporations' engineering and maintenance staff. If their output is measured by CTMs their productivity shot up by something between 3 and $3\frac{1}{2}$ times between 1958 and 1968. This was an extremely important gain because the engineering and maintenance departments account for such a high proportion of employment.[15]

In contrast to air transport, railways are often regarded as a technologically stagnant industry, yet it is evident that the replacement of steam by modern forms of traction has resulted in major savings in manpower. In comparison with diesel and electric locomotives steam engines were highly labour intensive. They required not only firemen but also a large body of workers behind the scenes to light their fires and prepare them for work. In March 1958, if attention is confined to adult male employees, British Rail employed nearly 39,000 firemen and supporting workers, which represented about 8 per cent of its total labour force.[16] Besides those who were engaged in the day-to-day running and servicing of steam engines, a large number were employed on their repair and maintenance at the railway workshops. An important characteristic of diesel and electric locomotives is that they require considerably less maintenance per mile.[17]

Similarly in the fuel and power industries there have been major technological changes which have helped to increase their productivity.

In electricity there has been a remarkable increase in the size of generating sets. During 1958 the CEGB commissioned its first set with a capacity of over 100 MW and even this was only 120 MW, but by March 1969 sets of between 120 MW and 500 MW accounted for about a quarter of its capacity, and sets of 500 MW and over represented a further 17 per cent.[18] Because a large set does not require proportionately more attention than a small set this has led to a far more economical use of labour. In fact the amount of capacity per worker is about $3\frac{1}{3}$ times greater at generating stations where 500 MW sets have been installed than it is at those with 60 MW sets. This obviously helps to explain the rise of approximately 75 per cent in the productivity of the CEGB's power station workers over the period 1958–68 as measured by electricity sent out per man hour.[19]

Again in the coal industry new machines, and in particular power-loaders and self-advancing pit props, have boosted productivity. Some idea of the contribution which power-loading has made can be gained from the fact that in the early sixties OMS underground was about 70 per cent higher at pits with fully mechanized faces than at other pits. This, however, gives a rather exaggerated impression of its importance, partly because power-loading was introduced first at the pits where productivity was already high, and partly because it smashes up the coal and reduces its value. Nevertheless the increase in the proportion of output which was power-loaded from 28 per cent in 1958 to 90 per cent in March 1968 obviously explains a considerable part of the rise in the industry's productivity.[20] More recently the introduction of self-advancing pit props has been making a substantial contribution to the rise of productivity. According to Lord Robens the OMS on faces with Anderton Shearers which are equipped with power supports is on average 50 per cent greater than on those with ordinary supports.[21] This explains why the NCB has been pushing ahead so rapidly with the introduction of power supports. In mid-1962 only 184 faces had self-advancing pit props but by March 1968 the number of major faces so equipped had risen to 732, and faces with power supports accounted for 71·2 per cent of all output from faces where power-loading was in use.[22]

Although it is not difficult to point to major technical developments which have had an important impact on productivity, the more the performance of the nationalized industries is studied, the more evident it becomes that productivity gains have been made over a broad front. This is true even of the airways, where the dramatic increase in the size and speed of planes has made a striking contribution to productivity. Although, for instance, the rise in the productivity of engineering and maintenance workers, in terms of CTMs, has been largely due to the introduction of more advanced planes, that has not been the only force at work. There has also been a substantial rise in terms of aircraft miles, which probably gives a better indication of the maintenance work load. Between 1958 and 1968 the number of aircraft miles per maintenance worker grew by about 50 per cent. There has also been a substantial increase in the productivity of ticketing and sales staff in terms of the number of passengers carried, which gives a better indication of their work load than CTMs. Measured in this way BEA's output per worker rose by 65 per cent largely due to the mechanization, and now the computerization, of seat reservation.[23]

The story is the same on the railways where, although dieselization and electrification have certainly helped to improve productivity, savings in manpower have been made in almost every direction. Except for the London underground and for white collar workers there have been large reductions in all categories of employment. For instance the number of workers employed on track maintenance, on signalling, at passenger stations or on terminal operations for freight, such as road collection and delivery, fell between the beginning of 1958 and the beginning of 1968 from almost 200,000 to only about 105,000.[24] This clearly had nothing to do with the introduction of new forms of motive power. It was due partly to other less important forms of modernization and technical progress such as the mechanization of track maintenance and the spread of power signalling, which has enabled many of the old manually-operated signal boxes to be closed. It was due partly to rationalization of the railway system which involved, for example, the closure of 30 per cent of the route and 55 per cent of all stations. And finally it was due partly to the pruning of staff which the use of work study has facilitated.[25] An examination of the other nationalized industries which have made large productivity gains would show that they also have made progress over a broad front.

Technical Progress: Coal and Gas

Even if it had been shown that productivity gains within the public enterprise sector have been the consequence of a few major developments, it would not necessarily follow that its performance is less creditable than it appears. This depends on whether the industries have themselves played a significant role in innovation and have rapidly adopted the techniques which others have pioneered. As Britain is only a small part of the world economy it is clearly unreasonable to expect that our industries, whether publicly or privately owned, should be the only or even the major source of innovation. However, there is no reason why they should not quickly utilize new practices and new machinery which have been developed abroad. The nationalized industries must be awarded high marks if they have quickly adopted or adapted innovations pioneered abroad, whereas their productivity gains will seem far less impressive if they have taken years to copy the best foreign practice.

It is evident that some of the nationalized industries have played a major part in the development of the new machines and techniques which have transformed their operations. For instance, in coal, the NCB and its officials made an important contribution to the development of power-loading. The early work on this was undertaken in the United States, where already by the time of the second world war a substantial proportion of output was being loaded by mechanical means. Unlike the machines which are now in use, the early American equipment did not simultaneously cut the coal and load it on to a conveyor but only picked up coal which had already been cut. Moreover it could only be operated under extremely favourable geological conditions where what is known as the room and pillar system of mining was in use, and for this reason the attempt by the British Government during the war to introduce American machines and boost coal production was an almost total failure. These experiments did, however, stimulate interest in power-loading and in the later stages of the war the Meco-Moore cutter loader was developed on the Government's initiative. Although this was important because it was the first real step towards the introduction of power-loading in this country the machine could only be used where mining conditions were very good. A further difficulty both in the use of the Meco-Moore and the development of improved machines was the fact that the existing coal conveyors were rigid and hence difficult to move forward as the face advanced. This problem was overcome with the development by the Germans of a flexible conveyor, the Panzer Forderer, which could be snaked forward. It was by mounting an adapted version of the standard coal cutter on a flexible conveyor that Mr Anderton constructed his revolutionary power-loader in 1952.[26] This was the machine which, as we have seen, was the basis for the general introduction of power-loading in this country.[27]

It can be seen that, like many other innovations, power-loading had a complicated history and a large amount of work on its development had already been undertaken before Mr Anderton and the Coal Board arrived on the scene. Successful power-loading machines were developed at about the same time on the continent; these were coal ploughs which were better suited to continental mining conditions due to the softness of their coal. Nevertheless Mr Anderton and the NCB deserve considerable credit for developing the first really satisfactory power-loader for use in Britain. The Board also deserves praise for having pushed forward from 1955 onwards so rapidly with the introduction of power-loading. The proportion of output which was power-loaded shot up from 11 per cent in 1955, when the power-loading drive was launched, to 28 per cent in 1958 and over 90 per cent in 1968. By any standard this must count as rapid progress and power-loading has, if anything, been introduced faster in Britain than in the European Coal and Steel Community. Up to 1961 the proportion of output obtained in this way was very similar in Britain and the continent, but since then we have steadily drawn ahead. By 1966, for instance, 84 per cent of our coal output was power-loaded compared with only about 71 per cent in the Coal and Steel Community, though the continental figure would be slightly higher but for coal fields like South Belgium where mining conditions are very difficult.[28]

The process of speeding up the rate at which the coal face advances created the need for a system of roof support which could be set and withdrawn more rapidly. This had already been recognized before nationalization and new types of prop which could quickly be released and reset because they were telescopic had been invented. Even when these props had been fully developed, which took several years, it was difficult to advance the support system as fast as the face. The Coal Board therefore developed, in co-operation with the mining machinery industry, roof support equipment which was able to follow under its own power. Although it took a decade to perfect this system so that it could be introduced on a large scale the Coal Board nevertheless stole a march on the continental coal producers. This was largely because the latter concentrated on what are known as friction props which have to be set by hand while the Board preferred hydraulic props. Because these were already semi-automatic the British coal industry was able to move forward to power supports.[29] Not only can it take the credit for this innovation but it has also introduced self-advancing pit props more rapidly than the continental producers. By the spring of 1968 64 per cent of the Coal Board's output was produced at faces equipped with power supports. In Holland during 1968 only 21 per cent of output was produced with the assistance of power supports, in Germany the proportion was even lower at 18 per cent, in France it was only 14 per cent as late as May 1969, while in Belgium very little use had been made of this form of mechanization.[30]

In gas, as in coal, the British industry has made a substantial contribution to the developments which have been taking place. This is true both of the importation of liquefied natural gas and of the revolutionary new processes for making gas from light oil. The pioneering work on the transportation of liquefied natural gas was undertaken in the United States where by 1953 sufficient progress had been made for it to be proposed that liquefied gas should be shipped in a specially constructed vessel from the Gulf of Mexico to Chicago. This scheme languished for lack of support but attracted the attention of the British gas industry which, after investigating the situation, arranged in 1957 for the trial importation of liquefied natural gas into this country. A ship was converted for this purpose and during 1959 and early 1960 a number of cargoes of liquefied gas were delivered successfully. This led to the full-scale importation of natural gas into Britain from Algeria and its distribution through the natural methane grid.[31] Although the spadework on the transportation of natural gas was carried out in America the British gas industry can be seen to have assisted in its development by grasping its commercial possibilities and providing the necessary support.

Before the first consignment of gas had arrived from Algeria the industry's prospects had been transformed by the advent of new processes for producing gas at a very low cost from light distillate which is a refinery by-product. This innovation had been preceded by a considerable amount of work on the manufacture of gas from petroleum products. First processes were developed in France (Onia-Gegi) and by the South Eastern Gas Board (Segas) for making gas from a wide range of feed stocks. They both had the disadvantage that the cost of production was high, that the production of gas was not continuous and that the gas came off at a low pressure, which meant that it could not be distributed over any distance without pumping. Later Shell developed a process which produced gas continuously at a high pressure and at a slightly lower cost.[32] But it was not until 1962 when ICI announced its process for making gas from light oil that a method for producing cheap oil-gas became available; not only were capital and running costs low but the gas also came off at a high pressure. For this important development the gas industry can obviously take no credit. What it did contribute at about the same time were two methods for producing a high quality gas which could be used to enrich the lean gas made by the ICI process. These were the gas recycle hydrogenator and the catalytic rich gas process. The latter could also be used or adapted to produce gas of the normal quality, and another method of making gas from light distillate was developed by Haldor Topsoe in Denmark. Thus what happened, in fact, was that a number of different techniques were discovered more or less simultaneously for doing the same thing.[33] The British gas industry cannot claim any exclusive title to the development of the new processes for making cheap gas from light distillate, but it played a creditable part.

Once they had been developed, the Gas Boards made swift progress in introducing the new types of plant. In 1968–9 73 per cent of the gas which the industry produced was made from oil compared with only 6 per cent in 1962–3.[34] The figure would by now have been considerably higher but for the discovery of North Sea gas.

Technical Progress: Railways

For a long period after nationalization the railways' record for technical progress was distinctly poor. As we have seen, it was not until 1955 when the Modernization Plan was published, that British Rail started to make up for lost time and to introduce equipment which had already been adopted on a large scale abroad. Only then did the BTC embark on a large programme of dieselization and electrification, decide to install power brakes on its wagons, and take the first step towards the introduction of long welded rails. Moreover, the modernization plan suffered from the serious weakness that it did not propose the new operating methods which were called for, although the need for them was dimly perceived.[35] The movement of freight continued to be based on the marshalling and remarshalling of wagons and it was not until the early sixties that a drive to shift goods in full train loads was launched. Again it was not until this period that plans were made for the transport of coal by merry-go-round trains and for the introduction of liner trains for general merchandise.

It seems possible from these developments that British Rail has by now managed to make up for lost time. To discover whether BR has caught up or perhaps overtaken the continental railways, let us examine the relative progress which has been made in the provision and maintenance of the track, the extent to which rolling stock has been modernized, and the degree to which new operating methods have been introduced. As British Rail started laying long welded rails so long after the continental railways it is hardly surprising to discover that the latter still enjoy a considerable lead. At the beginning of 1968, the great bulk of the German running track was equipped with long welded rails; in Switzerland the figure was 27 per cent (in 1965), in France it was 20 per cent, but in Britain the proportion was only 12½ per cent.[36] However, after its late start British Rail is now making rapid progress, and now appears to be laying a greater mileage of long welded rail each year than the French railways. The revolutionary new machines for maintaining the track which have been devised in recent years have been introduced by British Rail, and there is no reason to believe that in this field we are behind the continental countries. Indeed BR claims that it is further ahead than any other railway in the world.[37]

Despite the comparatively late stage at which the replacement of steam engines by modern methods of traction was decided upon, steam has been eliminated more quickly in Britain than in many other countries. In 1967 steam engines accounted for 17 per cent of total train mileage in Germany, for 9 per cent in France, but for only 4 per cent in Britain, where steam traction was eliminated during 1968.[38] It is true that here steam engines have largely been replaced by diesels, whereas on the continent electrification has played a far more important part. However, both the financial estimates for the London-Midland electrification scheme and the disruption and loss of traffic which it caused suggest that British Rail was right to concentrate on dieselization.[39]

The progress which has been made towards the modernization of the wagon fleet has been less impressive. In 1956 the BTC announced that it was planning to complete the fitting of power brakes by the end of 1966, but in 1958 the conversion of mineral wagons was more or less halted because of the technical difficulties which were encountered. The railways found that as originally designed the brake gear collided with some of the devices for tipping mineral wagons which were in use. Worse than this, the continental coupling which had been adopted for use with power brakes involved the laborious and time-consuming work of screwing and unscrewing the device; there was opposition both from the railways' customers and their own staff, and it was found that, even where they were used, power brakes did not save any time – the higher speeds and shorter transit times were offset by the extra time needed for marshalling and terminal operations. The technical answer to this problem was the adoption of automatic couplings, which took place in 1961, but due to their expense it was decided that it was not worth fitting them to many of the railways' obsolescent mineral wagons. As a result, although unbraked merchandise wagons had either been converted or scrapped by about 1963, a large part of the fleet of mineral wagons has not yet been fitted with power brakes. So far only about 28,000 or 12 per cent of all mineral wagons have been fitted and it is not expected that loose-coupled wagons will be eliminated for at least another decade. Nevertheless the proportion of freight train mileage which is worked by trains which are fully or partially fitted with power brakes has been steadily increasing and by the end of 1968 totalled 81½ per cent. Ten years earlier the figure had been only 35 per cent.[40]

Again little progress has been made towards remedying the other principal historic weakness of British wagons: their diminutive size. Between the end of 1958 and the end of 1968 the average carrying capacity of BR wagons only increased from 14·9 tons to 17·1. In contrast the average continental wagon had a capacity of 25·3 tons at the beginning of the year.[41] The low capacity of its wagons is one of the longstanding weaknesses of the British railway system which has been recognized for almost half a century but has never been put right.

The Samuel Commission on the Coal Industry urged as long ago as 1926 that the 20-ton wagon, on which the continental countries had already standardized, should be brought into general use for mineral traffic. Despite further inquiries virtually nothing was done and in 1948, when the railways were brought into public ownership, the average mineral wagon had a capacity of only $12\frac{1}{2}$ tons. The Railway Executive could have built 20-ton wagons, for much of the equipment for loading and tipping was able to accommodate wagons of this size. However, it was found that, although the cost of providing capacity tends to decline as the size of the wagon increases, a 16-ton wagon was more economic than one of between 16 and 22 tons. It was therefore decided to construct 16-ton wagons because, although the Executive would have liked to standardize on $24\frac{1}{2}$ tons, which they believed to be the optimum size, wagons of this size could only be handled at a few collieries. Although at a comparatively early date the Coal Board decided that all the collieries sunk and re-constructed henceforth should be able to accommodate $24\frac{1}{2}$-ton wagons, progress was very slow due to the time it took to complete any significant part of the Board's modernization programme.[42] When in the mid-fifties the Transport Commission started building $24\frac{1}{2}$-ton wagons, it found that they could only be handled at a limited number of pits.

Perhaps, despite the heavy cost, it would have been worth launching a crash programme to modernize the coal industry's coal-handling facilities and probably British Rail should from the beginning have built the 21–22 tonners adopted when it was found that wagons of $24\frac{1}{2}$ tons could only be used on a restricted scale. Nevertheless it is important to recognize that history had erected formidable obstacles to progress that could only be slowly or expensively removed. Unfortunately by the time they had been more or less overcome, the railways found that, due to the reduction in coal traffic and the tightening up of wagon control, they had a surplus of wagons and that it was unnecessary to build many new ones.[43] But for this, there would have been a substantial increase in the average size of mineral wagons because of the Modernization Plan's programme of new construction. But it was a weakness of the plan that it did not recognize the scope for the construction of larger wagons for general merchandise. This was because it was framed on the assumption that the traditional pattern of operations would persist and that the railways would go on moving freight in small wagon loads. Now that the emphasis has shifted to train load traffic, the railways have started to build very much larger wagons. For instance, freightliner flats are able to carry 51 tons, and wagons able to carry up to 60 tons of steel coil are being designed. On the mineral side 32-ton coal wagons are being built for the new merry-go-round services. Mention should also be made of the enormous tank wagons which the oil companies have built, some capable of carrying up to 100 tons.[44] There is no doubt, therefore, that the railways are alive to the importance of developing high-capacity wagons and it seems likely that there will be a swift increase in the average size once wagon building starts again in earnest. British Rail has already applied to the Government for permission to launch a wagon-building programme but so far the necessary expenditure has not been sanctioned.

Considerable progress towards the adoption of new operating methods for moving freight in train loads rather than wagon loads has been made during recent years. In 1967 43 per cent of all freight tonnage was shifted in train loads and in 1968 the proportion must have been significantly higher due to the build-up of the freightliner system. Although British Rail was slow to grasp the importance of eliminating marshalling and introducing through-train working, it appears to have made at least as much progress as the continental systems. In Germany, for instance, block trains account for 50 to 55 per cent of all goods train mileage, but in Holland they only carry about 25 per cent of the freight traffic.[45] The rise in the proportion of British Rail's freight traffic moved in train loads has not been due to an increase for coal, where the percentage was already substantial, but in other types of traffic. Here the proportion of the tonnage carried by block trains increased from 33 per cent in 1961 to 47 per cent in 1967, whereas in coal it remained about 40 per cent. The increase in the percentage of other freight moved in train loads has been partly due to the efforts British Rail has been making to attract suitable traffic – hence the increase in its carryings of oil, cement and cars – and partly to the reorganization of existing traffic, such as steel, which used to move in wagon loads, into train loads.[46] The scope for carving out further block trains must be more or less exhausted by now and the future increase in through-train working will have to come largely through British Rail's own contribution to modern railway working: the freightliner.

It was not until the second half of the fifties that the BR started to devote serious attention to the possibility of introducing through trains carrying containers or road trailers.[47] This of course was no new idea. The first piggy-back trains for road trailers were introduced in the United States before the war but piggy-backing did not catch on until the period 1955–60, and there were two formidable obstacles to introducing it in Britain. First the British loading gauge is too restricted to permit ordinary road trailers to be carried on flat wagons and, second, piggy-back operations are only economic where the rail haul is 150 miles or over. This is because it involves the use of two expensive pieces of equipment, a railway wagon and a road trailer. Moreover the tare weight is high in relation to payload. These disadvantages might have been at least partly overcome by use of the Chesapeake and Ohio Railways' ingenious dual-purpose trailer which, due to its retractable wheels, can be run both on road and rail. However, British Rail ultimately rejected this and decided to opt for its freightliner system of containers and flat wagons. There was nothing original about containers as such, but what did represent an innovation was the combination of through-working, large containers and the fact that these could be transferred efficiently and smoothly to ordinary lorries. The last feature, for instance, distinguished the freightliner concept from some American systems such as Flexi vans which require special road vehicles.[48]

British Rail's first step towards the development of the freightliner was the introduction in 1959 of a fast but otherwise conventional container service between London and Glasgow. Condor, as this service was called, was followed in 1963 by Speedfreight. This ran between London and Manchester and represented an advance because of the use of large but lightweight containers and the introduction of wagons capable of higher speeds. Finally in November 1965 the first freightliner service was introduced between London and Glasgow, a year later than originally intended. This delay is usually blamed on the National Union of Railwaymen who were opposed to the delivery and collection of freightliner containers by private hauliers. But the delay was, in fact, due to teething troubles with the new equipment which had to be modified and although the dispute over open terminals dragged on until early 1967 there is no reason to believe that it significantly delayed the development of the freightliner system. By the end of 1968 the network included 45 routes and traffic, as measured by ton miles, had built up to about 10 per cent of all freight traffic apart from coal.[49]

Although British Rail was slow to develop fast and efficient through services it was ahead of the continental countries. In France and Germany, where the loading gauge is less restricted than in Britain, a limited amount of progress was made with piggy-backing but it is only comparatively recently that they have started to build up freightliner networks. Indeed as late as 1968 the German Federal Railway had not even investigated the potential market for a freightliner service in detail, although they were having liner trains forced upon them for port traffic.[50]

Freightliners have already made a limited contribution to the rise in British Rail's productivity but their full impact will not be felt for a number of years. The same is true of merry-go-round working which is the other up-to-date operating method which is now being introduced. During 1968 only about 7 per cent of coal traffic was being transported by this method, but by 1975 the proportion will have increased to around half. Although the introduction of circuit working for the delivery of coal to power stations seems an obvious step which should have been taken long ago, British Rail has been no more tardy in adopting this practice than the American railroads. The first British merry-go-round trains for coal were introduced in 1966 whereas in America the first shuttle trains of this type started running in about 1964. However, they were an even more obvious development in the United States than in Britain due to the enormous output of some American collieries and opencast sites.[51]

From this survey of coal, gas and railways, it is evident that the nationalized industries have made a significant contribution to technical progress. The NCB helped to develop power-loading and power supports; the gas industry sponsored the experimental trans-shipment of liquefied natural gas and played an important part in the discovery of the new processes for making gas from light distillate; and the railways have the freightliner to their credit. It is true that in no case did the British nationalized industry make the innovation single handed but this was hardly to be expected. So far as the adoption as opposed to the discovery and development of new techniques is concerned, the coal and gas industries have excellent records. Power-loading is almost universal and power supports are being introduced far more quickly in Britain than they are on the continent. In gas other countries which could benefit from the importation of liquefied natural gas are only now beginning to think about the possibility and the British industry, prior to the discovery of North Sea gas, was switching over to the new oil-based processes at an extremely rapid rate. The railways' record appears to have been less satisfactory because of the time which they took making what seem in retrospect to have been obvious steps. But in many cases foreign railways were no quicker off the mark and in most areas modern equipment and techniques are used as extensively on British Rail as they are abroad. The only important exceptions appear to be the adoption of power brakes and the introduction of large wagons. Nevertheless, as will be seen when a detailed comparison is made with the principal continental systems, BR has not yet tightened its efficiency up to that of the French and German railways.[52]

The record of the other nationalized industries which have not been considered in detail is in no way inferior to the record of those which have. We shall see, when we come to examine economics of scale, that the electricity industry, despite the criticisms made against it, has had a good record in the construction of large generating sets, which is perhaps the most important technical development of the last decade.[53] As for BEA and BOAC the Edwards Committee on Air Transport states that

> Both Corporations have admirable records as innovators, particularly in technical and operational areas. A complete list of all developments in which BEA or BOAC can claim to have been the leading airline would be extensive and we shall only mention here their outstandingly important achievements. BOAC was well ahead of the rest of the world in the operational development of jet aircraft, when it first introduced the Comet I in 1952. Its perseverance with Comet development, after the tragic failures of this aircraft, was rewarded by being, in 1958, the first airline to introduce jet aircraft on the North Atlantic route. Amongst other technical 'firsts' by BOAC, we rate highly the introduction of TRACE, an advanced method for diagnosis of faults in electronic equipment. BEA's reputation as an innovator of high standing rests partly upon being first with the introduction of turbo-prop aircraft. BEA's work in the field of automatic landing (and BOAC's as well) may well prove to be one of the really major technical advances of the 1970s. BEA has already achieved (in 1966) the distinction of being the first airline . . . to make a fully automatic landing in a dense fog.[54]

To this impressive list, marred only by the knowledge that the corporations have paid a heavy price for flying advanced (and not so advanced) British aircraft, must be added BOAC's work in the application of computers to seat reservation and other aspects of airline operations. In this field the Corporation has a lead over the rest of the world.[55]

Future Technical Progress

Not only have the nationalized industries had a good record for technical progress in the past but it seems likely that in coming years this will be maintained or perhaps even improved. So far mention has only been made of those developments which have already made some contribution to the industries' performance, although in some cases, such as the liner train, the main rewards have still to be reaped. However, it is evident that a number of innovations are in store which have so far made no contribution or virtually none. The most obvious examples are mining by remote control and the advanced passenger train. In coal the next logical step after the introduction of power-loading and power supports is full mechanization so that the team of workers at the face, who at present control and steer the equipment, can be replaced by a single worker who controls from a remote position in the roadway which serves the face. Once power-loading had been developed and the development of power supports was in an advanced stage, the NCB began during the mid-fifties to investigate mining by remote control. The most difficult problem here has been the development of some means of steering the coal cutter so as to keep it cutting coal and prevent it wandering into the roof or floor. Although this problem has not yet been completely solved, and thus is holding up the general introduction of remote control mining, a considerable amount of progress has been made and a number of steering devices have been developed and tried out in a series of experiments which began in 1960. When all the difficulties have been finally overcome, as they should be during the next two or three years, remote control mining should bring about a large improvement in productivity.[56]

The first of British Rail's advanced passenger trains are planned to be in service by about 1974. These trains, which should be able, through the use of hydraulic suspension, to give passengers a smooth ride at speeds of up to about 150 miles per hour, seem likely to have a revolutionary impact. Although some track and signalling work will be necessary before these speeds can be attained the expense will be modest while the pay-off in terms of extra traffic will be large. From experience with electrification and from detailed marketing studies it has been calculated that for every mile per hour by which average journey speeds exceed 60 miles per hour the volume of traffic increases by 1 per cent. It was the French Railways which in a series of celebrated tests in the mid-fifties showed that high-speed trains are possible, though with existing systems of suspension uncomfortable, but it is British Rail who is actually developing a high-speed train which will run smoothly over the existing route. Unlike foreign projects for hovertrains and monorail, the advanced passenger train will not require a new and expensive route system but will nevertheless achieve a decisive improvement in inter-city timings.[57]

Mention should also be made of the swift conversion to natural gas which the Gas Council and the Area Boards are planning. Conversion will take place at a faster rate than in other countries such as Holland where natural gas has been discovered.

CHAPTER 5

Productivity Bargaining
and Labour Relations

DURING recent years, as Britain's economic difficulties have become more acute, increasing attention has been paid to methods by which a more effective use of labour can be secured. The most recent innovation has been productivity bargaining but this, of course, is only the latest of a long line of managerial techniques. The traditional method has been payment by results which in one form or another has been used for centuries. Payment by results has recently been subject to considerable criticism and seldom works as well in practice as in theory it should. The negotiation of piece-work rates is frequently a time-consuming and contentious process because of the multitude of jobs to be covered and because of the disturbing impact of technical change. Moreover, the earnings of different groups of workers tend to get out of step because productivity does not increase everywhere at the same rate, and for this and other reasons there is a tendency for incentive schemes to degenerate and for management to lose control of their labour costs. Nevertheless it is clear that payment by results usually has a beneficial effect on productivity when first introduced and that some of its disadvantages can be avoided where it is possible to measure the time and effort which each job involves.

Work Study

Incentive schemes which are based on work measurement have the great advantage over ordinary piecework that money values are not negotiated with each task. What happens is that a money rate is agreed for a standard effort expended during a given time. This not only has the advantage that the amount of haggling is reduced but also that the danger of earnings getting out of step is reduced since the rate remains the same even when tasks alter. Although work measurement involves an element of judgment, it generally produces standards of acceptable consistency where it has been carefully carried out. A survey by the Prices and Incomes Board suggests that a relatively low proportion of workers in private industry are in jobs covered by work study. However, according to the Board, work study 'is often imperfectly applied. A frequent fault, for instance, is that method study, which in theory should precede all work measurement, is omitted or done only sketchily'.[1] Method study, it should be explained, is the branch of work study which seeks to develop more efficient methods of work whereas work measurement is concerned only with the assessment of the time and effort which a given method involves.

The nationalized industries have made extensive use of work study. The railways and the coal industry were the first part of the public enterprise sector where work study was applied on a large scale. The systematic use of the technique began in 1955 when the BTC with the blessings of the railway unions set up a work study training centre at Watford. By the beginning of 1966 about 76,000 staff had been covered by study schemes, over a third of those whom BR had estimated that it was profitable and practicable to cover. In addition a considerable number of clerical staff had been covered by work study or similar techniques. The field in which most advance has been made is the maintenance and renewal of track where by the end of 1962 85 per cent of all employees had been covered. However some progress has been made in every section of the railways, including latterly the workshops where the existence of a decayed piecework system and local opposition to work study had long impeded its introduction. Although British Rail have had particular difficulty with the workshops, this is by no means the only field of operations in which it has had to overcome opposition, despite the generally co-operative attitude of leading union officials. As the railways are a declining industry in which the more efficient use of labour means, at least in the short run, less work for railwaymen and an increased risk of redundancy, this is hardly surprising. There has indeed been determined opposition to work study even in industries, like engineering, which are expanding. What is remarkable about the railways is not the amount of opposition which British Rail has faced but the extent to which it has steadily been overcome. As the Select Committee reported in 1960, when the railways had made less progress than they have now, 'the Commission's efforts in introducing work study into the railways have been undertaken in the most difficult conditions and reflect credit on them'.[2]

When work study was first introduced on the railways the main emphasis was on work measurement. This is the simplest aspect of work study which inevitably tends to occupy work study staff during the early stages of its introduction before standard times have been built up.

However, in 1963, British Rail began a five-year programme to build up a bank of standard data. In this way it hoped not only to achieve greater consistency in work measurement but also to release staff for more rewarding work in the field of method study. Over the years the emphasis has, therefore, switched from work measurement to method study and indeed wide-ranging investigations of the railways' efficiency.[3] This development places British Rail ahead of a large part of private industry which is still preoccupied with work measurement.

The National Coal Board has from the beginning concentrated on method study rather than work measurement. This was partly because the coal industry's system of wage payment was by long tradition based on haggling at pit level and partly because it is almost impossible to lay down standard times due to the way in which mining conditions vary from one face to another and change as time goes by. As a result the coal industry's piece-work system was, despite the improvements which nationalization brought about, of the lowest order.[4]

It was almost impossible to abolish payment by results so long as productivity at the coal face was largely dependent on physical effort, but once power-loading had been introduced, the industry was able to switch over to time rates without this having too damaging an effect on output per manshift. This change, which is now almost complete, was accomplished as a result of the National Power-Loading Agreement of 1966. Although the elimination of piece-work led to a small, once and for all, reduction in OMS there is little doubt that the long-term effect on productivity has been highly beneficial. Labour relations have been improved as the marked reduction in strikes indicates; managers do not have to waste time negotiating and renegotiating piece-work lists and then checking week by week the amount to which workers are entitled; and colliery officials report that whereas they used to assume that increases in productivity would automatically be forthcoming due to payment by results they now work harder to create the conditions for success. Managers, they say, can no longer avoid having to manage.[5]

Although there has been little scope for work measurement in coal mining there is ample room for method study as the Coal Board long ago recognized. The Board's efforts in this field date back to 1952 when it commissioned a firm of industrial consultants to investigate the possibilities of employing method study in mining. The consultants' report was favourable and the training of method study engineers was put in hand. As the Board was starting from scratch this inevitably took time, but by the end of 1959, 370 trained engineers were at work and during that year method study teams carried out nearly 2,300 investigations, though in subsequent years the figure seems to have been rather lower presumably because the inquiries tended to be more extensive. These investigations have covered a wide field including the underground transport of coal and materials, machine utilization with a view to improving running time, and manning standards at faces covered by the Power-Loading Agreement. Colliery reconstruction projects are vetted by method study experts. Precisely what contribution this activity has made to productivity it is impossible to tell, but it seems likely that it has been significant. The Coal Board's examples of the type of savings which have been secured are impressive, even if it selected the best of the bunch.[6]

Although British Rail and the NCB are the nationalized industries which have so far made the greatest use of work study, it has been or is now being introduced in other parts of the public enterprise sector. In BOAC, for instance, a productivity deal made in 1964 has enabled it to apply work study to engineering and maintenance staff which had previously been impossible due to the lack of an agreement permitting time and motion study to be used.[7] The gas industry has also made some progress with the introduction of work study. By April 1968 14 per cent of the gas industry's manual workers were covered by incentive schemes which were based on work study and they are being extended rapidly. Moreover, it is clear that payment by results, which at that time covered 18 per cent of all manual workers, has led to some impressive productivity gains. 'In general,' states the Prices and Incomes Board, 'schemes appear to be kept under good control and the necessary data are systematically obtained to keep them under surveillance. They are helping to raise both the performance and the pay of gas workers, while reducing unit labour costs and so benefiting the industry and the consumer.' As, however, the industry believes it will eventually be possible to cover 80 per cent of its manual employees by incentive payments schemes its progress has so far been relatively limited.[8]

But it is in electricity, where work study has scarcely been used in the past, that the most dramatic schemes are afoot. In 1968 agreement was reached with the unions for the introduction of incentive payments based on work study for manual employees throughout the industry. Work study is being used to establish standards of performance for each task and thereafter employees receive a bonus if their performance is not less than 65 per cent of the standard level. The size of this bonus increases step by step as the standard performance is approached. When the norm is reached workers receive a maximum payment equivalent to one-third of their basic pay. As the general level of performance is at present below 65 per cent it seems probable that the agreement will lead both to considerable gains in productivity and to a significant reduction in labour costs. If the average worker has a performance of, say, 60 per cent and, as a result of the incentive bonuses, the figure gradually increases to 95 per cent the industry's productivity will rise by about a third. Chickens must not be counted before they are hatched and, as the Prices and Incomes Board has pointed out, there are a number of difficulties to be surmounted but the success which the industry has made of productivity bargaining gives ground for confidence in its ability to make the best of its new agreement.[9]

It is evident, therefore, that work study has been or is being introduced on a very wide scale in the public enterprise sector. Indeed it is only in odd corners such as the vehicle maintenance works of BRS and of the nationalized buses that little or no progress has yet been made.[10] Although the gas and electricity industries were slow to introduce work study, the extremely rapid progress which is now being made will almost certainly push the public enterprise sector ahead of the rest of British industry, if it is not already ahead.

The Extent of Productivity Bargaining

Having considered the traditional method by which management has tried to improve the performance of its workers, we can now turn to the latest technique: productivity bargaining. Following the Prices and Incomes Board definition, a productivity bargain may be defined as 'one in which workers agree to make a change or a number of changes in working practice that will lead in itself – leaving out any compensating pay increase – to more economical working; and in return the employer agrees to a higher level of pay or other benefits'.[11] How much use, it may be asked, have the nationalized industries made of this device, what gains in productivity have been secured, and have the financial savings been at least sufficient to cover the cost of the agreement?

It is evident that productivity bargaining has been practised on a large scale within the public enterprise sector. Indeed it can be claimed that productivity bargaining was discovered, or to be more accurate rediscovered, within the public enterprise sector. As long ago as 1957, when the speed limit for heavy lorries was increased from 20 to 30 miles per hour, British Road Services reached an agreement by which operations were rescheduled throughout the undertaking so as to reduce the normal working day by an hour. Although the agreement contained a provision to prevent earnings falling, opposition at a local level prevented the new scheme from being put into operation until 1960 and when it was introduced a serious strike occurred.[12] However these initial difficulties had already been overcome by the time that the first stage of the celebrated Fawley agreement, which although it had more impressive results covered far less workers, had been negotiated let alone implemented.[13] Moreover to some extent the agreement put BRS ahead of other road haulage operators who, as late as 1965, had not fully rescheduled their operations. By then the speed limit had again been increased and in 1968 BRS made a new productivity deal which provided not only for scheduling at 40 miles per hour but also for flexibility of duties.[14]

Despite BRS's early agreement it was not until 1964 that extensive progress in productivity bargaining was made within the public enterprise sector. In that year a number of important agreements were negotiated, of which the electricity industry's status agreement must take pride of place. The negotiations which led up to the bargain were both difficult and protracted. At one stage the Minister of Labour had to set up a Court of Inquiry to prevent industrial action and to re-start the negotiations. But what is important is that an agreement was eventually reached on what the Court had described as 'a project of great magnitude, complexity and novelty' which was 'admirable and imaginative in conception'.[15] As a result of the status agreement, which was concluded in three stages between June 1964 and September 1965, the unions agreed first to the flexible use of labour, regardless of the old boundaries between jobs, provided that workers were paid the rate for the job and were not temporarily up-graded to craft duties. Second, it was agreed that new patterns of work should be adopted so that workers would be available automatically at the times when they were needed and excessive overtime could be avoided. For instance, maintenance workers at power stations need to be available at week-ends when electricity consumption falls off and plants can be shut down. In return workers received financial compensation for the disturbance or inconvenience to which the new work patterns gave rise, payment to cushion workers against a fall in their earnings due to the reduction in overtime, and payments for their co-operation in increasing the flexibility of labour. Workers also received staff status which meant that they were put on annual salaries and their sick pay was brought into line with that of other staff.[16] Other more limited agreements were made in 1964 and 1965 by the air corporations and, as we shall see, by London Transport.[17]

During this period while the other nationalized industries were announcing the agreements which they had concluded, British Rail was trying by means of a productivity bargain to extend single manning on diesel and electric locomotives.[18] Ultimately, in October 1965, after negotiations had broken down and a Court of Inquiry had considered the matter an agreement was reached. The railways have often been blamed for giving in to the unions but it is difficult to dissent from the Court's

D

verdict that the railways were 'to be commended for their determination that productivity payments to footplate mea should be made in return for clearly established contributions to higher productivity by their staff'. After the agreement the only unnecessary restrictions on single manning were that locomotives had to be double manned during the deep night hours and that British Rail had committed itself not to declare its surplus firemen redundant or move them from their existing depots against their wishes.[19]

This agreement has been overshadowed by the far-reaching productivity bargain which was, with great difficulty and after more than two years of discussions and negotiations, concluded in August 1968. The agreement provided for the extension of single manning to the deep night hours, for more flexible use of labour through a substantial reduction in the number of grades and the easing of demarcation lines, and for the adoption of a new pattern of work. Railwaymen were to move from an orthodox working week of 40 hours split into five eight-hour shifts, to one of four ten-hour shifts. As the great bulk of railway work takes place during the 20 hours from four in the morning to midnight, this would enable British Rail to switch from a three-shift day to a two-shift day and to avoid a large part of the overtime which now has to be worked. In return railwaymen's rates of pay were increased by an average of about 8 per cent, though allowing for the reduction in overtime it was estimated that their weekly earnings would increase by only 4·6 per cent.[20]

Major productivity deals for the nationalized buses, which had been preceded by years of haggling punctuated by limited agreements, also came in 1968. The first step towards the introduction of one-man buses, which has been the main field for productivity bargaining, was taken as long ago as 1960 when an agreement was reached for Tillings and Scottish and the other company buses. By providing a 15 per cent bonus for those operating one-man buses, this enabled a little progress to be made.[21] In 1964, after several years of deadlock, a limited agreement was also negotiated by London Transport. This provided for the extension of single manning on its country buses, and for the experimental use of standee buses in central London.[22] The agreement of July 1968 allows for the general switch-over to one-man operation which London Transport is planning.[23]

The Results of Productivity Bargaining

The progress in negotiating productivity agreements has been impressive but what impact have they had on output per worker? In the electricity industry the status agreement has had a dramatic result. Average weekly hours, which had previously been stable, dropped from 49$\frac{1}{3}$ in April 1964 to 41$\frac{1}{2}$ in April 1966, a reduction of 16 per cent. This gives an exaggerated impression of the gains which productivity bargaining brought about, mainly because the reduction in hours led to some extra workers being taken on.[24] Nevertheless the aggregate hours worked by all manual workers was 9 per cent lower in April 1966 than it had been in April 1964. As there had been a rise of 5 per cent during the previous two years from April 1962 to April 1964 it seems evident that on balance the status agreement had a highly favourable effect on the industry's productivity.[25]

In the other industries where major agreements have been concluded the gains in productivity, though less marked, have nevertheless been clearly visible. For instance BRS's productivity deal of 1957 led to a modest reduction in the average working week although it has remained very long. In 1957, which was an extremely difficult year, average hours stood at 59$\frac{1}{2}$. In 1967, when traffic was far from buoyant, they were 55·7, though in 1966 and 1968, which were good years, they were slightly higher. It appears, therefore, that the productivity bargain may have cut average hours by around 5 per cent. Despite the agreement, however, the average working week in BRS seems to be just as long as it is in the private sector of road haulage.[26]

Similarly in road passenger transport the gains through productivity bargaining have been perceptible but fairly modest. London Transport managed to increase the number of one-man buses from 261 at the beginning of 1965 to 1,052 at the end of 1968. As it employs about 2·2 conductors per bus this increase represents a staff saving of 1,750 or 4 per cent of its road transport labour force. London Transport is hoping that during coming years spectacular reductions in employment will be secured as a result of its 1968 agreement. It reckons that it will be able to save some 12,500 road passenger jobs by 1975, or about a quarter of the present total, as a result of its bus re-shaping plan which is based on one-man operation.[27]

The results of British Rail's productivity deal on the single manning of locomotives were disappointing. Between the spring of 1965 and the spring of 1968 the number of firemen fell from 16,585 to 11,340. However, a large part of this reduction was due to the reduction in the number of trains rather than to the introduction of single manning. From the decline in the number of drivers, due to the fall in the amount of work, it appears that the saving in manpower, which the extension of single manning brought about, totalled only about 1,760. This represented less than $\frac{1}{2}$ per cent of British Rail's work force at the beginning of the period. Substantial economies in manpower are, however, being made as a result of the productivity deals which were negotiated in 1968. British Rail estimated at the time of its agreement that there would be a saving in costs of £13·3 million per annum before allowing for the higher wages which it would have to pay in return for union agreement. As most of this potential saving represented labour costs, some idea of the economy in manpower which the railways were hoping to achieve can be obtained by comparing the figure of £13·3 million with British Rail's total staff expenses.[28] This calculation suggests that British Rail expected to be able to cut its employment by 4 per cent as a result of the deal. However, it was stated at the time that the financial savings had been estimated conservatively and this has turned out to be the case.

Counting the Cost

The final question about the nationalized industries' productivity bargaining which needs to be answered is whether it has been financially worth while. Obviously there is little or no merit in concluding productivity agreements if at the end of the day costs are higher than they would otherwise have been. At first sight it appears that the way to discover this is to compare an estimate of the savings involved with the cost of the deal in terms of higher pay and other benefits. A moment's reflection, however, shows that this is not so because, in the absence of the deal, some increase would have had to have been conceded. What therefore is required is an estimate of the net cost of the bargain after deducting that part of the pay rise which was unavoidable. Fortunately, it is not necessary to make this difficult calculation when the savings involved exceed the gross cost of the settlement before any deduction has been made. As the net cost is bound to be smaller than the gross cost the deal must, in this case, be financially worth while from the undertaking's point of view.

This commonsense point tends to be ignored when the nationalized industries' productivity bargains are under discussion. For instance, the *Economist* strongly criticized the railways' agreement of 1968 on the ground that the cost of the wage concessions at £13 million per annum would almost entirely swallow up the £13·3 million of savings which British Rail hoped to achieve, which meant that, as the savings would not be achieved until 1970, whereas the cost had to be paid immediately, the deal should never have been approved. 'Even on British Rail's own accounting,' the *Economist* thundered, 'the full saving after 1970 will be only £0·3 million a year more than the present pay-out; it could take the railways up to 40 years to recoup the pre-productivity £13 million or so that may have been paid out in the meanwhile . . . the Government should not allow this deal to go through in its present form'.[29] This is muddled thinking. Not only has the *Economist* failed to take account of the fact that some increase in railway wages was inevitable, but it has made the extraordinary assumption that the savings through higher productivity would suddenly become available in 1970 without any build-up. If it is assumed that the economies would be secured bit by bit from the date of the settlement to the final quarter of 1969, when British Rail was hoping that they would offset the gross cost, then it appears that the latter would total only about £6½ million during the first year of the agreement instead of £13 million as the *Economist* supposed. Which is the more reasonable assumption, that the full savings would suddenly become available with a wave of the wand after a year had elapsed, or that there would be a gradual build-up? When the increase in pay which the railways would anyway have had to concede is brought into the picture it becomes apparent that they struck a good bargain. As there had been no general wage award since early in 1967 when the railwaymen had received an increase of 3½ per cent, which would have been paid in September 1966 but for the prices and incomes standstill, it is evident that in the normal way a substantial pay rise would have had to have been granted. Indeed, according to one contemporary estimate, the cost of a settlement of the conventional type based on comparability might have totalled £12 million a year, or only slightly less than the cost of the productivity deal.[30]

The electricity industry's productivity bargain has been reviewed, and reviewed more impartially, by the Prices and Incomes Board. The electricity industry provided the Board with an analysis of its labour costs in April 1964 and April 1966 which suggested that, on an annual basis, they were £0·8 million lower than they would have been in the absence of the agreement. This estimate included the relatively small costs of transitional payments to workers for loss of previous earnings but excluded some other non-recurring items which the industry had had to bear in the meantime, such as the cost of the status agreement during the interval before overtime fell. These once-and-for-all costs totalled about £4–5 million. The industry's calculations allowed for changes in the volume of work and the amount of sub-contracting but, according to the Board, may not have fully taken into account the increases in efficiency which would have been secured in the normal course of events. On the other hand, the Electricity Council did not allow for the wage increases which it escaped by negotiating the agreement. The Board considered that these would have been considerable and 'would have outweighed any savings from improvements in efficiency which might reasonably have been expected; and this implies that the status agreement brought an overall saving to the industry'.[31]

So far there seems to have been only one productivity bargain of any importance within the public enterprise sector where there is evidence that the cost may have outweighed the savings.[32] This was the agreement for the partial elimination of firemen which the railways concluded in the autumn of 1965. British Rail estimated at the time that this would lead to staff savings of over £6 million a year, and that the cost of the productivity payments would be only about £3 million. However, in the autumn of 1967 BR disclosed that up to that time there had been a loss of £3·3 million and that no cumulative net saving was expected before 1971. What had happened was that the Board had failed to foresee that the rate of wastage of footplate staff would slow down and that the number of trains was going to decline. As the Board had pledged itself not to declare any footplate staff redundant, or to move them to other depots against their wishes, this meant that its surplus firemen were not eliminated through promotion and natural wastage as it had planned. The Court of Inquiry under Professor Donald Robertson, which investigated the working of the manning agreement when the unions were pressing for more generous treatment, rightly concluded that 'the Board gravely miscalculated in 1965 and did not sufficiently analyse probabilities which would appear to have been within the realm of prediction'.[33] Moreover in this case the cost of the deal was as high as it appeared because, after it had been concluded, footplate staff also received the same increases as other railwaymen.

But in general, it appears that the nationalized industries' calculations of the likely payoff from their agreements have been cautious and that their bargains have proved a financial success.[34] Nor does it seem likely that the nationalized industries could have negotiated better terms. As we have seen, agreement with the unions has usually been reached only with great difficulty. In most cases the negotiations have broken down, the unions have resorted to industrial action, and a Court of Inquiry or some dramatic move has been necessary in order to bring them to a successful conclusion.

After reviewing the evidence on the extent and consequences of productivity bargaining in the public enterprise sector, it is impossible not to be impressed with the progress which is being or has already been made. Nevertheless, it would be wrong to be starry-eyed and to ignore the fact that the nationalized industries have considerable scope for future advance. This is true even in the railways and electricity where major productivity bargains have already been negotiated. British Rail has not managed to merge drivers and guards into a single grade so that they can be used more flexibly, or to eliminate guards entirely from vacuum-braked freight trains where they are unnecessary. As fully braked freight trains account for a large and increasing proportion of all goods trains and British Rail employs 7,700 freight guards, it is clear that worthwhile savings in manpower could be made.[35] But although further economies are certainly possible and, indeed, are being planned, it would be wrong to jump to the conclusion that, if British Rail had a free hand, it could slash its labour force by, say, one-third, which is the figure frequently quoted in the Press. No reason is ever given for believing that the figure is anything like as large; except, that is, for the splendid argument produced by the Institute of Economic Affairs that because the railways have (due to modernization and rationalization) managed drastically to cut back their labour force they must be a hotbed of restrictive practices.[36] In the electricity industry there has, as a result of the status agreement, been a significant relaxation in demarcation lines, but progress has been uneven and can go much further.[37]

If this is the position in those nationalized industries which have already concluded important productivity agreements, it is hardly surprising to find that there is also scope for advance in those which have not. For instance, in the gas industry, a large amount of overtime is worked, and in October 1968 average weekly hours were $2\frac{1}{2}$ longer than in manufacturing industry. According to the Prices and Incomes Board, some of this overtime is necessary, but its inquiries suggested that 'some of the overtime is worked, or paid for, mainly as a means of augmenting earnings. This implies inadequate control by management over the allocation and performance of at least part of the labour force.' However, the Chairman of the Gas Council reports that although some scope exists for the easing of demarcation lines they are not a major problem.[38]

The Importance of Negotiating Machinery

The question naturally arises why the nationalized industries have been able to make such swift progress in the field of productivity bargaining. One possible explanation is that, unlike the majority of private firms, almost all nationalized undertakings have their own negotiating machinery. It seems likely that membership of an employers' association which conducts wage negotiations inhibits productivity bargaining. These associations are usually too unwieldy and remote to take the initiative themselves and, like the Confederation of British Industry, have in general regarded productivity bargaining with suspicion.[39] It is surely significant that a high proportion of the most important deals within private industry have been the work of firms which do not belong to their employers' federation. Either they have already negotiated for themselves, like British Oxygen, ICI, the Steel Company of Wales and Esso at Fawley, or they found it necessary to resign, like Alcan and Esso at Milford Haven. Perhaps the most striking illustration of the incompatibility of productivity bargaining and membership of an employers' association is provided by oil distribution where, in the words of the Prices and Incomes Board,

> Up to 1964 the Employers' Panel of the Oil Companies Conciliation Committee (which dealt only with distribution – not refining) bound its members to pay no more and no less than was prescribed in its agreement with the union. The Panel was willing to discuss arrangements for increasing efficiency, but Esso, which had for some time been questioning the Panel's value, could not see how the proposals which it was evolving could be compatible with continued membership and gave notice of withdrawal. Other companies which were then developing plans of their own also withdrew one after another . . .[40]

The case for believing that membership of an employers' association inhibits productivity bargaining is strengthened by the fact that when the nationalized industries have attempted to negotiate deals jointly with these associations they have been unsuccessful and that when they have been members they have not tried. The productivity bargains which BRS negotiated in 1957 for the rescheduling of operations at the new 30 miles per hour speed limit was preceded by an abortive attempt to negotiate a deal in conjunction with the Road Haulage Association.[41] According to BRS: 'Attempts were made to reach agreement with the Road Haulage Association on some arrangements which could be applied to the industry as a whole and under which drivers would share in the increased productivity. This unfortunately proved impracticable and BRS had to initiate separate negotiations with the unions.'[42]

British Road Services already possessed its own negotiating machinery but the Tillings and Scottish bus groups have always negotiated through the National Council for the Omnibus Industry. Significantly Tillings and Scottish have displayed less interest in productivity bargaining and work study than almost any other part of the public enterprise sector, though it is in buses that the scope for productivity bargaining has been most obvious. London Transport, which has its own bargaining structure, began to negotiate seriously on the introduction of one-man buses far more quickly than the National Council. It is difficult to avoid the conclusion that the nationalized industries have been successful at productivity bargaining because they do not, for the most part, try to negotiate through employers' associations, but possess their own machinery. This is no accident, but a consequence of the way in which the nationalized industries have been unified through public ownership.

The Climate of Labour Relations

Another possible explanation for the success of the nationalized industries in productivity bargaining is the climate of industrial relations within the public enterprise sector. Because productivity deals involve the modification of traditional practices they are unlikely to be accepted in undertakings where labour relations are poor, because the management's proposals will be seen as tricks by which it hopes to induce its workers to surrender their rights. Unless labour relations are good, and there is an atmosphere of mutual trust and respect, the deal is bound to be seen as a Trojan horse. Yet trust is particularly important in productivity bargaining because it is a largely uncharted sea and it is almost impossible to tell in advance precisely what the consequences of any agreement will be. It almost seems safe, therefore, to conclude that labour relations must be reasonably satisfactory in those nationalized undertakings which have successfully made agreements because, if they were not, this would have been impossible.

Yet this argument is unsatisfactory as it stands because it is circular. What is required is some independent evidence about the state of labour relations in the public enterprise sector. The most obvious guide to the state of industrial relations is the presence or absence of strikes. The incidence of strikes is by no means a perfect yardstick. Industrial discontent can, for instance, express itself in other ways, such as overtime bans, absenteeism or high labour turnover. Again, an undertaking may only be strike-free because it is willing to tolerate restrictive practices, high overtime, or a generally inefficient use of labour. Nevertheless it can hardly be denied that strikes are an important sign of industrial discontent and that where strikes occur frequently labour relations are unhealthy, even if they are sometimes poor where there are few disputes. Moreover, it can hardly be said that an enterprise which has few strikes and concludes a productivity bargain is only strike-free because it tolerates inefficiency. If this were so the mere suggestion of a productivity agreement would be the signal for the outbreak of hostilities. It can, therefore, be assumed that strikes do provide a rough and ready guide to the state of industrial relations.

In Table 6 figures are presented year by year for the number of days lost per thousand workers in the nationalized industries and in manufacturing. The strike statistics for manufacturing, for coal, and the main

Table 6

DAYS LOST IN STRIKES PER 1,000 WORKERS[1] 1949–68

	Electricity	Coal	Railways	Gas	BEA and BOAC	Nationalized Buses	BRS	Public Enterprise Sector Excluding Coal	Public Enterprise Sector	Manufacturing
1949	55	1,000	35	70	2	190	..	60	440	50
1950	1	600	10	300	75	320	40	80	280	65
1951	340	470	60	—	25	150	950	160	280	65
1952	55	850	5	—	3	35	65	20	350	110
1953	6	500	3	—	—	110	60	20	210	180
1954	15	600	45	1	25	700	95	110	310	90
1955	—	1,500	1,500	1	35	120	40	800	1,100	95
1956	1	650	2	35	—	30	120	15	270	160
1957	6	650	8	—	2	3,800	60	430	500	700
1958	15	600	5	6	800	13,500	650	1,500	1,100	75
1959	25	500	5	4	8	8	40	10	210	550
1960	15	750	65	2	70	130	1,100	90	350	200
1961	9	1,200	30	5	330	40	220	40	460	180
1962	9	500	600	6	240	55	75	300	380	550
1963	4	550	25	8	10	35	55	20	220	110
1964	15	550	20	60	55	100	50	35	220	160
1965	45	800	30	8	110	320	60	70	330	220
1966	10	250	25	1	—	80	100	25	100	110
1967	30	230	210	15	50	230	200	130	160	180
1968	30	140	40	5	700	80	180	75	95	430

[1] Rounded to nearest 5 between 10 and 100, to nearest 10 between 100 and 500, to nearest 50 between 500 and 1,000 and to nearest 100 over 1,000.

part of the railways were obtained from the *Ministry of Labour Gazette* and the *Employment and Productivity Gazette*. Information on the other nationalized industries and the railway workshops was extracted from the Department's records. For most industries information about industrial stoppages is supplied by the Department's regional manpower advisers and employment exchange managers as a result of day-to-day contacts with employer's, and supplemented by information from the press. As there is no obligation on industry to notify the Department of disputes or stoppages, some strikes may escape its notice. However, in the case of the coal industry and British Road Services the Department receives data from the undertakings in question. Thus the Department's statistics for nationalized industries tend to be more comprehensive than its figures for private industry, so that, if anything, the Table makes the strike record of the public enterprise sector appear less satisfactory in relation to that of private industry than it is.

Even so, it can be seen that the sector's record now compares favourably with that of manufacturing. In 1968 less than 100 days were lost per 1,000 workers as against 430 in manufacturing; that is, the strike rate in manufacturing was four and a half times as high as it was in the nationalized industries. Too much weight should not be attached to this because the number of working days lost fluctuates considerably from one year to another and because 1968 was an exceptionally bad year in manufacturing, largely because of the one-day national stoppage of engineering workers. But it does seem significant that the nationalized industries have been less strike-prone than manufacturing since 1966. This has not always been the case. Indeed up to 1958 the public enterprise sector's record was consistently worse than that of manufacturing.

Between 1949 and 1958 three times as many days were lost per 1,000 workers in the public enterprise sector as in manufacturing. But, here as elsewhere, the late fifties represented a turning point. Between 1959 and 1965 the rate at which working days were lost was more or less the same in the nationalized industries as in manufacturing, and between 1966 and 1968 the rate was twice as high in manufacturing as it was in the public enterprise sector. This switch has been primarily due to the large reduction in the number of days lost by the nationalized industries while the number lost in manufacturing has been higher since 1958 than it was before. In the public enterprise sector the number of days lost each year averaged nearly 500 between 1949 and 1958; between 1959 and 1965 the figure was down to just over 300; and between 1966 and 1968 it dropped to 120. In contrast, the rate in manufacturing increased from 160 during the period 1949–58 to 270 between 1959 and 1968.

It is natural to suppose that the reduction in the number of days lost in the public enterprise sector, and its favourable showing in relation to manufacturing, has been largely or even exclusively due to the well-known transformation of coal from a strike prone to a comparatively peaceful industry. At first sight, it appears likely that coal has been a special case and that the number of days lost has remained about the same in the other nationalized undertakings, or perhaps increased in line with those in the rest of industry. As usual, however, it is important not to jump to conclusions and to take a closer look at the figures. There is no doubt that there has, during recent years, been a spectacular reduction in the strike rate in the coal industry. Between 1966 and 1968 the number of days lost per 1,000 workers averaged only about 200 each year compared with nearly 750 during the period 1949–58 and 700 between 1959 and 1965.

But coal is by no means the only part of the public enterprise sector to show an improvement. In the other nationalized industries the average number of days lost per 1,000 workers declined from 320 between 1949 and 1958 (or 175, ignoring the provincial bus strike which took place during the last year of the period) to only 80 during the second decade of nationalization. There has, it is true, been no improvement (or deterioration) during recent years, but as the strike rate was already an exceptionally low one, this is hardly surprising. To describe the strike rate in any of the nationalized industries as exceptionally low when their industrial troubles are celebrated almost daily in the Press and on television must seem like exaggeration. But it is a matter of cold statistics. Excluding coal the number of days lost per 1,000 workers was between 1959 and 1968 only 30 per cent as great as the number in manufacturing.

Turning from the general picture to the individual industries, it appears that, coal apart, each one lost fewer days in relation to its labour force than manufacturing and that, with the exception of the airways, their strike rates were lower during the second decade of nationalization than they had been during the first. The undertaking which during the period 1959–68 had the worst record was BRS. On average, about 210 days per 1,000 workers were lost each year although but for the major strike in 1960, which resulted from its productivity deal, the figure would have been only half as great. Next came the airways with an average of 160 and the buses with about 110. For the railways the figure was 100 but the figure would have been less than half as large had it not been for the one-day stoppage during 1962 in protest at British Rail's proposals for rationalizing its workshops. Finally there was electricity, which lost an average of only 20 days per 1,000 workers, and gas which lost a mere 10.

It must be concluded that, when judged by the presence or absence of strikes, labour relations in most parts of the public enterprise sector are now tolerable and that this may help to explain why the nationalized industries have been able to make such progress in the field of productivity bargaining and work study. It would, however, be unsatisfactory to leave the argument at this stage. What one wants to know is why labour relations in most of the industries now compare favourably with those of private enterprise. A number of possible explanations spring to mind. One of these is that certain of the nationalized industries appear by their nature to be relatively strike-free. International comparisons have shown that railways and, to a lesser extent, gas and electricity typically have few disputes.[43] On the other hand, they show mining to be a very strike-prone industry. It is not difficult to find reasons as to why the situation should be changing here; for instance it has been suggested that the reduction in strikes is due to the difficult position in which the coal industry is placed. The mine workers know, so the argument goes, that their bargaining power is weak and that if they strike the only effect may be to hasten the closure of their pit. Their discontent expresses itself in other ways, such as higher absenteeism, which is unlikely to have the same dire results.

This line of argument has been given forceful expression by Mr L. J. Handy.

> Absenteeism, strikes, labour wastage and accidents [he argues] are all to some extent indices of morale, and reflections of worker dissatisfaction. And in coal-mining they appear, over the post-war period, to be alternative expressions of discontent. Thus, while in numbers strikes in coal-mining, even when deflated by employment indices, have declined dramatically since 1957, absenteeism, accidents per 100,000 manshifts and voluntary wastage have all tended to increase (and particularly so in more recent years) since then.[44]

Apart from the fact that the number of men killed per 100,000 manshifts has declined and the number seriously injured has been more or less stable since 1959, the difficulty with this argument is that there has been a dramatic reduction in strikes even in those parts of the country where the profitable pits are concentrated. Thus between 1957 and 1968–9 the tonnage lost as a result of stoppages and restrictions of work in Yorkshire and the Midlands fell by 80 per cent. It is true that in other coalfields, where the NCB's unprofitable collieries were mainly situated, the reduction was slightly greater at 84 per cent, but in view of the enormous reduction which took place in the profitable districts, it seems likely that there were other factors at work besides the industry's declining fortunes.[45]

For instance, the progressive abolition of piece-work under the Power-Loading Agreement has obviously been responsible for a large part of the reduction in strikes because it has removed the principal bone of contention in the industry – price lists. Prior to the agreement, disputes about these lists and other aspects of the piece-work system accounted for up to three-quarters of the stoppages and restrictions of work which took place. The enormous number of disputes which used to occur inevitably suggests that labour relations in mining were extremely bad. Before nationalization, this was certainly the case, but after nationalization there seems to have been a gradual improvement which was not reflected by a reduction in the number of strikes.[45] Haggling over price lists had become an ingrained habit which it was difficult to break. However the reduction in the demand for coal seems to have at last broken the custom. The industry's economic difficulties were probably the occasion rather than the cause of the reduction in strikes which has taken place.[46]

As the experience of the mining industry suggests, and as evidence from other industries confirms, it would be wrong to regard labour relations as an act of God which, if bad, cannot be changed by deliberate action and, if good, will continue this way however foolishly management behaves. It is, for instance, often assumed that the reason why the British car industry has an exceptionally large number of strikes is the boring and repetitive nature of the work. There is no convincing evidence that this is the case, and even if it is true that the industry is particularly liable to strikes the tendency for strikes to occur cannot be so strong that management is helpless. This is shown not only by the fact that in Germany, Sweden and France the motor industry is relatively free from strikes, but also by the wide variations in the extent to which the different manufacturers are strike-prone in Britain.

The prevalence of strikes in some parts of the car industry is readily explained by its chaotic wage structure, its defective bargaining system, and its weak management. Earnings in the motor industry vary enormously from job to job, and from factory to factory, even when they are in the ownership of the same company. These differentials are not fixed, but wax and wane owing to the difficulty which management has in controlling the earnings of workers who are paid by results, and to the varying impact of the fluctuations in activity to which the industry is subject. It is hardly surprising that in this situation grievances arise and that the attempt to remedy them creates new stresses and strains, especially as management has usually been ready to buy off trouble.[47] The cure to these ills is to be sought in a reform in the industry's bargaining system. What happens at the moment is that although national negotiations have some influence on the general level of earnings, their structure is the outcome of negotiations at factory level.

Industry-wide Bargaining

The motor industry's troubles illustrate in an extreme form the difficulties which exist over a large part of private industry. What has happened, as the Donovan Commission has argued so cogently, is that the traditional system by which wages were fixed through industry-wide negotiations has largely broken down because, under the pressure of full employment and the regional shortages of labour which have developed, earnings have risen high above the national wage rates. Although these rates still help to determine the level of earnings, in many industries pay is crucially affected by local work-place bargaining in what the Commission terms the informal system of industrial relations.

Nevertheless [the Commission argues] the assumptions of the formal system still exert a powerful influence over men's minds and prevent the informal system from developing into an effective and orderly method of regulation. The assumption that industry-wide agreements control industrial relations leads many companies to neglect their responsibility for their own personnel policies. Factory bargaining remains informal and fragmented, with many issues left to custom and practice. The unreality of industry-wide pay agreements leads to the use of incentive schemes and overtime payments for purposes quite different from those they were designed to serve. Any suggestion that conflict between the two systems can be resolved by forcing the informal system to comply with the assumptions of the formal system should be set aside. Reality cannot be forced to comply with pretences.

Accordingly the Commission recommends that the pretence that pay and conditions of work are fixed through industry-wide agreements should be given up and that the informal system of industrial relations should be formalized. In this way it hopes that the present disorder in factory and workshop relations and in pay structures can be brought to an end.[48]
Even if the bargaining system develops in the way in which the Commission hopes, it is questionable whether order will be re-established and industrial relations will improve. The Commission has become the prisoner of its own terminology. It does not follow, if local bargaining became more formal, that the wage system would become more orderly. The Commission has mistakenly assumed that orderly procedures produce orderly results. But surely the reason why wage structures have

become anarchic is not the disorderly methods by which they were determined but the fact that they were largely fixed at branch level rather than centrally. It is an inevitable feature of local bargaining, unless it is centrally monitored, that its results will be untidy because the bargains struck will differ from place to place. Hence it is to be expected that even if plant bargaining becomes more formal the state of industrial relations will remain much the same because the principal cause of industrial conflict will continue to be present. It is significant that it is those countries whose wages are fixed nationally that have the fewest strikes. Wage bargaining is highly centralized in Sweden, Holland and Germany and these are the countries at the bottom of the international strike league. On the other hand the United States, where company bargaining predominates, is almost at the top.[49]

The nationalized industries have escaped the general decay in industry-wide bargaining. In the public enterprise sector it has not only survived but has recently been extended to the only important group of workers whose wages used to be largely determined at plant level. These were the former piece-workers in the coal industry whose price-lists were, prior to the Power-Loading Agreement, negotiated separately for each face. The survival and development of industry-wide bargaining in the nationalized industries is no accident. It is the consequence of their unified ownership. This has enabled a firm grip to be maintained from the centre and has prevented the negotiated rates from being supplemented, and ultimately subverted, through local bargaining. In most of the nationalized industries these rates are fixed at a national level and even in gas where the rates for most jobs are fixed at area level, the key rates for gas fitters and labourers, which provide upper and lower fixed points for the wage structure, are determined nationally. Once rates have been fixed within the public enterprise sector they are more or less adhered to and it is this which marks the nationalized industries off from most of the private sector. In the nationalized industries it is the exception and not the rule for workers to receive more than the standard rate, except of course where incentive schemes have been established.[50]

Because of the difficulty of introducing incentive schemes and then of controlling them they involve the danger that they will disrupt the wages structure and produce stresses and strains which the bargaining system cannot handle. These dangers have not been entirely avoided in the public enterprise sector. In the railways, as the Prices and Incomes Board discovered, the average excess of earnings over basic rates varied in October 1965 between one centre and another from as little as 15 per cent to as much as 121 per cent.[51] However, the risks inherent in incentive bonus schemes seem for the most part to have been kept to the

minimum through the use of work study and the control which is exercised over them.[51] Certainly the wage structures of the nationalized
industries have not been allowed to degenerate into chaos like those of so
many private industries and this helps to explain why the public enterprise sector has relatively good labour relations.

Model Employment Practices

Another possible reason, or set of reasons, is that the nationalized
industries try to be model employers. This is well illustrated by the way
in which they have handled the problem of redundancy. Despite the
massive run-down in employment in coal and railways, remarkably few
workers have had to be sacked and most of these have refused alternative
employment. For instance, during 1958 and 1959, for which figures
happen to be available, British Rail's labour force declined by about
55,000, but less than 3,000 workers had to be dismissed due to redundancy and most of those had been offered other work.[52] In coal
employment was cut by 270,000 between the end of 1958 and the spring
of 1967 but only 25,000 were declared redundant.[53] This has been the
result not of good luck but of careful planning. Recruitment has been
firmly controlled so that the greater part of the reduction has been
achieved by means of natural wastage, and transport is often arranged
for workers whose local colliery has closed but who are within travelling
distance of a pit with vacancies. A scheme has also been in operation
since the spring of 1962 to assist miners who are prepared to leave the
declining coal fields and move to Yorkshire and the Midlands.[54]

Not only have the nationalized industries taken great pains to keep
redundancy to the minimum, but they have all adopted procedures to
ensure that when workers were dismissed for misconduct or incompe-
tence, justice should not only be done but be seen to be done. In contrast
a high proportion of private firms have not introduced machinery of this
type. Indeed a survey by the Ministry of Labour suggests that well
under 20 per cent of all firms have adopted formal procedures, although
the proportion seems to be higher among large firms. Yet it is important
that clear procedures should exist because dismissals can arouse hard
feelings and strikes over this issue account for a significant proportion of
all industrial disputes.[55]

The fact that the nationalized industries are model employers is also
shown by the way in which the public enterprise sector has become a
miniature welfare state. For instance, by 1963 about 80 per cent of all
those who worked in the nationalized industries were covered by
occupational pension schemes, compared with only about 40 per cent in

the private sector. By the early sixties virtually all manual workers in the nationalized industries were covered by sick pay schemes as against only about a third in the private sector. The provision which public enterprise makes for the welfare of its employees is perhaps best shown by figures for expenditure. A survey by the Department of Employment and Productivity shows that in 1964 the nationalized industries spent £32 per manual worker on all forms of private social welfare. In manufacturing the figure was only £13.[56] Although it is impossible to buy good industrial relations, as the motor industry has found to its cost, it is difficult to believe that the nationalized industries' regard for the welfare of their employees has not contributed to their good industrial relations.

Some of the nationalized undertakings have taken considerable pains to make their industrial relations less autocratic. This is by no means universally true, as a recent study of British Road Services indicated. Although its conditions of employment are superior to those of most private firms, and this is appreciated by BRS employees, Dr Peter Hollowell reports that they resent the emphasis on rules and regulations and the pettifogging behaviour of its managers and office staff. Too much weight should not be attached to his findings, as they were based on a very small sample, but it does seem likely that BRS remains a somewhat paternalistic undertaking.[57] In contrast the electricity industry has devoted great efforts to making its industrial relations less authoritarian and joint consultation a success. It has become part of the conventional wisdom that joint consultation has failed but it does appear that over the years the electricity industry has made real progress in this field. Indeed Mr R. D. V. Roberts of the Electricity Council claims that its extensive experience with joint consultation was one of the factors which explains the success of the status agreement.[58]

In the coal industry there has been a marked improvement in the relations between management and men and joint consultation now appears to be working reasonably well. Professor Clinton Jencks, who spent nine months making a first-hand investigation of the industry's labour relations, found that 'All mineworkers and management representatives who were interviewed claimed that the most important change since nationalization has been the improvement in industrial relations'. Although by no means all rank-and-file workers were aware of the work of their Consultative Committees he reports that their members 'were emphatic and positive in their declarations that the committees are important, of practical value in accomplishing needed changes, and contribute to a good feeling of shared responsibility of mineworkers towards the industry and safety'.[59] Though in some ways disappointing this is in other ways a most heartening finding because the key men on the union side are always members of their Committees. Moreover, since Professor Jencks made his investigation there has been a move to consult ordinary workers and to provide them with information. For instance 'teach-in's' may be held when new coal faces are being opened up, or after they have been in operation some time, in order to see what difficulties have arisen and how working methods can be improved.

It is perhaps the process of productivity bargaining and the introduction of work study which best illustrate the way in which the nationalized industries tend to handle their labour relations. Their approach is generally democratic rather than autocratic. Each step is carefully agreed with the unions even if this takes months of difficult negotiations and then, at a local level, the implementation of the agreement is preceded by consultation and explanation. Here, for instance, is an account of the way in which the gas industry set about introducing work study.

> In all the boards studied [states the PIB] the trade unions concerned were fully consulted before any action was taken and the agreement of their local full-time officials was obtained. Next, the shop stewards and work people involved were invited to a preliminary meeting in which the scheme was explained and any questions answered. A programme of work study was generally the next step, covering such matters as organization, the provision of tools and other equipment and the establishment of standard times. Finally, a further meeting with all those involved has generally been held, where the results have been explained. Bonus schemes have thus been introduced in a correct way and one which treats the workers involved as responsible participants.[60]

In electricity the implementation of the status agreement was handled in much the same way. Professor Sir Ronald Edwards observes that the statement on employee co-operation, which was the first stage of the agreement, 'was followed by what was probably the most extensive and detailed exercise in consultation that this industry has undertaken – consultation which began with senior managers and trade union officers, continued down the line and finally involved many hundreds of informal meetings between departmental heads and working groups of employees'.[61] In coal, as the 'teach-in's' show, the Power-Loading Agreement has been followed up by an extensive programme of consultation and information.

However, it is in British Rail that the most interesting developments have taken place. In the past, relations between the rail unions and management were always formal and sometimes frigid. The Railways

Board and the Transport Commission were jealous of the supposed prerogatives of management and were unwilling to justify their proposals in detail and refused to disclose the facts and figures on which they were based. The final stage of the productivity deal of 1958 was, however, conducted in a very different manner from previous negotiations. For a period of a week the BR team, headed by Len Neal, and the executives of the NUR and ASLEF, withdrew to New Lodge, Windsor, where they stayed until they had talked out their differences. Not only was the atmosphere less formal and less divisive than before – there were easy chairs instead of divisive tables – but what was more important was that Neal was ready to explain his plans and the Board's accountants were present so that their figures could be discussed. Moreover, the agreement reached made provision for the joint assessment of its results. This bargain was followed up in the autumn of 1969 by a new agreement which has not previously been mentioned because, since it provided for the negotiation of local deals, it is difficult as yet to say much about its consequences. But what is clear and of relevance is Mr Neal's aim. He was motivated partly by the belief that since conditions differed from one region to another local bargaining made economic sense. However, he was also hoping that, as a result of the local bargaining and the accompanying programme of local consultation, the workers' feeling of alienation from the decision-taking progress could be reduced. Stage 2 of the railways' productivity bargaining was intended therefore as a step towards industrial democracy. Local bargaining within an industry obviously involves the danger that it will do more harm than good because the wage structure will degenerate and become unfair. Provision is, however, made in the rail agreement for the monitoring of all local deals.[62]

CHAPTER 6

Productivity in Perspective

THE purpose of this and the two succeeding chapters is to assess the performance of the nationalized industries by means of productivity comparisons. This is a simple object but it will prove a difficult and lengthy undertaking. It will also be a rewarding one, for the comparisons do enable us to evaluate the gains in productivity which the nationalized industries have made and to tell whether the level of their productivity is higher or lower than it is reasonable to expect.

Productivity Growth in Public and Private Enterprise

The most obvious question to ask is whether output per man within the public enterprise sector has been growing faster or slower than it has within the private sector. The answer is provided in Table 7 where productivity growth rates are given for each of the nationalized industries, for the sector as a whole, and for manufacturing. The comparison has been made with manufacturing partly because reliable figures are available and partly because it is here that the scale of operations and the methods of production appear most similar to those in the public enterprise sector. There is no danger that by comparing the nationalized industries with manufacturing they will be shown in too favourable a light. Output per man in the manufacturing industries has been growing considerably faster than it has in the rest of the private sector.

During the post-war period as a whole output per man hour in the public enterprise sector increased at a slightly faster rate than in manufacturing. Between 1948 and 1968 the nationalized industries' productivity increased by 3·4 per cent per annum as against a rise of 2·8 per cent in manufacturing (and 2·5 per cent in the private sector as a whole). In the air corporations and electricity output per man hour increased at a much faster rate than in manufacturing, and in gas and BRS it increased somewhat faster. The air corporations' productivity rose by 11·4 per cent per annum; the electricity industry's increased by 6·3 per cent and the gas industry's productivity grew by 3·6 per cent each year. Information on BRS is not available for the whole period, but between 1950 and 1966 its output per man hour increased by 3·1 per cent per annum. The coal industry's rate of increase was, at 2·8 per cent, the same as that of manufacturing but the railways' rate of 2·3 per cent was significantly lower, and productivity on the nationalized buses fell.

Table 7

LABOUR PRODUCTIVITY GROWTH RATES FOR
PUBLIC ENTERPRISE AND MANUFACTURING[1]
(*Per Cent Compound Per Annum*)

	1948–68	*1948–58*	*1958–68*
BEA and BOAC	11·4	14·0	8·9
Electricity	6·3	4·6	8·0
Gas	3·6	1·6	5·5
BRS	3·1[2]	0·8[2]	4·9
Coal	2·8	0·9	4·7
Railways	2·3	0·3	4·3
Nationalized Buses	−1·0	−0·6	−1·4
Public Enterprise Sector	3·4	1·5	5·3
Chemicals			6·9
Textiles			5·2
Bricks, Cement etc.			4·9
Vehicles			4·0
Clothing			3·8
Engineering			3·5
Other Manufactures			3·4
Paper, Printing, Publishing			3·3
Metal Manufacture			2·6
Food, Drink, Tobacco			2·5
Timber and Furniture			2·2
Shipbuilding			1·3
Miscellaneous metal goods			1·0
Leather and Fur			0·7
Manufacturing	2·8	1·9	3·7

[1] Output per man hour except for nationalized buses and prior to 1963 railways where figures are for output per man year.
[2] 1950–68 and 1950–58.

It is evident that the nationalized industries' performance was much better during the second half of the period than it had been during the first. During the first decade of nationalization, output per man hour in the public enterprise sector increased at a somewhat slower pace than in manufacturing. Between 1948 and 1958 public enterprise productivity grew by 1·5 per cent per annum compared with a rise of 1·9 per cent in manufacturing (but only 1·7 per cent in the private sector). Among the nationalized industries only the air corporations (14·0 per cent per annum) and electricity (4·6 per cent) did better than manufacturing, and even the gas industry (at 1·6 per cent) failed to keep pace.

During the second decade of nationalization output per man hour increased considerably faster within the public enterprise sector than in manufacturing. Between 1958 and 1968 the nationalized industries' productivity rose by 5·3 per cent each year compared with 3·7 per cent in manufacturing (and only 3·4 per cent in the private sector). This means that the nationalized industries' productivity has been growing about 40 per cent faster than productivity in manufacturing. The only nationalized industry which did not outstrip manufacturing was the buses, where productivity fell. Even the railways' rate of 4·3 per cent was significantly higher than that of manufacturing and the other public undertakings were even further ahead. The air corporations led the field at 8·9 per cent, next came electricity at 8 per cent, followed by gas at 5·5 per cent, BRS at 4·9 per cent and coal at 4·7 per cent.

Within manufacturing, different industries increased their productivity by different amounts. The industry with the largest increase in output per man hour between 1958 and 1968 was the chemicals group (at 6·9 per cent). But this was the only major industry which chalked up a larger rise than the public enterprise sector as a whole. Even textiles, which (at 5·2 per cent) came second to chemicals, fared slightly worse than the nationalized industries. It is obviously a severe test to compare the whole of the public enterprise sector with the leading private industries, but even when judged by the best which the private sector has to offer the nationalized industries appear to have performed well.

Despite their interest, simple comparisons of this type can be misleading. In assessing the performance of public enterprise it is necessary to take the numerous factors which contribute to the growth of labour productivity into account. On the one hand, it is possible that the nationalized industries have enjoyed some advantage which explains why they have managed to secure larger gains than manufacturing industry. On the other hand, it is conceivable that they have laboured at a disadvantage and that their performance is even better than it appears. What does not seem likely is that the nationalized industries' fast rate of advance since 1958 is a temporary phenomenon. Although it is impossible to be certain about the future, there is reason to believe that their output per man will go on increasing at a rapid rate.[1]

Table 8

OUTPUT AND PRODUCTIVITY RANKING FOR PUBLIC ENTERPRISE AND MANUFACTURING
(% Change 1958–68)

		Output	*Output per Man Hour*[1]	*Product-ivity Ranking*
1	BEA and BOAC	+247	+135	2
2	Electricity	+112	+115	3
3	*Chemicals, etc.*	+86	+87	4
4	*Bricks, cement, etc.*	+73	+64	8
5	*Miscellaneous manufactures*	+71	+40	18
6	*Electrical engineering*	+69	+44	15
7	*Glass*	+60	+67	6
8	*Oil refineries, coke ovens, etc.*	+58	+144	1
9	BRS	+55	+62	9
10	Gas	+55	+71	5
11	*Paper, printing, publishing*	+53	+39	19
12	*Mechanical engineering*	+51	+43	16
13	*Drink and tobacco*	+36	+41	17
14	*Timber, furniture, etc.*	+33	+24	22
15	*Vehicles and aircraft*	+32	+48	13
16	*Non-ferrous metal manufacture*	+30	+28	21
17	*Pottery*	+30	+51	12
18	*Textiles*	+29	+66	7
19	*Clothing, footwear*	+25	+46	14
20	*Ferrous metal manufacture*	+24	+31	20
21	*Food*	+21	+24	23
22	*Miscellaneous metal goods*	+21	+10	25
23	*Leather, leather goods and fur*	−7	+7	26
24	Railways	−13	+52	11
25	Nationalized buses	−24	−13	27
26	Coal	−27	+59	10
27	*Shipbuilding and marine engineering*	−29	+14	24

[1] Except for nationalized buses and the railways for the years 1958–63, where the figures are for output per man year.

Source: Table 4 for public enterprise. Manufacturing production from CSO. Employment for SIC orders from AAS 1960 p 104, 1967 p 109, 1969 p 120; for sub-orders AAS 1960 Tables 135 and 142, *Monthly Digest of Statistics* July 1967 Table 15, *Statistics on Incomes, Prices, Employment and Production* March 1969 Table E 4. Hours for adult men from MLG/EPG April and October surveys.

Production and Productivity

One of the most important factors to be taken into account is the speed at which production has increased in manufacturing and in the public enterprise sector. As a number of studies have shown, there is usually a close relationship between changes in output and changes in output per worker. Those industries which have the largest increases in production usually show the largest increases in output per worker and vice versa.[2] This has come to be known as Verdoorn's Law after the Dutch economist who first noticed the phenomenon. Britain has been no exception to the Law because over the period 1958–66 the correlation coefficient between the increase in output and in output per worker in 23 manufacturing industries was +0·79.[3]

Like other correlations this does not tell us anything about causation. Where an industry had a large rise in both production and productivity this could have been due to an initial increase in productivity which, through its beneficial effect on the relative price of the product, stimulated demand and so led to a large rise in production. Alternatively the process may have begun on the demand side. An autonomous increase in demand could have led to higher production which, in turn, led to higher productivity because it enabled the industry to secure economies of scale and encouraged its management to be more enterprising. Unfortunately the figures do not tell us which process was at work, though it is normally true that industries with large gains in productivity do show a reduction in their relative price. This is because the increase in average earnings does not vary greatly from one industry to another and because large productivity gains tend to be accompanied by a reduction in the relative cost of materials.[4] No doubt in practice the association between increases in productivity and production is due partly to the supply and partly to the demand side, and to their interaction. But it is probable that the demand side will usually have the more important role in the expansion of production and productivity because it is doubtful whether demand is very responsive to price when whole industry groups are under consideration.[5] Even if this presumption is wrong and the supply side does play the leading part, it seems highly likely that, once production has started to rise, further gains in productivity are more likely to be secured.

It is, therefore, interesting to observe that between 1948 and 1968 productivity within the public enterprise sector increased slightly faster than in manufacturing despite the fact that its output only grew about 40 per cent as fast. This comparison may be criticized on the ground that the contraction of the coal industry was partly responsible for the slow rise in production and, whatever may be true of the other national-ized industries, there is no reason to believe that rising output has a beneficial effect on coal productivity. Higher production, the argument proceeds, will almost certainly mean that inferior seams have to be worked.

This has some force although the historical evidence on the relation-ship between output and productivity in coal is by no means clear cut. But the contrast between manufacturing and the public enterprise sector remains even if coal is excluded, though the difference between the rates of increase in production certainly becomes narrower. Excluding coal, the rise in the output of the public enterprise sector between 1948 and 1968 was about 90 per cent as large as that in manufacturing. But the gap between the productivity gains is increased if coal is left out because out-put per man has grown less in coal than in the remaining part of the sector. Excluding coal, the nationalized undertakings' rate of produc-tivity growth was about 30 per cent higher than that of manufacturing.[6]

This contrast between the performance of manufacturing and public enterprise persists even though their production is now growing some-what faster. Between 1958 and 1968 the increase in productivity in manufacturing (44 per cent) was only slightly greater than the growth in its output (42 per cent). But in the public enterprise sector the rise in productivity (74 per cent) was very much greater than the increase in output (53 per cent). It remains true none the less that during the past decade the nationalized industries' output has grown slightly faster than manufacturing output and that this helps to explain why their produc-tivity has increased more rapidly.

When the relationship between production and productivity is con-sidered industry by industry there is very little which can be said about the air corporations, electricity or buses. Electricity and airways both had very large gains in output and output per man hour. In Table 8 the nationalized undertakings have been ranked with 20 manufacturing industries by the rise in their production and productivity between 1958 and 1968. It can be seen that airways are top of the output list and second in the productivity league. Electricity comes second in the production league and third in the productivity league. Again the buses' produc-tivity position is more or less what would be expected from its output ranking. It was at the bottom of the productivity league but there was only one manufacturing industry which had a larger reduction in output.

What is significant is that the railways and gas secured larger rises in productivity than was to be expected from the increase in their output. Shipbuilding was the only manufacturing industry which between 1958 and 1968 had a larger fall in output than the railways but whereas it had a tiny increase in productivity the railways managed to obtain a bigger increase in output per man year than 14 manufacturing industries which had the benefit of a larger increase in production. Gas secured a greater productivity increase than four of the six manufacturing industries whose production rose faster but none of the industries whose production rose more slowly was ahead of it in the productivity league.

Calculating Residual Productivity

Statistics showing the way in which output per man hour has changed in a particular industry or undertaking suffer from the obvious weakness that labour is the only input taken into account. Any change in the amount of capital is simply ignored. However, this weakness of labour productivity as a measure of efficiency is usually more important in theory than in practice. As a number of studies have shown, industries whose output per man has increased most tend also to show the largest increases in residual productivity. (Figures for labour productivity are obtained by dividing the quantity of output by the amount of labour involved in its production, measured in, say, man hours, to obtain output per man hour. Similarly residual productivity is calculated by dividing the quantity of output by an estimate of the labour and capital involved in its production to obtain output per composite unit of labour and capital.) In a study covering the period 1948–54, Professor W. B. Reddaway and Mr A. D. Smith found that there was a close relationship between the change in overall productivity and the growth of output per man hour. The manufacturing industries with large increases in labour productivity normally had large increases in residual productivity and vice versa.[7] An inquiry by Professor R. C. O. Matthews, which used a slightly different procedure and covered the periods 1924–37 and 1948–62, produced the same result. According to Matthews 'conclusions to be drawn about the relative performance of different industries on the basis of the residual conform quite closely, but not perfectly, to the conclusions that would be drawn on the basis of the more familiar concept, rate of growth of productivity per man'.[8]

It is possible that the public enterprise sector may be an exception to the rule and that it may owe its greater rise in labour productivity to the substitution of capital for labour. It is all the more necessary to investigate this as it is widely supposed that the nationalized industries have a particularly voracious appetite for capital. Estimates of productivity, which allow not only for the amount of labour used but also for the amount of capital employed, have therefore been made. This raises the difficult problems of how to measure the amount of capital in use and how to determine the respective contributions of labour and capital to the process of production.[9] How in the automobile industry, for instance, are we to decide the share of production which is attributable to the car workers and the share which should be attributed to the machinery they use and the factories in which they work?

Although this question may appear to be unanswerable, it can be answered at least in principle. If the market mechanism works in text-book fashion the remuneration of labour and of capital will reflect their contributions to the process of production. The contribution of the workers will be indicated by the amount they are paid, which collectively is the wages and salary bill, and the contribution made by capital will be indicated by the flow of interest and profits. Under conditions of perfect competition there can be no more than a temporary divergence between the contribution of labour and its remuneration. This is because firms will take on extra workers or install new machinery so long as it pays them to do so, and it will pay them up to the point at which the value of the extra output they obtain is equal to the extra cost involved in its pro-duction. Hence they will take on extra labour until the extra wages they have to pay are just equal to the value of the extra output they obtain after deducting any other costs which are incurred. Similarly they will employ additional capital until the extra interest they have to pay is just equal to the extra output they obtain after deducting any other costs.

However, for a number of reasons traditional theory is a poor guide to what actually happens. This is especially true in the case of the national-ized industries because the profits which they earn on their capital appear to be exceptionally low and the railways make a loss.[10] Hence, if the contribution of capital is measured by its remuneration, too little allowance will be made (or for the railways a negative allowance) and residual productivity will consequently be overstated. However, the theory of perfect competition does suggest a rough-and-ready method by which allowance can be made in productivity calculations for the contri-bution which capital makes to production. The contribution of capital will be the remuneration it would receive in the absence of distorting factors.

Therefore, following the example of Reddaway and Smith, a 'guessti-mate' was made of what the rate of return on capital ought to have been. This was then applied to the CSO's estimates of the net fixed assets at replacement cost for the nationalized industries and for manufacturing.[11] The notional figures for profits which were thereby obtained were then, together with the CSO's estimates of replacement cost depreciation, assumed to represent the contribution of capital while the actual wage and salary bill was assumed to represent the contribution of labour.[12] The indices of the gross stock of capital and the quantity of labour were then spliced together, year by year, using notional gross profits as the capital weight and labour remuneration as the labour weight. The figures so obtained were divided into output to obtain output per composite unit of labour and capital. The CSO's capital stock figures were used for manufacturing and the air corporations; its estimates for electricity and coal were used, after adjustment, for capital work in progress and pit closures; and independent estimates (which, unlike the CSO figures, allow for the exceptional scrapping of assets) were made for railways and gas.[13] The rate of return was assumed to be 10 per cent, i.e. about the rate of return which manufacturing earned during the base year 1958, when its depreciation and net assets are calculated at replacement cost.[14]

Residual Productivity Results

It is apparent from the figures for residual productivity which are given in Table 9 that the year to year fluctuations are greater than the fluctuation in labour productivity, and that the latter has been increasing more rapidly than the former. Neither of these facts is in any way surprising. The growth of residual productivity is less steady than the growth in labour productivity because firms cannot adjust their capacity to short-run fluctuations in the growth (or decline) of output to the extent to which they can tailor their labour force. That residual productivity has been increasing more slowly than labour productivity is explained by the way in which most industries have been deepening their capital and installing labour-saving machinery. It was only to be expected that this would turn out to have been happening in the nationalized industries. It would, however, be significant if the abnormally large gains in productivity, which public enterprise appears to have made when this is measured by output per worker, were to disappear when the use of capital is taken into account.

Over the full period of nationalization the airways, electricity and gas have had relatively large increases in residual productivity. The air corporations' output per unit of labour and capital grew by 8·4 per cent per annum over the period 1948–67, in electricity it increased at an average rate of 3.4 per cent between 1948 and 1968 and for gas the figure was 2·2 per cent. In contrast residual productivity in manufacturing increased by no more than 2 per cent. This, however, was a faster rate of progress than was obtained in coal or railways. The coal industry's rate, at 1·7 per cent, was not all that much lower than that of manufacturing

Table 9

INDEX NUMBERS AND GROWTH RATES FOR OUTPUT PER UNIT OF LABOUR AND CAPITAL 1948–68

(i) *Index Numbers (1958 = 100)*

	Electricity	Coal	Railways	Gas	BEA and BOAC	Manufacturing excluding textiles
1948	69·9	96·4	100·6	93·6	47·0	85·9
1949	69·6	101·4	102·2	95·6	53·3	89·1
1950	73·9	104·0	103·0	100·7	65·8	91·9
1951	78·4	104·2	106·8	100·9	83·5	93·2
1952	78·0	101·9	104·8	97·0	89·0	90·9
1953	80·9	103·2	106·6	99·5	93·4	93·2
1954	86·7	103·0	105·9	104·0	92·1	96·5
1955	90·6	101·4	104·5	102·3	98·2	100·1
1956	94·4	100·5	106·7	101·2	104·3	98·6
1957	95·4	98·7	107·7	98·5	106·1	100·2
1958	100·0	100·0	100·0	100·0	100·0	100·0
1959	103·7	102·7	101·2	100·5	108·9	103·8
1960	112·8	103·4	105·6	103·1	126·7	108·7
1961	116·8	105·7	102·5	105·7	131·8	107·1
1962	124·8	111·7	98·5	111·1	132·4	108·0
1963	128·1	115·8	102·8	113·0	148·7	112·3
1964	128·7	117·2	111·9	118·3	169·7	117·8
1965	133·8	119·6	112·7	125·7	193·7	120·1
1966	130·8	121·1	116·1	131·2	213·9	121·9
1967	130·1	125·1	116·0	139·7	218·5	122·2
1968	135·9	135·2	126·3	144·0		126·8

(ii) *Growth Rates (Per cent compound per annum)*

	Electricity	Coal	Railways	Gas	BEA and BOAC	Manufacturing excluding textiles
1948–68	3·4	1·7	1·1	2·2	8·4[1]	2·0
1948–58	3·6	0·4	—	0·7	7·8	1·5
1958–68	3·1	3·0	2·4	3·7	9·1[2]	2·4

[1] 1948–67.
[2] 1958–67.

but the railways, at 1·1 per cent, were a long way behind. As usual the first decade of nationalization turns out to have been a bleak period for the public enterprise sector. The railways' residual productivity was no higher in 1958 than it had been in 1948 and in coal and gas it was only slightly higher. Moreover, in all of these industries residual productivity was lower in 1958 than it had previously been. Their productivity increased fairly rapidly during the earlier years of nationalization, but in coal it then drifted downwards and in railways it slumped so far during 1968, owing to the reduction in traffic, that what progress had been made was wiped out. In manufacturing the rate of productivity growth (at 1·5 per cent), though by no means fast, was much greater than in any of these industries, and between 1948 and 1958 was only exceeded by that of electricity (3·6 per cent) and airways (7·8 per cent).

During the second decade of public ownership the nationalized industries' general performance has been vastly better than its own record during the previous ten years, and much superior to that of manufacturing. Between 1958 and 1968 residual productivity in manufacturing grew by 2·4 per cent per year. This rate was equalled by the railways and exceeded by the other nationalized industries. In coal output per unit of labour and capital rose by 3 per cent per annum, in electricity by 3·1 per cent, in gas by 3·7 per cent and in airways by 9·1 per cent. Electricity was the only one of these industries in which the rate of productivity growth was slower during the second decade than it had been between 1948 and 1958. This is because, during recent years, the growth of electricity sales has fallen away. In 1967 the industry's output per unit of labour and capital was, due to the slow growth in sales, somewhat lower than it had been in 1965. However during 1968 it recovered sharply, and it seems likely that the slow rise in productivity between 1965 and 1968 will turn out to be no more than a temporary setback.

It can be seen that the exceptionally large gains in productivity which statistics of output per man hour suggest the nationalized industries have made, are by no means entirely illusory. However, during the first decade of public ownership, the nationalized industries' relative performance appears even poorer in terms of residual productivity than in terms of labour productivity. Electricity was the only nationalized industry which over this period did not, relative to manufacturing, make smaller gains in residual productivity than in labour productivity. Electricity's productivity growth rate for both output per man hour and output per unit of labour and capital was about two and a half times the manufacturing figure, but whereas the gas industry's rate for labour productivity represented 85 per cent of the manufacturing figure, its rate for residual productivity was only about half that for manufacturing.

Similarly coal productivity grew about half as fast as manufacturing productivity in terms of output per man hour, but only about a quarter as fast in terms of output per unit of labour and capital. And whereas the railways had a small increase in labour productivity their residual productivity was no higher at the end of the period than it had been at the beginning.

However, during the second decade of public ownership, the industries' relative performance has been nearly as good, when measured by output per unit of labour and capital, as it has in terms of labour productivity. The record of gas and coal has been as good, while the airways actually made larger gains in residual than in labour productivity. Electricity and the railways appear, in contrast, to have done relatively less well, if the use of capital is taken into account, than they have when it is ignored. Between 1958 and 1968 the electricity industry's output per worker increased well over twice as fast as that of manufacturing, but its residual productivity only increased about a third faster. Moreover, while the railways did slightly better than manufacturing in terms of labour productivity they did no better in terms of residual productivity. As, however, the railways have been operating under conditions of declining demand, when the utilization of their capacity inevitably tends to decline, their gains in output per unit of labour and capital are, in reality, more impressive than their gains in labour productivity.

Although these results have been stated boldly, they should be regarded as very tentative, for the calculation of residual productivity is a hazardous undertaking. In particular it is extremely difficult to measure the stock of equipment which industries are using. This is especially true of coal, for which only a rough and ready estimate can be made due to the difficulty of allowing for the effect of colliery closures. However, even if no allowance is made, the rise in residual productivity for coal since 1958 appears to have been as large as it has in manufacturing.

Because of the difficulty of calculating overall productivity, our estimates have very little independent value but corroborate rather than cast doubt upon what the labour productivity figures seemed to indicate. During the last decade their residual productivity turns out, like their labour productivity, to have been increasing at a rapid rate. Indeed, with the exception of electricity and railways, where special factors have been at work, their performance relative to manufacturing has been as good in terms of residual productivity as it has in terms of output per man hour. During the whole period of nationalization, allowance for capital does show the nationalized industries in a slightly less favourable light but the picture does not change beyond recognition.

Like with Like Productivity Comparisons

This is as far as it is possible to proceed by comparing the performance of the nationalized industries with that of manufacturing, but this, of course, is by no means the only type of comparison which it is possible to make. Instead of trying to compare different industries we can try to compare like with like. Unfortunately as long as attention is confined to Britain, it is impossible in most cases to make such a comparison because the whole of each industry is now in public ownership. Road transport is, however, an exception for here the performance of BRS can be compared with that of the road haulage industry as a whole. Over the period 1958–68 BRS output per man hour appears to have increased by almost exactly the same amount as it has in the industry of which it is a part.[15] However, in both cases the estimates of output are crude.

A comparison between public and private enterprise can also be made for buses. This is particularly interesting because, as we have seen, the record of the nationalized buses has been a dismal one. However the performance of British Electric Traction, which was by far the largest privately-controlled bus group, was no better. Between 1958 and 1966 its productivity and that of the nationalized Tillings and Scottish bus groups, as measured by journeys per man year, declined by almost exactly the same amount.[16]

Unfortunately road passenger and road freight transport are the only industries where this type of comparison can be made. For the other nationalized industries it is possible to compare their performance before they were brought into public ownership with their performance since. The productivity of all the public sector heavyweights has increased much faster since 1948, and especially since 1958, than it did between the wars. The Census of Production shows that in the gas industry output per man year was no higher in 1935 than it had been in 1924.[17] On the railways productivity increased by 1·2 per cent per annum between 1924 and 1935 compared with a rise of 2·3 per cent between 1948 and 1968 and of 4·3 per cent over the more recent period 1958–68.[18] In the coal industry there was an average increase of 1·9 per cent in output per manshift between 1924 and 1938. However, between 1948 and 1968 the figure was 3·1 per cent, with an average of 5 per cent from 1958 to 1968.[19] Electricity was the only one of the industries which had a fast rate of productivity growth before the war. Between 1924 and 1935 output per man rose by 5·5 per cent per annum but between 1948 and 1968 it grew by 6·3 per cent and over the period 1958–68 the figure was 8 per cent.[20]

It should be recognized that in some of these industries the picture

E

would have appeared rather different if the inter-war periods had been altered by a year or two. This is not true of gas and electricity. Between 1935 and the war there was no significant increase in gas productivity and output per man in electricity seems to have gone on rising at a swift rate.[21] But for coal and railways a slightly different impression could have been created by choosing a different terminal year. If 1936 or 1937 had been chosen the railway companies would be shown in a more favourable light as over the period 1924–37 their productivity grew by 1·5 per cent per annum. But if 1938 had been selected their performance would appear less satisfactory. The rise and fall of rail productivity between 1935 and 1938 was due to the growth of traffic during 1936 and 1937 and its sharp decline in 1938. Changes in output have a marked effect on rail productivity and for this reason 1935 is probably the fairest terminal year. Between 1948 and 1968 British Rail was handicapped by falling traffic whereas the private companies had the advantage of stable traffic between 1924 and 1936 and rising traffic between 1924 and 1937. Even the choice of 1935 places British Rail at a marked disadvantage as its traffic declined by 1·2 per cent per annum between 1948 and 1968 compared with an average fall of only 0·5 per cent between 1924 and 1935. In coal, output per manshift reached a peak in 1936 and then declined. As, however, this decline was not due to the state of trade and continued after 1938 the latter seems to be the most reasonable terminal year. It should be borne in mind that at the start of the inter-war period the industry's productivity was considerably lower than it had been at the turn of the century.

It is possible that the reason why the coal, gas and electricity industries have been increasing their productivity faster than they did between the wars is that they have invested more. After our previous findings, this type of argument can be treated with scepticism, but it cannot be dismissed out of hand. In this particular case it may provide the explanation. Estimates of residual productivity were prepared for the inter-war period by the method which has already been described. Figures for depreciation and the return on capital (at 10 per cent) in 1935, to serve as the renumeration of capital, were derived from Dr Charles Feinstein's study of capital formation during the inter-war period. This was also the source for estimates of capital stock.[22]

Once again the statistics for overall productivity show broadly the same picture as those for labour productivity; gas, railways, coal and electricity appear to have had a better performance since 1948 and especially since the late fifties, than they did before they were nationalized. Between 1924 and 1935 the overall productivity of the gas industry fell by 0·4 per cent per annum compared with a rise of 2·2 per cent per year between 1948 and 1968 and of 3·7 per cent between 1958 and 1968. The railways' residual productivity rose by 0·4 per cent per annum between 1924 and 1935 compared with an annual rise of 1·1 per cent over the period 1948–68 and of 2·4 per cent over the period 1958–68. For the coal industry there was a rise of 1·2 per cent between 1924 and 1938 and a gain of 1·9 per cent between 1948 and 1968 and of 3·3 per cent between 1958 and 1968.[23] Electricity is the only industry in which the post-war rate of productivity growth has been about the same as the pre-war rate. Between 1924 and 1935 its residual productivity increased by 3·2 per cent each year compared with a rate of 3·4 per cent between 1948 and 1968 and one of 3·1 per cent between 1958 and 1968.

Although statistics of overall productivity tell the same story for the nationalized industries as those for labour productivity, they tell a very different tale for manufacturing. This, too, has had a faster rate of increase in labour productivity since 1948 than it had before the war. For instance, between 1924 and 1937 output per worker increased by 2·0 per cent per annum, whereas between 1948 and 1968 output per man hour increased by 2·9 per cent each year and between 1958 and 1968 by 3·7 per cent.[24] However, as Professor Matthews has pointed out, this was entirely due to a higher rate of investment and consequently to a faster growth in capital stock.[25] Between 1924 and 1937 residual productivity in manufacturing increased by 2·2 per cent per annum compared with 2·0 per cent between 1948 and 1968 and with 2·4 per cent between 1958 and 1968. It would thus be wrong to imagine that manufacturing has, like the nationalized industries, increased its rate of progress in comparison with the pre-war period and to belittle the latter's performance on this account. Allowing for higher capital expenditure manufacturing productivity has only been increasing at about the same rate as it was between the wars.

It would obviously be foolish to attach too much weight to the fact that the nationalized industries have had a better productivity performance under public than under their former ownership. Technical progress has provided them with opportunities for increasing their output per man which they did not possess during the inter-war period. Nevertheless, at that time, most of the industries which were subsequently nationalized had considerable scope for increasing their productivity which they failed to exploit. In gas, coal, and railways the rate of progress could have been considerably faster than it was. The gas industry could, had it possessed a more rational structure, have made greater progress towards integration and the closure of small and inefficient works.[26] The coal industry, as the Reid Committee established, was technically backward.[27]

Between the wars the continental producers increased their productivity much faster than Britain. Over the period 1925–36 output per man shift underground increased by 130 per cent in Holland, by 104 per cent in the Ruhr, by 68 per cent in Belgium, by 63 per cent in France, but by only 34 per cent in Britain. Poland and Czechoslovakia also made much larger gains than Britain. Moreover, the picture remains the same even if these comparisons are taken back to 1913 or indeed to the 1880s: the British coal industry was falling behind.[28] By 1937 our OMS, which had once been the highest in Europe, was significantly lower than that of Holland, Germany, Poland and Czechoslovakia.[29] This does not mean that a decisive increase in productivity could easily have been won. As the Coal Board's experience during the first decade of nationalization was to show, the industry would first have to be reconstructed.[30] But, as its experience also proves, reconstruction ultimately yields handsome results.

Although the inefficiency of the railways was never exposed by an official committee in the same way as that of the coal industry, it is almost certain that larger gains in rail productivity were possible. First, the pace of electrification could have been faster. Even the Weir Committee's conservative estimates indicated that substantial savings, mainly in labour, would result from electrification.[31] However, the railway companies were wedded to steam and were happily engaged on building bigger and better locomotives which they hoped would match the new diesel expresses which the Germans were introducing.[32] Secondly, the companies failed to follow the continental example of introducing power brakes on wagons which would have led to a general speed-up of operations. Thirdly, there was the unnecessary shunting and empty running because empty coal wagons had to be returned to the collieries which owned them.[33] Fourth, there was ample scope for the rationalization both of the railway system and of operating methods. Even then, for instance, a large part of the route failed to pay its way.

CHAPTER 7

International Productivity Comparisons for Fuel and Power

Has the NCB Fallen Behind?

It has been asserted that our coal industry's record does not compare well with that of other countries. According to Professor Duncan Burn: 'The early years of the coal industry were extremely discouraging. Since 1957, when competitive pressures from oil and natural gas stirred the fuel industries, the record is better. But not better than the record in other countries.' Professor Burn goes on to compare the increase in output per manshift underground in the European Coal and Steel Community countries and in Britain from 1957 to 1963. He concludes that 'Britain did much less well than the other countries, excepting France . . . We are told the automatic mine is on the way, faster than elsewhere, but so far other mining areas have had better overall productivity increases.'[1]

If this is true then it is obviously a most important discovery. However, closer examination shows that Professor Burn ignored a number of factors which ought to be taken into account. For instance, he made no allowance for changes in the length of the shift. There were, however, a number of important changes during the period he used for his comparison. Shifts were lengthened in Germany and France and reduced in Britain.[2] If we use figures which allow for changes in shift length it appears that between 1958 and 1968 Germany was the only leading European coal-producing country which had a larger increase in productivity than Britain. It can be seen from Table 10 that in Germany OMS underground almost doubled and that in Britain it rose by 78 per cent. Belgium followed close on Britain's heels with an increase of 77 per cent. After Belgium came Poland with a rise of 63 per cent, Holland with a rise of 59 per cent, France with an increase of 36 per cent and Czechoslovakia with one of about 42 per cent between 1956 and 1968.

However, Belgium owed part of its productivity gain to the extensive pit closures in the southern coalfield where production slumped by well over 60 per cent. As productivity is exceptionally low in the southern

Table 10

INDEX NUMBERS OF LABOUR PRODUCTIVITY IN THE EUROPEAN COAL INDUSTRIES[1]

1936–68 (1958 = 100)

	Germany	Britain	Belgium	Campine	Poland	Holland	France	Czechoslovakia[2]
1936	121	94	103	..	158[3]	176	78	..
1952	84·2	96·9	90·9	..	107·8	105·9	80·6	..
1957	96·0	97·4	99·4	104·1	96·4	98·6	100·1	..
1958	100·0	100·0	100·0	100·0	100·0	100·0	100·0	..
1963	142·4	137·3	144·3	137·9	135·4	132·8	113·2	..
1964	147·6	143·1	139·8	130·2	140·4	136·2	118·3	..
1965	152·8	150·3	148·6	138·2	145·3	139·8	117·9	(101)
1966	165·3	153·8	158·3	148·8	150·9	142·8	121·6	(112)
1967	184·4	161·9	165·6	155·2	156·5	150·8	129·5	(125)
1968	199·2	177·6	176·7	168·0	163·2	159·0	135·7	(142)

[1] Tonnage per underground man shift allowing for changes in shift length.
[2] 1956 = 100; figure for 1968 is for January–September.
[3] 1937. Assumed that a shift of 7¼ hours was being worked.

Source: 1936–52 from OEEC *Industrial Statistics 1900–55* p 27; 1952–68 from NCB except that Campine from EEC *Energy Statistics*; Poland 1938–58 from UN/ECE *Quarterly Bulletin of Coal Statistics for Europe*; Czechoslovakia from UN/ECE/P p 163 and UN/ECE *Quarterly and Annual Bulletin of Coal Statistics for Europe*. For the length of Polish shifts see UN/ECE/P p 180; ILO *The World Coal Mining Industry*, 2 p 352 and International Labour Conference 1939 *Reduction of Hours of Work in Coal Mines* p 68. Elsewhere it appears that shift length remained the same between 1936 and 1952.

coalfield this obviously helped to boost productivity. In the north Belgium coalfield – the Campine – OMS underground increased by only 61 per cent between 1957 and 1968. Moreover, according to the High Authority of ECSC, productivity at the Belgian pits has been improved by cutting down on preparatory and maintenance work and by excessive skimming of seams.[3] But there can be no dispute that since 1958 Germany has increased its productivity considerably faster than we have. Although 1958 has been used as the starting point for most of these comparisons the picture would have been much the same if 1957, which Professor Burn favours, had been used.

What may be questioned is whether 1957 or 1958 is a really satisfactory base line for assessing the NCB's comparative performance. If, as Professor Burn says, the Board's previous performance was discouraging, that of most of the continental countries can only be described as disastrous. In 1958 OMS underground was below the pre-war level in every country except France. In Germany, for instance, it appears to have been about 20 per cent higher in 1936 than it was in 1958, whereas in Britain it was about 7 per cent above the pre-war level. The best starting point for any comparison which goes back to the pre-war era is 1936 because productivity almost everywhere reached a peak during that year and then declined. Hence it does not make much difference if 1937 or 1938 is used as the base year.

Over the period 1936 to 1968 our underground OMS increased by 90 per cent, which was the largest increase anywhere in Europe. The country with the next largest increase was France, whose productivity increased by 74 per cent; Belgium was close behind with a rise of 72 per cent, and then came Germany with one of 65 per cent. In Poland OMS was only slightly higher than it had been in 1937, and in Holland it was 10 per cent below the 1936 level.

Although it is not intended to explore the development of European productivity in detail, it is important to know why it took so long for Germany, Belgium and Poland to regain their best pre-war level and why Holland has not yet succeeded in doing so. If the answer is war destruction or deteriorating geological conditions then the comparison between Britain and the continental countries is unfair. The amount of investment must also be taken into account.

In France, according to the Economic Commission for Europe, there was a considerable amount of war damage and in the Ruhr a third of the pits were damaged or destroyed. The necessary repair work appears to have been undertaken remarkably quickly. France was the only major European producer to have regained its 1937 level of production by 1946, and in Lorraine, which had been particularly hard hit due to flooding, output in 1950 was already 50 per cent higher than it had been before the war. Moreover, as we have seen, France, despite its war damage, has had a large rise in productivity. In the Ruhr, as an OEEC report shows, only a small proportion of the pits were still out of action in 1949.[4] It is clear, therefore, that war destruction does not explain why it took most of the continental countries so long to get back to their pre-war levels of OMS.

Nevertheless their experience during the immediate post-war period does provide an explanation. In 1945 coal production in the continental countries had fallen to a very low level and there was an acute shortage of fuel. The principal reason was the depletion of the mining labour force; by the end of the war the industry was, to a considerable extent, manned by conscript workers who left when peace was declared. For instance in the Ruhr the work force, which was already down from 400,000 to 100,000, was mainly composed of foreign workers taken from the former occupied territories.[5] In this situation a desperate effort was naturally made to increase production by recruiting extra workers, especially as productivity was low and only recovered slowly.

> During the next three years [states the ECE] the labour force in the mines was restored and, in all producing countries except the United Kingdom, exceeded the pre-war numbers by the end of 1948 . . . However, . . . again with the exception of the United Kingdom, productivity remained very far below the pre-war rate. This is partly attributable to the higher average age of the workers in most countries, but it also appears that in many instances the attempt to expand production has resulted in crowding more workers into the mines than could be employed with maximum efficiency, thus causing an apparent reduction in output per worker.[6]

The number of underground workers in Poland was in 1949 about 50 per cent higher than it had been in 1937; and in the other continental countries it was between 20 per cent and 30 per cent greater. This forms a sharp contrast with Britain where, despite the NCB's best efforts, the figure was 10 per cent smaller.[7]

The association between the expansion of the mining labour force and low productivity, to which the UN and other observers have drawn attention, was no temporary phenomenon.[8] As late as 1958 those countries which had increased their productivity above the 1936 level were those which had reduced their work force below the 1936 level, and those countries whose OMS had fallen were those whose labour force had risen. Employment had fallen and productivity had risen in France and Britain, whereas the reverse had occurred in Holland, Poland, Germany and Belgium. Moreover, the two latter countries, which had a smaller labour increase than Holland and Poland, experienced a smaller productivity reduction than they did.[9]

What appears to have happened, although it was not the only factor at work, is that the generous standards of manning which had been adopted when coal was required at any price were never seriously revised. It was not until 1957, when the market turned sour, that a shake-out began. France was the exception because at an early date it started to prune its labour force and concentrate on higher productivity.

The main reason was that there was never a serious shortage of coal in France after 1949. This was due to the industry's success in increasing its production which, in turn, owed much to the large programme of capital expenditure it put into operation almost immediately after nationalization. In 1948 French colliery investment per ton produced was at least three times as great as it was in Britain. Charbonnages de France was, therefore, able to concentrate on improving its efficiency rather than its production. Indeed it was forced to do so because the industry ran into marketing difficulties during 1950 and again in 1953 and 1954. In the second modernization plan higher productivity became a main objective and after the 1953 recession it became the principal object. By 1957 a considerable amount of rationalization had already taken place and the French investment programme, which reached its peak around 1950, had already borne fruit.[10] This helps to explain why productivity has increased so little in recent years. Professor Burn's explanation – nationalization and protection – is wide of the mark.

Preoccupation with the problem of higher production does not fully explain the drop in Dutch productivity between 1936 and 1958. As we have seen, OMS in Holland is still considerably lower than it was before the war although the industry has, during recent years, cut back its production and made great efforts to improve its efficiency, which by technical standards has always been high. The explanation is the deterioration in geological conditions due to the exhaustion of the best seams. Between 1938 and 1955 the thickness of seams worked in the Dutch State Mines fell from $48\frac{1}{2}$ inches of coal to 39 inches or by a fifth. The position has probably improved somewhat now as production has been concentrated where working conditions are least difficult.[11]

The adverse effect of these developments was intensified during the years of coal shortage by the Dutch policy of extracting as much coal as possible from each deposit in order to husband their reserves. This led not only to the exploitation of seams which were lean and dirty but also of those where, due to faulting or some other reason, the coal could only be worked on a short front. As a result there was a large fall in average output per face which was one of the main technical causes of the high

OMS which Holland enjoyed before the war.[12] The switch from a policy of conservation to one of concentration must explain a considerable part of the rise in Dutch productivity since 1958.

Apart from Holland, it does not appear that productivity comparisons between Britain and the other continental producers are invalidated by changing geological conditions. Despite numerous assertions to the contrary, all the evidence suggests that conditions only change at a glacial speed in the large producing nations. This is illustrated by the remarkably slow increase in the proportion of British coal mined from thin seams. In 1900 18 per cent of our output came from seams which were less than three feet thick; 65 years later the figure was, believe it or not, 18 per cent.[13] It is therefore hardly surprising that, during the period with which we are concerned, there has been only a small change in the average thickness of seams worked. In 1938 the figure was 52 inches and in 1965 it was 50 inches, though it is true that dirt bands seem to have become rather wider.[14]

There is evidence that mining conditions have also been remarkably stable in the Ruhr. In 1963 the average seam being worked contained 49 inches of coal as against 45 in 1933 and 46½ in 1941.[15] This slight improvement may have been offset by a decline in the proportion of coal obtained from relatively flat seams.[16] For France and Poland information is only available for a comparatively short period, but there does not appear to have been any significant change in average seam thickness in Poland between 1955 and 1964 or in France between 1955 and 1966. Belgium is the only country, apart from Holland, where conditions do seem to have altered, though again information is only available for a short period. Between 1960 and 1967 the average seam thickness improved considerably from 46 inches to 53 inches. This was almost certainly due to the rundown of the southern coalfield where the seams are relatively thin, and are much more heavily folded and faulted than they are in the north.[17]

Geology and Productivity

Hitherto the discussion has centred on the pace at which productivity has been changing in different countries and coalfields. We must now examine their present positions in the productivity race. In coal, snapshot comparisons of this type are quite easy to make but very difficult to evaluate. The reason is that geological conditions vary from one place to another and the ease with which coal can be worked obviously helps to determine output per man. If productivity comparisons are to throw any light on the relative efficiency of mining operations, it is necessary to know both the way in which geology affects output per man and the extent to which mining conditions vary from one country or coalfield to another. Our first task, therefore, is to examine the influence of geology on productivity.

Although no systematic investigation of this problem appears to have been made it seems clear that there are a relatively small number of geological factors which are likely to have a decisive effect. This is apparent both from the numerous references to the subject which have been made in print and from discussions with mining engineers.[18] The five big factors which emerge are, as might be expected, the thickness of the seams being worked, their inclination, their depth, the composition of their roofs and floors, and the prevalence of faults. The National Coal Board has collected information on a number of these topics which it kindly made available. By analysing this it is possible to see what relationship they had with productivity.

When the figures for seam thickness and productivity are examined, a clear pattern emerges. The pits with the thinnest seams have the lowest OMS underground.[19] In 1965–6 it was 17 per cent below the national average at the 34 pits where the weighted average seam thickness was less than 30 inches and 8 per cent below at the pits where it was between 30 and 40 inches. Productivity rose to a high point where the seams were of a moderate thickness: OMS was 8 per cent above the national average at the mines where the seams were between 40 and 50 inches thick. It then slowly fell away until it was slightly below the national average at the pits with the thickest seams. Thus it was 99 per cent of the national figure at the 35 pits where the seams were 70 or more inches thick.

The fact that the pits with the thickest seams did not have the highest OMS need cause no surprise. Mining engineers report that as seams become thicker the condition of their roofs and floors tends to deteriorate because the pressure on them increases.[20] What is startling about the relationship between productivity and seam thickness is the small influence which seam thickness appears to have. It is only at pits where the seams are very thin that OMS differs markedly from the national average. The pattern is clear but its colours are not very bright.

This is also true of the relationship between productivity and seam inclination. Because very little coal is mined in Britain from steeply inclined seams it was necessary to obtain information from abroad on this topic. Statistics for West Germany show that productivity is highest at the flattest seams. In July 1967 OMS at the face was 4 per cent above the national average at seams which slope by 0–18 degrees. It was 8 per cent below average where the seams were inclined by 18–36 degrees. At seams which sloped by 36–54 degrees and 54–90 degrees productivity was 11 per cent below the average figure.[21] However, the relationship between seam inclination and the productivity of all underground workers was almost certainly less marked than the relationship at the face.

Analysis of British data on the depth at which coal is mined does not reveal any significant relationship with productivity. Output per man shift was considerably below the national average at very shallow pits, but that was all. To be more precise OMS during 1965–6 was 20 per cent below the national figure at the 21 pits where the weighted average depth at which coal was mined was less than 250 yards below the surface when a survey was conducted at the beginning of the year. Except for these pits no clear relationship between OMS and depth can be discerned. For instance, OMS was 1 per cent above the national average both at pits where the coal was mined at a depth of between 250 and 500 yards and at the 29 pits where it was over 2,250 yards and the depth was greatest. In between productivity fluctuated in a seemingly random manner from 4 per cent below the national average (at a depth of 1,500 to 1,750 yards) to 8 per cent above it (at a depth of 1,000 to 1,250 yards).

These results are somewhat surprising because pressures become greater as depth increases and this might be expected to have an adverse effect on productivity. For instance extra workers may have to be employed on maintaining underground roadways which deteriorate as the pressure pushes the roof and floor towards each other. The fact that productivity does not fall away could be due to the tendency for the thickness of the seams being worked to increase with depth. However, further analysis of the figures taking seam thickness into account did not reveal any general tendency for OMS to fall as depth increases.

The last geological factor for which there is any firm statistical information is the composition of seam roofs. Within the industry, sandstone is regarded as being probably the worst type of roof because, among other reasons, it fails, due to its strength, to collapse in a convenient manner but holds up for a considerable period thereby straining the support system only to crash down later *en masse*. The difficulty of working under these conditions is confirmed by an examination of the productivity at pits where there are sandstone roofs. It is slightly, but only slightly, below the national average. In 1965–6 OMS was about 5 per cent below the national average at the 19 pits where 75 per cent or more of the output was produced at seams with sandstone roofs, when a survey was conducted at the beginning of the year. Once again the pattern is clear but the colours are dull.

The condition of roofs and floors is also affected by the extent to which the strata are faulted. Naturally roofs tend to be weak where the ground is disturbed and this increases the difficulty of mining. This is not the only way in which faulting has an adverse effect on productivity. Although the whereabouts of major faults is usually known, minor faults are an unpredictable hazard. When they are encountered they bring operations to a halt and time and effort have to be devoted to crossing or getting behind the disturbed area; the task is all the more difficult because the seam will be at a different level on the other side of the fault. No wonder faulting is frequently regarded within the industry as the most important geological influence on productivity apart from seam thickness.[22]

Unfortunately, due to the absence of statistics it is impossible to form any clear idea of the impact which minor faults have on productivity. However, the position is by no means hopeless so far as major faults are concerned; although no direct information is available the problem can be approached indirectly. The chief way in which these faults will affect productivity will be to restrict the area of coal which can be worked, thereby depressing OMS because an excessive amount of labour will have to be devoted to opening up fresh faces.[23] Moreover, where faulting restricts not only the distance which can be advanced but also the length of the face, the effect will be particularly severe. OMS is considerably higher where faces are long because relatively little work then has to be devoted to advancing the side roads and cutting stable holes – the apertures into which the coal cutter is inserted so that it can begin a new traverse. A survey by the Coal Board during 1966 revealed that OMS at the coal face was 78 per cent higher where the length was over 250 yards than at short faces of between 50 and 100 yards. Furthermore, the productivity of those who work elsewhere underground is much higher where faces are long. As figures are available on the length of faces in different countries it is possible to tell whether they are shorter abroad than they are in Britain. Where they are as long or longer it is unlikely that major faults have a more adverse effect on their productivity than they have on our own.

How Mining Conditions Vary

Having examined the influence which the various geological factors have on productivity we can now turn our attention to the way in which they vary from place to place. As the object of the exercise is to discover in which countries or coalfields mining conditions are approximately the same as in Britain, we can start by ruling out those in which they are decidedly better or worse. There is no doubt that conditions are considerably more favourable in America than they are in Britain and the United States has therefore been excluded from the comparisons.[24] In contrast, the coalfields of south Belgium and northern France have been ruled out because their mining conditions are decidedly inferior to our own.

In south Belgium the seams are about as thick as they are in Britain but they contain a large amount of dirt. But what makes this area particularly difficult to work is the prevalence of faulting and the fact that the seams are surrounded by unstable heaving ground. Because conditions are so difficult it has been possible to introduce power-loading on only a limited scale. In the adjacent coalfields of northern France the position appears to be somewhat similar.[25] The Lorraine, which is the other main French coalfield, has also been excluded. Conditions in this field are quite different from those in Britain. The seams are both very much thicker and far more steeply inclined; 38 per cent of its output comes from seams which slope by more than 45 degrees whereas only $3\frac{1}{2}$ per cent of British production comes from those which have an inclination of more than 18 degrees. Nor can it be assumed, as it usually can, that sloping seams are a disadvantage because where they are very steep conditions may become easier.[26] This will be the case if the seams have been tilted *en bloc*, as when a telephone directory is rotated bodily from the flat to the vertical. If however the seams slip against each other, as when a telephone directory is held firm at one end and then bent, conditions become difficult due to the faulting which this will cause. In south Belgium the seams have in some places been bent in this manner whereas in the Lorraine they have not. Here, due to the steep inclination of the seams, it is possible to simply dislodge the coal and let it slide down into a line of tubs at the bottom.

In the other principal coalfields of Europe conditions appear to be similar enough to those in Britain to be worth investigating in detail. How does their seam thickness compare with seam thickness here? On the one hand, a relatively high proportion of British output comes from thin seams where productivity is low. In 1965–6 about 27 per cent of our output came from seams less than 40 inches thick. This compared during the early sixties with 7 per cent in Poland, 17 per cent in the Ruhr and 20 per cent in the Campine. Only in Czechoslovakia was the proportion of output from these seams (34 per cent) higher than in Britain. On the other hand, a relatively low proportion of our production comes from thick seams where productivity is past its peak. About 11 per cent of our output comes from seams of over 70 inches thick compared with 17 per cent in the Campine, a third in the Ruhr and Czechoslovakia, and 64 per cent in Poland.[27] The advantage of working relatively few thick seams which Britain enjoys appears to be cancelled out by the disadvantage of working a relatively large number of thin seams.

On balance mining conditions in Britain appear to be remarkably similar to those in the continental coalfields in which we are interested. This can be shown by calculating what British OMS would have been if the distribution of our output by seam thickness had been the same as that of each of the European producers. If our output had been distributed in the same way as in the Ruhr, Poland or the Campine our productivity would have been within 1 per cent of the actual figure. Only if it had been distributed as in Czechoslovakia would it have been significantly different. In this case it would have been 4 per cent lower because the bulk of Czech production comes from seams which are either very thin or very thick. Holland has had to be omitted from these comparisons because the distribution of its output is not readily available but in the early sixties the average seam thickness was about 8 per cent less than our own.[28]

Unfortunately, this is not the end of the story because no allowance has been made in these calculations for the fact that seams often contain bands of dirt and that some countries have dirtier seams than others. British seams are relatively clean by continental standards. In Germany they appear at first sight to have taken up a considerably higher proportion of the seam. But further inquiry shows that this is partly explained by the different ways in which seams are measured in the two countries. In Britain that part of the roof and floor which is extracted during the course of mining is not regarded as forming part of the seam whereas in Germany it is. Because of this difference in statistical conventions it is difficult to know how much dirt their seams would contain using British definitions. If it is assumed, however, that roof and floor dirt represent 40 per cent of the total thickness of dirt extracted (which is the portion in Holland), it appears that in 1968 dirt bands comprised $8\frac{1}{2}$ per cent of the average German seam. In the Netherlands during 1961 the figure was 13 per cent and in the Campine during the early sixties it is stated to have been 18 per cent. This seems very high and it is more than likely that roof and floor dirt has been included. Nevertheless we shall work on the assumption that it has not. No direct information is available for Poland and Czechoslovakia, but it seems likely that Polish seams are at least as clean as those in Britain and that Czech seams are only slightly more dirty.[29]

Turning from seam thickness to seam inclination, Britain and North Belgium possess the flattest seams in Europe. In Britain about $96\frac{1}{2}$ per cent of output comes from seams which are inclined by less than 18 degrees and in the Campine the proportion is about the same. They are also very flat in Holland where the figure is 84 per cent and in Poland and Czechoslovakia where it is around 80 per cent. However, in the Ruhr, where seams tend to be more inclined, the proportion is only 65 per cent.[30]

Except in the case of the Ruhr the advantage which Britain enjoys over the continental producers through flatter seams is hardly significant. This can be shown by calculating what our productivity would have been if the distribution of our output by seam slope had been the same as that of the various European countries. The calculations were made with the German figures for the relationship between face OMS and seam inclination. They showed that if our output had been distributed in the same way as it was in the Campine our productivity would have been unchanged, and that if it had been distributed as in Poland, Holland and Czechoslovakia, it would have been respectively 1 per cent, $1\frac{1}{2}$ per cent and $2\frac{1}{2}$ per cent lower. Even if our seams had been as steeply inclined as those in the Ruhr our productivity would have been reduced by no more than $4\frac{1}{2}$ per cent. Moreover, the use of statistics for the relationship between face OMS and seam inclination probably gives an exaggerated idea of the effect of seam inclination.

For faulting and for roof and floor conditions we have to rely on what the experts, and in particular those who have visited different coalfields, have to say. Holland appears to have the least favourable conditions. The Reid Committee described its seams as being often badly faulted, and a Coal Board team which visited Holland reported that the seams were disturbed by major and minor faults and severe undulations, and considered that mining conditions were more difficult than in Britain.[31] The Dutch told the ECE that 'the geological conditions compared with those of the basins in the adjacent coal-producing countries [i.e. the Campine and the Ruhr] are considerably less favourable. Tectonic disturbances occur frequently and the overlying stratum is waterlogged in places . . . Although the condition of the roof and floor of the older coal seams in the south-east is better than that of the younger seams in the north-west, it may be said in general that special measures in working the seams are necessary.'[32] Nevertheless faulting has not been so heavy that the length of Dutch faces has been seriously restricted. In 1966 their average length was 209 yards compared with just under 188 in Britain.[33]

The Reid Committee described the Ruhr as being more heavily faulted than Britain where in this respect conditions were perhaps somewhat easier.[34] A mining engineer from the Ruhr who has some acquaintance with conditions in Britain says that 'the relatively frequent occurrence of faults and the often rather friable roof makes the mechanization of coal mining and supporting operations much more difficult'.

He also says that 'undulating seams and fluctuating thickness occur much more often in West German mines than in British ones. Needless to say, this causes additional strains on the coal-getting machines, and also difficulties with the supports.'[35] The high level of mechanization achieved in the Ruhr suggests this may be an exaggerated account of the geological difficulties which are encountered. Furthermore floor conditions in the Ruhr appear to be reasonably good and hard. Indeed a British investigating team which visited the Saar and Holland, but spent most of its time in the Ruhr, reported that the roofs and floors at the seams it inspected were more favourable than the average in this country and that the degree of faulting did not differ greatly from that in Britain.[36] If our country had a decisive advantage over the Ruhr expert opinion would not differ in this way. Moreover, faulting has not been severe enough to have seriously restricted the length of German faces. In 1966 the average length was 200 yards which was rather higher than in Britain.[37]

It seems to be generally agreed that in Poland mining conditions are relatively easy. According to the Reid Committee the Upper Silesian coalfield is fairly free of faults and the roofs are generally good.[38] This is confirmed by an NCB technical mission which reported that although there were a number of fairly large faults there were no broken areas of large size. In contrast the incidence of faulting in the Lower Silesian coalfield was found to be very high.[39] But Upper Silesia accounts for over 90 per cent of Polish coal output.[40]

The Upper Silesian field continues into Czechoslovakia where, as the Ostrava Karvina coalfield, it accounts for about four-fifths of Czech production. An NCB technical delegation concluded that the geological conditions in this field are similar in many respects to those in Britain. It reported that at the two pits which it visited the roof conditions would be considered normal in this country but the floor was somewhat stronger.[41]

In Britain the coalfields of Yorkshire, the East Midlands, Northumberland and Durham, which are responsible for about two-thirds of our coal production, are fairly free of faults. However, the Scottish coalfields are fairly heavily faulted and in Lancashire and North Wales faulting is severe. In South Wales the roof is often broken or shattered but in Yorkshire and the East Midlands they are strong and in Northumberland, Durham and Scotland generally fairly good.[42]

It appears, therefore, that in Poland geological conditions both for faulting and for roofs and floors are at least as good as they are in Britain and that, if anything, they are better. In Czechoslovakia they seem to be much the same as in Britain, but in the Ruhr they are probably slightly more adverse though the difference cannot be very great. However, in Holland conditions are decidedly worse than they are in Britain.

We may sum up by saying that, taking all the different geological factors into account, mining conditions in Poland are about the same as they are in Britain but that in the other continental coalfields they are somewhat inferior. If the British coal industry was working under Czech conditions its OMS would probably be about 8 per cent less, mainly because the way in which output is distributed by seam thickness is less favourable in Czechoslovakia and because their seams are probably slightly more dirty. If the NCB was working under the conditions found in North Belgium its productivity might be as much as 14 per cent lower because of the extra dirt which its seams would contain, though this figure is probably on the high side. If our conditions were the same as those in Germany our productivity might again be about 10 per cent lower because of extra dirt (at 4 per cent); more steeply inclined seams (at say 2 or 3 per cent); a slightly greater amount of faulting; and slightly inferior roof conditions. This estimate squares reasonably well with Dr H. R. Sander's observation that 'geological difficulties, similar in some respects to those in West Germany, can be found in the North Western and Scottish Divisions of the National Coal Board'.[43] OMS underground is normally about 18 per cent below the national average in Scotland and 11 per cent less in the North Western Division.[44] If the British coal industry was working under Dutch mining conditions its OMS might be 20–25 per cent less. This is only a guess but it is clear that while geological conditions in Holland are considerably worse than our own, they are unlikely to have an adverse effect of more than about 25 per cent. Even in Wales, where mining conditions are notoriously difficult because of faulting, OMS is only about 25 per cent below the average for the whole of Britain.[45]

Coal Productivity in Britain and Europe

Having examined the way in which geological conditions affect productivity the final step is to discover how British OMS compares with that of the various European countries and coalfields. This, fortunately, is a relatively simple task. If attention is confined to underground workers, who account for the great bulk of the labour force, the coal industry has a firm boundary. There is a large quantity of information available on mining productivity, and a considerable amount of labour has been devoted to the preparation of comparable figures by a group of experts on coal statistics who meet under the auspices of the Economic Commission for Europe. The National Coal Board, which has taken a leading part in this work, regularly prepares standardized figures for OMS underground. These are accepted by the ECE as the best that can be done, and have, where possible, been used. The only further adjustment

Table 11

LABOUR PRODUCTIVITY IN THE EUROPEAN COAL
INDUSTRIES 1968

	Tonnage per Underground Manshift of 8 hours[1]	Per cent of Britain	Per cent by which OMS expected to be below Britain due to less favourable mining conditions
Germany	3·690	117·6	10
Britain	3·138	100·0	—
Holland	2·607	83·1	20–25
Poland	2·541	81·0	0
Campine	2·479	79·0	14 or less
Czechoslovakia	(2·415)	(77·0)	8
France	2·348	74·8	..
Belgium	2·228	71·0	..

[1] Metric tons.

found necessary was for Germany. For the Campine and Poland it was possible to prepare figures which were on the same, or almost the same basis, as the NCB's standardized statistics but despite adjustment the Czech figure may not be completely comparable.[46]

Germany is the only one of the countries and coalfields in which we are interested where the OMS is higher than in Britain. In 1968 it was 18 per cent higher; but in Holland it was 17 per cent lower than in Britain; in Poland 19 per cent lower; in the Campine 21 per cent lower; and in Czechoslovakia 23 per cent lower. However, when geological conditions are taken into account the comparison becomes somewhat less favourable to Britain. Germany is considerably further ahead than she appears because her geological conditions are somewhat more difficult. Indeed, if our 'guesstimate' of their influence is correct, productivity in Germany is about 30 per cent higher than in Britain. The Dutch coal industry may also have a higher technical efficiency than our own because although British OMS is higher, Dutch mining conditions are considerably more difficult. However, it does not seem likely that Holland is much ahead of Britain. Our lead over Belgium, in terms of OMS, appears to be slightly higher than was to be expected even if their seams really are as dirty as they appear. The Polish and Czech coal industries appear to be significantly less efficient than the NCB. Output per man shift is considerably lower in Poland although her geological conditions are no less favourable than our own and our lead over Czechoslovakia is considerably greater than was to be expected.

In 1884, after a pioneering attempt at international productivity comparisons, Mr J. S. Jeans told the Royal Statistical Society that the British coal industry had 'little need to fear or be ashamed'.[47] Today the British coal industry, due to the rise of alternative sources of energy, has reason to be afraid but it has little of which to be ashamed. After a long and dismal era, dating almost from the year in which Jeans spoke, during which the British coal industry fell behind in the productivity race, it has under the Coal Board's stewardship made up much of the ground which was lost, although the German lead remains substantial.

Productivity Changes in Electricity

How does the development of the British electricity industry's productivity compare with that of foreign countries? Unfortunately, figures on employment in electricity are not collected and published by any international organization and do not even seem to be available for a number of countries. However, information has been assembled for the American investor-owned utilities, for Electricité de France, and for Germany, Italy, Belgium and Norway. It is presented in Table 12.

Over the past decade the rise in productivity in Britain compares favourably with that in all but one of these countries. The exception is Belgium where between 1958 and 1967 sales per man hour increased by 144 per cent against 85 per cent in this country. In the other foreign countries, however, the rise in productivity was either about the same as or less than in Britain. In Germany sales per man hour in 1967 were 93 per cent greater than in 1958. This was a slightly larger increase than in Britain, but the British electricity industry secured so large a gain during 1968 that it seems doubtful whether German output per man hour can have risen faster between 1958 and 1968. Over this period our productivity rose by 110 per cent which placed us slightly ahead of the American private companies and Electricité de France. They both secured increases of just under 100 per cent. Although the French power workers did not come out on strike in 1968 EDF's performance in that year must, however, have been adversely affected by the strike wave. Therefore, it is probably fairer to disregard 1968 and restrict the comparison between Britain and France to the period 1958–67. On this basis EDF's productivity appears to have increased slightly faster but its lead was insignificant. After Germany, Britain and France, where productivity has been increasing at much the same rate, came Italy and Norway which trailed a long way behind. In 1967 sales per man hour in Italy were only about 57 per cent higher than they had been in 1958 and in Norway sales per man year were only 60 per cent greater.

Table 12

INDEX NUMBERS OF LABOUR PRODUCTIVITY AND
SALES IN ELECTRICITY FOR BRITAIN AND
FOREIGN COUNTRIES 1951–68 (1958 = 100)

	Belgium[2]	Germany	Britain	USA[3]	France	Italy[4]	Norway[5]
(i) Productivity[1]							
1951	..	..	68·7	63·0	63·2	..	..
1958	100·0	100·0	100·0	100·0	100·0	100·0	100·0
1966	220·2	187·0	178·2	178·3	181·0	150·5	151·9
1967	243·6	192·6	185·4	185·8	189·3	156·0	160·2
1968	..	..	210·4	199·3	199·4	..	..
(ii) Sales							
1951	..	..	60·2	59·9	59·2	..	..
1958	100·0	100·0	100·0	100·0	100·0	100·0	100·0
1966	203·1	202·9	187·1	181·3	194·9	177·6	178·5
1967	216·1	208·8	192·8	192·5	206·0	193·7	190·2
1968	..	..	207·4	211·5	217·0	..	..

[1] Sales to ultimate customers per man hour except where otherwise stated.
[2] Production and net purchases from industrial producers.
[3] Investor-owned utilities.
[4] Sales per manual worker hour.
[5] Sales per man year.

Source: UN/ECE *Annual Bulletin of Electric Energy Statistics for Europe* 1959 Table 4, 1968 Table 2; *Annuaire Statistique de la Belgique* 1967 p 299, etc; *Statistisches Jahrbuch für die Bundesrepublik Deutschland* 1962 p 254, 1969 p 229; Edison Electric Institute *Statistical Year Book* 1956 p 32, 1968 pp 31, 49; MDSD 1968–9 p 125 etc.; Table 5; MLG/EPG for hours; US Department of Labour *Monthly Labour Review* Table C1; EDF 1951 pp 37, 63, 1958 pp 67, 83, 1968 pp 20, 56; *Revue Français de Travail* January-March 1960 p 108; *Statistique Sociales* April 1969 Supplement p 87; information from the Italian Central Statistical Office; *Statistical Yearbook of Norway* 1963 p 127, 1969 p 113.

When assessing the comparative performances of the different countries, it is important to take a look at the extent to which sales have increased in each country because, in electricity, swiftly rising sales are a considerable advantage. It does not appear that Britain's favourable showing is explained by an exceptionally fast rise in sales. Over the period 1958–68, as can be seen from the Table, sales rose by slightly less in Britain (107 per cent) than in America (112 per cent) and France (117 per cent); and between 1958 and 1967 British sales increased by less (93 per cent) than German (109 per cent) and by the same amount as Italian and Norwegian consumption. Moreover in Belgium, which was the one country with a larger gain in productivity, the increase in sales was substantially greater (116 per cent) than in this country.

Although the British electricity industry's productivity performance seems, if anything, to have been slightly better than that of the American utilities, it has been argued that it is much inferior. Mr George Wansborough has produced figures which seem to show that since 1951 the American utilities have had a strikingly better record. He puts their increase in sales per employee at 181 per cent compared with a figure of only 119 per cent for Britain, excluding the North of Scotland Hydro-Electric Board.[48] But this comparison is misleading as he did not take the average hours worked into account. In the US they hardly changed but in Britain there has been a considerable fall. Allowing for this and bringing the comparison up to date the productivity gains become, for the period 1951–68, 216 per cent for America and 206 per cent for Britain. In reality, therefore, the gap between the two rates of advance was very small. It is also of interest that over this long period the growth of productivity here was much the same as in France. Between 1951 and 1968 EDF's sales per man hour rose by 216 per cent.

How British Productivity Compares with American

The electricity industry's critics have argued not only that productivity has been growing more slowly in Britain than it has in America, but also that our output per man is at a much lower level than that of the US investor-owned utilities. 'At present,' states Mr Robert Gilbert, 'the socialist experimenters have 57 per cent of US total [employment], while selling 18 per cent as much electricity, a padding of 216 per cent.'[49] Despite Mr Gilbert's quaint language, which is explained by the fact that he is an American, this is a serious charge. The only fault which can be found with the calculation, and it strengthens their case, is that Gilbert and his followers have ignored average hours and have mistakenly included the public utilities' sales to other electricity undertakings and foreign countries in their total sales. These outside sales are almost exactly offset by purchases from outside.[50] Excluding these sales and allowing for average hours it appears that in 1966 sales per man hour by the American private electricity sector were 260 per cent higher than they were in Britain.[51]

Although such calculations may be arithmetically correct it is possible, as the Electricity Council has argued, that they are misleading because the American utilities carry out less contracting and retail work. This is true, but it is offset by the fact that in the United States a higher proportion of employees seem to be engaged on capital work.[52] Nevertheless a comparison of units sold per employee is bound to favour the US companies because the level of consumption is much higher in America than Britain. In both countries there is a close statistical relationship between productivity and average consumption. In England and Wales sales per person employed by the South Wales Electricity Board, which enjoys the highest sales per consumer, are nearly 40 per cent greater than they are in the South Eastern Area, where the average consumption is lowest.[53] The association between productivity and sales is in no way surprising. The higher the level of consumption the more intensively the distribution system is used.

Although average consumption is about twice as high in the United States as it is in Britain there are some areas where it is approximately the same. In Massachusetts, Maine, New Hampshire, Vermont and Rhode Island, the five States where it is lowest, sales per consumer averaged 9,591 units in 1966. The corresponding figure for Britain was only slightly lower at 8,105. Moreover, in the five areas where the level of consumption is highest (the Midlands, South Wales, Manweb, Yorkshire and the North West) sales per customer were almost exactly the same as they are in the five New England States.[54]

A comparison of sales per employee in these selected areas should give a better idea of the extent to which the American electricity industry has higher productivity than a crude comparison between the two countries. In 1966 sales per worker by the investor-owned utilities of New England were 87 per cent greater than they were in the part of Britain where the level of consumption was about the same, excluding, in so far as possible, those engaged in retailing, contracting and capital work.[55] Although the productivity gap between Britain and America still seems formidable it now appears to be only about 40 per cent as large as a nationwide comparison suggests.

It is important to examine the New England utilities more closely to see whether they provide a proper basis for comparison. It is obviously possible that their relatively low level of output per worker by American standards is due not only to low consumption but also to low efficiency. However, the New England utilities seem if anything to be slightly above the average efficiency. W. Iulo, in his painstaking study of the comparative performance of American electric utilities, has examined the extent to which their unit costs are above or below average. Having discovered by means of regression analysis the principal factors which accounted for the variation in their costs he then found the extent to which each undertakings' costs diverged from the expected level. On this basis he classified them as 'relatively efficient', 'normally efficient', or 'relatively inefficient'. Fifteen of our New England utilities which account for over two-thirds of their total employment are covered by Iulo's study. Five are relatively efficient and two are inefficient. One of the inefficient utilities is a big concern but even so the efficient undertakings account for a somewhat larger proportion of all employees.[56]

Productivity in Europe

How does the British electricity industry's productivity compare with that of the continental countries? In 1967 sales per man hour seem to have been around 10 per cent higher in Germany than they were here. But the German supply authorities purchased a considerable proportion of the electricity which they sold from industrial producers. As measured by electricity generated and sent out per man hour, productivity in Germany was only about the same as in Britain.[57] Since, however, the distribution of electricity is considerably more labour intensive than its production, output per man would appear to be closer to the higher figure than to the lower one. These productivity estimates allow for the fact that the German electricity authorities undertake virtually no retailing and contracting work. 'Contracting and the sale of fittings,' reported a British Productivity Team which visited Germany in 1961, 'are left to private firms and the electricity supply service virtually ceases at the consumers' terminals'.[58] Therefore, in calculating productivity the 15,700 workers engaged in these activities in England and Wales were excluded from the British employment figure.[59]

In 1967 sales per man hour by Electricité de France were 23 per cent higher than they were in Britain. But like the Germans, EDF purchases large amounts of electricity from outside sources. In 1967 it bought 13 per cent of the electricity which it distributed chiefly from Compagnie Nationale du Rhône, which is a large hydro-electric producer; from the coal industry's pithead power stations; and from the railways. In terms of output per worker EDF's productivity was only 8 per cent higher than our own. These estimates allow for the fact that EDF does little selling or servicing of appliances but no allowance has been made for the advantage which it may enjoy as a large hydro-electric producer.[60] The last continental country for which a productivity comparison has been made is Italy. In 1967 Britain and the Italian Electricity Agency, ENEL, had approximately the same level of sales per employee, but in 1968 ENEL's productivity appears to have been 12 per cent lower than our own.[61]

Although our sales per consumer are low by American standards, they are considerably higher than they are in Germany and France, and three times as large as they are in Italy. This is because domestic consumption is very low in these countries, largely due to the fact that electricity is not used to any appreciable extent for home heating.[62] There are a number of reasons for this. Winters tend to be severe in Germany and northern France and this has led to the installation of central heating or large boilers. On the other hand in Italy and the south of France winters are usually too warm for space heating to be necessary. The tendency for consumption to be low is intensified by the high domestic tariffs which are necessary if electricity undertakings are to cover their (average) costs which are always high where consumption is low.

Perhaps the continental producers should, like the British electricity industry, have adopted promotional tariffs. What is clear is that if the level of consumption had been as low in Britain as it was in Germany, France or Italy our sales per employee would have compared even less favourably. It therefore seems likely that so far as the use of labour is concerned the British electricity industry is less efficient technically than a comparison of the crude figures for sales and output per worker may suggest.

It seems clear that the British electricity industry's general level of productivity is considerably below that of the United States even allowing for their advantage of higher average consumption. Nor is a comparison between Britain and the leading continental countries reassuring. Germany and France are slightly ahead of Britain in terms both of the amount of electricity sold and the quantity of electricity produced per worker although they appear to be at a disadvantage due to their low levels of consumption. The British electricity industry obviously has ample scope to economize in its use of labour. This indeed has been recognized by management and unions and the new productivity agreement should, in time, greatly reduce the gap between output per man in Britain and America.[63]

CHAPTER 8

International Productivity Comparisons for Transport

INTERNATIONAL productivity comparisons for railways are almost as difficult to make as those for coal. The main problem is the difficulty of measuring rail output. The solution which is usually adopted for international comparisons and other purposes is to add passenger miles and freight ton miles together to obtain what are usually described as 'traffic units'.[1] This is unsatisfactory because the amount of work involved in shifting a ton of freight from one place to another is generally greater than the amount involved in carrying a passenger. Not only do passengers weigh much less but unlike freight they load and unload themselves. This is reflected by the fact that the European railways generally charge more for transporting a ton of goods over a given distance than they do for carrying a passenger. It is, therefore, possible to construct rough production indices for the continental railways by adding passenger and freight ton miles with revenue weights. This is, of course, the normal method for constructing a production index and is the one which has been used in this study for the period 1958–68.

Although this method should produce a more accurate result than the simple addition of ton and passenger miles it is still a relatively crude calculation. In particular, no allowance is made for changes in the composition of freight and passenger traffic. That this is a point of some practical importance is shown by the divergence for British Rail between the change in weighted passenger and freight ton miles and the movement of the more sophisticated index of rail production from the Central Statistical Office, even after London Transport railways have been knocked off. Over the period 1958–68 the crude index declined by 16 per cent compared with a fall of $12\frac{1}{2}$ per cent as indicated by the CSO's figures. Although this is not an enormous difference it does mean that British Rail's productivity performance appears somewhat better when the sophisticated index is used than when the crude one is employed. This can be seen from Table 13 which besides presenting productivity figures for the European railways, as calculated from the crude indices of production, provides figures for British Rail using both the crude and the sophisticated measures of output. Although the sophisticated production and productivity figures for Britain are in general to be preferred to the crude estimates, it seems right to bear the latter in mind when assessing the relative performances of BR and the continental railways, in case shifts in the composition of traffic have also led to their productivity gains being understated. It is, of course, possible that instead of understating the rise in productivity on the continent the crude estimates overstate its growth. Indeed on at least one European railway there is reason to believe that this is the case. The growth in rail traffic in Sweden seems to have been mainly due to increased shipments of Lapland iron ore.[2] As this is almost certainly a low value traffic the Swedish railway's output, and therefore its output per worker, have probably increased less fast than they appear to have done.

The trouble involved in making international productivity comparisons for railways is repaid by their interest. Surprising as it may appear, British Rail's productivity performance compares favourably with that of the continental railways whichever way its output is measured. Using the sophisticated production index it can be seen that British Rail's productivity increased by 56 per cent between 1958 and 1968. The only continental railways which on this basis secured as large or larger rises were the German and Swedish. In Germany productivity appears to have increased by about as much as it has here, but in Sweden it appears to have increased by 77 per cent, but, as we have just seen, this almost certainly exaggerates the progress which the Swedish railways have made. Although British Rail is, using the preferred index, equal with Germany, two other countries are only just behind. In Belgium and Switzerland rail productivity appears to have risen by 50 per cent between 1958 and 1968. British Rail's lead over these railway systems was obviously too small to be of any great significance. Moreover, it disappears when the crude estimates of production and productivity are used. What is significant, and what remains true, is that none of the continental railways, with the doubtful exception of the Swedish, had a superior performance, while some had an inferior record. In 1968 rail productivity in Austria was only about a fifth higher than it had been 10 years before and in Italy and France it was only about a third greater; though it must be remembered that in 1968 the French railways were adversely affected by the strike wave which disrupted the whole economy.

Previous international comparisons for rail have shown that there is usually a close association between gains in traffic and productivity.[3] Here, British Rail has laboured under the disadvantage of falling traffic, while all the continental railways had the advantage of an increase. This

Table 13

INDEX NUMBERS OF LABOUR PRODUCTIVITY AND PRODUCTION FOR EUROPEAN RAILWAYS
PRE-WAR TO 1968 (1958 = 100)

	Sweden	Germany	British Rail		Belgium	Switzerland	France	Italy	Austria
			Sophisticated Estimate	Crude Estimate					
(i) Labour Productivity[1]									
Pre-war[2]	72·8³	..	83·4³	87·7³	65·3⁴	59·8³	55·9⁴	61·0³	67·4³
1950	90·3	90·1	100	95·2	70·7	80·3	62·6	73·2	73·9
1958	100	100	100	100	100	100	100	100	100
1966	172	141	135	131	145	144	130	113	127
1967	165	141	139	135	142	148	134	127	123
1968	177	158	156	150	150	150	132	132	119
(ii) Production[5]									
Pre-war	55·0³	..	82·6³	86·9³	108·8⁴	43·7³	83·0⁴	59·4³	49·0³
1950	103	105	109·8	104·3	87·8	75·6	77·7	78·1	77·6
1958	100	100	100·0	100·0	100	100	100	100	100
1966	137	110	87·7	85·2	100	143	120	114	117
1967	126	105	82·9	80·1	98·3	145	129	119	113
1968	129	112	87·4	83·9	103	149	117	121	111

[1] Output per man hour but it has been assumed that average hours did not change on the continent during 1967 and 1968.
[2] 1929 or 1938 whichever was higher.
³ 1938.
⁴ 1929.
[5] For continental railways traffic units pre-war to 1958; weighted passenger and freight ton miles 1958–68.

Source: Pre-war to 1958 information from continental railways. BR production is the CSO index excluding London Transport railways and for traffic units AAS 1957 p 203, 1963 p 191; employment from Ministry of Transport. *Railways (Staff) Return* 1938 p 5, BTC Statement VIII–1. For 1958–68 continental traffic from *International Railway Statistics* 1958, 1966, 1967, 1968, Tables 2–2, 2–3; revenue weights from 1958 Tables 3–1, 3–2, BTC 1959. 2 pp 174, 190. Continental man hours for 1958–66 from continental railways; employment for 1966–8 International Union of Railways figures supplied by BR. BR output is the CSO index excluding London Transport railways and for traffic units AAS 1967 p 202; BRB 1953. 2 p 49, 1964. 2 p 37, 1968 p 117. Employment from BTC. 2 Statement VIII–1; BRB Statement 5–H; average hours from MLG/EPG.

ranged from nearly 50 per cent in Switzerland and 30 per cent in Sweden to something over 10 per cent in Germany and Austria. Even in Belgium, the continental railway which fared worst, traffic was slightly higher in 1968 than it had been in 1958. But in Britain it was 13–16 per cent lower. In contrast, therefore, to most of the continental railways, British Rail secured its productivity increase wholly through the painful process of shedding workers. British Rail cut its labour force far more drastically than any other railway in Europe. Between 1958 and 1968 its employment fell by 46 per cent. In Belgium, Sweden and Germany employment was cut by about a quarter, but in the other continental countries it either increased or fell by only a small amount. Therefore, in so far as the decline in British Rail's traffic has been due to developments which were largely beyond its control, its comparative productivity performance is even more impressive than it appears.[4]

It has been suggested that the decline in its traffic at a time when traffic on the continental railways was increasing shows that British Rail is to blame for its misfortunes. However, as we shall see, there is no evidence that British Rail's passenger services are on balance of lower quality than those provided on the continent. How the quality of British Rail's freight service compares with that of the continental railways it is difficult to say, but what is clear is that they have nothing which matches BR's liner trains.[5] Moreover, there is no reason to believe that the movement of freight charges explains the differing experience of the British and continental railways. Over the period 1958–67 rail charges, as measured by revenue per ton mile, fell by 5 per cent in Britain. In several of the continental countries there was an increase. In Italy there was a rise of 15 per cent and in Austria and France charges appear to have risen by about 30 per cent or more. In Germany, Switzerland, Belgium and Sweden freight rates seem to have been stable or to have fallen slightly. But in no case was there a reduction of more than 5 per cent.[6] Due to changes in the composition of traffic, the average length of haul and differences between countries in the speed of inflation, too much weight should not be attached to these figures, but they certainly do not suggest that British Rail lost traffic because its charges increased relatively to those of the continental railways.

The explanation for the differing experience of the British and European railways is to be sought partly in the greater natural and legislative protection which the continental railways have enjoyed. The distance between industrial centres on the continent, and the relatively long average hauls which continental railways possess, afford them a measure of protection against road competition which is absent in Britain. Furthermore, in Switzerland, competition is limited because the country's terrain is so difficult. The Swiss roads are inadequate and as a result there are severe limitations on the weight and dimensions of lorries.[7] In other continental countries competition has been deliberately restricted in order to protect the railways. For instance, as the Geddes Committee points out, strict control is maintained over road haulage concerns in France and Germany:

> [The] central government decides the number of vehicles that provincial authorities may license for long-distance haulage. The 'quotas' have been increased very little since before the war . . . At the same time the French and German Governments exercise close control over the charges made for road haulage in the same way as railway rates are controlled. Indeed, in Germany the rate schedule for long-distance road transport was until recently identical to the railway rate schedule.[8]

Moreover, transport on own account has been subjected to special taxation. Between 1955 and 1958 the German Government sharply increased the tax on the long-distance sector by 2d per ton mile with the object of safeguarding the railways. The extraordinary severity of this tax can be seen from the fact that in 1968 British Rail's average charge for freight was only 3·3d per ton mile. There has been some tendency during recent years for the continental railways to lose their privileged position (and their traffic). In Germany taxation has been substantially reduced and in Belgium the strict control which had previously been exercised over road haulage contractors in the interests of the railways was abolished in 1960.[9] Nevertheless, there is no doubt that many of the continental railways have enjoyed a substantial measure of protection against road competition.

Although the growth in British Rail's productivity compares favourably with that of the continental railways during the last decade, notwithstanding the disadvantage of declining traffic, it must be recognized that, if the comparison is taken back to 1950, BR's performance appears much less satisfactory. For the period 1950–8 passenger and freight ton miles were as before combined with (1954) revenue weights. A comparison of the results obtained in this way and by the traffic unit method shows that over this period, at least, there is no great difference. Employment figures before 1958 are somewhat dubious although there are reliable statistics for traffic units per man hour. It was, therefore, decided to fall back upon the latter measure. But, as before, a more sophisticated estimate of British Rail's productivity was derived from the official index of rail output. Table 13 shows that between 1950 and 1958 most continental railways secured worthwhile gains in productivity, whereas BR's output per man failed to rise when the preferred measure of output is used (and barely increased when rail production is measured in traffic units). As a result, although BR is near the top of the productivity league for the period 1958–68, it is at the bottom for the period 1950–68. In 1968 British Rail's productivity appears to have been around 57 per cent higher than in 1950 (and it does not make any difference how production is measured). The only continental country which did almost equally badly was the Austrian railways. In Germany, Italy, Switzerland and Sweden productivity appears to have been somewhere between 75 and 95 per cent higher than it had been in 1950, and in Belgium and France it seems to have more than doubled. It must, however, be borne in mind that all of the continental railways have had the advantage that their traffic has risen whereas BR had the disadvantage of a slump. It may also be questioned whether 1950 is a satisfactory basis for international rail comparisons, but for this industry, in contrast to coal, it appears to be a fair starting point.

Estimating Productivity Levels

Having examined the rate at which the different railways have been increasing their productivity we must now compare the level of output per man in the various countries. Despite the relatively swift progress which British Rail has been making previous studies suggest that our railways are still a long way behind those on the continent. According to D. L. Munby's estimates the volume of traffic per employee in 1959 was 55 per cent higher in Germany than in Britain, 90 per cent higher in France and 106 per cent greater in Italy. If these figures are correct then, even allowing for some narrowing of the gap since 1959, British Rail is desperately inefficient by continental standards. However, Mr Munby warns that

> comparisons of labour productivity are particularly difficult and can be very misleading, in so far as different railway systems do or do not employ their own labour to build and repair stock and track. We have made . . . no allowance for it (or for any of the other complications) in the case of these international comparisons, so that the figures must be treated with caution.[10]

This is a candid and disarming admission but it hardly inspires confidence in Mr Munby's findings. Mr Munby, as a pioneer worker in the field of international rail comparisons, may perhaps be excused for recognizing a problem, staring it in the face and then passing on, but the time has come to produce more reliable figures.

There are other complications, as Mr Munby suspected, besides the fact that some railways are more self-reliant than others, which further reduce the value of his findings. He measured the output of the different European railways by adding their passenger kilometres and their freight ton kilometres together. But, as we have seen, this is an unsatisfactory approach because the transportation of a ton of freight for one mile involves more work, and earns more revenue, than the transportation of a passenger. As the relative importance of freight and passenger traffic differs greatly from one European railway to another, this means that Mr Munby's figures are bound to be misleading. The rot goes deeper than this because short-haul traffic involves more work per mile and earns more revenue per mile than long-haul traffic. Because the proportion of short and long-haul traffic varies from country to country, it is necessary to allow for this fact.

This can be done along normal statistical lines by discovering the distribution of freight traffic by distance in each country and the average revenue per ton for each distance. The amount of freight traffic can then be calculated, country by country, by multiplying the tonnage carried by the revenue per ton, and summing up the results. Passenger traffic can then be calculated by multiplying the number of passenger miles by the revenue per passenger mile, and adding this to the figure for freight. In this way freight traffic in general, and short-haul traffic in particular, are given their due weight. This method was therefore adopted after British Rail had kindly supplied figures for a sample week during 1966, showing for coal and other wagon-load traffic its revenue and tonnage broken down by distance.[11] From this the necessary figures for revenue per ton were calculated.

It was necessary to take into account the fact that the composition of traffic varies from country to country. The ideal way of handling such differences would be to discover the way in which the tonnage of each commodity is distributed by distance and the appropriate revenue per ton. Unfortunately, it proved impossible to obtain from the various railways all the necessary information and the best which could be done was to distinguish between coal, general freight in wagon-load quantities, and part-load traffic, such as parcels and mail. However, for the Italian and German railways, where only the tonnage of coal was known, all wagon-load traffic was ultimately treated as if it was general freight.[12] This seemed justified because the Italian railways carry very little coal, and, when assumptions were made about the distribution of German coal by distance, it was found to make very little difference whether it was accorded separate treatment. For part-load traffic the tonnage carried (and no allowance was made for distance) was readily available for the three continental systems.[13] However, an estimate had to be made for British Rail so that it could be divided into British Rail's revenue to ascertain its receipts per ton for the purpose of weighting.[14]

Although it is impossible to be certain, it seems unlikely that the failure to go further and distinguish other categories of freight traffic has greatly affected our results. Once coal is excluded, the composition of goods traffic appears to be very similar in Britain, Germany and France. In all three, basic and bulky products account for the greater part of the tonnage carried. For instance in 1966 the steel, oil, chemical and building material industries were responsible for about 88 per cent of the tonnage in Britain, 70 per cent in Germany, and 63 per cent in France.[15] Allowance was made for the fact that the three continental railways carry large amounts of goods which involve relatively little work because they pass straight through the country or only have to be loaded or unloaded. However, their output turned out to be only slightly lower than it previously appeared.[16]

The final stage in the calculation of the comparative productivity of the different European railways is to allow for the fact that, as Mr Munby observed, some are more self-reliant than others. There appears to be a tendency for British Rail to undertake work and provide services with its own labour where the continental railways would use an outside firm. In Germany, for instance, the repair and renewal of the track and the manufacture of new rolling stock is carried out by private undertakings.[17] Fortunately the continental railways have, from time to time, provided the International Union of Railways with estimates of the extra workers which they would have had to employ if they had not relied on outside concerns in this way. It is, therefore, possible to adjust their employment figures to make them more comparable with those of British Rail.[18]

Table 14

OUTPUT, EMPLOYMENT AND LABOUR
PRODUCTIVITY FOR BRITISH RAIL AND THE
FRENCH, GERMAN AND ITALIAN RAILWAYS 1966
(*British Rail 1966 = 100*)

	Traffic Units	*Weighted Output*	*Adjusted Employment*	*Weighted output per worker*
French National Railways	190·0	167·3	110·5	151·4
German Federal Railway	169·7	168·1	133·0	126·4
Italian State Railways	80·6	62·3	61·5	101·4
British Rail	100·0	100·0	100·0	100·0

F

How BR Compares

The results of these computations are set out in Table 14, together with figures for the output of the different railways as calculated from traffic units. It can be seen that, in general, the crude addition of ton and passenger miles gives an exaggerated impression of the output of the foreign railways. In terms of traffic units SNCF's output during 1966 was 90 per cent larger than that of British Rail whereas our calculations show it as being around 67 per cent greater. Again the production of the Italian State Railways was only 19 per cent smaller than that of BR as measured by traffic unit, but about 38 per cent less in terms of weighed output. However, in the case of the German Federal Railway, the results of the two calculations correspond almost exactly. At 68 per cent above that of British Rail their weighted output is a mere $1\frac{1}{2}$ percentage points less than their output in traffic units.

There is nothing surprising about the fact that British Rail's output, relative to that of France and Italy, turns out to be somewhat greater than crude calculations make it appear. Indeed it is exactly what one would expect from the structure of their traffic. In both countries the proportion of short-haul (and high value) freight traffic is much smaller than in Britain, although for France this is partly offset by the fact that BR carries relatively more (low value) passenger traffic than SNCF. British Rail also carries considerably more than the Bundesbahn and this explains why, despite BR's somewhat greater proportion of short-haul freight, our calculations of the relative output of the Bundesbahn and British Rail give more or less the same results as estimates based on traffic units.

It can be seen from the Table that even when allowance is made for the differing patterns of traffic in France and Britain SNCF retains a large lead in output per worker. In 1966 the French railways' level of productivity was about 50 per cent higher than that of BR. The Bundesbahn's lead, at around 25 per cent, was less great than the French railways but was nevertheless a considerable one. However, in Italy the level of output per worker was only about the same as in Britain.

In contrast to the nationalized industries which have already been considered, it is possible to investigate in detail the reasons why British Rail occupies the position which it does. This is due to the considerable volume of information which is available on the work performed and equipment used by the different railway administrations. An investigation of why the French and German railways have a higher output per worker than BR is not only of great inherent interest but also necessary because of what has previously been said about British Rail and foreign railways. In our discussion of technical progress within the public enterprise sector, it was found that BR had, after a late start, made considerable progress by foreign standards towards the modernization of its equipment and the adoption of up-to-date operating methods. Though some weak spots, such as the small size of British wagons, were identified it also became clear that BR had with its freightliners played an important part in the development of fast and efficient door-to-door transport. What we must now try to discover is whether the technical and operating weaknesses which British Rail has not yet fully overcome explain why its productivity is somewhat lower than that of the German and much lower than that of the French railways; or what other explanations there may be.

The largest block of railway workers are employed on the maintenance and servicing of railway vehicles. In 1967 this work absorbed nearly a third of British Rail's manual employees. The maintenance and servicing of carriages and wagons appears to have been the task on which most workers were engaged.[19] The volume of maintenance work and the number of workers employed varies with the size of the carriage and wagon stock. The number of vehicles is, for instance, more important than their capacity because a large wagon or carriage does not require proportionately more maintenance than a small one. Although a vehicle which is intensively used will need more maintenance than one which is little used even this will have to be serviced from time to time. In 1967, despite the large cutback which had taken place, British Rail's carriages and wagons were still being used very much less intensively than those of the continental countries. In Italy carriage utilization, as measured by passenger miles per carriage was twice as great as in Britain, in France it was over 75 per cent greater, and in Germany it was over 10 per cent higher. On the freight side the contrast between the utilization of rolling stock in Britain and the continental countries was even sharper. In France wagon utilization, in terms of freight output per wagon, was nearly four times as great as in Britain, in Germany well over two and a half times as high and in Italy it was over twice as high.[20]

What is the explanation for British Rail's extremely poor showing? The British Transport Commission suggested to the Select Committee that it was partly due to seasonal fluctuations in traffic which were sharper in this country than in France or Germany. On the freight side an examination of monthly figures for the years 1964, 1965 and 1966 showed that British Rail's traffic was slightly more 'peaky'. However, BR's disadvantage was so small that it can only account for a small part of the difference in wagon utilization. On the passenger side, it is British

Rail which appears to enjoy the advantage of having less seasonal variation in its traffic. It is possible, and in the case of France probable, that the peak-hour problem is more intense on the British suburban services than it is in Europe, but it is difficult to see how this can account for more than a small part of our inferior carriage utilization.[21]

What does help to explain British Rail's depressing performance is that both our carriages and our wagons are smaller than their continental counterparts. For instance, in Germany, which has the largest wagons, the Bundesbahn's vehicles have well over 60 per cent more capacity than British Rail's; and in Italy, which has the largest coaches, they are 15 per cent larger than in Britain. The small size of our carriages is due to the fact that there is insufficient clearance on platforms and tunnels to allow for the way in which long coaches overhang the track on bends. The cost of providing extra clearance would be prohibitive. The low capacity of British wagons is, as we have seen, one of the long-standing weaknesses of our railway system, which has never been put right.[22] But the relatively small size of British rolling stock only partly explains why the continental railways get so much more use out of their carriages and wagons. For wagons the main factor seems to be that although British Rail has drastically and progressively tightened up its methods of wagon control since the early sixties its standards are still greatly inferior to those which have over the years been developed on the continent. The same is probably true for carriages despite the marked improvement in their utilization made during recent years.[23] Another explanation for Britain's inferiority is probably the relatively small loads which our passenger trains carry.

Whatever the explanation for the present state of affairs there is no insuperable obstacle to prevent British Rail from reducing the size of its carriage and wagon fleets and using the remaining vehicles more intensively. This in fact is exactly what the Railways Board is planning to do. It intends to reduce the number of coaches, which at the end of 1967 stood at 9,300, to about 5,000 and for freight vehicles an even more drastic cutback is in store. According to the Chairman of British Rail, Sir Henry Johnson, 'The existing wagon fleet, comprising more than 400,000 vehicles, restricted in speed and designed and built to Victorian standards, is the biggest and least efficient in Europe. It must be replaced by a modern fleet of, say, 100,000/150,000 wagons capable of running at least at 60 miles per hour, fitted with power brakes, and needing little maintenance.'[24] When these goals have been achieved British Rail's utilization of its freight and coaching vehicles should approximate to continental standards.

Train crews are another major group of railway workers. In 1967 drivers, firemen and guards comprised over a fifth of British Rail's manual employment. The productivity of these workers is largely determined by whether the goods and passenger trains which they operate are heavily or lightly loaded. Now one of the most striking features about British Rail is that, by continental standards, its trains carry very small loads. In 1967 output per train mile was about 85 per cent higher in France than in Britain, 50 per cent higher in Germany and 25 per cent greater in Italy.[25] Both our passenger and our freight trains are more lightly loaded.

In 1967 passenger trains carried an average of 163 passengers in France and 151 in Italy, compared with 96 in Britain and 94 in Germany. Our passenger trains would be more heavily loaded were it not for the stopping and suburban services. It appears that on suburban services the number of passengers per train is slightly below the general average and that on the stopping trains it is little more than half as great. In contrast British Rail's inter-city passenger trains carry an average of 150 passengers.[26] But even these appear to be relatively lightly loaded because, as we have just seen, the average Italian train carries as many passengers and French trains carry more despite the inclusion of stopping services.

The heavy loads which continental trains carry seem to be mainly explained by the fact that British Rail provides a more frequent service. In 1967 an average of 51 passenger trains passed daily over each mile of railway route which was open to passenger traffic. In France the figure was 22, in Italy it was 33 and in Germany 36.[27] It is significant that it is in Germany, the continental country where trains were most frequent, that the number of passengers per train was nearest to our own. There is nothing surprising about the discovery that British Rail provides a more frequent service than the other countries. It is the practice on the continent, and especially in France, to dispatch flights of trains during certain times of the day whereas British Rail strives to maintain a regular and frequent service.

British Rail's emphasis on regularity and frequency seems to be partly a matter of marketing policy. BR considers that in this way it can secure the optimum level of traffic. However, it is more necessary to provide a frequent fixed interval service in Britain than it is on the continent where the average length of journey tends to be longer. In 1967 the average was 54 miles in Italy, 38 miles in France, 22 miles in Germany and slightly less than this in Britain.[28] When journeys are short, due to reasons of geography, it is no use a railway scheduling trains to suit its own convenience if it is to secure traffic. Trains have to be timed to the requirements of the customers who cannot be expected, when they are only going to travel a short distance, to wait until the railway chooses to run a train or even to look up a time-table to see when it will do so.

Although the frequency of passenger trains in Britain is probably the most important reason why they are so lightly loaded there are other forces at work. This is shown by a comparison of suburban services in Britain and France. In Britain suburban services are relatively lightly loaded due to the way in which the bulk of traffic is concentrated during the rush hours with the trains running almost empty during the rest of the day. In France, however, the Parisian suburban trains are extremely heavily loaded. During 1967 they carried an average of 230 passengers which appears to be about two and a half times as many as British suburban trains. One reason for this may be that a large number of Parisian workers still go home to lunch.[29]

By continental standards our freight trains are, like our passenger trains, lightly loaded. In 1967 the amount of wagon-load freight per train mile was well over 50 per cent higher in Germany than in Britain, 40 per cent higher in France and slightly greater in Italy. British Rail attributes the small size of our trains to reasons of history. One of these is that Britain has for years been the only major industrial nation in which a large proportion of goods traffic is carried in loose-coupled wagons not fitted with power brakes. In the absence of a proper braking system trains obviously have to be short and light because of the difficulty of stopping if they are heavy. Moreover, the length of those trains which are equipped with power brakes often has to be restricted because of the limitations of the braking system in use.[30]

Another historical reason, or rather set of reasons, why British trains are so short is that in the past many marshalling yards were too cramped for larger trains to be assembled; that many lightly-loaded trains were run in order to pick up and deliver wagons at depots which handled little traffic; and that freight services were maintained over parallel routes which had once been under the ownership of different companies.[31] By the mid-sixties the marshalling yard system had been more or less modernized and hundreds of old-fashioned yards and little-used freight depots had been closed, but the traditional pattern of operations, and the habit of running short trains, to some extent survived. A National Freight Train Plan was, therefore, launched with the object of concentrating traffic and building up larger trains, a policy which had long ago been adopted in France and Germany. British Rail's campaign seems to have had a large measure of success. In 1963 the average train load was scarcely greater than in 1957, but by 1968 it had shot up by 45 per cent.[32]

It appears likely that this rise had other causes besides the concentration of existing traffic on to fewer trains. The rise must also have owed something to British Rail's drive to secure train-load traffic, the paucity of which constituted yet another of its historical weaknesses. No doubt if the Freight Train Plan and the marketing drive had been started earlier the average load carried by British freight trains would not in 1967 have compared so badly with that of the continental railways. As we shall see, however, when we come to examine the reasons why rail traffic has fallen, there is remarkably little train-load traffic for the railways to capture.[33] It, therefore, seems possible that freight does not move in bulk to the same extent in Britain as it does on the continent and that this helps to explain why our freight trains are so short.

The last major area of rail activity which warrants investigation is the operation and maintenance of the signalling and the maintenance of the track. In 1967 it accounted for a fifth of British Rail's manual employees. As Dr Stewart Joy has forcefully argued, standards of track maintenance and of signalling can be adjusted to the volume of traffic but it remains true that the number of staff required does not vary in proportion. Moreover, what is crucial is the number of trains which pass over the line rather than the loads which they carry. A railway which runs a large number of trains will require a high-quality signalling system even if they are all empty, and its trains would still be heavy and give rise to considerable track maintenance because of the weight of the locomotive.[34] It is evident, therefore, that the productivity of signalling staff and track maintenance workers largely depends on the quantity of goods and the number of passengers passing over the line although the standard of signalling which is necessary and the amount of track maintenance are largely determined by the number of trains.

Despite the Beeching closures British Rail's output per track mile is lower than that of the continental countries. In 1967 the figure was 50 per cent higher in Germany, about 45 per cent higher in Italy and a third greater in France. The productivity of our track maintenance workers must therefore be lower. However, in the case of signalling staff, output per route mile is the determining factor because the signalling system will be more or less the same regardless of the number of tracks. For once, British Rail compares fairly well with the three continental countries. In 1967 output per route mile was about a fifth greater in Germany but in France it was no higher and in Italy it was 7 per cent smaller.[35] Although the quantity of freight and passenger traffic which passes over British Rail's track is low by continental standards the number of trains which pass over its track is not, on balance, very different. The number of trains per mile of running track was about 25 per cent lower in France than in Britain during 1967, whereas in Germany it was 7 per cent greater and in Italy the number was about 10 per cent higher.[36] The seeming paradox that in comparison with the continental countries more trains than traffic pass over our track is, of course, due to the fact that by continental standards both our freight and our passenger trains are very lightly loaded. As we have seen, the shortness of our freight trains is due to a number of long-standing technical weaknesses which are now being overcome, and our passenger trains are lightly loaded partly because of the British policy of providing a frequent, high-quality service. It is passenger train operations which principally determine how intensively the track is utilized, because in Britain passenger trains account for over 70 per cent of all train miles. The fact that British Rail has a large amount of track in relation to its output is therefore partly a consequence of the high quality of its passenger service.

A number of important conclusions emerge from this area-by-area comparison between British Rail and the main continental systems. First, it is evident that British Rail has serious technical and operating weaknesses which have an adverse effect on productivity. They include the low capacity of our wagons and the excessive maintenance (and also marshalling and track repair) to which this gives rise; British Rail's inferior standards of wagon control which again results in the maintenance of an excessive number of vehicles; the lack of power brakes on so many of our wagons and, in consequence, the shortness of our freight trains; and the continued operation of branch-line services despite the low level of traffic. These weaknesses are no new development but have been obvious for half a century. Some of them, such as BR's inferior standards of wagon control, are in the process of being tackled while the final solutions of other difficulties, such as the inefficiency of the wagons themselves, are now being planned. Despite the progress which has been and is being made it none the less remains true that British Rail's historical weaknesses explain a large part of the gap between its output per worker and that of the German and French railways.

The second main conclusion is that British Rail labours under a number of disadvantages which are beyond or almost beyond its control. British carriages are somewhat smaller than those on the continent because of the lack of clearance on bends; commuter traffic is more 'peaky' than in France and what is far more important the average passenger journey is shorter because Britain is a small island country. In order to compete with the car over short distances, BR has to provide a more frequent service than the continental countries although this entails the running of a large number of lightly-loaded trains. This not only requires the employment of extra train crews but also necessitates the upkeep of a larger fleet of rail vehicles and a longer mileage of track than would otherwise be required.

The provision of a frequent and regular service is, however, more than a defensive reaction. It is, to some extent, an attempt on the part of British Rail to provide its passengers with a service of exceptionally high standard. Although the emphasis on regularity and frequency has some adverse consequences for the passenger it seems likely that British Rail does provide a superior standard of service to most of the continental railways.[37] The third main reason, therefore, why British Rail's production per worker is lower than that of the French and German railways is that its output is of somewhat higher quality. If allowance could be made for this the productivity gap would appear smaller than it does.

It seems likely that these factors more than explain why the level of productivity on the French and German railways appears to be higher than in Britain. Not only is British Rail's showing so poor in terms of the various operating ratios that a larger productivity gap would have been expected, but for Italy there is no gap although BR's operating performance is also greatly inferior. At first sight this appears to throw doubt upon our calculations of output per worker, but this is not really the case because the various operating ratios, such as output per wagon and per track mile, were derived from the same figures for production as the estimates of output per worker.

What does seem likely is that, although British Rail performs a large amount of work, which the continental railways avoid due to their superior operating performance, it does this work very efficiently. For instance, the fact that relatively little goods or passenger traffic passes over BR lines means that it is involved in more track maintenance than the continental railways. It is quite possible that it uses fewer men to undertake this work than the continental railways would require. In order to check this theory it would be necessary to have more information about the composition of the different railways' employment than appears to be available. The way, however, in which BR has ruthlessly pruned down its labour force makes it appear likely that this is the explanation. Moreover, when British railwaymen visit the continent they report that manning standards are more generous.

Productivity Growth in Aviation

The last part of the public enterprise sector for which international productivity comparisons can readily be made is the airways. Table 15 shows that over the period 1958–68 BOAC increased its productivity much faster than any other major international airline, whereas BEA was almost at the bottom of the league. As measured by passenger miles per employee, BOAC's productivity rose by 232 per cent over the period. This estimate allows for the loss of traffic caused by the pilots' strike which took place during the summer of 1968. However, even if no allowance had been made, the growth in BOAC's output per worker would (at 212 per cent) still have exceeded that of Lufthansa, which was its nearest rival, by a large margin. Between 1958 and 1968 Lufthansa secured a productivity increase of 177 per cent. It was closely followed by KLM and Alitalia, both of which had increases of about 172 per cent. Then, after a considerable interval, came Qantas and Pan American Airways at around 135 per cent. They were followed by SAS at 114 per cent; Japanese Airlines at 107 per cent; Air France, allowing very roughly for the effect of the 1968 strike wave, at about the same figure; and Swissair at 84 per cent. Finally there was BEA with an increase of 56 per cent and Sabena with one of 50 per cent.

Obviously BEA's performance leaves something to be desired. However if BEA and BOAC are treated as a single airline it can be seen that the overall performance of the British air corporations has been relatively satisfactory. Between 1958 and 1968 their output per worker increased by 144 per cent, allowing for BOAC's strike. This was somewhat less than the gain of between 170 per cent and 180 per cent which was secured by Lufthansa, KLM and Alitalia but it was a larger increase than the other seven foreign airlines managed to obtain.

It may be thought that these comparisons give an exaggerated idea of the progress which the air corporations have been making because of the exceptional scope for productivity gains which BOAC had at the start of the period. As we shall see later when we come to examine its finances BOAC's efficiency appears at that time to have been at a low ebb.[38] However if the comparisons are taken back to 1951, which is about as far as available statistics permit, it is found that BOAC had a larger increase in productivity than all save one foreign airline. Between 1951 and 1968 BOAC's productivity rose by about 440 per cent, compared with a gain of 480 per cent by Qantas, which was top of the league. After BOAC came KLM with an increase of 314 per cent; Pan Am at 287 per cent; SAS at 280 per cent and Air France with an increase of about the same amount, if allowance is made for the 1968 strikes. Next came BEA with a productivity gain of 228 per cent, followed by Swissair at 211 per cent and Sabena at 184 per cent. Therefore, British European Airways are again nearly at the bottom of the league. When their results are combined, however, the air corporations appear to have had an even better performance over the period 1951–68 than they have during the

Table 15

INDEX NUMBERS OF LABOUR PRODUCTIVITY AND PASSENGER TRAFFIC FOR BEA, BOAC AND OTHER INTERNATIONAL AIRLINES 1951–68 (1958 = 100)

	BOAC	Lufthansa (Germany)	KLM (Holland)	Alitalia (Italy)	BEA/ BOAC	Qantas (Australia)	Pan American	SAS (Scandinavia)	Air France	Japanese Airlines	Swissair	BEA	Sabena (Belgium)
(i) Passenger Miles per Worker													
1951	61·6	—	65·9	..	56·5	41·0	60·2	56·3	54·4	—	59·0	47·7	52·9
1958	100·0	100·0	100·0	100·0	100·0	100·0	100·0	100·0	100·0	100·0	100·0	100·0	100·0
1966	316·9	248·7	236·2	235·7	235·9	176·8[1]	219·1	163·8	181·5	138·8	165·1	156·3	138·1
1967	315·1	265·4	257·5	246·8	232·7	203·7	212·1	189·5	193·7	165·7	169·8	150·7	146·0
1968[2]	332·0	277·0	272·5	271·5	243·6	237·7	233·4	213·8	178·7[1]	207·3	183·7	156·5	150·3
(ii) Passenger Miles													
1951	52·6	—	44·3	10·8	44·7	30·8	43·4	32·0	39·9	—	19·5	32·8	23·1
1958	100·0	100·0	100·0	100·0	100·0	100·0	100·0	100·0	100·0	100·0	100·0	100·0	100·0
1966	338·1	695·5	195·6	608·5	311·8	321·8[1]	307·9	180·0	227·6	595·3	294·2	272·2	138·1
1967	361·7	846·5	215·5	677·0	328·1	390·3	341·9	210·7	254·3	767·7	327·8	277·4	163·1
1968	378·1[3]	904·3	229·3	763·2	342·3[3]	462·0	389·3	235·6	227·8	984·6	365·0	288·4	165·0

[1] Serious strike during year.
[2] Estimated from traffic and beginning of year employment.
[3] Allowance made for effect of BOAC strike on traffic (see BOAC 1968–9 pp 3, 49).

Source: ICAO *Digest of Statistics* 38, 81, 99, 131, 137, 142; allowance has been made for the fact that BOAC now excludes some engineering and catering employees from its staff statistics.

last decade. Between 1951 and 1968 their output per worker rose by 331 per cent which was faster than that of all save one of the foreign airlines.

Have the air corporations' productivity gains been accompanied by an exceptionally large increase in their output? If they have, their performance may be less impressive than it appears because, as we have seen, large increases in output are usually associated with large increases in productivity.[39] There is no reason to believe that air transport is an exception to this rule. Between 1958 and 1968 the six airlines which had the largest increase in passenger traffic obtained an average rise of 165 per cent in their productivity, whereas the productivity of the six remaining airlines grew by only 93 per cent. BOAC which had the largest increase in productivity did not enjoy by any means the largest increase in output but was sixth in the production league, with Swissair close behind. In contrast BEA occupied a slightly lower place in the production than in the productivity league. It ranked eighth in terms of output but eleventh in terms of productivity. However, when their results are combined it can be seen that the air corporations had a somewhat better productivity performance than was to be expected from the increase in their traffic. There were six foreign airlines which had a larger increase in production but only three which obtained a greater rise in output per man.

Productivity Levels in Aviation

Having considered the way in which the air corporations and foreign airlines have been increasing their output per man we can now examine the level of productivity at which they are operating. At first sight passenger miles (or load ton miles) per employee appears to be a suitable measuring rod. It has, however the major defect that short-haul airlines are inevitably at a disadvantage compared with long-haul airlines. The extent of the advantage which long-haul operators enjoy has been investigated in a number of studies. The latest and most thorough forms part of an inquiry by the Civil Aeronautics Board into the relationship between the costs and charges of American domestic airlines. What the CAB did was to calculate, from information which the airlines supplied for 1965, how the average costs per passenger mile varied according to the length of the passenger journey, where the airline was using jet aircraft suited to the type of work they were performing. From the figures of representative costs which the Board developed, and from other information which it provides, it is possible to calculate costs per passenger mile for any given length of haul and load factor.[40]

In its study the CAB used the load factors which American domestic carriers typically experience on different lengths of haul; in the United

States they decline sharply as the distance increases. But it would be unrealistic to make the same assumption for the international airlines in which we are interested. Examination shows that, in 1967, there was no relationship whatever between their average length of hop and their load

Table 16

TRAFFIC AND TRAFFIC PER WORKER FOR
BEA, BOAC AND FOREIGN AIRLINES 1967
(BEA/BOAC = 100)

	Weighted Passenger Miles	*Weighted Passenger Miles per Worker*	*Passenger Miles per Worker*	*Available Seat Miles per Aircraft hour*
Alitalia	41·1	170·2	170·3	88·7
Pan American	128·6	154·2	188·8	145·9
Japanese Airlines	33·7	138·3	153·7	132·4
SAS	36·9	116·9	99·7	82·1
Lufthansa	47·2	113·0	107·6	95·2
Swissair	25·5	106·6	100·1	101·9
BEA/BOAC	100·0	100·0	100·0	100·0
Air France	62·8	99·9	102·6	103·6
KLM	32·0	94·8	101·2	108·4
Qantas	16·7	69·1	94·6	129·3
Sabena	15·6	62·1	62·3	88·8

factor.[41] It seems best to assume a constant load factor so far as international operations are concerned. On this basis, it appears from the CAB study that the cost per passenger mile is about 30 per cent lower on medium length hauls of 750 miles than it is on hauls of only 300 miles, and that on long hauls of 1,750 miles the cost is 44 per cent less.

The CAB study, therefore, confirms that long-haul operators do have a considerable advantage over airlines with short hauls when output is measured by passenger miles. What is far more important is that the data on the relationship between costs and length of haul which it provides enables us to make allowance for the latter to develop a better measure of production. By discovering an operator's length of haul and the representative cost per mile for this distance, it is then possible, by multiplying the cost by the airlines' passenger miles, to obtain a figure for output which allows for the fact that short-distance traffic is more costly and more valuable than long.[42] For a number of reasons this procedure may not produce results which are exact. It is possible, for instance, that the variation between costs and distance is not exactly the same for international operations as it is for American domestic work. However, it should provide a rough-and-ready indication of the comparative production and productivity of the different airlines and has therefore been employed.

The results are shown in Table 16. In six of the foreign airlines output per man appears during 1967 to have been higher than that of the British air corporations. Alitalia was in top place with productivity about 70 per cent greater than that of the British air corporations. Next came Pan Am with a lead of about 55 per cent and JAL with one of 38 per cent. However BEA/BOAC's productivity compares less unfavourably with that of SAS whose output per man was 17 per cent higher, Lufthansa which had a lead of 13 per cent, and Swissair which was 7 per cent ahead. The air corporations in their turn are shown as having a higher level of productivity than KLM, Qantas and Sabena. KLM's output per worker was 5 per cent lower, for Qantas it was about 30 per cent less and for Sabena nearly 38 per cent lower.

It is of interest to see whether the results of our productivity calculations are in line with what would be expected if a more commonsense approach had been adopted. Long-haul airlines have the advantage that they are able to use larger aircraft and to fly them faster. This advantage shows up in the larger capacity which their aircraft generate when they are flying. This means that, as the Edwards Committee recognized, statistics of aircraft productivity can be used to identify airlines which are operating under similar conditions and should be able to achieve a similar level of labour productivity.[43] As the latter has been measured in terms of passenger miles, the relevant figure for aircraft productivity is the number of seat miles generated per aircraft hour. This has been shown for each of the airways in Table 16, together with passenger miles per worker. A comparison between the figures for seat miles per aircraft hour and passenger miles per worker on the one hand, and the estimates of weighted passenger miles per worker on the other suggests that the latter do give a reasonable indication of the productivity ranking of the different airlines. For instance those foreign airlines which have about the same number of passenger miles per worker as BEA/BOAC (SAS, Swissair, Air France and KLM) stand in the productivity league more or less where one would expect from the number of seat miles per aircraft hour which their planes produce.

Productivity Growth Reviewed

Now that international productivity comparisons have been made for coal, electricity, railways and airways, a number of important conclusions can be drawn. First, it may be useful to summarize our findings on the growth of productivity. Productivity growth rates for the four industries and the various countries are presented in Table 17. In addition the rate of growth in manufacturing productivity has also been included for the nations which figure in the comparisons. In general the British national-ized industries have a favourable showing. During the period since 1958 the Coal Board's OMS increased more rapidly than that of all save one of the major continental producers; British electricity's productivity has increased at a faster rate than all save one of the foreign suppliers for whom figures are available; British Rail has outstripped or kept pace with all except one of the continental railways; and the air corporations, when their results are combined, had a faster rate of productivity growth than 7 out of 10 major international airlines.

If a comparison is made over a longer period, the air corporations' performance remains good. Indeed, over the period 1951–68, output per man in BEA/BOAC increased more rapidly than that of all but one of the other international airlines for which figures are available; while between 1936 and 1968 the British coal industry pushed up its OMS faster than any of the continental producers. In contrast British Rail, despite its favourable showing during the past decade, was outstripped by all the continental railways when the comparison is taken back to 1950.

To be at or near the bottom of the league is of course the normal position for British industry, and it can be seen that in manufacturing our productivity grew more slowly than that of almost every other country. For instance in Italy output per man hour increased by 7·8 per cent per annum between 1958 and 1968, in Sweden it rose by 6·9 per cent, in Germany by 5·9 per cent, in Belgium by 5·4 per cent, and in France by 5·2 per cent. However, in the UK, the figure was a mere 4 per cent and there were only two countries whose productivity grew at a still slower rate. In the United States output per man hour increased by 3·6 per cent each year and in Australia output per man year rose by approximately 3 per cent. The poor showing of British manufacturing is not explained by the malfunctioning of a few particularly backward industries but by a general tendency for productivity to rise at a slower rate than abroad. Indeed, there are probably only one or two British industries outside the public enterprise sector which are at or near the top of their productivity leagues, and chemicals – the one British indus-try to have made larger gains than public enterprise – is not among them.[44]

On the other hand the fact that the nationalized industries have a better comparative performance than British manufacturing industry suggests that their fast rate of productivity growth cannot be explained

Table 17

LABOUR PRODUCTIVITY GROWTH RATES FOR UK AND FOREIGN MANUFACTURING AND FOR INDUSTRIES NATIONALIZED IN BRITAIN 1958–68

	Manufacturing: Output per man hour	Airlines: Output per man year and league position	Electricity: Sales per man hour and position	Railways: Output per man hour and position	Coal: Output per man hour and position
Japan	9·3	7·6 (9)	..	..	..
Italy	7·8	10·5 (3)	5·1[1] [2] (7)	2·8 (7)	..
Sweden	6·9	7·9 (7)	..	5·9 (1)	..
Holland	6·8	10·5 (2)	..	..	..
Germany	5·9	10·7 (1)	7·6[1] (3)	4·7 (2)	4·7 (5)
Austria	5·7	..	..	1·7 (8)	7·1 (1)
Belgium	5·4	4·2 (11)	10·4 (1)	4·1 (5)	..
Norway	5·4	..	5·4[3] (6)	..	5·3[4] (3)
France	5·2	7·6[1] (8)	7·3[1] (4)	3·3[1] (6)	..
Czechoslovakia	4·8[1]	..	..	..	3·1 (6)
Switzerland	4·6[2]	6·3 (10)	..	4·2 (4)	3·0[5] (7)
Poland	4·5[1]	..	..	..	5·0 (4)
UK	4·0	9·8 (4)	7·7 (2)	4·6 (3)	5·9 (2)
USA	3·6	8·8 (6)	7·1 (5)	..	..
Australia	(3·0)[3]	9·0 (5)	..	..	..

[1] 1958–67.
[2] Output per wage earner hour.
[3] Output per man year.
[4] Campine.
[5] 1956–68.

Source: Tables 10, 12, 13, 15 and for manufacturing National Institute *Economic Review* November 1969 p 77; UN *Monthly Bulletin of Statistics* November 1969 Tables 6, 7, 10; UN *Statistical Yearbook* 1967 Table 23 and (for Polish Employment) 80; UN *Statistical Yearbook* 1968 Tables 23, 53 and (for Polish and Czech employment) 82.

by the ease with which advances can be made in the industries which happen to have been nationalized. If it had been found that, although the nationalized industries' productivity had risen faster than that of manufacturing, it had increased more slowly than that of the same industries abroad it would have been legitimate to conclude that the public enterprise sector was operating under especially favourable conditions. It might, for instance, be the case that the industries which have been nationalized have turned out to be those in which technological progress has been especially fast.

Another and more rigorous proof that our public enterprise sector is not situated in a part of the economy where the rate of progress is exceptionally high is furnished by a comparison of the rate at which output per man is increasing in other countries' manufacturing sectors and in the industries which have been nationalized in Britain. If productivity gains could be secured with particular ease in these industries it might be expected that their productivity gains would almost everywhere be substantially greater than those in manufacturing. In civil aviation and electricity this does seem to be the case. In air transport the only countries where the principal international airline had a smaller increase in productivity than manufacturing were Belgium and Japan. In the other countries, however, the airlines were a long way ahead. For instance, in Holland KLM's output per worker rose on average by 10·5 per cent each year between 1958 and 1968 as against an average productivity increase of 6·8 per cent per annum in manufacturing. In electricity productivity has been increasing less fast, relative to that of manufacturing, than it has in aviation. But Italy is the only country for which figures are available where output per man hour in electricity has increased less than in manufacturing.

In railways and coal, however, productivity has tended to increase less fast than in manufacturing. In not one of the continental countries for which calculations have been made has the growth in output per man hour on the railways outstripped the growth in manufacturing and in most it has been significantly slower. In fact rail productivity only increased about two-thirds as fast as manufacturing productivity. In the case of the coal industry the contrast appears at first sight to be much less striking. In both Germany and Poland, the rise in OMS underground exceeded the rise in manufacturing productivity. In Belgium, as represented by the Campine, the rates of advance were about the same, and only in Holland, France and Czechoslovakia was the growth of productivity significantly slower in coal than in manufacturing industry.

However, the rise in OMS gives an exaggerated impression of the growth of productivity. It seems likely that on the continent, as in Britain, there has, over the years, been an increase in the proportion of low grade coal. If so, production has fallen faster than is indicated by the crude figures of tonnage output from which OMS is calculated. The growth of output per man shift for underground workers also exaggerates the rise in coal productivity because the number of underground workers has everywhere been falling faster than the number of surface workers. If surface workers are taken into account it appears that in Germany the *tonnage* of coal produced per man shift rose at the same rate as manufacturing productivity. In the Campine the *tonnage* per man shift seems to have increased by about 3·9 per cent, which was slightly less than the rise in manufacturing productivity in Belgium.[45] Moreover, if proper production indices, which allowed for the growing proportion of small coal, were available for Germany and the Campine the rise in the industry's productivity would almost certainly have been shown to have been smaller than that of manufacturing. Hence the increase in output per man has in all the continental countries been smaller in coal than in manufacturing, and that in most countries it has been substantially less.

We are now in a position to make some judgment about whether the industries which have been nationalized in Britain have secured larger increases in productivity in foreign countries than their manufacturing sectors. In Britain these industries have, on average, had a better productivity performance than manufacturing – has this been true abroad? The position in foreign countries is that since 1958 the increase in productivity in coal and railways has without exception been lower than in manufacturing and that in most countries it has been substantially less. In contrast the rise in productivity in aviation and electricity has, with one or two exceptions, been higher than in manufacturing. Coal and railways, however, form a substantially greater part of the public enterprise sector than electricity and aviation. This is reflected by the weight which they have been assigned when calculating the general rise in the productivity of the nationalized industries. For the last decade coal and railways have, in virtue of their net output in 1958, been given a combined weight of 61 per cent whereas electricity and the air corporations have a weight of 23 per cent. As coal and the railways (where in other countries productivity has been increasing less than in manufacturing) weigh heavy while air transport and electricity (where productivity has increased faster) carry far less weight, it is difficult to see how in other countries the overall rise in productivity of the industries in which we are interested can have been greater than that of manufacturing. Thus foreign experience does not suggest that productivity gains are particularly easy to secure in those industries which happen to be in public ownership in Britain. This suggests that public enterprise deserves full credit for having increased its productivity faster than that of British manufacturing industry.

Although it suggests this it does not prove it, because it is possible that British manufacturing has laboured under some special disadvantage in comparison with foreign industry which has not handicapped the nationalized industries. It is often argued that the relatively slow rate at which British output has increased explains why our productivity has increased so little. As we have seen, there is usually a close relationship between the rate of increase in production and the rate of increase in productivity and when comparisons are made between countries this relationship is found to hold good.[46] But it is far from clear whether swiftly rising production leads to a rapid increase in productivity or whether the causal process runs in the other direction. Let us nevertheless assume that production influences productivity and see whether this explains the contrasting positions of manufacturing and the nationalized industries in the international productivity leagues. Have the nationalized industries had the advantage that their output has been rising more rapidly or dropping more slowly than the output of their foreign counterparts?

This is certainly not true of British Rail, which has laboured under the disadvantage of declining traffic while none of the continental railways has experienced a fall and most have had the benefit of a significant increase. Nor is it the case that the British electricity industry has been in an advantageous position. On the contrary, during the past decade the sales of all but one of the foreign suppliers have increased at a more rapid rate. Again the air corporations secured a somewhat larger increase in productivity than was to have been expected from the growth in their traffic. Over the period 1958–68 there were six foreign airlines which had a larger increase in traffic than BEA/BOAC but only three which obtained a bigger rise in output per man.

Productivity Levels Reviewed

What conclusions can be drawn about the level of productivity in the nationalized industries and in the same industries abroad? Hitherto attention has been confined to the pace at which productivity has been growing, but what we must now try to decide is whether their level of efficiency is relatively high or relatively low. It is clear that as measured by, say, American standards the nationalized industries have a low output per worker and are comparatively inefficient, but this is hardly surprising in view of the fact that the general level of productivity is so much higher in America. What we therefore need to find out is whether the nationalized industries' productivity, relative to that of other countries, is better or worse than that of the rest of British industry.

Some rough estimates of output per worker in the non-agricultural sectors of the leading industrial nations have been made by Dr Angus Maddison. These and our estimates for coal, railways and the airways are given in Table 18. The air corporations' productivity, relative to that of other countries, appears to be somewhat higher than that of British industry as a whole (a position which will henceforth be referred to simply as better than average or above par). It can be seen that, assuming that the general level of productivity is considerably higher in Switzerland and Australia than it is here, there were eight cases where BEA/BOAC's productivity was above par. However Alitalia and JAL had much higher productivity than the British air corporations although, according to Dr Maddison's figures, the general level of output per worker in their parent countries is lower than in Britain.

But it must be borne in mind that both Italy and Japan are dual economies in which handicraft production, and industries in which old-fashioned methods are used, continue to exist along with modern industries where productivity is high. In the advanced factory sector of the economy Japanese productivity is probably higher than it is in Britain. For instance in the Japanese steel industry output per worker must by now be considerably higher than it is in the British steel industry. In Italy the same contrast exists and there is little doubt that in the advanced sector of the economy its productivity is significantly higher than in Britain. For instance in steel, output per man hour was, in 1959, about 47 per cent greater than in Britain. Again in motor vehicles it appears that output per employee was in 1964–5 about 17 per cent higher than in Britain.[47] Nevertheless, it is clear that both Italy and Japan have a considerably greater lead over Britain in aviation than they do in the other industries which comprise the advanced sector of their economies. On balance, however, the air corporations' performance is above average. If the figures are to be trusted there are only two countries where their performance is below par compared with eight where it is better than that of industry as a whole. Moreover, the average gap between BEA/BOAC's productivity and that of the 10 foreign airlines appears to be considerably smaller than in industry as a whole.

It seems likely that for coal, as for aviation, productivity compares more favourably with that of other countries than it does in British industry as a whole. There is no case in which, allowing for geological conditions, the NCB's level of OMS appears to be below par and there are several countries for which it seems to be above. These, as can be seen from the Table, include Belgium, as represented by the Campine,

Table 18

LABOUR PRODUCTIVITY IN UK AND FOREIGN NON-AGRICULTURAL SECTORS AND THE INDUSTRIES NATIONALIZED IN BRITAIN (UK = 100/Base line)

	Output per man year in Non-agricultural Sector 1965	Output per man year in Aviation 1967	Output per man year in Railways 1966	Output per man hour in coal Allowing for Geological Conditions 1968
USA	188·1	154·2	..	..
Switzerland	..	106·6	..	..
Norway	133·7	116·9[1]	..	..
Germany	132·7	113·0	126·4	Somewhat higher, say 30 per cent
Australia	..	69·1	..	..
France	126·1	99·9	151·4	..
Belgium	116·9	62·1	..	A little lower, say 10 per cent or more
Holland	116·8	94·8	..	A little higher, say 5–10 per cent
Czechoslovakia	..	..	..	Slightly lower, say 15 per cent
UK	100·0	100·0	100·0	..
Italy	98·9	170·2	101·4	..
Japan	80·7	138·3	..	Somewhat lower, say 20 per cent
Poland	..	..	..	..

[1] SAS.

Source: Tables, 11, 14, 16; A. Maddison, Royal Commission on Trade Unions and Employers Associations *Selected Written Evidence* p 644.

and Holland, (where Maddison's statistics may well give too favourable an impression of British industry's relative efficiency).[48] It also seems likely that, as compared with Czechoslovakia, the NCB's productivity is above average. Output per worker is probably somewhat higher in Czech industry than in British industry but in coal the reverse is true.[49] In comparison with Germany the NCB's productivity is only about average.

It is difficult to know whether British Rail's productivity, relative to that of other countries, is better or worse than that of the rest of British industry. It has only been possible to make comparisons for a few countries and they do not fall into any clear pattern. The level of output per man year in Italy during 1966 appears to have been about the same as in Britain. If so British Rail's productivity was probably somewhat above par, when the comparison between Britain and Italy is confined to the modern sector of the economy. Again, in the case of Germany, British Rail's productivity seems to be above average although the difference is unlikely to be very great. Productivity on the railways may be about 25 per cent higher in Germany than in Britain whereas in industry as a whole the lead was, according to Dr Maddison, about a third. But when Britain is compared with France, BR's productivity is found to be considerably below par. SNCF's productivity was about 50 per cent greater than that of British Rail although the general French lead over Britain is only about 25 per cent.

However if, as has been argued, the quality of service which British Rail provides is, at least on the passenger side, somewhat higher than that on the continent then BR's productivity rating compares slightly more favourably. It would not have been so far below par when compared with that of France and it would have been further above par in comparison with Germany and Italy. If so it seems likely that British Rail's output per worker is slightly above average, though this must only be regarded as a provisional conclusion. There is certainly no reason to believe the widely accepted view that British Rail's efficiency is exceptionally low.

In the case of electricity the only country with which a full comparison was possible was the United States. Here it appeared, when attention was confined to those parts of the USA and Britain where the level of consumption was the same, that our productivity was just about average. It is difficult to see from the limited comparisons which could be made with France, Germany and Italy how our productivity could be above par for those countries. Indeed it seemed possible that it was below. All that can be said therefore is that the level of productivity in the British electricity industry is about as far behind in America as it is in

British industry as a whole and that there is certainly no reason to believe that, if the comparison was extended to additional countries, it would be shown in a more favourable light.

It may, however, be questioned whether it is legitimate, when comparing British and American productivity in electricity, to adjust for the difference in electricity consumption but not to allow, when making a general comparison, for the advantage which American firms enjoy due to their larger markets. This, of course, assumes that it is in practice an advantage for an industry to serve a large market; but this cannot be taken for granted as the various investigations which have been made into the relationship between output per worker and market size show different results. L. Rostas, in his classic study of British and American productivity, found that in several of the industries where the US productivity lead was greatest the American market was exceptionally large. But, this apart, he found little association between the two variables. In contrast Marvin Frankel, in his later but more limited investigation, found that there was a fairly strong relationship.[50] Yet even if the evidence was more conclusive its relevance would be open to doubt. For what has been allowed for in our comparisons of output per worker in electricity is not the difference in total sales but the variation in the quantity sold to the average consumer, and it seems doubtful whether the relationship between productivity and sales per customer is anything like as strong in industry as a whole as it is in electricity.

Having reviewed the level of productivity in most of the nationalized industries to see whether their productivity ranks high or low by British standards, it is possible to form some impression of the general position. No evidence has been found that the industries are exceptionally inefficient in their use of labour. On the contrary it appears that in coal and air transport productivity compares slightly better with that of other foreign countries than it does in British industry as a whole. The same is probably true of railways but this is less certain. Finally the electricity industry's productivity is about average in comparison with America. If anything, therefore, the nationalized industries' productivity seems to compare more favourably with that of the same industries abroad than that of the rest of British industry.

It should be recognized that the comparisons which have been made are probably slightly unfair to the nationalized industries. This is because for industry as a whole the comparison of output per worker related to the year 1965 and since then most foreign countries have drawn ahead. Because of the speed at which productivity has been increasing abroad this is a factor of some importance. For a considerable number of countries the productivity advantage which they enjoyed over British manufacturing industry increased by around 6 per cent between 1965 and 1968. This was true of Germany, France, Italy and Belgium. In a few countries the productivity gap widened appreciably more than this. In Holland and Sweden it increased by around 10 per cent and Japan increased its lead, presuming it to have existed at the beginning of the period, by about 30 per cent. Only in the case of the United States and Australia did the productivity gap narrow slightly.[51] It can be seen, therefore, that in general the productivity comparisons which have been made probably show the nationalized industries in too unfavourable a light. This makes their favourable showing all the more significant.

PART TWO

Finances

CHAPTER 9

Prices, Wages and Profits

IN previous chapters we have examined the technical efficiency with which the nationalized industries use labour (and capital) to produce goods and services. We must now consider the financial side of their operations and in particular the profits and losses they have made. We shall start by taking a brief look at their prices and the earnings of their workers or, to be more exact, at the way in which they have changed over time. Besides their inherent interest and importance prices serve as a convenient link between the physical side of the nationalized industries' operations with which we have previously been concerned and their financial side. The price of a commodity is equivalent to its revenue per unit of output, and output is a physical affair while revenue is a financial matter. The justification for taking a glance next at earnings is that, if profits constitute the reward of capital, wages are the reward of labour, which is the other factor of production. Having dealt with prices and wages we can then turn to profits and losses, and the rest of the chapter will be taken up by a general survey of public enterprise's financial performance. The other chapters in this part of the book will be devoted to an examination of the large losses which two of the nationalized industries have incurred. The rail deficit is examined in Chapters 10 and 11 and BOAC's losses are discussed in Chapter 12.

Prices

The criticism of the nationalized industries most frequently heard among economists is that their prices ought to be higher because their return on capital is too low. But among the general public the criticism is almost the exact reverse: the prices of the nationalized industries have increased, are increasing and ought to be diminished. At the same time the public also blames the nationalized industries when, sometimes in the interest of price stability, they make losses. As usual, however, the facts remain obscure. Incredible as it may seem, there is, with the exception of coal, no comprehensive price index for the goods or services provided by any of the nationalized industries. The Department of Employment and Productivity of course prepares what the casual observer, or the over-enthusiastic politician, may take to be price series for the nationalized industries and for the public enterprise sector as a whole.[1] These figures are of doubtful value because not only are they constructed by a method which is almost bound to show the nationalized industries' prices as having risen faster than those of private industry, but also because they are confined to goods and services sold to the general public. As about half of the nationalized industries' production is sold to industry there is obviously a serious danger that a price index confined to consumer goods and services will give a misleading impression of what has been happening. This is, in fact, the case because the nationalized industries have raised their industrial prices less than their consumer prices. In Table 19 price series are given which cover both industrial and consumer sales, and which, it is hoped, give a fair impression of the way in which the nationalized industries have been increasing their charges. They were obtained by dividing the nationalized industries' production into their sales revenue to obtain the amount they charged per unit of output.[2]

As our examination of the nationalized industries' production, productivity and employment revealed, the economic history of the public enterprise sector can be divided into two periods because the late 1950s seem to constitute a natural watershed in their development. The nationalized industries' price history is certainly no exception to this rule. During the first decade of public ownership their prices increased rapidly whereas during the second decade they have been increasing relatively slowly. Thus between 1948 and 1958 the public enterprise sector's charges increased by 59 per cent compared with a rise of about 47 per cent in industry as a whole. However, between 1958 and 1968 the nationalized industries' prices increased by 16 per cent as against a general rise of 25 per cent. Over the full period of nationalization public enterprise charges have risen by almost the same amount as those of industry as a whole.

During the first decade of public ownership the airways and electricity were the only nationalized industries which did not make spectacular increases in their charges. Between 1948 and 1958 the air corporations' prices rose by 12 per cent and the cost of electricity increased by 30 per cent. In contrast coal, gas, railways and the nationalized buses were all increasing their prices at a rapid rate. The coal industry led the field with an average increase of 81 per cent, and gas and buses were close behind, with increases of 74 per cent and 73 per cent respectively. The rise in railway charges was, however, more modest at 52 per cent. BRS appears to have increased its prices by 35 per cent between 1950 and 1958, though too much reliance should not be placed on this figure.

Table 19

PRICE INDEX NUMBERS 1948–68 (1958 = 100)

	Electricity	Coal	Railways	Gas	BEA and BOAC	Nationalized Buses	BRS	Public Enterprise Sector	All Goods and Services[1]
1948	76·9	55·3	65·7	57·5	89·1	57·7	..	62·9	67·8
1949	79·0	55·8	63·3	58·5	94·0	57·7	..	63·0	69·6
1950	77·6	55·5	67·3	60·4	95·5	58·5	74·3	64·2	69·2
1951	79·0	60·0	71·9	64·7	96·1	62·5	82·2	68·5	73·8
1952	84·5	67·2	79·7	73·0	99·6	70·0	88·1	75·8	80·9
1953	88·6	71·6	82·3	75·9	96·9	72·3	91·0	79·3	83·0
1954	89·7	74·3	86·8	77·8	97·8	75·7	88·8	81·9	84·6
1955	90·0	81·1	90·4	82·8	96·7	81·1	93·4	86·2	87·4
1956	94·4	91·9	94·3	91·1	97·7	87·5	97·8	93·3	91·9
1957	97·4	97·6	98·0	96·7	96·0	96·2	109·0	97·9	95·7
1958	100·0	100·0	100·0	100·0	100·0	100·0	100·0	100·0	100·0
1959	97·8	99·4	98·5	100·5	99·2	101·0	101·9	99·1	101·2
1960	94·8	101·8	100·4	103·1	93·7	106·9	105·3	99·7	102·3
1961	97·6	107·9	103·9	106·2	89·3	115·6	112·1	103·3	105·5
1962	98·8	110·6	109·3	107·6	87·9	120·1	118·4	105·5	108·8
1963	100·4	111·1	110·3	109·0	88·0	123·3	121·4	106·4	110·5
1964	102·6	111·3	107·4	109·8	82·8	134·8	125·5	106·7	112·4
1965	106·5	111·4	111·8	108·9	79·3	147·1	122·0	108·2	116·1
1966	109·6	122·1	115·0	107·5	77·1	159·0	120·5	111·5	119·2
1967	110·0	123·3	115·2	105·3	80·2	165·0	119·7	111·7	122·8
1968	118·0	122·7	114·2	107·7	89·3	173·2	125·0	115·7	125·2

[1] Excluding those provided free of charge by the State, the effect of indirect taxation, and imports of all types, ie GDP at current factor cost, excluding public administration and defence and public health and education services, per unit of output.

During the second decade of nationalization only the buses have increased their prices by more than the rise in industry as a whole. Between 1958 and 1968 the nationalized buses raised their charges by 73 per cent. The public enterprise with the next largest increase was BRS with a rise of 25 per cent; the same figure as for industry in general. However, once again it is doubtful whether the figure for BRS gives more than a rough indication of what has been happening to its charges, and it should be borne in mind that private hauliers' prices have been increasing at a rapid rate.[3] The nationalized industries whose prices increased less than average were led by coal with a rise of 23 per cent and then came electricity, where prices have risen fairly rapidly since 1963, at 18 per cent. Rail charges rose by 14 per cent which was little more than half as fast as in industry as a whole. In gas the figure was only 7 per cent and the increase was concentrated during the earlier years of the period. The air corporations' charges declined by 11 per cent.

Wages

Both the opponents and the supporters of nationalization have argued that, due to public ownership, wages have risen faster than they would otherwise have done. The right-wing view, as stated by the Federation of British Industries, is that 'under all Governments political considerations, and the fact that the taxpayer can be called upon to meet deficits, have weakened the control of labour costs'.[4] The left-wing position is that nationalization, by eliminating private profit, makes it possible to attain higher wage standards than can be wrung from capitalist firms. This view is seldom heard now, and it has indeed come to be argued that wages in the nationalized industries, and in particular on the railways, have lagged behind those paid by industry in general.

Statistics of average earnings do not lend any firm support to either of these positions. The movement of average earnings in manufacturing and those nationalized industries for which information is available are shown in Table 20. The figures mostly refer to adult male workers, who are, of course, by far the largest group, and they are for hourly earnings, with the partial exception of British Rail where weekly earnings have had to be used prior to 1963. In the index for the public enterprise sector, or rather that part of it for which there is information, each industry was assigned an importance commensurate with the total amount of wages it paid to the workers in question during 1958.[5] The series for manufacturing has in contrast been calculated each year by dividing its total wage bill by the number of workers. Over the whole period of nationalization from 1949 to 1968, wages in the public enterprise sector appear

Table 20

INDEX NUMBERS OF AVERAGE EARNINGS OF MANUAL WORKERS[1] 1948-68 (1958 = 100)

	Electricity	Coal	British Rail	Gas	Air Transport[2]	Public Enterprise Sector	Manufacturing
1948	56·2	53·8	..	56·6	..	(55·1)	54·7
1949	58·5	55·5	58·7	57·3	..	56·8	56·7
1950	60·4	56·9	59·4	58·8	..	58·0	58·9
1951	65·7	61·9	66·6	64·6	..	63·7	63·8
1952	70·4	69·3	70·6	71·0	..	69·8	69·3
1953	74·2	73·2	75·2	73·7	..	73·9	73·3
1954	77·4	77·0	79·1	77·5	71·9	77·6	77·8
1955	85·2	81·3	87·6	85·9	80·1	83·7	84·4
1956	92·4	89·7	95·7	93·8	93·6	91·9	91·1
1957	97·5	96·0	96·3	98·7	100·2	96·4	95·6
1958	100·0	100·0	100·0	100·0	100·0	100·0	100·0
1959	104·0	102·6	103·0	103·1	106·2	102·9	104·0
1960	115·3	105·8	118·7	110·5	115·8	110·7	112·7
1961	119·6	115·2	122·6	118·4	124·4	118·0	119·9
1962	126·5	120·3	126·4	123·7	124·4	122·8	124·9
1963	133·9	124·1	(131·8)	132·8	131·5	127·7	130·1
1964	144·9	132·4	135·7	139·8	141·5	134·9	139·8
1965	169·0	139·2	150·1	154·8	153·8	145·8	152·1
1966	183·2	146·3	169·5	167·8	166·8	147·7	163·5
1967	188·1	152·7	177·2	175·2	167·1	164·1	169·4
1968	195·8	160·3	180·9	185·7	181·5	170·8	181·1
1969							

[1] Average hourly earnings of adult males for electricity, gas, air transport, manufacturing and British Rail since 1963. Prior to this average weekly earnings for BR, average earnings per shift (including youths) for coal, allowing for the reduction in shift length in 1961.
[2] The bulk of these workers are employed by BEA and BOAC.

Source: MLG/EPG April and October surveys for all industries except railways where figures relate to the Spring survey as reported in MLG/EPG or AAS.

to have increased by 6·0 per cent per annum compared with an average rise of 6·3 per cent in manufacturing.

During the first decade of nationalization earnings seem to have risen by almost exactly the same amount in public enterprise and manufacturing, earnings in coal having increased a shade faster than average and those in gas, electricity and railways a trifle more slowly. During the second decade of public ownership earnings have, if anything, increased slightly less fast in public enterprise than in manufacturing. In the airways, railways and gas they have risen about as fast, and in electricity somewhat faster, but in coal they have lagged far behind. Over the period 1958–68 earnings increased by 81 per cent in manufacturing, by almost the same figure in air transport and for British Rail, by 86 per cent in gas, by 96 per cent in electricity but by only 60 per cent in coal. The exceptionally large rise in electricity is explained by the industry's productivity bargains of 1964–5 which led, in effect, to a large reduction in overtime in return for a large increase in hourly earnings. However, the increase was not large enough to prevent the rate of increase in weekly earnings in electricity falling behind that in manufacturing. As a result weekly earnings increased significantly less fast in electricity between 1958 and 1968 than in manufacturing. In coal the slow rise in hourly earnings has probably been due to the industry's depressed condition. The miners lagged even further behind manufacturing in terms of the increase of weekly earnings than they did in terms of hourly earnings. This was due to the very large reduction in average hours in coal due to the fall in the number of shifts worked and the growth of absenteeism.

Profits and Losses

The final stage in our general survey of the financial side of the nationalized industries' operations is an examination of their profits and losses. It is widely believed that their profits resemble snakes in Ireland: there are none. For instance the Radcliffe Committee declared that 'at present the nationalized industries are in total getting no net return on capital employed.'[6] The belief that the nationalized industries have been unprofitable rests largely upon the fact that in most years both the public enterprise sector as a whole and the majority of the separate undertakings have failed to cover their interest charges.[7] But the question arises of whether it is right only to count a nationalized industry as having made a profit when it has a surplus after interest. It is true that when the financial performance of private undertakings is under discussion their profits are usually measured after both depreciation and interest charges. In practice, however, interest charges are usually small because the great bulk of the capital of most privately owned concerns is in the form of equity shares on which a variable dividend is paid.

In contrast the public enterprise sector makes large interest payments because, with the exception of BOAC, it is financed wholly on a fixed interest basis. It is therefore highly misleading to compare the surpluses or deficits which the nationalized industries show after interest and depreciation with the net profits earned by private concerns, or to ignore the fact that when a public enterprise breaks even it would, if it were a private firm, show a considerable profit. Yet, although this has been pointed out many times, it is frequently ignored. For instance even those papers which should know better, such as the *Financial Times*, almost always headline the nationalized industries' surpluses or deficits after interest; and the Conservative Campaign Guide for 1964 showed their 'financial results' without even explaining that their figures were net of interest charges.[8] This is hardly surprising but what is extraordinary is that there are professional economists who imagine that a nationalized undertaking which just covers its interest charges has a zero return on its capital and who, when statistics for the surplus after interest are not available, will go to the trouble of calculating them in order to have figures which they mistakenly believe to be on a private enterprise basis.[9]

Not only are statistics for the nationalized industries' final surpluses or deficits misleading, unless carefully qualified, but they are also uninformative. It is important to know whether they cover their running costs and their depreciation charges, but what help is it to know that they do or do not cover their interest charges? It might be thought that they indicate the extent to which taxation has to be raised to meet, on behalf of the nationalized industries, the interest payments which they cannot meet for themselves. Except in the case of the railways deficits are normally covered by borrowing. It may then be imagined that the deficits show the amount which the nationalized industries have to borrow from the Exchequer. But these deficits form only a small part of their borrowing requirements which are primarily for the purpose of investment. Finally it might appear that the presence of a surplus or deficit tells us something about the return which the industries have earned on their capital. It does, but it is best to measure this directly and to calculate the rate of return, because even where an industry has a large surplus it may have a relatively low yield on capital employed. The nationalized industries' results after interest will therefore be ignored and we shall first examine their profits before interest and then at a

G

later stage in this chapter consider the rate of return which they have earned on their capital.[10]

Figures for the nationalized industries' profits are presented in Table 21. As usual there is a sharp contrast between their performance during the first and the second decade of public ownership. During the first period the sector's profits fluctuated but showed no marked tendency to increase. It can be seen for instance, that in 1958 they totalled only about £95 million compared with around £80 million during 1948. However, the second decade of nationalization has seen a spectacular increase in the sector's profits. By 1968 they had risen to about £410 million. What happened during the first decade of nationalization was that rising profits in electricity, and to a lesser extent gas, were offset by falling profits and then mounting losses on the railways. Between 1948–9 and 1958–9 the electricity industry's profits shot up from about £20 million to £100 million, and in gas they increased from about £10 million to £20 million. However British Rail which, including the subsidiary activities which it now controls, had a surplus of £27 million in 1948 was by 1955 only just covering its working expenses. Thereafter it showed a rapidly mounting loss which in 1958 stood at £46 million.

The spectacular rise in public enterprise profits during the second decade of nationalization has been due to the fact that British Rail's losses have been more or less contained, that losses have been replaced by profits in BOAC and that profits have gone on rising in electricity and gas. Between 1958 and 1962 British Rail's loss increased from £46 million to just on £100 million. By 1964, due to the combined effect of economic recovery and the Beeching reforms, the figure was down to £65 million. Thereafter it has fluctuated according to the state of the economy, but has never been as high as it was during the early sixties or as low as in 1964. During 1968 it stood at £83 million, although if redundancy payments, which ought perhaps to be regarded as capital expenditure, are excluded the figure was £78 million. In electricity, to turn to the industries which have contributed to the rise in the sector's profits, the surplus has mounted rapidly from £100 million in 1958–9 to well over £350 million in 1968–9; and in gas there has been an even more spectacular rise from £20 million to £90 million. In 1958–9 BOAC had a deficit of £11 million but after some heavy losses in the early sixties its financial position improved dramatically and in 1968–9 it earned a profit of £28 million and, but for the pilots' strike, the figure would have been about £8 million higher.[11]

It should be explained that the timing of the Corporation's losses, which were largely due to the premature retirement of aircraft, partly depends upon what accounting conventions are adopted. What happened was that the Corporation decided in 1961–2 to provide £31·7 million of extra depreciation on those of its aircraft which it anticipated having to withdraw before they had been fully depreciated. This obviously makes the year appear far blacker than it was and correspondingly presents in too favourable a light the Corporation's results during the years in which insufficient depreciation was provided. The extra depreciation has therefore been spread over the years during which the planes to which it relates were in use.[12] A number of other changes have also been made to the published figures so that they reflect more accurately the Corporation's year-to-year financial performance. For instance the group profit for 1968–9 is considerably smaller than that shown in BOAC's accounts because the provision of £7·5 million for pensions which was found to be unnecessary, and for which credit was taken, has been transferred to the years in which it was set aside.[13]

The profits of the remaining nationalized industries, though they have in some cases fluctuated, have displayed no marked or persistent tendency to rise or fall. For instance in coal, which is the most important undertaking, they stood at £18 million in 1948, at £19 million in 1958 and at £30 million in 1968. However, despite the widely held belief that it has made large losses, the Coal Board turns out, when profits are defined in private enterprise terms, to have had only one deficit. This was in 1947, its first year of operations, when it made a loss of £8 million. This was due to a special reason, namely the control which the Government exercised over its prices. What happened was that the NCB, having introduced a number of benefits for the miner to which the Government had already agreed in principle, found that the Minister would not permit it to increase its prices as much or as soon as it had hoped.[14] Although the coal industry has not had a deficit since then it has, during recent years, had the benefit of Government support and of a capital reconstruction which has reduced its depreciation charges.

In most of the other nationalized industries deficits have also been few and far between, and when they have occurred have been due to special factors. Besides electricity and gas the Tillings and Scottish bus groups and the London Transport railways have never shown a loss. Moreover, BRS has only once made a loss and this took place during its early days and was due to exceptional causes.[15] In the remaining part of the public enterprise sector losses have been more serious, but with the major exception of British Rail the undertakings in question have not been persistently in deficit and in most cases are now financially healthy. Thus BEA, which incurred a deficit up to 1953–4 has never since made a loss and BOAC which made heavy losses up to 1950–51, and again during the late fifties and early sixties, has since made a dramatic recovery. The

Table 21

PROFITS AFTER DEPRECIATION BUT BEFORE INTEREST 1947–68 (£million)

	Electricity[1]	Coal[2]	British Rail[3]	London Transport Railways	Gas[1]	BEA[1]	BOAC[1]	Tillings and Scottish Buses	London Transport Buses	BRS	Public Enterprise Sector[2][4]
1947	22·6	−7·9	..	..	..	−3·6	−7·1	..	..	..	(81·1)
1948	20·9	17·6	27·2	2·4	..	−2·7	−6·3	4·4	5·0	1·2	78·9
1949	25·8	27·2	13·5	1·6	9·4[5]	−1·1	−8·0	4·5	3·6	1·5	94·5
1950	28·6	26·2	27·5	1·4	11·8	−0·8	−4·6	3·7	1·7	−1·1	101·1
1951	28·4	14·9	35·9	1·3	13·9	−1·3	1·7	4·1	−1·4	3·3	108·7
1952	39·3	5·8	40·5	2·0	17·5	−1·2	0·4	4·1	−0·3	1·7	140·3
1953	50·3	22·7	35·1	1·4	15·6	0·7	2·1	5·1	0·6	8·9	129·0
1954	59·2	16·2	17·4	1·8	16·8	1·2	0·7	5·3	2·0	8·7	104·4
1955	60·7	2·0	3·3	2·0	18·6	0·9	1·5	5·7	3·0	4·3	131·0
1956	69·7	39·7	−14·9	2·0	22·8	2·2	1·0	5·3	2·5	1·8	112·9
1957	81·1 *92*[6]	19·9	−25·1	1·9	23·3	1·8	−2·9	5·0	3·8	2·8	96·5
1958	100·9 *118*	19·1	−45·9	2·6	20·1	3·9	−11·4	6·0	−0·8	2·0	124·2
1959	110·7 *135*	13·1	−37·7	2·0	20·6	1·9	−1·1	6·6	4·0	3·1	117·0
1960	113·5 *143*	20·2	−64·3	2·4	26·7	3·1	−2·1	6·5	5·4	1·8	116·9
1961	138·2 *171*	27·1	−82·2	3·7	28·9	..	−17·2	6·2	4·0	3·4	148·9
1962	166·6 *202*	45·4	−99·0	3·0	31·1	..	−12·9	6·7	5·0	3·5	..
1963	206·2 *246*	58·0	−78·1	3·4	37·3	7·2	−10·8	6·5	3·8	4·7	228·0
1964	217·3 *265*	46·6	−64·8	4·6	46·7	5·2	16·8	7·2	2·1	7·3	280·3
1965	262·9 *316*	10·9[7]	−73·9	3·1	46·1	5·1	24·1	6·8	−2·1	7·0	280·1
1966	223·7 *286*	21·4	−72·7	4·4	46·5	4·8	27·5	7·5	−4·1	4·9	275·8
1967	291·4 *366*	33·1	−88·9	2·2	43·7	3·1	25·3	6·8	−6·7	3·0	301·0
1968	356·7 *446*	30·1	−82·6	2·2	90·4	2·8	28·3	8·0	−5·4	3·8	408·9

[1] Financial year beginning during the year shown.

[2] Where necessary financial year figures have been roughly adjusted to a calendar basis.

[3] Includes the Board's present subsidiary activities except non-operational property.

[4] Includes BR and London Transport receipts from non-operational property and for 1948 gas at £9.4 million.

[5] Eleven months at annual rate.

[6] Estimated profits if the English and Welsh Boards had followed American depreciation practice and written off their assets over a longer period, etc. (see pp 195, 196).

[7] Depreciation charges were in 1965–6 reduced by £14.1 million due to the financial reconstruction under the Coal Industry Act, 1965, and in subsequent years there were further reductions. (Neither the Railways' nor BOAC's financial reconstructions affected the size of their profits before interest.)

Source: Annual Reports.

London Transport buses incurred small deficits in 1951 and 1952 due to the tardiness of the Transport Tribunal in dealing with an application for higher fares and there was also a deficit in 1958 due to a strike. Between 1965 and 1968 there has, once again, been a deficit and during the last two years of the period it was for the first time large enough to outweigh London Transport's rail profits and produce an overall loss. These losses have been largely due to the control which the Government has exercised over fares.[16]

Where BR Loses Money

British Rail is the only part of the public enterprise sector which is in a dire financial position. However, even the railways make a profit on some of their regions and activities, the bulk of its deficit being concentrated on a comparatively small part of its business. In 1968 it earned a profit of £5·3 million on its subsidiary undertakings to which its shipping services contributed £4·6 million and its hotels £0·8 million. The only one of these activities which made a loss was the hovercraft company, which was having teething troubles. On the railways themselves BR made a loss of £83·5 million after allowing, on the one hand, for net receipts from advertising (£0·7 million) and the letting of property which was in operational use (£6·5 million), and on the other hand for the tiny deficit on catering.[17] This overall loss conceals the fact that some of the regions make a profit. During the mid-sixties for instance the Eastern Region made a profit of about £3 million per annum and the Southern Region had a surplus of about £1 million. The North Eastern Region lost an average of about £6 million, though during 1966 it showed a small profit. In the Western Region the loss was rather larger at about £9 million but even here the deficit was equivalent in 1966 to only 8 per cent of its revenue. The grossly unprofitable regions were Scotland where the loss averaged about £14 million, and the London Midland where it was about £53 million. In 1966 the Scottish deficit was equivalent to about a quarter of its revenue and the Midlands' to nearly a third.[18]

These figures should not be pressed too far as regions have been credited with all the revenue they receive and some regions export more than they import. This was the objection which the Transport Commission always used to give to the publication of regional accounts. However it seems to be more important in theory than in practice, though it is probably true that the loss incurred by the Midland region is not quite as high as it appears while the losses made by the Scottish, Western and North Eastern regions are somewhat larger. Nevertheless, it is probably safe to say that during the mid-sixties British Rail would have come near to breaking even had it not been for the wildly un-profitable Midland and Scottish regions. Yet these regions accounted (in 1959) for only about 40 per cent of the railways' revenue.[19] Why the Midland Region has such an enormous deficit is by no means clear. It is probably due to a number of factors including the disruption and loss of traffic which resulted from electrification work, the existence of a large amount of duplicate route, and the fact that the region's costs have never been systematically pruned like those of the Western Region (by Sir Stanley Raymond and Gerald Fiennes), and those of the Eastern Region (by Sir Reginald Wilson and Fiennes).[20]

The rail deficit can also be analysed according to the profitability of the different types of traffic. In order to do this it is obviously necessary to allocate the railways' costs. This is a reasonably simple task with the exception of track, signalling and administrative expenses. It is, however, impossible, even in theory, to apportion a large proportion of track costs because of the heavy fixed cost which has to be incurred regardless of how intensively the track is used or of the type of traffic it carries. Nevertheless it is clear that a considerable part of these costs should be attributed to passenger traffic because standards of track maintenance have to be higher and signalling has to be more elaborate than they would have to be in the absence of passenger trains; and since passenger trains account for the bulk of all train miles it seems likely that they impose most wear on the track.[21] However, due to lack of information on the precise and proper allocation of track and other overhead expenses, attention will have to be largely confined to the surplus or deficit after direct costs. In 1966 British Rail made what appears to have been a handsome surplus on four categories of traffic, namely its principal inter-city passenger trains (£31 million), coal (£32 million), oil in train loads (£3 million) and Post Office mail (£11 million). On all of these the surplus was equivalent to well over 40 per cent of the allocated expenses, which was the overall margin it needed to earn in order to cover its track and other overhead expenses. It also seems likely, as the Southern Region's profit suggests, that the London suburban services had a con-siderable surplus. The only other category of traffic where there appears to be a satisfactory surplus is goods traffic which moves in train-load quantities.[22]

However, with the possible exception of its secondary inter-city services, British Rail does little more than break even on any of its remaining types of traffic and in many cases does not even do this. In 1966, for instance, it sustained a direct loss of £10 million on its stopping services and £16 million on its freight sundries – consignments which have to be bulked to form wagon loads. And this was only the tip of the iceberg for there must have been large losses on suburban services in the provinces and on freight which moves in wagon but not train loads.[23] Moreover, a considerable part of the railways track costs must be attributed to its stopping services because many of them run along lines which would otherwise be shut.

The Adequacy of Original Cost Depreciation

When the nationalized industries' accounts are put on a private enterprise basis and their interest payments disregarded, it appears that most of the industries have been earning profits, but it has been argued that these are illusory. It is widely believed that public enterprise makes too little provision for depreciation because the amount which it sets aside is based upon what its assets originally cost, and not upon their current replacement value. Because the purpose of depreciation is, from an economic point of view, to keep capital intact, it is the cost of replacing plant and equipment which is important, and in times of inflation this will normally be considerably higher than its historic cost. As a result undertakings which base their depreciation charges upon the latter are likely to give an exaggerated impression of their profitability.

In the main, the nationalized industries do calculate their depreciation by the original cost method. What they do is to spread the cost of the assets which they have acquired in equal instalments over their estimated lives.[24] The plant and equipment which were taken over when the industries were transferred to public ownership after the war are, however, a partial exception to the rule. In the case of BRS and the nationalized buses, vehicles were brought into their books at their estimated replacement value, and for the coal industry the compensation price greatly exceeded the written-down value of the assets which were acquired. As a result, the industry's transfer to public ownership was followed by a large increase in the amount of depreciation being set aside and the Coal Board believed that initially it was sufficient to cover its depreciation at replacement cost.[25]

Whatever the position may have been in the early days of nationalization it was officially stated in the early sixties that the nationalized industries' depreciation provisions were inadequate to cover their capital consumption. The White Paper on the Financial and Economic Obligations of the Nationalized Industries declared that 'The total retained income of all these industries taken together . . . has not been sufficient to provide for the replacement of assets used up in the production process, and this is also the case in most of the individual industries concerned'.[26] If so, their depreciation provisions must obviously have been insufficient. The CSO's estimates of the public corporations' capital consumption, which are in effect estimates of depreciation at replacement cost, have frequently been quoted in support of this view. They suggest that there is an enormous gap between what the corporations actually provide and what they ought to provide. For instance in 1968 there was a difference of nearly £300 million between the CSO's estimate of replacement cost depreciation and the sum which was set aside for depreciation. If so, the bulk of the profits which the nationalized industries show in their accounts are a statistical mirage.[27]

The CSO's estimates of capital consumption will, however, give a misleading impression of replacement cost depreciation under certain circumstances. As the CSO itself warns, 'Capital consumption should be valued at the cost of replacing capacity but so far it has only been possible to value it at the estimated cost of replacing existing fixed assets with identical assets. Consequently, the capital consumption estimates fail to allow for technical change.[28] If an industry's rate of technical advance is sufficiently rapid, then the cost of replacing a given amount of capacity with up-to-date equipment could, despite inflation, be lower than the cost of the original plant, let alone the cost of replacing it with modern equipment of old design.

In some parts of the public enterprise sector, and in particular electricity, this is exactly what has happened. The Electricity Council estimates that in 1960–1 and 1969–70 depreciation provisions were respectively £24 million and £35 million higher than they would have had to be in order to cover replacement cost.[29] However, in earlier years, the industry's depreciation provisions were inadequate by replacement cost standards. In 1954–5, for example, they appear to have been about £17 million too low.[30] The swing from inadequate to excessive depreciation is explained partly by the extremely short period over which generating plant has been written off since 1958–9 but mainly by the way in which, despite inflation, the cost of constructing a given amount of generating capacity has fallen as sets have become larger.[31]

Gas is another industry in which technical advance has tended to reduce replacement cost depreciation below what it would otherwise have been. Prior to the discovery of the new processes for making gas from light oil there appears to have been a gap of £6 million to £10 million between the industry's depreciation provisions and full replacement cost depreciation.[32] This estimate, however, was based on the replacement of like-with-like and the new techniques which became available in 1962 had a much lower capital cost than the old coal-based processes. Indeed the cost of capacity fell from £50–£60 per therm day for the traditional process of deriving gas from coal to only about £10. As a result replacement cost depreciation on the industry's gas-making plant fell to about £6 million, which appears to have been about half what the industry was providing.[33] Hence it seems doubtful whether the Gas Boards' depreciation provisions have, ignoring the effect of North Sea gas, been seriously deficient since the early sixties. The discovery of gas in the North Sea has substantially reduced the amount which the industry needs to cover the replacement cost of its gas distribution and storage system. Because natural gas has twice the calorific value of coal gas, the thermal carrying capacity of mains and the storage capacity of gas holders is virtually doubled when natural gas is substituted for coal gas.[34] As a result, it would obviously cost considerably less, now that natural gas has been discovered, to replace the existing mains and holders by physically smaller facilities but with the same capacity. There seems little doubt that the gas industry's depreciation provisions, based as they are upon what the distribution and storage system originally cost, are now more than sufficient to cover the replacement cost of its assets.

In aviation the rate of technical progress has again been very rapid and the introduction of larger and faster planes has, despite inflation, brought down the cost of replacing capacity. Both the air corporations report that their historic cost depreciation exceeds the amount which it would be necessary to set aside if they were working on a replacement cost basis, and BOAC adds that this has been so for a decade or more.[35] It also appears unlikely that there has been any serious under-provision in British Road Services. Lorry prices have been relatively stable, which means, of course, that replacement cost depreciation cannot be very different from depreciation at historic cost.[36]

The final nationalized industry where technical and economic progress has possibly reduced replacement cost depreciation is the railways. This may appear surprising in view of British Rail's estimate that it would in 1967 have had to provide £21 million more depreciation in order to cover replacement cost. But what this calculation, almost certainly of the like-with-like variety, ignores is the virtual certainty that a high proportion of the existing assets will not have to be replaced even in the absence of further rail closures. Despite the enormous cutback which has taken place since the early sixties, the railways are still using far more equipment than they will need in a few years' time. British Rail which at the end of 1968 possessed 430,000 wagons, hopes ultimately to be able to reduce the number to between 100,000 and 150,000, and during the next few years substantial progress towards this target is expected. It is also planned that by then there will be a fairly substantial reduction in the number of locomotives, and anticipated that the carriage fleet will be reduced from just under 8,400 at the end of 1968 to about 5,000.[37]

Quite apart from the general tightening-up in efficiency, the new operating methods which have been devised, or are being planned, will lead to a far more intensive use of equipment. Freightliners and merry-go-round working will have this effect and so will the new scheme for wagon-load traffic and the advanced passenger train. The new rolling stock will, of course, be more expensive than the old but it will be used so much more intensively that it seems unlikely that its cost per unit of capacity will exceed that of the railways' existing equipment. For instance it appears from the estimates for freightliners given in the Beeching Report that their depreciation charges are only about half as great, per ton mile, as those which British Rail provided for its ordinary freight trains during 1967.[38] However, it should be recognized that the case for believing that the railways' depreciation provisions were (prior to the financial reconstruction) more or less adequate is more debatable than it is for the electricity, gas and airways.

Coal and buses are the only nationalized industries where depreciation provisions seem to be on the low side and the question arises of whether private industry is, like the public enterprise sector, on balance providing sufficient depreciation to meet the replacement cost of its plant and equipment.[39] There is a considerable amount of evidence to suggest that in the private sector depreciation provisions are inadequate. The Monopolies Commission has, for instance, made estimates of profits after replacement cost depreciation for quoted companies. When these are expressed as a proportion of the companies' net assets at replacement cost the rate of return on capital appears to be significantly lower than the rate shown by the companies' own figures for profits and capital. In 1963 the latter was 12·7 per cent whereas the Monopolies Commission estimated that the rate was only 10·7 per cent at replacement cost. If these figures are correct the companies must have been failing to provide sufficient depreciation to cover the replacement cost of their plant and equipment, although the gap between the yield on capital at replacement cost and on the book value of their assets had narrowed considerably over the years. The Commission's estimates of the cost of replacing assets suffer however from the same weakness as those of the Central Statistical Office: they make no allowance for technical and economic change.[40] It is therefore possible that the companies' depreciation provisions are, like those of the nationalized industries, more satisfactory than they appear.

The estimates of replacement cost depreciation which companies have from time to time prepared do not suggest that this is the case. For instance, in their submissions to the Monopolies Commission, firms frequently argue that due to rising prices their depreciation provisions are on the low side and their rates of return on capital are not as high as they appear. Thus British Oxygen calculated that although during 1954 it showed a return of 23 per cent on the basis of historic cost, the figure was only 16·5 per cent at replacement cost; for ICI's fertilizer business it was found that whereas the rate was 17·3 per cent in 1955–6 using historic cost, it was only 12·9 per cent when partly adjusted to replacement cost; for Fisons' fertilizers the historic and replacement cost figures were respectively 21·6 per cent and 13·8 per cent; and for Kodak, which based its estimates of replacement cost on the amount for which it insured its assets, they were 20 per cent and 13 per cent for 1963. These estimates must be treated with care as it was obviously in the firms' own interests to be as cautious as possible in their figures. On the other hand they must have known that the Commission would be on the look-out for unrealistically low figures and in the case of ICI the company had already, prior to the Commission's inquiry, revalued its assets and increased its depreciation. Nevertheless the firms' estimates are persuasive rather than conclusive.[41]

What is of greater significance is that some firms, such as the London Brick Company, appropriate part of their profits to a special reserve because they recognize that their normal depreciation provisions are inadequate. Even more conclusive is the fact that when firms reply on a confidential basis to inquiries where they have no incentive to understate their profits they say that the figures which stand in their books are unrealistic. A number of companies provided Professor Reddaway with figures of replacement cost for their overseas subsidiaries. From these it appeared that, in 1964, the net replacement cost of the assets exceeded their book value by 26 per cent. Moreover, despite the fact that some companies had revalued their assets, the gap between replacement and book value appeared to have risen significantly since 1955, though this finding should be treated with caution as only a small number of companies were able to provide figures for the earlier years.[42] The conclusion must be that, whereas the nationalized industries' depreciation provisions are for the most part sufficient to meet the cost of replacing their assets, those of private industry are inadequate. As a result private enterprise's profits are appreciably smaller than they appear, whereas those of public enterprise are not.

The Rate of Return on Capital

Although the nationalized industries have, with the exception of British Rail, mostly earned profits, and although they have not been overstated, it is widely believed that their profits have been exceptionally low. This belief rests partly upon the mistaken notion that they only have a profit when they show a surplus after interest and upon the erroneous supposition that their depreciation charges have been inadequate. But the main source for the belief is the comparatively low rate of return which the industries appear to have earned on their capital. Comparisons between the rates of return in private and public enterprise were presented and popularized by the White Paper on the Financial and Economic Obligations of the Nationalized Industries and subsequent figures which the Government has made available. In Table 22 the official figures are given for the NCB, the gas industry, the air corporations and in the first of the two columns shown for electricity.[43]

The nationalized industries appear, even when the highly unprofitable railways are left out of the picture, to have earned only a modest rate of return on their assets. Over the period 1959–68 the Coal Board's profits have only averaged about $3\frac{1}{2}$ per cent on the capital invested in the business: BOAC has earned about $4\frac{1}{2}$ per cent; BEA around 5 per cent; the Gas Boards approaching 5 per cent; and the Electricity Boards in England and Wales, which are slightly more profitable than the two Scottish Boards, about 6 per cent. In contrast to these industries with their rates of around 5 per cent, the Transport Holding Company, which owned BRS and the Tillings and Scottish bus groups, earned just under 9 per cent between its establishment in 1963 and its dismemberment at the end of 1968. However, even this does not appear very high when set against the Government figures for private industry. These show that during the period 1956–65 – the latest ten-year period for which official figures seem to be available – quoted companies in manufacturing and distribution earned about $14\frac{1}{2}$ per cent on average.[44] Even when the railways are ignored public enterprise is, at first sight, only about a third as profitable as private enterprise.

It is widely believed, and has been argued by Mr George Polanyi, that this shows that the nationalized industries are inefficient.[45] But their rate of return on capital indicates little or nothing about the level of technical efficiency at which they are operating. It is obviously possible for an industry which is technically very efficient, and has the lowest possible operating costs, to earn a low rate of return on capital. This will happen if it decides to hold its prices down, and forgo profits which it would

Table 22

PROFITS AS A PERCENTAGE OF NET ASSETS 1955-68

	Official Series	Electricity[1,2] Private Enterprise Accounting Conventions	NCB[3]	Gas[2]	BEA[2]	BOAC	Tillings and Scottish[4]	BRS[4]	Manufacturing[5]
1955	4·6	..	0·4	3·6	7·8	3·3	16·5	13·0	16·0
1956	4·7	..	6·7	4·1	4·6	2·9	15·3	5·8	14·3
1957	5·0	5·1	3·5	4·0	7·6	-1·2	14·2	8·5	14·0
1958	5·6	6·0	2·6	3·3	4·8	-7·1	16·6	5·6	14·0
1959	5·5	6·1	1·6	3·3	7·7	3·4	17·8	8·7	14·7
1960	5·0	5·8	2·3	4·0	6·5	2·7	17·3	4·7	14·8
1961	5·5	6·3	3·2	4·3	0·7	-26·5	15·9	8·9	12·6
1962	6·1	6·7	5·2	4·6	2·1	-12·1	16·1	9·6	11·5
1963	6·9	7·5	6·7	5·2	8·3	-6·6	12·6	9·5	11·9
1964	6·5	7·2	4·9	5·9	5·8	15·2	13·6	14·4	13·2
1965	7·0	7·6	0·1	5·4	5·4	9·6	12·8	13·2	12·0
1966	5·1	6·1	3·7	4·8	4·8	21·7	13·9	8·4	10·8
1967	6·1	7·0	4·6	3·7	2·7	17·1	12·2	4·5	9·1
1968	7·1	7·9	4·0	6·5	6·5	21·1	13·2	5·3	11·4

[1] England and Wales.
[2] Financial year.
[3] Financial year from 1963–4.
[4] Net fixed assets 1955–62; net assets excluding goodwill 1960–8.
[5] Net assets excluding goodwill; profits after stock appreciation.

have earned, in the interest of higher sales. Conversely it is possible for an inefficient undertaking which is operating under conditions of imperfect competition to earn a high rate of return by restricting its sales – and increasing its prices. As many of the nationalized industries possess a significant degree of monopoly power, a high rate of return could certainly be earned in this way even if their costs were excessively high. This invites the reply that although rates of return may tell us little about technical efficiency they provide valuable information about allocative efficiency. If the nationalized industries earn a low rate of return on their assets, it appears that capital has been drawn away from industries where it could have been used more profitably and more productively. However, this assumes, first, that if the nationalized industries had not invested, the capital expenditure would have taken place elsewhere and, second, that there is a close connection between the prospective rate of return on capital, when calculated correctly, and profits as a proportion of net assets. There is no guarantee, as we shall see, that if the nationalized industries reduce their investment a compensating rise will take place elsewhere, or that a firm which earns a high rate of return in economic terms – i.e. when the yield on prospective investment is calculated by the correct (dcf) method – will have a high yield on net assets. Even if its forecasts are realized this is the case because, as Professor G. C. Harcourt has shown, accounting rates of return are of dubious economic value.[46]

Nevertheless in default of any more reliable statistics these continue to be quoted, especially when the nationalized industries are under discussion, and cannot therefore be ignored. Although the official statistics of the rates of return in public and private enterprise are constantly mentioned they have not been subjected to detailed investigation. Most commentators have simply accepted the Government's figures at their face value.[47] No heed has been paid to the warning which is buried away at the end of *The Financial and Economic Obligations of the Nationalized Industries* that the valuation of assets cannot be obtained on a uniform basis because it depends on the date and price level at which they were bought and the way in which they have been depreciated and written down.[48] Yet both the way in which the nationalized industries originally acquired their assets and the depreciation policies which they have adopted have affected the book value of their assets and the apparent level of their profits.

When the coal industry was nationalized about £277 million was paid for the fixed assets which were taken over from the colliery companies and this was the value at which they were set down in its books once compensation had been determined. The basis on which compensation values were fixed need not concern us but what is important is that they must have greatly exceeded the value at which the assets stood in the companies' books. Dr Charles Feinstein has estimated from a sample of company accounts that in 1937 the net book value of their fixed assets totalled only £181 million.[49] By adding on the amount which the industry invested between 1938 and 1946, and then deducting an estimate of the depreciation which was provided, it is possible to discover roughly what the book value of the colliery companies' net assets was just before nationalization. It appears that by vesting date the book value of the companies' net assets had declined to £153 million. It would be wrong to jump to the conclusion that as £277 million was paid for the assets which the Board took over, compensation was excessive, because the book value of companies' assets is a poor guide to their market value.[50] The difference between the net book value of the colliery companies' fixed assets and the compensation price (£124 million) is nevertheless the figure with which we must start in order to put the Coal Board's accounts on more or less the same basis as those of industries which remained in private ownership, and did not have the value of their assets marked up, due to acquisition by the State.

If the property which it took over had been set down in its books at what it stood at in those of the colliery companies, but everything else had been exactly the same since vesting day, the value of the NCB's net assets would obviously have been £124 million lower than the figure which is given each year in the Board's accounts. In this situation the industry's rate of return on its assets would have seemed more respectable. Alternatively, it would not have been necessary for the Government to enable the Coal Board to write down the value of its assets by such a large amount. By the spring of 1969 the NCB had, under the Coal Industry Act of 1965, written £284 million off the value of its fixed assets, excluding a small contribution which it had made from its own funds.[51] If, however, its assets had not been revalued when the industry was nationalized, the sum need not have been so large, because the book value of the Board's assets would have been £124 million smaller when the capital reconstruction came to be made. Whether this has any economic significance is open to doubt, but so long as attention is paid to accounting figures and rates of return it must be borne in mind that the NCB's financial performance would have appeared somewhat better if the assets which it took over had been set down at their existing book value.

When it calculated the Transport Holding Company's rate of return the Treasury included not only tangible assets but also goodwill in the Company's net assets. It is very doubtful whether goodwill should be included. In the case of Tillings and Scottish where goodwill is a particularly large item there was a considerable difference between the price which was paid for those companies by way of compensation and the subsequent purchase of shares, and the value of their assets. This difference, which was termed goodwill, presumably reflected the security which bus undertakings enjoy due to the difficulty which new operators have in securing the necessary road service licences from the Traffic Commissioners. However, it would be wrong to regard goodwill of this type as forming part of an undertaking's assets on which it should be expected to earn a rate of return, because the only way in which it can do this is by exploiting its monopoly power. Goodwill must, therefore, be excluded when calculating the return which the Tillings and Scottish bus groups have earned. When their profits are expressed as a proportion of their tangible assets, as they have been in Table 22, it becomes apparent that their rate of return has been considerably higher than it appears.[52] For instance, Tillings and Scottish turn out to have earned about 13 per cent in 1968 compared with about 9 per cent when goodwill is included in their assets.

The book value of British Road Services also includes an element of goodwill. When long-distance road haulage was brought into public ownership the transport operators received not only the estimated market value of their vehicles and buildings but also an additional sum equivalent to between two and five times their average profits. This was, among other things, intended to reflect the value of their licences to ply for hire. Here again it would clearly be wrong to treat the so-called goodwill which BRS acquired as part of its assets. During recent years BRS has acquired Tayforth, Harold Wood and a number of smaller concerns at a price which exceeded the value which has been placed upon their assets. This may, in part, have been due to their customer connections, and as such have constituted goodwill in the normal commercial sense, but a large part of the difference between asset values and the takeover price must have been due to the value of the licences which they possessed. Thus it seems best to calculate the rate of return for BRS simply upon its tangible assets. The results are shown in Table 22.[53] In 1968 BRS earned a return of 5·3 per cent compared with 4·4 per cent if goodwill is included in its net assets.[54]

If the financial performance of coal and nationalized road transport has been slightly better than it appears, due to the price at which they acquired assets from the private sector, that of the electricity industry has been affected by the prudence of its depreciation policy. In 1958 the CEGB substantially reduced the periods over which its assets are written off, and this has depressed the profits and the rate of return which the industry has shown.[55] That the life-span adopted for the purpose of depreciation is extremely short is shown by a comparison with that used by the privately-owned American electricity undertakings. A study by the Federal Power Commission reveals that in 1961 the American utilities were writing off their generating stations, with the exception of hydro-electric plant, over an average period of 35 years or more. The CEGB 'in contrast' was depreciating its conventional stations over 25 years and its nuclear power stations over 20. For transmission plant the American companies were assuming a service life of over 40 years but the CEGB was assuming that it would be 25–30 years. Only in the case of distribution investment, where the Area Boards had not reduced their depreciation periods in 1958, were the British and American electricity industries writing their capital expenditure down over a similar period. In fact, the CEGB and the Area Boards write off their capital expenditure even more rapidly than a comparison of depreciation periods may suggest. This is because the British electricity industry starts depreciating its investment in the financial year following that in which the expenditure is incurred, whereas the American companies wait until the investment has come to fruition and plant is in service.[56]

As the American commentator Robert Gilbert puts it, in his own inimitable way, by private enterprise standards 'the British Socialists are over-depreciating'.[57] In order to make a fair comparison between the British electricity industry's rate of return and that of private industry it is necessary to calculate what it would have been if the CEGB and the other Boards had followed the best private practice, as represented by the American investor-owned utilities. As American firms generally write off their plant and equipment faster than British firms, the use of American depreciation periods is most unlikely to lead to the Board's profits and rate of return being overstated in comparison with that of the rest of British industry. In theory, it seems desirable when recalculating the British electricity authority's depreciation and assets to obtain the fullest possible breakdown of its capital expenditure, and then to write down each type of investment over the life which the American utilities assume. However, not only would this have involved a great deal of work but it also seemed unnecessary, partly because the pattern of investment is likely to be similar in both countries, and partly because the life-span is not very different for the main classes of investment. It was, therefore, decided to depreciate the British electricity industry's capital expenditure over the average period during which the American companies write off their investment. From the Federal Power Commission's study this appears to be about 37 years. To avoid any risk of depreciating over too short a period the industry's investment was written off over 35 years, commencing in the case of the CEGB's investment from the time at which the plant and equipment came into service.[58]

What the electricity industry's profits would have been if it had calculated its depreciation on this private enterprise basis is shown in the column of Table 21 which has been printed in italics. It can be seen that in 1968–9 a profit of around £450 million would have been declared. As the Electricity Boards' aggregate profit appears from their published accounts to have been £357 million (which is the figure given in the previous column) the extreme prudence of their depreciation policy led to about £90 million of potential profit being hidden from view.[59] This makes less difference to the industry's rate of return than might be expected, because if its investment had been written off more slowly its assets would have appeared greater. Nevertheless, it can be seen from the third column of Table 22 that the Electricity Boards in England and Wales would, in 1968–9, have had a return of 7·9 per cent if they had depreciated their assets in the same manner as the American utilities. This compares with a figure of 7·1 per cent which is the return as calculated from their accounts.

While the official figures tend to understate the nationalized industries' rates of return they tend to exaggerate the profitability of private industry. The most obvious reason is that no allowance has been made for stock appreciation: the apparent financial gain which firms make when the book value of their stocks increases due to rising prices. However, an allowance has been made from the estimates of stock appreciation which are published in the Bluebook.[60] This was not necessary in the case of the nationalized industries as their stock appreciation is negligible. According to the CSO it totalled only £7 million in 1968 for all public corporations.[61] When stock appreciation is eliminated, quoted manufacturing companies turn out to have had an average rate of return of about 12 per cent over the period 1959–68. It appears, therefore, that during the past decade private enterprise has been about twice as profitable as public enterprise, and not, as usually believed, three times as profitable.

Moreover, it can be seen from Table 22 that the returns have been falling in manufacturing. During recent years profits have only represented about 10 per cent on net assets compared with nearly 15 per cent in the second half of the fifties. In contrast, there has been some tendency for returns to increase within the public enterprise sector. The most striking case is BOAC where, during the late fifties and early sixties, the rate of return was negative but in recent years has been around 20 per cent. In electricity there has been a far less spectacular but fairly steady increase in profitability. A decade ago the Electricity Boards in England

and Wales were earning 6 per cent or less but, on a private enterprise basis, they earned nearly 8 per cent in 1968–9. The gap between the rate of return in electricity and in manufacturing has therefore become quite narrow. In gas also returns have been increasing, although they are still significantly lower than in electricity. During the second half of the fifties the gas industry earned between 3 per cent and 4 per cent but by 1968 the figure had reached 6½ per cent. It must be concluded, therefore, that the gap between public and private enterprise rates of return is far smaller than usually supposed, that it has narrowed considerably as the years have gone by, and that it is now quite small in the case of electricity, which accounts for so much of the nationalized industries' investment.

Profit Comparisons

Although it is customary to compare the financial performance of public enterprise with that of the private sector, it is more instructive to compare like with like, and see what rates of return have been earned by private firms in the same industry or, where there are none, by the same industries abroad. In road haulage, road passenger transport and perhaps air transport there is no need to look abroad because the industries have been only partly nationalized. Unfortunately, the amount of information which is readily available on the profitability of private road haulage contractors is somewhat limited. The best overall comparison which can be made is to calculate the share of gross trading profits in value added for BRS and for all road haulage companies. This is the nearest which can be got to calculating profits as a percentage of turnover, but as pay and profits constituted 63 per cent of BRS's turnover in 1964 it is fairly near. In that year BRS's gross profits represented about 26 per cent of its value added as against 30 per cent for all road haulage companies during 1964–5.[62] This was, it should be noted, an exceptionally good period for BRS, although the same may be true for the rest of the industry.

The State air corporations have, during recent years, earned higher rates of return than the private British airlines, though BEA's advantage has not been very great. According to the Edwards Committee during 1962–7 BOAC earned 10·3 per cent on its net assets, BEA earned 5·6 per cent, but the private sector only made 5·2 per cent. BOAC's rate would have appeared much higher but for the losses which it incurred during the first two years of this period, before it had sorted out its financial difficulties. Too much significance should not be attached to these comparisons because the corporations and the companies tend to undertake different types of work; BEA and BOAC earn almost all their revenue from scheduled services whereas the bulk of private airline revenue comes from charter operations. But it is interesting to observe that in 1966, which was the only year for which the Edwards Committee was able to obtain detailed figures, the private sector made a loss of about £400,000 on its scheduled services.[63]

Nevertheless, the private and the state airlines are such different animals that it is probably best to compare BEA and BOAC with their foreign competitors. During the period 1958–67 BEA came fifth and BOAC sixth in the rate of return league for the international airways for which figures are readily available. The airlines with the highest rates were Pan Am with an average of 12·1 per cent, Swissair and Qantas with 6·1 per cent, and Alitalia with 5·2 per cent. Then came BEA with 4·7 per cent and BOAC at 2·4 per cent. The airlines which earned even lower rates of return were KLM with 1·8 per cent, Aer Lingus at 1·6 per cent, Air France with 0·8 per cent and Lufthansa with −0·2 per cent. In assessing the performance of BOAC and BEA two important qualifications need to be made. First, BOAC earned a relatively high rate of return during the second half of the period. Over the five years 1963–7 Pan Am was the only airline which was ahead. It had a rate of 15·7 per cent compared with BOAC's 11·4 per cent, but the gap was probably narrower than it appears because the Corporation has been writing off its assets faster than Pan American. Second, it must be borne in mind that BEA has shorter hauls than any of the other airlines and that short-haul operations are, the world over, less profitable than long-haul work. If BEA's domestic routes, where hauls are extremely short, are excluded from the picture the corporation's rate of return compares favourably with those of its competitors. For instance in 1966–7 the rate of return on BEA's international services was roughly 7½ per cent.[64]

In electricity, comparisons can readily be made between the nationalized British undertakings and the privately owned utilities in America. Over the five-year period 1962–6 the CEGB and the Area Electricity Boards in England and Wales had an average return of 6·3 per cent whereas in the United States the electricity companies earned 9·7 per cent.[65] Not only is the difference between the two figures comparatively small but it is partly due to the fact that the British electricity industry has been pursuing a far more cautious depreciation policy than the American utilities. Between 1962 and 1966 the Electricity Boards would have shown a return of 7 per cent if they had been following American depreciation practice, and in 1968–9 the figure would have been nearly 8 per cent. That American electric companies earn only a low rate of return on their assets need cause no surprise. It is due partly to the fact that they are subject to regulation in order to prevent them from exploiting their monopoly power and earning unduly high profits. But this does not explain why the American utilities are content to go on operating, or how they are able to raise capital, when the rate of return on their assets is so low. The reason is that the degree of risk is very low. American experience, therefore, suggests both that the normal rate of profit in electricity is considerably below the general average, and that the rate of return which would have been earned if these industries had been in private ownership in Britain might not have been very much higher than it has been under public ownership.

The remaining nationalized industry where it is possible to make an international profitability comparison is the railways. As is well known, railways everywhere tend to make losses. In Europe only the Swiss railways make a profit. In 1967 its working surplus was equivalent to 6 per cent of the revenue it received. However, the Swiss railways were in an exceptionally favourable position because of the restrictions imposed on road goods traffic.[66] In Germany Bundesbahn's loss represented about 5 per cent of revenue, in Sweden about 10 per cent, in Holland the figure was 14 per cent and in Italy it was around 35 per cent.[67] Similarly in 1968 the Belgian National Railways' deficit was equivalent to a third of their revenue, though this may exaggerate their true losses as their pension payments were exceptionally heavy, presumably because they have been cutting their staff unusually fast by continental standards. However, even if pensions are entirely ignored the Belgian railways had a sizeable deficit.[68] The Bundesbahn's deficit is slightly lower than it appears because it is not fully compensated by the Government for the pensions burden in which it was involved when Germany was divided. The financial arrangements of the continental railways are extremely complex and the figures which have been given should only be regarded as approximate. Nevertheless they do seem to indicate that British Rail's deficit, which was equivalent to 18 per cent of its revenue in 1968, was about average. In Germany and Sweden the deficit as a proportion of revenue was much smaller than in Britain, in Holland it was only slightly smaller and in Belgium, Italy and France it was considerably greater.

CHAPTER 10

British Rail's Loss of Traffic

In the years up to 1955 British Rail consistently made an operating profit, though it was small in relation to its turnover or the amount of capital employed. A larger surplus would have been earned but for the obstacles which the Transport Commission faced in adjusting its charges. The BTC estimated that the delay or modification of price increases by the Transport Tribunal or the Minister cost it over £50 million between the autumn of 1949 and the end of 1955. The Commission also argued that, because it was prevented from obtaining any margin against future inflation, it had to bear about £50 million of extra costs in the intervals before an application for a new increase in charges could be made. A small part of the £100 million of potential revenue forgone would have accrued to London Transport but the bulk of the loss was sustained by British Rail.[1]

To this extent British Rail's financial position was stronger than it appeared. On the other hand, in the early fifties, large amounts of maintenance expenditure was charged to a special account. During the war a considerable sum had been set aside to cover maintenance which was being postponed. As a result the BTC was, during its early years, able to treat part of its maintenance as a war-time arrear. For instance, in 1953 it charged £21 million of rail expenditure against the reserves which it had inherited. The partial exhaustion of these balances and the growing unreality of the procedure led the Commission to discontinue the practice in 1954. As maintenance expenditure continued at about its previous rate during 1954, and increased thereafter, this had the effect of reducing the railways' profits.[2] This accounting change was, therefore, partly responsible for the swing from profits to losses.

Of more fundamental importance was the growing intensity of competition from road transport. In 1954 the volume of rail traffic, which had hitherto been more or less stable, started its long decline and the same appears to be true of the railways' share of inland goods transport.[3] In 1956 the railways were barely in surplus though this was partly due to special factors, such as the rail strike which lost the Commission about £12 million. During the following year the railways had a deficit of £16½ million.[4] Once again the Commission's disappointing financial performance was partly due to special causes. Early in 1956 the BTC asked the Government to sanction a 10 per cent increase in rail freight charges and said that it was going to apply to the Transport Tribunal for permission to increase passenger fares. But the Government, which did not wish to prejudice discussions on price stabilization which it was about to hold with the FBI and other bodies, only permitted a 5 per cent increase in freight charges and persuaded the Commission to delay its application to the Tribunal. These restrictions were imposed for a period of six months, and, according to the Ministry of Transport, they cost the Commission about £8½ million of revenue.[5]

More important, the Government's action led to a reassessment of the Commission's economic and financial position. Its weakness could no longer be glossed over as it had been in the past. The report of the working party which drew up the Modernization Plan during 1954 had warned that, allowing for interest, losses might be incurred in the period before modernization had borne fruit,[6] but this warning was omitted from the published version of the Plan. In the discussions on the railways' financial future in 1956 and in its Memorandum to the Minister, the Commission argued that they would damage their commercial position if they tried to eliminate the deficit by jacking-up charges. The Commission believed that, although this would increase revenue in the short run, the rise would be purchased at the expense of a substantial contraction of traffic in the long run. It forecast that in 1961 or 1962 its surplus would be large enough to cover all capital charges except for interest on deficits. By then modernization would have started to pay off and the corrective measures it was proposing would have taken effect. However, the Transport Commission believed that in 1957 and 1958 there would be still worse losses, even before interest, and proposed either a financial reconstruction or that it should be relieved temporarily of part of its interest burden.[7] The Government agreed to the latter proposal.

The Commission's deficit in 1957 was considerably higher than in 1956: the rail loss increased from £16½ million to £27 million. This was only slightly greater than the figure which the BTC had forecast and was still at a manageable level.[8] In 1958 the railways' finances completely collapsed. The deficit soared to £48 million, which was much more than had been intended. This disastrous result was due to a staggering fall in rail traffic, which declined by 8 per cent. Although they rallied slightly during the boom years of 1960 and 1964, rail carryings have continued to decline. In 1968 they were 20 per cent lower than they had been in 1957.[9]

Falling Traffic and Stable Charges

There is no mystery about the cause of British Rail's insolvency: the basic reason has been the fall in traffic. In particular its ruin has been due to the decline in freight carryings and freight revenue. The profitability of the passenger side of the undertaking had already collapsed by 1954 when the railways were still in surplus. Between 1949 and 1954 the margin of passenger revenue over direct expenses fell from £30 million to £5 million. One reason for this was the difficulty which the BTC had in adjusting its fares, due to the operations of the Transport Tribunal. On the freight side the margin over direct expenses rose from £35 million in 1949 to £90 million in 1954. In 1957 the figure was slightly lower, at £80 million, but after this the margin slumped disastrously. By 1966 it had fallen to a mere £20 million. There has, in contrast, been some improvement in passenger finances. Between 1957 and 1966 the margin over direct costs rose from £5 million to £35 million.[10]

If the railways' traffic had not collapsed and if they had been able to increase their charges in line with the general rise in prices they would almost certainly be making a profit by now. If British Rail's output in 1968 had been as high as it was in 1957 it would have had 24 per cent more traffic. On the assumption that revenue would also have been 24 per cent greater BR's receipts would have totalled £567 million, compared with the actual figure of £457 million. Between 1957 and 1968 rail charges increased about 13 per cent. Meanwhile the general level of prices rose by 31 per cent. If rail charges had risen in step they would, by 1968, have been 16 per cent higher than they were and BR's revenue would have totalled £658 million. Against this must be set the extra costs which the additional traffic would have involved. A large part of the railways' costs are 'fixed costs' which do not vary directly with the volume of traffic. This category includes the cost of providing signalling (£39 million in 1968); the cost of maintaining the track (£57 million); the cost of maintaining sidings, stations and other buildings (about £15 million); the pay of porters and ticket collectors (about £15 million); and administrative and general expenses (£82 million). Altogether, the railways' fixed costs appear to have totalled about £208 million in 1968. Although fixed costs were large British Rail's variable costs were still larger at about £339 million.[11] If with 24 per cent more traffic fixed costs had been the same but variable costs had been 24 per cent higher, aggregate working expenses would have been £628 million. This means that British Rail would have had a surplus of £30 million before interest.

It is not entirely realistic to assume that the railways' 'fixed costs' would have been no higher. Although the cost of track maintenance, for example, does not increase in line with traffic, it does tend to rise as the track is used more intensively. According to British Rail the cost of track maintenance increases by up to 20 per cent when traffic doubles and as a result the figure for fixed costs is probably slightly too low.[12] But the figure for variable costs is certainly too high. British Rail almost certainly has a considerable amount of spare capacity. If its traffic increased it would not have to run proportionately more trains; the loading of existing services would improve. More seats would be occupied on passenger trains and more wagons would be hitched on to freight trains. As we have seen, our trains are lightly loaded by foreign standards.[13] Moreover by assuming a general increase of 24 per cent in variable costs it has, in effect, been assumed that British Rail would have accepted 24 per cent more traffic whether good or bad, but it is possible that the railways would have been more willing to shed unprofitable traffic if there had not been a general decline in the demand for rail transport. It seems probable that one reason why British Rail has been so slow to eliminate unprofitable activities has been the feeling that at all costs it had better hold on to what traffic remained. The railways' financial difficulties may have increased the pressure to cut costs and have led to some economies which would not otherwise have been made, but such gains may well have been offset by the deadening effect on management which the decline in business and the slide into deficit must have had.

After reviewing the available evidence it is difficult to avoid the conclusion that British Rail would today have a comfortable profit but for the decline in traffic and the fact that rail charges have risen less than prices in general. At this stage two fundamental problems arise. First, there is the question of how far the fall in traffic has been due to circumstances beyond the railways' control and of whether British Rail could have taken steps to prevent it happening. Second, there is the problem of why the railways did not act more promptly and more firmly to cut their costs and eliminate loss-making activities. The remainder of this Chapter will be devoted to answering, or at least trying to answer, the first question, while in the next Chapter we shall examine why those in charge of British Rail did not do more to cut the system down to size.

The Erosion of Coal Traffic

The explanation for the decline in rail traffic which springs most readily to mind is the increase in competition from road transport. Between 1957 and 1968 the volume of rail freight, as measured by ton miles, fell by about a quarter; but meanwhile the volume of road traffic appears to have increased by 90 per cent.[14] At first sight the growth of road transport and the decline of the railways appear to be different sides of the same coin.

This view has, however, been challenged. For instance, the Geddes Committee argued that 'a substantial part of the fall in the total volume of rail traffic arises from decline in the transport needs of traditional rail users. The growth in road transport equally owes much to the development of industries for whose work road is specially suitable. In the overall change which has taken place there must have been an element of transfer of traffic from rail to road, but this element is probably a minor part of the whole.'[15] If this is correct the decline of the railways has been due to economic developments even more fundamental, and even less reversible, than the rise of road transport. The railways have been hit, not by competition, but below the belt where they have little chance of defending themselves. Owing to a change in the structure of the economy the demand for their services has simply dried up.

The most obvious case where this has happened is the transport of coal although it also appears to be true of iron and steel products and materials. The railways have always been heavily dependent on the coal industry for traffic and have, therefore, been dealt a heavy blow by its contraction. Between 1957 and 1968 rail carryings of coal and coke fell from 167 million tons to 123 million tons, which is a reduction of over a quarter. A large part of this reduction was the inevitable consequence of the decline in coal sales. It seems possible however that, if British Rail had been more enterprising and efficient, the decline in its coal traffic would have been less great. It was claimed in the Beeching Report, on the basis of a detailed investigation of the coal which passed by road, that no less than 17 million tons was suitable for rail conveyance. But a close examination of the figures given in the Reshaping Report shows that a large part of the traffic which was described as suitable for rail was of a very poor nature. Nearly half of the total was hauled less than 26 miles and only about four million tons passed in sufficient quantities to be carried in block trains.[16]

Not only has there been an unavoidable reduction in the quantity of coal shifted by rail but there has also been a substantial decline in the average distance it is carried. Because coal is tending to be consumed nearer and nearer its point of production the average length of haul for rail-borne coal declined by 13 per cent between 1957 and 1968.[17] This has been due to changes in the pattern of coal consumption. In particular the amount of coal consumed by the electricity industry, where the rail haul is only about half the general average, has been rising fast. As a result of this and other factors deliveries to power stations in England and Wales have increased as a proportion of all railborne coal from 13 per cent in 1958 to 33 per cent in 1968.[18]

Are Rail Charges Competitive?

The catastrophic but largely inevitable decline in the railways' staple traffic in coal and steel made it all the more vital that there should be a corresponding rise in their other business. This has not taken place. Indeed the volume of general goods traffic, in ton miles, declined by roughly 15 per cent between 1957 and 1968. All of this reduction took place during the first half of the period and in 1968 rail carryings were significantly higher than they had been at any time since the early sixties.[19] Even so, British Rail's lack of success in this field has been striking and requires explanation.

In order to understand what has happened it is necessary to bear in mind the position at the start of the period. It seems likely that at that time British Rail was carrying a large amount of traffic which could have been sent more expeditiously and at a lower cost by road. Reference has already been made to the investigation by Professor Walters and Mr Clifford Sharp in which they worked out what it would have cost those firms in the Birmingham area which used rail to have let BRS carry their goods, and vice versa. They found that the average rail charge for goods passing by rail over a distance of between 75 and 100 miles was higher than the estimated average amount which British Road Services would have charged. Again the average cost by rail for rail consignments of between one and six tons, and possibly also of ten tons and over, was as high or higher than the prospective road haulage charge. For a number of other categories of traffic the average cost by rail was only slightly lower than the estimated cost by road. Indeed, only where consignments were very small or hauls were very long did rail users appear to obtain a decisive price advantage by continuing to patronize British Rail. Except, therefore, for traffic of this type, which represented only a small part of the total, there must have been large numbers of rail users who would have been charged less if they had let BRS transport their goods.[20]

My experience [reported the Transport Manager of Stanton Ironworks] is that road rates are almost always lower than rail, whether for short distances or long. It is noteworthy that even when the railways quote exceptional rates with the object of attracting or retaining traffic they still do not actually undercut their BRS competitors. I think it true to say, speaking for my own Company at least, that the whole of our finished products could be transported by road cheaper than by rail, with a saving of many thousands of pounds.[21]

Professor Walters and Mr Sharp say that sometimes the reverse was true and that a substantial proportion of the traffic which BRS handled could have been carried more cheaply by rail. However, their figures strongly suggest that the proportion of rail traffic which BRS would have carried more cheaply was much higher. It is significant that the only types of consignment, by weight, carried by BRS for which on average the rail price would have been lower were those between half a cwt and three cwt. For consignments in the other weight groups the potential rail charge was significantly higher than the actual BRS price. Moreover it seems likely that where traders used BRS, although the railways would have done the job more cheaply, there was often a rational explanation for this, such as faster delivery. From the records which one Birmingham firm maintained it appears that in 1954 the average transit time for parcels which travelled by goods train was about five and a quarter days as against three and three-quarter days for consignments which passed by road, although the average distance was about the same.[22] For general merchandise traffic BRS was usually able to provide overnight delivery within a radius of 200 miles of all main centres whereas a high proportion of railway rail freight took three or more days to arrive.[23]

Although the quality of the service seems to explain the use of BRS when the railways would have charged lower rates it makes the continued use of rail, where the BRS price was lower, all the more surprising. When trying to explain the continued use of rail for consignments weighing between one and two tons, where the average rail charge was much higher than the prospective BRS price, Walters and Sharp make the following instructive comment:

> Partly it is explained by 'routineering' on the part of some traders; they sent all or certain of their goods by rail irrespective of price. Some traders used the railway for most of their consignments because it was cheaper, and also for the odd consignment which would have been cheaper if sent by road. Hiring another haulier was just not worth the trouble. Partly it is explained by the lag in transferring traffic to a less expensive agency.[24]

If so, it was to be expected that British Rail would over the years lose more and more of its traffic as firms gradually adjusted their routines and found that the convenience of using rail as their single carrier no longer outweighed the cost. It is clear from the Birmingham survey that routines were gradually changing. A considerable amount of traffic had already been transferred from rail to road and further transfers were being planned.[25]

In 1957, as we have seen, the railways obtained a considerable measure of commercial freedom and were at last able to set about recasting their charging system so as to secure traffic which could be carried at a low cost and discourage high-cost traffic.[26] And this was what the Transport Commission said that it was planning to do. In *Proposals for the Railways* the Commission announced that it would use its new freedom

> to reorganize their freight charging arrangements towards the following ends: the encouragement of traffic consigned in larger quantities and good wagon loads; the encouragement of regular traffic for which economical services can be arranged; the attraction of good loading traffic, now passing by road, for long and medium distances; the avoidance of loss on some of the shorter distance rail traffic.[27]

A reorganization of the pricing system along these lines was long overdue because British Rail, due to the perverse charging structure which it had inherited, tended to receive the traffic it was least fitted to carry.[28]

It has been asserted by the Prices and Incomes Board that what in practice has happened is that the railways have continued to make general and unselective price increases and have priced themselves out of the market. 'General increases in fares and charges,' the Board declares, 'have diminished total traffics, and increased unit costs, the increase leading to increased fares, with each turn of the screw aggravating the problem.' Yet the Board discovered that British Rail's average revenue per ton mile had been declining: It commented that: 'Whilst some of the decline in average receipts in recent years may have been due to changes in the composition of products carried, and to more efficient methods of transit, the fall in average receipts for traffics other than coal and steel during a period when road rates were rising suggests insufficient control over salesmen.'[29] Surely the Board cannot have it both ways: either the railways have lost traffic due to general price increases or they have lost revenue due to price cuts because they do not control their salesmen properly. But they cannot have generally raised and generally lowered their prices at the same time. The Prices and Incomes Board, in its enthusiasm to find fault with British Rail, has passed beyond the bounds of reason. No doubt the railways are always to blame but they cannot, whatever the Prices and Incomes Board may say, always be to blame for everything.

If we turn from the Board's contradictory commentary and examine the available figures, it appears that British Rail has since 1957 reduced its prices. For all goods other than coal and coke the charge per ton mile fell by about 28 per cent between 1957 and 1968. Moreover, for general goods traffic, excluding in so far as possible iron and steel products and materials, there appears to have been a fall of almost 35 per cent. But this is only a rough estimate because, among other reasons, British Rail altered the scope of its figures for general merchandise in the early sixties.[30] Moreover, figures for revenue per ton mile probably exaggerate the reduction in prices which took place because the average length of haul for non-coal traffic increased by 14 per cent over the period. Because railway rates taper off as the distance grows an increase in the average haul will tend to reduce the revenue per ton mile even though rail charges remain unchanged. Nevertheless, *other things being equal,* there must have been a large reduction in charges because revenue per ton declined by 18 per cent for all traffic other than coal and by 25 per cent for general goods. And this, of course, tends to understate the reduction in charges because on average each ton was carried farther.

Unfortunately, other things may not have been equal and it is possible that the apparent reduction in rail prices was due to changes in the composition of traffic. If the proportion of traffic which is carried at a low charge per ton (or ton mile) has increased then revenue per ton (and per ton mile) will fall even if a railway's rates remain the same. This is shown by a simple example. In 1960 the Banana Island Railway carried ten tons of bananas, which are squashy and difficult to handle, at a charge of £2 per ton and ten tons of oranges, which are firm and easily handled, at a rate of £1 per ton. The average revenue per ton was, therefore, £1 10s. By 1965 a disease had killed all the banana trees but the railway still carried the same quantity of oranges the same distance at the same rate. The railway's revenue per ton had fallen to £1 creating the false impression that it had cut its prices by a third. As this example shows, the alteration in the composition of traffic has to be very marked, and the variation in rates between commodities very large, in order to bring about any appreciable change in average revenue per ton. On the Banana Island Railway it only declined by a third although the proportion of bananas in its total tonnage had fallen from half to zero, and though the rate for carrying bananas was twice as great as the rate for oranges.

There have certainly been changes in the composition of traffic by commodity which, other things being equal, would have served to reduce the average revenue per ton. There has, for instance, been a considerable increase in rail carryings of oil and cement for which the rate per ton is low. However, it seems very doubtful whether the variation in the composition of traffic has been sufficient to explain, by any means, all of the apparent reduction in the railways' prices. What information is available for separate commodities also suggests that British Rail has been cutting its charges. Figures for revenue per ton are available for eight separate commodities or product groups which account for a considerable proportion of all merchandise and steel traffic. Between 1962 and 1966 two showed rises (timber and drinks); for two the charges were about the same (animal feeding stuffs and iron ore); and for the remaining four there were significant reductions. The rate per ton fell by about 4 per cent for finished and semi-finished steel, by 15 per cent for cement, by 33 per cent for fertilizers and by 43 per cent for petroleum products. These can only be regarded as approximations but they do suggest that British Rail has been cutting its charges for many types of traffic.[31] The introduction of freightliners also seems to have involved a reduction. In 1968 the average revenue for general goods traffic was 3·35d per ton-mile but for the liner trains it was only about 2·4d. This is a very low rate even if allowance is made for the fact that the average length of haul for freightliner traffic was about twice that for general goods.[32]

While rail charges have been falling road haulage rates have been rising. The only period for which firm figures are available is 1962–6. A survey carried out by Mr Brian Deakin and Miss Thelma Seward of the Department of Applied Economics in Cambridge disclosed that by 1966 the average charge per ton mile had increased by about 20 per cent.[33] It seems unlikely from the price increases which the Road Haulage Association recommended prior to 1962 that charges were declining, and probable from its estimates of increased costs that rates have risen since 1966. Between 1957 and 1962 the RHA recommended that rates should be increased by 20 per cent, excluding the temporary surcharge which was recommended at the time of the Suez crisis. It estimates that during 1967 the industry's costs increased by about 7 per cent, that in 1968 they increased by around 11 per cent, and that during 1969 the rise was up to 15 per cent. These figures give an exaggerated impression of the way in which charges have actually risen because the RHA makes no allowance for the extent to which increased costs are offset by gains in productivity.[34] Nevertheless, there has certainly been a substantial rise since 1957. This is confirmed by the way in which BRS's prices have risen. These appear to have risen by about 25 per cent between 1958 and 1968.[35]

As rail charges have fallen while road haulage rates have increased it seems possible, or even likely, that although rail prices used to be on the high side they have become highly competitive. That they are now competitive is borne out by the study by Mr Deakin and Miss Seward. They obtained information from British Rail for a sample week in 1966 and conducted a survey among road haulage contractors to discover what charges they made. As a result they were able to calculate the average rate per ton mile for 28 commodity groups apart from coal and coke. Where the average rail haul was shorter than the average road haul it was to be expected that even if the rail tariff was the same as the road tariff the railways' rate per ton mile would have appeared somewhat higher, due to the tapering of charges with distance. However, there were six commodities where the rail haul was lower but the road charge per ton mile was higher. Road hauliers charged nearly three times as much for carrying petroleum products; about 70 per cent more for transporting iron ore and scrap iron; about 45 per cent more for non-ferrous ores and also for other crude materials; nearly 40 per cent extra for coal tars; and over 22 per cent more for finished and semi-finished iron and steel products. In addition there were three products where the rail haul was slightly longer but where the road haulage charge per ton mile was so much higher that there is no real doubt that the rail prices were lower. The road charge was about 30 per cent higher for general chemicals and plastics, over 55 per cent greater for flour, and 85 per cent higher for fertilizers. For none of these commodities was the rail haul more than 7 per cent longer than the average road haul.[36]

Where the rail haul was considerably longer it was to be expected that the rail charge per ton (but not of course per ton mile) would be higher than the road charge because the railways had the extra work, and its customers had the extra benefit which resulted from the longer journey. Despite this, the railways' rate per ton was either lower or no higher than the road charge for four commodity groups. In the case of tobacco and miscellaneous foods the road haulage rate was about the same as the rail but for animal feeding stuffs, lime and cement the road haulage charge was from 20 per cent to 65 per cent higher. Yet for these four commodities the average distance by rail was between 55 per cent and 90 per cent longer than the average distance by road. There were four other commodities where the rail haul was longer where it seems reasonably certain that the railways' price was no higher than the road price and may well have been lower. For these products the rail charge was only slightly higher than that of the road hauliers although the rail haul was very much longer. In the case of dairy produce and eggs, sand and other crude minerals, meat and poultry, and cereals the railways' charge per ton was around 15 per cent higher than the road hauliers'. On the other hand, British Rail's average haul was between 55 per cent and 170 per cent longer.

In all, there were 18 products for which the rail tariff was lower than the road haulage price. In contrast, there were only four commodities where road haulage was the cheaper mode of transport. For the remaining six product groups, it is impossible to be certain which mode was cheapest but it seems likely that rail either had the edge over road or that their prices were much the same. 'In freight transport,' conclude Mr Deakin and Miss Seward, 'the railways appear to have had a more competitive price structure in 1966 than road haulage contracting for transporting most of the 29 commodities.'[37]

Appearances can, of course, be deceptive and it may be objected, for instance, that rail would no longer appear the cheapest mode if allowance was made for the expense of collection and delivery by road. So far as the railways' existing traffic is concerned, this objection does not carry much weight because the great bulk of rail freight either does not have to be collected or delivered or the railways provide this service with their own vehicles and the cost has already been included. It can be calculated from the Reshaping Report that in 1961 only 10 per cent of the tonnage of steel and general traffic which British Rail carried was collected and delivered at their customers' expense. This is because the great bulk of rail traffic was loaded at private sidings or unloaded at sidings and docks, and because a large part of the remainder was collected and delivered by rail vehicles.[38]

Whatever the situation may have been in the past it is evident that where liner train services have been introduced the railways are competitive even where road collection and delivery is necessary. This is best shown by examining some sample routes and some specimen rates. For the journey between London and Glasgow the standard charge per ton, where the largest 30-foot container is used, works out at about 82s including collection and delivery at both ends within a radius of 20–24 miles of the terminal. Where the customer regularly sends one or more containers per day and/or where there is a return load the rate drops. The freightliners' lowest rate, where there is both a return load and five or more containers are dispatched each day, works out at only about 69s 6d per ton. In each case the exact figure will depend upon the type of goods which are being sent since the charge depends on the size of the container and not upon the weight of goods which are packed into it.[39] It has, however, been assumed for these calculations that 80 per cent of their tonnage capacity is utilized, which is about the average proportion.

How does this compare with the cost by road? A survey of the rates which were being paid by large firms in 1966 showed that the average charge for heavy loads was about 80s 6d per ton. Since then there has been a large increase in road haulage rates[40] and this means that freightliners must be competitive even for the traffic for which they make the highest charge when they are four-fifths full. For 20-foot containers which are the other most widely used type, the freightliners' rates work out at between about 90s and 106s per ton. The average road haulage

H

charge for loads of a similar size was found to be about 86s per ton in 1966. Allowing for the increase in road haulage rates this suggests that liner trains are competitive with road for most, though not all, types of traffic. Freightliners Ltd believe that, in practice, their prices are as low or lower for virtually all traffic between London and Glasgow.

Between London and Manchester, to take a medium-distance freightliner route, the rate works out at between 39s and 44s 6d per ton for a 30-foot container carried by road for up to ten miles at both ends. The corresponding charge by road was 43s in 1966. For a 20-foot container the freightliner charge ranged in effect from about 52s to about 58s 6d as against the road charge of 49s. It can be seen that, allowing for the rise in road haulage rates since 1966, the freightliner charges were competitive for traffic originating fairly near the railhead. However, it seems unlikely that they are competitive when the distance rises to 20–24 miles except for the type of traffic for which freightliners are best suited, and where the goods are moving from places to the north of Manchester and the south of London.

Over relatively short-haul routes as illustrated by London–Birmingham liner trains are probably only competitive for goods in 30-foot containers which originate within ten miles of the railhead. For this type of traffic the freightliner charge works out at between 33s 6d and 37s. This compares with a road haulage rate of about 32s 6d in 1966.

The Standard of Rail Services

If, as seems probable, the decline in the railways' general goods traffic has not been due to the price they charge, the next most likely explanation is the quality of the service. As survey after survey has shown, traders regard the service which British Rail provides as being distinctly inferior to that of road transport. For instance Mr Clifford Sharp, in an investigation in the Birmingham area, found that by far the greatest amount of criticism for poor quality service was directed against the railways. In particular, they were criticized for taking a long time over delivery and for having a bad loss and damage record.[41] And yet, poor though the railways' general standard of service may be, it seems clear that there has, over the years, been a significant improvement. Between 1957 and 1968 the number of train miles per engine hour rose by 38 per cent.[42] Unless this was offset by an increase in the amount of time which wagons stand idle between their loading and their delivery, and there is no reason to believe that it was, there must have been a noticeable reduction in transit times.

The principal step British Rail has taken to improve the quality of its service has been the development of train-load working which, including liner trains, accounted, by 1968, for about half of its steel and general freight traffic. Company trains which, as their name implies, carry the traffic of a particular customer, have formed the spearhead of British Rail's drive to increase its train-load operations and win new traffic. By the end of 1968 about 1,500 company trains were being run each week as against only 600 at the end of 1963. The largest group carry petroleum products and a few years back British Rail was running about 400 trains for the oil companies. Other products for which company trains have been introduced on an extensive scale are cars and vehicle components where there were about 120 trains, and chemicals, limestone and cement for each of which there were about 100.[43]

Where flows of traffic are large enough to enable company trains to be run and their customers possess private sidings, the railways can in this way provide a tailor-made service of high quality. The advantages of company trains are that they run at regular times which can be adjusted to meet customers' requirements, that purpose-built rolling stock can if necessary be used, and that the damage level is likely to be very low. This is because goods do not have to be transferred from lorries on to railway wagons and because there are no shunting shocks. The main causes of damage on the railways are therefore avoided. That the potential advantages of company train working are secured in practice is suggested by the fact that Fords' company trains have been dependable and that the level of damage is probably lower than it would be if road haulage had been used.[44] 'The success of this method of transporting vehicles,' says one leading transporter company which operates several car trains, 'has surpassed even our most optimistic expectations. During a severe winter we did not miss a single delivery by train but our road transporters were scattered all over the country.'[45]

To cater for traffic which is not sufficiently heavy and regular to be carried in company trains, and for firms which do not own private sidings, British Rail has developed the liner train.[46] On the routes where they are available they provide a service of an extremely high standard in terms of speed, reliability and the absence of damage. How quick freightliners are is illustrated by the services between London and Glasgow. The train leaves London at 10.10 in the evening and arrives in Glasgow at 4.30 the following morning. Containers are normally expected to arrive about an hour before the train departs and are not ready for collection until about half an hour after the train arrives. Even so, the service is far swifter than road transport, though the latter is of course more flexible. The timekeeping of the liner trains is as good as that of passenger trains which means that, while they do not always arrive exactly on time, only a small proportion are seriously late.

So far as damage and loss are concerned the freightliner organization only receives claims in respect of a tiny proportion of the containers it carries. During the first half of 1969 the proportion was only 0·4 per cent. They are usually able to establish that the damage did not occur while the container was in their care and claims were paid in respect of only 0·06 per cent of all containers carried.[47] By any standard, this is an extraordinarily low figure and liner trains are a far safer mode of transport than road transport. A survey for the Ministry of Transport disclosed that even where firms use their own vehicles 1·1 per cent of all consignments are damaged.[48]

Although the volume of freightliner traffic is increasing very rapidly, it only accounted in 1968 for a relatively small proportion of all steel and general goods traffic; and, as we have already seen, about half of the total was still shifted by means of wagon-load working. This tends to be less efficient from the customers' (and the railways' own) point of view than train-load operations. Where the wagon is the primary unit of movement, it becomes necessary to marshal them into trains which is a time-consuming process and tends to cause damage due to shunting shocks.

Although wagon-load working, even when it had to some extent been modernized and improved, continued to produce relatively long and unpredictable transit times the quality of service which the railways were able to provide was not as low as might be expected. The railways' traditional operating methods were castigated in the Beeching Report with its reference to 'the slow and semi-random movement of wagons'. However, as a table in the Report shows, the average delivery time was to be measured in days rather than weeks. Indeed it can be estimated that, excluding mineral wagons, the average transit time was only one and three-quarter days and that for containers it was less than one and a half.[49] This probably gives too favourable an impression of the railways' standard of service, because journey time was almost certainly measured from the point when the wagon was collected by a pick-up train from the yard or siding at which it had been loaded. As it might already have spent some hours waiting before the pick-up train arrived, the total transit time must have been longer than it appeared. Even so, since nearly every freight station was served by a daily train to remove and deliver wagons it seems unlikely that the average wagon spent very long waiting to be collected.[50] Of course average transit times may and to some extent do obscure the fact that there was a wide dispersion around the mean. However about 65 per cent of wagons, even when company and other

through-train services are excluded, arrive within 48 hours of their dispatch. It is clear, therefore, that the great bulk of wagon-load consignments have a reasonably fast journey. But for a significant minority
transit times are very long, with 7 per cent of wagons taking more than
a week to arrive.[51]

The proportion of goods which were lost or damaged was also smaller
than might have been supposed from the complaints of traders. The
extent to which goods were lost was inquired into by the Central Transport Consultative Committee in 1957. It discovered from British Rail
that, during the previous year, 15,400 loaded wagons went temporarily
astray and that in 1,350 cases the identity of the consignment was never
established owing to the loss of the destination labels which are clipped
on to the wagon. As about 19 million wagons of steel and general goods
traffic were dispatched in 1956 the railways lost under one wagon in
every 1,000 and the great bulk of these were ultimately rediscovered.[52]
Nor, to judge from compensation figures, does the problem of damage
appear in general to be very serious. In 1962, which is the last year for
which detailed information is available, the compensation which British
Rail paid for lost or damaged goods represented only 1·3 per cent of
their freight revenue, excluding coal. This is a remarkably low figure
when it is remembered that the cost of transporting goods usually
represents only a fraction of their value. However, the railways do seem
to do more damage than road haulage, due presumably to the frequent
need for double handling. In 1963 claims for loss and damage in road
haulage, as represented by BRS, constituted only 0·8 per cent of traffic
revenue.[53] Moreover, there is probably some tendency for firms to avoid
using the railways for goods which are easily broken.[54]

Though higher than might be expected, there is no doubt that the
general standard of rail service for wagon-load traffic is inferior to that
provided by road transport. The railways' wagon-load service is like the
curate's egg good in parts and it is possible for firms which are discriminating and moderately well informed to have their goods transported in
a speedy and reliable manner. By 1957 most regions were publishing
freight train time-tables and providing for the overnight delivery of full
wagon-load traffic between some main centres. Also, the Green Arrow
service, which had been withdrawn during the war, was once again in full
operation; traders were able on payment of a small fee (2s 6d per consignment in 1967) to have a special watch kept on traffic in full wagon
loads to ensure that it reached its destination with all possible speed. As
railway modernization proceeded and trains were fitted with power
brakes, overnight delivery was considerably extended. For instance by
the end of 1960 the railways' Export Express Service, which had only

been started in 1956, covered ten ports and nearly 350 inland centres. Some idea of the coverage of the general overnight delivery service which British Rail had built up can be gained by considering a town such as Liverpool. In 1967 British Rail was, in normal circumstances, able to provide overnight delivery to 25 towns if the traffic was in wagon loads and was received by 5.30 in the afternoon. Besides relatively near-by places such as Manchester, Birmingham and Leeds, these towns included Edinburgh, Glasgow, Newcastle, York, Leicester, Cardiff and Carlisle.[55]

In general, British Rail's special services appear to be reliable. The Central Transport Consultative Committee, when it made its investigation in 1957, did not find any complaint about Green Arrow or the special services for livestock and perishable commodities. The Rochdale Committee reports that it heard a good deal of praise for the railways' Export Express Service, and the Associated British Chambers of Commerce expressed its appreciation and said that it could not be faulted on service or price. There is nothing incredible, therefore, about British Rail's claim, when the service had been running for almost two years, and over 28,000 wagon loads of export traffic had been carried, that not a single shipment had been missed due to the failure of the service. Mr W. R. Cook was told by the Birmingham firms he interviewed during the mid-sixties that two or three days was the normal transit time but that for the special services such as Export Express and Green Arrow it was 24 hours or less.[56]

The rail expert Freeman Allen argues however that although by 1964 'BR were proclaiming next-day delivery between almost any pair of industrial centres in England and Wales, and not a few Anglo-Scottish pairs as well, trip-working or yard delays gave these claims the lie too often for peace of mind'.[57] It is possible that the run-of-the-mill overnight services are not as reliable as Export Express and Green Arrow. Nevertheless it seems clear that over large parts of the country and for certain categories of traffic, British Rail does provide a fairly reliable and fairly quick service for its wagon-load traffic.

Although the railways' service is good in parts, it is also bad in parts. This is true, or at least was true, of freight sundries, i.e. consignments which travel by goods train in quantities too small to be treated as a single wagon load. The quality of service provided by the railways never appears to have been very high for this type of traffic. As we have seen, one Birmingham firm, which kept careful records, found that in 1954 the average delivery time by rail was one and a half days longer than it was by using BRS.[58] During the first half of the sixties there was a serious deterioration in the railways' standard of service, and traffic was subject to serious delays. In the Beeching Report sundries were identified as one of the areas in which large losses were being made and savings had to be achieved. Examination showed that the return on the investment necessary if the service was to be thoroughly modernized and re-organized was unattractive. It was, therefore, decided to rationalize operations without undertaking any large-scale capital expenditure. When the National Sundries Plan, as it became known, was put into effect it was found that some of the depots on which traffic was being concentrated were, due either to inadequate facilities or shortage of staff, unable to handle the extra work. Another cause of delay was that the Plan was implemented piecemeal, which meant that staff became confused and demoralized due to the constant stream of re-routing instructions as depot after depot was closed.[59]

Gradually difficulties have been overcome and the system has settled down; delays have lessened and transit times improved. For instance, when National Carriers, which is now in charge of sundries, made a survey in the autumn of 1969 it found that the average delivery time was three and three-quarter days.[60] This may sound a long time but is, in fact, a reasonably creditable performance for the type of traffic which National Carriers handles. Moreover guaranteed overnight delivery has, under the title Yellow Diamond, been introduced between London and a number of provincial centres and this service is being extended. Despite the high standards now being set there is no doubt that in the past they were generally low, and around 1965 abysmal. This helps to explain why British Rail has, so far as the quality of its service is concerned, a reputation which is worse than it deserves. Although freight sundries only account for a small part of its traffic, they represent a high proportion of all consignments and are the only type of rail service which many firms use.

The Rail Sales Effort

It is often said that railways' salesmanship is poor and that they treat their customers in a bureaucratic and high-handed fashion. Is this part of the explanation for their decline and fall? In the past, insufficient attention was paid to marketing and to customer relations. The long period during which they had a virtual monopoly of transport is likely to have produced an attitude of take it or leave it. The railways were also inhibited in the field of marketing by the statutory and other restrictions which prevented them from tailoring their charges.

From 1957, when the railways gained a substantial measure of commercial freedom, a more vigorous and more positive approach became possible. However, it seems likely that British Rail's sales drive would have been more effective had its managerial structure not been so decentralized. This meant that the relatively small number of large concerns which account for the bulk of the railways' revenue, and whose needs are nationwide, did not for the most part have the necessary contact with headquarters. Instead they tended to have contact with, and to be contacted by, relatively obscure and powerless local officials. The railways' marketing effort was further weakened by the absence of a separate commercial department whose sole task it was to obtain, or at least retain, suitable traffic. During the second half of the fifties the formerly separate commercial, operating and motive power departments were thrown together into a hotchpotch Traffic Department.[61]

The railways' defective marketing structure was put right after Dr Beeching took charge. During 1962 the commercial and operating departments at the railways' national and regional headquarters were separated. At both levels the marketing and sales organizations were strengthened and during 1963 and 1964 a system was adopted by which each of the railways' 300 largest customers is looked after by a senior railway commercial manager. He has been made personally responsible for their welfare and acts as a channel of communication in all important matters.[62]

A case study of Ford's transport requirements throws some light on the way in which this system has been working and on the railways' sales effort. The numerous references to British Rail's Liaison Officer show that he has been extremely enterprising. He has succeeded, for instance, in capturing a considerable share of Ford's steel traffic, although the firm at first displayed no interest in his scheme. The proportion of steel arriving at Dagenham by rail has risen from virtually zero to 38 per cent. Another illustration of British Rail's salesmanship has been its readiness to develop new types of rolling stock to meet Ford's requirements. Wagons have been converted so that they can carry sheet steel, and carry it in larger quantities than is possible by road; experiments were in progress with wagons for carrying strip as part of the drive to obtain more steel traffic; special vans were built to Ford specifications for the transfer of components between Dagenham and the new Halewood factory; and BR has at Ford's request developed a double-decked car transporter called the Cartic – a difficult undertaking due to the railways' restricted loading gauge.[63]

No doubt British Rail has been making an especial effort to secure Ford's traffic because it is so large, but it seems clear that the general level of British Rail's salesmanship is now of a high order. In his study of Birmingham firms, Mr Cook found that all save one had been approached about contracts. He reports that many transport managers were impressed by the railways' efforts to regain traffic, although they were not always successful.[64] This picture is confirmed by Mr Clifford Sharp's survey of firms in the Birmingham area. He reports that the railways appeared to have publicized their proposed freightliner service very effectively, and found that a considerable number of the firms in his sample had been visited by BR representatives.[65] In fact, British Rail makes an extremely thorough investigation of the potential traffic before liner trains are introduced. Road hauliers plying over the prospective route are, for instance, canvassed to discover the amount of traffic which they are handling and to find out whether they are likely to use the new service for their trunk haul. In this, and many other ways, the railways have followed up the enormous survey described in the Beeching Report which sought to identify all regular wagon-load traffic which did not pass by rail and to sift out all that was suitable.[66]

To some extent the railways' marketing efforts have been blessed with success and a considerable amount of new traffic has been secured. The most spectacular gains have been in oil where, largely as a result of contracts signed up with the oil companies from 1963 onwards, rail carryings have shot up from about five million tons in 1961 to over 14 million tons in 1968. By that time they accounted for well over a fifth of the railways' ton mileage of general traffic although they represented a smaller proportion by revenue. Important agreements were also concluded with the cement companies which were reflected in an increase in rail carryings from just over one and a half million tons in 1961 to just under three million tons in 1966. Again the railways have succeeded in capturing a large amount of new business from the car industry where the business has been built up from almost nothing to the movement of about 300,000 cars per annum. The freightliners are, of course, still in their infancy but even so they accounted, by 1968, for about 10 per cent of the ton mileage of general freight. Not all of this is new business but probably about 70 per cent of it is.[67]

The Railways' Potential Market

Nevertheless the railways' gains seem very small beer when set against the estimates given in the Reshaping Report of the amount of traffic which British Rail had some chance of capturing. In so far as possible information was collected on all regular wagon-load traffic which, during 1960, did not pass by rail, and 223 million tons of iron steel and general goods traffic was identified; of this 93 million tons were initially judged to be potentially good rail traffic. In the Beeching Report's own words,

All of the flows making up the total 223 million tons of non-railborne traffic were examined to determine their potential suitability for rail haulage. As a result, 130 million tons had to be judged unsuitable on first inspection, mainly because the length of haul was too small, but also because of terminal considerations, irregularity of flow, requirements for special vehicles, etc. . . . The 93 million tons of traffic which was left after this first sieving was judged potentially suitable for rail haulage by virtue of its physical characteristics and the distance over which it moved. It represents a very large part of the total longer distance road freight of the country.[68]

It was recognized that not all the 93 million tons was really suitable for rail movement. However, the Report summed up by saying that

there is a considerable tonnage which is potentially good rail traffic. This includes about eight million tons which could be carried in train-load quantities, and a further 30 million tons which is favourable to rail by virtue of the consignment sizes, lengths of haul, and terminal conditions. In addition, there is a further 16 million tons which is potentially good traffic for a new kind of service – a Liner Train service – for the combined road and rail movement of containerized merchandise.[69]

If so there was 54 million tons of really favourable traffic which British Rail should have been able to secure, granted sufficient marketing effort and improved methods of operation. As at the time the Report was published, the railways' steel and general goods traffic totalled only around 85 million tons per annum, it appeared that there was a relatively large pool available and that they should have no great difficulty in increasing their carryings by a substantial amount.

The more closely the Beeching Report and its figures are studied the less clear it becomes that this is the right conclusion to draw. In fact a number of contradictory statements are made as to the amount of really worthwhile traffic available to the railways and in some places it is implied that it may be quite small.[70] It seems best to ignore the general statements which are made in the text of the document and to concentrate on its tables. These show that in 1960 there was eight and a half million tons of traffic which could have been carried in full train loads from one private siding to another. This British Rail would be able to carry at a very low cost and should have been able to secure unless, as seems likely enough, part of it was moved by ship at a charge the railways could not hope to match. There was a further five million tons of potential siding-to-siding traffic which, although it would not make up a full train load, would nevertheless occupy a block of wagons. This, too,

British Rail would be able to carry cheaply and ought to have been able to obtain, except perhaps where the haul was very low. Making some allowance for this by knocking off all traffic passing for less than 50 miles there was some three and a half million tons which the railways could hope to get. The only other type of traffic which, unless it was suitable for liner trains, British Rail might find it profitable to carry was long-distance traffic moving in bulk where there was a private siding at one end. According to the Reshaping Report the railways would be able to cover their direct costs where the haul was over 150 miles and there was a potential train load or block of wagons. Traffic of this type totalled four million tons.[71]

In all, therefore, there seems, ignoring liner trains, to have been only about 16 million tons of really favourable traffic. However, seven and a half million tons which was included in the Report's figures of suitable traffic was carried by coastal shipping and a further three million tons was carried by inland waterways.[72] As the railways would probably find it impossible to capture some of this traffic, and as a large part would almost certainly be included in the potential train or block-load traffic, it seems unlikely that British Rail could expect to capture all 16 million tons of really suitable traffic. Indeed it is probably safe to assume that the available pool did not contain more than 10 million tons, if it contained that.

It was estimated in the Beeching Report that there was $15\frac{3}{4}$ million tons of liner train traffic among the consignments which were in 1960 carried by road and sea. However two and three-quarter million tons of this was on hauls of between only 70 and 100 miles where it seems doubtful, even on the basis of the figures given in the Report, whether the railways could be competitive and hope to cover their costs.[73] It is thus probably right, when adding up the railways' potential traffic, to include only the 13 million tons of potential freightliner traffic where the haul was greater than 100 miles. If so, what the Beeching investigations really showed was not 93 million tons of potentially good rail traffic, or even 54 million, but merely something over 20 million.

It was evident, or at least it should have been evident, that a large part of this could not be secured easily or quickly. Obviously the 13 million tons of traffic suitable for liner trains could only be obtained when the system had been created and sufficient time had elapsed for traffic to build up. It was estimated in the Beeching Report that this would only take about five years and that by 1968 freightliners would be carrying 30 million tons, of which about half would be entirely new traffic and half would be existing traffic which was suitable for liner trains.[74] It is hardly surprising that this has proved to be a wildly over-optimistic forecast.

Liner trains were still on the drawing-board at the beginning of 1963 when the Reshaping Report was published and it was not until early 1965 that a prototype liner train had been built and that test runs could begin. Some modifications proved necessary and it was not until November 1965 that the first service was introduced. The extension of the system has been delayed, not by the opposition of the National Union of Railwaymen to open terminals as is usually supposed, but by the time the manufacturers have taken to deliver the cranes for use at the freightliner depots.[75] Although the amount of progress made with liner trains has been slower than was hoped, it has probably been as fast as it was reasonable to expect.

Transport Users' Knowledge and Attitudes

Another reason why it was unlikely that British Rail would secure all of the potentially good traffic quickly was that a large part of it was being carried by firms in their own vehicles. It was found that out of the 93 million tons which was initially judged to be suitable for rail, 40 per cent was being conveyed in 'C' licence or 'A' contract lorries.[76] There are various obstacles which make it difficult for the railways to win back traffic which traders carry themselves even where they can offer a cheap service of high quality. One important obstacle is that a large proportion of firms have so little knowledge about their transport costs that they must have difficulty in recognizing a good bargain when the railways offer it.

Just how ill-informed many firms are is evident from the various transport inquiries which have been carried out. The first and in many ways the best of these investigations was that by Professor A. A. Walters and Mr Clifford Sharp, which has already been referred to on a number of occasions.[77] They found in the mid-fifties that, of the 217 traders which could be classified, firms which accounted for 31 per cent of total expenditure on 'C' licence vehicles, lacked any precise information on the costs of operating their lorries because they did not even distinguish this item in their accounts. Firms which knew the overall cost of their vehicles but nothing more accounted for 47 per cent of expenditure. The next group of firms in the spectrum ranging from ignorance to knowledge had some idea not only of their costs but also of the overall volume of work performed by their vehicles. They were, therefore, able to calculate such figures as their average cost per ton mile. It was only the final 10 per cent of firms which had made detailed costings, and knew their costs per ton mile on some or all of their traffic flows, which were in a position to make a more or less informed choice between the different modes of transport.[78]

One explanation why so many firms did not trouble to compare costs, state Walters and Sharp,

> might be that these firms are using a form of transport, the charges for which are far below the charges for any other service. However, even the most cursory examination of their traffic showed that this was not the case; in fact from a small sample of these which were examined, it seemed that they had at least as much as the others to gain by acquiring knowledge of relative costs. The principal reason for this lack of knowledge was that some traders, especially those with large 'C' licence fleets, would never consider permitting the goods to be handled by a public haulier.[79]

There is little doubt that, as the years have passed, firms have become somewhat better informed. Nevertheless, the pace of change does not appear to have been so fast as to have more than modified the situation which Professor Walters and Mr Sharp described. The dawn light is now slightly stronger than it was but the long night of ignorance has by no means passed. This is shown by the repeat study which Mr Clifford Sharp has recently made. In it, a large number of the firms which had provided information during the previous survey were re-interviewed. Once again information was sought about the knowledge which 'C' licence operators had about their costs. Of the 96 firms whose answers could be analysed almost half had no more than a general knowledge of the total costs of their road haulage fleet. A further 14 per cent appeared to have some broad estimates available of their average cost per ton. The third group, which contained a fifth of the firms, were thought to have made detailed costings for some of their vehicles or for part of their traffic. The tests which firms had to satisfy in order to be included in this category were scarcely stringent. A firm whose manager merely said that costs were kept was, for instance, included. It seems likely that this was a less exclusive category for which it was easier to qualify when the second survey was carried out than it was at the time of the original survey. The fourth and final group contained 18 per cent of the undertakings and comprised those which possessed detailed and up-to-date knowledge of their operating costs. According to Mr Sharp: 'Only the firms in class 4, and perhaps some of those in class 3, possessed the essential data to enable them to compare what they were paying for their 'C' licence operation with the costs of outside hauliers'. It seems likely that the proportion of firms able to make a more or less informed choice between the different transport agencies had risen from about a tenth in the mid-fifties to about a fifth in the mid-sixties.[80]

It would obviously be wrong to place too much weight upon Mr Sharp's figures, derived as they were from a relatively small-scale inquiry, and involving as they did a considerable element of judgment. However, there is no reason to doubt his general finding that there is an extremely widespread ignorance of costs among 'C' licence operators. This has been confirmed by Mr W. R. Cook's investigation of 33 of the largest firms in the Birmingham area.

> It was clear [states Mr Cook] that transport managers were not very much aware of the importance of transport in the cost of the various products they were moving. Where they had an idea of transport cost, it was a general average which masked wide deviations. . . . Some transport departments had very little cost information available and saw their work as organizing the moving of certain physical tonnages, making up loads, and keeping customers satisfied. Even where transport managers did take account of cost, they tended to see it in relation to the total budgeted cost of their department rather than in relation to particular consignments of traffic . . . Subsequent questions showed that even amongst those managers who spoke of cost there were several who lacked the information to assess the cost of their decisions.[81]

A dissident note has, however, been struck by Mr B. T. Bayliss and Mr S. L. Edwards in the study of the demand for transport which they conducted for the Ministry of Transport. As part of the investigation which they carried out during 1966 and 1967 they obtained cost data for 5,472 consignments which were dispatched by a sample of manufacturing firms. Messrs Bayliss and Edwards summarize their findings as follows:

> Of the firms covered by this . . . investigation a proportion which varied between one-third and one-half according to the nature of the industry, knew the costs by alternative modes for some or all of the consignments about which they were asked. The questions put to firms were specific and tied to individual consignments; firms were not asked, for instance, whether they had made a general investigation of the costs and other attractions of the various modes available to them.[82]

But this is rather misleading because the firms were able to provide estimates for using another method, which may or may not have been accurate, for only 22 per cent of the consignments which they dispatched in their own vehicles. But, even where they had a reasonably accurate knowledge of the cost of alternative methods, it cannot be assumed that they were well informed or in a position to make a rational choice. In order for this to be the case they would also have to know the costs of using their own vehicles. To what extent they did the investigation by Messrs Bayliss and Edwards does not tell us because no questions were asked about this. It was decided not to do so on the ground that since most 'C' licence operators would not know the answer there was no point in asking.[83] It is apparent from the other and more informative studies which have been made by Professor Walters, Mr Clifford Sharp and Mr W. R. Cook that this is a fair assumption, and clear also that the investigation by Mr Bayliss and Mr Edwards provides no evidence to modify this conclusion.

Even where firms assemble the information necessary for rational decision-taking, it cannot be assumed that they use it intelligently. As none of the transport surveys discuss the problem of how firms set about comparing the cost of providing their own transport with that of using the railways, one can do little more than speculate about this. It seems likely that what a large number of firms do is to compare the rates which the railways charge with the running costs of their own vehicles. For the short run this is obviously the correct comparison to make but for the long run, since it is always possible for a firm gradually to dispose of its 'C' licence fleet and to avoid the overhead costs of its transport department, what firms should compare are rail charges and their total costs. These, of course, should include capital charges on vehicles. Yet it seems probable that firms sometimes ignore these because they argue that their transport department should not make a profit as this will only be at the expense of the concern as a whole. Vauxhalls, for instance, appears to work on this assumption. It reports that when it was considering the best way of transporting components and sub-assemblies between its existing plants at Luton and Dunstable and its new factory at Ellesmere Port, various alternative methods

> were examined in detail. These included doing the job with a Vauxhall-owned transport fleet. Finally this latter method emerged as the most efficient and the most economic way of tackling the job. It offered many advantages over all other means. In the first place, it was the cheapest – one obvious reason being, of course, that a Vauxhall-owned fleet, unlike other methods, would not in itself be operating for profit.[84]

Not only are a large proportion of firms ignorant of their transport costs where they use their own vehicles, but there is also reason to believe that they are by no means entirely free of bias. When he surveyed Birmingham firms Mr Cook found evidence of irrational hostility towards the railways.

> There is still [he reports] a large amount of 'bad will' towards the railways. Some of this is rational, being based on experience of trouble and of the inconvenience of slow and unreliable deliveries, but more than one

transport manager described some of his customers as 'cranks' . . . This antipathy to the railways suggests that, when British Rail modernize their freight services and improve speed and reliability, it is likely to be some time before they get all the traffic which might be expected.[85]

Just how 'cranky' and prejudiced against the railways some firms are is illustrated by some of the replies which Aims of Industry received when it carried out a survey among those who receive its newsletter. Here are a few examples:

Reversion to rail transport [declared a company at Letchworth in Hertfordshire] could ruin our business. The percentage of damage, *approximately 60 per cent,* is crippling, and so are the charges.

Our goods [claimed a North-West London firm] are *usually* damaged if sent by rail.

A firm at Aldershot said: Delivery to Scotland approximately one week by passenger train, *four weeks* goods trains, whereas by road two days maximum.

A Derbyshire engineering concern reported that by rail delays, damage and loss are *ten* times greater than would normally be expected with private road transport.[86]

To these comments may be added that of an undertaking from which I received some bottles of wine. They had been carried by goods train and arrived intact, and out of interest I wrote to the concern inquiring what proportion of their customers reported that bottles arrived smashed. Its Joint General Manager replied that during September 1968 1,184 cases containing either six or 12 bottles had been dispatched by rail and that claims were made for 33 broken bottles, which was about average. The railways seem, therefore, to have only smashed about 0·3 per cent of the bottles which were entrusted to their care: a remarkably low figure for such a fragile commodity. Nevertheless the Manager was very dissatisfied with the quality of British Rail's service mainly, it appears, because he considered that it was slow. This may or may not have been justified, but what is significant is that in the last part of his letter he launched into a general diatribe against the railways. 'The trains,' he wrote, 'which we see passing by on the main line 400 yards from this building look like a motley collection of junk, no two carriages ever being the same colour and all being filthy. Nothing short of scrapping and starting from scratch can save British Rail.' One must always beware of basing generalizations on a few striking but possibly exceptional cases. Nevertheless, these and other examples of irrational hostility to the railways do tend to confirm Mr Cook's finding that there is a considerable amount of ill-will towards the railways.[87]

Passenger Traffic

Having examined British Rail's freight traffic we must now turn to its passenger traffic. In 1957 the volume of passenger traffic, as measured by the number of passenger miles, was at its post-war peak. By 1968 it had fallen by 21 per cent, almost every year having seen a reduction. Information about the number of passengers using the various types of rail service is none too plentiful, but it is known that there has, over the period as a whole, been some increase in the amount of commuter traffic into London. Between 1957 and 1967 the number of passengers entering central London between seven and ten in the morning increased by 7 per cent. But it seems likely that total traffic on the London suburban services has been stagnant or declining, and that what happened was that a higher proportion of traffic was concentrated during the rush hours.[88]

For the railways' other services, it is possible to make some rough estimates of the volume of traffic from their total receipts and from average revenue per passenger mile. It appears that between 1961 and 1967 the volume of traffic on the railways' express and semi-fast services declined by about the same amount as passenger traffic in general. However, on the branch line and other stopping services, traffic declined by around a third compared with an overall reduction of 14 per cent.[89] This exceptionally large fall was obviously due to the Beeching cuts but, despite appearances, these can have been responsible for only a small part of the total reduction in rail passenger traffic. If traffic on branch line and stopping services had moved in line with traffic on express and semi-fast services between 1961 and 1967 British Rail's total passenger traffic would, at the end of the period, have only been 3 per cent higher than it was.

The railways' passenger traffic has obviously been adversely affected by the spread of car ownership and the growth of private motoring and, to a large extent, this was an inevitable development which would have taken place whatever British Rail had done. But it would be wrong to regard the railways as having been entirely at the mercy of fate and to assume that the volume of their traffic is entirely insensitive to the quality and the price of the passenger service they provide.

Although it is widely believed that trains are slower now than they were before the war, there has been a marked improvement in the general standard of the railways' passenger service. This is evident from the gains which have been made in speed, punctuality and frequency: the holy trinity of a high quality service. However, it was not until a comparatively late date that pre-war standards of speed were regained and then surpassed. In 1939 there were 116 runs between stations each weekday where the train averaged 60 miles per hour or over, but no improvements in decisive speeds had taken place since 1850.[90] During the war, track maintenance was neglected and speeds had to be restricted. And, due to the shortage of steel, it was not until the early fifties that arrears of maintenance were made good.[91] By 1958 the railways were again running over 100 mile-a-minute trains, though more progress may have been made than this suggests as the old companies concentrated on running a few flyers whereas British Railways was securing a general speed-up.[92] The number of runs averaging 60 miles per hour or over then soared up and by 1969 there were about 1,575 each weekday. This was largely due to the switch from steam to diesel traction. With the introduction of electric services between London, Manchester and Liverpool in 1966 there was a dramatic increase in trains travelling over 75 miles per hour. In 1969 there were 127 which means that there are now more trains averaging 75 miles per hour than there were averaging 60 miles per hour before the war.[93]

Contrary to popular belief the speed of British express trains does not compare too badly with that of other countries. This is shown by a comparison between British Rail and SNCF which is celebrated for its speed. By the summer of 1969 trains with an average speed of 60 miles per hour or over between stops were covering a total distance of almost 64,000 miles each week-day. A few years earlier, the French National Railways were claiming that their long-distance passenger trains were covering 75,000 miles each day at an average speed of over a mile a minute. By 1969 the figure was probably slightly higher. However, it must be borne in mind that since France is a larger country than Britain, and its towns tend to be farther apart, British Rail may well provide more station-to-station runs at over 60 miles per hour than SNCF. Where the French railways do have a significant lead over BR is in the provision of super express trains running at around 75 miles per hour and over. In France during the summer of 1969, SNCF was providing 188 start-to-stop runs each day at average speeds of over 120 kilometres, or 74·6 miles per hour, and they covered a total distance of just over 22,000 miles. The corresponding figures for Britain were about 134 runs and 12,500 train miles.[94]

The French lead is probably explained by two factors. First, SNCF has the advantage, purchased at a heavy price in terms of capital expenditure, that a far higher proportion of the track has been electrified. That electrification facilitates high speeds is shown by the fact that the bulk of the British trains scheduled at very high speeds run over the Midland Region's electrified routes. Over these lines, moreover, British Rail provides a service which is, if anything, better than the French. According to Mr Cecil Allen, a well-known rail expert, 'In its combination of speed, frequency and even interval timing this has no equal in the world other than the Tokaido line in Japan.'[95] The second reason why SNCF runs more trains at over 75 miles per hour is that, unlike British Rail, it does not try to provide a fixed interval service, but dispatches groups of trains during certain parts of the day. This makes it easier to run fast trains because, since they are concentrated at certain times, freight trains do not have to be held up so frequently to let them pass. But it is not true as has been suggested that to prevent its freight operations being disrupted too severely British Rail tends to restrict the pace of its express passenger trains.[96]

The increase in British train speeds has not been achieved at the expense of punctuality which over the years has tended to improve. The proportion of express trains arriving within five minutes of time increased from 63 per cent in 1948 to 71 per cent in 1953. During the rest of the fifties, no further improvement occurred largely because of the disruption caused by modernization. In the early sixties time-keeping improved again and in 1968 76 per cent of express trains arrived within five minutes of their scheduled time, although during 1969 the proportion fell back to 73 per cent.[97]

By continental standards time-keeping on British Railways leaves something to be desired. In Germany 89 per cent of main-line trains during 1967 arrived within five minutes of time.[98] And the proportion of French express trains which arrived more than 15 minutes late was slightly lower than the proportion of British expresses which were over 30 minutes late.[99] The fact that, unlike most of the continental systems, British Rail provides a regular interval service helps to explain why fewer of its express trains arrive on time. They do not have certain parts of the day set aside for their exclusive use, but have to mesh with slower types of traffic which, if anything goes wrong, will impede their progress. There is a conflict between the provision of a frequent express service and the punctuality and speed of the trains.

It is arguable that British Rail has placed too much emphasis on frequency but what cannot be denied is that this is an important factor in the overall quality of the service it provides. During the past decade BR has made important gains in this direction because it has progressively shifted over to a fixed-interval time-table. Originally this was confined to the Southern Region where a frequent and regular service had been introduced when its lines were electrified. However, in 1959, the time-table of much of the Eastern Region was recast on the same principle and somewhat later the Western Region started to redraft its entire main-line time-table along the same lines. A fixed-interval service has also been provided on the newly electrified London–Midland routes.[100]

In other respects besides speed, punctuality, and frequency there has been a considerable improvement in the quality of service which British Rail provides. The introduction of long-welded rails on a considerable proportion of the main line has made trains smoother; the elimination of steam traction has led to an improvement in the standard of cleanliness; railway catering has greatly improved; new facilities such as motorail have been introduced; and as regards comfort, particularly in the matter of cushioning, modern British second class coaches are superior to any in Europe.[101] No doubt there is scope for still higher standards especially in time-keeping, but the general quality of British Rail's passenger service is already a high one by international standards, and there is no reason to believe that a small improvement in quality would have produced a large improvement in traffic. It is significant that the fall has taken place during the period in which the improvement in speed, punctuality and general performance has been greatest. The car has advantages in terms of convenience which the railways cannot match, however hard they try, and over long distances air transport has the advantage that it is considerably faster.

What part have prices played in the decline in rail travel? During most of the post-war period the trend of costs has moved sharply in favour of the private car and against rail travel. Between 1957 and 1968 rail fares increased by 79 per cent, whereas the running costs of motor vehicles only increased by 34 per cent and the purchase price of cars and motor cycles actually fell by 11 per cent. The cost of motoring has been so stable partly because car manufacturing is an industry with rapidly rising productivity and partly because there are usually no wage costs in driving a car.[102] The main reason for the exceptionally large rise in rail fares is that, since 1959, British Rail has been trying to improve the profitability of its passenger services by jacking up its charges. Prior to this the passenger services, taken as a whole, barely covered their direct costs and made scarcely any contribution to track, signalling and general administrative costs.[103]

Although passenger fares have risen so much faster than the price of motoring it has been authoritatively argued that this had very little effect on rail travel. According to Messrs G. F. Ray and R. E. Crum of the National Institute of Economic and Social Research

> it would probably be wrong to suggest that . . . price trends explain much of the shift from the railways to private motoring. From 1952 to 1961, the railways' loss of their share of passenger traffic seems to have continued

without any visible connection with the movement of relative prices . . . It is not the cost of rail travel which leads people to buy cars; and once the car is bought, the owners will tend to use it wherever it is more convenient, without elaborate cost calculations. The fact that the total cost per mile of car travel is usually – for one or two persons – much higher than the railway fare is no deterrent; for car travellers, if they work out the cost of their proposed car journey at all, will tend just to calculate the cost of fuel, and ignore any additional depreciation and maintenance.[104]

This argument probably contains a large element of truth but it seems doubtful whether relative price changes have had quite so little influence as Messrs Ray and Crum seem to suggest. Calculations by Mr Richard Lecomber, which were derived from regression analysis, suggest that each 1 per cent increase in the relative cost of travelling on British Rail ultimately leads to a decline of 1·1 per cent in the volume of traffic. This figure may be on the high side because it is derived from figures of consumer expenditure; and travel on business account, which is probably relatively unresponsive to changes in price, accounts for a significant proportion of rail travel. As British Rail appears to derive about a fifth of its passenger revenue from this source, and as season tickets account for a similar proportion, a substantial proportion of all passenger traffic is likely to be more or less unaffected by an increase in prices.[105] Nevertheless as Mr Lecomber's estimates of elasticity suggest, the volume of traffic would not have fallen so far if British Rail had not increased its prices so much.

Conclusions

To sum up, there is little doubt that if British Rail's traffic had remained stable instead of having collapsed, and if its charges had not lagged behind the general rise in prices, it would today be earning a comfortable profit. The reduction in its traffic is not explained by an excessive increase in its charges. On the passenger side there has been a swift rise in fares and this probably explains some, though by no means all, of the reduction in carryings; but on the freight side charges appear to have fallen and for general merchandise traffic there has been significant reduction. In contrast there has been a large increase in road haulage rates, and a comparison of road and rail charges suggests that the railways' charges have become highly competitive. Nor does it appear that their sales effort has been inadequate. Nevertheless British Rail has continued to lose traffic partly because they were, back in the mid-fifties, carrying a substantial amount of general merchandise traffic where they were hopelessly uncompetitive both in service and price, and which traders were on the point of transferring to road. Even more important, there have been changes in the structure of the economy which have eroded the railways' staple traffic in coal and steel. Similarly on the passenger side the railways have inevitably been hit by the spread of car ownership. Not only were the railways bound to lose a substantial part of their old traffic but their opportunities for gaining new traffic are more restricted than is usually supposed. A careful reading of the traffic surveys which formed part of the Beeching Report shows that British Rail's potential market was quite small and since then BR seems to have secured a considerable proportion of the goods traffic which it is fitted to carry. But there is obviously some suitable traffic which the railways have failed to attract. The quality of service which they provide is now of a high order for train-load traffic and where freightliners have been introduced, but BR's wagon-load operations, though better than sometimes supposed and good in parts, leave much to be desired in terms of reliability. Despite this, it seems reasonably certain that the railways are not receiving all the traffic they ought to. A number of studies suggest that many traders are prejudiced against the railways and fail to make careful cost and quality comparisons between the different methods of transport. As a result they may be slow to recognize that the railways are now much more competitive in price and quality than in the past.

If so, then the question obviously arises of whether the nation can afford to wait while firms slowly revise their opinions, or whether the Government is not justified in taking steps to steer traffic back to the railways. This is hotly denied both by private firms, who are opposed to state intervention in a field they regard as their own concern, and by the large body of economists for whom free markets are an article of faith. This is evident from the almost hysterical opposition with which the quantity licensing provisions of the Transport Act, 1968, were greeted. This is not the place for an extended discussion of that measure but the time has surely come for a second and cooler look at the case for legislation.

CHAPTER 11

The Rail Deficit

ALTHOUGH British Rail has been operating under extremely adverse demand conditions the question still arises of why it has not done more to cut its costs. The steps taken to increase the railways' general level of efficiency and bring costs under control have already been described. It is evident that considerable progress has been made as a result of dieselization and other forms of modernization, and that the railways have made extensive use of work study and productivity bargaining to slim down their labour force. British Rail was slow to adopt some forms of modernization such as long-welded rails, and some expensive mistakes were made, such as the choice of an unsuitable type of braking system for wagons. Moreover there is no doubt that BR could have done more to tighten up its efficiency and prune its labour force, if only by beginning earlier.[1] Nevertheless so much has been achieved in this direction that it seems unlikely that the railways could, by attacking the general level of their costs more vigorously, and by modernizing more effectively, have eliminated their deficit. Solvency could not have been reached by travelling faster along this path but might have been attained if British Rail, instead of trying to bring down the general level of its costs, had started earlier and done more to cut its system down to size and to rationalize the part which was retained. By eliminating those of its lines where the traffic was too light to yield a profit and squeezing the surplus capacity out of the rest of their operations British Rail's financial débâcle might have been avoided.

The questions which we shall try to answer in this Chapter are why there was so little rationalization before Dr Beeching arrived on the scene and why, despite his activities, the railways are still in deficit. Is it because his Plan has never been fully carried out, or because it was inadequate?

Rail Ignorance

It has been suggested that until the arrival of Dr Beeching the railways were hamstrung because they did not know where they were losing money. The Reshaping Report gave currency to this type of explanation when it said that 'there had never before been any systematic assembly of a basis of information on which planning could be founded'.[2] When the Select Committee on Nationalized Industries investigated the railways in the pre-Beeching era it reported that, although it had tried to discover where the railways' loss was being made,

> this proved very much more difficult than might have been expected. It appeared that neither the accounting system nor the costing techniques, which are now being developed by the Commission, have yet been developed enough to show precisely where the loss is being caused. 'We find one of the most difficult things in the Ministry is to discover where money is actually being lost,' said the Permanent Secretary to the Ministry of Transport, 'it is very difficult to get an answer to that.'[3]

The railways' ignorance was by no means as black as these statements suggest. The Beeching Report itself states that the Commission's Traffic Costing Service had, for a number of years, prepared figures showing the revenue and direct costs of each main class of traffic.[4] The date of the first reasonably reliable statistics is not entirely clear but the financial results of the different categories of passenger train were known by 1953. The committee which, during that year, prepared the first tentative plans for rail modernization was armed with estimates of the revenue and movement costs of express, suburban and other passenger services. These showed that expresses earned £33 million more than movement costs, that suburban services made a contribution of £7 million towards overheads, but that the remaining passenger services failed by £14 million to cover their movement costs. This meant that on balance passenger revenue exceeded passenger train costs by £26 million. Since station and other terminal expenses were estimated at £25 million, it appeared that the passenger services barely covered their direct expenses, and made no contribution to general administrative expenses or the costs of providing the route system.

In order to obtain more detailed and reliable information a census of passenger traffic was undertaken during a week in October 1952. This, together with supplementary information, enabled the Traffic Costing Service to make rough estimates of the annual revenue of each train service. Estimates of movement and terminal expenses were then derived from cost studies and from information on the train mileage and characteristics of the individual service. When costs and revenues were brought together it was confirmed that the inter-city services covered their allocated expenses by a comfortable margin but that the stopping services were incurring an enormous loss. The survey which broadly reflected the situation in 1953 indicated that British Rail's fast and semi-fast services contributed £31 million to track, signalling and administration costs. On balance suburban trains just covered their direct expenses but the stopping services failed to meet theirs by £41 million. Moreover, on the great majority of these services the revenue represented less than two-thirds of the train costs, which means that it formed less than half of their total direct costs. When the results of all these highly unprofitable services were totted up it was disclosed that their allocated expenses exceeded their revenue by £40 million and that they accounted for over 90 per cent of all stopping train miles.[5]

On the freight side the Transport Commission was again well aware of the facts. It had, at least by the time of the preliminary discussions on rail modernization, broken down its expenses in such a way as to reveal that trunk haulage accounted for a relatively small part of the total and that the great bulk was absorbed by trains to pick up and deliver wagons, by shunting and marshalling and, as had long been known, by the cost of providing and maintaining wagons. By the mid-fifties surveys had disclosed that a high proportion of depots handled very little traffic and could, with financial advantage, be closed. The need for rationalization and the large losses being incurred on some sections of freight business were also shown by a detailed costing investigation similar to the one described in the Beeching Report. This inquiry, which was undertaken during the mid-fifties, showed, like the Beeching investigation, that traffic handled at stations tended to be unprofitable whereas the traffic from private sidings was generally profitable.[6]

The Beeching Report made great play not only with the fact that for certain types of traffic revenue was insufficient to cover its direct costs, but also with the way in which over large parts of the system the value of the traffic was less than the cost of maintaining the track and providing the signalling. The announcement, following one of Dr Beeching's traffic surveys, that half the route carried a mere 5 per cent of the traffic was greeted with amazement. But the railways had known for years that the bulk of their traffic was concentrated on a small part of the route. This had been shown, for instance, by a survey in 1949 carried out in order to determine which lines were worth electrifying.[7] It also followed from the passenger train profitability survey, which was based on the census of 1952, that almost all branch lines were unprofitable.

The Transport Commission certainly possessed sufficient information to outline plans for rationalization, but it might be said that they lacked the detailed information necessary if such plans were to be executed. This is a more plausible suggestion and it would be foolish to pretend that the Commission was armed with perfect knowledge. But why, if the Commission had sufficient information to make general policy decisions, did it not see that detailed investigations were carried out so that these plans could be put into effect? Once it is conceded that the Commission possessed enough information for planning purposes, the reason why the Commission failed to rationalize their services and their route system must be sought elsewhere. Moreover, it is clear that a number of surveys which were adequate for the purposes of detailed planning were carried out. For instance, the passenger train profitability study provided details for each service which the railways provided. This inquiry was followed up by further surveys. In 1958 the Southern Region carried out a passenger traffic survey in which it ascertained, during representative weeks revenue and movement costs train by train, and terminal costs station by station. In 1960 there was a similar survey covering freight. In the Eastern Region a series of passenger train censuses were carried out to ascertain the profitability of its services, and some extremely detailed work had also been done on the freight side.[8]

If the railways were fairly well informed about the profitability of their services why did the Beeching Report, the Ministry of Transport and the Select Committee say that they were not? The explanation is probably that Dr Beeching was anxious to create the impression that a new and more scientific era of rail management had at last dawned and that Ministry officials, when asked about rail losses, did not want to reveal their own ignorance. As for the Select Committee, it was misled by the words of the Chairman of the BTC, Sir Brian Robertson, who said that services were making a full contribution to track and other overhead expenses when they were only covering their direct costs.[9]

The Branch Line Story

It seems possible that, although the British Transport Commission knew where it was incurring losses and where scope for rationalization existed, it failed to act because it believed that it had an obligation to maintain loss-making services or because it did not realize that prompt action was necessary. It does seem likely that the Commission would have acted with greater determination if it had realized in the mid-fifties that its finances were about to collapse. But the Commission did not foresee, and could not be expected to foresee, the way its coal traffic would slump, and the traffic forecasts prepared at the time of the Modernization Plan were not unreasonable at the time they were made. Nevertheless the Commission was, later on, guilty of over-optimism about its financial prospects. In particular it went on expecting an increase in its general freight traffic when it was obvious that it was falling, and it failed to make proper allowance in its financial forecasts for the increase in wages which it would have to meet.[10] But it is difficult to believe that this is the full explanation for the lack of progress with rationalization. It had been recognized as early as 1954 by the Modernization Planning Committee that the Commission's finances were going to come under severe strain, and after 1955, with a large and growing deficit staring it in the face, the Commission cannot have been oblivious of the need for economies. Nor does it seem likely that the Commission was motivated to more than a minor extent by the belief that loss-making services should be retained in the national interest. It recognized that the passage of the Transport Act, 1953, had removed the duty and restricted the scope for cross-subsidization; and on the freight side, where it seems implausible to suppose that it was motivated by social service considerations, there was no more rationalization than there was in passenger operations.[11]

However, the main reason for supposing that the BTC was aware of the need to take action and prepared to withdraw unprofitable passenger services is shown by the policies which it adopted. In order to understand its policy towards the stopping services, it is necessary to go back to the Committee on railway motive power which was set up soon after the railways were nationalized. This had reported in 1951 that diesel railcars might well be suitable for use on secondary services, and their introduction which was expected to lead to a dramatic saving in costs was quickly put in hand.[12] But it was recognized within British Rail that dieselization was no wonder cure and that many stopping services were hopelessly uneconomic. As the Transport Commission explained at the time the characteristics of diesel traction

> do not necessarily make diesel trains economic on branch lines. Apart from anything else the potential traffic and therefore the service required seldom call for the intensive working which is necessary if full advantage is to be taken of the first and dominant characteristic of the diesel engine – its great availability. The quicker acceleration, greater cleanliness and lower cost per unit mile are advantages which register in branch line operation but they are advantages in comparison with steam traction, not to the road coach or bus by which so many who were formerly passengers on railway branch lines now prefer to travel.[13]

Consequently when the tentative plan for rail modernization was drawn up during 1953 it was contemplated that a substantial proportion of the stopping services would be withdrawn. At first it was considered that almost 50 million train miles or well over half of all stopping

services should be eliminated and that 5,750 miles of route, which represented 30 per cent of the total, should be closed. In a later draft these
targets were reduced and it was anticipated that 24 million train miles of
stopping services would be withdrawn. But by the time of the Modernization Plan the results of the passenger train profitability survey were
available and it seems likely that a substantial cutback was considered
necessary. The Plan itself declared that there would be 'a marked reduction in the stopping and branch-line services which are little used by the
public and which, on any dispassionate review of the situation, should be
largely handed over to road transport'.[14] Certainly at the beginning of
1956 the Commission warned the Central Transport Consultative
Committee that a large number of proposals for the withdrawal of
passenger services would be submitted to it in the near future.[15]

After this there was silence and 1956 and 1957 turned out, like 1955,
to be years when very few closures took place. Between 1955 and 1957
services were in fact withdrawn from only 465 miles of the system and the
estimated annual saving was a mere £650,000. From 1958 the pace began
to quicken slightly and over the period 1955–61 the saving from the
closure of lines and stations to passenger and/or goods traffic and withdrawal of services built up to a level of about £4 million per annum.
Nevertheless, this was a trivial sum compared with the enormous loss
which British Rail was incurring on its branch-line services.[16] Moreover
the mileage performed by stopping trains appears, if anything, to have
been slightly higher in 1961 than it had been in 1954.[17]

The reason why so little was done when so much was intended is by
no means entirely clear. What seems to have happened is that the preparation of closure schemes was left to the initiative of the regions but that,
with the partial exception of the Eastern, none was forthcoming.[18] Not
only did the regions fail to act but they also succeeded in muddying the
waters. This they did by arguing that although branch-line trains did not
appear to pay they contributed to the profits which the inter-city services earned because they fed them with traffic. Although this was a
theoretical possibility it was of little practical importance.[19] But the
argument was difficult to refute at the time because there does not appear
to have been any information on the number of passengers transferring
from branch-line to main-line trains. Nevertheless, it should have been
evident that the regional talk about contributory revenue was little more
than a delaying tactic. The losses on most stopping services were so
large that it was unreasonable to suppose that the Commission would not,
on balance, save by withdrawing the bulk of its loss-making trains.
Moreover, if it was really true that the inter-city services were only
profitable because of the traffic they were fed by the branch lines, then

this was an argument for withdrawing the main-line services and not for retaining the branch lines. This followed from the fact that by the mid-fifties the losses on the stopping services outweighed the profits on the inter-city routes.

Unfortunately, it was conceded by the Commission's working-party on the future pattern of services that the withdrawal

> of services which act partly or solely as feeders to main-line trains involves considerable risk of losing main-line business. In such cases arrangements should be made to ensure that, wherever possible, the alternative road services feed into the rail junctions and that suitable connections are maintained between the local road services and the main-line trains. The ideal arrangement would be to bring these road and rail services under co-ordinated management locally.

This argument was then repeated to the Commission by the regions in more emphatic tones, and became a formidable obstacle to rationalization.

> It is recorded [one region commented on the working party's report] that the withdrawal of services which act partly or solely as feeders to main-line trains involves considerable risk of losing main-line business. This risk cannot be underrated on the [Barset] Region and in the case of any project affecting branch lines not already closed it will be imperative for any alternative road services to have really satisfactory interchange facilities and connections with the main-line trains . . . We still believe, on [Barset] region territory at any rate, that all types of service can be developed and indeed are complementary to each other.

In effect this meant that there could be no rationalization, for however sensible they may sound in theory, it is very difficult in practice to provide bus feeder services.

On many branch lines there was so little traffic that, allowing for some loss when trains were withdrawn, a substitute bus service would not pay its way. Except for the few routes where no bus service existed, there was therefore no question of introducing a new feeder service and it became a problem of whether the timings of the main-line trains and the local bus service could be co-ordinated. The failure to achieve this is usually attributed to the obscurantism of local bus and rail officials, but it is in reality due to the fact that co-ordination usually involves inconvenience to the majority of bus travellers who do not wish to transfer from bus to train or vice versa. To give time for passengers to alight, buy their tickets and get on to the platform, the bus would have to arrive some time before the train, and it would then have to wait until the train has come in and its passengers have had time to collect their luggage and board the bus. As a result there would be a delay of between 10 and 15 minutes, and if the train was late the bus would be kept hanging around even longer.

What happened therefore was that the closure programme got bogged down, due to regional inertia, in futile discussions about contributory revenue and the co-ordination of bus and train services. If the Commission had taken a stronger line with the regions more progress would have been made. Unfortunately, it was in a weak position due to the policy of maximum decentralization which the Government had wished upon the railways. It is significant that the Commission did not feel strong enough to prevent the Western Region from going ahead with diesel hydraulic locomotives, although it realized that this was a mistake.[20] Similarly under pressure from the regions the Commission opted for vacuum brakes, though it was advised by its experts at headquarters that its wagons should be fitted with air brakes.

It would, however, be wrong to imagine that there was a clear-cut division of opinion over the withdrawal of stopping services between the regions and the centre. Although the Commission recognized that some stopping services would never be made to pay and would one day have to be withdrawn, it was hoping that dieselization would turn out to be a success and that the number could be kept to the minimum. It was not prepared to insist upon the closure of lines which the regions wished to keep open until there was some practical experience with the new multiple units and the impossibility of dieselizing out of deficit was clear beyond doubt. As a result, a large number of stopping services were placed in limbo and no steps were taken either to withdraw them or to try to make them financially viable. In addition the Commission approved the purchase of multiple units for many services which were losing heavily and where it knew that dieselization was a gamble. 'Any plan for refashioning the railway system to suit modern transport conditions,' the Commission declared in the autumn of 1956, 'must first explore alternative methods of operation. Thereafter, those services which cannot possibly be made economic by modern rail methods but can be better catered for by road transport must be eliminated.'[21]

Once the Commission had committed itself to the policy of waiting to see whether and to what extent the stopping services could be made viable it took several years to discover the answer. It was not until the end of 1957 that a substantial number of multiple units were in service and it obviously took a year or two after they had been introduced in any area to know what financial effect they had had. If there had been no effect this would have been a simple matter, but the introduction of diesels resulted in a very substantial reduction in unit costs and a considerable increase in the volume of traffic. It was found that in 1957 movement costs per train mile were 63 per cent lower where stopping services had been dieselized than where they were still operated by steam. The BTC provided the Select Committee with information on 22 modernization schemes covering stopping and suburban services outside London in which it compared the last year of steam working with a subsequent year of diesel operation. For these schemes, which were drawn from all over the country, and must have accounted for a high proportion of all mature dieselization projects, there was an overall increase in passenger receipts of 34 per cent.[22] Since the introduction of diesels was usually accompanied by an improvement in the frequency of service, this was less impressive than it seems. Indeed, it is doubtful whether dieselization was followed by any permanent or general increase in revenue per train mile. In one region for which details are available earnings per mile on stopping services were, during 1961, 25 per cent lower for diesel trains than they were for the remaining steam trains.

Nevertheless only the most hardened sceptics within the BTC can have been unimpressed by the gains in traffic to which some of the earlier diesel schemes led, and would have written off the possibility that traffic would go on increasing as the services became more widely known and better appreciated.[23] If only because of the large reduction in costs it seems clear that where dieselization took place there was a significant improvement in the financial position. In one region where steam traction had been cut to 28 per cent of all stopping train mileage, the excess of movement costs over earnings had been reduced on these services from £3 million in 1953 to £0·6 million in 1961. Moreover, the remaining steam trains were responsible for the bulk of this loss. On those stopping services for which the region was solely responsible the steam trains failed to cover their movement costs by about £650,000, but the multiple units had a surplus of roughly £350,000. When allowance was made for station costs this surplus was transformed into a deficit of around £800,000. Nevertheless, during the early stages of the diesel revolution, it cannot have been altogether unreasonable for this region to hope that it would be able to make most of its stopping services self-supporting. Although this region made far better use of its multiple units than the rest of British Rail, it appears from what information is available that dieselization did lead to a general and substantial reduction in the losses which the stopping services were incurring. In 1953, as we have seen, their direct cost exceeded their earnings by around £40 million but by 1961 the figure had been cut to around £20 million.[24]

This does not mean that the Commission's policy towards its branch-line services was anything other than a failure, and a predictable failure at that. Yet once the mistake of introducing multiple units on an extensive scale had been made, it was some years before it was apparent that dieselization was no solution, and during the interim period when costs were tumbling and revenue increasing it must have been remarkably difficult to keep a grip on reality. By 1959 the Commission had come to recognize that a substantial withdrawal of stopping services could no longer be avoided and was beginning to put pressure on the regions to make cuts. At the time of the Re-appraisal of the Modernization Plan it was anticipated that by 1963 10 per cent of the route would be closed and that stopping services which accounted for 33 million train miles would be withdrawn. This represented about 38 per cent of the mileage performed by stopping trains and about half of the cuts which were announced in the Beeching Report.[25] The Commission was at last moving in the right direction, but it was moving too slowly.

The Theory and Practice of Freight Rationalization

Just as the Commission was from an early date aware of the need to rationalize its stopping services so also it had good intentions about its freight operations. In particular it made tentative plans for the closure of little-used freight depots and for the consequent reduction in the number of pick-up trains, and for a considerable reduction in the size of the wagon fleet. Although an increase in traffic was expected, the Modernization Plan estimated that the number of wagons would be reduced from about 1,100,000 at the end of 1954 to about 750,000 in 1974. This was to be brought about partly by the introduction of larger mineral wagons but mainly by using the wagon stock more intensively. It was hoped that turn-round time, which is the average period from one loading to another, would be cut by 30 per cent with a consequent saving of 250,000 wagons. The reduction would, in turn, be partly due to the modernization of the railway system and the speed-up it would bring about. But it would have to be mainly achieved through better wagon control since, as the Modernization Plan recognized, wagons spend only a small proportion of their time on the move. It was also announced in the Modernization Plan that the depot system would be rationalized and, after a survey had revealed that 60 per cent of stations dealt with less than 20 wagons in a week, it was stated in *Proposals for the Railways* that there were 'conclusive arguments for closing many goods stations and the concentration of rail freight at a smaller number of modern freight terminals served by road'.[26]

Despite this, very little was accomplished. Between 1954 and 1961 the number of freight stations was only cut by 12 per cent and this was offset by the reduction in traffic. In fact, there was a small decline in freight tonnage per station. By the end of 1961 the number of wagons had been cut to about 940,000 but this was more than counterbalanced by the reduction in traffic. In 1961 the average turn-round time was 15 per cent worse than it had been in 1954.[27] As with the failure to curtail stopping services, it is by no means entirely clear why so little rationalization took place. But it appears that the lack of progress with the closure of depots was a compound of regional inertia and the fear that if freight stations were closed the railways would lose the traffic which they handled. To some extent this fear was genuine, and even justified, but it became all too often a convenient excuse for going slow.[28] The Commission's failure to improve the utilization of its wagon fleet was partly due to the inevitable difficulty of keeping wagons in intensive use at a time when traffic was falling. There was naturally a tendency for wagons to stand waiting for slightly longer than usual because there was less traffic to be carried. This could only have been prevented by reducing the wagon fleet in line with the reduction in traffic, which is no easy matter. A railway would naturally be reluctant to scrap valuable freight vehicles which it might require if and when traffic recovered. At the time it was hard for British Rail officials to see what was happening because traffic did not fall smoothly and because the swift reduction in traffic after 1957 appeared to be largely due to the recession.

But when every allowance has been made the Commission still appears to have been unnecessarily slow to adjust the size of its wagon fleet. It was not until 1959 that it was cut back, although traffic had fallen almost every year since 1953. That it is possible to improve utilization even when traffic is falling is shown by British Rail's achievements during the sixties. Between 1961 and 1968 wagon turn-round time was improved by 25 per cent and, what is more significant, ton miles per ton of wagon capacity was increased by 90 per cent. This was brought about by slashing the wagon fleet from just over 940,000 at the end of 1961 to just under 430,000 at the end of 1968.[29] Some had advocated a drastic reduction in the size of the wagon fleet in the days of the British Transport Commission. But this was strongly opposed by other rail officials who argued that there was little scope for reduction and pointed to the wagon shortages which all too often developed. Paradoxically the reason for this was the very fact that the wagon stock was excessively large. The railway system was choked with wagons and as a result it was difficult to sort them out and move them to where they were wanted.

But the basic reason, apart from the lack of central initiative, why

I

wagon utilization was so poor and becoming poorer was that the system of wagon control was defective. It was, as rail officials themselves recognized, markedly inferior to the system which had been developed by the German railways. In particular, the Bundesbahn ensured that the reports which were transmitted to the centre on the whereabouts and use of its wagons were comprehensive and accurate. The British Transport Commission did not. The stock reports which were transmitted day by day by each loading point only showed the whereabouts of between a quarter and a third of the railway's wagon stock. Moreover, it seems likely that the reports were none too accurate.[30] The Commission, therefore, lacked the essential first requirement of a proper system of wagon control: accurate information.

The weaknesses of the system were both exacerbated and explained by the fact that although the Commission was nominally in charge of wagon control day-to-day administration was in the hands of a complex and inefficient regional machine. The defects of the old system and the advantages of the new have been well described by Mr Freeman Allen. British Rail, he explains, was in the pre-Beeching era

> operating a wagon control system inherited from the wartime Railway Executive Committee. This left the Regions, as approximate successors to the pre-1948 'Big Four', to manage wagon affairs within their own boundaries. For the most part these boundaries had been drawn arbitrarily, of course, so that control limits sometimes separated closely adjoining areas of empty wagon supply and demand. Apart from the reservation of detailed supervision of some special types of wagon, such as banana vans, to the BR Wagon controllers, the latter's functions were confined to the organization of mass-inter-Regional wagon movements to balance Regional surpluses and requirements; and here, as in other matters, the decentralizing 1953 Act tended to weaken the centre's effectiveness of control. When a Line stratum was added to the Regional chain of command, the transmission of wagon states to the centre became intolerably devious . . . The defect of the old system was not merely the time and staff it consumed, but that the high degree of independent Regional control sometimes led to ridiculously wasteful cross-purpose working of empty wagons . . . Today's BR wagon control system cuts out the Regional and Line staging points in the transmission of information and links the BRB's Central Wagon Authority direct with 36 Districts or Divisions by Telex. Each day the Districts and Divisions report their net wagon positions to the centre at 15.00; and at 16.30 the same day the headquarters' controllers, having shuffled the spares reported by each area to meet the nearest call for empties, issue their orders for empty wagon distribution during the ensuing 24 hours. Under the new

system, however, considerably less empty wagon movement is left to await decision-making on the basis of District and Divisional returns. It has been made cardinal policy that spare empty wagons should automatically be switched from stations or depots regularly unloading more than they load to places where the outgoing traffic consistently outweighs incoming.[31]

The Workshops and the Need for Central Planning

The absence of firm central control and the presence of regional methods and regional thinking was one of the principal explanations for the railways' financial débâcle. The same pattern of too little central control and too much regional autonomy is to be observed in many other areas besides the administration of the wagon fleet. The failure to cut-back the stopping services was, as we have seen, largely due to the fact that the initiative was expected to come from the regions but that none was forthcoming. However, the clearest example of the need for central initiative and the dangers of regional thinking is provided by the railway workshops.

Prior to 1962, the workshops were controlled by the regions and each region was virtually both self-supporting and self-governing. As a result no real attempt was made to plan their future on an industry-wide basis. There was, indeed, very little planning of any sort. This is shown by the failure to modernize the workshops and adapt them so that they could cater properly for the new forms of traction and new types of freight and passenger vehicle which were being introduced. Sometimes the results were comic; in some works diesel locomotives had to have their wheels removed before the power unit could be lifted off because of the inadequate headroom in the old buildings.[32] But there was no amusement when the attempt to service and repair diesel locomotives alongside steam engines led, among other reasons, to the faulty running which marred the early years of British Rail's diesel revolution. As the railways should have learned from their early experience with diesels, their maintenance can only be successfully undertaken in conditions of absolute cleanliness. In some regions, such as the Eastern, this lesson was learned and proper preparations were made for the reception of diesel locomotives, but others made virtually none. The prize example was the Midland Region which at one time was getting such a poor performance out of its diesels that it had partly to revert to steam traction.[33]

The need for planning, and central planning at that, became even more pressing as British Rail's Modernization Plan began to bear fruit. One of the major consequences of modernization was the reduction in the railways' maintenance requirements. Diesels required much less maintenance than steam and so did the railways' new wagons, which were larger and constructed of steel instead of wood. The fall in traffic and the consequent decline in the number of rail vehicles led to a further reduction in maintenance. Yet it was not until the late fifties that any attempt was made to plan the reduction in maintenance facilities. In 1959, it was announced that a considerable number of workshops would be closed or partly closed and that their labour force would be reduced by 11,000 by the end of 1961. Although the programme sounded impressive only the smaller workshops were involved and the planned reduction in capacity was quite inadequate. By 1962 under capacity working had become widespread and a further reduction in the work load was in prospect. As Miss Lesley Cook says, the workshop plan of 1959

> was based on Regional thinking. This is most clearly demonstrated by the fact that it was planned to retain new building of locomotives at four works and the new building of both carriages and of wagons at five works each. This, despite the fact that the economies of scale are greatest in the new building activity. In the 1962 Plan only two works are retained for each of the three main building activities.[34]

The Disadvantages of Decentralization

Looking back, the chief defect of the railways' administrative structure in the pre-Beeching era is seen to be not, as often supposed, over-centralization but, on the contrary, too much decentralization. For this the Transport Act of 1953 and the associated Railways Reorganization Scheme were largely to blame. The Act abolished the Railway Executive which, under the general direction of the Transport Commission, had run the railways using a functional system of management with each of the Executive's full-time members responsible for a separate department. Each of these departments had a regional office which was responsible to it, though there was a Chief Officer in each region charged with the duty of co-ordination. This centralized system of administration was replaced by a much looser structure. The old headquarters departments were abolished and the regional departments became fully responsible to the chief regional officers, or Regional Managers as they became known. These in turn were responsible to the part-time Area Boards which the 1953 Act brought into being. Some link between the Boards and the Commission was provided by the fact that the Area Chairmen were members of the Commission, though mostly on a part-time basis. Another link was the periodic attendance of the Regional Managers at the Commission's meetings to report on their activities.[35]

It seems clear that the abolition of the system of departmental responsibility to headquarters, the elevation of the Regional Managers and the interposition of the part-time Area Boards in the chain of command deprived the Commission of effective control. Like the God pictured by Mr Justice Holmes, the Commission was an omnipresence brooding in the sky. According to Mr D. W. Glassborow, the BTC's former economist, the 1953 Act, by abolishing the Railway Executive, 'created the need for the Transport Commission to take day-to-day management decisions and at the same time imposed on them the obligation to refrain from taking such decisions and from ensuring their implementation. Their formulation of policy was made ineffective by the lack of an organization for carrying it out.'[36] It is significant that in 1959 the British Railways Central Staff numbered only 225 although it dealt with such important matters as financial control, commercial policy and charges, relations with Government Departments, and wage negotiations.[37]

The decentralization of the railways was not confined to the transfer of power from the centre to the regions. Decentralization has often been described as an attempt to get back as nearly as possible to the company set-up which had existed before the second world war, but it would be more accurate to regard it as an attempt to return to the situation which existed prior to the formation of the GWR and the other regional companies in 1923. Each region was divided into lines or divisions, each of which was placed under a Traffic Manager who was responsible for commercial and operating matters. This was a far more profound revolution in rail management than nationalization. The old railway companies had, with the partial exception of the LNER, been organized on a departmental rather than a geographical basis and this system of management was retained and extended after nationalization.[38] The new decentralized system of organization involved a major upheaval, and in some places had no sooner been created than it had to be changed because it was obviously inefficient.[39] The difficulty of creating the new system is shown by the time which it took to bring it into being. Although the changeover began in the mid-fifties it was not completed until the autumn of 1961, by which time Beeching was already re-centralizing railway management.[40]

The justification given for decentralization within the regions was that it would bring the railways into closer touch with the firms which used them.[41] This was a ridiculous idea for the railways' chief customers are not small local traders but large national concerns. As their transport requirements extend over the whole country they do not want to contact a divisional nonentity but need a direct channel of communications with railway headquarters. This is shown by the fact that more than half the freight revenue is derived from 30 major customers and that the railways have now established a system by which each of the 300 largest customers, which account for three-quarters, is looked after by a senior railway commercial manager.[42] The most ironic feature of the whole exercise was that the genuine possibilities for decentralization were ignored. There was considerable scope for decentralizing the railways along functional lines by, for instance, separating the main workshops and the shipping services from the regions. This has now been achieved but was rejected during the regionalization mania of the fifties.[43] From whatever angle it is viewed the decentralization of the railways seems to have been a mistake.

Not least among its disadvantages was the time and energy which it must have absorbed. When those in charge of the railways should have been thinking about more important matters they were engaged in a senseless attempt to restore the status quo ante-nationalization. 'In my 21 years in public transport . . .' Sir Stanley Raymond reflects, 'at least half my time has been devoted to organization, reorganization, acquisition, denationalization, centralization, decentralization, according to the requirements of the now regular political quinquennial revaluation of national transport policy.'[44] The cumulative and manifold effect which these organizational changes had on the railways' financial position must have been considerable. The administrative upheavals of the early fifties deprived the railways of leadership at a time when they required it most while regionalization of the railways deprived the Transport Commission of the machinery for command and reduced it largely to the role of spectator. Finally the continuation of decentralization and administrative upheaval during the second half of the fifties diverted the Commission and railway officials at all levels from the vital task of rationalizing the system and making it pay.

Just when the Commission might, if placed under new leadership, have got down seriously to the task, a further administrative revolution began. By 1960 it was clear that the attempt to make the stopping services pay had partly failed and the Government had decided that rationalization was necessary.[45] Instead of ensuring that this was put in hand, the Government appointed a committee under Sir Ivan Stedeford to investigate the position of the railways and then decided that the abolition of the British Transport Commission was the first priority. 'As a result,' states the Beeching Report, 'it was not until the later part of 1961, after the first steps had been taken to give effect to the structural reorganization . . . that positive steps were taken towards planning the future shape of the railways.'[46]

The Beeching Report

The rationalization of the railways did not begin in earnest until the publication of the Beeching Report in the spring of 1963. This contained proposals which it was estimated would produce a net saving of £115–147 million a year, ignoring interest charges. However, as some of the proposals involved capital expenditure, and therefore an increase in interest charges, the overall benefit would be somewhat smaller.[47] The principal saving was expected to come from the withdrawal of stopping passenger services and local freight services, the closure of stations, and the closure or partial closure of lines. It was estimated that up to £41 million would be saved in this way. The other major rationalization proposals were the reduction of the carriage and wagon fleets and the closure of workshops which were expected to reduce costs by up to £19 million, and the reorganization of the service for freight sundries and the shedding of unprofitable freight traffic through higher charges which was expected to reduce losses by up to £26 million. Apart from these rationalization measures it was estimated that the conversion from steam to diesel traction would save up to £20 million and that liner trains and new freight business would produce net earnings of up to £27 million.[48]

Despite the Reshaping Plan, British Rail has come nowhere near breaking even: indeed, it has not even managed to reduce its deficit. In 1965, the year in which Dr Beeching left the railways, there was an operating deficit of £73 million and in 1968 it was £83 million.[49] Why has the Beeching Plan failed? One possible explanation is that the Plan has not been fully implemented. The progress which British Rail has made is shown by the extent to which it has fulfilled the rationalization targets which it set itself. It was planned in the Reshaping Report to close 5,000 miles of railway route to passenger traffic. Between the beginning of 1963 and the end of 1968 3,450 miles had been closed to passenger trains and over 5,000 had been closed completely. The railways said they wanted to close 2,128 passenger stations; 1,690 have been shut. The number of depots handling freight sundries was to be drastically reduced; it has been slashed from 950 in 1961 to 266 at the end of 1966. It was intended that the wagon stock should be cut to 500,000 by the end of 1965. By the end of 1968 it was down to 430,275. The immediate target was to reduce the stock of coaches by 7,575; it has been cut by 14,330.[50] Under the plan for the workshops it was intended by the end of 1967 to close 12 of the main works and to reduce the workshops' wages staff to 35,000 by the end of 1967. By the appointed day the works had been closed and wages staff had been reduced to 34,776.[51] When the

National Plan was drawn up the railways estimated that their employment, excluding the workshops, would have fallen from 390,000 in 1964 to 277,000 in 1970. By mid-1968 it was already down to 291,000.[52]

It can be seen that, with the partial exception of the withdrawal of stopping services, British Rail has achieved its rationalization targets. Moreover, the loss the railways are incurring on the passenger lines which they had hoped to close only accounts for a small part of the total rail deficit. According to British Rail:

> The delay in the closure of unremunerative services is not a major railway problem ... The cost to the Board of the service and line closure proposals which the Minister has not yet been able to approve from the time of publication of the Reshaping Report in March, 1963, to the end of 1967, is about £4 million a year. In addition, cases which are still at some stage in the closure procedure account for an annual loss of about £4 million, making £8 million in all which the Board have to find each year.[53]

The fact that a considerable number of proposals are still being considered is not the railways' fault. It is due to the length of the official pipeline along which the proposals have to pass.[54]

The fact that only a small part of the railways' continued deficit has been due to the failure to implement the Beeching Report casts doubt on its estimates of the savings which rationalization would produce. One possibility is that the Plan's figures bore no relation to reality. The Reshaping Report may simply have over-estimated the extent to which costs would be reduced. Although this charge is often made it does not appear to be true. Since the Reshaping Report there has been a very large reduction in the railways' working expenses in real terms. Between 1962 and 1967 rail costs were cut by about £138 million at constant prices.[55] Not all of this saving was due to the implementation of the Beeching Plan but it seems clear that a considerable part of it must have been.[56] Where the Reshaping Report went wrong was to ignore the effect which rising prices and, in particular, higher wages would have on rail costs. No less than £112 million of the saving of £138 million which the railways achieved during the period 1962–7 was absorbed by wage and other price increases.[57] Dr Beeching made no allowance in his calculations for the rise in wages which would inevitably cancel out much of the saving which he hoped to secure. If the likely increase in wages had been taken into account in the estimates given in the Reshaping Report it would have been evident from the beginning that its proposals were not sufficiently radical.

It would be quite wrong, however, to dismiss the Reshaping Report as being a modest mouse of a programme; it was one of the most drastic rationalization schemes which has ever been put into effect. Yet the fact remains that, in relation to the financial problem which the railways faced, it was inadequate. The Reshaping Report's moderation is well illustrated by the surprisingly small part of the railway system which was marked down for closure, although it is popularly supposed that it was here that Dr Beeching was particularly brutal. The Report proposed that passenger services should be completely withdrawn from 5,000 route miles though only about 4,300 miles of withdrawals are shown on the relevant map. Even if it was planned that 5,000 miles of route were to be completely closed this would have represented only about 29 per cent of the total route mileage and 39 per cent of the route open for passenger traffic.[58]

Yet one of the surveys on which the Reshaping Report was based showed that during a sample week in the spring of 1961 half the route mileage carried only $7\frac{1}{2}$ per cent of all rail traffic. If it accounted for the same proportion of railway revenue then this traffic was worth £36 million in 1961.[59] However the cost of providing this part of the route was stated in the Reshaping Report to be about £40 million.[60] This means that the revenue from the traffic did not even cover the cost of providing the track over which it passed, let alone the cost of operating the trains in which it travelled.

It may be objected that the traffic which passed over the least used half of the route was not average traffic. Indeed it was not. On the passenger side it comprised passenger trains which failed to cover their direct costs by a large margin and on the freight side traffic of the poorest type. It may also be argued that although the overall revenue associated with half the route was insufficient to cover the total cost of providing it, the revenue from its best sections may have been sufficient to cover track costs. This is true, but only just. If we disregard the least used third of the railway route and confine our attention to the next 17 per cent it can be estimated that revenue (at £24 million) only just exceeded route costs (at £20 million).[61]

How the Government Stopped Rationalization

Although it is clear today that the Beeching Report's proposals were unduly modest it should be recognized that it was intended only as the first instalment of railway rationalization. It was stated in the Report that the stopping services which it was not proposed to withdraw immediately would be reviewed and, if they were found to be uneconomic, would then be proposed for closure.[62] During the next few years a number of additional services were added to the list and no doubt more would have been if the official machinery for considering closures had not already been clogged up, and but for the increasingly adverse political climate. From early 1966 British Rail was for a period prevented from making further proposals for the withdrawal of stopping services because the Ministry of Transport was, in conjunction with the Board, conducting a review of the railway system to decide what part should be retained for development. The results of this review were published in March 1967. The Government decided that some 11,000 route miles should be retained. This meant that about 2,700 miles of route which was open at the beginning of 1967 might be proposed for closure, though before services could be withdrawn the Board had to comply with the normal laborious vetting procedure.[63] In effect the railway system was fixed at about the same size as it would have reached if the Beeching proposals had been carried out in full, although the lines were somewhat different.

The suggestion that the railway system should be reviewed and then stabilized originated from Sir Stanley Raymond, who was then Chairman of British Rail. But it is clear that the proposal was only made because the Labour Government was obviously not prepared for the drastic rationization which was necessary if the railways were to break even.[64] British Rail had been preparing a second rationalization scheme as the publication, early in 1965, of the second Beeching Report on the Development of the Major Railway Trunk Routes shows. This was a more tentative document than the Reshaping Report in that no hard and fast proposals for the closure or partial closure of lines were put forward, but potentially it was a far more radical scheme. The Trunk Route Report started from the fact that there are a large number of main-line routes which run more or less parallel to each other and serve the same centres of population, although they pass through different small towns on the way. Routes which run more or less parallel to each other account for two-thirds of the trunk route system, if such it can be called. Most of these 'parallel' routes run only two abreast but triplicate and quadruplicate routes represent nearly a fifth of the total mileage. These parallel routes are an inheritance from the Victorian era of competitive railway building but the problem of surplus line capacity has become more and more serious as rail modernization has proceeded and the railways' financial position has deteriorated.[65]

The second Beeching Report proposed that traffic should be concentrated on a limited number of routes and that surplus track capacity should be eliminated in order to secure the very considerable savings which were to be had. According to the Report only about 3,000 of the existing 7,500 miles of main-line route were necessary to handle the traffic passing between the main centres of population and, by implication, it was suggested that the remaining line should be wholly or partly closed. This, it was estimated, would reduce the direct cost of providing the trunk route, which then totalled about £85 million per annum, by about half, and there would also be important savings in other directions.[66]

The saving in track costs were possible because when the traffic on a line is doubled the cost of maintaining the track, and of maintaining and operating the signalling, is increased by 20 per cent or less.[67] This is due to the fact that a high proportion of route maintenance costs are incurred with the passage of time rather than the passage of trains. For instance the cost of maintaining cuttings, embankments, tunnels and bridges, drainage and fences is essentially a time cost because the effects of the weather and the natural deterioration of the materials far exceed those of passing trains. In the case of signalling equipment, maintenance is mainly based on a system of regular inspection designed to spot chance faults and is therefore scarcely affected by the amount of traffic on the line. Similar considerations apply to the maintenance of sidings, depots and stations, although their costs were not included in the Beeching figures showing the relationship between route costs and traffic.[68]

The full financial savings which are possible because maintenance and signalling costs do not rise in line with traffic can only be secured by concentrating traffic on some routes and closing others. But some savings will arise where routes can be partly closed by, say, reducing them from double to single track. They are not as large as might be expected because a number of important costs such as the maintenance of cuttings and embankments will be the same irrespective of the number of tracks. Also the conversion of a line from double to single track is both a costly and a complex operation. For instance, it is often necessary to install new signalling and to re-lay and re-align the track. Indeed British Rail believes single tracking yields a relatively poor rate of return on the necessary capital expenditure.[69]

What is probably even more important is that if the decision is taken to preserve two alternative routes it may be possible only to single track one of the lines and not both. This is because the capacity of a single-track route carrying trains in both directions is considerably less than that of a double-track line where one track is reserved for trains moving in one direction and the other track for trains moving in the opposite direction, and as a result the attempt to save money by reducing both routes to single track may well, by unduly restricting capacity, prevent a railway from providing a high-quality service. Similar considerations apply to the decision to reduce a three or four-line route to double track rather than to close an alternative line entirely. Full, as opposed to partial, concentration of traffic has the further advantage that the level of traffic on the selected routes may be so dense that it becomes worth while to electrify them, to install sophisticated signalling, or to reduce curves and gradients.

Despite the manifest advantages of reducing surplus railroad capacity by eliminating alternative routes, it has now been decided to keep them open but to reduce the number of tracks. This policy follows from the Labour Government's decision to preserve a route system of some 11,000 miles including virtually all the 7,500 miles of through route covered by the second Beeching Report. It is this which is preventing British Rail from completing the rationalization of its track system. This has been officially denied. According to the report of the Joint Steering Group, British Rail's surplus capacity 'is not mainly related to the route mileage of the system or to the decision to retain and develop a basic network of 11,000 route miles. It is almost wholly to be found in the shape of excess *track* mileage (e.g. four tracks, where two would suffice to carry the traffic).'[70] But no attempt was made to justify this claim and it seems very unlikely that the matter was given any careful attention. What was the point, seeing it had already been decided to retain 11,000 miles of route whether it was surplus or not? The significant point is that the Committee, which contained railway representatives, believed that by eliminating surplus track capacity, only about £15 million of expenditure on maintaining the track and on maintaining and operating the signalling, could be saved, whereas the second Beeching Report put the figure at over £40 million.[71]

The last Government not only restricted the scope which the railways have for rationalization, but also somewhat delayed its progress. One important cause of delay has been the lengthy period which its policy took to mature and the difficulty which British Rail obviously had in taking action before the Government had taken the fundamental decisions about the shape and size of the railway system. The elimination of surplus track capacity is an obvious case in point. Another important instance, which has cost British Rail dear, was the long interval which elapsed before the Government decided what to do about the rail sundries service and the further interval which elapsed before its plans, which required legislation, could be carried through Parliament. This was one of the topics considered by Lord Hinton during his inquiry into transport during 1965. Subsequently it was decided by Mr Tom Fraser, who was then Minister of Transport, that the rail service should be merged with BRS Parcels to provide a joint organization. However, it was not until January 1969 that the proposal to transfer rail sundries came into effect in accord with the provisions of the Transport Act 1968.[72]

Throughout this Chapter it has been tacitly assumed that the social benefits which the railways confer when they provide loss-making services are outweighed by the loss which they incur by running them. This cannot be taken for granted and will be examined later, although, to anticipate our conclusions, it will be found that there is a case for withdrawing most stopping services even when the likely social costs are taken into account.[73] This is hardly surprising in view of the enormous losses which they incur. What is puzzling is the furious opposition with which the suggestion that the route network should be cut back is greeted by the Labour Party. One of the principal purposes of nationalization was that the railways should be re-shaped, and this, in effect, was what the party was proposing when it advocated co-ordination. As long ago as 1933 Herbert Morrison argued in *Socialization and Transport* that the Government should 'pursue the sensible course of enabling each form of transport to serve in the field where it is best fitted to serve. There are transport needs for which the railway is not the best medium: for example light traffics, branch routes connecting sparsely populated areas, or rural areas with the great towns; door-to-door deliveries for moderate distances; and so on. There is a field within which road transport is unquestionably superior to the railways, just as there is a field within which the railway is superior to road transport.'[74] Furthermore it might have been expected that a party which is sceptical of the virtues of competition, and used to lay great stress on its wasteful nature, would be favourably disposed towards the elimination of the duplicate routes which resulted from competitive railway building in the Victorian age, though it would, before sanctioning the closure of any part of the trunk route, naturally have wished to discover by means of cost benefit studies whether there was a genuine case for retention.

CHAPTER 12

BOAC Losses

1945–51 : Uneconomic Aircraft

THERE is no mystery about the cause of the large deficits which the air corporations incurred during the immediate post-war period: they were mainly due to lack of suitable aircraft. Nearly all the planes initially available to the corporations were thoroughly uneconomic. BOAC and BSAA (British South American Airways) had to make do with obsolete planes most of which were military conversions. Until 1949, the only satisfactory aircraft which BOAC possessed were six American Constellations and BSAA did not have any. Yet their operating fleets included up to 146 planes. The first year in which BOAC's passenger fleet consisted wholly of modern aircraft was 1951 and, significantly, it was the first year in which the Corporation made a profit. The main reason why the operating costs of the old converted military planes were so high was that their carrying capacity was very low in relation to their size. In March 1948, the average seating capacity of BOAC planes was only 19 compared with 41 in March 1952.[1]

BEA was in a similar but somewhat easier position. Although some of the planes with which it commenced operations were wildly uneconomic, the Vikings and Dakotas, which from 1948–9 accounted for the great bulk of its mileage, were relatively satisfactory stop-gap aircraft. The Viking was, for instance, able to seat up to 27 passengers. But it was not until these stop-gap aircraft were replaced by modern planes that BEA started to make a profit.[2]

The reason why it took so long for the air corporations to obtain satisfactory aircraft is once again no secret. It was due to the Government's policy that they should fly British aircraft. This was laid down in the White Paper on British Air Services, published at the end of 1945, which set the framework for civil aviation in the post-war period.[3] However, the policy was already over 20 years old. The agreement of 1924, by which Imperial Airways, BOAC's private predecessor, received a government subsidy, obliged the company to use only British equipment. In view of post-war experience, it is interesting to observe that despite its assured market the British aircraft industry was even then relatively unsuccessful. Only one of the planes taken by Imperial Airways was sold to other users. On the other hand aircraft built in Holland, Germany and America and, to a lesser degree, in Italy, were being ordered by airline companies all over the world.[4]

During the war Britain concentrated entirely on fighter and bomber aircraft while the production of transport aircraft was left to the Americans who built large numbers of transport aircraft of types designed originally for civil use. It was obvious that at the end of the war they would be able to revert readily to making airliners, which was exactly what they did.[5] The British aircraft industry was not in this fortunate position but when, during the war, plans for the future were drawn up it was hoped that between 1948 and 1950 a new generation of advanced British airliners would become available. As a stop-gap measure it was eventually decided that a number of interim types based on combat aircraft should be introduced when the war ended. It was recognized from the beginning that at least some of these makeshift planes would not be economic but it was decided that BOAC must, at any price, fly British.[6]

This policy largely came to grief and was certainly a financial fiasco for the air corporations. The advanced British aircraft either did not become available till well into the fifties like the Comet or turned out to be duds like the Brabazon.[7] When the interim types became available they either crashed or flew at a loss. Where they did not become available, the corporations had to make do with converted military planes which were hopelessly uneconomic. BOAC was in the latter position. It was originally intended that in the immediate post-war years it should be equipped largely with Tudor aircraft which were based on the Lancaster bomber, but when the long-range version for use on the North Atlantic routes failed to arrive on time, BOAC was permitted to buy five Constellations. This was a lucky escape as the Tudor would have incurred heavy losses. When the medium-range version for use on Empire routes failed to materialize, and proved less economic than had been anticipated, BOAC had to make do with converted military aircraft all of which were obsolete from the start, and some of which BOAC had great difficulty in getting into service.[8]

The type of difficulty with which BOAC had to contend is illustrated by the case of the converted Halifax bombers which it agreed to use as a stop-gap for the Tudor. According to the Corporation's report for 1946–7

it was stipulated that the aircraft should be delivered between May and June 1946, complete in all details for operation on the Empire routes. The first six aircraft were delivered without de-icing equipment, and the promised spares were not forthcoming. At Bovingdon, the base provided for these aircraft, the hangers were unheated and no living accommodation was available at the station. Despite these handicaps, a limited service was started in September 1946, but after six weeks the aircraft had to be grounded for failures in the hydraulic system. The aircraft were returned to the manufacturers for fitting of de-icing equipment and did not operate again in the year under review. The maintenance of the base with approximately 400 personnel for nearly 12 months was, therefore, almost completely unproductive.[9]

Ultimately BOAC managed to get hold of American aircraft. In particular, after what Sir Miles Thomas describes as 'a rousing battle with the Ministry and the authorities' BOAC was given permission to buy 22 Canadairs or Argonauts, as they became known. This was the plane which enabled the Corporation to get out of the red; it was fitted with Rolls-Royce engines and other British equipment to save dollars.[10]

British South American Airways, like BOAC, had to rely at first on converted military planes because its Tudors were not available. But it did at last obtain them and this was its undoing because, after two had mysteriously disappeared into the sea, they were withdrawn from service and the Corporation was merged with BOAC. The continued use of converted military aircraft on the South America routes instead of the Tudor involved BSAA and BOAC in an operating loss of over £2 million, and in addition there was a capital loss of just under £1 million.[11]

The air corporations' operating costs were so high during the immediate post-war period not only because their planes were inherently uneconomic but also because they had to operate so many types. BOAC in particular laboured under this disadvantage. The Corporation was, from the beginning, well aware that a standardized fleet consisting of no more than two or three main types was what it required. Yet in the spring of 1947 it was operating with ten different models and the number only fell gradually. Even in 1951 BOAC was still using five types of aircraft, though one of these was used to carry freight. The large variety of planes which BOAC operated involved heavy training costs for air and ground crews, necessitated the stocking of a large assortment of spares and resulted in the number of accounting, administrative and maintenance staff being much larger than the Corporation would have required with a unified fleet.[12]

Poor Maintenance Facilities

The air corporations' maintenance costs were swollen still further by the lack of suitable facilities. This indeed ranks with the lack of satisfactory aircraft as a major cause of their deficits. Once again it was BOAC which was in the most difficult position. As it explained in its Annual Report for 1946–7 what was required was

> a well-equipped maintenance base at or near to the main terminal aerodrome. At the end of the war there were few buildings available at the aerodromes designed for civil use. Maintenance therefore had to be carried on either in the open air or in hangars and workshops which were for the most part unheated and widely dispersed. London Airport was opened for operations in May 1946, but as there were no hangars or workshops available to the Corporation, the landplanes based in the United Kingdom had to be maintained elsewhere . . . involving high costs for dead flying. In order to ensure that aircraft would be in position for scheduled departures, they often had to be positioned the evening before departure, especially during the bad weather months, resulting in reduced utilization and higher costs of flying crews . . . During the year the Corporation was obliged to use eight maintenance bases which meant multiplication of administrative staffs, capital equipment and various ancillary services.[13]

It was estimated that if the whole of the Corporation's landplane fleet had been maintained at London Airport there would have been a saving of nearly £1 million per annum and this was after some temporary hangars had become available.[14]

The Corporation was, however, unable to obtain the facilities which it needed so badly because of the stringent control which the Government exercised over building work and the capital cuts which delayed the completion of London Airport. Furthermore, to save dollars, BOAC had to give up its best-equipped base at Dorval in Canada and move to temporary premises in Britain. The cost of the move accounted for about £400,000 of the Corporation's losses. Nevertheless, BOAC's difficulties gradually eased as accommodation became available at London Airport, and by 1951–2, the year in which BOAC first made a profit, maintenance had been concentrated at only two main bases. Not until 1954 was maintenance concentrated entirely at London Airport.[15]

The last major reason for the air corporations' deficits in the early post-war period was that they continued operating routes on which exceptionally heavy losses were being made, and where it was hopeless to expect profits in the near future. This was largely the result of Government policy. It was the air corporations' duty, as laid down in the White Paper on British Air Services, to provide essential but unremunerative services in the public interest. BOAC had to operate some services of this type and BSAA, at Government request, purchased two highly-unprofitable companies which operated in the West Indies although it knew that they were a doubtful commercial project.[16] But it was BEA that had to bear the heaviest burden. Because it was Government policy the Corporation provided what it termed social services to the Highlands and Islands on which it made a loss of about £300,000 per annum.[17] Although the loss on these routes was particularly heavy none of BEA's domestic routes made a profit. The loss on the domestic routes was indeed more or less responsible for the Corporation's deficit. For instance in 1950–51 BEA made a loss of about £1 million on its internal services, but had a profit of about £200,000 on its continental services.[18] It seems likely that, even in the absence of Government pressure, BEA would have continued to operate its main domestic routes either because it hoped that they would one day be profitable or because it regarded them as essential if the goodwill of the public was to be maintained. But clearly BEA was by no means a free agent. According to Mr John Longhurst:

> The opening during 1949 of the first air service in Wales, and the first British air service connecting the North and the Midlands direct with Paris were, in fact, the result of the personal intervention of the Minister of Civil Aviation between British European Airways and the local authorities who had been pressing for these facilities to be provided. BEA had come to the conclusion that these services were not warranted commercially but the Minister considered that their operation for a trial period at least was worth while.[19]

Was BOAC Inefficient?

It will not have escaped the eye of the critical reader that most of the evidence on the disadvantages under which the air corporations laboured has been taken from their own reports. As these are almost the only source for detailed information this was inevitable. Reliance upon what the corporations said in their own defence does, however, involve the risk that a one-sided picture has been obtained. Naturally they would not have drawn attention to the contribution which inefficiency may have made to their deficits. Yet it was widely believed at the time that BOAC's operating costs were excessive, due to over-staffing.[20] Fortunately, it is possible to calculate roughly what the Corporation's costs would have been if it had possessed up-to-date aircraft and proper maintenance facilities. It is therefore possible to see whether BOAC exaggerated its difficulties.

Regardless of the general position there was one part of the Corporation which, even during the early post-war period, operated under favourable conditions. This was the Atlantic Division which had Constellations and was based at Dorval. If the Corporation was as badly handicapped as it made out, we should expect that its costs would be significantly lower in the Atlantic Division, where modern equipment was available, than in the rest of the undertaking. This was, in fact, the case. During 1947–8 BOAC's expenditure per capacity ton mile was 31 per cent lower in the Atlantic Division than it was in the rest of the undertaking, and during 1948–9 it was 22 per cent lower. It is true that in 1949–50 the figure was only 7 per cent less, even when expenditure on the move from Dorval is excluded, but this seems to be explained by the adverse effect which devaluation had on operating costs in the dollar area.[21] If during 1947–8 and 1948–9 BOAC's unit costs had been as low on its eastern and southern routes as they were in the Atlantic Division, the Corporation's operating loss would have been only about £4 million compared with the actual figure of about £12·7 million. It, therefore, seems likely that the difficult conditions under which BOAC laboured explained about two-thirds of the losses incurred during the early post-war years.

It may be thought that inefficiency and over-staffing accounted for the remaining third of the corporation's deficit, for even in the Atlantic Division where conditions were favourable, BOAC lost money. For instance, in 1947–8 and 1948–9, there was a total deficit of £1·2 million.[22] It seems very doubtful whether this was primarily due to bad management. Even BOAC's critics were impressed with its performance in this area. According to Mr John Longhurst

> throughout 1948, BOAC's Western Division, running the North Atlantic service, was getting over one hour a day more utilization out of each of its Constellation air liners than any of its three American competitors, Pan American Airways, American Overseas Airways and TWA. And during 1948 the same Division carried a higher average number of passengers and a higher total payload per flight than any of its seven American and European competitors.[23]

As might be expected BOAC's operating costs for the Atlantic area were lower than those of her principal American rival, Pan-American. In 1948, at the post-devaluation rate of exchange, which probably gives a fairer impression as the pound had previously been over-valued, the figures were about 34 cents per CTM for BOAC and about 41 cents for Pan Am.[24]

At first sight it seems surprising that Pan American made a profit on the Atlantic routes whereas BOAC incurred a loss. The explanation is that the American airline was subsidized through the very high rate which it received from the United States Post Office for carrying mail. During 1948 the Civil Aeronautics Board estimates that American international carriers, of which Pan Am was by far and away the largest, received a subsidy equivalent to £11 million at the post-devaluation rate of exchange. Other things being equal they would, but for this subsidy, have incurred a loss of about £7 million. Indeed, their subsidy exceeded their profits in every year up to 1954 and during the period 1946–58 American international carriers received total aid of just under £100 million.[25]

As BOAC's operating costs compared favourably with those of Pan American Airways on the Atlantic routes, where they were operating under similar circumstances, it seems most unlikely that BOAC can legitimately be described as grossly inefficient or that weak management was an important cause of her deficits. The closer the evidence of BOAC's inefficiency, produced by such critics as Mr John Longhurst, is studied the less convincing it appears, though it is unnecessary after our comparison between the Corporation and Pan Am to go into detail. This does not mean that BOAC's staff was perfectly adjusted to the work load. Although it was not a major cause of the Corporation's losses, there was almost certainly some over-staffing during the early post-war years. This is shown by the highly successful purge of unnecessary administrators which Sir Harold Hartley initiated when he became Chairman in mid-1947 and which his successor, Sir Miles Thomas, intensified.[26] The fact that the cost of administrative staff was cut by about £½ million between 1946–7 and 1951–2, although there was presumably a considerable rise in salaries over this period, must have been at least partly due to this economy drive.[27] By 1951 however general and administrative expenses formed a significantly smaller proportion of total costs in BOAC than they did in Pan Am's Atlantic Division, than in TWA's international services or in SAS. KLM was the only airline, for which comparable details are available, where the proportion was lower than in BOAC.[28]

BOAC's 1957–63 Deficit: Excessive Costs?

After their early difficulties the air corporations seemed, during the first half of the fifties, to be entering a period of prosperity. The policy of flying British which, as we have seen, was largely responsible for their initial losses, appeared at last to be paying dividends. In 1953, BEA introduced the world's first turbo-prop airliner, the Viscount, which was the foundation for the Corporation's Commercial success. What appeared even more significant at the time was that BOAC had, during the previous year, introduced the Comet, the world's first jet-propelled airliner. Its speed and comfort had great passenger appeal, and during 1952–3 it had a load factor of 87 per cent compared with a general average of 63 per cent for the passenger routes over which BOAC was operating. As a result, it earned a profit up to the time that it had to be withdrawn from service in 1954, although its operating costs per seat mile were very much higher than those of conventional piston-engined airliners. Its withdrawal was due to two disastrous crashes caused by technical weaknesses which could not have been foreseen when it was designed. This, together with its early commercial success, makes it appear that, except for bad luck, BOAC would, as the only airline flying jet aircraft, have been in an extremely strong position. However, it seems doubtful whether the Comet I would have had a very long life even if it had not crashed. Because at the time it was built the available jet engines had a relatively low power the Comet had to be a very small plane, which explains its high operating costs. This meant that it was only viable so long as it retained its extremely high load factor and that it was highly vulnerable to competition, yet this competition would have been provided by the later and larger versions of the plane for which foreign airlines were waiting. The early version of the Comet was not, therefore, the magnificent plane dogged by ill-luck which it is popularly supposed to have been, but a premature and somewhat foolhardy venture.[29]

The sudden withdrawal of the Comet in the spring of 1954 disrupted BOAC's operations, and involved the Corporation in a capital loss of £3 million.[30] Despite this, it continued to make a profit which seemed striking evidence of the Corporation's resilience and efficiency. However, during the late fifties and early sixties, BOAC's good record was marred by some extremely heavy losses. Between 1957–8 and 1963–4 there was a total deficit of no less than £58½ million. The year-by-year figures are shown in Table 21.

One possible explanation for the Corporation's large losses is that it was inefficient and badly managed. In its report of 1959 the Select Committee concluded that 'in recent years BOAC have been operating with less efficiency than most of the airlines to which they can fairly be compared'. What particularly disturbed the Committee was the corporation's high operating costs which in 1956 and 1957 were higher than those of six foreign airlines, and were only exceeded by Air France. This, in turn, was largely due to BOAC's excessively high aircraft maintenance expenses.[31]

The Select Committee suggests that this was an example of gross inefficiency. It says that when the corporation eventually discovered that its maintenance costs were excessive, this

> bore out . . . the opinions which had been expressed to the Board, unavailingly, by the financial side of BOAC as far back as 1952. In these circumstances, it surprised Your Committee that the major investigation by BOAC into their excessive engineering costs should not have begun until mid-1957, although the annual statistics published by IATA and ICAO had some while previously shown that something was wrong.[32]

This is a highly misleading account of what happened as the evidence received by the Select Committee shows. An official from the Ministry of Transport and Civil Aviation testified that when in 1955 ICAO first published statistics comparing the costs of different airlines, they showed that 'the engineering costs of BOAC compared fairly favourably with the other airlines'. It was not until 1956, with the publication of figures for 1954, that they had any figures which showed that BOAC's were higher than those of most other operators. When the Ministry approached the corporation it found that it was already investigating the problem. After an expert team had visited three European airlines in the second half of 1956, the time taken for an engine to pass through the overhaul shops was approximately cut in half during the following year.[33]

Although the Select Committee paints too black a picture there is no doubt that BOAC's maintenance costs had got seriously out of line. When, after a delay which BOAC attributed partly to the serious difficulty which its engineering department was having with the Britannia, a team investigated KLM, Pan Am and another American airline in the second half of 1957 it was found that BOAC employed over twice as many engineering staff per flying hour.[34]

The Select Committee was again highly critical of BOAC in its report of 1964 concluding that the Corporation's progress in reducing its maintenance costs had been unduly slow. Yet the figures which the Ministry of Aviation provided showed that between 1957 and 1962 BOAC had reduced its maintenance costs faster than any of the eight foreign airlines for which comparative details were given.[35] However, the Ministry used specious arguments to cast doubts on the improvement which had been achieved; and the Select Committee unfortunately devoted almost all its attention to maintenance and hardly discussed BOAC's overall operating costs. BOAC's progress was clearer in the field of operating costs as a whole than it was for maintenance costs alone. Air France was the only foreign airline which had been found to have higher operating costs than BOAC in 1957, but between 1957 and 1962 BOAC's overall costs were reduced faster than those of any of the other airlines. By 1962 only three operators had lower costs than BOAC, and in 1963, though the Select Committee did not know this, it was only Pan American and TWA.[36] Because BOAC is a long-haul airline it was to be expected that its costs would be lower than those of the short-haul airlines. But as the Ministry of Aviation told the Select Committee 'some of the cost differences are so large as to leave little or no doubt of BOAC's greater efficiency'.[37] Though the Committee quoted the Ministry's criticisms of BOAC at length, it failed to mention this grudging tribute to the Corporation's efficiency.

It seems evident that the large operating losses which BOAC incurred during the early sixties were not due to inefficiency in the sense of exceptionally high operating costs. During the late fifties BOAC's costs were excessive but over most of this period the Corporation itself had an operating surplus, ignoring the extra depreciation which had later to be set aside. The only exception was 1957–8 when there was a small deficit of £$\frac{1}{3}$ million. Of course if BOAC had had lower costs during the late fifties, when there was scope for saving, its operating surplus would have been larger and its financial difficulties less serious. But it is clear that these difficulties were not themselves due to the Corporation's excessive costs.

Unprofitable Subsidiaries

Although by the early sixties there is no reason to believe that the overall level of BOAC's costs was excessively high, there was one unnecessary burden on its revenue. This was the loss made by the Corporation's subsidiary companies. Here perhaps is evidence for the charge, made in the White Paper of 1963 on BOAC's financial problems, that the Corporation was badly managed and that its system of financial control was weak. According to the White Paper: 'The Corporation's motive for investing in local airlines has been to secure feeder traffic for the main trunk services and to protect transit and traffic rights'.[38] This is a highly misleading account of the way in which these companies were acquired. What the White Paper failed to mention, with the exception of Kuwait Airways, was the part which the Government had played in the process. The two West Indian concerns which BOAC had inherited from BSAA had also been bought at Government request although they were known to be doubtful commercial prospects. Government influence also played some part in the acquisition of Middle East Airlines, though it seems that in this case commercial motives may have been more important.

Once they had been purchased it was difficult for BOAC to disengage from some of these concerns. For instance in the case of Kuwait Airways, which had been bought in 1958, BOAC was bound by a five-year contract from which it was unable to gain release.[39]

Although BOAC never made a profit on its subsidiary companies the loss had, during the first part of the fifties, been quite modest; in 1954–5 it totalled only £25,000. After this the position rapidly deteriorated and very considerable losses were incurred. During the period from 1957–8 to 1963–4 BOAC's subsidiaries lost over £9 million out of the Corporation's aggregate deficit of over £58 million. The bulk of this loss was incurred by subsidiaries which BOAC would not have acquired but for Government pressure, and a considerable part was due to the 1958 revolution in the Lebanon which had a devastating effect on Middle East Airlines.[40] Nevertheless, when all the mitigating circumstances have been enumerated, it remains true that BOAC went on losing money on its subsidiaries and associates year after year; that it continued to make optimistic assumptions about the future despite past losses, that its financial and managerial control over the companies was weak; and that only in 1961 or 1962 did it start making detailed assessments of the value of the feeder traffic which it received from the companies, though this was one of the principal arguments used to justify their retention.[41]

By the early sixties these deficits had largely been remedied and unprofitable holdings were at last being jettisoned, though this involved a capital loss of nearly £1½ million. In 1963 Mr J. T. Corbett, who had investigated BOAC on behalf of the Minister of Aviation, was able to report that although there was room for further improvement, 'positive steps have been taken within the last two or three years not only to reduce the Corporation's commitment in associated and subsidiary companies but also to exercise managerial control and take steps to prevent uneconomic schemes'.[42] These efforts were not without avail and, in 1963–4, BOAC made a profit on its subsidiaries for the first time.

Another criticism which has been made of BOAC is that it misjudged the demand for its services. The White Paper described the rate at which the Corporation had expanded its capacity and frequency as unduly optimistic.[43] There is no doubt that, during the late fifties and early sixties, BOAC was increasing its capacity at an exceptionally rapid rate. This was due to the strategy adopted after the Comet disaster which, at a blow, had deprived the Corporation of a large part both of its existing capacity and of the additional capacity which it had planned for future years. The Corporation made desperate efforts to find replacement aircraft. It even managed to buy the private plane of an American airline magnate who, since he was a most elusive person, had to be tracked down and the deal negotiated at three o'clock in the morning on the steps of a hotel.[44] Nevertheless BOAC's production, in terms of capacity ton miles, fell slightly during 1954–5, and though it rose in 1955–6 was 9 per cent below the original target. The delay in the delivery and introduction of the Britannia further aggravated the position, and it was not until 1958–9 that BOAC began to overtake the setbacks in its programme. The policy which BOAC had adopted was to increase its rate of growth substantially above the normal level during this and the following few years in order to recapture the ground which had been lost to its competitors. Its normal rate of growth was 10 to 15 per cent a year but during 1958–9 it was stepped up to 18 per cent; then to 24 per cent; next to 32 per cent in 1960–1; and finally, it was planned, to 34 per cent in 1961–2. After this spurt it was planned that the rate of advance should drop back to the more normal rate of 10 per cent per annum in 1962–3 and 1963–4.[45]

Up to the end of 1960–61 this programme appeared to be a success. The volume of business did not increase as fast as capacity, and consequently there was a drop in the load factor, but this had been largely expected. What was significant was that during 1960–61 the Corporation's revenue was only fractionally below the level which had been forecast and that, disregarding the results of subsidiaries, BOAC showed an operating surplus of £4¼ million which made it almost the best year in BOAC's history.[46] However the following two years, 1961–2 and 1962–3, were a financial disaster. First, the large increase in BOAC's capacity during 1961–2 coincided with an exceptionally large increase of 27 per cent in that of other international airlines. Second, the rate of increase in international traffic was much slower than in previous years. Third, the reduction in the rate at which traffic was growing was particularly sharp on the routes between Britain and the United States. Traffic had previously been increasing at 20–30 per cent per annum on these routes, and it was here that BOAC was expanding its capacity by the greatest amount. In 1961–2 there was an increase of only ½ per cent and in 1962–3 the figure was 14½ per cent. This fall, which came quite suddenly, was due to the American recession and the new non-stop jet services from America to the Continent. The advent of the long-range jet had reduced the advantage which the Corporation had derived from London's position as an essential staging post in trans-Atlantic air travel. As a result of these developments BOAC's passenger load factor fell catastrophically from 59·8 per cent in 1960–1 to 49·6 per cent in 1961–2 and 47·6 per cent in 1962–3.[47] This largely explains the Corporation's operating loss of £7·7 million, though BOAC estimated that a strike during the height of the 1961 traffic season cost it about £3 million.[48]

There may, as the Ministry of Aviation alleged, have been an element of bad planning in this deficit.[49] Perhaps BOAC should have made greater allowances for the large increases in capacity which other operators were providing in 1961, and increased its production less fast that year but faster in 1962 and 1963. However, it seems clear that BOAC's long-term strategy was sound and that the deficit was largely due to plain bad luck. By 1963–4, revenue was once again in line with the forecasts which had been made in 1959 and the corporation had an operating surplus.[50] During recent years, as can be seen from Table 21, some extremely handsome profits have been earned.

One question which suggests itself is whether BOAC, when it found that it was running at a deficit, could have done more to keep the figure within bounds. The Ministry of Aviation, ever ready to criticize, told the Select Committee that BOAC appeared reluctant to consider drastic measures to secure improved results.[51] But as the Committee discovered, BOAC in mid-1961 and again in mid-1962 examined the possibility of drastically reducing its fleet and cutting out unprofitable routes. It also considered whether it should try to save money by reducing the frequency of its services. There were a number of powerful arguments against either course. It was found, for instance, that the cost of contraction in terms of redundancy payments to staff and, even more serious, cancellation charges for aircraft would be extremely heavy. Nor was any great benefit to be secured by reducing frequencies because travellers would not wait for a BOAC plane but catch the next one to their destination.[52] Another possible step which the Corporation could have taken was to step up its sales effort. However, it was difficult for the Corporation to make much further progress in this direction. According to the White Paper, management consultants who investigated BOAC found that 'the Corporation's effort on sales, advertising and publicity has been at about the right level and well directed'.[53]

Flying British with the Britannia

Although BOAC lost considerable sums through its subsidiaries and incurred a heavy operating loss during the early sixties, the bulk of its deficit did not arise in this way. Before the provision of extra depreciation there was, on balance, a net operating profit over the period 1957–8 to 1963–4 which was more than sufficient to cover the losses made on subsidiaries.[54] Most of its losses were due in one way or another to the policy of flying British aircraft.

The Britannia was the largest source of loss. Not only was the plane delivered late but it was also found that certain parts were liable to become dangerously iced-up during flight. Their introduction was delayed by two and a half years and it was not until early 1957 that the medium-range Britannia 102 started to come into service.[55] Even after it had been introduced the aircraft was plagued by a series of electrical and mechanical faults. At the end of 1958 when operations were still being crippled, the Managing Director of BOAC told the Select Committee that 'teething troubles in the Britannia have gone on for a longer time than with any other aircraft. We have a bad reputation for irregularity on the eastern routes . . . and we have suffered in consequence on our general load factor on those routes.'[56] This helps to explain the damaging fall in BOAC's load factor during 1957–8 and the poor financial result to which this led. Another contributory factor was the late delivery of the long-range Britannia 312, which meant that out-moded aircraft due for retirement had to be retained in service.[57]

The difficulties with the Britannia meant that its introductory costs were exceptionally high. By the time the plane went into service BOAC had spent £5¾ million on development flying and on training personnel. The cost of introducing the American DC-7C which went into service at about the same time was very much smaller. For the same number of planes it would have been only about £2¾ million. In addition BOAC had to spend very large sums correcting the faults which developed after the Britannia had been introduced. For instance, a considerable part of its electrical system had to be replaced at a cost of £25,000 per aircraft and this was only a fairly small example of the expense to which BOAC was put. But when, in November 1957, the Corporation tried to refuse delivery of Britannias which it regarded as sub-standard Harold Watkinson, the Minister of Transport and Civil Aviation, instructed it to take them.[58]

Because of the difficulties with the Britannia, BOAC was forced to buy a fleet of ten DC-7Cs in order to make sure that it was not left without advanced aircraft.[59] This meant that BOAC was put to the expense of flying another type of aircraft although it has been shown that the way to keep costs down is to keep the number of types down. But this was a minor difficulty compared with the problem of obsolescence which BOAC soon had to face. As Mr Stephen Wheatcroft says, 'when the rapid transition to jet aircraft in 1959 and 1960 caused non-jets to become obsolete, BOAC had a double problem on its hands because it then had fleets of both Britannias and DC-7Cs'.[60] In the event BOAC was forced to retire these planes prematurely, thus incurring an enormous capital loss.

Their early retirement was inevitable because the big jets, as represented by the Boeing 707, were so much cheaper to operate. Due to its size and speed the Boeing 707 produced about 10,500 CTMs per hour compared with only about 4,300 for even the biggest version of the Britannia and a mere 2,700 for the Douglas DC-7C. As a result during 1961–2 it cost BOAC about 1s 11½d to provide a ton of capacity over a distance of one mile using a DC-7C, over 1s 6d using a big Britannia, but less than 1s 1d by flying a Boeing. The Comet 4 at 1s 9½d per CTM was also uneconomic because although it was a jet, and an improved version of the earlier Comet, it was a smaller and technically less advanced plane than the Boeing.[61]

BOAC was therefore forced during the early sixties to retire its Britannia 102s and DC-7Cs after an average of less than five years' service per aircraft; and by the mid-sixties had to retire its Britannia 312s and Comet 4s after six years of service. Moreover, it was anticipated that these would be a very poor market for them when they were disposed of. As it had been BOAC's practice to depreciate its aircraft over seven years and to assume that they would have a residual value of 25 per cent, the Corporation was involved in a huge capital loss when in 1961–2 it provided the extra depreciation which was necessary. During that *annus horrendus* it wrote £31·7 million off the value of its fleet; of this the Britannia accounted for £22·4 million, the Comet for £4·7 million and the DC-7C for £4·6 million.[62] Obviously, a large part of this loss would have been avoided but for the Corporation's commitment to British aircraft with their habit of arriving late and going wrong. BOAC only purchased DC-7Cs because the Britannia was delayed. If the Britannia had been introduced up to two and a half years earlier, as originally planned, far more of its value would have been written off by the time it had withdrawn from service.

But why, it may be asked, did BOAC order Britannias in the first place? Could it not have foreseen that the plane would become obsolete before its normal life had expired? The initial order, which was for 25 aircraft, was made as far back as July 1949. Subsequently a larger version of the Britannia was developed and, in 1953, the order was revised to 15 of the original version and ten of the new. By the summer of that year negotiations had begun for the purchase of further big Britannias and these led to the development of a long-range version. Ultimately in 1954 BOAC increased its order from 25 to 33, including 11 of the long-range version, of which three took the place of aircraft already on order. In October of the following year Pan American Airways startled the world by announcing that it had opted for big jets and ordered Boeing 707s and Douglas DC-8s.[63] BOAC's initial order for the Britannia was therefore made at a time when the big jet was only a pipe-dream but its final order took place only about a year before Pan Am's historic decision. This strongly suggests that the Corporation was being shortsighted when it increased its order. But, although BOAC cannot be given high marks for perspicacity, it must be remembered that it was already both morally and intellectually committed to the Britannia. The negotiations for the purchase of extra aircraft had been going on for many months and a new version of the Britannia was being developed on the Corporation's behalf. What was perhaps equally important was that BOAC had, due to the length of time which it had taken to develop and the problems which were encountered, become so preoccupied with the Britannia that it was difficult for those in charge to make an impartial assessment.

Moreover, ideas were changing very rapidly in the world of aviation during the mid-fifties. In their study of aircraft innovation Ronald Miller and David Sawers give this illustration:

> As late as 1954, just a year before the airlines began buying the 707 and DC-8 and a year after the 707 prototype flew, two engineers from American Airlines argued that manufacturers were going from designs that were too small to be economic to designs that were too big. The airliners of 180,000–200,000 lb gross weight that were then being proposed would, they said, have too high an initial cost and make amortization 30 per cent of the direct operating cost . . . The 707 and DC-8 are larger than the 200,000-lb airliners that were held too expensive – though the 707 prototype weighed 190,000 lbs and obviously inspired these remarks . . . another indication of how fast ideas changed is that this 1954 paper says that it may be possible to extend the range of jets to get non-stop trans-oceanic flights; a year later airplanes were being ordered that could operate non-stop across the Atlantic.[64]

The interval between BOAC's final order for the Britannia and Pan Am's initial order for big jets must therefore be regarded as a comparatively long time. BOAC's decision to order the Comet 4 was taken about the same time as it placed its final order for Britannias. Once again the Corporation was already heavily committed to this aircraft and determined that it would not be beaten but would make the aircraft a success. It had the satisfaction in October 1958 of being the first airline to introduce a jet service between Europe and North America, though it was only a few days ahead of Pan American with its Boeings.[65]

The premature ordering of aircraft by what may appear a short interval but what was in reality a disastrously long period, was the inevitable consequence of flying British. Almost all foreign airlines buy their aircraft off the peg rather than having them made to measure. What usually happens is that one of the major American operators gives the lead and that other airlines then follow its example. But even the US concern which sets the fashion does not have to place its order up to a decade or more in advance of delivery. Pan American Airways was able to introduce its Boeing 707s only three years after their order had been announced. This was an exceptionally short period, but American aircraft are normally developed more quickly than British planes.[66]

There is a further disadvantage which BOAC suffers through being tied to the British aircraft industry. Not only does it have to order years and years in advance, but it also has to commit itself to buy a large batch of planes. This is because the initial design and tooling costs are so heavy in the aircraft industry that the cost of producing only a few planes of a given type would be prohibitive. If the manufacturer is to have any hope of finding a general market for the plane he must be assured of a large initial order. In practice, this will have to be a home order because foreign airlines are reluctant to buy aircraft which have not been ordered by the domestic airlines.[67] Thus British aircraft manufacturers are dependent for their initial order on either BOAC or BEA and the order will have to be sizeable. The danger in a rapidly changing situation of placing large orders years in advance has been underlined by the VC 10 which, like the Britannia, has been responsible for a large part of BOAC's losses.

The VC 10

Early in 1956 the corporation started to consider their requirements for an aircraft to replace their fleet of Comets and Britannias on their eastern and southern routes in the mid-sixties. At that time it was thought that the American big jets would be unsuitable mainly because the runways were too short for them to land. BOAC started to sound out the British aircraft manufacturers to see which of them was prepared to construct a suitable plane; because of its duty to support the aircraft industry it had no other option. It was certainly left in no doubt that this was the Government policy. At one point in the negotiations between the Corporation and the industry the Government went so far as to insist that, subject to certain conditions, BOAC should engage de Havillands. When in October 1956 the Government announced that the Corporation was to be permitted to buy Boeing 707s for its north Atlantic services, its obligation to fly British in future was reaffirmed. In the event, the negotiations with de Havillands fell through because the company said that it would not proceed until it had secured orders for at least 50 aircraft, which seemed highly improbable.[68]

BOAC then began discussions with Vickers whose VC 10 was the only suitable British aircraft on offer. The Corporation tried to place an order for 25 planes with an option for ten more, but when Vickers stood out for a larger number they agreed to place an order for 35 aircraft with an option for 20 more. There is no doubt that BOAC thought that they would be required. However, the Corporation's Chief Engineer, C. Abell, told the Select Committee that BOAC

> were most loth to place an order for that number of aeroplanes so far ahead, this being early 1957, and we were asked to forecast our aircraft requirement as far ahead as 1966–7. This in the transport industry, which we are in, is a very difficult thing to do. What we would have very much preferred was to have a very much smaller order initially and then order them in small batches later on, as the need arose.[69]

None of the airlines which had a free hand over the aircraft they purchased had committed themselves this far ahead because of the obvious risk involved. Unless BOAC was for some obscure reason obsessed by a passion for forward commitment, the Government's policy that it should fly British must explain the Corporation's decision. What other explanation could there be?

The Select Committee has argued that:

> The Board may have been unduly influenced by the Minister's condition that future purchases of aircraft had to be from British sources. They do not seem to have appreciated that there was another course open to them. If they thought that either the size or financial terms of the order were commercially unacceptable, it was open to them to return to the Minister and request a contribution to the development costs of the aircraft as a condition of their proceeding with the order. As a Ministry witness pointed out, things never came to that point. If, he argued, it had proved impossible to negotiate a contract for British aircraft a new situation would have arisen. In fact the question of what might happen *in extremis* – whether, for example, the purchase of more Boeings would have been authorized – never arose because BOAC accepted Vickers' offer.[70]

It is evident that the Corporation would have found it very difficult to take any other line. First, in the Select Committee's own words 'The negotiations on the number of aircraft to be ordered were concluded in the knowledge that the Government were not prepared to contribute in any way to the project for the VC 10'.[71] Second, BOAC could not have argued either that they did not need so large a number of planes or that they should buy a smaller number of Boeings. At that time it was widely believed that Boeings were unsuitable for the routes in question and the Corporation expected that it would require at least 35 aircraft. If BOAC had used the general argument that it was commercially unwise in a rapidly changing industry to place so large an order so far ahead it would, in effect, have been announcing that it would probably never again want to fly British as these were the only terms which the industry was able to offer. With the wisdom of hindsight it is evident that the Corporation should have put up a fight, but the pressure which it was under can readily be appreciated, and it is the Government which must take the blame for Government policy.

Although the agreement between BOAC and Vickers was reached in the spring of 1957 it was not until 1958 that the contract was signed. By this time both parties had come to want a plane which was somewhat larger and more powerful. However, serious doubts arose within BOAC as to whether the plane would be an economic proposition. Vickers argued that its guarantees of performance were conservative and urged that those of the Boeing, with which the VC 10 was now being compared, were over-optimistic. After Vickers' opinion had been confirmed by the Royal Aircraft Establishment at Farnborough, which had been called in to help resolve the dispute, the Corporation's Board over-ruled its Engineering Department and signed the order for 35 planes. Once again, the pressures on BOAC were formidable. Not only was Vickers' supported by the RAE but it was believed that the VC 10 was the only available aircraft. According to the Select Committee, the Corporation's documents make it clear that the Boeing was regarded only as a yardstick for assessing the VC 10 because 'they would not be allowed dollars to buy aircraft for use on the Eastern routes in any case, or in all probability, for the western routes over and above the 15 Boeings already ordered.'[72]

As time passed, the disadvantages of having been rushed into a premature decision in a rapidly changing industry gradually became evident. For instance modifications to the Boeing and extensions to runways, which were partly financed by the American Government, meant that it could now be used on the Corporation's eastern and southern routes. Experience was also to show that the doubts which its Engineering Department had expressed about the comparative performance of the VC 10 and the Boeing were fully justified.[73] In 1960 the Corporation were again called upon to sacrifice their commercial freedom in the interests of the British aircraft industry with what proved to be catastrophic results. What happened was that in 1959 Vickers found that it had got its sums wrong and that the VC 10 was going to cost more than the company had expected. In this situation it did the obvious thing and tried to get hold of some public money. Or, as the Plowden Committee puts it, 'Vickers, faced with heavy losses on the Vanguard and rising costs on the VC 10, sought from the Government in 1959 a substantial subvention towards their civil aircraft programme'.[74] Hopeful that financial assistance would be forthcoming, as of course it ultimately was, to the tune of £10¼ million, Vickers tried to persuade BOAC to take a further 10 aircraft which would have the effect of spreading the costs over a larger volume of production. What Vickers proposed was that BOAC should agree to take a new and larger version which had become known as the Super VC 10.[75]

According to the Select Committee 'BOAC were clear (in November, 1959) that they should not increase their order for either version of the VC 10'. However, the Corporation soon came under strong pressure from the Ministry of Aviation to take the planes. The order was crucial to the Government-sponsored merger which resulted in the formation of the British Aircraft Corporation. According to the Select Committee

> BOAC's confidential documents show that the rehabilitation of Vickers and their merger . . . was constantly in the minds of BOAC's Board, and in particular of their Chairman, Sir Gerard d'Erlanger, in the discussions that followed. Just before Sir Matthew Slattery became Chairman of BOAC in July 1960, he asked Sir Gerard d'Erlanger not to commit himself to these aircraft until he (Sir Matthew) had had an opportunity to take stock. Sir Gerard's reply was that it was too late; he had been under strong pressure and it had been necessary for the Minister's plans for the formation of the British Aircraft Corporation.[76]

The official view of this affair is that BOAC acted of its own free will, and that the Minister refused to consent to the purchase of the planes until he had been assured by the Corporation that they were commercially necessary. But even those like Mr M. Custance, of the Ministry of Aviation, who take this view admit that 'We were very anxious they should act in this way.'[77] Clearly, as BOAC's records show, the Minister managed to transmit this anxiety in an acute form to Sir Gerard, which in the British context is what is meant by bringing pressure to bear. Obviously he was not manhandled or even bullied in an ungentlemanly way; if he had been, no doubt the attempt to apply pressure would have backfired. Although there can be no real doubt that the Minister brought pressure to bear on Sir Gerard to take the VC 10s, it seems unlikely that he put up much of a fight. He shared the official view that the first duty of the air corporations is to assist the British aircraft industry. He told Sir Matthew Slattery that he 'never believed that it was the Corporation's job to make profits. The Corporation was there to support the British aircraft industry'.[78]

BOAC was able to assure the Minister that the Super VC 10s were commercially necessary because it appeared at the time that it would require extra planes. But it was obviously bad commercial practice for the Corporation to tie its hands so many years in advance. This was

K

obvious to the Board as its November decision shows, and it was obvious to the Corporation's prospective Chairman as his request to Sir Gerard indicates. The high price of being rushed into an order for the new VC 10 soon became apparent. First it was decided, at Sir Matthew Slattery's instigation, that the Super VC 10 was, as originally conceived, unsuitable for general use on the Corporation's routes because it was too large. As a result, a modified version of the new VC 10 was developed and it was also decided that the corporation's order should be changed from 35 Standard and ten Super VC 10s to 15 Standard and 30 Super. To keep the order within the financial limit which had been agreed with the Treasury the number of Standard VC 10s was reduced to 12 at a cost of £600,000 in cancellation charges; but this was a mere bagatelle.[79]

Second, it became obvious that the Super VC 10 was a considerably more expensive plane both to buy and to fly than the Boeing. According to BOAC's estimates of the break-even load factor the cost of the VC 10 was 14 per cent higher per seat mile than the Boeing when operating under the same conditions. This estimate was made before there was any operating experience with the VC 10, but this has only confirmed that it is a more expensive plane to fly. Because of the British aeroplane's high costs Sir Matthew Slattery proposed to the Ministry during 1962 that BOAC should buy Boeings in place of at least some of the VC 10s.[80]

Third, it became clear that BOAC would not require all the planes which it had on order because it could get the same amount of work out of a smaller fleet. By the early sixties BOAC was already utilizing its aircraft far more intensively than other large airlines. It was, therefore, misleading of the Minister of Aviation to suggest that the Corporation was inefficient when it reported that it could do still better. Nevertheless, the recognition that this was possible meant that BOAC had too many aircraft on order. Accordingly in the spring of 1963, having discussed the matter informally on several occasions Sir Matthew proposed to the Minister that 13 Super VC 10s should be cancelled.[81] Ultimately after a long delay, after protracted negotiation, after Sir Matthew had been fired and after the new Chairman, Sir Giles Guthrie, had also proposed cancellation, 13 VC 10s were cancelled (three of the thirteen were taken by the RAF). This cost BOAC £7½ million in cancellation charges.[82]

It is pleasant to be able to record that since the early sixties, BOAC has made a striking financial recovery. During recent years it has been one of the most profitable international airlines in the world. Indeed in 1967, the latest year for which figures are available, the Corporation earned a far higher rate of return on capital than any of the international airlines for which figures are to hand. While BOAC earned 17·1 per cent, Pan Am had a return of only 11·6 per cent, KLM of 9·6 per cent, Qantas of 7·6 per cent, Swissair of 7·2 per cent, Alitalia of 7 per cent, Lufthansa of 4 per cent, and Aer Lingus of −1·9 per cent.[83] The Corporation must again have been at, or near, the top of the profitability league during 1968.

Its critics have been quick to suggest that BOAC has only managed to jack up its rate of return by restricting the rate of growth in its capacity. This thesis appears to receive some confirmation from the fact that the Corporation's share of the traffic passing between Britain and the United States shrank from 38 per cent in 1961–2 to 31 per cent in 1966–7. The main reason for the drop was that BOAC withdrew its services from the London–Washington and London–Los Angeles routes because of the heavy losses which it was incurring. On the other routes the Corporation more or less maintained its share of the market, except for the UK to Chicago route where special factors were at work. It can, of course, be argued that if BOAC had been more efficient, it would have been able to make a profit on the two routes from which it withdrew. This does not seem a very strong argument, partly because there is no general reason to believe that the Corporation is inefficient, and partly because the private British companies, who are usually prepared to commence operations and hope for the best, have not provided services to Los Angeles or Washington.[84]

However, the main weakness of the argument that BOAC's high profits are due to the restricted amount of capacity which it has provided is that the overall growth in its traffic has been satisfactory and that its load factor has not been excessively high. The year 1960 appears to be the most satisfactory starting point for a comparison between the growth of BOAC's traffic and that of other airlines, because in the preceding period the Corporation was increasing its capacity exceptionally fast in an attempt to recapture the ground which it had lost as a result of the Comet disaster. Between 1960 and 1967 the overall rate at which ten major airlines increased their capacity on international routes was 16·2 per cent per annum, which was slightly faster than BOAC's rate of 15 per cent. But it was to be expected that the Corporation's traffic would grow less than average, because such airlines as Lufthansa, JAL and Alitalia, whose traffic was at the beginning of the period very small in relation to the size of their parent countries, have been able to secure enormous increases. If attention is confined to the major operators which had already reached maturity by 1960 (Pan Am, KLM, Qantas, Air France, SAS, Swissair, and Sabena), it is found that their international traffic rose by only 14 per cent per year.[85] It may be concluded, therefore, that BOAC's financial results are as excellent as they appear.

The Economic Consequences of Flying British

Now that the air corporations' losses have been examined in detail we are in a position to see whether they have had a common cause. The answer is that they have: the corporations' losses have in the main been due to the fact that they have flown, or at least tried to fly, British aircraft. This is not to say that BOAC has in other respects been perfect. Its engineering and maintenance costs were, during the late fifties, higher than those of most other airlines and it was slow to disengage from its loss-making subsidiaries. But these were relatively minor weaknesses which accounted for only a relatively small part of the Corporation's deficit. The short answer to the question of what has been wrong with the British air corporations is that there has been very little wrong with them but a lot wrong with British aircraft.

The only remarkable point about this conclusion is that the numerous official and semi-official inquiries on aviation have shied away from stating the obvious, and have taken it for granted that the air corporations should in general go on flying British. For instance, Mr Corbett having discovered that half of BOAC's accumulated deficit was due to the capital losses which had been incurred on (British) aircraft, failed to inquire whether they would have been avoided if foreign aircraft had been purchased, but found time to discuss at length the relatively trivial question of whether the Corporation should, by providing extra depreciation, have revealed its loss earlier.[86] The Minister of Aviation, in his White Paper on the Financial Problems of BOAC, followed Corbett's example and concentrated his attention on the Corporation's depreciation policy. In this way the impression was created that, apart from pure bad luck, all that was wrong was that too little had been set aside for obsolescence. The Select Committee's report on BOAC was a great advance on these shallow documents because the Committee made a serious attempt to discover what had gone wrong, and revealed the pressure to which the Corporation had been subjected when ordering the VC 10. However, the only moral which the Select Committee drew was that BOAC should have offered firmer resistance and, despite its findings, accepted the orthodox view that it was 'obviously desirable both for industrial and political reasons that, as far as possible, the air corporations should fly British aircraft. There have been a number of instances where it has been a big commercial advantage to have an aircraft tailor-made for their routes; airlines and manufacturers alike have benefited.'[87]

Is this true and have the corporations obtained an important commercial advantage from flying British which outweighs the disadvantages they have manifestly suffered? In the case of BOAC this view is wholly implausible because it is evident that, while the bulk of the Corporation's losses have been incurred as a result of flying British aircraft, the greater part of its profits have been earned with American planes. For instance, the large profits of recent years seem to have been primarily earned with Boeings and would probably have been higher but for the Corporation's relatively high-cost VC 10s. This scarcely supports the claim of a former Minister of Aviation, Julian Amery, that 'The smaller airlines of the world will, naturally, find it to their advantage to buy the best aircraft they can at the cheapest price off the shelf when they need them. A great airline like BOAC will find, I think, that over the years its interest is best served by being first in the field with a new aircraft built by its own national industry.'[88] Even if it were true that being first with new aircraft conferred any large or lasting advantage, which seems unlikely, it does not follow that BOAC should buy British. Although it may seem heresy to say so, there is nothing to prevent the Corporation from being first with American aircraft!

British European Airways, on the other hand, does appear at first sight to have benefited from flying British. This is because of its experience with the Viscount which was largely responsible for the corporation's swing from losses to profits in 1954–5 and formed the backbone of its fleet until 1961.[89] BEA was able to earn a profit with the subsequent British aircraft which it used and cannot, therefore, be said to have suffered greatly from flying British aircraft. Nevertheless it would have paid the Corporation to have bought foreign aircraft. For instance, instead of buying the Trident BEA should have purchased the Boeing 727 or possibly the French Caravelle. Although the Trident is a larger, faster and more economical aircraft than the Caravelle, the latter was already in service by the time the Trident was ordered, and could have been made available years before the British airliner, which was still on the drawing board and arrived late: a fact which cost BEA dear.

Indeed Hawker Siddeley and their predecessors were so slow to construct the Trident that although it had its first flight two years before the Boeing 727 the American plane was available first. Although a similar type of aircraft, it has the advantage of a better take-off performance, higher passenger capacity, greater range and probably slightly lower operating costs. If BEA had not been committed to the Trident, the Boeing 727 would have been the better buy and when in 1966 the Corporation found that it required extra jet aircraft it applied to the Government for sanction to purchase Boeing 727s and 737s. This was refused. As a result BEA has been obliged, at considerable extra expense, to purchase British aircraft, i.e. Trident 3 Bs and BAC 1/11s. Some measure of the extra cost is provided by the fact that the Government is providing BEA with £25–37½ million of compensation.[90] It must be concluded that, despite the Viscount, BEA's finances have been harmed by flying British aircraft or, in the case of its latest purchases, would be harmed but for the compensation which is being provided.

The British aircraft industry has not only been supported at the expense of the air corporations but also, as the case of the Trident 3 Bs and BAC 1/11s illustrates, out of money provided directly by the Exchequer. Between 1946 and 1958 the Government contributed £88 million to civil aircraft and aero-engine projects of which only about £25 million has been recovered. For a short period it was hoped that the industry could, with the air corporations as a crutch, stand on its own feet; but within a year the industry was struck by a financial crisis. As we have seen when examining the VC 10, Vickers was faced with heavy losses and the other aircraft manufacturers were beginning to encounter similar difficulties. In 1960 it was therefore decided to provide the industry with further public assistance. By mid-1967 the Government had either made or committed itself to an expenditure of £50 million of which it hoped to recover the £10 million which had been invested in engines but expected that most of the remainder would be a write-off. As the Plowden Committee reported 'Civil aircraft projects, with only few exceptions such as the Viscount and the Dart engine, have lost money both for the manufacturers and the Government.'[91]

This is not the place to make a full examination of whether the Government has been right to support the aircraft industry despite the heavy cost which this policy has imposed on the air corporations and the taxpayer. It is sufficient in a book on the nationalized industries to call attention to the devastating effect which the use of British aircraft has had on the finances of BOAC and the high price which is now being paid in order that BEA should fly British. This calls in question the policy of supporting the aircraft industry but does not by itself provide conclusive proof that the policy has been misguided. Nevertheless it is perhaps worth investigating briefly whether the financial well-being of the air corporations need have been sacrificed in the process of providing the aircraft manufacturers with a market. It is possible that the industry has required support, not because of the inevitable disadvantages under which it labours, but due to remediable weaknesses in its organization and policy. Indeed, it is conceivable that what has been wrong with the aircraft manufacturers is that they have been provided with too much assistance and too ready a market.

The aircraft industry itself takes what is more or less the opposite view and attributes its difficulties to the fact that its production runs are short, due to the small size of the British market. There is no doubt that long runs are a great advantage in aircraft production because they enable development costs to be spread thin and because, due to the complexity of the manufacturing process, it takes time to learn how to produce efficiently. To point to America's longer runs does not constitute a full defence against the charge of inefficiency. There is evidence not only that our manufacturers learn more slowly than the American but also that their productivity is about three times greater than our own. If British productivity were not so abysmally low we should, because wages are so high in the United States, be able to undersell the Americans despite their initial advantage of a large home market and long production runs.[92]

Moreover, the British industry's principal competitive weakness is not the high price of its aircraft, but the excessive time it takes to develop new projects, its failure to keep delivery dates and the protracted teething troubles which British planes so often encounter. That British aircraft arrive late and defective has been shown time and again by the treatment which the air corporations have experienced at the hands of the industry. None of the interim types of the immediate post-war period arrived on time and some of them did not arrive at all. Similarly, almost none of the modern aircraft which the corporations received in the fifties was able to be introduced on schedule. Turning to aircraft which have been introduced during the sixties, the Vanguard was about a year late into service, and the Tridents were delivered between six and 12 months behind time.[93]

The late delivery of British planes is only one aspect of the general tendency for the industry to be slow in developing and manufacturing aircraft. According to the Plowden Committee:

> The Americans are not necessarily quicker to initiate new projects; indeed, in the civil field they have started some recent aircraft later than comparable British aircraft. Thereafter, the statistics show that on average they develop and clear an aircraft for service in about a year less than British manufacturers. This ability to overtake a competitor after he has committed himself to an enterprise has proved a formidable advantage.[94]

It means, of course, that at any given time American planes will tend to be the most up-to-date aircraft on the market and that even if British aircraft appear to be superior, foreign operators can have some confidence that if they wait a year or two a more advanced American version will become available. Those who buy British will, on the other hand, run the risk of acquiring an inferior product especially if, like the British air corporations, they commit themselves years in advance. As the financial difficulties of BOAC show, the penalties in an extremely fast-moving industry of buying outmoded aircraft are considerable. This lesson has not been lost on foreign airlines such as Qantas, which long ago decided as a general policy not to fly British.[95]

Although by the time they finally arrive on the scene British aircraft have often been overtaken by events, it must not be imagined that our industry has been technically backward. Indeed what has tended to be wrong with British aircraft is that they have been too adventurous. This is illustrated by the Comet and the Britannia. It is doubtful whether the early Comets would long have remained a commercial proposition because they were designed at a time when jet engines were still at an early stage of development.[96] What happened with the Britannia was that Britain went ahead and built a long-haul turbo-prop aircraft at a time when the Americans did not consider that they had developed their engines sufficiently to construct one. Because of their greater caution the US manufacturers, by more or less avoiding the small jet and the large turbo-prop airlines, did not get stuck half-way towards the construction of the large jet in the same way as the British industry.[97] On the contrary, when the time was right, Boeings built their 707. This re-established America's decisive lead because the British manufacturers were unable to offer any convincing alternative.

Vickers, it is true, had with its V-1000 constructed a large jet and BOAC has been criticized for having refused to buy it. Yet BOAC was obviously right in believing that the V-1000 was no world-beater. Not only was it slower than the Boeing but it was much heavier per unit of capacity. As Messrs Miller and Sawers conclude in their authoritative and impartial study 'there is little reason to believe that the V-1000 could have been commercially competitive with the American airplanes . . . It might have been sold to BOAC instead of the 707, but the most likely outcome of its development would have been that this airline would have found itself operating a less efficient airplane than its competitors.' Fortunately the Corporation was spared this fate because the Government, presumably because it recognized that the Boeing was a superior plane, refused to give Vickers further assistance in developing the V-1000.[98]

One reason why British manufacturers rushed into the development of small jets and of large turbo-prop aircraft was their natural anxiety to establish a technical lead in a new field because the Americans already had a dominant position in the construction of conventional aircraft. However, it seems possible that the industry's lack of caution was also due to the fact that the air corporations were a captive market for its wares and

that the Government was contributing so generously to its development costs. The British industry could afford to make mistakes whereas
the American companies were restrained by normal commercial disci-
plines. If so, the large-scale support which the British aircraft manufacturers have received has had the perverse effect of reducing their
efficiency. That the industry has been inefficient and poorly managed is
scarcely open to doubt. Its productivity is disgracefully low, its development times are excessively long, and its delivery dates are more honoured
in the breach than the observance. If the industry had been more
efficient, it would have been better able to face American competition.
Even if it had been unable to dispense entirely with support from the
Government and the air corporations the aircraft industry would have
been a lighter burden for them to carry.

Instead of taking action to make the aircraft industry more efficient,
the Government has preferred to pay its bills with public money, to get
the air corporations to buy its inferior products, to hope that if the
companies were merged the sum would be greater than the parts and,
finally, to seek a European solution. Although joint ventures with the
European countries seem attractive the Concorde project suggests that
they have serious drawbacks. As one perceptive American observer has
commented: 'Concorde has the disadvantage of what appears to be the
higher cost of international collaboration. International collaboration
means the work must be divided between contractors in the two countries not only on the basis of efficiency but also on the basis of "fair shares".
Furthermore, in the Concorde project there are two final assembly lines,
one for each country.'[99] Moreover, international collaboration is likely,
as with Concorde, to mean the construction of highly advanced aircraft
which delight the eye of the politician and the aircraft designer. Their
justification is that they may put us a jump ahead of the Americans but
their danger is that they may be premature. It would be tragic if international collaboration led to a repetition of past mistakes. What is clear
is that joint projects with the European countries are unlikely to obviate
the need for a more efficient aircraft industry. As all else has failed, the
Government should put the industry under new management and stop
sacrificing the efficiency of the air corporations to the inefficiency of the
aircraft industry.

PART THREE

Investment

CHAPTER 13

Investment and Demand

IN this Chapter we begin, in earnest, our investigation of the nationalized industries' allocative efficiency by embarking on an examination of how they have framed their investment programmes. By way of introduction a brief look will be taken at how their capital expenditure and share of national investment have changed over the years. This is shown in Table 23. It is evident that the public enterprise sector has been exceptionally capital intensive and that the nationalized industries' investment policy demands the detailed attention which it will be accorded in this part of the book. In 1968 the nationalized industries produced about 7 per cent of the national income but they were responsible for 14 per cent of national investment and in the previous year the figure was 16·7 per cent.

These overall statistics are, however, somewhat misleading because they obscure the enormous variation in the capital intensity of the different nationalized industries. On the one hand, there were the nationalized industries whose investment was exceptionally large in relation to their output, i.e. gas, which in 1967 invested £1·19 for every £1 which it contributed to the national income; electricity, which invested £0·88; and the air corporations, which spent £0·36 and about double this amount during the following year. On the other hand, there were those nationalized industries whose capital expenditure was relatively small in relation to their production; British Rail invested only £0·2 for every £1 which it contributed, and the Coal Board a mere £0·14.[1] These figures should not be pressed too far because the industries' investment fluctuates widely; for instance the gas industry's figure was abnormally large because its programme for converting to natural gas was at its height. Nevertheless, the figures do give some idea of the capital output ratios of the various undertakings.

Although during 1968 the public enterprise sector's share of national investment was a high one it was lower than at any time since 1948. Furthermore, it was lower than that of the same industries before the war. During the first decade of public ownership the sector's proportion of total investment crept slowly upwards as the industries' modernization and expansion programmes got under way.[2] By 1958 they were accounting for 18·2 per cent of total capital expenditure and in the following year their proportion rose to an all-time high of 18·7 per cent. After this the proportion fell back and fluctuated around 16 per cent. With investment in coal and railways past its peak it was only sustained at this level by the upsurge in electricity investment between 1962 and 1966, and more latterly by the natural gas conversion programme. With electricity investment falling sharply and gas investment, though still high, already in decline there was a considerable fall in the volume of public enterprise investment between 1967 and 1968, and a slump in the sector's share of the national total.

This was no freak result but a trend which will continue for some years. Electricity investment will go on falling until about 1971 and in gas capital expenditure will fall away gradually. As a result the nationalized industries' capital formation will probably decline from about £1,100 million in 1968 to around £900 million in 1974–5. By 1973–4 it will, due to an upturn in electricity investment, be somewhat higher but will probably only total around £1,050 million. As national investment will go on rising, the nationalized industries' share will fall sharply. In 1974–5 it will probably be only about 10 per cent though the figure is subject to a wide margin of error.[3] Thereafter the proportion may, though this is little more than a guess, start to rise as investment by the electricity industry gets back into its stride. However, it seems improbable that the public enterprise share of national investment will fully recover to its past level.

The fact that the public enterprise sector's share of investment is lower now than it has ever been does not prove that it is economically justified; but it does suggest that statements about the misuse of investment by the nationalized industries should be treated with caution. They are usually made in the belief, and indeed often seem to rest upon the supposition, that their capital expenditure had been rising exceptionally fast. For instance Aims of Industry, in a memorandum presented to the Select Committee, prefaces its criticisms of the nationalized industries' investment with the declaration that 'The public corporations are taking an increasing share of the available resources. In 1956 it was 19 per cent. In 1966 it was 22 per cent. It is reasonable to ask whether this trend should be allowed to continue.'[4] But it is also reasonable to ask whether this really is the trend. What among other things Aims of Industry overlooked, or ignored, was that in the National Income and Expenditure Bluebook, from which it took its figures, the Post Office has only been treated as a public corporation since 1961 and that its inclusion accounts for most of the apparent rise in the corporations' share of national investment over the period 1956–66. Including the Post Office, but excluding nationalized steel, the public corporations' share rose from 21 per cent

Investment and Demand

Table 23

GROSS FIXED INVESTMENT 1938–68 (£ million)

	Electricity	Coal	Railways	Gas	BEA and BOAC	Public Enterprise Sector[1]	Per cent of Total UK Fixed Investment
1938	42	8	24	11	1	91	14·9
1948	97	22	40	25	9	205	14·4
1949	120	28	42	29	13	250	15·9
1950	135	26	44	33	9	266	15·6
1951	146	27	44	40	8	283	15·0
1952	156	40	40	46	9	316	15·0
1953	177	55	54	47	13	388	16·4
1954	211	70	65	53	12	448	17·6
1955	243	77	69	59	20	492	17·4
1956	243	82	89	51	26	514	16·6
1957	260	91	124	53	41	592	17·5
1958	292	96	138	51	39	635	18·2
1959	336	105	167	46	27	698	18·7
1960	333	79	171	44	46	692	16·8
1961	360	86	153	42	37	698	15·1
1962	406	81	118	57	25	704	14·9
1963	503	75	96	81	29	804	16·4
1964	600	83	107	86	40	937	16·0
1965	645	75	120	102	36	1,003	15·9
1966	707	76	109	186	22	1,130	16·8
1967	681	79	95	283	45	1,211	16·7
1968	584	58	99	221	99	1,092	14·0

[1] Includes BRS, Nationalized Buses and the NCB's investment outside the coal industry.

Source: C. H. Feinstein *Domestic Capital Formation in the United Kingdom 1920–1938* pp 82, 90, 177, 244, 245; NIE 1969 p 72 etc.; MDSD 1968–9 p 114 for deduction for Northern Ireland's electricity investment; Information from CSO on Air Corporations; THC 1968 p 67 etc.; LTB 1968 pp 68, 70 etc.; NCB 1968–9. 2 p 16 etc.

in 1956 to 21·6 per cent in 1966, but then fell to 20·1 per cent in 1968.[5]

We can turn now to the question of how the nationalized industries have fixed the level and distribution of their investment. Investment planning is a difficult undertaking because so many factors are involved and because they are all inter-dependent. As the National Coal Board explained in its first plan for the industry, it was faced at the outset

> with a series of circular arguments. Thus the future demand for coal depends on price, for export sales to a large extent and for home sales to a less extent; price turns on costs of production and delivery; costs on how much coal has to be produced, of what kinds, and where, which in turn depends on the demand. The circle is complete. Similarly, costs of production depend on wages, but wages may depend among other things on manpower needs; they in turn depend on production plans which themselves depend on costs of production in the future. Costs, again, depend on production techniques, production techniques on capital investment and capital investment on costs.

If anything the NCB made the problem of investment planning sound too simple because it did not mention the coal industry's dependence on the rest of the economy. For instance, as the Coal Board was well aware, the demand for coal would depend on what happened to its customers and to its competitors.[6] The planning problems which the Board faced were not only circular but also circuitous.

The Coal Board recognized that it was necessary to break the circle and make certain key estimates which could later be reviewed in the light of other calculations. The NCB began by making an estimate of the future demand for its product, and demand forecasts seem also to have been the starting point for the plans of the other nationalized industries. Our first task, therefore, will be to review the demand estimates which the various nationalized industries have made. How accurate have their forecasts been? Were they reasonable in the situation in which they were made? These are some of the principal questions which we shall try to answer. Because of the amount of ground to be covered and for other reasons, such as the availability of information, it seems best to confine our attention to three of the nationalized industries – coal, railways and electricity.

Sales Forecasts for Coal

In *Plan for Coal*, which was published in 1950, the NCB forecast that sales would increase from 215 million tons in 1949 to around 240 million in 1961–5. This gives a rather misleading impression of the rise which was expected because much more coal could have been exported in 1949 if it had been available, and but for rationing the demand for house coal would have been somewhat higher. According to the Ridley Committee's estimates the demand for British coal totalled up to 240 million tons in 1951. The Board's estimate for the early sixties was based partly on estimates of demand provided by the main consuming industries, such as electricity and steel, and partly on an analysis of past trends. These were extremely difficult to interpret. If home demand continued to rise as it had since the war for only another five years it would reach 215 million tons, but pre-war trends suggested an inland demand of not more than 190 million tons in the long run. The range of demand for which the Board finally plumped was 205–15 million tons. Export prospects were even more difficult to judge but these were guessed at 25–35 million tons.[7] In view of the export drive the Board could hardly have suggested a lower figure.

In the event the NCB's estimate turned out to be much too high. During the period 1961–5 the demand for British coal averaged only 195 million tons and the figure would have been lower in the absence of the support which the industry received.[8] Yet it is difficult to see how, at the time, a better forecast could have been made. Although with the wisdom of hindsight the Coal Board's forecasts may seem over-optimistic, they were considerably more realistic than other authoritative estimates made at about the same time. Far from being criticized for having set its sights so high the Board was blamed for being so cautious. For instance, in 1952 the Ridley Committee forecast that in 1959–63 the overall demand for coal would be somewhere between 257 and 267 million tons. It thought that inland demand would, at 232 million tons, be considerably higher than the Board's estimate but agreed that export demand would total between 25 and 35 million tons. The Committee concluded that 'in order to be able to meet prospective demands over the next decade in full, the National Coal Board may have to accelerate and expand their plans for future output'.[9] The Ridley Committee's estimates seemed pessimistic in comparison with other forecasts. The Federation of British Industries in its evidence to the Committee argued that the demand for coal would reach 283 million tons in the early sixties and concluded that 'on present trends, a true shortage which is now 10 to 20 million tons will by 1960–5 have grown to some 50 million tons.[10] Like Ridley the FBI was 'pessimistic' about exports.

The dispassionate academic view was that export markets would expand. 'It is difficult not to conclude,' wrote Mr Ian Little, 'that the estimate of 25–35 million tons foreign demand in 1961 is very conservative.

Allowing for the same rate of economic growth in Europe as in England, it is not unlikely that we could sell twice as much as this if we could produce it.' There was, he concluded, 'little or no risk of producing too much coal for as long as one cares to think'.[11] Another prophet from Oxford was Mr Anthony Crosland. In *Britain's Economic Problem* he described the National Coal Board's export forecast as 'disturbing' and found its projection of internal demand 'even more curious'. A further sustained rise in demand was certain, and all the indications were that demand would be 'much nearer to 300 million tons than to 240 million'. He ended by calling for 'a clear directive to the Coal Board . . . to ensure that its long-term investment plan, already behind schedule, shall be not merely maintained but enlarged'.[12]

The Coal Board made much greater allowance than these 'experts' for fuel saving and the competition which it would have to meet from the oil industry.[13] For this it deserves considerable credit. What was less creditable was the NCB's gradual conversion to the view that there would always be a ready market for whatever it was able to produce. By 1956 the process was complete: 'Even in the longer term', the Board declared, 'the problems of over-production for the coal industry can scarcely arise'.[14] Save for a brief interval, the Coal Board's production target remained at 240 million tons. In 1954 after the publication of the Ridley Report, and after the electricity industry had increased its estimates of future demand, the Board had tentatively increased the figure to 250 million tons. This was the maximum amount which the Board thought that it would be able to produce. But when a full-scale revision of the plan was made, the results of which were published in *Investing in Coal*, it was decided that an output of 250 million tons could not be attained before 1970.[15] Although the Coal Board was foolish to rule out the possibility of over-production it was in distinguished company. The German coal industry, which is largely in private ownership, was expecting a very large rise in output. In 1957 the Ruhr coal owners' association reported that the colliery undertakings were planning to increase their capacity from 125 million tons in 1956 to 165 million tons in 1975, which represents an increase of a third.[16] Moreover, the experts who were saying that over-production was impossible at the beginning of the fifties were shouting it by the middle of the decade. *Investing in Coal* appeared almost at the same time as the report of the OEEC's Hartley Commission which called upon member countries to increase their coal production as a matter of urgency. The Commission foresaw a growing shortage of coal and was seriously concerned that large imports of oil would be necessary in order to bridge the gap between energy requirements and coal supplies.[17]

Only a few years after the Hartley Commission had spoken the demand for coal started to decline, and in 1958 it became evident that the coal shortage was over for good. The industry had, therefore, to prepare new forecasts of its sales and these were published during 1959 in the Board's *Revised Plan for Coal*. It was estimated that in 1965 demand would total about 206 million tons. This was almost the same figure as in 1958 when the industry sold rather less than 208 million tons. However, the estimate was largely based on information provided by the main consuming industries, and the division of sales expected in 1965 differed considerably from the actual division in 1958.[18] Until about 1963, when 201½ million tons were sold, this estimate appeared reasonably accurate, although the industry was by this time receiving considerable support. But after 1963 demand again started to decline rapidly and by 1965 it was down to 188 million tons. The Board's estimates turned out too high for each of the main categories of demand except electricity, which increased its coal consumption even more than had been foreseen. The iron and steel industry on the other hand wildly overstated its consumption. If the NCB had not been misled by the Iron and Steel Board its estimate of consumption would not have been too wide of the mark. It was assumed in the *Revised Plan* that in 1965 the production of coke would require 35 million tons of coal but the figure turned out to be only about 26 million tons.[19] The steel industry's estimates of its needs have, over the years, been consistently excessive and explain a large part of the failure of successive demand estimates for coal.[20] Moreover, the Coal Board was led into an expensive but abortive programme of constructing coke ovens, so as to be able to supply the steel industry.[21]

Although the Coal Board's forecast that demand would not fall below 200 million tons by 1965 proved wrong it is again difficult to criticize the Board for having been over-optimistic. Not only was this figure largely based on estimates supplied by other industries which appeared reasonably trustworthy but it was endorsed by expert opinion. Only a few months after the *Revised Plan* was published the OEEC's Robinson Commission reported that demand could be expected to lie between 205 million and 220 million tons in 1965, though it considered that it would probably be closer to the lower figure.[22] As late as 1963 NEDC concluded that although the coal industry would have a hard struggle to reach its sales target of 200 million tons in 1966 it might well get fairly close.[23] Even later Mr G. F. Ray in his contribution to the National Institute's authoritative forecast of the British economy in 1975 argued that it was 'reasonable to assume that the coal industry will succeed in maintaining a home market of around 190 million tons a year, and total output, including exports, of around 200 million tons a year.[24] It was not only the experts who failed to foresee the coal industry's débâcle. The oil companies do not even appear to have seen what was coming although it is they who have obtained the lion's share of the market which coal has lost. They certainly failed to appreciate how fast the demand for their products was rising. In 1966 domestic consumption of petroleum products was 12 per cent higher than the oil companies had forecast in 1962 and total sales, including exports, were about 20 per cent greater.[25]

The Coal Board has, during recent years, continued to predict a high demand for coal despite the way in which its sales have been falling. But the Board's target figures cannot be regarded as a serious forecast of what is likely to happen. They have been part of its campaign to maintain morale within the industry and to obtain greater support from the Government. The Board have adopted Marx's dictum and are trying to change the world rather than to understand it. This would be very worrying if there was reason to believe that the industry's investment policy is affected by the optimistic sales targets which it puts forward; but this is no longer the case because the Board's capital expenditure is not designed to increase its capacity and is concentrated on a relatively small number of pits which have good prospects.[26] Demand forecasts have become a minor element in the Board's investment planning.

The Railways' Demand Estimates

The Railway Modernization Plan of 1954 assumed that there would be a modest increase in traffic. It was expected that rail freight receipts would, allowing for some reduction in charges, increase by about 6 per cent during the following 15 to 20 years.[27] On the passenger side it was forecast that receipts would rise by about 10 per cent between 1953 and 1974.[28] The estimates for freight, which were said to have been based on consultations with many branches of industry and trade, assumed that industrial production would increase by not less than 2 per cent per annum and that there would be a progressive increase in the overall demand for freight transport. However, little or no increase in rail carryings of general merchandise was expected. 'On balance,' concluded the Planning Committee of Chief Officers, 'it has not been considered wise at this stage to contemplate an increase in the tonnage of general merchandise by rail. There will certainly be changes in the composition and flows of traffic, with an increase in the relative importance of longer-distance movements.'[29] On the other hand, it was believed that there would be some increase in coal and steel traffic. It was expected that coal production would increase from 224 million tons in 1953 to about 250 million tons in 1964 and that rail carryings of coal and coke would increase roughly in line from 175 million tons to 190–95 million tons. On the basis that steel production would increase from $17\frac{1}{2}$ million ingot tons in 1953 to 25–28 million ingot tons in 1974 it was thought that rail carryings of raw materials would increase from 26 to 40 million tons and that traffic in steel products would rise from 19 to 20–22 million tons.[30]

Although these estimates are turning out to be badly wrong it is difficult to accuse the railways of having been guilty of over-optimism. In 1953 the volume of rail traffic in ton miles was 5 per cent greater than it had been in 1948 and the railways had, during recent years, just about maintained their share of inland goods transport. It is true that their carryings of general merchandise had fallen by $4\frac{1}{2}$ per cent since 1948 and that road competition could be expected to intensify with the denationalization of road haulage. However, the railways were hoping that in future their own competitive power would be greater partly because modernization would improve the quality of their service and partly because the new Railway Charges Scheme would enable them to bid more effectively for the traffics which it was remunerative for them to carry.[31] In the circumstances it would certainly have been unreasonable for the BTC to expect any large increase in their general merchandise carryings but, as we have seen, they did not. The railways' forecast that their coal traffic would increase somewhat was certainly not over-optimistic granted the Coal Board's plans for higher coal production. These have, of course, turned out to be wrong but it is hardly fair to criticize the Transport Commission for not having foreseen this when scarcely anyone else did.

Nor were the Commission's forecasts of higher steel traffic visionary. They were based on an estimate of steel production which has already turned out to be too low. In 1965 the industry produced 27 million ingot tons compared with the Transport Commission's figure of about $26\frac{1}{2}$ million by 1974. Even at the time this must have appeared cautious. In 1952 the British Iron and Steel Federation had forecast that demand would reach 21 million tons in 1957–8. This estimate was already beginning to look inadequate by the time of the Planning Committee, while its own forecast implied that production would only rise by about 2 per cent per annum between 1953 and 1974.[32] The Transport Commission was again cautious when it came to translating its figure for future steel production into rail carryings of steel products. Though it expected that production would increase by about 50 per cent over the next 20 years it only forecast a 5–15 per cent growth in rail traffic. In contrast rail carryings of raw materials were expected to increase roughly in line with production. This was rather surprising as the Commission's Planning Committee foresaw a number of developments, such as the increased use of high-grade ore from abroad, would restrict the railways' opportunities. But, on balance, the Committee's estimates for steel traffic do not appear to have been wildly over-optimistic. It is easy enough for Mr Christopher Foster with the wisdom of hindsight to attribute the financial failure of the Modernization Plan to faulty demand analysis, but could he have done better at the time?[33]

Where the Transport Commission can legitimately be criticized is for not recognizing that their traffic was in decline when in 1959 they prepared their Re-appraisal of the Plan. It was forecast that freight receipts in 1963 would be about the same as in 1957 because although a reduction in general merchandise charges was anticipated it was expected that there would be a small increase in the overall volume of traffic. The use of 1957 as the starting point gave, however, a misleading impression of the increase which was expected because the volume of freight traffic in ton miles was 12 per cent lower in 1958 than it had been in 1957. Moreover since it was expected that there would be a slight fall in coal traffic between 1958 and 1963, the Commission must have been expecting a very considerable rise in carryings of minerals and general merchandise. This was surely unrealistic: the volume of rail traffic had decreased every year since 1953 with the exception of 1956, when the railways were assisted by the fuel restrictions due to the Suez crisis. General merchandise was for instance down by 23 per cent.[34] One of the reasons for the railways' optimism was that they hoped that when the recession which had hit them so hard came to an end their traffic would bounce back to its old level. But experience had already shown that a ratchet process was at work and that once traffic was lost it tended not to return. This is not merely being wise after the event. As I wrote at the time: 'The Re-appraisal with customary optimism estimates that in 1963 the amount of freight which the railways carry will be slightly higher than in 1957. The railways will do well if they regain their 1957 position.'

On the passenger side the Re-appraisal was equally unrealistic. It assumed that there would be a 17 per cent increase in the volume of passenger traffic between 1958 and 1963. Past experience suggested that it was over-optimistic to expect such a large increase. Since 1953 there had been an increase of only $7\frac{1}{2}$ per cent.[35] Moreover, future prospects were not bright. As I commented:

The fact that the railways will have to face increasing competition from cars indicates that the estimate is over-optimistic. Doubtless as the Re-appraisal argues the railways will become cleaner and more reliable as modernization proceeds. But however good the railways become, families will continue to purchase cars. In late 1957 only 24 per cent of families possessed a car. By 1965 the figure will probably be about 45 per cent. The Re-appraisal states that in making its estimate full allowance has been made for the growth in private cars. This statement is not credible.

Far from increasing between 1958 and 1963, rail traffic declined both for coal and for other traffic. Of course 1963 was a year of industrial recession, but even if we compare the boom year 1964 with the recession year 1958 it appears that, even when coal is excluded, traffic failed to increase.[36] Yet the railways remained hopeful that the tide would soon turn. They forecast for the National Plan that between 1964 and 1970 there would be an increase of 17 per cent in freight ton miles and 3 per cent in passenger miles, though the latter figure includes London Transport where the opening of the Victoria line was expected to generate extra traffic.[37] The estimate that freight traffic would increase by as much as 17 per cent was from the start wildly over-optimistic. As British Rail was expecting a decline in its coal traffic it must have been hoping for a very large increase in its iron and steel and general merchandise business. Indeed, a rise of about 40 per cent seems to have been expected.[38]

It is evident that the railways' forecasts have, over the years, become less and less realistic. The estimate of future traffic which was made at the time of the Modernization Plan was cautious although it has turned out to be wrong; the forecast given in the Re-appraisal was clearly over-optimistic; and the estimate prepared for the National Plan was a flight of fancy. The explanation for this retreat from reality is that the future has become too unpleasant for the railways to face. As their prospects have deteriorated so those in charge have engaged in more and more wishful thinking because they have been unwilling to recognize that the industry was in decline. This explains in particular why, as the outlook for coal traffic has become more gloomy, their forecasts for other goods have become more and more optimistic, although past experience has offered less and less hope for the future. In 1954, when some increase in coal traffic was to be expected, little or no increase in carryings of general merchandise were forecast; in 1959 when it was clear that coal traffic would not rise, a considerable increase in general merchandise was expected; in 1965 when the prospects for coal were even more gloomy it was hoped that there would be a large rise in carryings of merchandise. Obviously a compensatory process was at work.

Yet it would be wrong to take too critical a view of the railways' forecasting. Although their more recent estimates of general merchandise traffic were unrealistic it was not unreasonable for them to expect some increase in their carryings, although they had been falling. At the time of the Re-appraisal the railways were hoping that the improvement in the quality of their service which modernization would bring about, and the reductions in their charges which they planned to make, would produce extra traffic. In view of the way in which their general merchandise had been falling, it was obviously unwise of the Transport Commission to assume that there would be a large increase. But was it, on the other hand, reasonable to expect that the ton mileage of all traffic apart from coal would fall, as it did, by 6 per cent between 1958 and 1963?[39] Again the railways were foolish to expect that in 1970 this traffic would be up to 40 per cent higher than in 1964, but who would have forecast that, despite the manifest improvement in standards of service and the apparent reduction in charges, its volume would during 1968 be 2 per cent lower than in 1964?[40] Moreover, while guilty of wishful thinking so far as their general traffic is concerned, it is difficult to convict British Rail of over-optimism about their carryings of coal. They did not foresee the way in which the demand for coal would collapse, but then who did?

Electricity Forecasts

The electricity industry prepares estimates of future demand each year. In the days of the British Electricity Authority the programme of new generating plant was fixed by the Authority in the light of demand estimates made independently by the Area Boards and by its own staff. Since the creation of the Electricity Council three sets of forecasts have been made. The Generating Board makes a forecast based on past trends; the Area Boards make estimates which, though largely based on past trends, also take into account local developments in industry and housing; and the Electricity Council makes a forecast after examining past trends and the way in which the economy is likely to develop. These estimates are then brought together and discussed, and a final national estimate for which the Electricity Council takes responsibility is prepared. Although the forecast covers a number of years the most important figure is the estimate of maximum demand five years ahead because this is the time which it takes to commission new plant and because it is the maximum demand on the system which determines the amount of plant which is necessary.[41]

In the case of this crucial estimate there was an average error of 7·7 per cent in the forecasts which the industry prepared each year from 1947 to 1961. This was the average amount by which the maximum demand, adjusted to standard weather conditions, was above or below the estimated demand. With the exception of the last of these estimates, made in 1961, the forecasts were consistently on the low side.[42] In the earlier post-war years the industry may have partly discounted the recent growth in its sales, attributing part of it to temporary factors, such as the shortage of coal, and the exceptional rate at which industrial production was growing. The fact that the amount of plant which the industry could install was restricted may also have affected its forecasting. But the main reason why demand was persistently underestimated was the general belief, within the industry, that sales could not go on increasing indefinitely at the enormous rate at which they had in the past.[43] Demand forecasts were therefore pitched somewhat below the long-term trend. For instance it was assumed, in 1958, that maximum demand would increase by about 6 per cent per annum although the average increase since 1948 had been 7 per cent.[44]

During 1959–60 and again in 1960–61, 1961–2 and 1962–3 peak demand increased by about 9 per cent after adjusting for weather conditions. This led to the adoption of progressively higher forecasts of the long-term increase in demand. By May 1962 the industry was basing its plans on the assumption that it would rise by about 7·9 per cent each year. This was below the rate of increase during the recent past and only slightly higher than the average increase during the preceding decade of 7·6 per cent.[45] The industry's forecasts were also based on the assumption that the rate of economic growth would be stepped up. In 1962, after consulting the Treasury and the Ministry of Power, the Electricity Council assumed that the national income would increase at an average rate of 3·3 per cent between 1960 and 1970 compared with the figure of 2·5 per cent during the previous 10 years. The National Economic Development Council had, of course, just been appointed and was already studying the implications of a 4 per cent rate of growth. In 1963 after this target had been adopted the industry agreed, at the Government's request, to base its forecasts on this rate. As a result it was now assumed by the Council that demand would rise by $9\frac{1}{2}$ per cent per annum. This barely satisfied the Neddy growth men who thought that demand might rise even faster.[46]

In the event, the four fat years of booming demand were succeeded by five lean years. Between 1962–3 and 1968–9 the maximum demand increased at an average rate of only 4·2 per cent per annum allowing for the weather. As a result the forecasts made during the early sixties are turning out to be over-estimates. The crucial five-year forecasts made in 1961 and 1962 for 1966–7 and 1967–8 were too high by 7·6 per cent and 20·8 per cent respectively. The estimate made in 1963 for 1968–9, which Neddy inspired, was still more excessive. It was a third above the actual figure.[47] Although its forecasts have proved wrong the electricity industry does not appear to be open to serious criticism. The assumption which it made in the fifties that the growth in sales would slow down looked ridiculous in the early sixties when electricity sales were booming, but it seems less foolish today. Yet it is difficult to blame the industry for abandoning this assumption after a succession of estimates had proved to be on the low side, and when the growth of demand seemed, if anything, to be increasing. Had the Electricity Council assumed that demand would increase at a much faster rate than it had in the past it would have been guilty of over-optimism. But even in 1962 the Council's estimates were pitched only slightly above the long-term trend. It was not until Neddy came on the scene that forecasting became wild but the industry cannot be held responsible for this episode.

The Select Committee on Nationalized Industries has suggested that errors in forecasting may have been due to lack of information and defective methods. The Committee reported that

> when the Generating Board was set up in 1958 Sir Christopher Hinton introduced the method of forecasting by projecting the curve of demand on a basis of compound interest. It is said that, if this method had been used in the past, the shortages of capacity would not have been nearly so marked. Thus the forecasts made in 1953 governing the generating capacity for 1959–60 were rather more than 10 per cent below actual demand. If the Generating Board's method had been used, the error would have been less than 2 per cent.[48]

No wonder the industry has got its estimates wrong if it did not even discover compound interest until 1958! This is nonsense. All that happened was that Sir Christopher adopted one out of a number of mathematical techniques for discerning the trend of demand. In forecasting there is no *a priori* way of knowing which is the best method to employ and no guarantee that the technique which, had it been used in the past, would have given the best results, will be the most accurate in the future. The fact that the industry underestimated demand was not due to its inability to see how demand had been increasing in the past, but to its assumption that it would increase at a slower rate in years to come. Correspondingly the way in which the CEGB over-estimated the growth of demand in the early sixties, despite Sir Christopher's wonder method, was due to the failure of the premise on which all such methods are based: the assumption that the future will be like the past.

The Select Committee's other criticism of the industry was that its forecasting was poor because there had been too little market research.

> During the years in which the 'explosion' of domestic sales was happening [the Committee concluded] the industry was not in close enough touch

with consumers to learn of the big change in the nature of demand that was taking place. Consequently the industry's forecasts of demand did not take account of the changing character of the rapidly rising domestic consumption nor of the extent to which it was contributing to the peak demand.[49]

The Committee seems to be assuming here that peak demand was increasing faster than total demand and that it was the industry's failure to foresee this that was responsible for its bad forecasting. This was not true. What the industry failed to foresee was the explosion of domestic sales rather than the extent to which this explosion would contribute to peak demand.[50] Whether the industry's forecasts would have been much better if it carried out more research is open to doubt. The Committee was much impressed by the fact that between 1955 and 1961 there was no major survey of domestic demand, which it regarded as a major omission.[51] The large investigations which the Electricity Council undertook from 1961 did not enable it to foresee that the growth of electricity consumption would slow up. No doubt the Council should arm itself with as much information as possible and no doubt surveys ought to have been carried out more frequently, but the Select Committee was a little naïve to imagine that information about the past is a crystal ball for the future.

Although there have been intelligible reasons for the forecasts which the electricity industry has made, and although some of the criticisms of its methods have not been well directed, it nevertheless seems possible that its estimating could have been better. This is suggested by the fact that the American electricity industry's forecasting has been perceptibly more accurate than that of the British electricity authorities, although the difference has not been dramatic. The Federal Power Commission has analysed the forecasts which American utilities reported between 1951 and 1960 for peak demand four peaks ahead. For instance, in January 1951, the utilities reported their forecasts for the peak during 1954 which would mainly have occurred in December. The amount by which the forecasts were above or below the actual figures averaged 3·6 per cent. In contrast the estimates by the Electricity Council and its predecessors, which were prepared between 1951 and 1960 for the fourth winter ahead, showed an average error of 4·9 per cent; and over the period 1947–62 the deviation was almost exactly the same. Moreover, the American estimates were probably rather better than they appear because the forecasts were compared with the crude figures for maximum demand before allowing for the state of the weather. For Britain the figures for maximum demand were adjusted to standard weather conditions.[52]

It is, of course, possible that it is more difficult to estimate the future demand for electricity in this country than it is in America. The year-to-year variation in the growth of demand might, for instance, be greater here than it is in the United States. If so, this would make estimating more difficult because it is obviously harder to take aim on a boat which is rocking up and down than on one which is sailing calmly along. But, over the period 1951–60, the increase in maximum demand compared with the previous year ranged only from 5·9 per cent to 9·2 per cent after allowing for the state of the weather. Unfortunately, there do not seem to be any temperature-corrected figures for the United States but it is difficult to believe that the year-to-year variation can have been much less than it was in Britain.

Conclusions

One of the most striking points which emerges from this Chapter is that the predictions of outside experts and organizations have tended to be even less accurate than those which the industries have prepared for themselves. Although the Coal Board's estimates have been far too high, it was more realistic and cool-headed than the numerous academics, committees and international organizations which tried to forecast the demand for coal, although the Board gradually fell under the influence of these false prophets. Again, in electricity, the excessive forecasts which the industry made during the early sixties would have been even more wild if it had listened to the NEDC. The railways appear to be an exception to the rule that outside experts are able to foretell the future even less accurately than those in the industry itself. Here it could be seen, and to some extent was seen, that the railway's estimates were over-optimistic. This was almost certainly because those who were in charge of the railways were reluctant to admit that their industry was in decline because the truth was too painful for them to bear. In contrast, those outside the industry were in a better position to see the obvious because they were not personally involved. This is confirmed by the Coal Board's apparent refusal to recognize how fast and how far the demand for coal is falling. The one circumstance, therefore, in which the outside expert or the Government may be able to read the future more accurately than the industry itself is where it is in decline. Although this conclusion has been stated boldly, it is nevertheless only a tentative judgment because a far more extensive investigation would have to be undertaken before one could be at all certain that this was the right interpretation, but it does seem likely that a study of other industries would confirm what has been said. Instances can readily be found of declining industries which have refused to recognize what was happening. Examples can also be found of centrally-controlled industries whose demand forecasts seem to have been reasonably accurate. In contrast, the estimates of outside experts and planning bodies have tended to be wide of the mark.

This has been partly but only partly because they have, like the NEDC and the old Department of Economic Affairs, been trying to change the future rather than to predict it or, like the Cambridge Growth Project or the Beckerman team, to see what a faster rate of growth would imply. No doubt if the NEDC and the DEA had succeeded in persuading businessmen to follow their plans the gains from extra growth would have outweighed the losses from any reduction in the efficiency with which resources are allocated. However, this defence of the British experiment in planning is more convincing in theory than in practice for what should have been obvious from the beginning was that the Government had almost no means by which it could induce private firms to raise their sights. In practice, therefore, planning degenerated into an attempt to talk up the rate of growth and to hope that if the electricity industry based its plans on 4 per cent growth the rest of British industry would do likewise. Both these hopes were naturally disappointed and the only practical result, apart from the discrediting of planning, was the over-expansion of the electricity industry. If this had simply meant excess capacity the results would not have been too dire, for the industry would have been able to scrap some of its old high-cost generating plant. But this has not been possible because the industry's attempt to provide capacity for 4 per cent growth appears to have disrupted its entire investment programme, and has led to serious delays in the completion of new power stations.[53] The lesson to be learnt from this episode is the impossibility of planning the economy by directing the nationalized industries. If the economy were more mixed than it is and if the nationalized industries included the 'commanding heights' the situation might be different, but at present any such attempt to plan through the nationalized industries is foredoomed to failure.

The most obvious conclusion to be drawn from the failure of the planners to see the future any more clearly than the nationalized industries is the extreme difficulty of making accurate forecasts. Although as outsiders they may not, except where demand has been declining, have been in the best position to see what was going to happen, the extent to which they have been in error has nevertheless been impressive. It is not only the outsiders who have been unable to see what was going to happen. The plans made by the German coal owners have proved no more realistic than those of the National Coal Board and the collapse of coal demand was not even foreseen by the oil companies who have been the chief beneficiaries. There is therefore no reason to believe that if the coal industry had been under different management or, like the German coal industry and the oil companies under private ownership, its forecasting would have been any better. The British coal industry failed to foresee the future not because it was blind or in public ownership but because the future was unforeseeable. As coal forms an important part of rail traffic it must also be concluded that British Rail should be partly excused for not having seen how its carryings were going to slump. And the estimates for other traffic which lay behind the Modernization Plan were reasonable in the situation in which they were made, even though they have proved wrong. What was less excusable was the optimistic estimates which the railways subsequently made for their non-coal traffic at a time when it was declining. Although the railways were foolish to forecast a large increase, there were grounds for supposing that the decline would be reversed and they cannot be blamed for not having seen how dismal their prospects were.

CHAPTER 14

Capital and Yield

ALTHOUGH estimates of future demand are usually the first stage in investment planning they do not, by themselves, provide an undertaking with any clear guidance as to how much capital it should spend. The need for extra capacity, for instance, is by no means the only reason for investment. Capital expenditure will be desirable if large savings in costs can be made by replacing old and obsolete equipment by new, or by substituting machinery for men. For this and other reasons it is vital that firms should not only estimate the likely demand for their products but also try to calculate what return is to be had from investing in plant and machinery. This may seem too obvious to need saying but both in public and private enterprise the obvious has often been ignored.

The Costing of the Coal Plans

Indeed it has been argued that some of the nationalized industries have even failed to prepare satisfactory estimates of the cost of their investment projects. Our first task, therefore, will be to discover how accurate have been the nationalized industries' forecasts of the costs of their schemes. It is clearly impossible to make calculations of the rate of return on capital expenditure if you do not even know how much you are going to spend!

Yet the Select Committee on Nationalized Industries has drawn attention to what it described as 'the early and substantial failure of the 1949 *Plan for Coal*'. According to the Committee it had been

> planned to produce 240 million tons of coal (not including open-cast coal) a year in 1961–5, at a total cost of £635 million at 1949 prices . . . By 1956, the difficulties facing the industry could be better assessed, and in that year a new programme – *Investing in Coal* – was brought out . . . The new plan still envisaged an output of 240 million tons of coal (but, this time, it included open-cast production of 10 million tons) in 1965, but the total cost was expected to be £1,350 million at 1956 prices. Even allowing for the different money values of 1949 and 1956, this showed a very considerably increased cost for 4 per cent less production.[1]

The Committee did not give a figure for the increase at constant prices but it has been suggested by some observers that it was well over 50 per cent.[2]

It does not appear, however, that the Coal Board's forecasts were so badly wrong or that *Plan for Coal* can be said to have failed. According to the NCB the rise in prices between 1949 and 1956 had added about £400 million to the cost of the plan as originally conceived. Furthermore, the cost of the modifications and additional schemes included in the revised plan was about £100 million higher than it would have been in 1949. Some new schemes were included because *Investing in Coal* covered expenditure on projects which would not be completed until after 1965 whereas *Plan for Coal* did not. The Board estimated that this accounted for about £120 million of the extra capital expenditure shown in the revised plan. The fact that this covered open-cast mining explained a further £25 million of the apparent increase in costs.[3]

Up to £640 million of the £715 million jump in investment between *Plan for Coal* and *Investing in Coal* appears, therefore, to be due to factors other than poor forecasting; though under-costing was slightly more important than this suggests because there is some overlap between the items included in the £640 million. However, it seems unlikely that under-costing accounted for more than 15 per cent of the rise.[4] If so, the estimates given in *Plan for Coal* were nothing like as bad as is sometimes suggested. Instead of 4 per cent less production for 50 per cent more capital expenditure *Investing in Coal* showed 4 per cent less production for an increase of about 15 per cent in the volume of investment.

The fact remains that the Coal Board's original estimates were too low and the question thus arises of what went wrong. Part of the answer is that the Board simply underestimated the cost of the projects which it was planning. But more important, the NCB underestimated the number of projects which it would have to undertake because it did not realize what a large amount of capacity was worked out each year. It must be remembered that when the Plan was drawn up the industry was acutely short of men with any experience or knowledge of investment planning.[5] Moreover, because of the industry's fragmented ownership, even those who had some experience did not have the right type of knowledge.

As the Board's Economic Adviser has explained:

> Each company knew very well that sooner or later this or that pit would come to the end of its life, that in many pits the distance underground would become longer, that shafts often had to be deepened at great cost, and that when the best seams had been worked out inferior seams had to be tackled.

But these tendencies affected different companies in very different ways, and no attempt was made to ascertain the position for the industry as a whole.[6]

Due to the collapse in the demand for coal it is impossible to know for certain whether the Coal Board would have succeeded in increasing deep-mined output to 230 million tons by 1965, though it seems likely. What is clear is that capital expenditure has not exceeded the forecasts given in the *Revised Plan for Coal* and that the Board's estimates of the cost of individual schemes have proved reasonably accurate. Because it was now estimated that deep-mined output would total no more than 198–213 million tons the *Revised Plan* stated that considerably less investment would be necessary than had been contemplated in *Investing in Coal*. According to the new Plan the Coal Board would need to spend £440 million on its collieries during the period 1960–65 and this was almost exactly what it spent allowing for the rise in prices. Production, it is true, was considerably less than had been expected. By 1965 deep-mined output was down to 180 million tons.[7] However, a large amount of capacity was potentially available and it is almost certain that if the demand had been present and if the necessary labour had been available the NCB could have met the production target which had been set in the *Revised Plan*.[8]

The Board's more recent estimates of the cost of its investment projects have turned out to be reasonably accurate. The final cost of the 15 major colliery projects which were completed during 1967–8 was about 10 per cent higher than the estimated cost after allowance had been made for inflation. As these estimates were made before tenders had been sought and as forecasting is naturally a difficult task, this must be regarded as an acceptable result.[9]

The Costing of Rail Modernization

In railways, as in coal, it appears at first sight that the modernization programme was very badly costed. According to its Plan of 1954 the Transport Commission intended to spend £1,240 million on the modernization and re-equipment of British Railways by about 1970. However, by the end of 1957 the Commission had re-assessed the cost at £1,660 million and the cost of certain projects, such as the London Midland electrification scheme, appear to have shot up.[10] What is the explanation for the large increase in the price of the Plan?

The increase in the overall cost of the modernization programme was due mainly to rising prices. The cost of railway vehicles seems to have

L

been rising exceptionally fast, and it appears that inflation added roughly £260 million to the cost of the Plan and to the bill for the extra projects which were included when it was re-assessed.[11] If so, the real increase in the cost of the modernization programme between the original plan of 1954 and the revised version of 1957 was 13 per cent. This rise was partly due to the addition of extra projects and partly due to the fact that some of the original items had been under-costed. For instance, little or nothing had been included in 1954 for the construction of depots in which the new diesel locomotives could be maintained.[12]

But, although some mistakes were made, the global estimates of the cost of modernization given in the Plan seem to have been reasonably accurate. This is shown by a comparison of the estimated cost and of the actual bill for modernization. It was forecast in 1954 that £590 million would be spent on new railway vehicles.[13] Not all of the rolling-stock which it was originally intended to introduce has been acquired. But it appears that roughly £435 million of the Plan has been put into effect. This represents the value at 1954 Plan prices of the new rolling-stock which had been introduced between the start of the modernization programme and the end of 1967. For instance, it was envisaged in the Plan that during the period 1956–70 255,000 wagons would be built at a cost of £150 million or £588 per wagon. By the end of 1967, 206,000 new wagons had been added which at £588 per wagon represents an expenditure of about £121 million at 1954 Plan prices.[14] Similar estimates were made for carriages and for diesel and electric locomotives and multiple units.[15]

The railways should have spent about £435 million on the new rolling-stock which they have acquired if the Modernization Plan was properly costed; what have they spent? As the price of rolling-stock has risen since the Plan was drawn up the relevant figure is what they would have spent if prices had remained at the level of 1954. If the official price index for railway vehicles is correct British Rail invested £535 million at 1954 prices on rolling-stock from the beginning of the modernization programme until the end of 1967, excluding expenditure on steam locomotives, and other items which the Plan did not cover but including a substantial amount of expenditure on power brakes.[16] It would obviously be wrong to attach too much significance to this figure but it is probably safe to conclude that although the Commission's estimates were on the low side they did not greatly understate the cost of modernizing its rolling-stock.

It is clear that the BTC over-estimated the amount of new equipment which it would require. This is because the railways use their new vehicles very much more intensively than the Modernization Plan assumed that they would. It was considered in 1954 that about 12,800 locomotives would be required in 1970, of which about 5,650 would be diesel and electric and about 7,150 would be steam engines. However, at the end of 1968 the railways had a fleet of only 4,650 locomotives.[17] The railways had managed to eliminate steam traction but had had to acquire slightly fewer diesel and electric locomotives (4,560) than they originally planned (4,800) in order to do so.[18] This must be due to the fact that British Rail is getting considerably more work out of its new engines than it anticipated because the amount of work performed does not appear to be very different from what had been expected. The distance covered by passenger trains, which account for the bulk of the total mileage, was about the same in 1968 as had been predicted for 1970. Similarly at the end of 1968 British Rail possessed only 19,550 coaching vehicles compared with the 36,200 which the British Transport Commission had considered necessary.[19] This again is due to a better utilization of equipment than had been expected. As a result the railways have purchased only about the same number of multiple units as had been anticipated, and considerably fewer new carriages than they expected. Yet they have, as planned, eliminated about 13,600 obsolete carriages which did not have corridors.[20]

The fact that the Transport Commission underestimated the amount of traffic capacity which could be obtained from new rolling-stock means that its estimates of the cost of modernization were too high. Although its estimates of the average cost of the new vehicles were probably on the low side, it has needed to acquire fewer than it anticipated but has nevertheless been able to provide a greater amount of capacity with new equipment. The Commission forecast in the Modernization Plan that the railways' capital expenditure on rolling-stock would total £665 million but, up to the end of 1968, they had spent only about £510 million at 1954 prices. Yet they had managed to eliminate steam traction which was not expected when the Plan was drawn up. The only place where the railways had achieved less than they had intended was in fitting wagons with power brakes. It had been planned that this should be completed by 1966. However, as we have seen, a large part of the wagon fleet has not yet been fitted.[21] Nevertheless, on balance, the railways have accomplished more than they expected but have spent less. Although their estimates of the cost of modernizing their rolling-stock were wrong, they were wrong in the right direction.

Unfortunately, it is impossible to check the accuracy of the Modernization Plan's estimates for capital expenditure on buildings, track and fixed equipment because it is not clear how much work the Plan covered. However, the rapid increase in the estimated cost of the London–Midland electrification project seems to suggest that the British

Transport's Commission's figuring was very poor. It was stated in the Modernization Plan that the scheme would involve an expenditure of £40 million on structures and £35 million on rolling-stock. The latter figure did not cover multiple unit vehicles which were included in the general item for expenditure on new passenger carriages. It was disclosed later that £12 million had been included for multiple units for the London–Midland route. The total bill for modernization and electrification appears therefore to have been estimated in 1954 at £87 million.[22]

Five years later in 1959 the Commission estimated that the cost would be no less than £161 million and even higher figures were quoted subsequently. This has been widely regarded as evidence that the cost of electrification was greatly under-estimated. However, it is clear that much of the apparent rise was due not only to inflation but also to an increase in the mileage of route which it was planned to electrify, and to the inclusion of items which were shown under other headings in the Modernization Plan. For instance, in 1959 it was intended that 13 per cent more route should be electrified and the costs of signalling (£41 million) and track work (£13 million) were now included.[23]

Although the rise in the cost of electrification was not as large and alarming as it appears, it would nevertheless be wrong to conclude that the project was properly costed. For example, it seems that the cost of the signalling which electrification would involve was greatly under-estimated.[24] What is far more important, the Transport Commission had no clear idea of the total cost of electrification until the work was well under way and thus was in no position to judge the relative merits of electric and diesel traction. Although having decided to electrify the Commission made a careful investigation of the different systems of electrification which were available, no such study was made of the overall capital costs of dieselization and electrification. As we shall see later this was part of a more general failure to weigh up their respective merits.[25]

Fortunately, the railways' estimating has become considerably more accurate since the days of the Modernization Plan. British Rail's capital expenditure on the major investment projects approved between May 1965 and April 1966 turned out to be about 4 per cent higher than was estimated.[26] Allowing for inflation the Board's forecasts must have been almost spot on.

The Costing of Electricity Expansion

In the electricity industry an extremely high standard of financial estimating had been set before the war by the old Central Electricity

Board. In 1933 when the original grid had been completed the Board reported that the cost of construction was within $2\frac{1}{2}$ per cent of the estimated figure.[27] Almost 30 years later the Central Electricity Generating Board were able to claim that its forecasts of the cost of the power stations completed between the spring of 1958 and the end of 1960 had been accurate to within $1\frac{1}{2}$ per cent![28] What happened was that their cost, in terms of the prices ruling when the estimates were made, was about 10 per cent lower than had been expected, but that this was just about offset by the rise in prices which had taken place. The main reason why the original forecast was on the low side seems to have been that the economies of scale which were secured turned out to be larger than had been expected. The Board's estimates of the cost of its power stations have continued to be reasonably accurate. At the end of 1968 the Generating Board disclosed that six major stations and six gas turbine plants which had recently been completed would cost $12\frac{1}{2}$ per cent more than had been estimated, but the bulk of this increase was accounted for by price increases. Allowing for inflation the cost was $5\frac{1}{2}$ per cent higher than had been expected.[29]

It must be borne in mind that during recent years serious delays have occurred in the completion of power stations, so that the CEGB's interest charges on the capital it has tied up in partly completed work have been heavier than it anticipated. As these charges should be regarded as part of the cost of its capital projects their total cost has risen considerably more than the Board's figures show it to have done. At the present time the commissioning programme for power stations is running about 18 months late and further delays are occurring before stations are brought into full commercial operation.[30] Exactly how much these delays will add to the cost of the stations has not been revealed but it must be a substantial amount.

Why, it may be asked, are these commissioning delays occurring? As their cause has been investigated by an official Committee under Sir Alan Wilson one naturally turns to its report for enlightenment. It states that the accuracy of the demand forecasts on which the industry's investment programme was based

increased until 1957, while thereafter the discrepancies became considerably greater. It was therefore decided in 1959 and subsequent years to increase the plant programmes very substantially, and at the same time to standardize on 500 MW units, the economic advantage of which had become apparent. This large increase in the volume of plant ordered, combined with the difficulties associated with the rapid advance in technology, overwhelmed the technical, production and managerial resources of the manufacturers and put an excessive strain on the staff of the CEGB . . . The primary cause of the difficulties in constructing power stations efficiently has been a failure in long-term planning. The construction of a power station is such a lengthy process that circumstances can alter substantially between the time when a plant is ordered and when it is completed, and it would be unrealistic to suppose that fluctuations in the plant programme can be avoided. But in the past the fluctuations have been excessive. They have at one time resulted in the country being short of electric power, at another time in the capacity of the capital goods industries being violently overstrained . . .[31]

Although the Committee does not tell us why the estimates of demand were so badly out or who, if anyone, was to blame, the impression conveyed is that the electricity industry was at fault. Naturally it is to be presumed, unless otherwise stated, that the industry is responsible for its demand forecasts and for their accuracy or inaccuracy.

What the Committee failed to discuss in its somewhat tendentious report was whether the industry could have been expected to make an accurate forecast of the future demand for electricity during the early sixties in view of what can now be seen to be the abnormally fast rate at which it was then growing.[32] Perhaps even more surprising was the way in which the Committee omitted to mention that the industry's forecasts had been increased in conformity with the Government's policy of 4 per cent growth, and its failure to discover how far the consequent rise in the plant programme was responsible for the delays in the completion of power stations. Yet this is a most important question because it is obviously possible that it was the rise associated with 4 per cent growth which finally disrupted the manufacturers and contractors who construct power stations. The increase in the plant programme for which the Government was responsible was certainly the last of the series and as the manufacturers were already under strain, would have had a disrupting effect out of proportion to its size. This, moreover, was considerable. Unlike the figurative last straw the increase was a heavy burden in its own right. The electricity industry estimated for Neddy that the adoption of 4 per cent growth would mean that by 1966 it would have to step up its capital investment from £574 to £690 million, which represented a rise of no less than a fifth.[33] It is unfortunate that the Wilson Committee did not investigate whether, as seems likely enough, it was this which was mainly responsible for the damaging delays in power station construction which have occurred, for it had access to the detailed information necessary before a firm conclusion can be reached.

Careful Yield Calculations for Coal and Rail?

After this examination of the estimates of capital expenditure which three of the leading nationalized industries have prepared, we shall now try to discover whether careful estimates of the pay-off from investment have been made within the public enterprise sector. It is clear that from the beginning some of the nationalized industries have taken great pains to calculate the likely return from their investment. This is true, for instance, of the coal industry.

In *Plan for Coal* the NCB made a broad estimate of the saving in costs which the modernization of the industry would produce. This was based on the one hand on the forecast of demand, which has already been examined, and on the other hand on estimates of the cost of supply. These, in turn, were based on an examination of the costs and prospects of each colliery which showed how much it would cost to supply varying amounts of coal. The estimates of supply and demand were then brought together and it was found that with demand at 240 million tons there would be a saving to the country of 7s per ton at the wage and price levels of 1949. This reduction in costs was the consequence of the increase in productivity which was expected. It appears to have been estimated that between 1949 and 1961–5 this would increase by about a third. The Board said that its productivity calculations were cautious and this they have certainly proved. By 1965 output per manshift was over 50 per cent higher than it had been in 1949.[34] Although the industry's plans have gone awry this was due neither to the absence of careful estimates of the savings which modernization would yield nor to wishful thinking about the gains in efficiency it would be able to secure.

The fact that *Plan for Coal* was based on draft colliery modernization projects did not mean that they were approved along with the Plan. At an early date the Coal Board established a clear procedure for the vetting of capital projects. This required that when schemes were submitted for approval a detailed appraisal of the likely financial return should be included along with the technical plans. The Fleck Committee reported that projects were often submitted to headquarters in an unsatisfactory form and were not being examined properly. This was one aspect of the lack of firm central control and the growth of insubordination during the period when the Coal Board was under pressure to decentralize to the maximum. Fortunately, as a result of the Committee's recommendations, this period soon came to an end.[35]

The thoroughness with which investment projects are prepared and appraised within the coal industry has been confirmed by an investigation by the Ministry of Power.

There is no doubt [Ministry officials concluded in 1963] that the National Coal Board's method of preparing investment projects for approval is extremely thorough. We are confirmed in this view both by our study of the Board's rules, and by the records of cases which we have inspected. The Stage II submissions of the Divisional Boards are supported by full statistical and other data as required by the standard forms which the rules provide. At Headquarters these submissions are critically examined by the Departments concerned and the attention of the National Coal Board is drawn to any particular in which the Divisional Board seems to have been over-optimistic. It is clear that projects are now subjected to severe scrutiny. The arrangement whereby schemes are discussed at large at Stage I and in detail at Stage II, and expenditure is sanctioned at Stage III on the basis of tenders or detailed estimates, seems entirely sound. Our conclusion is that the submission of projects leaves little to be desired.[36]

Not all the nationalized industries have made such careful and detailed estimates of the pay-off from their investment. The railways are the obvious example. The report of the Modernization Committee on which the Plan was largely based did not contain any estimate of the overall financial benefit to be expected from modernization. Indeed, the only important estimates which it gave were for wagons and power brakes. It was calculated that there might be a saving of £27 million in working costs partly due to the introduction of larger wagons and the consequent reduction in costs as fewer would have to be moved about; and partly to a general reduction in the number of wagons, and the consequent savings in maintenance and depreciation charges. The installation of power brakes was estimated to yield sufficient savings to cover at least the interest charges on the £75 million of capital involved; and it was thought that the figure would be much higher.[37] Moreover, it is clear, from a paper which the Chief Operating Officer of the Railway Executive presented to the Institute of Transport, that in the past a considerable amount of study had been devoted to the financial and operating consequences of introducing power brakes. The paper also shows that detailed financial calculations had been made to determine the optimum size of wagon.[38]

The forecasts of the likely pay-off from the other major items of expenditure under the Modernization Plan are not given in the Planning Committee's Report. The reason appears to be that they were prepared separately. Unfortunately, we do not know exactly what the financial working papers contained and how carefully the return on investment had been calculated. But it is clear that the likely saving in costs from introducing diesel multiple units on the stopping services had previously been studied in some detail. The subject had, as we have seen, been investigated by a committee on railway motive power.[39] It seems evident that the BTC did, by the time of the Modernization Plan, have a reasonably clear idea of the effect upon its net revenue of dieselizing branch-line services.

However it seems very doubtful whether the Commission was anything like as well informed about the financial consequences of introducing diesels for main-line work, which was the most important proposal of the Modernization Plan. Hitherto British Rail had had virtually no experience with this form of traction, and although the question of dieselizing main-line services had been considered in general terms by the motive power committee, it seems doubtful whether British Rail had much detailed information about its likely financial consequences. The Committee had, after all, recommended that there should be a large-scale experiment with diesels in order that the advantages of this form of traction might become better known.[40] Moreover, the decision to use diesels for main-line work was taken very hurriedly. During the preliminary stages of drawing up the Modernization Plan it was taken for granted that electrification would be the order of the day and the decision to opt for diesels was taken during a few hurried months in 1964.

There are two further reasons why it is difficult to regard the railways' financial estimates as being of a very high order. First, the Commission does not appear to have made any clear distinction between the financial consequences of investment and the benefits which could be secured by rationalization and the adoption of better operating methods. Its calculations of the likely financial consequences of modernizing the wagon fleet are a case in point. Secondly, the Commission does not appear to have made any real attempt to discover which of its main-line services should be dieselized and which electrified. It appears to have decided that available resources would only permit the electrification of one or two lines and to have selected those where traffic was heaviest; although the London–Midland scheme was in fact only added at the last moment as a result of regional pressure.[41]

No serious attempt was made to investigate the comparative advantages of the two forms of motive power, or even to see whether those routes which it was considered possible to electrify should be dieselized instead. When Mr John Ratter of the Transport Commission was questioned about the decision to electrify the London–Midland route he disclosed that 'there was no attempt made in the earlier estimates to make a precise calculation of the return on electrification. It was done on the basis of a yardstick of the return that comes from a given tonnage carried over the line. This was, however, well over the tonnage which is normally assessed as being that above which electrification is profitable.'[42]

What Mr Ratter did not reveal was that when, after the scheme was well under way, a detailed comparison of the cost of electrification and dieselization was made, the BTC had discovered that electrification was only slightly more economic. If the comparison had been made when the Plan was being prepared dieselization would have shown the highest return because the original scheme was for electrification with direct current which is less expensive than the alternating current method which was ultimately used.[43] The railways appear therefore to have hit by luck on what was probably the right policy: the electrification of one or two key routes. Perhaps there is an unseen hand which guides the nationalized industries!

It may be replied that, in most cases, the unseen hand appears to have led the railways astray and that if their estimates of the savings from modernization had been better their deficits would have been smaller. However, it does not necessarily follow that because the Transport Commission's estimates were crude they were also over-optimistic. As we shall see later when we come to examine the pitfalls of profit forecasting, the Commission made some serious mistakes which obscured how desperate its financial position had become.[44] But it seems very doubtful whether the figures for the cost savings from modernization included in the published version of the Plan were too high. For instance, very large economies have in practice been obtained through dieselization. For instance, between 1958 and 1968 the railways' bill for fuel and power was alone reduced by £37 million.[45]

The Transport Commission, however, ran a serious risk when it failed to make a careful calculation of the likely financial consequences of modernization, and if its methods had been better it might not have embarked on the mistaken policy of dieselizing its branch lines. Although the Commission knew that it was losing tens of millions each year on its stopping services it decided to try to dieselize them out of deficit with some idea of the likely savings in costs but no estimate of whether, at the end of the day, they would pay their way.[46] No doubt estimates of savings were required from each line before their conversion from steam to diesel traction was sanctioned. This was certainly the position where main-line locomotives were to be introduced.[47] However, the usual procedure was to calculate the extra revenue and the savings which diesels would produce without recording whether the diesel service would even cover its direct costs, let alone make a contribution to track, signalling, and station overheads.[48]

Since the Plan was published the railways' calculations of the rate of return on investment have gradually become more thorough, although their progress was by no means as fast as it should have been, and their economic methods, as we shall see, for a long time left much to be desired. However by 1967–8, if not before, British Rail appears in the case of all its major investment projects to have been carefully assessing the return which it would obtain, and the bulk of the expenditure which the projects covered was being assessed by highly sophisticated methods.[49]

The Evaluation and Non-evaluation of Electricity Investment

In electricity, which is the last industry which will be considered in detail, it is necessary to distinguish clearly between the financial estimates which have been made by the industry and those for which the Government was primarily responsible. It was the Government which, together with the Atomic Energy Authority, was mainly responsible for the first nuclear power programme. Early in 1955 the Government announced a provisional ten-year programme for the construction of 1,500 to 2,000 MW of nuclear capacity. The Central Electricity Authority had no part in the detailed preparation of this plan though, on the information available, it accepted it as a reasonable approach. It was stated somewhat ominously in the White Paper in which the programme was outlined that the decision to go ahead did not depend on precise comparisons of cost. Nevertheless, it was argued that the cost of electricity from the first of the nuclear stations to be constructed would, at around 0·6d per unit, be about the same as the cost of electricity generated at new coal-fired stations. But the estimate for nuclear energy was crucially affected by the size of the credit included for the sale of plutonium which was a by-product, for in its absence the estimated cost of electricity would have been about 0·9d per unit.[50]

It was recognized in the White Paper that the value of plutonium would fall as time went by, but it was argued that this would be offset by the fact that the later stations would be more efficient than the earlier ones. But as the efficiency of these early stations would remain about the same this meant that as the plutonium credit declined their costs would rise. It therefore seems doubtful whether a comparison of the expected lifetime costs of nuclear and conventional stations would have shown the early nuclear plants in such a favourable light. Moreover, the plutonium credit was placed at an unrealistically high level. It was known in 1955 that three large plants for enriched uranium were being built in the United States and that extensive world exploration for uranium was being undertaken. Both of these developments could be expected to result in lower prices for plutonium. It should therefore have come as no great surprise when in 1956 the United States Atomic Energy Commission reduced its prices for enriched uranium, and large new discoveries of uranium were made in Canada. As a result the British Atomic Energy Authority (AEA) was forced to reduce the plutonium credit from about 0·3d to less than 0·1d per unit.[51]

Thus during 1956 it became even clearer that nuclear power was not competitive with electricity generated by conventional means. Despite this the Government agreed to the AEA's proposal that now that uranium supplies had become more plentiful there should be a considerable expansion in the nuclear power programme. What happened was that the AEA's suggestion was examined by a committee which considered three possible levels to which the existing programme should be expanded. Although the Central Electricity Authority, which this time was represented, would have preferred the middle level the highest figure was adopted. This involved trebling the existing programme to 5,000–6,000 MW within the original period to the end of 1965.[52] This extraordinary decision, which cannot have been supported by any careful calculations of the cost of nuclear and conventional power, is explained by a number of factors. The proposal to expand the original programme was considered in the flush of enthusiasm following the commissioning of the experimental nuclear power station at Calder Hall, and the Ministry, so I have been told, was under pressure from the private consortia responsible for constructing nuclear stations to build more.

However, the main reason for the expanded programme was Suez. Ever since the fuel crisis of 1947 the Government had been haunted by the fear that insufficient supplies of coal would be available to meet our growing needs for energy. This helps to explain the anxiety to press ahead with the original nuclear programme. At that time, it was expected that the electricity industry would be able as an interim measure to obtain substantial supplies of oil. When at the time of the Suez incident doubt was thrown on its availability the Government decided that it was necessary to speed up the construction of nuclear power stations. As Sir Christopher Hinton, who was involved in the events, has commented: 'Without Suez it is inconceivable that the 6,000 MW programme for 1957 would have been given approval.' What happened was that the Government acted in a panic of its own making and failed to count the cost of expanding the nuclear programme. Unfortunately, this has turned out to be even heavier than was evident at the time.[53]

The original nuclear programme apart, extremely thorough estimates have been made by the CEGB and its predecessors of the saving in costs which will be achieved if investment schemes go forward. For major extensions of the national grid and for the replacement of old generating plant this has long been the practice. It is clear, for instance, that the construction of the supergrid, which was one of the British Electricity Authority's first major decisions, was based on a careful analysis of the likely savings in capital and operating costs which would arise. The same was true of the decision, taken in 1960, to reinforce the supergrid and to convert it to a higher voltage.[54] To see whether it could reduce its costs by replacing old plant a series of highly elaborate investigations have been carried out.

For instance in 1959–60 the CEGB examined the financial consequences of scrapping 500 MW of old plant and replacing it by new, and found that the investment was marginally uneconomic. In order to discover this the Board had to estimate what use would be made of each of the industry's generating stations year by year if the old plant was replaced and if it was not. This was necessary because power stations are run as an integrated system, and because the introduction of a new plant affects the operation of every other station. To be more specific, plants are operated in order of merit; their position in the league being determined by their relative operating costs. The figure by which a station is judged is its fuel costs per unit of output since fuel is only burnt when the station is actually being run. What happens is that plant with the lowest fuel costs will work as continuously as possible while the plant with the highest fuel costs may be brought in for only a day or two each winter. New plants will start at the top of the merit order and then drop down year by year as they become older and are gradually superseded by plants of more recent construction with lower costs. The pace at which they drop will, therefore, depend on the amount of new plant which is installed. This in turn will primarily depend on the rate at which the demand for electricity expands, but it will also be affected by the construction of new power stations to replace old plant.[55]

In order to see whether it was worth replacing old plant by new, the Generating Board had in principle to estimate its merit order, and its system costs, year by year, over the estimated lives of the replacement stations which it was thinking of building. This would obviously have been an enormous task and the CEGB decided that a sufficiently accurate result could be obtained by working out the system costs for two years and then, by interpolation and extrapolation, estimating what the savings would be in the other years.

The Board has continued to carry out exercises of this type to see whether it is worth replacing old plant and has, for some time, used a similar procedure to calculate which type of plant will minimize system costs; although it now calculates the costs for the first three and then every fifth year of the station's life.[56] It is necessary to calculate system costs here because conventional generating stations will, as time passes, slide down the merit order and be used less, whereas nuclear plant, which has low fuel costs, is likely to stay near the top of the merit table and continue to be used intensively. Simple comparisons which assume that both types of plant operate at the same load factor are therefore misleading, and are likely to give an exaggerated impression of the contribution which conventional plant will make. Nuclear plant will continue to make a large contribution because it will enable high-cost plant to be operated less than it would otherwise, whereas conventional plant will itself become costly to operate and a burden to the system.[57]

There is no doubt that the CEGB now makes an extremely thorough investigation of the financial consequences of pursuing different courses of action, but why did the industry not adopt its present methods earlier? The explanation appears to be that it was almost impossible for it to do so until computers became available. As the Ministry of Power says in a report on the CEGB's investment procedures:

> The simulation, year by year over the lives of the projects under consideration, of the capacity and loading of all other plant on the system in which the new plant will find itself is a heavy arithmetical task which could not have been accurately performed before the advent of computers. These methods have been developed and refined by the Board's staff over the last ten years, and the interest they continue to take in these matters gives ground for confidence that this development will continue as opportunity offers.[58]

Although the CEGB takes great pains to minimize its system costs when considering investment in new power stations it ignores the revenue side of the picture and does not try to calculate the rate of return which it will earn. There is, therefore, a risk that the Board will undertake investment which does not yield an adequate profit. (In the language of economists the Board ensures that it is operating somewhere on its long-run cost curve but there is no guarantee that it will be operating at the right point which is where the demand curve intersects it.) The Board argues that because the electricity industry is run as an integrated system, and because its prices tend to decline due to its exceptionally fast rate of technical progress, it would be worse than useless to try to attribute revenue to an individual station and then calculate its profitability.

When a station is new it will be run intensively and there will be a large margin between its costs and the price of electricity, which is based on the industry's average costs of production. As a result a new station will appear to show a large profit. But as the years go by, and more advanced stations are introduced, the industry's average costs will fall and its prices will be reduced. Consequently when the new station has become old, its costs will be above average and it will make a loss on every unit which it produces. The station will appear to make a large loss because, although it will not be called on to produce very often, when it does there will be a considerable gap between its costs and its revenue, and because even when it is not producing it will have to be staffed and maintained. However, appearances are deceptive because the system could not operate without the old station unless a new one was built to replace it and this would increase system costs. The Board concludes, therefore, that it is misleading to try to calculate the profits which a new station will earn because in its early years they will be overstated, and when it is old they will be understated.[59]

This argument shows that the revenue which a new station will earn cannot be calculated from its output, but this does not mean that it is impossible to estimate the contribution which it makes to the revenue of the system. What must be discovered is how much revenue the industry would forgo if the station were not constructed. At first sight the answer appears to be that it would lose virtually none because, except at peak periods, the industry has spare capacity. All that would happen, it might be argued, would be that the industry would not be able to meet the demand for a few hours each winter and that power cuts would become more frequent. A moment's reflection shows that the CEGB could not pursue this policy for very long without inflicting heavy social costs and losing demand throughout the year because consumers would switch to more reliable sources of energy. Whether the CEGB should pursue such a policy at all, and let the security of the system decline, depends on whether it is higher or lower than it needs to be. This is a difficult question to answer, but fortunately it does not have to be answered, because it is a separate issue. Once the CEGB has decided upon the standard of security it wishes to maintain it can, in principle at least, calculate the revenue it would have to forgo if it failed to install additional generating capacity to meet the growth in demand.

What it must try to discover is how much its consumption would fall throughout the year if it had, presumably by higher prices, to choke off the extra demand which it would be unable to satisfy at the peak period without letting its standard of security deteriorate. By calculating this loss, year by year, throughout the life of the power station which was under consideration, and by estimating what its tariffs would be each year of this period, the CEGB would be able to tell roughly what revenue it would lose if the station was not built. (In practice the Board might not lose anything because of the monopoly profits which it would earn by putting up its prices to choke off demand, but this is irrelevant because monopoly profits should be avoided.) That this is the right approach can be seen from the fact that, unlike the method of calculating revenue from output, it would not produce paradoxical results. A new station would not show enormous profits during its early years, because it would not be credited with the output diverted to it from less efficient plants, and it would not show enormous losses during its latter years, because it would be credited with the output diverted from it to more efficient plants.

Although in theory the industry could, and should, calculate the revenue and rate of return which new power stations will earn, it seems doubtful whether this would be a useful undertaking. The calculation would obviously involve a large number of extremely hazardous assumptions about the characteristics of the consumers who would be choked off. Even if there were no practical problems of this type it is questionable whether the calculation would add anything significant to the CEGB's knowledge. If the industry's estimates of future demand are right, it knows whether extra capacity needs to be built and if its estimates of the savings which it can achieve through scrapping old stations are correct, it knows whether existing capacity should be replaced. If these calculations are wrong an imposing superstructure of estimates of revenues and rates of return will be built on sand, however much it might delight the economist's eye.

Although the railways and some of the other nationalized industries have in the past failed to make careful calculations of the rate of return on their capital expenditure, or of the savings in costs which it would produce, it appears that they all do so now and that this has been the general practice for a number of years. The Coal Board has almost from the start required that detailed estimates should be made project by project. In gas, as we shall see, elaborate estimates of the profitability of investment have been made for a number of years. In the past some investment was regarded as obligatory and no calculation of the yield was made, but even here the alternative ways of undertaking the work appear in most cases to have been carefully investigated.[60] In BRS painstaking estimates of the rate of return are prepared for depot schemes, as examination of a typical project revealed, and the age and mileage at which it is financially desirable that vehicles should be replaced have been investigated. In the air corporations estimates of the rate of return have become steadily more detailed and thorough and have now, as the Board of Trade has explained, become extremely refined.[61]

The practice of estimating the rate of return on investment projects appears to be far more widespread within the public enterprise sector than it is in private industry. A considerable proportion of private firms did not, at least until a few years ago, make any serious attempt to calculate the likely yield from capital expenditure, as a number of surveys which have been conducted both in this country and abroad have shown.

An inquiry, by Robert Nield, during 1964 which covered 133 establishments, mainly in engineering, showed that only half regularly made written estimates of the probable savings in operating costs when the replacement of machinery and equipment was up for decision. Moreover, about half of those which did not make regular estimates made them for less than a third of their replacement expenditure. Yet this survey may well give a flattering picture of industrial practice because the inquiry was addressed to firms which had attended a conference on replacement policy.[62] In the late fifties Professor Tibor Barna interviewed directors or leading officials of 35 firms engaged in electrical engineering and food processing which together had a labour force of over 500,000. He found that 'only in two-thirds of the firms in the sample were projects supported by written evidence. In one-third, including not only some smaller firms where decisions are arrived at informally but also some large firms, there were no documents with profitability calculations.'[63] A small but intensive inquiry by Professor Bruce Williams and W. P. Scott into a number of substantial investment decisions made by a number of leading British concerns revealed a similar picture.[64] It is not only in Britain that a significant proportion of private firms fail to make careful calculations of the pay-off from investment. For instance, investigations by Professor Erik Lundberg among about 100 large firms in Sweden disclosed 'the relatively low frequency of more exact profitability calculations for new investments'.[65]

CHAPTER 15

The Evaluation of Investment

IT is essential not only that undertakings should calculate the rate of return on their investment but also that they should calculate it in the right way. During recent years most of the nationalized industries have adopted sophisticated techniques which take into account the timing of profits and investment. But before examining their present procedure we must consider their past practice. Until a few years ago the correct techniques were only used by a handful of British firms, and even in America the proportion of top companies which allowed for the timing of profits was very small.[1] It would, therefore, be wrong to judge the nationalized industries' performance by ideal standards. What must be seen is how far they measured up to the principles of commonsense economics. Although these principles are unsatisfactory as they stand, they are better than nothing.

A firm may be thinking of buying new capital equipment because demand is expanding and it does not have the capacity to produce the extra goods which it could sell; because its existing equipment is physically worn out; or because its existing equipment, though still serviceable, is becoming technically obsolescent. If demand has outrun capacity the firm should compare the profits it can expect to earn each year on its extra sales with the cost of the extra equipment it will need. If the net revenue, after meeting depreciation and the other costs of production, when expressed as a rate of return on capital exceeds the rate of interest by a sufficient margin the investment should be undertaken. The size of this margin will depend partly on the amount of risk involved. If the firm's existing equipment has worn out the calculation will be almost exactly the same: the net revenue expected from the new equipment must be expressed as a rate of return on its cost.

When the firm is thinking about replacing obsolescent equipment the calculation is different. In this case it must compare the avoidable costs it will incur if it continues to use the old equipment with the total costs it will have to bear if it installs new equipment. Obviously it is the total costs, including depreciation and interest charges, which are relevant in the case of the new machinery because this is what the firm will escape having to pay if it decides to go on using its old equipment. For the old machinery the relevant figure is for the costs excluding depreciation and interest charges, because the latter will have to be borne whatever decision is taken. If the total costs when the new equipment is in use will be lower than the avoidable running costs of the old equipment then it should be scrapped and new installed. These calculations will, however, give a misleading result where a loss is being earned. A reduction in costs, and therefore in losses, due to the installation of new equipment is not equivalent to a profit if the losses can be avoided by closing down. With these 'commonsense' principles in mind we can now examine how the nationalized industries have in the past set about the task of calculating the rate of return on their prospective investment.

Past Methods of Investment Appraisal

It appears that the CEGB has been using the right methods. This is shown by the important exercise which was carried out to see whether it was worth replacing old plant by new. The fuel and labour costs the industry would save if the old stations remained in operation were compared with those which they would have to bear if a corresponding amount of new capacity was installed. The savings which were shown to arise were then, in effect, compared with the extra depreciation and capital charges which the industry would have to meet. This procedure was obviously equivalent to comparing avoidable costs on the old plant with total costs on the new. In this particular case the capital costs of the old plant had already been written off so that the avoidable and the total costs on the old plant were the same as each other. As the whole exercise was an extremely sophisticated piece of work, which, as we shall see, even took account of timing, it seems clear that the correct economic method was being used by design and not by accident.[2]

Until the early sixties, at least, the Coal Board calculated the rate of return on its investment projects by two methods which were used in harness. First, it estimated the improvement in financial results and expressed it as a proportion of the extra capital involved. Second, it calculated how profitable the pit would be after the project had been completed by expressing the current profit and the estimated improvement as a percentage of the total investment, including the existing book value of the colliery, the new capital expenditure proposed and the working capital required.[3] Although the first formula seems more or less correct the second appears, at first glance, to lack any economic justification because what has been invested in the past has no bearing on what should be invested in the future. Economists have not failed to point this out and to make fun of the Coal Board's investment criteria. For instance, Dennis Munby in an amusing piece of knock-about refers to 'the introduction of irrelevances such as the book value of collieries' and says that the Board's method of relating total profits to total investment seems to have no economic justification, at least, at first sight.'[4]

However, a second look shows that there was method in the Coal Board's madness. What the Board was really asking itself was whether the colliery at which capital work had been proposed would end up by making a profit. Had the NCB's approach been more sophisticated, it would not have had to ask this question, because its investment rules would have been so framed that investment in a colliery which would end up making a loss would be automatically ruled out. But the Board was not very sophisticated and its first method for calculating the profit-ability of new investment might, in the case of a pit making heavy losses, show a handsome return (due to their reduction) even though the pit would never make a profit. The Board guarded against investment schemes of this type by expressing profits as a proportion of the capital which had been and was to be invested in the pit. For it is clear that where the rate was negative and the pit was going to continue, or to start making a loss, investment was not usually allowed. The Coal Board gave the Select Committee details of the major investment projects which it approved in 1956. These show that the pit which after invest-ment would be least profitable was expected to show a $6\frac{1}{2}$ per cent return on capital new and old. The NCB confirmed that capital expenditure on major reconstruction at its loss-making pits had only been sanctioned when it would make the colliery profitable.[5] A few years later the Ministry of Power informed the Select Committee that at none of the collieries where major schemes were sanctioned in 1959 and 1960 was the return on the total capital estimated to be less than $7\frac{1}{2}$ per cent.[6]

Nor does it appear that the minimum rate of return on new capital which the NCB in effect demanded before major investment should take place at unprofitable pits was exceptionally low. For the projects sanc-tioned in 1956 the lowest possible figure was $6\frac{1}{2}$ per cent which, as we have just seen, was the lowest return which the NCB expected on old and new capital, taken together (and for those approved in 1959 and 1960 the return must have been over $7\frac{1}{2}$ per cent). Obviously it must have been as high as this even in the limiting case where the value of the existing capital had been written down to zero. In fact the prospective return on *new* capital at the colliery where in 1956 a $6\frac{1}{2}$ per cent return was ex-pected on old and new was 10·7 per cent, ignoring losses avoided. The lowest return expected on new capital invested at a profitable pit appears to have been only $4\frac{1}{2}$ per cent. It is, therefore, possible that the NCB in allocating investment actually discriminated against pits which were making losses. But this may not have happened because in calculating the figure of $4\frac{1}{2}$ per cent the Board did not allow for the fact that in the absence of capital expenditure profits would have fallen.[7] The prospective return was therefore higher than the Board made it appear.

Unfortunately the railways, unlike the coal industry, did not guard against investment which, although it would cut losses, might not eliminate them. Before considering the mistakes which the Transport Commission did make we must dispose of the sins for which it has been blamed but did not commit. According to Mr Christopher Foster the Commission miscalculated the prospective rate of return on capital in the Modernization Plan, because it excluded from its calculations the £400 million of capital which it would not have to borrow but hoped to provide from its own resources. Mr Foster sums up his argument by referring to the Commission's 'failure to impute interest or an income to the £400 million'.[8] Now it is certainly true that the Commission did not impute interest to the £400 million for the simple reason that it would not have to pay it, but it does not follow, and it is not true, that the Commission wrongly attributed all the benefits of modernization to the £800 million of capital which it planned to borrow. What the Modernization Plan said, as Mr Foster reports accurately enough, was that the Commission hoped for a return of at least £85 million on its investment of about £1,200 million.[9] However, as the Commission would have to meet the interest on the new capital which it borrowed, and was unable to cover its existing interest charges, it was naturally anxious to show that the Modernization Plan should enable it to do so. Therefore, later in the Plan, it argued that the yield from modernization would be sufficient both to eliminate its existing deficit and meet the extra interest charges which it would incur.[10] But the fact that the Commission tried to show that it would be able to meet its statutory obligations and pay its way, hardly proves that it had forgotten about the £400 million which it was investing from its own resources.

Where the Commission did go wrong was that it tacitly assumed that the losses which it would avoid through modernizing or curtailing its loss-making activities, and in particular through dieselizing its branch lines, were the equivalent of profits earned. The return on modernization was therefore somewhat lower than it appeared. The Modernization Plan was, of course, only a general statement and it could be true that the Commission guarded against investment in lines which ought to be closed when their dieselization came up for detailed consideration. It is apparent from the instructions issued at the end of 1959 about the way in which the rate of return was to be calculated, that this did not happen. It was laid down that the estimated improvement in financial results was to be expressed as a percentage of the capital expenditure involved. However, no estimate was required of whether the line where the project was to be carried out would be profitable at the end of the day, and the method proposed was extremely curious. For major schemes such as dieselization and electrification details were to be given of all the receipts and expenses affected by the project, comparing what was expected when it was in full operation with the estimated position if existing assets were renewed like-with-like. Capital expenditure was treated in a similar fashion: the outlay which would be necessary if existing assets were renewed was to be deducted from the cost of the equipment which it was proposed to acquire. The net financial benefit so defined was then to be expressed as a percentage of the additional outlay.

Presumably the Commission justified this extraordinary procedure on the ground that one day the existing equipment would wear out, and what it was discovering was whether it was financially worth while simply to renew it or to install the latest type of equipment. However, the time to make this calculation, if ever, was when the existing equipment, say steam engines, was worn out. If these engines were still serviceable, the correct method of determining whether they should be prematurely retired was to compare the avoidable costs of operating them with the total costs of running diesels, including capital charges.[11] This the Commission's method certainly did not do, first because depreciation charges were being included in the costs of operating steam engines, secondly because the cost of buying diesels did not appear in full, and thirdly because the calculation was based on the hypothetical costs of operating new steam engines instead of the actual costs of continuing to operate with old ones. The first two factors would lead to the rate of return from dieselization being overstated, while the third would lead to it being understated. But, on balance, it seems clear that the Commission's method must have led to a very exaggerated view of the financial gain from introducing diesels.

But this was a minor disadvantage compared with the fact that it did not enable the Commission to see whether its investment would restore a loss-making line to profitability. This was because no estimate was required of what the total expenses would be after dieselization or electrification had taken place. All that had to be submitted was an estimate of the expenses affected by the scheme, which in practice meant train costs. Only in the case of lines where the heaviest losses were occurring, and revenue would not even cover movement costs, can the Commission have been able to see that something was wrong. Until it issued its instructions for the control of capital expenditure even this must have been hidden from its eyes. Up to that time the usual practice, when schemes were submitted, was to show only the estimated change in receipts and train costs.[12]

It was not until the arrival of Dr Beeching that steps were taken to prevent capital expenditure being wasted on services which were incurring heavy losses. Not only was a review of capital expenditure programmes made and the decision taken to eliminate loss-making parts of the system, but more information was required on the profitability of the facilities which were to be replaced or improved.[13] The investment criteria which British Rail adopted in 1965 laid down, for instance, that where the investment was more or less self-contained, as with wagons for a specific traffic flow or new coaches for particular passenger services, a special examination of the profitability of the traffic or service was essential.[14]

The gas industry has, for a considerable period, used more or less the correct procedure for calculating the rate of return on new investment. A description of the industry's methods which the Gas Council presented to the Select Committee at the beginning of 1961 contains only one obvious mistake. Although most of the Area Boards used the correct procedure when deciding whether to replace plant which had not been fully depreciated, a few Boards appear to have made the mistake of spreading the balance of capital expenditure on the old plant over the life of the new and then deducting this charge when calculating the rate of return. This is obviously wrong as the depreciation charges on the old plant have not been incurred due to the installation of the new plant. As a result of this error new plant was made to look less financially attractive than it should. A survey by the Ministry of Power in 1965, besides confirming that this was the only gross error that was being made, revealed that it was confined to three or four Area Boards. These subsequently fell into line and adopted the correct procedure as a result, no doubt, of the Ministry's comments.[15]

Although the deduction of excessive depreciation appears to have been the worst mistake which was being made within the industry, at least one Gas Board was, until 1964, calculating the return on investment by a method which produced a somewhat misleading result. The West Midlands Board treated the profits which arose jointly from the introduction of new plant and the construction of new grid mains as if they were due to the investment in mains, thus overstating the rate of return. But although the Board's method gave an exaggerated impression of the profitability of constructing new grid mains it was unlikely to show a profit where none existed (since capital charges on the new plant were allowed for in the cost of the gas).[16] It may be concluded that although mistakes have been made within the gas industry they have been relatively minor in nature or, where serious, confined to only a few of the Boards.

It is difficult to generalize about the methods of investment appraisal which the nationalized industries have employed. They range from the electricity industry's highly sophisticated approach to British Rail's fallacious procedures, with the Coal Board and the gas industry occupying a middle position because, although their methods have been far from perfect, they seem for the most part to have avoided the most serious pitfalls. Although the standards of the public enterprise sector have not, on average, been very bright, they have probably been no dimmer than those of the private sector. As an investigation by Professor G. Lawson has shown, private industry's methods for calculating the rate of return on new investment have been remarkably poor. When, during the early sixties, he conducted a sample survey among quoted companies he discovered, for instance, that a large number included a proportion of their existing overhead expenses in the running costs of new plant and machinery when calculating the rate of return which the investment would yield. Two-thirds of the firms included the existing overheads of the factory, about half included existing administrative overheads and one-third included existing selling and distributive overheads. It is also interesting to observe that 10 per cent of the companies made a similar mistake to that of some of the Gas Boards because they added the remaining book value of an asset which was to be scrapped to the capital cost of plant and equipment which would replace it.[17] However, he did not try to discover whether any other firms were, like the Gas Boards, spreading the balance of capital expenditure on the old plant over the life of the new and then deducting this charge when calculating the rate of return. The proportion of British firms which used the correct procedure, and confined their attention to avoidable costs, may have been smaller than Professor Lawson's inquiry suggests. An investigation of leading American companies by Professor D. F. Istvan, which appears to have been conducted in about 1958, revealed that, in one way or another, a quarter of the firms took the remaining book value of an asset into account when considering its replacement.[18]

The 'Discounted Cash Flow' Revolution

During recent years there has been a revolutionary change in the methods used within the public enterprise sector for assessing the rate of return on new investment. Not only have those nationalized undertakings which were making elementary mistakes ceased to do so, but there has been a widespread switch to sophisticated methods of investment appraisal. One of the principal weaknesses of the old common-sense methods of investment appraisal, even when correctly applied, was that they made no allowance for the way in which the profits expected from a project would be distributed through time. Yet this is of crucial importance since it is obvious that a pound to be earned in the near future is worth more to an undertaking than a pound to be earned in the distant future. A pound in the hand can be reinvested so that it yields an extra return whereas a pound in the bush cannot. Correspondingly, expenditure which will not occur for some years is a less serious burden than it appears, because it does not constitute an immediate drain upon the resources of the enterprise.

Because distant receipts are worth less than they appear and distant expenses are less of a burden than they appear, it is necessary for undertakings to calculate their present value. This can be accomplished by the process of discounting the future. If the rate of interest is 5 per cent then the enterprise must discount its future receipts (and expenses) by at least this amount for every year that they are expected to be delayed. If, for instance, it is expected that a certain investment project will earn a revenue of £100 three years hence, then with a 5 per cent rate of discount this will have a present value of about £85·7 (i.e. £100 less 5 per cent for the first year = £95; less 5 per cent for the second year = £90·25; and less 5 per cent for the third year = £85·7375). By calculating the present value of all receipts and deducting the present value of all expenses the enterprise will then be in a position to compare investment projects whose profits will be distributed differently through time. This, in essence, is the so-called 'discounted cash flow' method of investment appraisal which the nationalized industries have now adopted.[19]

The CEGB was the first public enterprise to adopt dcf techniques. As long ago as 1959–60, when it carried out its exercise to see whether it was worth replacing some of its old plant, it calculated the present value of the savings which were expected to arise.[20] During the mid-sixties most of the other nationalized industries switched over to dcf after the Treasury had taken the initiative in getting this technique adopted within the public enterprise sector. For instance, in 1965, British Rail laid down that henceforth dcf was normally to be used for all projects.[21] The Gas Boards started, at the suggestion of the Ministry of Power, to experiment with dcf in early 1965 and by early 1967 the technique appears to have been in regular use.[22] The air corporations also switched over to dcf at about the same time. In mid-1967 the Financial Director of BEA told the Select Committee that in all 'calculations – I can think of no exception – the dcf method of assessment has been used during the past few years, particularly in connection with aircraft purchases where we have gone to tremendous lengths to produce a very large number of dcf calculations for a wide variety of alternatives'. As the Board of Trade had confirmed, this is true not only of BEA but also of BOAC.[23]

The Select Committee on Nationalized Industries has expressed concern that although British Rail appears in theory to be fully committed to the use of dcf it is not being employed as widely as it should be. It was told by the Ministry of Transport that of the 57 major investment proposals which BR submitted between the beginning of 1965 and the end of 1966 only ten were accompanied by a dcf assessment when they were received, though three more were added at the Ministry's request. As British Rail does not submit its original investment calculations but prepares special documents for the Ministry, this does not necessarily mean that the railways had failed to calculate the dcf return for their own use. However, there does appear to have been some opposition to the use of dcf within British Rail and it seems likely that the technique was not being used to the full extent.[24] Fortunately the situation appears to have been improving rapidly. Between January 1967 and September 1968 the railways submitted 29 major projects which were estimated to cost £138 million. Of these 13, worth £104 million, were accompanied by dcf assessments, which means that although the number had not increased the proportion had and that at least 75 per cent of all the capital expenditure was covered by dcf calculations.[25] The situation now is reasonably satisfactory and by no means as disturbing as the Select Committee supposed.

The last industry to switch over to dcf was coal. Although the NCB had for some years used this technique to help evaluate capital expenditure on its subsidiary activities, it was not until 1969 that it was adopted for colliery projects. Even though it has now been adopted, at least in principle, the Board continues to use its old methods of appraisal for both colliery and ancillary projects which appear worthwhile on a dcf basis. A further restraint which has been placed on colliery investment is that the Board's total capital expenditure on collieries should not exceed the money available through depreciation provisions, without recourse to borrowing.[26]

Despite the Coal Board's somewhat anomalous position it is clear that the dcf revolution is now more or less complete and that the use of dcf techniques is now more widespread within the public enterprise sector than in private industry. It is ironic that the Treasury started by thinking that it would get the nationalized industries to adopt dcf like private industry and has ended by placing them ahead.[27] When the

Treasury first became interested in methods of investment appraisal only a handful of private firms were using dcf. About 2 per cent of the companies covered by Professor Lawson's survey were found to be employing discount cash flow, and Professor Nield's inquiry, which was slightly later, suggested that the proportion was only about 5 per cent.[28] Over the years the proportion of firms using dcf has gradually increased. A recent survey, which covered 83 quoted companies, disclosed that about 30 per cent used dcf as their principal method of evaluating capital projects. If however the smaller companies are excluded it appears that between 35 and 40 per cent of the larger firms placed most reliance on dcf.[29] Another inquiry which was carried out by the Ministry of Technology and the Manchester Business School during the first half of 1970 suggests that the proportion of company investment appraised by dcf is also somewhere between 35 and 40 per cent.[30] Although this is a substantial proportion there is little doubt that the public enterprise sector has a clear lead over the private sector in the use of dcf.

Allowing for Price Changes

Although it is important that undertakings should use the correct methods for calculating the rate of return their results will be no better than the estimates and assumptions which have been fed in. This does not mean, as is sometimes suggested, that dcf is worthless because unless it is used return calculations will be less reliable than the estimates and assumptions on which they depend. But it is important to recognize that dcf is not an automatic passport to successful estimating and that it must be handled with care. One area in which firms may easily go astray is in the assumptions which they make about future changes in prices. When calculating the prospective return on investment, undertakings will obviously have to make some estimate, both of the price which they will receive for their output, and of the price which they will be charged for the labour and materials they will require.

The problem here is not inflation but changes in relative prices. Firms will usually be able to assume that, when faced with an inflationary increase in costs, they will be able to increase their prices because their competitors will be forced to do the same. It may happen that an undertaking's competitive position is so weak that it cannot pass on the increase in costs which it has to bear even though they have not increased by more than the average amount. The railways, for instance, found themselves in this unenviable position.[31] Despite appearances, the problem here is not inflation but competitive weakness, because what is happening is that the undertaking's prices are falling relative to those of other products. To put the point another way, the undertaking would, due to its weak bargaining position, probably be forced to accept a lower price for its products in the absence of inflation.

Although an enterprise should try to allow for changes in the prices it will be charged by other firms they are usually difficult to foresee.[32] This is partly because of the number of products involved and partly because of the difficulty of knowing what developments are likely to take place in other industries. Fortunately such price changes are likely partly to cancel each other out. What is vital is that the nationalized industries should allow for what can be foreseen with confidence, and what is unlikely to be offset by other price changes, namely the increase in the price of labour. Obviously this tends to increase faster than the cost of other goods and services as the steady rise in real wages and in living standards shows. Those who are trying to calculate the rate of return on investment should build the assumption that the price of labour will increase into their estimates of the working expenses which will be incurred (and, in the case of a scheme for replacing old equipment, will be saved) if the project goes forward. If this is not done the desirability of economizing in the use of labour by using capital intensive methods (or by scrapping old labour intensive equipment) will be obscured.

It is necessary for the nationalized industries to do more than this because they must also allow for the effect which rising wages will have on their general financial position. If they fail to make any allowance, they run the risk that, if the rise in wages is not offset by higher productivity, they will need to increase their prices, in which case the industry may need to carry out less investment than it was planning. If it decides to increase its prices the demand for its products may rise more slowly, or fall faster, than its initial demand forecasts suggested, and if it decides not to make an increase (because the elasticity of demand for its products is greater than one) the least profitable parts of the business will start to incur losses and have to be closed. Either less investment in extra capacity will be necessary or less capital expenditure on replacing old plant will have to be carried out. The nationalized industries must, therefore, try to discover how far the tendency for their costs to rise, due to increased wages, will be offset by higher productivity, and what will happen to demand if they keep their prices in line with costs. This is extremely difficult, because the extent to which productivity increases will largely depend on how much investment is carried out, and because the extent to which demand is sensitive to price will depend on how much competition they will face from other industries.

Investment planning is a circular process in which the original demand estimates, if it is here that the circle is broken into, must later be modified when it is discovered how much investment appears to be necessary and what the implications for productivity will be. What we must now try to find out is whether the nationalized industries have allowed for the prospective increase in wages in their calculations of the rate of return on investment; whether they have made realistic forecasts of their future financial position which allow, on the one hand, for rising wages and, on the other, for higher productivity; and finally whether they have examined the consequences which this, and the development of competition from other industries, will have on the prices they charge and the demand they can expect. Unfortunately, there is less information available on these questions than on those which have previously been discussed. However, there is sufficient to arrive at tentative answers to at least some of these questions.

It is clear that for a long period the coal industry consistently failed to take rising wages properly into account and that the railways sometimes failed to do so. As we have seen, the NCB estimated in *Plan for Coal* that modernization would reduce the industry's costs by 7s 0d a ton at 1949 prices. However, the Board recognized that 'not all the saving will benefit the consumers of coal; the men employed in the industry will also share in it, since over the years their earnings are expected to increase with rising productivity'. Where the NCB went wrong was that it ignored the fact that wages would rise, regardless of what happened to productivity, and wrongly assumed that only a small rise in earnings was likely. For instance, it was estimated in *Plan for Coal* that 'Earnings per manshift would rise, with increased productivity, by an average of nearly 9 per cent for the country as a whole'.[33]

It is by no means clear how this figure was arrived at, but it seems likely that this was the automatic rise in the industry's wage bill which it was expected that higher productivity would bring about through the renegotiation of price lists, and the award of higher wages to time workers so that they would not fall behind.[34] What is clear is that the Board's allowance for higher wages was quite inadequate. This is probably explained by the fact that its main interest was the effect which higher wages would have on the relative costs of the different coalfields. The gains in productivity due to modernization, and the increase in earnings which this would entail, were not expected to be uniform. As a result the Board needed to know how relative costs of production would be affected, because this helped to determine what tonnage each coalfield could be expected to produce. Having made a calculation of the increase in earnings which was appropriate for the limited purpose which it had in mind, the Board appears to have assumed that it did not have to worry about higher wages because they were only going to increase by about 9 per cent. It seems that it came to believe that the price of coal would decline relatively to that of other products, although the size of the productivity gains which were envisaged made this extremely unlikely.[35]

The Ministry of Power's survey of the Board's methods of investment appraisal during 1963 revealed that the allowance which it made for higher earnings still only covered the automatic increase due to the rise in productivity which the project would bring about. By this time the Board could argue that increases in productivity would be great enough at least to offset the rise in wages which would take place. If the Board was right this meant that its prices would not have to be increased relative to those of other products, in which case the danger that it would invest in pits whose demand had been choked off would be less than it would otherwise. Furthermore, to guard against investment in pits which would become unprofitable, the Board had recently started to calculate the effect which likely wage increases would have on pit finances up to the date of the completion of the project, because presumably gains in productivity might, up to that point, be insufficient to cover higher wage costs.

Nevertheless the Board's Finance Department was wrong to argue that, because wage increases would take place irrespective of investment, the return on its projects would appear still higher, if wage increases were taken into account, as costs would rise but for the gains in productivity which investment would bring about.[36] What the Finance Department was assuming was that a pit would receive the higher profit which would arise if wages did not increase and investment reduced its costs; and that it would avoid the reduction in profits which would occur if wages increased and its costs rose without any compensating gains in productivity. Obviously both advantages cannot be obtained at the same time. Either wage rates will remain the same, costs will fall as productivity rises, and profits will increase; or alternatively wage rates will increase but productivity gains will hold costs down, and a reduction in profits will be avoided. The Coal Board was not understating the profitability of its projects as it imagined but, through failing to take account of higher wages, was running the risk of not investing sufficiently in labour-saving devices, which if the price of labour is going to increase are more attractive than they appear. It may be replied that the Coal Board was well aware of the importance of securing higher productivity. This is of course true, but undertakings should wherever possible avoid the risk of being led astray.

The railways' treatment of wages was inconsistent. On some occasions they may have allowed for rising wages, whila at other times they certainly did not. The BTC began in the Modernization Plan by making no allowance for the adverse effect which higher wages would have on the savings which it expected to secure.[37] However I have been told on good authority (although I remain slightly sceptical) that in 1956 the Commission started to allow for rising wages, and that the financial forecasts which were presented in *Proposals for the Railways* were based on the assumption that there would be an increase of about 2 per cent per annum. Similarly the estimates given in the Re-appraisal of the Plan are said to have been based on the same assumption, except that a special allowance of 6 per cent was made to cover the wage award which it was expected that the Guillebaud Committee would recommend. In fact the Committee was more generous than had been expected and the award turned out to be 10 per cent for salaried staff and 8 per cent for manual workers which immediately imperilled the BTC's forecast that the railways would have a working surplus by 1963.[38] Despite this object lesson in the importance of allowing for wages, the Beeching Report, which in this respect was a step backwards, made no allowance at all. This was one of the major reasons why it has been a financial failure. The savings which were expected have been more or less achieved but they have largely been absorbed by the increase in the pay of railwaymen which should have been foreseen.[39]

To what extent the other nationalized industries have in the past allowed for increases in wage rates and other changes in relative costs is not entirely clear. It seems doubtful whether any of them made any allowance in their calculations for the costs which they would incur or avoid if particular projects went forward. Even in the electricity industry, whose estimates were in other ways extremely sophisticated, no account appears to have been taken in its calculations of the desirability of replacing old plant, of likely changes in the price of labour or the cost of fuel.[40] It is possible that some of the nationalized industries for some years may have been allowing for rising wages in their general estimates of their financial prospects or their revenue budgets as they have come to be known.

During recent years there has been a marked improvement in the nationalized industries' methods. Some of them, at least, now allow for higher wages when estimating the rate of return on their projects and all appear to base their general financial forecasts on the assumption that earnings will increase. The railways are an interesting example of the way in which the correct financial procedures have been adopted. The instructions on investment appraisal which the Board issued in 1965 stated that, although estimates should be made initially at current wage and price levels, an alternative calculation should normally be made on the assumption that real wages would rise. Moreover, it is apparent from the Board's memorandum that considerable thought has been devoted to the problem of making the allowance for higher earnings as realistic as possible.

> A reasonable basis [the Board concluded] would be an average increase of about 4 per cent a year reduced by increased productivity from causes other than the investment itself to 2 per cent in the case of maintenance staff and to 3 per cent for most other staff, but for certain staff, e.g. signalling, increased productivity must depend mainly on investment. Where the price of alternative commodities, e.g. electricity or oil, are important the effect of differing changes in prices should be illustrated.[41]

British Rail has also started to allow for the impact of higher earnings in its revenue budget. For instance, the financial forecasts which the railways prepared for the Joint Steering Group in 1967 were based on the assumption that real wages would rise by 3 per cent per annum. At that time no allowance was made for other changes in relative prices but in its report the Group stated that detailed consideration would be given to the problem.[42]

Information on the way in which changes in relative prices are now handled is less plentiful for the other nationalized industries than it is for British Rail. However it is known that the CEGB tries to estimate, after considering past experience, the way in which relative fuel prices will change when it is comparing different types of plant.[43] It is also clear that the Gas Boards and the NCB allow for increased earnings in their revenue budgets.[44]

Once the nationalized industries have estimated their future costs, by allowing on the one hand for higher productivity and on the other for higher earnings, they should modify their initial estimates of demand in the light of what they discover. It is evident that in the past there was no feed-back of this type. In coal and to some extent railways there could not be any proper feed-back because the industries' estimates of their future costs were so unsatisfactory; and in electricity, where it might have been possible, little attention was paid to the possible relationship between demand and price.[45] This does not mean that the nationalized industries made no assumption about changes in relative prices or the effect they would have on the demand for their products. When, for instance, they based their estimates on past trends they were, among other things, assuming that relative prices would go on changing in the future as they had in the past.

It is not entirely clear to what extent the nationalized industries now try to modify their demand forecasts in the light of likely changes in their costs and their competitors' prices. We do know that the Electricity Council has recently undertaken a considerable amount of work on the responsiveness of the demand for electricity to factors such as price, and that the Gas Council, and the Ministry of Power, have been making an intensive study of the impact which cheap North Sea gas will have on the demand for the different fuels.[46] The way in which the problem of allowing for changes in relative prices is now being tackled within the public enterprise sector provides further evidence of the swift progress which the nationalized industries are making in the field of investment appraisal and the high degree of sophistication which they have now reached.

A Case Study of Investment Appraisal

After this general discussion of the revolutionary changes which have been taking place in the nationalized industries' methods of investment appraisal, a brief case study of the process in one part of the public enterprise sector may be of interest. During the winter of 1964-5 when I was investigating the capital development programme of the West Midlands Gas Board, I had the good fortune to observe the dcf revolution from the inside. At that time the Board was busy constructing a super-grid to link up the local distribution networks which had already been constructed, and was switching over to the new gas-making process based on oil which had recently become available. From vesting date until about 1960 the West Midlands Gas Board (WMGB) had, like the rest of the industry, adopted a policy of linking up the old gas undertakings and closing small and inefficient works.[47] The rate of progress had been comparatively slow and in 1961 the Board's area contained two main grid systems and a number of networks, whereas integration had already been completed in some parts of the country.[48] According to the Board this was due to the extraordinary difficulty which it had had in finding a suitable site and then obtaining planning permission for a Lurgi plant. The Board's plans for integration hinged upon the construction of this plant, which unlike the traditional processes for making gas from coal had the advantage that the gas is produced at high pressure. This means that it can be distributed over long distances without the expense of pumping.

At last at the end of 1958 the Board received permission to go ahead with the Lurgi plant and it came into operation in mid-1963.[49] By this time the new processes for making gas from light oil had become available. These were highly attractive not only because they too produced gas at high pressure but also because of their low capital and operating costs. As a result the Board had started to push ahead with integration and the closure of its carbonization plant. Moreover in 1961 the Board had come under the vigorous direction of Mr C. H. Leach and the team which he had brought with him from the Southern Gas Board, where

M

integration had already been completed with impressive results.[50] Before that, Mr Leach and his colleagues had been at the North Western Gas Board, and their transfer from area to area is an interesting example of the way in which managerial expertise can be deployed to the best advantage within the public enterprise sector.[51] The drive and initiative of the Board's new management is well illustrated by the completion and occupation of the largest open office in Europe only 12 months after the project had been proposed.[52] Certainly no description of the Board would be complete without a reference to its extraordinary but highly efficient headquarters building.

By the spring of 1964 not only had the Lurgi plant been brought into operation at Coleshill, which is just outside Birmingham, but the Board had also constructed part of its projected super-grid, which radiated from Coleshill. At this point the Board's grid was linked to the national methane pipelines, although the rich natural gas, which was to be used to enrich the lean Lurgi gas, was not received until late in the year. The WMGB had started work on a plant, also at Coleshill, for making gas from light oil which was to come into operation by the end of 1964. Due to the rapid increase in gas demand and the great commercial attraction of the new gas-making processes five more projects were planned for construction by the spring of 1969. This, it was thought, would permit the closure of a large number of works, although it was expected that coal gas produced by traditional methods would still account for 28 per cent of sales during 1967–8. So that this programme could go forward the super-grid system was to be greatly extended in order that the integration of the area would be complete by about the end of 1966.

The financial justification for this plan was contained in the Board's Capital Development Review for 1964, which was submitted to the Ministry and the Gas Council in February. The Review contained the following explanation of the Board's economic method:

> The avoidable annual costs of existing plant i.e. excluding depreciation and interest, are compared with the annual costs of alternative plant including depreciation but excluding interest. Any resultant saving is then converted to a percentage return on the capital cost of the new plant. This return, therefore, represents the margin to cover the payment of interest and to provide a contribution to net surplus. The minimum return looked for on this basis is 7 per cent . . . In making an economic assessment about whether an old installation ought, or ought not, to be replaced, any charge for obsolescence arising on the old plant is not taken into account.

The WMGB, therefore, followed the principles of commonsense economics and avoided the mistake, which a few of the gas boards made of trying to allow for obsolescence when calculating the return on new plant.[53]

Details were given of the estimated costs of gas production, including capital charges, at each of the works where capital expenditure would be incurred between 1964–5 and 1968–9 which was the period covered by the Review. For instance it was expected that at the Lurgi plant the cost would be 10·67d per therm if it was operated at a load factor of 93 per cent, and 13·26d at a load factor of 52 per cent. But at the new oil-based plant the costs would be only around 6·5d per therm at a load factor of 60 per cent and 7·3d for a load factor of 40 per cent. The Board did not compare these latter figures directly with the avoidable costs of producing gas at its old works. As it recognized, the installation of the new plants involved the construction of the grid system, the costs of which must be taken into account. Instead of treating the new plants and the new grid as a joint project the WMGB tried to calculate the rate of return on the grid alone.

What it did was to compare the avoidable costs of producing gas at the works which were to be closed with the total costs of the replacement gas from the Lurgi plant and the new oil-based works. It was estimated that the avoidable costs were £10,302,000 (230 million therms at 10·75d per therm), and that the cost of the Lurgi gas was £4,135,000 (93 million therms at 10·67d per therm) and that the cost of the gas to be produced from light oil was £4,281,000 (137 million therms at 7·5d). Ignoring for the moment the cost of the new grid the Board would therefore save itself £1,886,000 by replacement, though it is apparent that virtually all of this would arise through the installation of the oil-based plant despite the assumption that the Lurgi would operate at a 92 per cent load factor. Next the Board made an estimate of the financial consequences of meeting the increase of 99 million therms in demand for gas which was expected by 1968–9. It multiplied this by 2·58d per therm, which was the difference between what its production costs would be at the plant using light oil (7·5d) and what they had been in 1962–3 (10·08d) when the integration scheme was in its early stages. On this basis the financial benefit from the increase in sales appeared to be £1,064,000. Including replacement gas (at £1,886,000) there would, therefore, be a gross saving of £2,950,000. However, as the capital charges and other costs of the new grid main were put at £682,000 the net annual benefit on the integration scheme was stated to be £2,268,000. When this was expressed as a proportion of the capital which had been or would have to be invested in the new grid main (£7,073,000), a return of 37·5 per cent was shown.

Though better than nothing this was a somewhat curious calculation. The financial benefit which would be obtained by constructing extra plant to meet the increase in demand was, for instance, calculated wrongly. What the Board should have done was to compare the extra revenue it would earn with the extra costs which would arise. These would have consisted partly of the cost of producing the gas at the new works and partly of the distribution costs which it would incur, apart from the cost of the grid as this was included elsewhere. Instead the Board compared the costs of production at its existing works with those at the new works which were planned. Another curious feature of the calculation was that the Board credited the grid with all the saving which would arise from the closure of high-costs works and the introduction of new gas-making plant. What the WMGB should have done was to relate the saving to the total capital expenditure which was necessary if it was to be secured. As it was estimated that the grid would cost £7,073,000 and that Lurgi and the light oil plants to be completed by 1968–9 would cost £26,727,000, the total investment appears at first sight to have been £33,800,000.

However, this ignores the indirect consequences of scrapping old plant and of producing extra gas. If it closed down its high-costs works the Board would be able to realize about £2 million by disposing of their sites, and it would be able to avoid the heavy and growing expenditure on repairs which would be necessary if its old plants were to be kept in operation. Although the Board did not make any allowance for this in its calculations it was one of the reasons which it gave to justify scrapping. Not all of the indirect consequences of the Board's plans were financially favourable. In order to supply increased quantities of gas the WMGB would, besides having to install extra plant and construct a grid, need to reinforce its local distribution network. It was planning to extend gas supplies to new housing estates and new towns and these would obviously account for part of its extra sales. Although it is impossible to tell from the 1964 Capital Development Review just how much capital was to be devoted to reinforcement and extension, the figure must have been considerable. It must, therefore, be concluded that the rate of return calculation presented in the 1964 Review was misleading partly because the profit from selling extra gas was estimated in the wrong way, and partly because so much of the investment which ought to have been included was not taken into account.

The WMGB did provide other estimates in which it tried to assess the rate of return on all its investment. In its Revenue Budget it gave estimates of its revenue and its expenditure for the next five years. These included an allowance for the increased earnings which its employees would receive on the assumption that they would rise by $3\frac{1}{2}$ per cent each year. The Board's estimates showed a surplus after interest and depreciation on capital had been deducted, and it was expected that it would rise rapidly over the period. Finally this surplus was expressed as a rate of return on the net capital which would be employed. Although there was going to be a considerable increase in the book value of the Board's assets a sharp increase in the rate of return was forecast. This did not show what the return would be on new capital because the book value included past investment and the surplus included profits attributable to past investment. However it was clear that the rate of return on new capital must be high and that the Board was right to push ahead with its investment programme. Providing that the Board's basic figures were right, what other explanation, except perhaps a rise in prices which was not assumed, could there be? If, on the other hand, a decline in the surplus and in the rate of return on net assets had been shown the Board would presumably have been put on its guard. The Revenue Budget did, therefore, provide a valuable function and the mistake of not allowing for the increase in real wages was avoided.

Having examined the methods used in the West Midlands before the dcf revolution, we can now examine the switch-over to sophisticated techniques of investment appraisal. The Ministry of Power initiated the process. In the spring of 1964 when Ministry officials paid their annual visit to the Gas Boards to discuss their Capital Development Reviews, there was some discussion of whether Boards could provide an assessment of the profitability on their investment programme considered as a whole. In June, at a meeting between the Ministry and the Gas Council, it was agreed that the subject should be investigated and, as a result, five Boards prepared estimates for the Ministry. The Boards did not all use the same methods so that the Ministry devised a standard procedure which was then discussed with the industry.

The object of the assessment was to show the benefits to be derived from investment designed to meet the growth of demand or to reduce costs. All investment on projects which would be completed during the next five years was to be included, taking into account the money which had already been spent. The only exception was capital expenditure of a purely replacement nature such as renewals of mains, meters and vehicles. Allowance was to be made for interest during construction, for increases in working capital, and for the disposal value of old plant. The benefit from this investment, so far as additional sales were concerned, was the extra revenue which was expected less the extra production and distribution costs which would be incurred. For gas produced at plants which were being replaced the benefit was the costs of production at the old works at the beginning of the period, excluding capital changes, less the costs of production at the new plants. The total financial benefit was then to be shown as a rate of return on the capital involved before depreciation and interest, after depreciation alone, and after both depreciation and interest.

It is evident that this method of investment appraisal was a great improvement on the Board's old procedure. Most of the mistakes made by the Board had been avoided. For instance, whereas the Board had expressed the financial benefit from replacing old plant and supplying extra gas as a return on grid investment, the Ministry adopted the correct procedure and expressed it as a return on all the capital expenditure involved. However, the Ministry did make two serious mistakes. First, it was laid down that no allowance was to be made for increasing wages, and for other changes in relative prices, except where an increase was expected during the next few months. Secondly, in calculating the saving by replacing old plant, Boards were told to assume that their costs of production would remain the same although their continued operation might well necessitate heavy repairs and be accompanied by increased maintenance costs. Fortunately these mistakes were likely to lead to the profitability of new investment being understated and not overstated.

As part of its Capital Development Review for 1965 the West Midlands Board duly calculated the rate of return on its programme of new investment using the Ministry formula. The details of the calculation need not detain us as our primary concern is the methods which were employed, but a return of 11·8 per cent was shown after depreciation (on an annuity basis). Since the Lurgi plant had already been constructed this represented the return which the introduction of oil-based plant, and of course other developments such as the grid, had made possible. If Lurgi had been included the rate of return would have appeared somewhat lower. Disregarding this plant, whose construction had been delayed by factors beyond the Board's control, the rate of return it was expecting on its new investment appeared respectable, though not dramatic. According to the Gas Council, the West Midlands' figure was lower than that of most other Boards so that the prospective return on the industry's investment must have appeared even more attractive.

But, of course, these calculations took no account of the way in which future profits would be distributed through time, because dcf was not yet being used. This method started to be employed in the West Midlands almost immediately after the Ministry's new and more sophisticated formula had been adopted. What happened was that dcf and the Ministry's method were brought together, and that the return on capital expenditure on projects to be completed during the next five years was estimated. For the purpose of this calculation, it was assumed that unit costs and unit revenue would not change over the period of the assessment. This was taken as 15 years and the net book value of those assets with a probable life of more than 15 years was brought in at the end of the period as an additional item of revenue. Provision was included for the replacement of equipment which would wear out during the course of the period. On this basis it was estimated that the dcf or internal rate of return would be 14·7 per cent, i.e. this was the rate of discount at which the present value of the Board's net cash receipts would be zero.

The most obvious weakness of this calculation was that the West Midland Board, like the Ministry of Power, made no allowance for the rise in earnings which would occur at its old plants if they were not replaced or at the new plants which it planned to construct. Nor did it take into account the way in which maintenance costs would increase at both types of plant. By not allowing for these factors the Board understated the profitability of its investment programme. This was partly because the old plants which were to be scrapped were considerably more labour intensive than those which were to be constructed. Indeed the Board estimated that its total employment would fall by about a fifth over the period covered by the Review. As a result higher earnings would have less impact on costs if old plant were scrapped than if it were retained. The other reason why the financial benefits of new investment were understated was that the rise in maintenance costs would almost certainly be larger and sharper at the old plants than it would at the new. There was no danger that by failing to allow for changes in unit costs in its dcf calculations the Board would be encouraged to over-invest.

It is clear now that the problem of risk should have received more attention. In particular, the impact which North Sea gas would have if it was discovered in large quantities should have been thought out. If it was discovered in small quantities there would be no problem because it would, as the Board's officials argued, be used for enrichment purposes, but its discovery in large quantities would make redundant some, or all, of the new plant which they were planning to construct. The risk that this would happen does not seem to have been squarely faced up to. Even if it had been, it seems very doubtful whether it would or should have led to any significant alteration in the Board's plans. Most of the plant which was being installed was required if the growth in demand was to be met. If the Board had decided not to construct this plant because of the risk that it would be rendered redundant, its only course of action would have been to have choked off demand by sharply increasing prices. Even if the risk that large amounts of natural gas would be discovered had been a certainty, this would not have been justified, because the market would have been spoilt for North Sea gas when it arrived, and the industry's future profitability would have been impaired. The Gas Board would have fallen into the error of setting its prices high above its long-run marginal costs.

CHAPTER 16

Target Rates of Return

Now that we have considered the way in which the nationalized industries plan their investment and calculate the prospective rate of return, our next task is to try to discover whether they have aimed at a proper rate or been content with too low a yield. But what is the minimum rate of return which the nationalized industries should require before they approve a capital project? At first sight the answer appears to be obvious: the nationalized industries should seek to earn at least the minimum rate which private companies demand before they invest. If they do not, projects will be approved in the public enterprise sector although they show a lower rate of return than some of the schemes which private firms reject. As a result resources will be misallocated. The available evidence suggests that the rate which private firms require is a very high one. For instance, a survey conducted by the Centre for Business Research at Manchester University showed that many firms apparently look for a rate of return of 15 per cent and sometimes more.[1] If only because of the widespread failure within the private sector to make detailed profitability calculations, too much weight should not be attached to such findings. Nevertheless it does seem likely that the rate of return at which most private firms aim is considerably greater than the rates with which the nationalized industries have been content.

Before concluding that the nationalized industries should raise their sights in future, and that they have been a cause of misallocation in the past, it is necessary to take a closer look at the argument for believing that public enterprise should follow private practice. This argument assumes either that the reduction in the nationalized industries' capital expenditure which takes place when they increase their minimum rate of return to the private level will be offset by an increase in private sector investment, or that the general level of investment is already more than adequate. Clearly if the general level of investment is excessive, it is desirable that the low yield projects which are being approved in the public enterprise sector should be disallowed. However, far from being too high the British level of investment has almost certainly been too low. As is well known, Britain invests a much smaller proportion of its national income than most other industrial nations.[2] It would therefore

347

be wrong to insist that the nationalized industries should, by requiring a 'commercial' rate of return, restrict their investment unless it is reasonably certain that the fall will be made good by a rise in private investment.

The financial mechanism by which the necessary switch from public to private investment should be brought about is the rate of interest. Ever since they were brought into public ownership a large part of the nationalized industries' investment programmes have been financed by Government borrowing. If these programmes are reduced, Government borrowing will fall, and because this constitutes such an important part of the demand for loanable funds the rate of interest will tend to decline. But numerous investigations have shown that private investment does not readily respond to changes in the rate of interest. It would, therefore, be most unwise to assume that lower interest rates will automatically lead to a rise in private investment. There is no other reason why a cutback in public investment should, in the absence of deliberate Government action, be expected to have this result. The cutback is not in itself going to make private businessmen more disposed to invest. If anything, it will have the reverse effect because the reduction in public investment will, by lowering the general level of demand, make private firms feel less confident.

It might be possible for the Government to induce the private sector to increase its investment by the amount by which the nationalized industries' capital expenditure has fallen. Whether this is the case depends on the efficacy of the various fiscal tools by which the Government tries to adjust the rate of private investment. These include a reduction in company taxation, tax concessions such as investment and initial allowances, and the new investment subsidies by which the latter have been largely replaced. The difficulty with these devices is that their effectiveness partly depends on whether firms take tax into consideration when calculating the return on their investment. The available evidence suggest that they do not and that investment incentives are generally ineffective.

Almost all the businessmen consulted by the Richardson Committee stated that the possible changes in taxation discussed by the Committee, including the elimination of profits tax, would have no effect on their investment programmes, and they were broadly agreed that factors other than taxation largely determined investment decisions.[3] That firms do not respond strongly to changes in investment incentives has been confirmed by a number of surveys. When asked whether their investment decisions have been effected by favourable changes in the tax treatment of capital expenditure only between a fifth and a third of firms say that it has.[4] Although it is possible that firms will gradually become more responsive to changes in taxation as they become more sophisticated and adopt dcf, it would clearly be wrong to assume that as of now the Government can determine the level of private investment by altering the rate of taxation. If this were possible it would long ago have seen that the level was stepped up in the interests of a faster rate of growth.

If the Government wished to bring about an increase in private investment to counterbalance a fall in the nationalized industries' capital expenditure it would have to fall back, like so many Chancellors in the past, on the policy of stimulating demand. There is no doubt that private investment tends to rise when demand is high and production is increasing at a rapid rate. All the empirical studies which have been made show that it is demand and production, rather than profits, which determine private investment, although the way in which manufacturing investment follows manufacturing output makes elaborate investigations almost unnecessary.[5] Nevertheless, it is unlikely that the attempt to raise private investment by stimulating consumption will be a great success because the resources which the reduction in public investment has freed will be more or less absorbed in the process. Unless a very small increase in consumption brings about a very large increase in private investment, which seems improbable, most of the available resources will obviously have to be devoted to extra consumption and will not be available for extra investment. As a result the amount by which private investment rises will be considerably less than the amount by which the nationalized industries' capital expenditure has fallen. Thus it is almost certain that any fall in their investment, because they are seeking higher rates of return, will tend to depress national investment and the rate of economic growth.[6]

This will be met by the counter-argument that a little investment in the private sector goes a long way. Because the industries in private ownership are less capital intensive than the nationalized industries, less capital expenditure is required to increase the capacity of the private sector by 10 per cent than is required to increase public enterprise capacity by the same amount. It is unnecessary for private investment to rise by the amount which public investment falls in order that the rate of growth should be maintained. What this ignores is that just because the nationalized industries are capital intensive they require relatively little manpower and that this is a positive advantage in times of full employment. It is by no means obvious that the necessary manpower would be available to provide the extra output which a partial switch from public to private enterprise investment would make possible. The position might, of course, be different if the extra private investment was primarily of a labour-saving rather than of an output-increasing type. But why should it be supposed that an increase in demand will encourage private firms to install labour-saving equipment? It is surely more reasonable to suppose that their investment will be primarily designed to increase their capacity, though due to technical progress it will no doubt be somewhat more productive than existing equipment.

It must be concluded that the minimum rate of return which public enterprise should seek to earn on its capital expenditure should be relatively low, even if this means that projects are approved which would be rejected by private enterprise. This, despite the arguments which have been put forward, may appear to violate the normal rules for the efficient allocation of resources. What these rules assume is that the general level of investment is right and will stay right, but this certainly cannot be taken for granted. As Britain's high pre-war rate of unemployment showed, and as our slow post-war rate of growth has confirmed, national investment can be too low. In this situation it is wrong to make public enterprise dance to the tune called by private firms. What ought to happen is that this tune should be altered, if necessary by placing the pipe in other hands. Once private firms have stepped up their investment, a process which will itself tend to increase prospective rates of return, the ideal rules for the allocation for resources can be adopted without the likelihood that they will do more harm than good. This means that the existing nationalized industries should be expected to seek the same minimum return as the rest of industry. However, until the rate of investment is considerably higher than it is now the nationalized industries should not be expected to earn a 'commercial' rate of return on their new investment, unless, of course, it can be shown that if the nationalized industries reduce their capital expenditure the general level of investment will rise. But there is no reason to believe that this paradox would turn out to be true.

This line of argument should not be taken to mean that the nationalized industries should be prepared to accept a low overall rate of return on their investment unless this is the result of a number of projects all of which are just worth accepting. In most cases a low average rate should put them on their guard because it will mean that some projects are being approved whose profitability is so poor that they ought to be rejected. It would be wrong for public enterprise to create excess capacity, and use the profits which it will earn on the capacity which will be needed to meet its losses on the plant which will not be wanted. However it does seem right that the nationalized industries should be prepared to approve individual projects on which the prospective rate of return is considerably lower than the 15 per cent rate at which they might be rejected by a private firm.

The Test Rate of Discount

Although this general principle is satisfactory as far as it goes, it does not go far enough. For what the nationalized industries need to know in order to assess their investment projects, and we need to know in order to assess their performance, is the minimum rate of return at which capital expenditure should be sanctioned. There obviously comes a point where it is more advantageous to have a little private investment at a high rate of return than a lot of public investment at a low rate of return. During recent years the Government has devoted considerable thought to the minimum rate of return at which public enterprise should aim and in the 1967 White Paper in which the financial objectives of the nationalized industries were reviewed it laid down that the test rate of discount should be 8 per cent. In other words this was the rate at which they were instructed, when using the dcf method of appraisal, to discount their future receipts and expenses and so calculate their present value.[7]

The way in which the figure of 8 per cent was arrived at has been explained, and explained very clearly, by the Treasury. In its own words it seemed desirable

> with a view to getting the best possible allocation of investible resources between publicly owned and privately owned industries, to aim at a test discount rate for the public sector similar to the minimum return which would be regarded as acceptable on new investment by a private firm. It was plain that no single figure could be expected to apply to private companies of all sizes and types, but it seemed reasonable to set a rate for public corporations which corresponded to the cut-off rate likely to be used by a large private firm of good standing and engaged in low risk business. A study of some of the available writings on the subject, and discussions held with a number of large private sector undertakings, revealed some differences of opinion (as was to be expected); however most of those who had thought about the subject carefully, and used discounted cash flow methods of appraisal to calculate returns on investment, were of the opinion that the minimum return acceptable would be something between 6 per cent and 8 per cent after tax, at constant prices. On the basis of the tax arrangements in force at the time (before the change to Corporation Tax) we calculated that the corresponding gross of tax return would be below the range 12–16 per cent which would have been indicated by simply grossing up the range 6–8 per cent by a margin sufficient to allow for income tax and profits tax. This was because the combined effect of investment allowances, initial

allowances, and the common practice of calculating annual depreciation allowances at a constant proportion of the reducing balance of cash invested meant that little if any tax would become payable in the first years in which profits were earned, the effective rate of tax on a given profit level increasing steadily as the amounts allowed for depreciation diminished. Since profits earned in early years are weighted more heavily than those earned in later years when discounted cash flow methods of appraisal are used, the effect is to reduce the difference between rates of return before and after tax below what it would be if there were no investment allowances or initial allowances and if annual allowances were given only on a straight-line basis. Bearing these factors in mind, it seemed that a rate of return before tax within the range 8 per cent to 10 per cent would be appropriate. In the light of the Government's policy of encouraging investment that would lead to higher productivity and faster growth, it seemed appropriate to take the lower end of this range rather than the centre, and the figure chosen was therefore 8 per cent.[8]

At first sight it appears that the Treasury has fallen into the error of requiring public enterprise to dance to the mistaken tune which private industry calls. This is not really the case because the Treasury obviously confined its attention to large and sophisticated firms. What it should have discovered when it asked them about their cut-off rates was the cost of capital to large firms. A sophisticated firm should be prepared to sanction all projects where the prospective return is higher than its cost of capital. The latter and its minimum acceptable rate of return should be one and the same thing. It seems reasonably clear that the nationalized industries should not invest in projects where the estimated return is lower than the rate which large private firms have to pay. This, it is true, is higher than the rate at which the Government can borrow on behalf of the nationalized industries. But if public enterprise obtains large sums at this privileged rate for the purpose of investing in projects which have a low rate of return, less funds will be available for private firms and their cost of capital will be higher than it would otherwise be. This means that projects whose rate of return is just below this excessively high level will no longer be undertaken, even though they are more worthwhile than the low-yield investment which the nationalized industries are making. The cost of capital to private industry turns out to be (or at least to be closely related to) that elusive beast 'the social opportunity cost of capital,' i.e. what society would forgo by using the capital in the project under consideration rather than in the employment for which it would otherwise be used.

Now that we have identified the minimum rate of return which the nationalized industries should seek, we are almost in a position to see whether they have fallen below this norm. First, it is necessary to check the Government's figure of 8 per cent, which in the summer of 1969 was revised upwards to 10 per cent. This can be done by making a direct calculation of the cost of capital to private firms. This is the rate of return which they must provide for those who buy their shares and securities. Since expectations largely depend on experience, this rate is determined in the main by what shareholders have earned in the past. These earnings comprise not only the dividends which they have received but also the capital gains which they have made. Capital appreciation is sometimes ignored when the cost of capital to the private firm is under discussion.[9] However, it is clear that it must be included because the reason why capital gains arise is that only part of the profit which the firm makes on the investment it undertakes with shareholders' money is paid out in dividends. Consequently to ignore capital gains is to disregard part of the profit which firms need to earn on their capital expenditure and understate their cost of capital.

What then has been the return as measured by dividends and capital gains which equity shareholders have received in the past? A study by Professor A. J. Merrett and Mr Alan Sykes suggests that after allowing for the general rise in prices it has been no higher than 7 per cent net of tax. They found, for instance, that from January 1956 to January 1966 the return in dividends and capital gains on a lump sum invested in January 1956 was 5·9 per cent.[10] If the cost of equity finance has been about 7 per cent then, as Mr A. M. Alfred the chief economist of Courtaulds has shown, the overall cost to private firms has been just over 6 per cent. This is because a small part of their finance is raised by means of fixed interest stock which is a relatively cheap source of finance.[11] This suggests that the minimum acceptable rate of return in the private sector after tax was at or near the bottom end of the range of 6–8 per cent on which the Government based its calculations of the test rate of discount for public enterprise. If so, the rate before tax was also at or near the bottom end of the range estimated by the Government, which means that it was nearer 8 per cent than 10 per cent. Indeed Mr Alfred calculates that it was only about 7 per cent.[12] There is no reason to believe that prior to the introduction of Corporation tax the test rate of discount should have been any higher than 8 per cent, and this becomes a suitable bench-mark for assessing the rate of discount of those nationalized industries which were already using dcf.

As Corporation tax was brought in during 1965 this, in practice, means the electricity industry. Up to the early sixties the rate of discount which the CEGB used in its investment calculations was for most types of investment fixed in the light of what it had to pay on new long-term capital.[13] For example when in 1959–60 the Board carried out its exercises to decide whether it was worth replacing old plant, and at what voltage the new supergrid should operate, it assumed an interest rate of $5\frac{1}{2}$ per cent. This was obviously on the low side but after the industries' financial objectives had been agreed in 1961–2 the CEGB adopted a rate which was first 8 per cent but was later reduced to $7\frac{1}{2}$ per cent.[14]

For this it was roundly condemned by Professor Ronald Meek who believed that the figure had been arrived at by adding the percentage rate of surplus, which the Government was now expecting, to its borrowing rate. This, he thought, was an arbitrary procedure which except by accident would not lead to the opportunity cost of capital being adopted. To quote Professor Meek's own words:

> When the Secretary of State for Scotland instructs the North of Scotland Hydro-Electric Board to calculate comparative capital costs on the basis of a rate of interest of 8 per cent, or when a similar rate is used [by the CEGB] in the calculations upon which the current conclusions about the 'competitiveness' of nuclear power are based, it is not generally realized that the principles according to which this rate has been selected are arbitrary and ill-founded; that in all probability the rate is too high; and that the use of a rather lower rate is capable of altering the whole picture.[15]

Despite Professor Meek's strictures, the CEGB appears not only to have selected the right rate of discount but also seems to have chosen it for the right reasons. Certainly when Ministry officials investigated the Board's methods of investment appraisal, the CEGB used the correct economic arguments for using a rate of discount higher than the rate at which they could borrow.

> They take the view [the Ministry reported] that the prospective level of the Exchequer lending rate is insufficient for this purpose and that some addition ought to be made, partly on the ground that no prudent investor plans merely to recover the cost of borrowing; and partly also because the Board must have regard to the return which other low-risk undertakings, without the benefit of Exchequer lending, are expected to earn on their investment.[16]

When from the mid-sixties the other nationalized industries started to switch over to dcf they appear in the main to have adopted 8 per cent which was the rate which the Treasury was recommending.[17] For instance in 1965 British Rail laid down that its cut-off rate would be 8 per cent although it stated that projects would normally be expected to earn 12 per cent to 15 per cent. By the summer of 1967, the air corporations were using 8 per cent as their test rate of discount. It also appears that by that time the Gas Boards were using 8 per cent or more as the cut-off rate for their main investment projects. A variety of rates were, however, used in the appraisal of schemes to connect new housing estates. The Prices and Incomes Board disclosed at the beginning of 1969 that here the Boards used rates which ranged from $6\frac{1}{2}$ to $12\frac{1}{2}$ per cent.[18]

The long-awaited White Paper in which it was officially announced that the nationalized industries were expected to use 8 per cent was published in the autumn of 1967. By that time a powerful case could be made for the adoption of a still higher figure on the ground that the introduction of corporation and capital gains tax had raised private industry's cost of capital, for without an increase in the rate of dividends and capital gains there would be a decline in the net return which shareholders receive. Indeed Mr Alfred argued that if they are to continue to receive 7 per cent net of tax, companies now need to earn nearly 11 per cent before tax.[19] This figure is probably on the high side because the increase in tax on shareholders will probably lead to some reduction in their returns, the payment of capital gains tax can be avoided by only selling shares which have fallen in value, and Mr Alfred's calculation is for an ordinary location where the grants on new investment are at a minimum.

Nevertheless the tax changes have clearly led to some increase in the cost of capital to private firms, as the Government recognized when in the summer of 1969 it increased the nationalized industries' rate of discount from 8 per cent to 10 per cent. This raises the question of whether the rate should have been set at 10 per cent in the first place. The answer is that it probably should. Nevertheless, it seems unlikely that very much harm was done. Even sophisticated private firms are unlikely to have increased their cut-off rates immediately after the tax changes of 1965. Indeed it was probably some years before they had fully adjusted to the changed situation. If so, an 8 per cent rate of discount would not have been as much below the private rate as calculations of the cost of capital make it appear.

Investment Below the Test Rate

It seems possible that not only was the old test rate of discount too low but also that the nationalized industries have in practice been discounting at a rate even lower than 8 per cent. For instance the Prices and Incomes Board reports that in their investment appraisal some of the Gas Boards 'make no allowance for inflation in their estimates of future revenues and operating costs, but they include an allowance for inflation, usually at 3 per cent per annum, in their estimates of future capital costs.

Boards which do this and use a discount rate of 8 per cent are using an effective discount rate of between 5 and 8 per cent depending on the ratio of capital to other costs.'[20] This sounds most heinous but, as the Prices and Incomes Board admits, is a rather trivial point. What some of the Gas Boards were doing was to allow for the way in which rising prices would increase their initial capital expenditure on a project where this would be spread over a number of years. This led to their investment being slightly overstated or if, like the PIB, one prefers to regard their capital expenditure as remaining the same, in it being discounted at a rate lower than had been intended. Since it was their expenditure which was being exaggerated the Boards were making their projects appear slightly, but only slightly, less profitable than they really were.

The railways' investment appraisal has also come in for criticism. The Ministry of Transport has stated that 'many of the projects put forward for the Ministry's approval by the Board do not show that the investment will give an adequate return'.[21] Whatever the situation may have been in the past this is no longer true. Not only is the great bulk of the railways' investment expenditure now covered by dcf profitability calculations but all the major investment projects which are submitted to the Ministry in a dcf form show a rate of return higher than the test rate of discount. To quote the Minister of Transport's own words: 'All the investment proposals submitted . . . by the British Railways Board during 1969 for which a discounted cash flow assessment was appropriate showed a net present value surplus at the discount rate in use at the time.'[22]

Electricity is the only nationalized industry where there is evidence that during the time dcf has been in use large amounts of capital expenditure have been sanctioned, although the prospective rate of return was very low. The expenditure in question was mainly on atomic power stations and was the consequence of the Government's decision, against the industry's better judgment, to treble the nuclear power programme at the time of the Suez crisis. It was already evident by the time the new programme was announced that the generation of power by nuclear energy was considerably more expensive than generation by conventional means.[23] This dawned on Whitehall almost immediately after the fatal decision had been taken, and it was decided in the autumn of 1957, when capital cuts were imposed on the nationalized industries, to delay the completion of the programme by a year. This was only about seven months after the programme had been published.[24] That it was still much too large became more and more obvious as time went by and in 1960 it was decided that the completion of the programme should be further delayed. It was now decided that in 1968 there should be 5,000 MW of nuclear capacity compared with the Suez programme of 5,000–

6,000 MW by the end of 1965. Under the revised plan the electricity industry would continue to place orders for nuclear stations at the rate of roughly one a year. 'This,' stated the Government White Paper, 'should fully maintain the rate of development of our nuclear technology and should also sustain a nuclear plant industry capable of expanding to meet the higher level of our own future needs.'[25]

It is clear that the nuclear programme could have been cut back much more drastically if the advancement of technology had been the only consideration. Sir Christopher Hinton, the chairman of the CEGB, told the Select Committee in the summer of 1962 that

> ideally what I would aim at doing is to build one reactor every [two or] three years interposing perhaps a small model of a new type reactor, at the stage where I was satisfied that the new technology, or that the technology of the new reactor, had advanced to the point where this was justified. Such a programme would have to be expanded, perhaps about 1966, building up to a programme which in 1975 (on the basis of fuel availability) will have to be a considerable one.[26]

If the size of the nuclear energy programme of 1960 was larger than it need have been in order to secure technical progress, was it justified by the need to keep the nuclear plant industry in being. This was the second main argument used in the White Paper. Sir Christopher Hinton argued at the time that it was.

> A massive industry [he wrote in 1961] was created by and founded on the 1957 programme; it appears that a considerable industry will be needed in the 1970s when it is thought that coal supplies will not be sufficient to meet the requirements of the electricity supply industry and when it is believed that nuclear power will be cheaper than conventional on base load. One cannot expect to create a large industry by establishing a programme, to destroy that industry by slashing the programme and then to recreate it at one's convenience six or seven years later.[27]

But this argument is persuasive rather than conclusive because it does not tell us why nuclear engineering could not have been run down and then built up again. Two possible reasons spring to mind. First it is possible that research and design teams would have had to have been broken up and could not have been built up in time, if only because the industry would, due to its recent run down, appear a very risky business.[28] Secondly, it is possible that the obstacle was a political one. The Government and the CEGB may have felt unable to be so beastly to concerns which were in private ownership and would not have entered the industry but for the Government's nuclear power programme;

although the Government was under no real obligation to the nuclear consortia because it was partly as a result of their pressure that the original target was trebled in 1957.[29] Without a great deal of detective work it is impossible to say whether the Government and the CEGB were actuated by legitimate economic or illegitimate political motives. Probably both factors were involved.

Whatever the reason, the adoption and final execution of the nuclear programme which was adopted at the time of Suez has cost the electricity consumer dear. The CEGB estimated in 1965 that its costs would be between £25 million and £30 million higher than they would otherwise have been.[30] About a third of this can be regarded as necessary development expenditure but the remainder was pure waste.

The Return on Investment Before dcf

Attention has, hitherto, been confined to the adequacy or otherwise of the minimum rates of return which have been sought by the nationalized industries since they have been using dcf. But how adequate, it may be asked, were their rates of return during the long period before discounting was adopted, and how satisfactory have they been in the coal industry where the switch to dcf has only just been made?[31] This is an interesting and important question but it is one which is difficult to answer because unless dcf is in use rates of return do not have a straightforward economic significance. Nevertheless it is possible to say something.

An investigation which the Ministry of Power carried out in the mid-sixties disclosed that the Gas Boards normally refused to sanction projects where profits as a proportion of capital were less than 7–7½ per cent. However, the boards expected to have a return of at least 12 to 15 per cent unless the capital scheme in question was desirable for reasons other than its direct contribution to profits. The Boards based their rate of return calculations on their initial capital expenditure rather than upon the average depreciated capital over the life of the projects.[32] This method tends to make the yield appear lower than it would turn out to be if dcf were used.

But if the project involved an expansion in production the yield would be somewhat lower than it appeared because it would be necessary sooner or later to reinforce the local distribution system, and the Boards do not appear to have allowed for capital expenditure of this type when assessing the profitability of a new gas works and the associated grid mains. Moreover the boards did not allow for changes in working capital or for interest during construction, although some of them for such reasons as this required a higher return on major projects. Again the (annuity) method by which depreciation was calculated makes the rate of return appear slightly higher than the normal (straight line) method. A considerable number of factors were, therefore, involved some of which would have tended to raise a properly calculated dcf rate of return above the figures which the Boards obtained and others of which would have tended to pull it down. In practice these conflicting considerations may have more or less cancelled out and the Boards' figures may not have been too wide of the mark.[33]

At least they would not have been but for the fact that a detailed examination of the West Midlands Gas Board shows that it was expressing the profit which arose jointly from the introduction of new plant and the construction of new grid mains as a proportion of the grid investment, although when calculating this profit it deducted capital charges on the gas plant. This exaggerated the rate of return on its capital expenditure, except where it was the same as or lower than the return which it credited to its investment in gas plant when estimating the capital charges to which this would give rise. In other words, the rate of return was exaggerated except where it was around the kind of figure at which the Board might well decide that the project should not be sanctioned. As this was the crucial point, the Board's method did, despite its weaknesses, enable it to see where the rate of return would be unacceptably low. Moreover, as we have seen, when it came to make proper dcf calculations in the mid-sixties, the rate of return on its new investment turned out to be a high one. As the profitability of its investment does not appear to have been any higher, and may have been lower, than that of the rest of the industry, it seems doubtful whether the Gas Boards were carrying out any significant amount of investment at around that time on which the prospective rate of return was inadequate.[34]

What the position was during earlier times it is impossible to do more than speculate. It seems likely that the Boards had been requiring a fairly substantial rate of return since the early sixties when the industry was effectively set the target of earning $5\frac{3}{4}$ per cent on its net assets.[35] Although this target applied to all its investment, both old and new Boards would obviously have been reluctant to sanction investment which would make it more difficult for them to meet their targets.

When, during the early sixties, the Ministry of Power made a study of the NCB's methods of investment appraisal it found that it ordinarily looked for a return of at least $12\frac{1}{2}$ per cent from projects of major reconstruction. In the case of other schemes to improve efficiency a minimum of 15 per cent was normally required and for non-colliery projects the figure was 20 per cent. By 1969 these figures had, due to the rise in interest rates, been increased by a further percentage point. The rate of return was calculated by expressing profits as a proportion of the initial capital expenditure, including interest during construction. The projects often involved expenditure on underground roadways and other facilities which might be charged to revenue account unless they involved a substantial reduction in the colliery's profits. On the revenue side no allowance was made for prospective increase in real wages, but the effect of this must have been partly offset by the reduction in profits which would frequently have occurred unless the project took place. This was not allowed for in the Board's estimates though it was borne in mind.[36]

There were, as in the case of gas, a number of conflicting factors which may have led to the Coal Board's calculations either overstating or understating the dcf rate of return it was likely to achieve. But it seems unlikely that the Board would have undertaken much investment which, if it had estimated the return in the correct manner and used an 8 per cent cut-off rate, would have been seen to be uneconomic. Not only would the various conflicting tendencies have at least partly cancelled out but the minimum rates of return for which the Board looked were also very high. Indeed, at first sight, they appear to have been too high. As, however, coal had by this time become a risky business it was right and proper that the Coal Board should require a high rate of return before investing.

Some idea of the rate of return which the Coal Board hoped to achieve on the investment which it carried out during its first decade can be obtained from *Plan for Coal*. The Board estimated that if the Plan was carried out its costs would be reduced by 7s per ton. From this must be deducted the allowance which the Board made for the rise in earnings per manshift. This was put at 9 per cent which implied that wage costs were expected to rise by about 2s per ton. If so, the Board was expecting that if its programme of modernization was carried out its costs would be cut by approximately 5s per ton. As it produced about 200 million tons of saleable coal in 1949 the Board appears to have been hoping to achieve a saving of around £50 million. This represented a return of about 10 per cent on the £520 million of colliery investment which the Plan contemplated. If anything, this appears to understate the return which the NCB was expecting, because it had probably allowed already for interest charges at the rate of $3\frac{1}{2}$ per cent, and because a large part of the capital expenditure which was planned would be devoted to replacing exhausted capacity and increasing production.[37] The Board seems to have been hoping that there would be a substantial return on its investment in the form of lower costs which it would be able to pass on to the consumer, though this would reduce the apparent yield.

What was overlooked was that miners' earnings would rise by far more than 9 per cent over the period covered by the Plan and that it would be years before expenditure on reconstruction schemes would bear fruit. As a result, coal prices had to be raised by a considerable amount during the interval while modernization was in progress, and the industry's productivity was more or less stagnant. This contributed to the collapse of coal demand which in turn rendered part of the industry's investment abortive and reduced the yield on the remaining part of the Coal Board's investment programme. This would, anyway, have been less satisfactory than it appeared because distant profits are worth less than those which are quickly earned.[38]

The rate of return shown by the railway Modernization Plan was also less impressive than it appeared and for much the same reasons. The British Transport Commission claimed that the Plan was an economic venture of the most promising sort. Yet it was stated in the published version that since many of the projects were interdependent the full benefit from investment would not be reaped for many years ahead.[39] And the confidential report of the Planning Committee of Chief Officers had warned that 'During the period of fructification of the plan . . . it will be extremely difficult, if not impossible, to meet the additional interest burden.'[40] This was omitted from the published version. The Commission must, therefore, be convicted both of misleading the public and of engaging in wishful thinking. It should have been evident, even in the days before dcf, that investment which was going to take years to show results was less attractive than it appeared. This would have been seen if the Commission had made an estimate of the interest it would incur during construction and before its schemes had become fully profitable. By adding this to its figure for capital expenditure and then recalculating the yield it would have obtained an idea of the rate of return. It is by no means unreasonable to expect that the Commission should have made such an allowance as it was already common practice at the time the Plan was drawn up.

Not only did the Commission's figures tend to exaggerate the rate of return which would be earned, but they also failed to bear out the Commission's claim that the Plan was an investment of the most promising sort. Even if they are taken at their face value they suggest that it was running the risk that part of its investment would be unprofitable, or at best show a very low rate of return. The Commission estimated, or rather 'guesstimated', in the Modernization Plan that the financial benefit from this investment programme would be around £85 million. This, although the Commission did not give the figure, represented a return of only 6·9 per cent on the £1,240 million of investment which was contemplated. Moreover, as we have seen, part of the improvement of £35 million on the passenger side took the form of losses avoided rather than profits earned. The return was going to be somewhat less than the Commission's figures suggested, assuming them to be otherwise correct. What the Commission seems to have ignored is that, because it was an average return, the yield from investment in some parts of the system was going to be higher and elsewhere it was going to be lower. But if it was much lower it would be unacceptably low.

The Commission should have been put on its guard, and should ideally have refused to sanction the Plan *in toto*. However, it was obviously anxious after so much delay to press ahead with modernization and probably comforted itself with the thought that it had been extremely cautious in estimating the pay-off.[41] This may explain why the Commission was prepared to accept the Plan and excuse what appears at first sight to have been inexcusable. What was totally indefensible was the Commission's failure to ensure that when the individual modernization projects came forward for approval they were so calculated that it could see whether a reasonable rate of return would be earned.[42]

CHAPTER 17

Economies of Scale in Gas and Electricity

IF the nationalized industries are to use their capital expenditure to the best advantage they must do more than calculate the prospective yield in the correct manner. It is vital that they should secure the full economies of scale which are open to them and employ efficient techniques of production. The nationalized industries must not only get their sums right but they must be the right sums. For instance, it is no use the electricity industry using the correct methods of investment appraisal if it has decided to install plant which is too small. This may seem too obvious to need saying but it is a fact which economists have a habit of overlooking. They come to imagine that the economic mysteries in which they are skilled are more important than they really are. In this chapter we shall examine the extent to which the nationalized industries have reaped the economies of scale which have been available.

Gas : the Necessity for Rationalization

The gas industry was nationalized in 1949 on the recommendation of an official committee of inquiry under the future Lord Heyworth, the Chairman of Unilever. The Committee had in 1945 proposed that gas should be brought into public ownership because it considered that this was the only practicable way of rationalizing the industry's structure and so enabling it to reap the economies of scale which were to be had. According to the Heyworth Committee the cost of making gas fell progressively with the size of the plant up to a maximum of about 10 million therms per annum.[1] No figures were quoted but Dr B. H. Wormsley has calculated from the official returns that in 1950 the cost of production declined from just over 11d per therm in the smallest works, where the output was under 1 million therms per annum, to about $7\frac{1}{2}$d in those where it was over 10 million. This calculation, it should be explained, was confined to the cost of fuel and manufacturing labour and assumed that a uniform price was paid for coal and received for coke. The cost of distributing gas was not included, nor were capital charges though, as figures for new plant showed, the most striking economies of scale were in the use of capital.[2]

Despite the significant reduction in the cost of gas making which could be secured by installing big plants, large quantities of gas continued, up to vesting date, to be made in small works. In 1949–50 15 per cent of the industry's output was produced at works which made less than 1¼ million therms per annum; a further 15 per cent was produced at plants which made between 1¼ million and 5 million therms; and 20 per cent was produced at works which made between 5 million and 10 million therms. Therefore, half the industry's output was made at works which produced less than 10 million therms per annum.[3] In some places the level of consumption was too low to support a large plant and, in the past, the high cost of transmitting gas and distributing coke had frequently made large works uneconomic. However, during the inter-war period, new techniques were developed for transmitting gas through steel mains at high pressure.[4]

These developments were not exploited to the full.

> The evidence placed before us [the Heyworth Committee reported] suggests that in many instances transmission technique has not kept pace with carbonizing technique, and that substantial economies in this element of cost are still possible by a modernization of existing systems . . . Modern methods of high-pressure transmission have increased the range over which gas can be distributed at an economic price from a central station, and one or two striking examples of its application have shown the advantages to be derived from well-planned grids. Nevertheless there still remain too many small inefficient works well within the range of high-pressure mains.

The Committee gave the example of what it described as a typical area of high demand. Forty-two of its works, or over half the total, had an output of less than 1¼ million therms per annum although they were all within range of one or more larger plants.[5]

Apart from London, and one or two places like Swindon which had made enterprising use of high-pressure transmission, gas grids were confined to areas where coke-oven gas was available.[6] The purchase of large quantities of gas and the construction of the Sheffield gas grid was one of the most important developments of the inter-war period.[7] But even here it is doubtful whether the available opportunities were used to the full. 'It is unquestionably true,' PEP reported, 'that gas undertakings may be unwilling to accept the offer of a slightly cheaper and complete supply of coke-oven gas if it would involve closing their works.' This was shown by the failure of a grid scheme in Scotland, which, although it had been recommended by an official committee, fell through because Glasgow refused to co-operate.[8]

During the inter-war period some progress was made towards the larger groupings which were necessary if production was to be rationalized and gas grids were to be constructed. However, the pace of change was not very fast and some of the groupings which did emerge had serious limitations. One obstacle to desirable mergers was the industry's division between municipal and private ownership; another obstacle was parochialism. The local authorities, which in 1944 were responsible for 37 per cent of gas sales, were too jealous of their independence either to surrender control of their gas undertakings or to co-operate among themselves. Between the wars only 23 municipal undertakings were taken over by other local authorities or by private companies; and the Heyworth Committee found that there were only five joint concerns, the last of which had been set up in 1922.[9]

But it was not only in the municipal sector that parochial attitudes were to be found. According to Dr Wormsley

> there were many personal extra-economic reasons why potentially profitable amalgamations did not take place between companies. Many of the small undertakings had been family concerns for a long time, so that a pride of ownership was involved. By the very nature of the monopoly status enjoyed by these undertakings, and the statutory control of dividends, there was not much incentive for a small works which had been earning a reasonable dividend for many years to merge with other undertakings in order to improve profits or reduce prices.

After the Gas Undertakings Act of 1932, which removed the legal difficulties which had stood in the way of take-overs, holding companies started to develop. By 1944 they accounted for 11 per cent of all gas sales. Although these companies undertook a certain amount of rationalization the amount of progress which they were able to make was restricted because they could only extend their operations by consent and because the undertakings which they controlled were often scattered.[10] When they came to be nationalized it was found that six out of the ten holding companies controlled undertakings scattered over the territories of three or more of the Area Boards.[11]

When gas undertakings were compulsorily amalgamated into regional groups through public ownership it became possible for the first time to secure the full economies of scale available to the industry. We are indebted to Dr Wormsley for having made some extremely thorough estimates of the savings which could be made. As his study has never been published it may be useful to give a fairly full summary of his findings. His starting point was an estimate of the potential reduction in the cost of making gas as the size of plant increased which was prepared by two senior officials of the North Western Gas Board. Separate estimates were made for the three main types of carbonization plant on the assumption that it operated for 280 days per annum. Although transmission equipment was excluded, the cost of gas holders was included. The cost of production, allowing for the revenue from coke, totalled 11·1d per therm for an annual make of 1·4 million therms using the type of plant which had the lowest cost. There was a progressive reduction in the cost of gas making as the size of the plant increased. For the largest size of plant quoted with an annual make of 28 million therms the cost was only 7·6d per therm, once again using the type of plant which had the lowest costs. This estimate may possibly have understated the decline. It was based on the assumption that the quantity of gas and coke produced per ton of coal did not vary with the size of plant, though Dr Wormsley found that in existing plants the yield improved as output increased.[12] Even if the cost figures are accepted without query the economies of scale which they showed were of a significant order. This can be seen from the fact that in 1950–51 the industry's average charge per therm was 13d.

Unfortunately, the potential economies of scale in gas production could usually be secured only at the expense of an increase in the cost of distribution. Small works usually served small areas and before these plants could be shut integration mains would have to be installed. This would mean increased distribution costs not only because of the extra investment and higher capital charges but also because of the expense of pumping gas over a greater distance. However, integration would generally lead to some further economies on the production side which would help to offset the increase in distribution costs. If, for instance, the maximum demand occurred at different times in the places which were being linked there would be a saving in the amount of plant necessary.[13]

There were considerable economies of scale on the distribution side which, if they could be secured, would prevent the rise in distribution costs being prohibitive. Although it is very expensive to pipe a small quantity of gas anything but the shortest distance, it is quite cheap to transmit a large quantity a long way. One reason is that the cost of gas pipe does not rise in step with its capacity because the volume of any container increases faster than its wall area. It followed that the cheapest method of transmitting gas was to supply a number of small works by a single main rather than each singly.[14] This helps to explain why so many small works survived although they were quite close to large ones. Piping a supply might only be economic if a number of other small works could be linked at the same time to the same main. But this was only possible once ownership had been unified over a large area, which was unlikely to happen for the very reason that piecemeal expansion did not pay.

Dr Wormsley concluded that in districts where there were a number of small works within 20 to 30 miles of a large undertaking it would generally pay to close these in the not-too-distant future and give them a bulk supply rather than put up new small works. For instance, he estimated that even if only one plant could be linked up, it was more economic to lay pipe and transmit gas up to 35 miles when this could be done from a large plant producing about 20 million therms per annum and where the alternative was to build a small plant producing only 1·4 million therms. When several plants could be linked by a grid main it was more economic to pipe gas over 50 miles than to build a small works.[15]

These estimates assumed that the small works was going to be replaced because it was worn out or because its avoidable operating costs were so high that it was cheaper (even including depreciation and capital charges) to replace it by a new works of the same size. These assumptions could probably be safely made about a high proportion of the small works which the Gas Boards inherited. About a quarter of the capacity taken over at vesting day was over 30 years old. As comparatively little plant can have been constructed during the first world war the bulk of this plant must have been over 40 years old: the estimated life of plant adopted by the industry for depreciation purposes. Much of this obsolescent capacity was at small works and much of it was in a very bad state of repair.[16]

Finally, Dr Wormsley made some estimates of the financial benefit to be obtained from constructing grid mains and closing small works. Wherever there were a number of small works within about 30 miles of a large works he sketched out a grid scheme. Each was designed so that the maximum number of works was linked up by the minimum amount of pipe, though an extremely generous margin of 40 per cent was added to allow for deviations from the straight-line route and to cover contingencies. Altogether there were about 50 separate integration schemes involving the closure of over 500 works producing about 14 per cent of the national output. The capital cost of the grid was estimated at between £25 million and £35 million and the cost of extra capacity at large works at between £15 million and £40 million; though nearer the higher figures than the lower. In the absence of a grid Dr Wormsley estimated that it would cost about £60 million to replace small works which figured in his integration schemes. This figure, however, was likely to be an underestimate because it did not include certain indirect costs which would be incurred if, as he assumed, the cheapest method of production was employed. It appears from Dr Wormsley's estimates that integration would only cost about as much as replacement.[17]

As integration would lead to a reduction in operating costs the construction of a grid was well worth while. It was estimated that the cost of gas piped through the grids would be about 2d cheaper than that of gas made at small new plants after allowing for interest charges at 4 per cent on the investment, and that the overall saving through integration would total about £2½ million per annum. This figure is probably on the low side because Dr Wormsley's estimate of the capital cost of integration appears to have been on the high side. He also assumed in all his calculations that small plants would be operated as efficiently as large works. However, the Heyworth Committee found that many undertakings were too small to support the qualified staff necessary for high technical efficiency, as measured by the proportion of the available heat energy in the coal used which was extracted as gas and by-products. Hence the low efficiency of most small plants, though this was also due to the discontinuous methods of operation which they were forced to adopt.[18]

The Benefits of Integration

Although the gas boards were fully aware of the benefits of integration, the construction of grid mains and the closure of small works inevitably took time. Moreover during the early years of nationalization the industry was hampered by a serious shortage of iron and steel, and it was not until mid-1953, when the general rationing of steel ceased, that the industry was able to obtain adequate supplies.[19] By about 1960, integration of the type envisaged by the Heyworth Committee was more or less complete.

> Soon after nationalization [reports Mr Watson of the Gas Council] Boards began joining works that were not already linked within their 'divisions'. These were smaller semi-integrated areas that in many cases conformed to the areas served by former companies or local authorities. They then began to link divisions usually spreading outwards from the more concentrated to the less concentrated areas of demand. By the mid-fifties this had happened to a certain extent in all Boards and a study of their grid maps for this time shows octopus-like patterns of mains growing outwards from the main production areas. These could not be called true regional grids until the separate patterns were joined within a Board. By 1960 this had largely taken place within certain large geographical areas within Boards.[20]

As a result over 600 of the smaller works which had been taken over at nationalization had been closed down by early 1960; the proportion of gas made at works producing less than 1¼ million therms per annum had declined from 15 per cent to less than 3 per cent; and the proportion made at works producing more than 10 million therms had increased from half to over 70 per cent.[21]

It seems clear that, as expected, the Gas Boards obtained significant financial savings by means of integration. For instance in its Annual Report for 1953–4 the Gas Council quoted two Boards which, due to integration, had been able to avoid installing £7¾ million of plant which they would otherwise have required. After deducting the cost of the extra mains which were necessary there was a net saving of £4½ million of capital.[22] The details of three integration schemes which the North Eastern Gas Board provided for the Select Committee illustrate the saving in operating costs which could be achieved. In York and around Huddersfield, where small works were nearing the end of their lives, supply by means of a grid led to a saving of up to £125,000 per annum when the position after integration was compared with what it would have been if the existing plants had been replaced or reconstructed. In the Whitby area the Board was able by the construction of a grid to turn a loss of £50,000 before interest into a profit of £5,000 after interest on the new capital involved.[23]

The gains which the Southern Gas Board secured were far more spectacular. After negotiating a supply of refinery tail gas from Fawley it constructed a grid main system to which all save one of its gas works were linked. As a result it was able to reduce their number from 39 in March 1956 to six in March 1961 and to dispense with a large number of gas holders. The financial consequence was that the cost of gas, including the capital and operating charges on the new integration main, was slightly lower in 1960–61 than it had been in 1956–7. The Board estimated that had it not been for this grid scheme its costs would have been £900,000 higher than they were.[24]

These examples of the benefits of integration are persuasive rather than conclusive partly because they are only examples, and partly because in all but the last case the amount of information given is too meagre for us to be completely certain that something has not been left out of account. Nevertheless it does appear from other evidence that integration paid off. Between 1948 and 1958–9 the industry's technical efficiency rose from 72·0 per cent to 77·7 per cent, although before the war it appears to have been falling. This meant that the industry was consuming about 2½ million tons of coal less than it would have required had the output of gas and other products been produced at the efficiency of 1948. As the price of coal delivered to gas works was then about £15 15s per ton this represents a saving of about £14½ million.[25] A large part of this saving was due to the closure of small and inefficient works and the concentration of gas production in larger and more economic units. It was partly due also to the replacement of obsolete by modern plant, to better maintenance and to improved methods of working.[26] This too was an economy of scale if not of integration. Much of the obsolete and badly maintained plant was owned by small undertakings who lacked the financial and technical resources to replace it, or to put it in order, or to run it efficiently. The West Midlands Gas Board, for instance, had to spend no less than £13 million putting the plant and equipment which it had inherited from local authorities into good order; and the South Western Gas Board saved 20,000 tons of coal during the first year of nationalization by sending teams of technicians around the area to improve efficiency.[27]

The saving in labour which was made at gas works provides further evidence that integration and the closure of small works paid dividends. Between 1948 and 1958 the output of gas and coke per operative employed on their production rose by a third.[28] This was due to the reduction in employment from 54,000 to 44,300 and it seems likely that about two-thirds of the fall was due to the closure of small works where productivity was low and the concentration of production at large works where it was high.[29] If there had been no gain in productivity at gas works the industry's labour bill would in 1958 have been about £9 million greater than it was.[30] Of course both this saving in labour and the saving in fuel costs were purchased at the expense of some increase in the costs of gas distribution. But it seems clear that on balance the industry saved money through integration. The gain in productivity which the industry reaped on its production side was by no means entirely dissipated elsewhere.[31]

It is possible that although integration was generally beneficial it was sometimes carried too far. 'Both the Scottish and Welsh Boards,' declared the Prices and Incomes Board in 1965, 'invested heavily in rural grids without, apparently, using the appropriate methods of appraisal or rates of return. The current increases in costs spring in part from this fact.'[32] There is no doubt that both these Boards invested money which, from a narrow economic standpoint, should not have been spent. Faced with heavy and mounting losses at their small rural works both Boards decided to provide gas by extending the grid in order at least to reduce their losses. The latter point needs emphasizing. The Chairmen of the Welsh and Scottish Boards were absolutely clear in their evidence to the Select Committee that the grid was the cheapest way of providing gas. For instance Mr Mervyn Jones, the Chairman of the Welsh Gas Board, said that the cost of supplying gas to undertakings in central Wales 'is far less than it would have been had we not constructed the Mid-Wales Grid'.[33] It is difficult to see how the construction of rural grids, which in both areas had been largely completed some years before, can have led to a rise in costs as the Prices and Incomes Board asserted.

The decision to continue supplying gas at a loss appears to have been a decision of policy rather than the unintended consequence of sloppy accounting.[34] The Gas Boards argued that the industry had an obligation to go on supplying existing customers and to help keep rural communities alive. Because electricity would still be available this obligation does not appear to be a very strong one. A much more powerful argument, at which the Chairman of the Scottish Board hinted, was that the termination of supply would damage the industry's image and lead to a loss of public good will. If the Beeching proposals for withdrawing trains on which only a handful of passengers travel led to a storm of protest, what a tempest there would have been if the Gas Boards tried to deprive housewives of the gas by which they cook their children's meals! Whether, in financial terms, the gain would outweigh the loss it is almost impossible to tell if only because there has been no test case. But would anyone apart from the mandarins of the Prices and Incomes Board blame the Scottish and Welsh Boards for not providing one?

Whatever the answer the amount of debatable grid investment appears in general to have been limited. This is shown by the fact that in the early sixties, after a large amount of integration had taken place but before the grid link-up was complete, there were not many districts where a loss was being incurred. For instance in the North Eastern Board the only places which were making a loss appear to have been the small undertakings which had not yet been linked up to a grid. Similarly the only part of the North Western Area which was losing money was the Lake District where integration was far from complete.[35] The same pattern can be observed in Scotland. The places where costs have been high and losses have been incurred are not those served by a grid but the isolated undertakings which it has been too expensive to connect. According to Professor William Shepherd, who has made a study of the Scottish Area, the Board's grid schemes have been soundly based but there has been a rising tide of losses at the small plants in rural towns; and this despite the reduction in their number as integration has proceeded and the £1 million of capital expenditure which has been made. It is here that Professor Shepherd believes that misallocation may have occurred.[36]

This strongly suggests that had it not been for the construction of grids and the concentration of production a large number of smaller gas undertakings would have become insolvent. By the late fifties the whole industry was in a weak financial position due to the competition which it was facing and its dependence on coal, the price of which had greatly

N

increased. Gas was starting to price itself out of the market. The economies of scale which unified ownership made possible were the rock on
which the industry climbed to keep its head above water. There is
no need to exaggerate their size. They were modest in comparison with
the dramatic gains which the construction of the national grid made
possible in electricity. But they were sufficient for the industry to pass
through a period of adversity without damage. Mr C. H. Chester of the
South Western Gas Board, speaking about small undertakings with
which he was well acquainted, told the Select Committee that 'They
were old, and financially in difficulty, or quite a lot of them were. I
would hazard a guess that at least 75 per cent of them would have been in
the bankruptcy court long before now if they had not been taken over.'[37]
There is no reason to believe that this is an exaggeration.

It is possible that the industry would have regrouped but its division
into private and municipal sectors, and the lack in a regulated industry
of any pressing financial incentive for the strong to help the weak, do not
suggest that integration would have been pressed forward with the
necessary vigour. Foreign experience is instructive. In Denmark, where
co-operation is almost a way of life, gas undertakings have remained in
splendid isolation although they are close to each other and could have
been supplied from a few central gas works. In Sweden the position is
much the same. Yet in both countries the industry has been in difficulties.[38] A challenge does not always elicit a rational response.

Economies of Scale Increase

One of the most striking features about economies of scale in the gas
industry is that they have become progressively more important. During
the first decade of nationalization they were limited though, as we have
just seen, it was vital that the industry should secure them. But during
the sixties a series of developments has enormously increased the gains
to be had from the supply and distribution of gas on a large scale. First
there was the importation of liquid methane from Algeria and its distribution through the national methane grid. In practice supply had to
be organized on a national basis. Unless the gas was imported in bulk its
cost would have been prohibitive and although some of the Boards had
large enough markets to take bulk supplies this would have been far too
risky. They would then have become dangerously dependent on gas
from a source which, as experience has shown, is by no means wholly
reliable. The second development was the revolutionary new processes
which have been discovered for making gas from naphtha. Not only are
these subject to important economies of scale so far as capital and operat-

ing costs are concerned, but they have the great advantage that they produce gas at high pressure. This enables gas to be distributed without the expense of pumping which had previously reduced the gain to be had from installing large plants and supplying gas over a long distance. The third development which deserves a mention, though it is by no means as important as those which have already been listed, is the computerization of operations such as billing.[39] Because the initial cost of a computer is so high this will only produce a saving once accounting has been centralized and there is enough work to keep the machine busy.

The more rational pattern of organization which nationalization brought about has enabled the industry to exploit to the full the potential economies of scale which have become available. Moreover, the gas industry has itself played an important part in creating these opportunities. The industry's new organizational structure may have enabled it not only to reap more efficiently but also to sow more effectively. The pioneering work on the transportation of methane was undertaken in the United States but, as we have seen, it was the British gas industry which grasped its significance, and when the time was ripe arranged for the trial importation of methane into this country.[40] With the exception of France it is only now that the other countries, which could benefit, are starting to arrange supplies.[41] Moreover, the revolutionary new processes for making gas from oil have owed a good deal to the industry's own research effort.

The discovery of North Sea gas is the only one of the developments which have been transforming the industry to which it has itself contributed little or nothing; but paradoxically it is in this field that unification is likely to yield the most lasting benefit. Had the industry remained divided it would have been in no position to negotiate a satisfactory bargain with the monopolistic oil companies. It simply would not have possessed the necessary bargaining power. As the long and hard-fought negotiations have shown, it needed every ounce which it possesses. Bargaining power is not an economy of scale in the technical sense but about this the consumer is unlikely to know or care.

Electricity Before 1948

The gas industry has been shown to provide an example of the successful utilization of economies of scale; let us now examine electricity. This industry is of particular interest not only because of the large economies which have been secured in the past, and the way in which they were facilitated by the construction of the grid and by unified ownership, but also because it has fairly recently been attacked for having failed to make the most of its opportunities. The electricity industry is therefore a potential case study in light and shade.

Until the creation of the Central Electricity Board and the construction of the grid, the industry was forced to maintain a large amount of unnecessary generating capacity and was unable to minimize its running costs. The unnecessary generating plant existed because each undertaking had to have reserve capacity in case one of its plants broke down, some of which could have been dispensed with if they had been able to pool their risks through inter-connection. Another reason was that capacity is determined by the peak demand which has to be met during the year, and that as its timing varies from one part of the country to another, the peak for the industry as a whole is less massive than the sum of the peaks of the individual undertakings. Due to these factors the industry's margin of unnecessary plant was in the mid-twenties equivalent to about 45 per cent of the installed capacity.[42] In the days before interconnection the industry was not only forced to maintain unnecessary plant but operating costs were unnecessarily high. This was partly because power stations were not run in merit order. At any given time some undertaking would be running old high-cost plants, while in other places newer plants with lower running costs stood idle.

The margin of unnecessary generating plant before the grid was constructed was so extensive that the investment which the industry avoided having to make due to its construction was equivalent to a large part of its original cost. According to the Central Electricity Board

the progressive increase in the proportion of spare plant was arrested in 1930 (largely due to the temporary arrangements made by the Board during the construction of the grid) . . . a rapid decline in the proportion of spare plant followed the beginning of normal trading by the Board in 1933 and . . . by the end of 1936, the proportion had been reduced to a level appropriate to interconnected working . . . By the end of 1938, the total capital saving which had arisen from the programme of reduction in the proportion of reserve generating plant was approximately £22,000,000 – or nearly three-quarters of the capital expenditure on the construction of the grid and its extensions and reinforcements to date.[43]

It is hardly surprising, therefore, that the Board discovered that the cost of electricity was considerably lower than it would have been in the absence of the grid.

The real criterion of the contribution of the grid towards the national economy, is the extent to which the normal downward trend in production costs due to advance in technique, which was, of course, in evidence before the inauguration of the grid scheme, has been increased since the Board began operation. Changes in the level of prices, such as the abrupt rise in the cost of fuel, are outside the control of the supply industry and mask the effect of increased efficiency. However, it is possible to calculate, within reasonable limits of accuracy, the trend of the average cost of production at the generating stations of all authorized undertakers in the country since 1921 when corrected for variations in price levels. To discover this the annual data have been adjusted to the average price levels and load factors ruling in the period 1927–30 inclusive, during which period price levels and economic conditions were relatively stable . . . By the year 1937–8 . . . the adjusted average cost per unit sent out to local distribution systems was nearly 24 per cent below the figure which would have been reached if the normal trend of improvement prior to 1932 had continued. This calculation is based upon the units sent out to local distribution systems and, therefore, takes full account of the extra generating costs necessitated by the transmission losses of the grid. The only additional cost is the net amount paid by the undertakers to the Board to meet the expenses of the grid, and when this is added the annual net saving by 1937–8 still amounted to over 17 per cent.[44]

The advance, which due to the Central Electricity Board and the grid, had taken place in the production of electricity had not been matched by any corresponding progress on the industry's distributive side, although there were considerable economies of scale to be had. In many cases, the distribution system could not be laid out in the most efficient manner due to the industry's haphazard structure. Because the territories served by the multitude of separate undertakings were frequently small or curiously shaped, distribution lines and mains were often longer than they need have been. In some places two lines were built although one high capacity line would have cost less; in other places lines had to twist and turn according to district boundaries. By co-operation, neighbouring undertakings could often have obtained a higher loading on their distribution networks. This was possible where their periods of maximum demand did not coincide.[45]

In 1956 the Herbert Committee reported that

The amalgamation of many separate undertakings into a single large area of supply made it possible for the Boards to plan the development of each of their Areas comprehensively and to make significant economies relative to schemes which were restricted to the pre-vesting boundaries. The removal of these artificial boundaries also allowed the Boards to load the distribution system more evenly and efficiently.[46]

As an example of the savings which had been possible, it cited the case of the supply points at which electricity is fed into the distribution system from the grid. Their location and capacity had previously been determined largely by the separate requirements of the old undertakings. After nationalization it was frequently possible, by establishing new points, to secure a better loading of the existing distribution system and to avoid the need for its reinforcement. The industry estimated that during the first 10 years of public ownership they had saved £15 million by providing new points of supply in preference to developing those which already existed, as would have happened in many cases had the industry's structure not been rationalized.[47]

Because of the industry's division into private and municipal sectors, and the way in which even the smallest local authorities jealously guarded the independence of their undertakings, it is almost inconceivable that this rationalization would have been accomplished by voluntary means. The McGowan Committee on electricity distribution concluded that past experience demonstrated, beyond question, that any attempt to carry through by voluntary means the general reorganization, which it considered necessary, was bound to fail.[48] When the Government, following the Committee's advice, came forward with proposals for compulsory amalgamation there was a storm of protest from the industry and no legislation appeared. During the latter stages of the war, when the problem of reorganization again came under discussion, the best the industry could do was to propose a scheme based largely on the maintenance of the *status quo*, though it did not command much support since the municipalities considered it too radical; and this was at a time when the reforming spirit which the war had generated was at its height.[49]

The Advantages of Unified Ownership in Generation

Despite the construction of the grid and the lack of progress in distribution, it is in generation and transmission that the main scope for economies of scale has been found. Not only has the optimum size of generating set increased rapidly with the advance of technical knowledge, but the industry's structure prior to nationalization might well have impeded the industry's progress in the field of generation. As the Herbert Committee pointed out, the Central Electricity Board had to rely on the proposals of the existing authorized undertakers for the provision of new generating capacity.[50] Although this was not a statutory duty it was a practical necessity due to the weak position in which the Board was placed. In order to secure the extension of an *existing station* against its owners' wishes it was necessary to go to arbitration and, if the owners refused to abide by the verdict, the CEB had to persuade the Minister to lay an order for expropriation before Parliament. To secure the construction of a *new station* which the authorized undertaker was unwilling to provide the Board had to persuade the Electricity Commissioners to lay an order before Parliament for approval by both Houses.[51] The difficulty of exercising powers so circumscribed is apparent when it is recalled which of our two great political parties is normally in power. Moreover, because the successful operation of the grid depended on the co-operation of those who owned the selected generating stations, it was important that the Board should maintain their goodwill and avoid quarrels at almost any price.

It is true that once the selected stations had been designated and the grid had been constructed the CEB was in a somewhat stronger position than at first, but the philosophy of compromise and conciliation, which was a natural outcome of the Board's formative experience, was an important obstacle to it taking a firm initiative when the provision of new capacity was up for discussion. What is more, any determined attempt by the CEB to drag the industry along against its wishes, and where necessary to construct new plant for itself, would almost inevitably have prolonged the lengthy period it takes to plan and construct a generating station. During the post-war period, when there was an acute shortage of generating capacity, any further delay in the provision of new plant must surely have led the CEB to abandon the attempt to plan the industry on a national scale. Perhaps the Board's powers could have been strengthened though this might well have led gradually, through the construction of new power stations, to what in April 1948 was accomplished at a stroke: the public ownership of electricity generation. There was another powerful objection to the system of public control and private ownership which the Electricity Supply Act of 1926 had brought about, though it had little to do with economies of scale. The owners of the power stations had virtually no financial incentive to run them efficiently.[52]

In the pre-war period the disadvantages of electricity's mixed economy were not as serious as they might have been had it continued after the war, though according to the Herbert Committee they were already in evidence.

Because the Central Electricity Board were obliged to rely on the proposals of existing authorized undertakers for meeting the growth of load, the new power stations were not always sited to the greatest advantage from the national point of view . . . Before nationalization, even with the grid system, power stations were sited as near as possible to the centre of consumption. This happened partly because new power stations were constructed by the local authorities or companies, and partly because of the technical limitations of the grid system.[53]

These limitations were to some extent removed with the operation of the grid on a national as opposed to a regional basis. This took place on a limited scale from 1938 and then more fully under the impact of war. The grid's technical limitations were not completely removed until the construction of the super-grid which made possible the large-scale transfer of power from one part of the country to another. This had been considered by CEB committees from 1942 onwards but no firm decision appears to have been reached. An interim report, issued in November 1946, considered that a super-grid was unnecessary with the existing pattern of production, but did not reach any conclusion about the desirability of long-distance transmission of large blocks of power.[54]

The British Electricity Authority quickly made up its mind that even with the existing pattern of production a large increase in transmission was necessary to conserve capital expenditure; that the extra line capacity could be provided most satisfactorily by constructing a super-grid to operate at a somewhat higher voltage than the CEB had been considering (275,000 as against 264,000); that a super-grid would cost no more than the reinforcement of the existing low (132,000) volt system; and that it would have the major advantage of permitting long-distance transmission on a large scale which would enable the industry to alter its pattern of production and thereby achieve a further saving.[55]

It was estimated that the construction of the super-grid at a cost of £72 million would involve a net capital saving of £37 million. The saving in capital charges and in fuel costs through the siting of new power stations in the cheap coal-producing areas would total approximately £5 million per annum.[56] The policy of locating power stations on the coal fields instead of near centres of consumption has also led to a marked reduction in the average distance which the coal has to be hauled, though the consequent saving has presumably been included in the estimates which have just been quoted.[57] The benefit to be obtained through constructing the super-grid cannot have been so obvious before the NCB rationalized the price structure for coal.[58] However, it is difficult to avoid the conclusion that the CEB was dragging its feet, or to dissent from the Herbert Committee's verdict that 'The centralization of responsibility for ownership and operation of generation and transmission under nationalization enabled substantial gains in efficiency to be made.'[59]

These gains were by no means confined to the siting of generating stations but were secured over a broad front. For instance, according to the Herbert Committee, substantial economies were achieved throughout the industry as a result of the standardization of equipment.[60] Important savings in the cost of constructing power stations were also achieved by reducing the size of buildings required per unit of capacity. At power stations designed in 1937 the building volume was 51 cubic feet per kW, and in 1947 the figure was 58. But after nationalization there was a progressive reduction and by 1952 the volume was already down to 30½ cubic feet per kW. This was due to a number of reasons important among which was the construction of larger generating sets.[61] But economies of scale and technical progress were not the only factors at work.

According to the Beaver Committee on power station construction it was also due to the deliberate drive for economy which the British Electricity Authority launched and to its more cost-conscious approach. Hitherto power stations had tended to be monumental structures, often resembling large brick cathedrals. The British Electricity Authority was able to cut costs not only by eliminating wasted space but also by using cheaper methods of construction. In this way the Authority saved millions of pounds of capital per annum. Although this was not an economy of scale in the technical sense, the failure to minimize costs in the pre-nationalization era was certainly diseconomy of divided ownership. Under the old regime, power station owners had little or no financial incentive to keep their construction costs down. This was another reason why, even if the Central Electricity Board could have been given full control over the siting of stations, the industry's structure was in need of reform. It may be remarked in passing that the industry's standards of construction as measured by the volume of the main power station building in relation to its rated output appear to compare favourably with those abroad.[62]

The advantages conferred by unified ownership are shown by the experience of those electricity industries abroad which are still fragmented. The organization of the German industry is reminiscent of that of the British industry prior to nationalization. First, there are undertakings, including industrial companies generating electricity for their own use, which operate plants, large by German standards, and sell bulk supplies to other concerns. Some of these undertakings also distribute to individual consumers; others do not. Secondly, there are local distributors who purchase all or most of their requirements. Thirdly, there are the municipalities which usually aim, except in emergencies, to produce the power they need in their own stations. Even the biggest concern in the German supply industry has only about a quarter of the capacity of the CEGB.[63]

Because of their relatively small size the German undertakings have not been able to introduce really large generating plants. According to a British Productivity Team which investigated the German electricity industry in 1961: 'Federal German generating units are restricted in size to meet the requirements of individual undertakings. The largest units in operation, or under construction, are of 160 MW capacity as compared with the much larger units (300/550 MW) under construction for the British national system, and construction costs per kW installed are, therefore, higher.'[64] Another consequence of divided ownership and small scale operation is the absence of a proper national grid system with generation based on order-of-merit. It is true that the main transmission systems have been linked together and that there is a high degree of voluntary co-operation, but 'there is a duplication of transmission systems and load dispatch and control are exercised by each undertaking for its own purpose'.[65]

America provides another example of an electricity supply industry which labours under the disadvantage of divided ownership. There is a private sector which owns about three-quarters of all generating capacity; there is a public sector represented by federal, state and local undertakings; and finally there is a small co-operative sector, largely engaged in distribution. According to the Federal Power Commission's National Power Survey of 1964

> the large number of separate systems coupled with rivalries and controversies between segments of the industry has frequently resulted in economically meaningless boundaries for utility system planning and operation which undoubtedly cost the power consumers of this country millions of dollars every year in wasted opportunities for cost reduction.[66]

Many undertakings are still installing relatively small and inefficient generating sets because they are unable to support large plant. For instance units of 250 MW or less accounted for 28 per cent of all new conventional generating capacity installed during 1968, although it is evident from the Federal Power Commission's study that the continued construction of sets as small as this is seldom justified on economic grounds.[67] However, in America, the construction of really large generating sets has not been prevented by the industry's archaic structure as it has in Germany. Indeed, the United States can claim to have led the world in this respect. The American industry has been able partly to escape the limitations of its organization due to the extremely high level of electricity consumption which, given some degree of co-operation between undertakings, often provides a sufficient basis for the construction of large sets.

It is in the maintenance of excessive reserves of generating capacity that the industry's defective organization has in the main shown itself. It must not, of course, be imagined that American undertakings are not linked for the purpose of transmission. In 1964 about 97 per cent of the industry's generating capacity was interconnected in five large networks. However, according to the Federal Power Commission, 'In many interconnected situations . . . the depth of co-ordinated system planning has not progressed to the point of taking full advantage of joint planning of generating capacity.'[68] This has led to the maintenance of plant reserves which, by the early sixties, stood at 25 per cent or more above the peak load. The Federal Power Commission's study shows that with full co-ordination between undertakings the necessary reserve would only be about 15 per cent. The Commission estimates that if the industry's unnecessary reserves can be eliminated by 1980 the American industry will save itself nearly $9 billion of investment in generating capacity which would otherwise be necessary, even after allowing for the extra investment required in transmission lines. During recent years the margin of reserve capacity has declined but this appears to have been largely due to the serious delays which have occurred in getting new plant into operation rather than to any great progress with interconnection. Perhaps, goaded on by the Power Commission, the industry will during coming years achieve full co-ordination, but this should have happened years ago. As long ago as 1935 the Commission drew attention to the need for greater co-ordination between electricity undertakings and described the growth of interconnection as 'relatively haphazard, handicapped by intercompany rivalries and prejudices and by artificial barriers'.[69]

Is British Generating Plant Small?

This brief examination of the situation in Germany and America where the electricity industries are fragmented, appears to show the advantages of unified ownership. But during recent years some extremely adverse comparisons have been drawn between the performance of the British and foreign industries which we must now consider. F. P. R. Brechling and A. J. Surrey in a study undertaken at the National Institute of Economic and Social Research, published in 1966, argue that our electricity industry is technologically backward, having only partly secured the economies of scale which were to be had. They drew this conclusion from a comparison of the technical characteristics of the coal-fired electricity generating plant which had been or was being installed in Britain, France and the United States. The characteristics in which they were mainly interested were the capacity of the boilers and turbo-alternators, and steam temperature and pressure. As the size of boilers and turbo-alternators increases fuel productivity remains about the same but there is a progressive decline in the cost of each unit of capacity due to economies of scale. With higher steam conditions fuel productivity rises, though some additional capital cost is incurred. However, the decrease in cost with size is more than sufficient to cover the cost of higher temperatures and pressures.[70]

According to Brechling and Surrey

> the generating equipment which was installed in Britain over the whole period 1948 to 1963 has noticeably less advanced technical characteristics than the generating equipment installed in France and the United States – with, however, some catching up at the end of the period. In Britain the size of turbo-alternators and boilers has tended to be comparatively small, and this probably reduced capital productivity in the British industry. Moreover, in Britain steam temperatures and pressures have been comparatively low, . . . [these] technical characteristics probably contributed both to the comparatively low level, and to the comparatively slow rise, of fuel productivity in Britain.[71]

Messrs Brechling and Surrey went on to suggest that although we seemed to have more or less caught up in the technological field, we might be on the point of falling behind again. The CEGB had standardized upon 500 MW units with steam pressure at 2,300 lbs per square inch and steam temperature at 566C°.

> In the United States, however, 31 per cent of the additional capacity to be installed in the period 1964–8 consists of units larger than 500 MW and 27 per cent will operate at the supercritical pressure of 3,500 lbs per square inch. Examples of the very large units being installed in the United States include two 700 MW units at the Paradise plant (in service 1963) and one 900 MW unit at the Bull Run plant (in service 1965); both plants are owned by the Tennessee Valley Authority. Furthermore, Electricité de France plans to bring into service two 600 MW units in the next few years – one at Porcheville in 1967 and one at Le Havre in 1968. This evidence does not warrant firm conclusions, but it does suggest that the technical characteristics of the standard 500 MW British units may be surpassed in the late sixties by many units which will then be in service in America and perhaps a few units in France.[72]

This study has been quoted at length in order to avoid any risk of committing the same error as Messrs Brechling and Surrey: the selective quotation of information. It is perfectly true that in the period up to 1963 the average size of plant installed, and the average steam conditions used, were greatly inferior in Britain to those in the United States, and somewhat inferior to those in France. This was partly due, as Brechling and Surrey recognize, to the fact that between 1947 and 1950 the Government laid down that all sets for home use had to be of 30 or 60 MW. It was considered that, by concentrating production on these two types, it would be possible to produce the largest possible amount of plant, and so overcome the critical shortage of generating capacity without holding exports back. This policy may have had some success but it prevented the electricity industry from experimenting with larger units during the early post-war period and, since a power station takes five years to construct, prevented the British Electricity Authority from introducing larger sets until the mid-fifties. Moreover, the enforced concentration on sets of 30 MW and 60 MW seems to have led the British Electricity Authority to place too much emphasis on standardization and not enough on size, so that even when the restriction was lifted it failed to take the maximum advantage of its new freedom. What happened was that although it started to build a few units of 100 MW and then 120 MW and 200 MW, it continued to build a large number of standard sets. However, despite the industry's cautious approach, it had by 1960 caught up with France as Brechling and Surrey's charts, but not their text, indicate.[73]

It is also clear from other sources that, although Britain may have lagged behind America, we were by no means at the bottom of the technological league. The OEEC and OECD have published figures showing the size of electricity plant installed by member countries, year by year, since 1953. During the 11 years from 1953 to 1963 17 per cent of the thermal capacity installed in the UK was accounted for by sets of 200 MW or over, which were large by current standards. In France the figure was no higher, while in Germany and Italy, the other European countries where large amounts of conventional plant were introduced, the proportions were respectively zero and 8 per cent. Where France, though not the other European countries, was in advance of Britain was in having installed fewer small units of under 100 MW. During the period these sets accounted for only 6 per cent of new French capacity compared with half in the UK. In Italy the proportion was 56 per cent and in Germany 46 per cent.[74] It is unfortunate that Messrs Brechling and Surrey did not make use of the OEEC's readily available figures to paint a broader and less selective picture of international technical progress in electricity up to 1963.

The main weakness of their argument relates to the period since 1963. They suggest that France and America may once again be overtaking us in constructing large sets. So far as France is concerned this is nonsense. As OECD figures show, sets of 500 MW or over account for a higher proportion of all capacity installed, or to be installed in the UK, than they do in any other country in Western Europe. Between 1964 and 1972 these huge sets will form about 75 per cent of new British capacity compared with 15 per cent in France, and 8 per cent in Italy and Germany. Brechling and Surrey express their concern that our electricity industry should have standardized at 500 MW but do not even mention the fact that, with the exception of three large sets the French industry has standardized at 240 MW. Britain is not only ahead of Western Europe but also of Japan and probably Russia. Between 1964 and 1972 only 21 per cent of new Japanese capacity will take the form of sets of 500 MW and over, and although the Soviet Union seems to have built a few very large sets it appears to have standardized at 300 MW.[75]

America is the only country in the world where larger sets are being constructed than in Britain, although small sets certainly account for a higher proportion of their new capacity than of our own. In America sets of less than 500 MW account for 45 per cent of the conventional capacity which has been or will be installed during the period 1964–72, compared with only about 25 per cent in Britain. But whereas almost all of our large sets are of 500 MW and none is larger than 660 MW, a substantial proportion of the new American capacity takes the form of even bigger sets. Twenty-four per cent is accounted for by sets of 500–600 MW, and 30 per cent by still larger sets.[76]

The Advantages and Disadvantages of Giant Sets

How large are the economies of scale which the British electricity industry has forgone by not installing giant sets like the Americans? Messrs Brechling and Surrey fail to discuss this point but simply take it for granted that the bigger sets are the better they are. There is, of course, no doubt that the progressive increase in the size of units has in the past resulted in substantial savings. The cost of conventional generating stations constructed by the CEGB has fallen from £53·6 per kW for sets of 120 MW, to £36·6 per kW for sets of 275–375 MW and £34·4 per kW for sets of 500–50 MW. Moreover the reduction was somewhat greater than this suggests, as the smaller sets were constructed slightly earlier when costs were lower.[77] However, it is well known that the reduction in costs which can be achieved through an increase in the size of the unit becomes much less important above about 500 MW. Not only are the potential savings less substantial but in practice they are increasingly offset by diseconomies. The CEGB estimates that if it had constructed 900 MW sets instead of 500 MW units there would have been a direct saving of only £0·68 per kW at each coal-fired station. From this saving must be deducted the cost of the increase in the capacity of the transmission network and of the extra margin of reserve capacity which would have been necessary. Obviously, the larger sets and stations become, the stronger the transmission system has to be and the greater the reduction in capacity which the failure of any plant will cause. The CEGB estimates that, as a result of these factors, the saving in capital costs with the installation of 900 MW units would have been reduced from £0·68 to £0·61 per kW.[78]

This figure does not allow for the fact that, especially during the earlier years, the 900 MW sets would almost certainly be less reliable than those at 500 MW. According to the Tennessee Valley Authority which has constructed some of America's largest units they 'have needed more time than smaller units to reach maturity (time when maintenance stabilizes), and also have somewhat lower availability'. The proportion of time during which its units have been out of action when they should have been working, totals only 5·90 per cent for its sets of 300–30 MW and 8·19 per cent for those of between 550 and 575 MW. But its units of 704 MW have had a forced out age rate of 19·83 per cent, although their average age is slightly higher than that of the 550–75 MW sets. When scheduled maintenance is included, the reduction in availability, with the increase in the size of plant, was much less marked although it remained significant. The proportion of time during which the TVA sets were available fell from 81·7 per cent for those of between 300 and 330 MW and 79·7 per cent for those of 550–75 MW to 77·7 per cent for its 704 MW sets.[79]

The steady decline in the availability of plant as the size of sets has increased suggests that, if the TVA's experience is representative, an undertaking which installed 900 MW sets instead of 500 MW units would suffer a reduction of about 5 per cent during their early years. Once, however, the giant sets had settled down the difference in availability between the 500 MW and the 900 MW sets might be rather less, and even during their early years the loss in the availability of giant units might be reduced as experience was gained. Nevertheless, electricity undertakings should clearly allow for a significant reduction in the average availability of plant where they are contemplating the installation of giant sets. This means that if they opt for 900 MW units they will need to increase their reserve capacity and this will obviously involve extra expense. The CEGB estimates that if the installation of a large plant involves a reduction in annual availability of only 5 per cent then its cost is, in effect, increased by about £1·2 per kW.[80] Moreover the increase in breakdowns as the size of plant rises cancels out at least part of the operating economies which can, in theory, be obtained if large sets are constructed. 'In earlier studies,' concludes the report of a group of American experts, 'it was predicted that unit cost for maintenance would decrease with increasing unit size. This has not been the case because of the decreased availability of larger units. At present, the cost of maintenance material and labour per kilowatt hour is about the same regardless of unit size.'[81]

The TVA claims that on balance giant units are an economic proposition. According to Mr G. P. Palo and his colleagues

> TVA's experience shows continued economy in plant cost and operation as units increase to as much as 1300 MW. This economy is partly offset by increased system capacity reserve requirements, somewhat lower availability, and more difficult maintenance . . . However, it is believed that the net economy of each new unit will increase with greater understanding of its characteristics and that the decisions to install these units of continually increasing size are sound.[82]

It seems likely that the net advantage to be obtained from introducing giant sets is at best a small one. Mr Palo and the other American experts who investigated economies of scale for the Federal Power Commission found that there was 'very little economic incentive for units above 600 megawatts'.[83] It is possible that expert opinion may have changed since 1963, when this was written, but it was then that the giant stations which have been commissioned during recent years were being planned.

There is a further reason why the savings which American electricity undertakings have achieved through introducing larger sets than the CEGB cannot as yet have been large. In the United States a high proportion of the large units have been what is known as cross-compound machines, whereas in Britain virtually all have been of the single-shaft variety. Cross-compound machines are composed of two basic single-shaft units which have been linked together. Because of this, a cross-compound machine is considerably more expensive than a single-shaft unit of the same capacity. The CEGB estimates that a cross-compound set of 1,200 MW would have about the same cost per kW as a single-line unit of 600 MW and only £1·14 per kW less than a single-line unit with a capacity of 500 MW.[84] This suggests that a cross-compound machine costs about the same amount per kW as a single-line unit only half as large and that when economies of scale are under discussion the capacity of cross-compound sets should be divided by two to make it equivalent to that of single-line units.

If this procedure is adopted, sets of 500 MW and over are shown to have accounted for 60 per cent of all new capacity brought into service in the UK between 1966 and 1968 but for only 30 per cent of the new American capacity. Moreover, when allowance is made for the fact that the largest American sets were cross-compound, it turns out that as long ago as 1960 the British electricity industry had more or less caught up with the American utilities. In that year the sets of 200 MW which were commissioned in this country accounted for 18 per cent of the conventional capacity which was introduced. In America the proportion of new capacity in the form of sets of 200 MW and over was, at 22 per cent, only slightly greater. It is true that most of these large American sets had a capacity of more than 200 MW but even the biggest was less than 250 MW. In both countries sets of between 100 MW and 199 MW were predominant. In the United States they accounted for 68 per cent of the plant which came into service and for the UK the figure was 63 per cent. Where Britain did lag slightly, but only slightly, behind the American utilities was that small sets of less than 100 MW formed 19 per cent of our new capacity but only 10 per cent of their new plant.[85] These tiny units were among the last of the sets of 30 MW and 60 MW on which the British Electricity Authority standardized soon after the war.

After having examined in some detail the size of generating sets which have been and are being installed, it is possible to deal more briefly with steam conditions. There is very little which needs to be said about the steam temperatures which have been adopted. Messrs Brechling and Surrey's figures show that although during the fifties they were lower at the new plant being commissioned in Britain than they were in France and America, the CEGB had caught up by the early sixties. Moreover, OECD figures show that the temperatures which are being adopted for new sets remain much the same in Britain (566° C with a few at 538°) as in France (565°), or the USA (538°/565°). Nor have Italy (538°) and Japan (538°/566°) adopted higher temperatures.[86] As this virtual unanimity among the different power undertakings suggests, there does not appear to be any practical advantage from using still higher temperatures. According to American experts who advised the Federal Power Commission 'even the theoretical returns from increases in cycle temperatures decrease to a marked extent above 1050° Fahrenheit [or 566° Centigrade]. While the expected gain in thermal economy has been realized, its economic effect has, in many cases, been offset by loss of availability'.[87]

The position is slightly more complicated with respect to steam pressure. Here again Britain had caught up with EDF by about 1960. Moreover the pressures on which the British electricity industry has standardized (2,300 lb. per square inch in England and Wales and 2,350 in Scotland) are much the same as those being used by EDF (2,320), ENEL and the Japanese electricity undertakings (mainly something over 2,400). In contrast, in the United States supercritical pressures have, as Messrs Brechling and Surrey say, been adopted on an extensive scale.[88] But it would be wrong to jump to the conclusion that the British electricity industry is backward because it has failed to follow the American example. It seems likely that the economic case for adopting or not adopting supercritical pressures is so finely balanced that electricity authorities should receive neither praise nor blame for coming down on one side or the other. That the case is evenly balanced is indicated not only by the CEGB's calculations but also by those of EDF.[89]

It must be concluded that there is no real evidence that during the sixties the British electricity industry failed to secure the economies of scale which were available, and it does not appear that it will fail to secure them during that part of the seventies which is visible. It is only when we go back to the fifties that the industry's performance appears somewhat less satisfactory when judged by the best foreign standards, though this was by no means entirely its own fault.

Economies of Scale in Public and Private Enterprise

Although economies of scale are particularly important in gas and electricity, and it is here that the unification of the industries, through public ownership, has conferred the greatest advantages, nationalization also provided most of the other nationalized industries with significant opportunities. These will not be considered in detail but they deserve a brief mention. In the coal industry the closure of collieries and the working of their reserves from adjoining pits had been inhibited by its fragmented ownership, although concentration of this type can yield significant economies. As the Reid Committee saw, there was scope for the construction of plants, for such purposes as coal cleaning and the maintenance of machinery, which could serve a number of mines. For these and other reasons it concluded that it was not possible to provide for the soundest and most efficient development and working of an area unless the conflicting interests of the individual colliery companies working the area were merged together.[90] After the companies had been compulsorily amalgamated through nationalization, the Coal Board set about securing the economies of scale which were possible. It envisaged in *Plan for Coal* that 90 pits with an output of 22 million tons would be absorbed in schemes of concentration and reconstruction, and the Board has constructed central workshops and washeries.[91] The gains which have been obtained in this way cannot have been dramatic but they were obviously worth securing.

Similarly, in air transport economies of scale do not seem to be enormous but are nevertheless worth-while. For instance the Edwards Committee, after a very thorough investigation, concluded that a large airline with a fleet of 50 aircraft of the same type ought, if it makes the most of its opportunities, to be able to reduce its unit costs 10–15 per cent below those of a small airline with only five planes. These potential economies arise, among other reasons, because the large airline needs to hold a proportionately smaller quantity of spare parts due to the spreading of risks, and because it should be able to reduce its maintenance and overhaul costs as a result of repetition. In addition, the marketing effectiveness of an airline engaged on inter-continental work is greatly increased by the possession of an extensive route system and widespread sales outlets.[92] BEA and BOAC are large enough to secure most of these economies of scale, and the fact that their unit costs now compare favourably with those of their foreign competitors suggests that they have not wasted their opportunities.

Even in road haulage, though this is the most debatable case, it seems likely that there are advantages of large-scale operation. British Road Services is able to cater for the needs of firms with large-scale transport requirements and so save them the time and trouble of contacting large numbers of small hauliers. Through its depots BRS can operate its own clearing house system and arrange back loads. For this and other reasons BRS has been able to fill a very high proportion of the capacity which it provides. For instance in 1961 only 27 per cent of the tonnage capacity generated by its general haulage vehicles was not utilized – a remarkably high proportion when it is remembered that loads can be light but bulky. But small private hauliers do have the advantage, of which as the road check figures show they make considerable use, that they can run defective vehicles and flout the regulations which restrict drivers' hours, whereas BRS, a large publicly-owned concern, maintains exemplary but expensive standards.[93]

Although most of the nationalized industries seem to have obtained the economies of scale which have been available, the railways have been a partial exception. Their record has been somewhat disappointing, despite the marked improvement in recent years. A long period elapsed before large wagons began to be introduced and the average size of British wagons is still very small. Again the railways were slow to begin concentrating their traffic on to a limited number of routes and building up larger freight trains. These historical weaknesses are now being tackled in so far as this is possible granted the maintenance of the existing system of through routes. However, the substantial economies which could be secured by closing duplicate routes are being forgone, although this is not the fault of British Rail but a political decision.[94] Nevertheless, the general record of the nationalized industries in securing economies of scale is by no means a discreditable one. This, unfortunately, is more than can be said for a large part of the private sector.

The chemical industry has, by its own admission, failed to install large enough plant. According to a working party of the Economic Development Committee for the chemical industry which investigated a number of British and North American plants in 1966–7,

> A very significant difference between the chemical industries of Britain and America is in the scale of operations . . . The most important scale factor is the size of the individual unit of production, and here the American firms scored heavily. We found in nearly all cases that the basic unit of production was considerably larger than the corresponding unit in the British Company, in one case five times as large. This factor clearly has a very considerable effect on such crude measures of comparison as output per head . . . In each company whose works we visited, on both sides of the Atlantic, we made a close study of the process-manning of at least one particular process. From the data we collected we arrived at the conclusion that, on average, the production groups concerned with the American processes produced over twice as much per head as those concerned with the corresponding British processes. About two-thirds of this difference we estimated to be due to the effect of the well-known difference in scale of the production units themselves . . . This measure of the greater utilization of production manpower by the Americans would, in fact, be increased still further if due allowance were made for two factors. First, the American process worker, in general, undertakes a certain amount of 'first-aid' maintenance . . . Second, there is a higher proportion of actual product testing carried out by the American process worker . . . We are convinced from our investigations and from the statistics we have collected that, in relation to total output, the British chemical industry employs something like three times as many men as the American chemical industry. The greater part of this difference is caused by factors which can be controlled.[95]

Another British industry which has not obtained the full economies of scale which are available is the motor industry. In some of the processes performed during the manufacture of cars, such as assembly, the most efficient techniques of production can be employed even at relatively modest levels of output, but for the machining or pressing of the major components extremely expensive equipment is necessary, which requires a very large volume of output to justify its use. Just how large the annual output of an individual model needs to be in order to secure most, if not all, of the scale economies which are potentially available is by no means clear because the motor manufacturers on both sides of the Atlantic are so coy with figures, but it probably lies somewhere between 250,000 and 500,000 cars per annum. Yet in 1964, a year for which figures happen to be available, only two out of 13 leading British models approached the lower limit, despite the fact that it has been apparent for decades that the British car industry's production runs are too short.[96]

It is the steel industry which provides the most fascinating instance of the failure to reduce costs to the minimum by installing plant of the most efficient size. The relatively low capacity of British steelworks is a long-standing weakness which was quickly perceived by Mr Steven Hardie when he became Chairman of the British Iron and Steel Corporation after the industry had been brought into public ownership in 1951. He wrote in the following year:

> Whilst a limited amount of rationalization has become evident in recent years amongst some of the larger steel groups, it is only by developing this on a national basis that the full economies can be obtained which are so essential to the future of the basic industry. Pooling of raw materials, mining and ore-handling facilities, the elimination of overlapping capacity, the long-term planning and modernization of the industry to develop its maximum capacity with concentration of specific products into individual works, can be effectively obtained only if co-ordinated as a national programme.[97]

What this programme would have contained we do not know, but the general intention was clear enough: economies of scale were to be secured to the full. It is difficult to avoid the conclusion that, had steel remained in public ownership, the industry would at long last have been rationalized.

When the industry was denationalized the Government established the Iron and Steel Board to supervise it. The Board both lacked the power to rationalize the industry and failed, until its closing years, to see that this was necessary. Meanwhile steel companies were happily engaged on modernizing and enlarging their individual works regardless of the economies of scale which were being foregone. This is shown by the modest increase in the degree to which production was concentrated at large works and by the inadequate scale of so much of its plant. In 1965 the four largest steelworks accounted for around 26 per cent of crude steel capacity which was about the same figure as in 1957, and only slightly higher than in 1953 when the top four produced 21 per cent. The size of the average plant had, of course, been increasing but so also had economies of scale, and when the industry was renationalized only one or two of our works even approached the optimum size. In the mid-sixties the bulk of British steel output was produced at works with capacities of around a million ingot-tons or less and only 35 per cent of steel-making capacity was, during 1965, located at works capable of producing more than 1·3 million tons.[98]

Yet, according to an authoritative investigation by Messrs C. Pratten and R. M. Dean, unit costs for the production of crude steel are about 5 per cent less at a plant with a capacity of 2 million tons than they are at a 1 million ton plant; and at a 4 million ton plant they are about 8 per cent smaller. On finishing operations the economies are greater and at a works with a strip mill for sheet steel unit costs are about 15 per cent less at 4 million tons than they are at 1 million tons. The Benson Committee, which the steel industry set up just before it was nationalized, concluded that a steelworks which used the latest available techniques and equipment needed to have a capacity of 3½ to 5 million ingot-tons, the exact size depending on the type of product which was being made. Obviously it would be wrong to expect that the industry should have produced all its output in large modern works, but it is evident that it had failed to make any real effort to rationalize its structure and secure the available economies of scale. Incredible as it may seem, the industry had not even fully carried out the rationalization of railmaking, which had been proposed in the post-war modernization plan.[99]

PART FOUR

Allocative Efficiency

CHAPTER 18

Misallocation in Theory

IN previous chapters of this book it has been taken for granted that the welfare of the community is increased by technical efficiency and reduced when output is sold at a loss or when an undertaking invests in projects which are only likely to show a low rate of return. No attempt has yet been made to discover the relative importance of technical and allocative efficiency or to measure the damage which the nationalized industries may have inflicted by, say, producing at a loss. In the present chapter we shall try to answer these questions.

To do so it will be necessary to make a number of simplifying assumptions which will be held over for examination in the next chapter. One of the most important of these is the assumption that the contraction of those undertakings and activities which are losing money would not inflict any significant social costs on society. In particular it will be assumed that the resources which would be released could be swiftly employed at a profit elsewhere in the economy. If this is unrealistic and they would remain unemployed, society is better served if the nationalized industries continue to produce at a loss. It has the benefit of the goods and services which they provide, whereas it obtains no benefit from unemployed workers and idle machinery. Again, it has been taken for granted that an industry is able to reduce its costs and its capacity as its output falls. This may not be possible because, for instance, of the difficulty of reducing overhead expenses and the adverse effect on morale and productivity which the rapid rundown of an industry may have. These are by no means the only assumptions which have been made, but enough has probably been said to indicate that the analysis contained in this chapter is in some ways unrealistic and to help the critical reader to preserve his patience.

Losses and Efficiency

The most striking and important point about allocative efficiency is that, except in the most extreme circumstances, the waste of resources is likely to be relatively small. This has been shown time and again by economists in studies of the potential welfare loss which monopoly inflicts, and of the possible welfare gains which the abolition of tariff barriers would confer.[1] Despite the fact that the first of these studies was made by Professor A. C. Harberger as long ago as 1953 they have had remarkably little impact. Economists seem unprepared to face up to the fact that one of the most important discoveries of economic science is the unimportance of allocative efficiency. Nowhere is the recognition of this truth more overdue than in discussions of the nationalized industries.

It is almost a matter of common sense, once preconceptions are banished, that the waste of resources is quite small even where an undertaking incurs a large deficit and large sums of money appear to have been thrown away. In 1968 British Rail had a working deficit of £91 million, disregarding its net receipts from advertising and the letting of property in operational use. At first sight this appears to represent the value of the resources which were wasted.[2] However, the loss to society was very much smaller because most railway users would have been prepared to pay more than the railways charged. If all rail users had been prepared to pay what British Rail would have had to have charged in order to cover its costs, there would, other things being equal, have been no loss in welfare whatsoever. Although taxes would have been £91 million higher than they would otherwise, this payment would have been offset by the £91 million which the railways' customers would have been willing to pay but were not asked to. The general tax payer would have been poorer but the rail user would have been correspondingly richer. Of course, in practice, by no means all the railways' customers would have been prepared to pay a charge which fully reflected British Rail's costs, but to the extent that they would have been prepared to make a contribution to the difference between the railways' charges and the railways' costs no loss of welfare was involved.

What we need to know, in order to make a rough calculation of this loss, is the extent to which rail charges would have been increased and the degree to which the demand for rail services is responsive to changes in price. The necessary increase in rail charges is easily discovered: in 1968 British Rail would have covered its working expenses if it had had 20 per cent more revenue. For the railways' passenger traffic, which accounts for about 40 per cent of their revenue, it is possible to make an estimate of the extent to which demand is responsive to price by discovering what has happened to the volume of traffic when prices have been increased in the past. Calculations by Mr Richard Lecomber suggest that in the long run every 1 per cent increase in rail fares leads approximately to a 1·1 per cent reduction in the volume of traffic or, as economists would say, there is a price elasticity of 1·1.[3] (Correspondingly if every 1 per cent increase in price had led to a fall of 0·5 per cent in volume the elasticity would have been 0·5 etc.) Let us assume for sake of argument that the general elasticity for rail traffic is two. This does not seem too unreasonable and, due to the lack of information about freight, there is no way of obtaining a more reliable figure.

If, with an elasticity of two, British Rail had increased its charges by 20 per cent it would have lost 40 per cent of its traffic. As its revenue totalled £457 million in 1968 customers who used to contribute £183 million would have been lost, but those who remained would have contributed an extra £55 million of revenue. Those customers who would have been lost if charges had been increased by the full 20 per cent would have been prepared to pay something between 0 per cent and 19·9 per cent, or about 10 per cent more on average. If British Rail had been able to distinguish these customers and to charge them as much as they were prepared to pay, but no more, it would have collected a further £18 million of revenue which makes a total of £73 million. The difference of £18 million between this figure and British Rail's loss of £91 million represents the welfare loss, granted the assumptions on which the calculation is based. Thus only a fifth of the money which the railways lost was wasted because it was not matched by any benefit to the community; £18 million may sound a formidable sum but it represents only 3 per cent of British Rail's total working expenses, i.e. the resources which the railways used.

Had British Rail's technical and managerial efficiency been only slightly lower than it was, the social waste would have been very much greater. Let us see how much social waste there would have been if BR had broken even in 1968 but its costs had been 20 per cent higher than they should have been. If it is further assumed that the railways' customers had contributed £457 million of revenue (as they did), then they would have paid £78 million more than they would have done if British Rail had not been so inefficient. The resources corresponding to this £78 million would have been wasted because if the railways had been more efficient they could have been devoted to some other use. This diversion would not have involved any loss of welfare because the benefit which British Rail's existing customers received from using the railways would have remained the same. And if British Rail had been more efficient, and there had been a corresponding reduction in its charges, it would have had more customers. Its charges would have been 17 per cent lower (because 20 represents 17 per cent of 120) which means, with an elasticity of two, that the volume of its traffic would have increased by 34 per cent. Most of these customers would have been attracted even if charges had not been reduced by the full 17 per cent. For instance 2 per cent extra would have switched to rail even if prices had only been reduced by

1 per cent. If British Rail had been able to discover exactly how much each potential customer was prepared to pay, and had charged accordingly, it could have secured them by reducing its prices by an average of $8\frac{1}{2}$ per cent. The difference between what its extra customers would have paid if its charges had been reduced by the full 17 per cent, and what they would have been prepared to pay, represents a further welfare gain which the community would have secured if the railways had been more efficient. As this additional benefit would have totalled £11 million there would have been a total increase in welfare of £89 million.

This shows that it is more important that resources should be used with a high level of technical efficiency than that they should be allocated correctly. In 1968 the railways had an operating loss equivalent to 20 per cent of their revenue. If the elasticity of demand was two this involved a welfare loss of £18 million due to the misallocation of resources. But if their costs had been 20 per cent higher and the deficit had not existed, there would have been a welfare loss of £89 million.

The relative importance of technical and allocative efficiency can be neatly shown by means of supply and demand diagrams based on the assumptions about the railways which have already been described. Figure 1A on the opposite page illustrates the situation in 1968 in which British Rail's unit costs, as represented by C_2, were 20 per cent higher than its charges at C_1. The amount of traffic which the railways carried at price C_1 is shown by M_2, and the amount of traffic which they would have carried if their charges had been as high as their costs is shown by M_1. The rectangle OC_1AM_2, therefore, represents the railways' total revenue, which is the product of charges and traffic. Similarly the rectangle OC_2QM_2 shows British Rail's aggregate costs, which are the product of unit costs and traffic. The railways' deficit, which is, of course, the difference between its revenue and its costs, is shown by C_2C_1AQ. The welfare loss which the community sustained as a result of the deficit was very much smaller, because the railways' customers would have been prepared to make a contribution equal to C_1C_2TA in return for the services which they received at a price below their cost. The loss to the community was represented by the shaded triangle which, as can be seen, was only a fraction of the resources which the railways absorbed.

Figure 1B shows the waste of resources which would have occurred if British Rail had covered its costs but they had been 20 per cent higher than they were at C_3. Point M_1 is the traffic which the railways would have carried if they had broken even with their costs at the 1968 level, and M_3 the reduced traffic which they would have carried if it had been less efficient. The shaded rectangle C_2C_3XR represents the resources which the railways would have wasted if they had been less efficient than

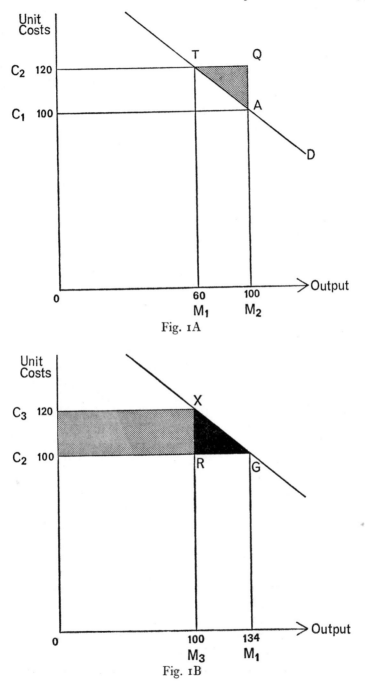

Fig. 1A

Fig. 1B

they were, and the black triangle XRG shows the additional loss which the community, in the shape of British Rail's potential customers, would have sustained. This triangle is the extra amount which the additional customers BR would have had if it had been fully efficient and had charged C_2 would then have been prepared to pay. It can readily be seen that the potential loss to the community through inefficiency C_2C_3-XG was very much greater than the waste of resources in Fig. 1A due to the railways' deficit.[4]

Taxation

So far, only the direct impact of the railways' deficit on the community's welfare has been considered. It will have some indirect effect if only because the Government will have to find the money to cover British Rail's loss. If, as a result, taxation is higher than it would otherwise be, there will be a further small loss in allocative efficiency. This is best shown by considering what happens if the burden of indirect taxation has to be increased. In this situation there is some loss in welfare because those consumers who would have been prepared to pay something above the old pre-tax price, but not as much as the new post-tax price, will now buy other products. The uncovenanted benefit which they would have enjoyed is thus lost to society. It cannot be made good by consumers re-arranging their purchases so as to concentrate their money on those products for which the benefit they receive is greater than the price they pay; if consumers are rational they will already have maximized their satisfaction in this way. (The effect of an indirect tax on consumers' welfare can be seen from Fig. 1B if this is assumed to represent the price and output of the commodity on which the tax is placed, instead as previously of an inefficient railway. If C_2 represents the pre-tax price, the difference between C_2 and C_3 represents the tax, and C_3 shows the post-tax price, then the rectangle C_2C_3XR indicates the tax revenue which the Government receives and the triangle XRG shows the reduction in consumers' welfare due to the tax.)

It may be more realistic to assume that, instead of having imposed new taxes to meet the railways' deficit, the Government has switched tax revenue from some other object for which it might otherwise have been used. It seems likely that Governments impose the highest taxes which they consider practicable, and then trim the expenditure which they consider desirable down to the sum which they expect to collect. If so, the relevant question is not how much misallocation has been caused by the taxation to pay the railway deficit, because it would have been levied in any case, but what benefit would society have had from the government expenditure which would otherwise have taken place. What we want to know is whether it is greater or smaller than the welfare benefit which society obtains as a result of the rail deficit. Unfortunately it is virtually impossible to answer this question, although the case for subsidizing British Rail is weak on distribution of income grounds.[5]

Protection

Although British Rail's deficit is the most striking case there are other ways in which the operations of the nationalized industries may have led to the misallocation of resources. The coal industry, unlike the railways, has not received large-scale financial assistance from the Government but it has been protected against competition from oil. In 1961 a tax of 2d per gallon was imposed on heavy oils and later the rate was temporarily increased to 2·2d. Although the tax appears to have been originally imposed for revenue purposes, its retention has been partly due to the desire of successive Governments to provide support for the coal industry while it carries through the reorganization which the contraction of demand has made necessary.[6] At the time when the tax stood at 2·2d per gallon the Ministry of Power stated that it represented 'an average loading of about 40 per cent on the delivered pre-tax price of fuel oil to large industrial users'.[7] If so, the tax formed 29 per cent of the price which the consumer had to pay. By now the figures may be slightly lower because the price of fuel oil has risen somewhat, owing to devaluation. It would probably be unrealistic to assume that if the tax was removed fuel oil prices would fall to the full extent of the tax. It appears that when the duty was imposed part of the burden was absorbed by the oil companies, which need cause no surprise in view of the ample profit margins which they seem to have been earning on fuel oil. During the early sixties a survey by the Iron and Steel Board showed that, excluding tax, the price was substantially higher in Britain than it was in the main continental countries apart from France.[8] It might not be too wide of the mark to assume that in the absence of the tax the price of fuel oil would be 25 per cent lower.

In order to calculate the loss in economic welfare which this involved, it is necessary to know how responsive the demand for oil is to changes in its price. Estimates which have been made by Mr Ken Wigley suggest that it is highly responsive and it has been assumed that the price elasticity for oil is about four.[9] If so, the loss in welfare which the community sustained can be calculated by the method which has already been described. As expenditure on heavy oil totalled about £350 million in 1967–8 there appears to have been a welfare loss of £45 million. This was equivalent to only 6 per cent of the coal industry's costs of production in 1967–8.[10] In other words the cost which the Coal Board would have imposed on the community if its costs had been only 6 per cent higher due to technical inefficiency, would have been as great as the loss in allocative efficiency which the community suffered as a result of the tax on fuel oil. Yet this tax represents about 25 per cent of the price of fuel oil! Once again it becomes apparent how much more important it is that resources should be used efficiently than that they should be allocated correctly.

Cross-Subsidization

Having examined the losses which the railways incur and the protection which the coal industry receives, the practice of cross-subsidization must be considered. When cross-subsidization takes place within an undertaking it makes a loss on one part of its operations which is financed out of the profits which it earns elsewhere. If it finds it necessary to raise the prices which the profitable part of the business charges then the firm is in effect taxing one group of consumers to subsidize another. Cross-subsidization thus appears to involve a double misallocation of resources: some products are sold below cost while the price of other commodities is unnecessarily high. The critics of the nationalized industries usually take it for granted that cross-subsidization has led to inflated prices. 'Suppose,' argues Professor J. Wiseman, 'the Coal Board decides against closing a high-cost pit because miners would become redundant and the Board cannot move them elsewhere (or is unwilling to bear the cost). Such a policy must raise the cost of coal, so that the social cost is borne by coal users.'[11] A moment's reflection shows that it does not necessarily follow that because an undertaking is practising cross-subsidization, it has inflated prices. This will not happen, for example, where its profits are already sufficient to cover the deficit on the undertaking's loss-making activities and it is prepared to accept a low overall rate of return on its assets. Professor Wiseman appears to have overlooked this simple point, or to have ignored it so as not to mar the symmetry of his argument for denationalization.

This is unfortunate as there is no reason to suppose that the Coal Board has been earning an excessively high rate of return on the profitable part of its business. The surplus of £66 million which in 1967–8 the NCB earned on its profitable pits represented a return of about 13 per cent on their assets.[12] Although cross-subsidization is less widespread within the public enterprise sector than is sometimes supposed, it is also practised to a significant extent by the nationalized buses and British European Airways. However, there is no question of BEA unilaterally jacking up prices on its international services to cover the losses on its domestic services, because international air fares are controlled by IATA. It does not seem likely that the nationalized buses have, during recent years, been earning monopoly profits on their remunerative services in order to meet the losses they make elsewhere. Too little information is available for it to be possible to calculate what rate of return Tillings and Scottish buses have earned on their profitable routes but it is very doubtful whether, during recent years, it has been very high. Between 1964 and 1968 they earned an average profit of £7¼ million, and had a rate of return of 13¼ per cent, which means that only if the losses on their unprofitable routes were very large can the profits on their remunerative routes have been excessive. Yet it is doubtful whether their losses were enormous. Tillings and Scottish estimated that in 1958 they lost £2½ million on their unprofitable routes which, although it is an out-of-date and somewhat dubious figure, probably does give some indication of the magnitude of their losses.[13] London Transport appears in 1964 to have made a loss of around £3 million on the unprofitable bus services which it maintained.[14] If so, it earned about £5 million on its profitable services which makes it seem unlikely that abnormally high profits were being earned there in order to cover up losses. During recent years, when the overall profit has been replaced by an overall loss, this seems even less probable.

It appears that cross-subsidization by the nationalized industries has not led to a double dose of misallocation. Although part, though a surprisingly small part, of their output has been sold below its costs of production, there is no evidence that the operation has been financed out of the monopoly profits which have been earned elsewhere. Indeed, the nationalized industries should not perhaps be regarded as having been practising cross-subsidization as this almost involves the notion that monopoly profits are being earned in order to cover up losses. If the term is restricted to this situation, as it sometimes is, the nationalized industries have not been practising cross-subsidization at all but have simply made losses on part of their business. If this is the case, it seems rational to suppose that their effect on the welfare of the community can be analysed in exactly the same way as British Rail's. This is the wrong approach, however, if the goods which are now produced at a loss could be produced more cheaply by the discontinuance of production at those of the undertaking's plants where costs are unavoidably high and the expansion of output where they are low. For instance, it may be possible for the Coal Board to close down its high-cost pits where geological conditions are difficult and to increase coal production at its low-cost mines where coal is easily won. If this can be done, society can go on consuming

o

the same amount of coal as it does now at a lower cost. In this situation it is illegitimate to try to discover, as we did for the railways, how much consumers would be prepared to contribute to the costs of the undertaking rather than to forego the output which is now produced at a loss. If it is possible to switch production from a high to a low cost part of the business then there is no need for the undertaking to incur the loss which it does and that is the end of the matter.

In the case of BEA and the nationalized buses it is not sensible to suppose that output can be shifted in this way because consumers would not, for instance, regard extra flights between London and Paris as an acceptable substitute for the withdrawal of services in the Highlands and Islands of Scotland. This means that the welfare effects of the losses which BEA and the nationalized buses incur on their unremunerative routes can be analysed in the same way as the rail deficit. But whether the Coal Board's losses can be treated in this way depends on whether the reduction in output at unprofitable pits could be made good by expanding production at those which are profitable. If this is possible then the entire deficit at loss-making pits must be regarded as a waste of resources. If it is impossible for the NCB to expand its profitable output, due for instance to the shortage of workers at its profitable pits, then its losses must be analysed in the same way as those of the railways, the buses and the airways. In this situation it is legitimate to ask how much consumers would be prepared to contribute to the Board's costs rather than to forego having the coal which is now produced at a loss. How far it is possible for output to be transferred from loss-making to profitable pits is discussed in the next chapter but let us, for the sake of argument, assume that it is impossible and calculate the welfare loss which is involved. If production can be shifted there is no calculation to make, for most of the £42 million lost at unprofitable pits during 1967–8 was wasted.

In 1967–8 the Coal Board's unprofitable output totalled about 60 million tons for which, to judge from the revenue per ton in the loss-making Areas, the Board would have received about £300 million. This means that the losses at unprofitable pits represented about 14 per cent of their revenue, which suggests, coal being an increasing cost industry, that prices would have to be raised by amounts varying from 0·1 per cent to about 28 per cent at the loss-making pits for their costs to be recovered. If price elasticity was roughly one and a half, which is what Mr Wigley's estimates suggest, it can be calculated that the deficit of £42 million at the unprofitable pits involved a welfare loss of 20–25 million.[15] If so, the social loss represented a substantial part of the Board's private loss, but nevertheless was only equivalent to 3 per cent of the total resources which the coal industry used. In 1966

BEA incurred a deficit of £1·3 million on its domestic routes and this was equivalent to 6 per cent of the £22 million of revenue which they produced.[16] Assuming an elasticity of one (the estimated figure for rail) the welfare loss was a mere £40,000. The loss which the nationalized buses make on their unprofitable services may in 1964 have been around £5½ million, while their revenue may have totalled about £45 million, assuming that a third of their mileage was unprofitable.[17] As Mr Lecomber's estimate of the short-term elasticity for bus travel was 1·2 there would, in this case, have been a social loss of only £¾ million.[18] Granted the assumptions which have been made, the total welfare loss as a result of cross-subsidization within the public enterprise sector totalled some £25 million, and represented only a fraction of the resources which the nationalized industries employed.

A Low Return on Investment for Expansion

The low rates of return which the nationalized industries are supposed to have earned on their capital expenditure constitute the final way in which their operations may have led to the misallocation of resources. It is usually assumed that nationalized industries should have aimed at the high return it is thought that private firms require, but as was argued in Chapter 16, the attempt to achieve a better allocation of resources between the public and the private sectors by requiring the nationalized industries to raise their sights may only result in a worse allocation of resources between consumption and investment. However, let us ignore this and assume for the sake of argument that any fall in investment in the public enterprise sector would be made good by a rise in private investment. Under these circumstances how much damage does an undertaking inflict on the community when it invests in projects which have a low yield?

Consider the case of an enterprise that is thinking about building a new plant to meet the growth in the demand for its products which will occur if its prices are not raised, and which goes ahead with the project although it expects that the rate of return on the capital involved will be only half the normal profit. If its forecasts turn out to be correct, it will be using some resources to provide output on which consumers place a relatively low value in the sense that they would not all be prepared to pay a price sufficient to yield a normal profit. Obviously these resources could have been used to better advantage providing goods which consumers value sufficiently highly to be prepared to pay a price which would yield at least a normal profit; or, to make the same point in another way, a relatively large amount of resources has been used to provide output for which consumers are prepared to pay a given amount of money. Hence the loss in welfare which the construction of the plant has involved is the difference between what consumers would have had to pay in order to yield the enterprise a normal profit and the contribution towards this profit which consumers would have been prepared to make by paying a higher price. The loss in welfare will therefore depend on the extent to which prices would have to be raised to earn a normal rate of return on the capital investment, and on the elasticity of demand. If, for instance, the plant costs £100 million and is capable of producing one million units of output at a cost of £200 per unit including a profit at 5 per cent on the capital employed, which is half the normal rate, prices would have to be increased by £5 per unit or 2½ per cent. (The additional 5 per cent on £100 million is £5 million, which represents 2½ per cent on the £200 million turnover.)

Although the welfare loss can be estimated from the increase in prices and from elasticity, this does not mean that prices should be raised if the plant has already been built. If prices are raised there will be a further welfare loss, partly because the rise in prices will deter some consumers from purchasing the product who would nevertheless have been prepared to pay something above the old price, and partly because productive capacity, which would have been used if prices had not been raised, will stand idle. In theory, an industry which has constructed too much capacity at too low a rate of return should delay the rise in prices until, in the absence of an increase, it will be forced to construct still more capacity at a low rate of profit. When the rise in demand to be expected as the national income grows has offset the temporary check brought about by the rise in prices, the industry can and should resume its construction of extra capacity, for this time it will be earning a normal rate of return on its investment.

This is a point of some importance because it is often assumed that if only the nationalized industries were required to earn a commercial return on their capital expenditure there would be not only a large but also a permanent reduction in their level of investment. This presumably is what Professor S. R. Dennison had in mind when he asserted that:

> In general, the rate of return on a piece of investment expected by the Boards (even when they follow an economic calculus) is much less than that required by private industry before undertaking expansion. . . . Thus it can be said that the level of investment in them has been too high in the sense that they have received a larger share of the nation's resources than would have come to them on the normal tests of the market.[19]

It is clear that, at least in the case of investment required for the con-

struction of extra capacity, which in fact accounts for the great bulk of
the total, an increase in the rate of return required by public enterprise
would lead, at most, to only a small and temporary reduction in the
nationalized industries' capital expenditure.

The only circumstance in which there would be a permanent reduction of any significance would be if a once-and-for-all rise in the
nationalized industries' profits led to a reduction in their long-term rate
of expansion. This, however, seems unlikely. Those who believe that if
the nationalized industries had sought a higher rate of return on their
investment there would have been a long-term reduction in their
capital expenditure, may have fallen into the trap of imagining that plant
and equipment which yield a low rate of return are permanent liabilities.
But this is not usually the case because if demand is expanding, the
investment would have had to have been undertaken sooner or later. All
that happens, when new capacity is installed in an expanding industry
although it shows a low rate of return, is that necessary capital expenditure has been undertaken prematurely.

A Low Return on Labour Saving Investment

Although most of the capital expenditure by the public enterprise
sector has been for the purpose of providing extra capacity, the nationalized industries have usually had the choice of adopting more or less
capital-intensive methods. The railways have, for instance, been able to
choose between dieselization, which involves relatively little capital expenditure, and electrification, where the initial outlay is much higher.
Similarly, in electricity a choice has had to be made between conventional generating stations, which have low capital but high running
costs, and nuclear power stations, where the position is the reverse. If an
undertaking is prepared to accept a low rate of return it seems likely that
its chances will be biased in favour of capital-intensive projects. To determine whether this has happened in the public enterprise sector it is
necessary to examine the facts. However, let us for the sake of argument
assume that this is the case and try to discover how large the waste of
resources is likely to have been.

At first sight it appears that investment in capital-intensive projects
which show a low rate of return inflicts permanent damage on the community. Capital, it might be argued, has been sunk irretrievably in
projects where the costs of production are high relative to the value of the
output which is obtained. They do not, of course, appear high to the
nationalized industry which is making the investment, but this is only
because it is underpricing capital in its calculations by being prepared to

accept a low rate of return. This particular argument is invalid because the damage inflicted on the community is unlikely to be more than temporary. The reason is that over the years capital intensive methods of production become more and more attractive due to the rise in real wages. It is, therefore, to be expected that a scheme for installing costly labour-saving equipment which does not quite show an adequate rate of return with labour at its current price will do so in a few years' time when the price of labour has increased. Capital will only be totally wasted if the project will never be worth while, or if the expected rise in wages has already been allowed for by the undertaking in its calculations of the likely rate of return. In practice the rise in wages will be sufficient, within a few years, to justify the project unless it has already allowed for higher earnings in its calculations. However, as we have seen, the nationalized industries have only just started to allow for changes in relative prices in their profitability estimates.[20]

Where an undertaking decides to scrap old but serviceable plant, although the rate of return from the project is only expected to be a low one, replacement should have been delayed until the rise in the operating and repair costs of the old plant was sufficient to justify its renewal. But as the costs of using old plant are likely to rise fairly fast, if only because there will be little scope for productivity gains to offset the inevitable rise in wage costs, replacement would probably have been worth while within a year or two.

It must be concluded, therefore, that where an undertaking invests in capital-intensive methods which show a low rate of return, or replaces equipment prematurely, the result is much the same as if it had invested in new capacity from which it expected a low yield: resources will not be used to the best advantage in the short run but, in the absence of further investment at a low rate of return, misallocation will become less and less serious as time goes by. The amount of misallocation will be smaller where the capital expenditure is for expansion, for the reason that most consumers would have been prepared to pay something above the price which will yield the undertaking a low rate of return. But where an undertaking is planning to use unnecessarily capital-intensive plant or to retire old plant prematurely it is illegitimate to raise prices in order to boost the rate of return. If it does this it will simply be exploiting its monopoly power and forcing consumers to pay an unnecessarily high price.

Counting the Cost of Low Yield Investment

This general analysis of the misallocation which is likely to occur when a nationalized enterprise undertakes investment from which it only expects a low rate of return strongly suggests that it will be relatively trifling. To discover whether this is the case we shall now try to quantify the possible loss in welfare. Its extent will, in practice, depend on how low the rate of return has been and, in the case of investment, to provide extra capacity upon the elasticity of demand. The great bulk of investment in new capacity within the public enterprise sector is undertaken by the electricity and gas industries and it is therefore their elasticities of demand in which we are primarily interested, assuming of course that their prospective rates of return on investment have been too low.

The sensitivity of the demand for electricity to changes in price has been studied by R. E. Baxter and R. Rees. Using quarterly data for the period 1954–64 they tried, by examining the relationship between changes in electricity consumption and prices in 16 industry groups, to discover the elasticity of demand. The main conclusion of their regression analysis was that

relative price changes are not unambiguously an important determinant of growth in industrial electricity consumption. The chief determinants are growth in output and changes in technology. Taken at face value, the results for the relative price variables suggest that in at least nine out of the 16 industry groups price elasticity of demand is zero; in a further two it is relatively inelastic; and in only five does there appear to be a marked responsiveness of demand to relative price changes.[21]

Messrs Baxter and Rees point out that their results may not bear the weight of this interpretation because, among other reasons, the price elasticity may not have been zero where they failed to obtain a statistically significant result. However, even if attention is confined to those industries where it was statistically significant, it appears that the general long-term elasticity was relatively low. The average for these seven industries was only 1·3.[22] For domestic electricity consumption Mr Lecomber estimates the long-term elasticity to be 2·9, which is probably on the high side. But even if this figure is accepted the overall elasticity for all types of consumption would only be about 2. Mr Lecomber's calculations for domestic gas sales, which have hitherto accounted for the bulk of the industry's output, suggest that the long-term elasticity was, at 4·3, a high one. As the (short-term) elasticity for commercial sales, which represent a large part of the remaining output, was low it is probably safe to assume that the overall elasticity for gas is somewhat lower than 4·3.

These estimates, if they are reliable, show what effect on demand a rise in gas or electricity prices would have. They do not show what would happen if gas and electricity prices were both raised together. In the simplest case where their prices were both raised by the same percentage it seems unlikely that there would be any switching between the two fuels. Their demand would only be affected to the extent that consumers changed over to coal and oil, or decided to spend their money on some entirely different commodity group such as extra food or warmer clothing. Estimates by Mr Wigley suggest that, so far as domestic consumption is concerned, the elasticities for gas and electricity are only about half as large when they both raise their prices in step as they are when they act in isolation.[23] No corresponding information is available for industrial consumption but it is probably safe to assume that here the demand for electricity falls almost as much when gas prices are raised simultaneously as it does when they are not; the reason being that the amount of gas sold to industry is only a fraction of industrial sales of electricity.[24] It therefore seems reasonable to suppose that the overall elasticity for electricity is about 1·5 when gas prices are raised in step compared with about 2 when they are not. For gas the elasticity may be about 2 when electricity prices are raised in step and around 4 when they are not. Obviously no great confidence can be placed on these figures, but they are the best that can be done without making a special study of the subject, and it is difficult to believe they are too low.

After these rough-and-ready estimates of elasticity, the next step in our calculation is to make some assumption about the gap between their prospective rates of return and the rate at which they should have aimed. This, of course, begs the question of whether in practice they have invested at too low a rate of return. Not only is it open to dispute whether the nationalized industries should aim at a commercial rate of return, but it has been shown that in the gas industry prospective rates of return have by any standard been respectable.[25] However let us assume that the prospective return on *all* gas and electricity investment has, during recent years, been no higher than the *minimum* rate of return which the industries adopted after the Government set their original financial targets. The gas industry was, in effect, set a target of 5¾ per cent on its net assets after depreciation and the target for electricity was 6¾ per cent. In practice the gas boards sought to earn a minimum of 7–7½ per cent and the CEGB started by requiring 8 per cent but later, when the rate of interest fell, reduced the figure to 7½ per cent.[26] To be on the safe side we shall take the figures at the lower end of the range and assume that the prospective return on the gas industry's investment has been 7 per cent and for electricity 7½ per cent. Let us further assume that if the industries had been privately owned they would have required prospective returns of 10 per cent before investing. Because gas and electricity are industries in which risks are low, or at least are generally believed to be, it would be difficult to make out a case for a higher figure. The American electricity companies have, as we have seen, been content with a rate of return on their assets of something under 10 per cent.[27]

Granted these assumptions, unfavourable as they are to the gas and electricity industries, the Gas Boards should have required a further 3 per cent on their capital expenditure and the Electricity Boards an extra $2\frac{1}{2}$ per cent. In order to discover the loss in welfare which the community would have sustained in this situation, we must next find out the rise in prices which the industries would have had to make in order for their investment in new capacity to have yielded the desired amount. It appears that during the past few years every 1 per cent increase in electricity sales has involved the industry in about £50 million of capital expenditure and yielded it £$10\frac{1}{2}$ million of extra revenue.[28] Thus, in order to step up its rate of return by $2\frac{1}{2}$ per cent, the industry would have needed to increase its revenue by £$1\frac{1}{4}$ million and its prices by 12 per cent. For gas only a very rough calculation is possible, but it appears that before the advent of natural gas a 1 per cent increase in sales necessitated about £9 million of investment and produced £$3\frac{1}{2}$ million of additional revenue. If so, the industry would have needed to increase its revenue by about £$\frac{1}{4}$ million on every 1 per cent of extra sales in order to step up its rate of return on the extra capital by 3 per cent. This, in turn, would have required a 7 per cent increase in prices.

Seven per cent of the increase in electricity prices would, therefore, have been matched by the rise in gas prices. With an elasticity of 1·5, which is the relevant figure when gas and electricity prices rise in step, there would consequently have been a fall of over 10 per cent in electricity consumption. For the remaining 5 per cent of the increase in electricity prices, which would not have been accompanied by a rise in gas prices, the relevant elasticity is 2. As a result there would have been a further reduction of 10 per cent in electricity consumption and an overall decline of about a fifth. Because the rise in gas prices would, at 7 per cent, be more than matched by the rise in electricity charges the elasticity would be 2 and the decline in sales would be 14 per cent. If so, the gas industry has over the years invested about £125 million more than it would have done with a 3 per cent higher rate of return (£9 million × 14). Correspondingly, the Electricity Boards have invested about £1,000 million more than they would have done had their rate of return been $2\frac{1}{2}$ per cent greater (£50 million × 20).

All that now remains to be done is to estimate the extent to which the community's welfare has been reduced through the investment of these sums at an unduly low rate of return. If we are right in supposing that private firms would have required 10 per cent on their capital when investing in projects with as low a risk as in gas and electricity, then it appears at first sight that the welfare loss in gas is 3 per cent on £125 million or £3¾ million per annum, and that in electricity it is 2½ per cent on £1,000 million or £25 million. What this ignores is that most gas and electricity consumers would have been prepared to pay more than they were asked. The amounts can be calculated by the usual method, and it turns out that those who consumed the gas corresponding to its £125 million of unnecessary investment would have been prepared to pay an extra £1¾ million, and that electricity consumers would have been willing to contribute £12½ million. If so, the welfare loss was only about £2 million for gas and £12½ million for electricity.

CHAPTER 19

Misallocation in Practice

THE discussion of misallocation in the previous chapter led to an important conclusion: the avoidable waste of resources within the public enterprise sector has been relatively trivial. Yet the analysis it contained was, in some ways, unsatisfactory because of the unrealistic and abstract assumptions on which it was based. The purpose of this chapter is to examine these assumptions and thereby throw some additional light on the extent to which the welfare of the nation has been reduced, or perhaps increased, by the actions of the nationalized industries and the fact that they are in public ownership.

Coal: The Problem of Feed-Back

One of the major weaknesses of the last chapter is that, like most conventional supply and demand analysis, it ignored the problem of feed-back. It was assumed, for instance, that, if the coal industry was drastically cut back so as to eliminate cross-subsidization and the need for protection, costs of production at the remaining pits would remain the same. This seems most unlikely and certainly cannot be taken for granted. Yet it is an assumption which is frequently made when the contraction of the coal industry is under discussion. It is now well over 30 years since John Maynard Keynes exposed the foolishness of ignoring the interaction of economic events when analysing the general level of economic activity, but the wider significance of this obvious point has not yet been fully grasped.

What would have happened to costs of production if the coal industry had not been supported and the Coal Board had closed its unprofitable pits as quickly as was administratively possible? The answer partly depends on the number of collieries which would have had to be shut. The higher the number of pits which would have been axed, the greater the amount of disruption which it seems reasonable to suppose the operation would have caused. It is evident that a large part of the industry would have been affected. In 1964 the NCB had about 150 grossly unprofitable pits where working expenses exceeded revenue by over 10s per ton which means that they failed to cover depreciation charges or make any contribution to the Board's overhead expenses. These mines had a labour force of 118,000 and an output of around 33 million tons. They accounted, therefore, for about a fifth of the Board's deep-mined output and a quarter of its employment. A few of these pits were unprofitable because they were under reconstruction but except for these it would, ignoring possible side effects, have paid the NCB to have shut them. In addition there were 114 pits which lost up to 10s per ton. They employed 94,000 workers and produced another 33 million tons of coal.[1]

Although this group made some contribution to the Board's overhead expenses, these were larger than they would have been if it had adopted a policy of drastic closure. Administrative and other costs may be fixed in the short run but can be avoided in the long run. If, therefore, the NCB had started to prune down vigorously its administrative apparatus in loss-making areas when, back in 1958, it became evident that the coal shortage was over, it would almost certainly have completed a large part of the task by 1964. This is not meant to imply that the Board made no progress towards slimming down its organization. Between the beginning of 1958 and the spring of 1965 the number of areas was reduced from 50 to 41, and this was presumably accompanied by a saving in expenses.[2] However, the Board was obviously unable to move as fast as it would have if it had ruthlessly closed all of its uneconomic pits as quickly as possible. Even so, it would have paid the NCB to keep open those of its collieries which, although they did not cover their full costs, made some contribution to the depreciation on that part of their assets which had no more profitable use and no significant scrap value. Yet even these pits, if the coal industry had been conducted by normal commercial standards, would probably have been on the point of closure. They would have been too poor a risk to warrant further capital expenditure, and without this they would soon have ceased to make any contribution to their depreciation.

It therefore seems likely that if the Coal Board had been bent on maximizing its short-term profits, it would already have closed or been about to close the great bulk of the 267 mines which failed to cover in full their depreciation charges and their share of overheads. Together these pits had a work force of 212,000, which represented 43 per cent of total colliery employment, and produced 66 million tons which was 36 per cent of deep-mined output. The position in 1964 has been examined in some detail because it is the last year for which full figures are available but, despite the large-scale closures during recent years, it seems likely that the proportion of output and employment accounted for by unprofitable pits is as great now as it was then. It is known, for instance, that in 1967–8 they produced 60 million tons which was about the same proportion of output as they had in 1964.[3] To have eliminated all its unprofitable pits by 1964 (or 1967–8) the Board would have had to greatly accelerate the substantial programme which it has put into effect. Between 1958 and 1964–5 277 pits with an output of 22½ million tons and a labour force of about 100,000 were shut.[4]

In order to get rid of all its unprofitable pits by the spring of 1965, the Coal Board would have had to speed up its closure programme by more than 200 per cent in terms of the number of employees affected, and by nearly 300 per cent as measured by the output involved. It seems unlikely that the amputation of so large a part of the industry so quickly would have had no effect on the Board's profitable pits. It is probable that if the NCB had swiftly shut down its loss-making collieries, it would have found it almost impossible to recruit new workers. Potential recruits would naturally have been reluctant to join a ship which appeared to be sinking, especially when the existing crew was being thrown overboard. By phasing the closure of unprofitable pits, the NCB has been able to avoid large-scale redundancy but if it had moved much faster large numbers of workers would have had to have been sacked.

Not only would it have been extremely difficult to find new workers but a large part of the industry's existing labour force might well have deserted. Those workers who were not declared redundant would surely have drawn the conclusion that it would be their turn next and decided to get out as quickly as possible. They would have feared that if they waited until they were sacked they might not, on the spur of the moment, be able to find suitable alternative employment partly because good jobs take time to discover at the best of times; partly because they would be looking at the worst of times when other redundant miners were also trying to find work; and partly because they would be older, less adaptable and less worth employing. It would have been the young and the enterprising who would have tended to leave while the old and the injured, who already formed a substantial part of mining labour force, would have remained. This, together with the difficulty of recruiting new workers, would have led to a rapid increase in the age, and deterioration in the quality, of the mining labour force. But, far more important, there would have been a rapid rundown in employment at profitable collieries, due to the combined effect of high wastage and inability to recruit. This would have led in turn to a reduction in their output and an increase in their costs because overhead expenses would have been spread over a smaller volume of production.

If retreat had become a rout and the industry's labour force had started to disintegrate, production would have been disrupted and productivity would have been harmed, which would have led to a further increase in costs. At this point, another round of closures would have become necessary because, as costs rose, another batch of pits would have become unprofitable.

That this is not merely a theoretical danger but a practical possibility can be seen from what has happened in the profitable central coalfields on which the industry's future depends. Between 1957 and 1968–9 employment in the Midlands and Yorkshire fell from 300,000 to 172,000. If the Coal Board had had its way there would probably have been some reduction but this was a far more rapid decline than had been planned. In 1963 the Board said that over the next few years it was seeking generally to maintain, and in some places increase, manpower in the central coalfields.[5] As there were at that time about 242,000 workers in the Midlands and Yorkshire, it appears that at least half of the reduction in employment in the central coalfields since 1957 has been unintentional.[6]

The rundown in the labour force in the Midlands and Yorkshire has been mainly due to a sharp fall in recruitment. Between 1955 and 1957, prior to the slump in coal demand, about 30,500 workers were recruited each year, including miners who transferred from other parts of the country. By 1964–6 the annual rate of recruitment had fallen to just under 17,000. Meanwhile there was only a small reduction in the amount of voluntary wastage, i.e. in the number of workers who left for reasons other than age, poor health, dismissal or death. During the period 1964–6 voluntary wastage in Yorkshire and the Midlands averaged just over 18,000 compared with about 20,500 during the years 1955–7. These figures give a slightly misleading impression because they suggest that there was some reduction in the rate of voluntary wastage; whereas if the number who left is expressed as a proportion of colliery employment it can be seen that the rate increased. During the period 1964–6 8·4 miners in every 100 quit the industry each year which was significantly higher than the rate of 6·8 between 1955 and 1957.[7]

This increase was all the more serious because predictably it was the younger workers who tended to leave. In the country as a whole the rate of voluntary wastage among workers under 40 increased from 9·4 per 100 between 1955–7 to 16·5 during 1964–6, but among workers over 40 it only rose from 2·0 per 100 to 3·6.[8] Although the NCB does not publish figures for the different coalfields there is no reason to believe that Yorkshire and the Midlands were atypical. There has certainly been a significant increase in the average age of their work force. Between 1957 and 1968 it increased from 40·6 to 43·8.[9]

Besides its direct impact on the size and quality of the labour force at profitable pits, it seems probable that the programme of colliery closures has also had an adverse effect on the morale of the miner. There is reason to believe that the rundown in the industry helps to explain the growth of absenteeism which has further reduced the Board's ability to step up production at its profitable pits. Not only has absenteeism led to a reduction in the number of shifts which each miner works but it has also had a disrupting effect. The case for believing that the rundown in the coal industry helps to explain the rise of absenteeism has been powerfully stated by Mr Handy. Since 1957

[he writes] pessimism has increased in the industry and it is particularly interesting to note how absenteeism fluctuates with the various economic forecasts for mining since 1957. Thus absenteeism increased in the spring of 1963 following the first NEDC report which forecast a very gloomy future for coal production. And the refusal of the Labour Government at the beginning of 1965 to underwrite the 200-million-ton target for coal was associated with a further rise in absenteeism. Later in that year the premature announcement of the forthcoming pit closure programme and the grading of pits as to their chances of survival induced even greater despondency in the industry and absenteeism continued to increase in the following months. And it is interesting also to note in which Coal Board Divisions the largest rates of growth in absenteeism have occurred. Thus South Wales and Scotland – divisions which in 1954 had the best absence records – have experienced 75 and 55 per cent increases in absenteeism respectively since 1954 (South Wales now recording the highest absence rate in the country) and the North Western Division an increase of 58 per cent. All these Divisions are suffering extensive pit closures, and there is local evidence that absence reaches remarkable heights in the months immediately prior to a pit closure, when the men feel they are fighting for a lost cause. It seems probable, however, that the effect of impending closures is not restricted to those areas where closures are most numerous. The Yorkshire miners, for example, have been as vocal in their protests against closure as those in South Wales and probably more so than the Durham miners. Indeed, a single pit closure on economic grounds often comes as a greater shock in areas unaccustomed to closures than in areas such as Durham where closure is not a new occurrence. Throughout many discussions in the coalfields the insecurity felt as a result of the unsettled future of the industry has loomed very prominently in the explanation of rising absenteeism. Absenteeism in the East Midlands – an area where the future of coalmining was, until recently, much brighter – has on the other hand only risen by 16 per cent since 1954.[10]

Would the East (and West) Midlands have escaped so lightly if closures had been still more extensive and had started to affect them more directly? Is it not likely that pessimism and discontent would have been expressed in other and more damaging ways if the industry had been run down at a still more rapid rate? So far the miners have co-operated readily in the drive for higher productivity and the introduction of labour-saving machinery. But can it safely be assumed that this co-operation would have been forthcoming if the Coal Board had declared hundreds of thousands of workers redundant? Even if organized obstruction had been avoided discontent might well have taken the form of a spontaneous go-slow. Indeed, it seems likely that this is why productivity stagnated during 1969 and that it was discontent at the large-scale colliery closures which the Government had forced on the NCB that lay behind the damaging strike which occurred during the autumn.

The large unplanned reduction in the number of workers in the central coalfields, not to mention the growth of absenteeism, has had a serious effect on the Coal Board's financial position. If the labour had been available there could have been a substantial increase in their production which could have been sold at a large profit. In 1965-6 the industry's 50 long-life pits, most of which were situated in Yorkshire and the Midlands, had an output of 35 million tons of coal per annum but were capable of producing a further 16 million tons. The Board estimated that if it had had the necessary manpower this could have been produced at a profit of about £2 per ton, which means that there would have been an increase of up to £32 million in the industry's profits.[11] It also follows that if the labour force in Yorkshire and the Midlands had contracted only slightly faster than it has, profits would have slumped. When marginal costs are low the benefits of increased production are great but so also are the penalties of lower production. When production increases costs do not rise in proportion and profits shoot up, but when production falls costs do not drop in proportion and profits collapse.

If during 1967-8 employment and output in the central coalfields had been only 10 per cent lower, there would have been 19,400 fewer workers and 9·6 million tons less production. At £2 per ton this would have reduced profits by £19·2 and in their coalfields they would have been eliminated. However, this probably understates the impact which reduced output would have had on profits because it seems doubtful whether the costs which have been treated as variable could, in fact, have been reduced in line with production. It seems unlikely, for instance, that the cost of repairs, heat, light, surface damage and pensions could have been cut back to the full extent. It, therefore, seems safe to assume that if production had fallen by 10 per cent in Yorkshire and the Midlands the Board's profits would have been reduced by say, £25 million. This alone would have been sufficient to wipe out a large part of the saving in avoidable costs which the Board would, in the absence of feed-back, have secured by closing down all its grossly uneconomic pits by 1967–8.

Indeed it is quite possible that the gains from eliminating unprofitable pits might have been more than offset by the financial penalties. In this case, the elimination of what appears, at first sight, to be unjustified cross-subsidization would not only have reduced the Coal Board's profits but might also have led to an increase in the price of coal. Far from having led to the waste of resources, the Board's policy of strategic withdrawal may have prevented the rundown of the coal industry from becoming a rout.

The Balance of Payments and Coal Protection

Those who believe that a free market offers a solution to every problem may reply that this risk should have been run, because if the industry had gone into a cumulative decline it would have been possible to secure supplies of cheap fuel from abroad. They would probably want to argue that they should have been obtained in any case, and say that if the coal industry had not been protected fuel policy would present no problem; it is only because supplies of cheap fuel have been shut out that there appears to be a conflict between the desirability of closing grossly uneconomic pits and the danger that if this happens the British coal industry may collapse and the price of coal increase. If coal and oil could be imported freely from abroad the Coal Board would not be able to jack up its prices. On the contrary, due to the availability of cheap coal and cheap oil from abroad, the Coal Board would have to bring down its prices. No doubt this would force it to close down its unprofitable pits faster, but this is precisely what it should do. Thus do the spectres which appear so realistic in the night of monopoly and protection melt away in the light of competitive day!

This thesis ignores the adverse effect which a large increase in our fuel imports would have had on the balance of payments. That there would have been a large increase is hardly open to doubt. If the present tax on fuel oil of 2d per gallon had not been imposed the price would have been at least 25 per cent lower. Moreover, there is reason to believe that the demand for oil is highly elastic.[12] The belief that, in the absence of the support it has received, the demand for coal would have been substantially lower is strengthened by the fact that, despite the tax on oil, it would have paid the electricity industry to have constructed oil rather than coal-burning power stations. However, the CEGB gave preference to coal partly because it was Government policy, partly because it feared that if it used too much oil the tax would be increased, and possibly because it was worried that if it did not help to support the coal industry this would go into a cumulative decline which, as it was the coal industry's largest customer, would be to its own disadvantage.[13] Similarly it would have paid the steel industry, or so the steel companies thought, to have imported coking coal from America. This, like a decision by the CEGB to switch to oil, would have had a considerable impact on the demand for British coal because the steel industry uses large amounts of coke and has been one of the few relatively stable markets which the Coal Board has had. Although the steel industry would have liked to buy foreign coking coal, the NCB was able to prevent this because of its legal monopoly over imports.

In view of these facts it would not be surprising if, in the absence of protection and support, the demand for coal had in 1967–8 been far below the actual figure of 166 million tons, and if the Coal Board had been unable to dispose of more than the 100 million tons of deep-mined output which it produced at a profit. Sufficient oil or foreign coal would have had to be imported to replace the 60 million tons of unprofitable output which would have been displaced. As each ton of oil is equivalent to about 1·7 tons of coal this represents about 35 million tons of oil, ignoring the fact that a small part of the domestic coal would have been replaced by imported coal. According to the Ministry of Power 'the foreign exchange content of home-refined fuel oil in 1965 was, on average, around £2·6 per ton, and of imported fuel oil around £4·6 per ton, an average of just over £3 per ton for all supplies of fuel oil'.[14] If so 35 million tons of extra fuel oil would have cost at least £105 million in terms of foreign exchange prior to devaluation.

This figure may well be on the low side because it seems doubtful whether the oil companies would have increased the capacity of their refineries in step with the increase in demand. In the past they have been slow to adjust their home-refining capacity to the growth in the British demand for oil probably because they have had plenty of spare capacity abroad due to the competitive investment which has taken place on the continent. They have been only too glad to export refined products to us and reluctant to build new refineries in Britain – a policy which as Professor Barna has pointed out imposed a considerable burden on the balance of payments.[15] There is a further reason why it is unlikely that much of the extra fuel oil, which might have been sold but for the protection of coal, would have been refined at home. In producing fuel oil a refinery also produces other petroleum products and the limits within which the output of fuel oil can be varied are fairly strict. If the oil companies had tried to refine a large quantity of extra fuel oil in Britain they would have had to produce a large quantity of other grades of petroleum. As there is no reason to suppose that the displacement of coal would automatically increase the consumption of these products they would have had to be sold abroad. This would have been extremely difficult, not only because of the existence of surplus capacity abroad, but also because the disposal of a large quantity of refined products from Britain would have upset refinery programmes in foreign countries.[16] In practice, the oil companies would have had to meet the extra demand for fuel oil, which would have arisen but for the protection of the coal industry, by an increase in imports.

The oil companies' stock reply to the suggestion that even fuel oil which is refined at home imposes a heavy burden on the balance of payments, is that the burden is by no means as large as it appears and that they make large contributions to the balance of payments. Both these claims are true. The Ministry of Power estimates that in 1965

> the net delivered cost of oil to the balance of payments was about £300 million . . . This is considerably less than the cif value of the oil, as shown in the Trade Accounts, which was about £500 million (after deducting exports of over £100 million). The difference is accounted for by the use of British tankers, inwards investment by foreign companies, and, in the case of British companies, items such as the costs of headquarters, research and other services and the companies' profit margin, all of which arise in or accrue to the United Kingdom. In addition, overseas oil business brings further benefits to the balance of payments. Although the overseas earnings – both profits and earnings from services – of British oil companies from producing and selling oil elsewhere are now lower in proportion to assets than a decade ago, they are still a major contribution to the balance of payments. Other overseas oil business is also carried on through London. The total net benefit to the balance of payments from all this overseas business is estimated in 1965 to have been around £200 million, including exports of capital equipment.[17]

Therefore, the net cost of the operations of the oil companies to the balance of payment is only about £100 million!

This is gloriously irrelevant because a large part of the oil companies' earnings of foreign exchanges are not affected one way or the other by the degree of protection which the British coal industry is afforded. In particular, the benefit of £200 million which the Ministry mentions would have been the same even if the coal industry had not been protected and would not rise if protection were removed. Obviously the profits which British oil companies receive from abroad, and the amount of British equipment which they install in foreign countries, depend upon how successful they are abroad and not upon how much oil they sell in Britain. The oil companies' other standard argument that the foreign exchange cost of imported oil is less than it appears from the trade returns is also irrelevant, because the Ministry allowed for this in its calculations. Indeed it seems possible that it made too large an allowance. Although the Ministry rightly deducts the amount which foreign oil companies invest in Britain there is no mention of it having added back the value of the foreign equipment which they import.

The free traders' reply to the argument that, but for the protection of the coal industry, the nation's import bill for fuel would be greater, is that if industry were able to buy cheap oil its costs would be lower and it would therefore be able to export more. This is true but not very important because the cost of oil forms such a tiny part of the cost of our exports. According to estimates prepared for the Cambridge Growth Project the oil content of our exports of goods and services totals only about 0·3 per cent excluding direct exports of oil.[18]

Since the duty on fuel oil represents about one-third of the final price, its abolition would, other things being equal, reduce the price of our exports by 0·1 per cent. If the tax on fuel oil were removed some consumers would find it advantageous to switch from coal to oil so that the total saving would be somewhat greater than 0·1 per cent, say about 0·15 per cent. If the elasticity of demand for our exports of goods and services is about 2½ per cent, which if anything is probably on the high side, the abolition of the fuel oil duty would increase their volume by 3·25 per cent and their value by £23 million (in 1967). It appears, therefore, that in the absence of the protection which the coal industry has received, and of its policy of cross-subsidization, our import bill would in 1967 have been at least £105 million greater, while our export receipts would only have been £23 million higher. Although these are only back-of-an-envelope calculations which must not be pressed too far, it is difficult to avoid the conclusion that, on balance, the taxation of fuel oil and the operation of loss-making pits has had a highly favourable effect on the nation's external account.

Social Costs and Pit Closures

The adverse effect which the removal of coal protection would have on the balance of payments is but one illustration of the fact that what suits part of the community may not benefit the nation as a whole. Another instance of a private advantage involving a social loss is where the resources which are released when an industry contracts do not find suitable alternative employment. It was a weakness of the previous chapter that its economic analysis implicitly assumed that the resources which are liberated when a nationalized undertaking reduces its output will be used elsewhere. For example, it was taken for granted when the welfare loss of subsidizing the railways was being calculated that the railwaymen who would be rendered redundant if the subsidy were removed would be employed elsewhere. It is obvious that if they were to remain unemployed society would lose what they now produce on the railways without obtaining any extra production elsewhere. In this case it would pay society to go on subsidizing the railways even though, in the absence of a subsidy, it would pay the railways to reduce their output. In practice this is probably a weak argument for continuing to meet the rail debt because it seems likely that most redundant railwaymen would quickly find alternative employment. They would be scattered over the country and in most areas work can normally be obtained relatively easily. In contrast, the coal industry's unprofitable pits are concentrated in areas where jobs are scarce, and for this and other reasons it seems probable that if the Coal Board's unprofitable pits had been shut as quickly as possible a significant minority of workers would have remained unemployed.

In 1964, 212,000 of the Coal Board's workers were employed at unprofitable pits which, if the Coal Board had been pursuing a normal commercial policy, it would already have closed or have been on the point of closing.[19] Of these workers 126,000 or nearly 60 per cent were concentrated in Northumberland and Durham (62,000), South Wales (39,000) and Scotland (25,000). A large number of those who were employed at unprofitable pits in other districts must have been situated in places such as Cumberland, North Wales and East Lancashire where employment prospects were far from bright. Not only did the Coal Board's loss-making pits tend to be located in regions where unemployment was well above average but within these districts they were concentrated at the places where the problem was most acute. In 1964 no less than 95 out of the total of about 150 mines which failed to cover their running costs were situated in what were euphemistically called Development Districts.[20]

Apart from the fact that so many of the Coal Board's unprofitable pits operated in places where jobs were scarce, the composition of the mining labour force makes it appear likely that substantial unemployment would have resulted if the Board had adopted a policy of ruthless closure. In 1964 just over 60 per cent of the mineworkers in Scotland, South

Wales, and Northumberland and Durham were over 40 years old and about a fifth were over 55.[21] As a study of pit closures in the Houghton-le-Spring area by J. W. House and E. M. Knight shows, redundant miners' prospects of finding new employment decrease sharply with age. All of those aged between 15 and 35 ultimately found new jobs, but over a third of those in the 36–55 age group were still out of work up to three years after they had been laid off. Among those aged 56 or more the proportion who had failed to find a new job was over four-fifths, even when allowance is made for those who, during the intervening period, had passed retirement age.[22]

If the Coal Board had declared redundant all of the 126,000 miners at its unprofitable pits in Scotland, South Wales and North-Eastern England and the same proportion of the age groups had been unable to get work, then approximately 45,000 of them would have suffered long-term unemployment. This represents over a third of the total. One reason why so many of the redundant miners in the Houghton-le-Spring area remained unemployed was that a large number suffered from some form of ill-health or disability. In fact, only a quarter of those who were still under 65 and had not found work were fit for more than light work.[23] If the NCB had resorted to mass sackings the proportion of healthy men among the redundant would probably have been higher. Yet it is evident that a substantial proportion of the workers on its books are sick and disabled, and that the proportion is exceptionally high in South Wales and the other areas where the unprofitable pits are concentrated. If the NCB were to close its loss-making pits as quickly as possible, it would not be able to find new jobs for so many of its damaged workers, a very high proportion of whom would never find outside employment.[24]

Even if the bulk of the young and healthy workers had been prepared to move to other areas in search of work it seems likely that a substantial number of older workers and some younger workers would not. House and Knight found considerable evidence of immobility. They report that:

> The most common attitude, especially among the older men [who failed to find new work], was that it would be difficult to obtain work which paid adequately enough to compensate for the severing of a lifetime's roots and connections. In practical terms there was the difficulty of obtaining new accommodation, notably since costs would probably be higher in places where employment vacancies existed, which was considered not to be worth it for the few remaining years. Of considerable importance here, was the fact that few men indeed possessed the financial backing to move. The

early exhaustion of savings and other capital and the reduction to a subsistence level completely hindered mobility. National Assistance might cover food and rent costs in an established home where replacement of furniture could be economized upon but it would not provide a surplus for expenses incurred in hunting for accommodation, removal or travelling costs while searching for work. Of equal importance was the consideration that even assuming a move could be made few well-paid jobs would be available in view of either the lack of complete health and of skilled trades among those concerned. In particular the younger men unwilling to move suffered from some form of disability and were clearly dubious about their ability to hold a full-time job in strange surroundings. The desire to hold on to the familiar community and way of life was extremely high, especially in view of the psychological shock many must have sustained upon redundancy after a lifetime's work. As a result even the relatively young were prepared to 'tighten the belt' rather than try where employment vacancies undoubtedly existed.[25]

Indeed many workers who remained unemployed had given up the search for jobs within travelling distance. House and Knight report that only about a third of this group were really concerned with finding new jobs.[26] As by this stage in the inquiry only a small number of redundant miners were involved these findings should be treated with a certain amount of caution. However, other evidence and previous investigations point to the same conclusion: coal miners are a relatively immobile group of workers.

One of the reasons why so many of the long-term unemployed had ceased to look for work was the belief that even if they obtained it the job was unlikely to be financially attractive, especially after travelling costs had been deducted. Two-thirds of the redundant miners who did manage to find jobs experienced a drop in income.[27] If the coal industry had been run down faster, not only would a substantial number of the workers displaced have become unemployed but the bulk of those who obtained work would have been forced to accept lower earnings. Miners are one of the best-paid groups in the country and in 1968 the average hourly earnings of manual workers in coal were about 30 per cent higher than the average for British industry in general.[28] Furthermore it seems likely that displaced miners would have had to be content with relatively low-paid work, so that it is doubtful whether their average earnings from their new jobs would be as high as the general average. Good jobs would obviously become extremely scarce in the areas where large numbers of coal miners had been declared redundant and were looking for work. It must also be remembered that although mining is a relatively skilled job most colliers, unless they were retrained, would only qualify for semi or unskilled work elsewhere, for the obvious reason that their skills have no general application. One of the most striking results of the Houghton-le-Spring survey was the small proportion of those who left the coal industry who obtained skilled work. The proportion was less than 10 per cent.[29]

It would be wrong to jump to the conclusion that because miners are likely to suffer a reduction in earnings when they transfer to new work, the welfare of the community is inevitably reduced. One of the reasons why colliers receive such high pay is that their work is exceptionally hard, dirty and dangerous. Allowing for this, miners' earnings are not as attractive as they seem or, as economists would say, the net advantage which miners obtain from their work is smaller than their relatively high wages seem to suggest. This is confirmed by the House and Knight survey which found that the ex-miners who had obtained work were generally satisfied with their new jobs despite the lower level of pay.[30] Nevertheless the reduction in earnings which would have occurred if mass redundancy had taken place would probably have been so considerable as to lead one to expect that there would have been some reduction in the net advantage from work.

If the rundown of the coal industry had led to a substantial amount of unemployment, a significant reduction in the purchasing power of those who found work locally, or to large-scale migration in search of jobs, this would have had an adverse effect on the mining areas over and above the initial loss. Miners who become unemployed or accepted low-paid work would have had less money to spend which would have reduced the income of local traders who would, in turn, have tended to have reduced their employment. When ex-miners moved to other parts of the country not only would their purchasing power have been totally lost, but it is to be expected that the younger and more vigorous members of the community would have left. There was the danger that if the coal industry had been run down much faster, secondary unemployment would have developed and the old mining areas would have started to go into a cumulative decline. To what extent this would have happened depends upon how large the primary increase in unemployment and reduction in earnings would have been, and it would require a detailed and far-reaching investigation for even a tentative answer. But it seems safe to assume that if the coal industry had been run down faster a significant number of miners would have remained unemployed, and that the possible welfare gain through closing loss-making pits is considerably smaller than it appears. Indeed it may well be negative.

Hardship and Closures

Our discussion of the social costs which a swifter rundown of coal and the railways might have inflicted on the community has not yet taken into account the hardship which this would have caused. Yet it is frequently argued that if the NCB had ruthlessly closed its unprofitable coal mines this would have caused distress among the miners who would have been thrown out of work, and that the withdrawal of branch-line services would have led to their passengers suffering hardship. We must try to discover whether the apparent disregard of hardship and distress constitute a further weakness of the economic analysis presented in the previous chapter and a further reason for believing that profits are a poor measure of welfare. This is a fair point in so far as a swifter closure of pits would have led to long-term unemployment among miners, for men who are out of work for long periods become angry and feel humiliated. Yet the distress which they experience is not measured by, and is additional to, the loss in welfare which the community sustains because it does not have the benefit of the output which the unemployed could have produced. Indeed, there is no way in which this distress can be translated into monetary terms and so incorporated into our analysis of the economic impact of continuing to maintain activities which run at a loss. It would be quite wrong, however, to disregard the suffering which unemployed miners would experience just because it cannot be expressed in pounds, shillings and pence.

This means that it may be impossible at the end of the day, when as many factors have been quantified as possible, to avoid making some judgment as to whether any net gain in welfare from ruthlessly closing unprofitable pits is likely to offset any consequent distress due to long-term unemployment. For what it is worth, my judgment is that even at its highest the potential welfare gain is so small that it has been right to avoid the risk of causing distress. But it is probably unnecessary to have to form a judgment because in practice it seems very doubtful whether there would have been a positive benefit even ignoring this risk.

At first sight the hardship which the closure of branch lines would inflict on passengers seems analogous to the distress which the closure of unprofitable pits would inflict on miners. However, this is not the case because the hardship which would be imposed on passengers can, in principle, be incorporated into welfare analysis by discovering how much extra they would have been prepared to pay above the price they were charged. Obviously those passengers who found that other means of transport were very expensive or inconvenient would have been willing to pay considerably more than they were asked, while those for whom the advantages of rail travel were marginal would not. The only rational objection which can be made to this argument is that the railways tend to be used by the poorer sections of the community who, although they would experience hardship if rail services were withdrawn, would not be prepared to pay more because they do not have the money.

It seems doubtful whether this objection has much practical importance because those with low incomes do not use the railways very much. This is shown by the Government's survey of family expenditure. In 1967 households with a weekly income of less than £15 comprised slightly over a fifth of all the sample families. They accounted for only 3½ per cent of the money which was spent by the survey households on rail travel. On the other hand those families which had an income of over £40 per week were responsible for nearly half of all rail expenditure, although they formed less than a fifth of all households. These affluent families accounted for a much higher proportion of spending on rail travel than they did for expenditure as a whole. Here their share was only about a third. In contrast families with low incomes were responsible for a much lower proportion of rail expenditure than they were for expenditure on all goods and services because those with incomes of less than £15 accounted for 10 per cent of total household expenditure.

The railways are not a necessity for the poor, who travel by bus and coach, but a luxury for the rich.[31] The benefit which rail users obtain from branch-line services, and the hardship which they avoid through branch lines remaining open, can therefore be measured in the normal way by asking what contribution they would be prepared to make towards the railways' costs. Similarly, it appears that this benefit will be partly or wholly offset by the loss in consumers' welfare, due to the fact that by no means all of those who use unprofitable rail services would be prepared to pay a price sufficiently high for British Rail to cover its costs. As a result the community seems to suffer a loss equivalent to the difference between what those travellers who would not be willing to pay the full cost would pay, and the value of the resources which British Rail has used on their behalf.[32] But in the case of a particular branch line it may be wrong to regard this as a loss because there may be no level of production at which BR is able to cover its costs. At first sight it may appear impossible that this should be so, for if all except the railways' marginal customers are prepared to pay more than they are asked, it seems evident that by reducing its output and raising its prices British Rail will be able to break even. But this is not necessarily true, because if the quality of service is maintained unit costs will rise since the same expenditure will have to be borne by fewer passengers, while if the frequency of service is reduced a large number of extra passengers may desert. If the track is already being lightly used it may be impossible to make any further reduction in signalling and maintenance costs when trains are withdrawn. Again if a service is already infrequent, it may be difficult, if it is pruned still further, to find alternative uses for the rolling-stock and train crews. So even where it is possible to provide a service of lower quality without losing too many passengers the saving may be severely restricted.

Although a branch-line service fails to pay its way and there is no way of remedying this, it may be economically correct to keep it in operation. Its retention will be justified where the extra contribution, which the passengers would be prepared to make, exceeds the amount which it loses. If it does, the welfare benefit to consumers (as measured by the actual payment and the potential contribution of rail users) exceeds the quantity of resources being used on their behalf (as measured by the railways' costs). In this case it is obviously right to go on providing the service at a loss because the 'hardship' which rail users would be caused if it were withdrawn is greater than the cost of providing the service. If so the line makes what can be regarded as a social profit even though it involves British Rail in a private loss. This, however, is not quite the end of the story because the Government has to find the money to pay the rail deficit; but there is no need to face this problem unless it is discovered that the welfare benefit from maintaining unprofitable branch lines exceeds their costs.

In 1966 British Rail's stopping services earned £28 million but had direct costs of £38 million. What share of the railways' track, signalling and general administrative expenses were incurred in providing these services is not known, but it must have been substantial because a considerable part of the route system was maintained for the exclusive use of stopping services. Despite the Beeching closures branch lines open to passenger traffic still represented at least a fifth of the total route mileage in 1966. If the stopping services accounted for only the same proportion of the railways' indirect expenses as they did of its direct expenses (10 per cent) they still cost the railways a further £15 million. The total deficit must therefore have been at least £25 million.[33] To discover if the extra amount which stopping service users would have been prepared to pay exceeded the sum which the railways lost, is a herculean task and so far the necessary cost-benefit analysis has been applied to only a few branch lines. Nevertheless these studies are extremely valuable because their findings can, granted one major assumption, be applied to branch lines in general.

Professor George Clayton and J. H. Rees, in their cost-benefit study, did not try to discover, by means of direct inquiry, what those who travelled on the line would have been prepared to pay. What they tried to find out was the value of the time which rail users on the Central Wales Line saved by travelling by a train at about 30 miles per hour rather than by bus at 13–15 miles per hour. The amount of time which the passengers saved was determined by asking all the passengers, who travelled on the line during a sample week, about their journeys and then estimating how much longer they would have taken if the trains had been replaced by a bus service. The relatively small group of passengers who were travelling during their working time were divided into manual, white collar, and self-employed, and then sub-divided by sex. The amount of time which they saved was multiplied by the average hourly earning for the workers in each of these groups to obtain a figure for its value. Leisure time was then valued at half the average rate of pay because research indicates that people value their leisure time at about half their rate of pay for normal working hours. On this basis the value of both the work and the leisure time which the rail passengers saved turned out to be equivalent to about 60 per cent of the amount they paid the railways.[34] This, in so far as it could be measured, was the benefit which passengers received over and above what they paid.

If it is assumed that passengers on other stopping services also received a free benefit equivalent to 60 per cent of the amount they paid, then since these services earned £28 million in 1966, it was worth £17 million.[35] As this welfare surplus was considerably smaller than the loss of £25 million or more which British Rail incurred in running stopping services, it appears that most of them should be withdrawn if a replacement bus service can be arranged. Although the railway preservationists are right in supposing that the benefits which the railways confer exceed the revenue which the railways earn, they are wrong in assuming that they are sufficient to make it desirable that stopping services should be maintained.

It may be thought that too much weight is being placed upon the results of a single inquiry into the closure of a single branch line. The doubt obviously arises that the Central Wales Line is atypical and that the welfare case for maintaining other stopping services may be stronger. For instance, it could be true that elsewhere there is a greater saving in time by using the railway. This, however, seems most unlikely because in central Wales the replacement bus service would have been unusually slow due to the hilly terrain and narrow winding roads. An investigation into the closure of three branch lines in other parts of the country (Sussex, Bradford–Huddersfield and Dumfries–Stranraer) showed that there was remarkably little increase in travelling time. According to the Ministry of Transport, who sponsored the investigation, 'In terms of increases in cost and times of journeys no widespread hardship resulted from the closures. About half the former regular travellers reported lower or unchanged costs, and about two-fifths reported shorter or unchanged journey time. Average increases in cost and time were small.'[36] It, therefore, seems likely that the central Wales study gives an exaggerated impression of the benefits which are generally to be had through keeping branch lines open.

It may be replied that what Messrs Clayton and Rees did not take into consideration were the other benefits besides the saving in time which stopping services confer. For instance, it might be argued that it is less tiring and more comfortable to go by rail than by bus. Although this is probably true it seems unlikely that the difference is sufficiently marked to warrant the retention of grossly unprofitable stopping services. Many of those interviewed in the course of the Ministry of Transport's inquiry 'complained that the general conditions of travel by bus were more tiring and crowded and less comfortable. For the majority, however, a change in the general comfort of travelling must be considered an inconvenience rather than a hardship'.[37] If so, it is unlikely that they would on this score have been prepared to make a substantial extra contribution to the railways' costs. There are a number of other benefits which the retention of branch lines might provide, such as the promotion of rural industry, but there is no reason to believe that they are of any great importance.[38]

The general case for withdrawing stopping services and closing branch lines appears to be so strong that it is very doubtful whether it is worth subjecting every proposal to a lengthy inquiry. Although a few lines might then be closed which should have been kept open, the welfare loss is likely to be more than compensated by the saving in resources which will be achieved through closing the other branch lines as soon as possible. Nevertheless before any part of the main line is closed to passenger traffic, it is desirable that a careful cost-benefit analysis should be made. Although there is no doubt that British Rail loses money on large parts of its trunk-route system these losses may be more than offset by the gain in welfare through keeping them open. The losses on the main line are less enormous in relation to revenue than they are on branch lines while the advantages of rail over bus travel in terms of time and comfort are probably much larger.

It also seems likely that the gains in welfare justify the relatively small losses which BEA makes on its social service routes to the remoter parts of Scotland, and which the nationalized buses incur in providing services in rural areas. It does not seem worth discussing this at length, partly because the losses are so small and partly because too little research has been undertaken for any firm conclusions to be drawn.

CHAPTER 20

Conclusions: The Irrelevance of Ownership?

THE two broad questions which we have been trying to answer in this book are whether the nationalized industries have contributed to the national welfare by being technically efficient, and what effect they have had on the national welfare through their impact on the allocation of resources. We are now in a position to see that these questions are by no means equally important. Although economists tend to ignore technical efficiency, it is a matter of elementary economics that society stands to lose more through technical inefficiency than it does through the maldistribution of resources. It is more important, therefore, that the output of an undertaking should be produced efficiently, than that the output should be at the right level and priced in the correct way. For instance in 1968 British Rail incurred an enormous deficit and its prices would have to have been considerably higher for it to have covered its costs, which makes it seem likely that resources were being misallocated on a large scale. However, the waste of resources was very much smaller than it appears because nearly all the railways' customers would have been prepared to pay something above what they were asked, which means that part of the BR deficit was offset by the benefit which rail users received but did not have to pay for. If, on the other hand, the railways' costs had been higher than they were, due to technical inefficiency, society would have been worse off by the full amount.[1]

Technical Efficiency

What, to consider first things first, do our investigations show about the technical efficiency of the nationalized industries? During the first decade of public ownership the nationalized industries' performance was on the whole disappointing. The rate of increase in their labour productivity (1·5 per cent per annum), though about the same as in the private sector as a whole, was slightly lower than in manufacturing (1·9 per cent). In railways and coal, which form an important part of the public enterprise sector, productivity increased very slowly.[2] Their slow

433

advance was due, among other reasons, to the restrictions which the Government placed on rail investment and the time which it took to modernize collieries. Since 1958 their investment programmes have borne fruit, which helps to explain the rapid rate at which their productivity has been increasing. During the second decade of public ownership the sector's rate of advance (5·3 per cent) has been much faster than that of private industry (3·4 per cent) and manufacturing (3·7 per cent). The only part of the public enterprise sector which has not secured a larger increase than manufacturing is the nationalized bus undertakings whose productivity has, like that of the private bus companies, declined. In contrast the only manufacturing industry whose productivity has increased faster than that of the public enterprise sector is chemicals.[3]

The nationalized industries' performance appears equally impressive if their productivity gains are compared with those which were secured when they were under private and municipal ownership. The productivity of the coal, gas, rail and electricity industries has increased at a faster rate since the war, and especially since 1958, than it did in the inter-war period. During the pre-war era, at least in the case of coal, productivity increased less in this country than it did abroad.[4] However since nationalization, the industries in the public enterprise sector have made productivity gains which compare favourably with those which have been achieved in foreign countries. During the period since 1958 the Coal Board's productivity has risen faster than that of all save one of the continental producers; British Rail, whose relative performance had previously been disappointing, has outstripped or kept pace with all but one of the continental railways; the electricity industry's productivity has increased at a more rapid rate than all except one of the foreign suppliers for whom figures are available; and, when their results are combined, the air corporations' output per worker has risen faster than that of seven out of ten major international airlines. While the nationalized industries' productivity has in general been increasing fast by international standards, that of private industry has been increasing slowly, and the same appears to have been true of nearly all the separate manufacturing industries for which figures are available, including chemicals.[5]

Nor does it appear that the nationalized industries have enjoyed any advantage sufficient to account for more than a small part of the exceptional productivity gains which they made during their second decade. If allowance is made for the use of capital, their performance, relative to manufacturing, turns out, during the first ten years, to be even worse than when attention is restricted to labour productivity. In contrast, during the period 1958–68 it appears that the airways, gas and electricity had larger increases in output per unit of labour and capital than manufacturing, while the railways kept pace with it. As was to be expected the nationalized industries' residual productivity tended to increase less than their labour productivity. But this was also true for manufacturing, and their relative performance appears little or no worse in terms of residual productivity than in terms of output per man hour. The airways had a relatively larger increase in residual productivity, and gas and coal had about the same relative performance in residual and labour productivity. Electricity and coal appear to have done relatively less well when the use of capital is taken into account, but here special factors have been at work. When allowance is made for capital it remains true that the nationalized industries' productivity has increased faster since the war than it did before the war. But the substitution of capital for labour does appear to explain why labour productivity in manufacturing has increased more rapidly since 1948 than it did between the wars.[6]

Another possible explanation for the nationalized industries' favourable results is that they are due to the advantage of rapidly rising production for, as numerous studies have shown, gains in production and in productivity tend to go together. Over the period 1958 to 1968 the airways and electricity had large increases in both production and productivity. The nationalized buses have had falling output and falling productivity. But the railways, gas and coal, though the latter as an extractive industry is a special case, have had much larger gains in productivity than was to be expected from the change in their production. This has also been true of the public enterprise sector as a whole even when coal is excluded.[7] Nor, when international comparisons are made, can the contrasting performance of the nationalized industries and of British manufacturing industry be explained in terms of production. Manufacturing has laboured under the disadvantage that its production has risen more slowly than it has abroad, but British Rail is the one European system whose output has been falling, all but one of the electricity suppliers have had larger increases in sales, and the air corporations have made larger productivity gains than was to be expected from the rise in their traffic.[8] An attempt is sometimes made to argue in a reverse direction and to ascribe the productivity gains which coal and the railways have made to the closure of unprofitable pits and branch lines where output per man was low. It is evident that this has accounted for a relatively small part of the increase in their productivity.[9] Moreover, the gains which coal has achieved through closures have not been easily won but have required careful planning and involved difficult decisions.[10]

The final argument which might be used to belittle the nationalized industries' achievements is that the rate of technical progress tends to be

P

faster in some industries than in others and that public enterprise happens to operate in fields where progress has been exceptionally fast. Aviation and electricity might be cited in support of this view because their productivity has in most countries been increasing faster than that of manufacturing. However in coal and railways, which form a large part of the British public enterprise sector, productivity has almost everywhere risen less than in manufacturing. For this reason it does not seem likely that in general productivity gains have been easier to secure in the nationalized industries than they have in manufacturing.[11]

Thus the pace at which productivity has been growing in the public enterprise sector has probably been due to causes other than very high investment, or the good fortune of rapidly rising production, or fast technical progress, and it is not difficult to identify some of these other causes. In general new methods of production have been introduced rapidly, e.g. power-loading and self-advancing pit props in coal, oil-based processes in gas and, after a late start, new forms of traction on the railways. The nationalized industries have themselves made an important contribution to the development of new equipment and techniques, e.g. liner trains, the transportation of liquefied natural gas and self-advancing pit props.[12] The nationalized industries have also secured most of the economies of scale which have been available while important opportunities have been neglected in the private sector.[13] Although the railways were slow to take action, the nationalized industries have on the whole had an impressive record in the field of rationalization and the elimination of surplus manpower. This is shown by the progress which British Rail has now made, by the efforts which have been made in gas, and by the way in which BOAC tackled its excessive engineering costs. Work study is now being used extensively within the public enterprise sector and is being rapidly extended. A large part of the public enterprise sector has now been covered by productivity bargains, though it will be some time before they have their full effect.[14] Again the rapid rise in the sector's productivity probably owes something to the care with which investment projects have been sifted. Until recently methods of investment appraisal have not been very sophisticated but, unlike many private firms, the nationalized industries have at least tried to calculate rates of return.[15]

After reviewing the evidence the conclusion seems irresistible that the technical efficiency of the public enterprise sector has been rising more rapidly than that of the private sector, and that this must in part have been due to the way in which it is organized and managed. This is not to say that the nationalized industries have always been as prompt at remedying weaknesses as they should have been or that their level of technical efficiency is as high as it could be. It is evident, for instance, that the railways have not yet succeeded in putting right their inherited technical deficiencies and, as the nationalized industries' productivity deals themselves indicate, there is some over-manning.[16] International comparisons suggest, however, that the general level of efficiency within the public enterprise sector is already somewhat higher than that in private industry.[17] As yet the difference does not appear to be very great but it seems likely that the nationalized industries will rapidly pull ahead because their productivity will go on increasing more rapidly than that of the private sector. Certainly there is no reason to suppose that the large productivity gains of the last decade are a once-and-for-all phenomenon. As investment in the public enterprise sector is, for some years at least, likely to remain relatively stable its future productivity performance relative to that of private industry may appear even better in terms of residual than of labour productivity.[18]

Allocative Efficiency

After technical efficiency we must now turn to the question of allocative efficiency. It is often argued that the industries' low profitability indicates that resources have been misallocated, supposed that cross-subsidization is a further source of misallocation and believed that they do not relate their prices to their costs, and that they have been prepared to invest at a low rate of return. If so, the public enterprise sector has absorbed a disproportionate share of national investment, and the national income has been reduced below what it would have been if it had adopted a more commercial approach. What light do our inquiries throw upon the contention that resources have been misallocated in this way?

The nationalized industries' profits have not been as low by private enterprise standards as is usually supposed. Because of their heavy interest payments the nationalized industries often appear to be making losses when, if they were financed on an equity basis like private firms, they would be shown to be profitable. Indeed the only nationalized undertakings which have, during the past decade, failed to cover their operating costs at any time have been BOAC, London Transport and British Rail, and only the last named has incurred both heavy and persistent losses.[19] Nor in general does it appear that the profits of public enterprise are overstated because depreciation provisions are, due to rising prices, insufficient to cover the replacement cost of their assets. Technical progress has held down the cost of replacing capacity in electricity, gas, aviation, road haulage and probably also rail transport, whereas in private industry depreciation provisions may well be inadequate.[20]

This is one reason why accounting figures for the rate of return on capital should be treated with scepticism. Such statistics are of little or no economic value because of the absence of any clear connection between profits as a proportion of net assets and the dcf yield. To make matters worse, the official figures for the rate of return show private enterprise in too favourable a light and make public enterprise appear less profitable than it has been. When the figures are adjusted to make them more comparable by, for instance, excluding stock appreciation from private industry's profits, it is found that the gap between the rate of return in manufacturing and the profitable part of the public enterprise sector is less enormous than usually supposed and that it has been shrinking. In 1968 manufacturing companies earned 11½ per cent whereas BOAC earned 21 per cent, Tillings and Scottish earned 13 per cent, and most of the other nationalized industries earned something between the Coal Board's rate of 4 per cent and the English and Welsh Electricity Boards' figure of 8 per cent.[21] In order to determine whether the rates of return which the nationalized industries have earned are abnormally low by private standards, it is more relevant to compare them with those of private concerns in the same line of business than with those of private industry in general. In America privately-owned electricity undertakings have been content to earn what appear to be relatively low rates of return because of the low degree of risk. Their rate is not very much higher than that of the British electricity industry.[22]

The nationalized undertakings where relatively large losses are incurred on some more or less physically distinct part of the business and covered by profits earned elsewhere are coal, buses and BEA. At worst this involves a single and not a double dose of misallocation because it does not appear that abnormally high rates of profit are earned on the profitable side of the business.[23] Furthermore the Coal Board can only be regarded as practising cross-subsidization if it is reasonably certain that the saving through closing down its loss-making collieries faster would not be offset by a reduction in the profits which it now earns at its remunerative pits. But in view of the danger that mass redundancy would harm the drive for higher productivity, and of the increasing difficulty which the Board has encountered in recruiting the workers its profitable pits need, it seems quite possible that the cure might be worse than the disease.[24]

The amount of information available on the returns which the nationalized industries have expected to earn on their capital expenditure is patchy and difficult to evaluate because, until recently, their methods of investment appraisal have not been very sophisticated. However it does not appear that, *granted the assumptions on which their calculations were based*, their prospective rates of return have on average been all that low or that rates on marginal projects have been negligible.[25] The railways are a partial exception to the rule because capital expenditure was sanctioned for lines and services which were making such heavy losses as to be financially hopeless.[26] But in coal, where it is sometimes supposed that the pattern of investment was distorted by cross-subsidization, the NCB took care to avoid investing in pits where there was no prospect of making a profit and the minimum rate of return which was, in effect, required before major schemes were sanctioned at loss-making pits seems to have been fairly high.[27]

In general the estimates of future demand on which the nationalized industries' investment plans have been based have turned out to be wide of the mark, and this, rather than the acceptance of low rates of return, has been the main reason why capital has been wasted in coal and railways. By no means all of this waste could have been avoided, or can properly be regarded as misallocation, because it was virtually impossible to predict what has happened. Although the estimates on which the Coal Board based its modernization programme have proved badly wrong, they were more realistic than those which outside experts were making.[28] As the collapse in coal demand was not foreseen by the German coal owners or the oil companies, there is no reason to suppose that if the coal industry had been under different management or private ownership it would have been more perceptive.[29] The demand estimates which underlay the rail Modernization Plan were not unreasonable in the situation in which they were made, though the railways' later forecasts were clearly over-optimistic. However, British Rail could not have been expected to foresee the extent to which its coal and other traffic would decline and can therefore be held responsible for only part of the capital which has been misinvested.[30]

With the exception of the earlier estimates of the pay-off from railway modernization it is evident that the nationalized industries have, on the whole, made careful calculations of the yield on their capital projects. In this respect standards have almost certainly been significantly higher within the nationalized industries than they have in the private sector where a substantial proportion of firms do not seem to make proper calculations.[31] Until comparatively recently the methods by which the nationalized industries estimated the rate of return were, except in the case of electricity, somewhat crude, but they were no worse than those which were employed in the private sector, and the only serious departures from economic common sense were that the railways did not try to

discover whether the lines in which they invested would become profitable, and the more general failure to allow for the effect of rising
wages.[32] Not only have these failures been remedied but the nationalized industries have during the past few years adopted sophisticated
tech niques such as dcf. As a result their standards are now considerably more advanced that those of many British and American companies.[33]

Nor does it appear that the minimum rate of return which the nationalized industries have required since their switch-over to dcf has been
very different from the minimum rate which private firms need to earn
if they are to obtain funds for investment.[34] There is therefore no
reason to believe that capital is being squandered by the public enterprise
sector. Yet it is widely believed that these industries are over-investing
because it is supposed that their share of national investment has
been steadily rising. In reality it has fallen rapidly during the past
few years, will go on falling for some years, and is now considerably
lower than in 1938 or any year since 1948.[35]

It is vital when evaluating the effect which the nationalized industries
have on the national welfare not to disregard social costs or to assume
that normal commercial behaviour will ensure that resources are allocated in the best possible way. For instance, it is often taken for granted
that the nationalized industries should require a high commercial rate of
return before they invest, and that resources have been misallocated
because they have for the most part been prepared to sanction projects
which show a lower rate. But it seems doubtful whether the investment
which would be forgone in the public enterprise sector if a higher
minimum rate of return were adopted would be offset by an increase in
private investment. The devices which the Government has used for
stimulating private investment seem to have been largely ineffective,
while, if it had to engineer an increase in consumption in order to get
private firms to invest more, the bulk of the resources liberated by the
reduction in public enterprise investment would no longer be available
for private investment. In a situation in which the general level of investment is already too low, there is a powerful case for instructing public
concerns to base their investment plans on a lower minimum rate of
return than would be considered normal in the private sector.[36]

Similar considerations sometimes apply in the case of current output.
Where production takes place at a loss within the public enterprise
sector, as it does at the Coal Board's unprofitable pits, it is all too easy to
jump to the conclusion that resources are being misallocated. This is
only true if those who are employed at loss-making pits rapidly found
alternative employment where they would contribute as much to the

national income as they do by working in the coal industry. If only because of the well-known immobility of the miner, and the concentration of the Board's unprofitable pits in areas where unemployment is already above the national average, it seems quite possible that the social loss through a faster contraction of the coal industry would outweigh the social gain.[37] It is also necessary to take into account the hardship which unemployed miners would experience and the impact on the balance of payments of replacing home-produced coal by imported oil. If the protection which the coal industry is afforded by the tax on fuel oil was removed, and the Board closed its unprofitable collieries forthwith, the import bill for oil might rise by about £100 million, while the potential reduction in export prices due to the abolition of the tax would be much smaller.[38] Remembering the disrupting effect which a still larger programme of colliery closures might have on productivity at the industry's profitable pits, it seems reasonably clear that the national welfare has been increased, and not reduced, by the Board's policy of 'cross subsidization' and the Government's tax on fuel oil.

This does not mean, of course, that every apparent act of misallocation in or on behalf of the public enterprise sector can be justified on the ground that there is a divergence between social and private costs. Each case must be judged on its merits and the arguments for, say, preserving loss-making branch lines on the railways turn out to be very weak. The loss which they make is so large that it seems very doubtful whether it is outweighed by the cost which would be imposed on their users, particularly in the form of extra travel time, if they made the journey by bus. In the case of British Rail's unprofitable main-line services, where the loss is smaller in relation to costs than it is on the branch lines, and where the alternative bus services are much slower, the social cost arguments are stronger, though not necessarily always convincing. For unremunerative bus services, where no alternative form of public transport exists, it seems likely that the social benefit will, in most cases, more than offset the operators' deficit, though again this was not investigated in detail.[39] It must therefore be concluded that the rail deficit has involved some misallocation of resources, but it seems unlikely that the welfare loss sustained by the community has been very great.[40] Furthermore, even if the arguments for the protection of the coal industry and for its phased rundown are rejected, the welfare loss as a result of these policies has not been enormous.[41]

Now that this book has been distilled down and the most important conclusions have been highlighted, we are in a position to reach a general verdict on the nationalized industries as economic institutions and the impact which they have had on the national welfare. On the one hand, the public enterprise sector has had a significantly better performance in respect of technical efficiency than the private sector. On the other hand, the operations of the nationalized industries have, when judged by ideal economic standards modified by what it was reasonable to expect, led to remarkably little misallocation. As technical efficiency is far more important than allocative efficiency the nationalized industries must, on the whole, be judged an economic success, and it seems likely that they have had a favourable impact on the national welfare. What would have happened if they had remained in the hands of their former owners it is impossible to know and for the most part unrewarding to speculate, but in view of the quality of their performance it is difficult to believe that it would have been of the same standard had they not been transferred to public ownership.

The Conventional Wisdom on Public Ownership

This conclusion is obviously in conflict with the generally accepted view that the ownership of an industry is largely irrelevant to its performance but that, if anything, the nationalized industries are probably slightly less efficient than those which are privately owned. The classic statement of the conventional wisdom was made in the mid-fifties by Mr Anthony Crosland in *The Future of Socialism*, but more recently Mr Christopher Foster has restated this view though he seems to retain a lingering faith in the efficacy of public ownership.

> Most authorities [he writes] agree that it has made possible the rehabilitation of the fuel and power industries, that the Atomic Energy Authority and the nationalized airlines and many of the fringe industries are not inefficient . . . But this achievement looks less impressive than it would have done between the wars, because private industries have made equal or greater strides in efficiency . . . Scarcely anyone would now claim nationalisation as a panacea for industrial inefficiency; on the contrary many would claim that nationalised industries tend to be less efficient than private firms.[42]

How are we to account for the general conviction, which is reflected in these statements, that ownership is irrelevant and that the economic performance of the nationalized industries has been undistinguished? One important explanation is that these views were formed during the early years of public ownership. At that time the new public undertakings were having to cope with the difficult problems of welding hundreds of separate concerns together and creating the necessary administrative machinery. During this period it was all too easy to form the impression that the managerial problems of the nationalized industries were more than transitional difficulties and bore witness to the supposed inherent disadvantages of large-scale organization. The nationalized industries overcame their teething troubles with surprising success, but this was obscured not only by the investigations of the public administrators in general, and of the Acton Society in particular, but also by the way in which these troubles were unnecessarily prolonged and intensified by the decentralization which the politicians encouraged or enforced. The nationalized industries were, for instance, criticized by Mr Crosland both for over-centralization and for the managerial weakness which the Fleck Committee identified and ascribed, correctly enough, to excessive decentralization.[43]

What was more important in forming attitudes towards public enterprise than its early administrative difficulties was its patchy economic performance. In one respect after another, as this study has revealed, the first decade of public ownership was a disappointing era. The nationalized industries' productivity increased less than that of the private sector and in coal and railways was more or less stagnant; technical weakness was more in evidence than technical progress; the nationalized industries' prices increased faster than those in the rest of the economy and there was an enormous rise in the price of coal; despite this, coal was in short supply and the quality of the service provided by the railways was low; there was no obvious evidence that nationalization had brought an improvement in labour relations and coal remained the most strike-prone industry in the land.[44] It is true, as this study has also made clear, that in the main these failures were due to factors beyond the control of the nationalized industries and that, although there was little to show on the surface, their transformation was already well under way; but this could only have been obvious to the most perceptive, dispassionate and industrious of investigators and these were notable by their absence.[45]

Unfortunately the hasty and superficial judgments formed during the earliest and most difficult years of nationalization soon hardened into unquestioning and unquestioned conviction. With the notable exception of Professor William Shepherd, there has been no serious or fresh contribution on the subject of the nationalized industries' performance. British economists have, like Mr Foster, been content to echo and repeat what has been said before and to take it for granted that 'private industries have made equal or greater strides in efficiency'. None of these declarations have been or, I believe, can be documented or supported by statistical comparisons. The belief that the nationalized industries have a mediocre record and that ownership is irrelevant to economic performance is a dogma which arose during the first and most difficult years of public ownership, and has lived on to become a serious obstacle to rational inquiry and rational conviction.

Efficiency by Coincidence?

It is, of course, possible that the efficiency of the nationalized industries is due to some other cause than public ownership. Different explanations might be found for the different industries and the fact that they happen to have been nationalized passed off as an irrelevant coincidence. However, such an approach appears implausible from the start because of the size of the coincidence which has to be explained away. It is a coincidence which extends to other countries and has been growing over time. The late fifties seem to have constituted a watershed in the development of the nationalized industries, and during the second decade of public ownership a marked contrast has emerged between the two sectors. Moreover, during 1965–9, which almost seem to be another turning point in the nationalized industries' development, not only has the public enterprise sector's productivity continued to outpace that of the private enterprise sector but the nationalized industries have switched over to sophisticated methods of investment appraisal, the way has been paved for a massive extension of work study, productivity bargains have been signed up which cover the bulk of the sector, except for coal in which the system of wage payment has been recast with highly beneficial results, striking new technical developments have come to fruition in coal and railways which have placed them ahead of the rest of the other European countries, and new pricing systems have been introduced in electricity and railways.[46] Some of these changes, such as the use of productivity bargaining, have in part been matched within the private sector, but the scope and speed of advance within the public enterprise sector has been so much greater that it must be regarded as a difference in quality rather than in quantity.

The most powerful reason for believing that the efficiency of the industries which are in public ownership is not a chance but a causal relationship is that the same pattern emerges in other developed countries. For instance in Italy the success of the state holding companies IRI and ENI has become a byword, and has even been recognized in the publications of the Institute of Economic Affairs.

> Much of the criticism about IRI's management [reports Mario Deaglio] has faded away in recent years. IRI does not generally attract the common complaint against nationalised industries that its management is not as good as in private industry. Nobody could seriously argue that IRI in recent

years has lacked vigour and enterprise: the drive to the south, the notable contribution to the new motorway network, the reform in Italy's telephone system, have left a deep impression that IRI's management is both competent and dynamic.[47]

Mention should also be made of the Italian steel industry which from very small and inefficient beginnings has, due to IRI's efforts, been rapidly built up into one of the most advanced in the world.[48]

The success of Italian public enterprise has been ascribed to the weakness of the Italian system of government and to the freedom from state control which IRI and ENI have enjoyed. In France, where the nationalized industries have been closely supervised by the civil service, public enterprise has been as successful as it has in Italy. According to Professor C. Kindleberger of the Massachusetts Institute of Technology, 'The public corporations especially in railroads, aviation and electricity, have been among the leaders in increasing efficiency and improving technology.' The record of the coal industry, as Professor Kindleberger acknowledges elsewhere, has also been impressive while that of Renault has been brilliant.[49] John Sheahan has observed that the enterprise and drive of the nationalized industries has been accompanied by an intense concern with the development of economically rational methods of determining prices and choosing between competing investment projects. Indeed the French nationalized industries have in many ways led the rest of the world in the sophistication of their investment appraisal and systems of pricing.[50] Again, in the United States public enterprise in the form of the Tennessee Valley Authority has been notable for its enterprise and technical prowess. The TVA's early triumphs are well known but more recently the TVA has taken the lead in the introduction of large generating plant.[51]

In view both of British and foreign experience, it must be concluded that the creditable way in which public enterprise performs is something more than a coincidence. The relationship between good behaviour and public ownership must henceforth be regarded as one of cause and effect. The question then arises of why nationalized industries tend to have a better economic performance than private industries. To provide a full answer it would be necessary to write another and a different book. The present book has mainly been concerned with the problem of evaluating and assessing the nationalized industries' performance rather than with the problem of why they have behaved in the way they have. This question has arisen from time to time but it has not been the focus of interest. Almost nothing has, for instance, been said about the motivation of those who direct nationalized industries and the way in which it may differ from those in charge of private concerns. Yet, in view of the differences in the performances of public and private enterprise, it is possible that significant differences exist. No apology needs to be made for the fact that such topics have not been investigated because it was obviously necessary to discover how the nationalized industries have performed before asking why. The danger of beginning with the wrong question is illustrated by the cautionary tale of the public administrators, who more or less took it for granted that nationalization was a failure and set out to discover the reasons, when what they should have been inquiring into was how and why public enterprise was managing to cope with the inevitable difficulties it faced.[52] Although it is impossible here to make a full inquiry into the reasons for the nationalized industries' distinctive performance, something can and indeed must be said.

New Management and Unified Ownership

The most obvious reason why the nationalized industries have performed so well is that their acquisition by the State led in most cases to a much needed managerial shake-up and clear-out. It is surely no accident that the least successful nationalized industries have been those in which it did not occur. The least progressive public undertakings have been the nationalized buses, as their continuously declining productivity and their long failure to introduce single-manning shows.[53] Yet it was here that the transition from public to private ownership was smoothest. The undertakings in the Tillings and Scottish bus group were acquired by voluntary agreement and the minimum of changes were made in their managerial structure and personnel.[54] The other nationalized industry where the transition from private to state ownership left the old managerial structure more or less intact, and the same men in the same seats, was the railways. The creation of the Railway Executive at the very top, composed of old railwaymen, did not constitute a sufficient break with the past. This was shown by its decision to go on building steam engines and by the regional counter-revolution which deprived the railways of effective leadership, and handed power back to those who were content to go on running the railways in the same inefficient way as they had in the day of the old companies.[55] It was not until the early sixties, when Dr Beeching took charge, that a managerial revolution took place. In the other nationalized industries, however, the break with the past came earlier and it is these which have on the whole been most successful. Paradoxically, the managerial upheaval which occurred in most of the nationalized industries, and which led to such acute short-term difficulties, may in the long run have been an advantage.

Another obvious way in which nationalization promoted efficiency was by rationalizing the structure of the industries which were affected. It created undertakings large enough to secure the full economies of scale which were to be had. This was particularly important in gas and electricity, where the fragmentation of the industries and their division into company and municipal sectors had become a serious obstacle to progress.[56] Quite apart from the scope for technical economies the unification of ownership and large-scale operation provided other advantages. With the exception of Tillings and Scottish buses, the different nationalized industries and undertakings handle their own collective bargaining and do not, like all save a few of the very largest private firms, leave the job to employers' associations. This has been one of the explanations for the progress which the nationalized industries have made in the field of productivity bargaining.[57] Because of their size the nationalized industries have been able to take an industry-wide view and to stop their wage structures degenerating into an irrational chaos due to the competitive bidding for labour at a local level, and to piecemeal concessions made in order to buy off trouble. They have, therefore, naturally avoided one of the main causes of industrial strife within private industry or where, as in coal, they inherited a bad system of wage payment, they have been able to remedy the situation and improve their industrial relations.[58]

The Coal Board as the sole employer in the industry has also been able to handle the problem of redundancy more effectively than separate colliery companies could have done. For instance, it has been able, through a careful control of recruitment, to provide jobs at the collieries which were continuing operations for the workers who have been displaced through closures.[59] Since it is responsible for the whole industry it has, and this is even more important, had the maximum incentive to minimize redundancies. If the different collieries and coalfields had remained under separate ownership, it would have paid the concerns which operated in the areas where loss-making pits are concentrated to have closed down as soon as they found that, due to the contraction of demand, they could no longer operate at a profit. This would have inflicted heavy costs not only on the miners who were thrown out of work and on the community which would have lost their output without the benefit of commensurate production elsewhere, but would also have had a damaging effect on those colliery concerns which operated in other parts of the country and in the more profitable parts of the declining coalfields. Mass sackings of miners in the areas where loss-making pits are concentrated would have had an adverse effect upon morale at the profitable pits and upon their ability to preserve their labour force.[60] If the ownership of the industry had remained fragmented this would have been yet another social cost of contraction, but because its ownership has been unified it is a private cost which the Coal Board avoids by keeping its loss-making pits open until they can be phased out.

Financial Constraints and Cost Reduction

The advantages so far mentioned which are enjoyed by the nationalized industries as a result of their transfer to public ownership have been the consequence of the change in their management and the unification of their ownership. They have not been the consequence of public ownership as such and could, at least in theory, have been secured if the industries had remained under, or, where they were partly under municipal control, had been transferred to private ownership. Whether the necessary consolidation of ownership and managerial clear-out would have taken place in the absence of nationalization is highly debatable, but the theoretical possibility must be recognized. There are, however, a number of beneficial effects of public ownership which, if they have occurred, must be regarded as the consequence of nationalization *per se*.

Public enterprise does not have the same financial freedom as private industry but operates under a number of important constraints. On the one hand, the nationalized industries are expected to cover their interest charges and to meet their financial targets, while, on the other hand, they are usually under pressure not to increase their prices in order to do so. The bulk of private industry's capital is in the form of equity upon which dividends are only paid if sufficient profits are available, whereas the capital of the nationalized industries is, with the exception of BOAC and steel, wholly in the form of fixed interest stock. Under the Nationalization Acts the industries only have a duty to meet their interest charges and cover their other costs over a period of years, or to use the statutory form of words 'taking one year with another'. But in practice they have to meet their interest charges every year, and, if they have not earned a sufficient profit they must borrow the money in order to do so. This they will not wish to do partly because it will be taken as a sign that the industry is badly managed and lead to unfavourable publicity and tighter financial control by the civil service machine, and partly because if they become burdened with dead weight debt they will find it more difficult to pay their way taking one year with another.

It is, of course, true that if their accumulated deficit becomes insupportable it will ultimately have to be written off, as it has been for British Rail, BOAC, the NCB and London Transport. But a financial reconstruction is not something which is lightly requested or easily granted.

It is an admission that those in charge of the industry have failed to fulfil their statutory duty; unless the extenuating circumstances are very strong the chairman and some of his colleagues are likely, one way or another, to lose their jobs; it will be accompanied by the public debate and adverse publicity which the nationalized industries shun; and it will require legislation for which the Government will show little enthusiasm.

It may be objected that some of the nationalized industries, and in particular electricity, have had no great difficulty in meeting their interest charges. Since the early sixties, however, the nationalized undertakings have been expected not only to break even but also to achieve the financial targets set by the Treasury. As a result even the undertakings whose economic position is strong do not escape the financial discipline to which public enterprise is subject. The nationalized industries would find their financial obligations less difficult to fulfil if, like those concerns in the private sector which possess significant market power or whose competitors are no more efficient, they were able, when faced with an increase in costs, to simply pass it on to the consumer. But the raising of prices is not a simple matter for industries which are in public ownership. When a nationalized industry increases its prices this always receives the maximum amount of publicity and is invariably greeted with cries of protest. Furthermore the industries have to notify the Government, or in some cases regulatory bodies, of the increases which they are proposing to make and obtain their approval. This has often, though not always, been difficult to secure and has frequently involved costly delays before charges could be raised.[61]

These are by no means the only constraints which affect the working of the nationalized industries. Also of great importance is that, unlike most private firms, the nationalized undertakings have been dependent on borrowing for the bulk of the funds they invest. Frequent reference is made by economists, especially when the nationalized industries are under discussion, to the discipline of having to borrow on the market. They fail to recognize that private industry is largely self-financing and, other things being equal, the nationalized industries will be under the greatest constraint. It will, of course, be said that other things are not equal and that, whereas the capital market is a discriminating mechanism, the Treasury and the Ministries give away capital with an open hand. During the earlier years of public ownership capital expenditure programmes were not always scrutinized as carefully as they should have been, but this is not true today and has not been the case for a long time. Something will be said later about civil service control but what needs to be observed here is the way in which it is constantly borne in upon the nationalized industries that capital is scarce and must not be wasted.

This is the message behind the capital cuts to which they are subjected at periods of national crisis, and also of the cuts for which they are instructed to prepare but are never called upon to execute. Again this point is reiterated time and again in letters they receive from the Ministries.

It seems likely, although it cannot be proved, that the financial constraints under which public enterprise operates have a significant impact upon its functioning. It would be surprising if the strong incentive which the nationalized industries have to pay their way and meet their financial targets without raising their prices did not result in their searching more vigorously for ways to cut their expenses. Cost reduction is the only way of escape from the difficult position in which they find themselves. This may help to explain the success which most of the nationalized industries seem to have had in increasing their productivity, the emphasis which so many of them have placed on work study and productivity bargaining, and the rapid rate at which most cost-reducing innovations have been adopted.[62] Is it altogether an accident, for instance, that the electricity industry's interest in productivity bargaining dates from the period when, due to the financial target which it had been set, it was searching for ways to cut its costs? Again it seems evident that the care with which most investment projects have been evaluated has owed something to the constraints which have been placed upon their capital expenditure. On the other hand the railways' financial collapse took place after they had persuaded the Government to suspend their obligation to pay their way, though this, of course, is by no means the full explanation for their financial ruin.

The Permanent Investigation

Besides the constraints under which the nationalized industries have had to labour, public ownership has resulted in their operations being subjected to detailed investigation. Although this has had some unfortunate consequences it has probably on balance made a significant contribution towards efficiency. There can certainly be no doubt that the nationalized industries have been inquired into far more thoroughly than any other part of the economy. The transfer of the fuel and power industries to public ownership had been preceded by official investigations which exposed their weaknesses and outlined the way they could be remedied.[63] And since the nationalized industries have been in public ownership, and especially during the past decade, there has been a stream of reports on their working. The Select Committee on Nationalized Industries, since it got down to work in 1957, has investigated the air corporations twice, and each of the other nationalized industries once, except for British Road Services and the provincial buses which have never been covered. In addition it has inquired into the subject of Ministerial control and the exploitation of North Sea gas. During the course of these investigations the Committee has asked 23,100 questions and has received almost 1,900 pages of written evidence and has gone on to produce reports containing nearly 1,100 pages.

During the period 1965–71 the Select Committee was joined as an organ of inquiry by the Prices and Incomes Board. In the autumn of 1967 it became Government policy that every major price increase in the nationalized industries should be referred to the Board, but this was already more or less standard practice, and while it was in existence it dealt at length with them in no less than 29 of its reports.[64] A wide range of topics were covered, including applications for price increases by the National Coal Board, British Rail and the Gas Boards; the pay of railwaymen and gas workers; the electricity industry's productivity deals; and the efficiency of the gas industry. The latter report deserves a special mention because it constituted what was more or less an efficiency audit. Besides the continuous work of the Select Committee and the PIB, there have over the years been a considerable number of *ad hoc* investigations into the operations of the nationalized industries. At a rough count there have been at least 21. Their scope has varied greatly. On the one hand, there have been broad and far-reaching inquiries such as the Herbert Committee on the electricity industry, the Edwards Committee on air transport, and presumably the Stedeford Committee on the railways; while, on the other hand, there have been detailed investigations into particular subjects such as the Fleck Committee on the Coal Board's administrative structure, the Wilson Committee on the delays in the commissioning of CEGB power stations, and the Pearson Court of Inquiry into the breakdown of the electricity industry's productivity negotiations.[65]

The quality of these reports has varied widely and not all of the proposals have been helpful.[66] Most of them have, however, been able to suggest ways in which the working of the nationalized industries could be improved or have drawn attention to shortcomings which might be remedied. For instance the Fleck Committee recommended that the coal industry's capital projects should be scrutinized more thoroughly and that firmer control should be kept on schemes which had been started to ensure that they were completed on time; the Chambers Committee found in 1955 that London Transport's workshops were inefficient and that the cost of maintaining its vehicles was excessive; the Select Committee on Nationalized Industries recommended in 1959 that BOAC should make an urgent and thorough review of the operations of its associated companies, and drew attention to the fact that the Corporation's maintenance costs were higher than those of most other operators; the Select Committee criticized British Rail for carrying out investment schemes without discovering whether the services affected would end up making a profit, and said that it was essential that the wagon fleet should be used more efficiently; and the Prices and Incomes Board recommended that the piece-work system should be replaced in mining and that British Rail should cease to base its passenger fares on a standard charge per mile but should adopt a more flexible system of pricing.[67]

Not all of the useful recommendations made by the various committees of inquiry have been promptly implemented. There was a delay of ten years between the Chambers Committee's suggestion that London Transport should begin experimenting with short-distance one-man buses in central London and the introduction of the first standee vehicles, and a decade also elapsed before the electricity industry followed the Herbert Committee's advice and began using work study.[68] However, in general the nationalized industries have taken action fairly quickly once a weakness has been exposed or a remedy proposed. It is significant that all of the major recommendations which were quoted in the previous paragraph were acted upon within a reasonably short period. Once the Fleck report had been published, the Coal Board tightened up its control over capital expenditure and launched a successful drive to speed up the completion of its modernization schemes, while between 1955 and 1963, as the Select Committee discovered, there was a considerable improvement in the efficiency of London Transport's vehicle maintenance.[69] BOAC has also taken firm action to reduce its unit maintenance costs, and by the mid-sixties KLM appears to have been the only major airline whose costs were significantly lower. Soon after the Select Committee's report, the Corporation began reviewing its associated companies and adopted the policy of disengagement.[70] Again, British Rail has, as the Select Committee recommended, improved the utilization of its wagons by drastically reducing their numbers and has for a long time now guarded against investment in hopelessly unprofitable traffic or routes.[71] Finally, the NCB is, under the Power-Loading Agreement, abolishing piece-work, and British Rail has adopted a more flexible system of charging for its passenger services.[72] Even if these were the only recommendations which the nationalized industries had implemented they would, due to their importance, constitute an impressive list, and they are by no means the only examples of implementation and the list could be made still more formidable.

No doubt some of these reforms would have been carried out by the nationalized undertakings on their own initiative. However, it seems clear that the outside inquiries into their operations have, in general, had the effect of speeding-up change and of ensuring that obvious cases of inefficiency are tackled in a determined manner. For instance, the railways were already thinking about switching over to a more flexible system of charging on the passenger side but according to British Rail the Prices and Incomes Board's recommendation hastened its introduction.[73] I have also been told by one of the gas industry's leading officials that the inquiries by the Prices and Incomes Board have led to the introduction of work study being accelerated. In the more distant past, it was the Fleck Report which enabled the Coal Board to overcome local opposition and to introduce standard costs and tighten up control over capital expenditure.[74]

Apart from these examples the pressure which is exerted on the nationalized industries to implement recommendations and to remedy the weakness which have come to light also makes it seem likely that the numerous reports on the nationalized industries have led to faster progress and more determined action. This pressure arises from the general publicity which the nationalized industries receive, from the prodding which the industries will get from their Ministries, and from the likelihood that some future inquiry will want to know what action has been taken. Thus the Select Committee checked up on the action which the Coal Board had taken on the Fleck Report, on the action which the electricity industry had taken on the Herbert Report, and on the progress which London Transport had made in implementing the recommendations of the Chambers Committee. In the case of a number of its reports the Committee has later made inquiries to discover how far its recommendations have been taken up. The fact that it has become the practice for the nationalized industries and Government Departments to make written comments on the Committee reports and say what action they are taking also provides some guarantee that they will not simply gather dust. So again does the way in which most of the Committee's reports have been debated in the House of Commons.[75]

The Benefits of Government Supervision

Another and related feature of public enterprise which has probably contributed to its above-average performance is the supervision and control which the Government has exercised. This, to a greater extent than the other consequences of public ownership, has been a mixed blessing. During the first decade of public ownership the nationalized industries were to a large extent left to their own devices. There were occasional and usually disastrous acts of Ministerial intervention, such as the requirement that the Coal Board should invest heavily in coke-ovens and the trebling of the nuclear power programme at the time of Suez, there was the restriction on rail investment; there were general capital cuts during periods of economic crisis; there was the control which was exercised over the price of coal and, from time to time, other goods; there was the close watch which was kept over the air corporations while they were being subsidized; but there was no sustained attempt to monitor their performance or scrutinize their plans.[76] This is illustrated by the history of the railways and the way in which, once the restrictions on their investment had been lifted, finance was made available almost without question. The Modernization Plan was approved after what can have only been the most cursory of inspections and the Government agreed, in 1956, without any proper investigation, to finance the Transport Commission's deficits. It was not until the railways' finances had completely collapsed that the Ministry of Transport began to ask probing questions or to start vetting their investment schemes with any thoroughness.[77]

Partly as a result of British Rail's financial débâcle, during the second decade of public ownership, there was a marked change in the Government's relations with the nationalized industries. Unfortunately Ministers have, from time to time, persuaded or compelled the nationalized industries to pursue policies which were not in their own best interest. For instance, BOAC was pressed into buying VC 10s which later had to be cancelled at great expense, the electricity industry was encouraged to plan for 4 per cent growth which has resulted in its over-expansion, and the railways have been prevented from pruning their trunk route system.[78] But what has also happened is that over the years the positive side of state ownership and Government control has been more and more in evidence, and a number of developments have now taken place which have made it more difficult for Ministers to meddle with nationalized industries.[79]

The positive side of Government control is illustrated by the crucial part which the Treasury and the sponsoring departments have played in the revolutionary improvement which has taken place in the nationalized industries' methods of investment appraisal. The Treasury began to devote serious thought to the criteria and techniques which should be employed during the early sixties. Advice on the proper methods to employ was obtained from the universities and industry and discounted cash flow, the technique that was suggested, was then discussed with the Ministries and tested out on the London to Bournemouth electrification project and another investment scheme. Early in 1965 the Treasury summoned a conference of representatives of the various departments and the nationalized industries to discuss the application of dcf. This was followed up by a series of smaller meetings under Treasury chairmanship at which the issues involved were discussed and a paper explaining the dcf method was prepared and circulated to the Ministries and the industries.[80]

Meanwhile, the Ministry of Power was, on its own initiative, undertaking a series of investigations into the procedures which the fuel and power industries were using. Although at first the Ministry's approach was not very sophisticated, these investigations were nevertheless of considerable value, for they exposed the more obvious mistakes which were being made, for example the way in which some of the Gas Boards were taking into account costs which had already been incurred when deciding whether to replace old plant. By circulating these papers to the boards and asking for their comments these errors were put right.[81] The Ministry also initiated a method for calculating the return on gas investment which covered both the installation of new plant and the construction of grid mains. This was a great advance on some of the procedures which were then in use and served as the basis for dcf.[82]

As this brief and by no means comprehensive account of the work of the Treasury and the Departments in the field of investment appraisal shows, it was they who took the lead in the adoption of new methods and the correction of old faults which began in the mid-sixties. Not only did the initiative come from the Ministries but it seems unlikely that the nationalized industries would, left to themselves, have adopted dcf anything like as fast as they have. At first there was some scepticism within the industries of the value of dcf which, but for the pressure exerted by the Ministries, would have delayed its adoption.[83] It is surely no accident that it is the public enterprise sector rather than the private sector in which dcf is most extensively used.

This revolution is the most clear cut and well-documented case of civil service initiative. It is by no means the only example of the beneficial effects of the supervision and control which the Ministries exercise over the nationalized industries. This is shown by the establishment of a uniform test rate of discount; it is shown by the way in which the nationalized industries have been encouraged to take movements in relative prices into account in their financial estimating; it is illustrated by the joint investigation of the railways' future prospects which has been made by the Ministry of Transport and British Rail; it is indicated by the way in which productivity bargaining has been encouraged; and it is evident from the way in which the Ministry of Aviation put pressure on BOAC to improve the efficiency of its aircraft maintenance.[84] But the most important way in which the Ministries promote and assist in the successful working of the nationalized industries is by asking questions and demanding explanations, and by ensuring that the industries plan ahead. In this way Government ownership and departmental supervision discourage ill-conceived policies and promote rational behaviour.

Has Supervision Become Excessive?

This view of the supervision which the Government exercises over the nationalized industries differs sharply from that of the Select Committee on Nationalized Industries, as presented in its report on Ministerial Control. The Committee concluded that there had been

> a failure to understand and to work towards the fulfilment of the basic purposes of Ministerial control in respect of the industries . . . these are, first, to secure the wider public interest – and secondly, to oversee, and if possible ensure, the efficiency of the industries. The implications of this demarcation, in the opinion of the Committee, were that it was the intention of Parliament that Ministers should be primarily concerned with laying down policies – in particular for the whole of their sectors of the economy – which would guide the operations of the individual industries, and should not intervene in the management of the industries in implementing these policies. The practice has revealed an almost reversed situation. Until fairly recently Ministers appear, on the whole, to have given the industries very little guidance in regard to either sector policies or economic obligations such as pricing policies or investment criteria; clear policies on some of these matters, including pricing, are still lacking. On the other hand they have become closely involved in many aspects of management, particularly in control of investment in some sectors . . .[85]

The Committee were greatly disturbed by the evidence which they had received of

> scrutiny which goes so far in pursuit of efficiency within the industries that it ceases to be effective in achieving this purpose and which indeed, as one witness [Sir Stanley Raymond] put it, creates an 'unnecessary defensive mechanism' on the part of the industries. They note that some Board Chairmen [Sir Ronald Edwards and Lord Robens] were also disturbed because detailed scrutiny had expanded, they said, to the limits of tolerability. One Chairman [Sir Stanley Raymond] complained of 'meticulous detail' and others [Sir Stanley Brown and Lord Robens] of questions which were 'relatively useless' and which asked for 'endless figures'.[86]

The Committee's conclusions would carry greater weight if they were more consistent and the Committee had not earlier conceded that a considerable amount of detailed questioning was necessary. Thus it accepted in the fuel and power sector 'with so much money at stake, the need for pretty meticulous checking of the industries' plans for investment and of their forecasts of demand. This must involve detailed questioning by the Ministry.'[87] Even in the case of transport where the Committee considered, probably rightly, that supervision had been carried too far they agreed that

> The concern shown by the Ministry of Transport in the details of investment is, to a large measure, inherent in the nature of the transport industries, particularly British Railways. Their total investment requirements cannot be closely related to demand, as can those of the fuel industries, especially gas and electricity, and so the size of the programmes cannot be considered separately from their components. And these tend to be numerous, relatively small, and largely unrelated to each other. Under these circumstances it is inevitable that the Ministry should concentrate on some form of scrutiny of individual projects.[88]

It is apparent that the Committee were by no means as critical of detailed questioning as their conclusions made them appear. Moreover, in summing up they played down the progress which has been made towards establishing economic obligations and investment criteria for the nationalized industries by describing it as fairly recent. Not only is this misleading in itself because by now an enormous amount of progress has been made, whether recent or no, but it also obscures the fact that the process began as long ago as 1961 when the Government published the White Paper on the Financial and Economic Obligations of the Nationalized Industries. But the main weakness of the Select Committee's report is that no real evidence is presented that the system of Ministerial control, which comes in for such heavy criticism, has had a damaging effect on the nationalized industries. The main yardstick by which the Committee judged Government supervision was not the impact which it had had on the industries, but whether their Chairmen were happy, and whether there was a clear division of responsibility between the Ministries and the Boards. In a word, the Committee's inquiry was an exercise in public administration and as such addressed to the wrong question. Instead of trying to discover what effect Government control had had, and then going on to suggest administrative remedies if these appeared necessary, the Committee tried to discover whether the administrative set up was good in itself. But this is a pointless inquiry because the excellence or otherwise of administrative machinery can only be judged by its results. It is the disregard of this simple point which makes public administration such a barren subject and why, as we have frequently had cause to observe during the course of this book, it has contributed so little to the understanding, and so much to the obscuration, of the way in which the nationalized industries have performed.

Apart from the weakness of the Select Committee's approach and its concern with happiness and tidiness instead of efficiency, it exaggerated in its conclusions the extent of managerial distress caused by Government supervision. While the Committee quoted the evidence of unhappiness and dissatisfaction which it found, it ignored the statements in which the chairmen of the nationalized industries said that they were reasonably content. Although the Committee quoted Sir Stanley Raymond's complaint that the Ministry of Transport went into meticulous detail, it ignored his later statement that he did not want

> any impression to be conveyed that so far as capital expenditure projects are concerned, we have an intolerable situation as between the Ministry and ourselves. That is certainly not the case. In fact, I think that we have one of the best machines for dealing with investment as between a nationalized industry and a sponsoring department that exists. We have very good relations with the Ministry as far as capital investment is concerned.[89]

While the Select Committee interpreted Sir Stanley Brown as having complained that the CEGB was asked quite a lot of relatively useless questions it omitted Sir Giles Guthrie's belief that 'the questions are relevant and I think they are intelligent'.[90] Nor did the Committee report Mr Anthony Bull's feeling that in general the questions which were addressed to London Transport were sensible or cite Sir Henry Jones' testimony that, so far as the submission of information by the gas industry was concerned,

> I do not think this has been deeply resented by the boards or by ourselves. I think we have found this (after all, we are using large sums of money) a useful way of keeping the Ministry informed . . . The people in the gas division now are experienced and have been there some time. They understand our problems and I personally would say, as far as the Gas Council is concerned that the questions are usually all right.[91]

It is not pretended that these statements fully reflect the nationalized industries' feelings about Ministerial control. They are merely intended to show that the Select Committee picked out the evidence of dissatisfaction it received but ignored the testimony which pointed in a contrary direction. It is, in fact, extremely hard to tell from the evidence it obtained how far those in charge of the nationalized undertakings are happy or unhappy. This is partly because some of the chairmen made contradictory statements and partly because of the difficulty of knowing whether their words should be taken at their face value. On the one hand, it is possible that some of the chairmen toned down their views about Ministerial control because this might make their relations with the Government still more difficult, while, on the other hand, it seems likely that some of them criticized Ministerial questioning when what they really objected to was Government policy. The Committee was naïve not to see that the real reason for Lord Robens' dissatisfaction was not the Ministry's request for endless figures but his objection to the Government's policy for running down the coal industry and his unwillingness to provide information which might be used to further this aim. The Coal Board's plans are not usually examined in detail – the last examination by the Ministry of a colliery project took place about six years ago – and the Board's officials are not distracted by endless questions for it is well known that, with Lord Robens' backing, they refuse to answer.[92]

Although it is almost impossible from the available evidence to know the degree to which Ministerial control causes dissatisfaction it does not appear that with the possible exception of Sir Anthony Milward of BEA, and Sir Reginald Wilson of the Transport Holding Company and the National Freight Corporation, it is so intense as to lead one to suppose that something is badly wrong. In both these cases it appears that the main cause of dissatisfaction was not Government supervision as such but the decision that BEA should fly British and the constant organizational changes to which the nationalized transport services have been subject.[93] Clearly there is a danger that supervision will be carried so far that the efficiency of the nationalized industries will be impaired, but there is no real evidence that this has happened, and the Select Committee by emphasizing the risk, has made it less likely that it will happen. Despite the criticisms which have been made the Select Committee's report on Ministerial Control is therefore timely and its very exaggerations are likely to increase its impact.

Ownership and Motivation

The final way in which public ownership may help to explain the nationalized industries' surprisingly good performance is that they have a different purpose and motivation from that of most private firms. In theory the main aim and driving force of private enterprise is to make a profit, although in practice many firms seem content to jog along, hoping for a quiet life and pursuing a policy of live and let live. What is important to recognize is that, regardless of the level of profit with which they rest content most private firms do not have any alternative aim to profit making.

In contrast, the aim of those in charge of the nationalized industries is to meet the needs of the consumer at the lowest possible price, to act as model employers and in general to help maximize the welfare of the nation. This does not mean that profits are irrelevant but in public enterprise they are a constraint and not a driving force. Those who manage nationalized industries are expected to end up earning a profit but this is not the object of the exercise but merely one of the rules of the game. This difference between the purposes of public and private enterprise has been forcefully pointed out by Lord Beeching who, because of the leading positions which he has occupied in both sectors, is eminently qualified to judge:

> The nationalised industries are expected to meet some need for goods or services, the nature of the need being judged, in part at least, not by them but by the Government. They are expected to meet that need in a manner which is judged to be socially desirable, and which is specified, in relation to the various aspects of their business, by the Government, but not always consistently so. At the same time, they are expected to pay their way by remunerating their capital, taking one year with another. In effect, therefore, the making of an adequate profit is not a primary objective, but it is a condition which they are nevertheless expected to satisfy after doing a number of other obligatory things. The primary objective of any company in the private sector, on the other hand, is to make the best possible return on the capital provided by the shareholders.[94]

Lord Beeching regards private industry's single-minded pursuit of profit as an advantage, but what needs to be stressed here is that those in charge of the nationalized industries cannot but be aware that their primary duty is to make the best possible use of the national assets entrusted to them, and in this way promote the welfare of the community in general and of their customers and employees in particular. This follows from the fact that the industries are owned by the nation and that their shareholders and the community are one and the same. In this situation profit maximization is no longer a credible objective, because it is clearly ridiculous to make the highest possible profit one can on behalf of the nation as shareholders if it is earned at the expense of these same shareholders in the guise of consumers or employees. It obviously makes no sense for a nationalized undertaking to earn an exceptionally high profit for the benefit of its shareholders as this will only mean that its shareholder-consumers are being compelled to pay unnecessarily high prices. This much must be clear, even to the managers of nationalized industries who are least given to reflection.

They can hardly be unaware that, since the industries over which they have charge are owned by the nation, they must do more than simply earn a normal profit in the least troublesome way which is open to them. For if costs are excessive and methods of production inefficient it is the public on whose behalf they are supposed to be managing the enterprise who will pay the price. They are therefore likely to set great store by the development of more productive machinery and more efficient techniques, to place great emphasis upon the modernization and rationalization of their industries, and in general to value anything which will serve to reduce costs. This helps to explain the rapid strides which public enterprise has made in the technical field both here and abroad. In contrast those who manage private firms are under no obligation to obtain their profits in socially desirable ways. Since their shareholders represent only a small part of the population, their interests may diverge from those of the community at large.

The social service orientation of the nationalized industries does not only derive from the fact of public ownership; it is reinforced by both expectations and institutions. None of those who are in charge of public enterprise, however averse they may be on ideological grounds to State ownership, can altogether escape being influenced by the high hopes for which the transfer to public ownership was brought about. Generations of socialist propaganda have inevitably entrenched the idea that the primary purpose of the nationalized industries is to serve the interests of the community. This ideal is constantly brought home to those who manage the nationalized industries by the machinery of public accountability.

Besides the official machinery for accountability there is the unofficial machinery provided by the Fourth Estate. As any newspaper reader or television viewer must be aware, the amount of attention which the nationalized industries receive is out of all proportion to their economic importance. Much of the discussion in the press and on television is of low quality, many of the criticisms are unfair, and the media give more prominence to the nationalized industries' failures than to their successes. But the very fact that, because they are nationalized, their doings are discussed so frequently and arouse such interest must constantly remind those who direct the industries of the special responsibility which they are felt by the community to bear.

The knowledge that they are public servants and have charge of industries which are expected to serve the community, would seem to provide those who direct the nationalized industries with an incentive which is lacking in private industry. It is this difference in the motivation of those who direct public and private enterprise which I believe explains much of the contrast between the performance of the two sectors. But although a strong *prima facie* case can be made out for believing that this is so, it should be recognized that it is no more than a *prima facie* case. No hard evidence has been produced to show that those who manage the nationalized industries do in fact regard their jobs any differently from those in similar positions in private industry. To leave the argument at this stage and pass on to other matters would in most circumstances be unsatisfactory, but in the present case it seems almost inevitable because of the great difficulty of discovering the motivation of those who direct public and private concerns and the impossibility, without a mammoth inquiry, of establishing what effect this has on the quality of their work.

The Danger of the National Interest

Although it seems likely that public ownership provides a valuable drive which is lacking in private industry, it is clear that service to the community is in some ways a dangerous principle on which to conduct industrial undertakings. In the past the nationalized industries have pursued ill-conceived policies because they, or more usually the Government, believed that the national interest should take priority over their commercial well-being. For instance in 1957 the Government committed the electricity industry to a financially disastrous programme of nuclear power although the Central Electricity Authority wanted a lower target and it was already becoming clear that nuclear stations were uneconomic.[95] Later in 1963, when the attempt was being made to talk up the rate of growth, the industry agreed, at the Government's request, to base its plans on the assumption of 4 per cent expansion. This led to excess generating capacity or would have done had not the vastly increased plant programme overwhelmed the manufacturers and led to costly delays in the completion of partly finished power stations.[96] Again BOAC and British South American Airways were pushed, in the supposed interests of British foreign policy but against their own better judgment, into purchasing a number of airlines which became a financial liability.[97] What was far worse, the air corporations have been expected to go on flying British long after it had become plain to the rest of the world that British aircraft are a bad bet. As a result the corporations have committed themselves to a series of planes which have, with the exception of the Viscount, turned out in one way or another to be inferior to American aircraft.[98]

Fortunately, the risks which are run when the nationalized industries disregard their own best interests are now better understood and it has become more difficult for the Government to get them to adopt policies which are likely to endanger their financial position. Hegel believed that the only lesson to be learned from history is that nobody learns anything from history. This is too cynical a view. One of the reasons why the Government established financial targets for the nationalized industries in the early sixties was the hope that by defining their financial obligations more clearly it would be less easy for them to pursue policies, or be loaded with duties, which could not be justified in commercial terms. It was not expected that the boards' non-commercial obligations would be eliminated, although a move in that direction was no doubt contemplated, but it was intended that henceforth the Government should decide, when setting the targets, exactly what those obligations were. Moreover, it was laid down that if unprofitable activities were subsequently imposed on any industry it would be entitled to ask for an adjustment of its financial objectives.

When the targets were originally set there does not appear to have been any thoroughgoing investigation of the cross-subsidization which was being practised in order to see whether the social gain outweighed the private loss.[99] The Government either turned a blind eye or, as in the case of railways, assumed that the social benefits were negligible, and that loss-making activities should be eliminated as quickly as possible. The setting of financial targets, no matter how they were arrived at, has provided the nationalized industries with some protection against unreasonable interference and backstairs pressure. It is natural for the boards of nationalized industries to want to keep on good terms with the Ministers who appoint them and supervise their activities. They have therefore been reluctant to force those Ministers who wish to exercise power without assuming responsibility into justifying their policies in public, but now that financial targets have been set boards find it easier to speak out and compel Ministers to take responsibility.

The existence of the Select Committee on Nationalized Industries makes it unlikely that Ministers will in future try to give 'lunch table directions' to the chairmen of nationalized industries. The Committee has been so successful at ferreting out under-cover intervention that Ministers can no longer hope that their actions will remain secret. The Select Committee has, however, done more than this for, as a result of its constant advocacy, it has helped to establish the principle that where the nationalized industries are required to do something which is against their own commercial interests they should be compensated by the Government. Although this was at no time formally adopted by the Labour Government, in practice it usually worked on the principle.[100]

Not only has the Government more or less agreed that it should bear the cost of the nationalized industries' social obligations but the boards have also become increasingly reluctant to pay the price and take responsibility for what are, or ought to be, Government decisions. Indeed the industries have both here and in other fields displayed a new and refreshing ability to stand up for themselves. BOAC, under Sir Matthew Slattery, was the first undertaking to show this new spirit of independence. Sir Matthew as an old Admiral was given to blunt speaking. He once described the Corporation's capital structure as 'bloody crazy'. The real reason for the Corporation's less deferential attitude was that it was now paying the price for having in the past bowed to Ministerial wishes and supported the aircraft industry through thick and thin. As a result BOAC started to press both for a clear recognition by the Ministry that its responsibility was primarily commercial and for the cancellation both of the deficit it had accumulated, and of some of the planes it had ordered in the 'national interest'.[101] Although Sir Matthew was forced to resign, the new Chairman, Sir Giles Guthrie, took the same line, the Minister was assumed by BOAC to have conceded that its fundamental responsibility was to act commercially and the unwanted aircraft and unfair debt were ultimately cancelled.[102]

The example of independence which the Corporation set has been followed increasingly by other boards. For instance the Coal Board under the leadership of Lord Robens has, as is well known, repeatedly stood up to the Government, over the speed and extent to which the coal industry is being run down. Again Sir Reginald Wilson, the Chairman of the Transport Holding Company and the National Freight Corporation, has protested in the strongest terms against the administrative reorganizations to which the nationalized transport sector has repeatedly been subjected.[103] It is not only in years but also in spirit that the nationalized industries have come of age.

The convention which grew during the sixties that public enterprise should act commercially unless the Government rules to the contrary and provides appropriate compensation, does not automatically prevent the nationalized industries from being forced to pursue policies which reduce the welfare of the nation. The Labour Government, for example, prevented British Rail from pressing on with the rationalization of its route system. The retention of some of the lines which BR would otherwise have closed may be justified on the ground that the social gain outweighs the railways' private loss. But no real attempt has been made to identify these by means of cost-benefit analysis and then close the rest, because the Labour Government believed, as an article of faith, that the existing route system should be preserved more or less in its entirety. This means that a loss in welfare is being sustained by the community, although its importance should not be exaggerated.[104] Yet there is no reason to believe that the Government would not have decided to halt closures and to subsidize the railways if they had remained in private ownership. They are being subsidized not because they are a nationalized industry but because the Labour Government regarded the railways as an essential public service. It may of course be said that it took only this attitude because they are in public ownership, but it seems more likely that the Labour Party's policy is the result of the railways' history. It regards them as essential because, until comparatively recent times, they were a great basic industry on which, despite their private ownership, public service obligations were laid.

So far as the other nationalized industries are concerned there seems little reason to suppose that the Government will be more prepared to pay them to engage in policies which reduce their profits than it would if they were privately owned. Indeed the eagle eye with which the nationalized industries are regarded may well mean that the Government will be less willing to subsidize them than it is to pay money to private firms. The increasing extent to which cost-benefit analysis is being used by the Treasury and other Departments to help determine policies towards public enterprise is also a reason for expecting that the nationalized industries will not be provided with indiscriminate doles or forced to act in ways which reduce their profits without increasing the welfare of the nation. Indeed it would be surprising if during years to come cost-benefit analysis was not gradually applied to the railways which are the only nationalized industry where misallocation appears to be occurring on a significant scale. Some progress has in fact already been made within the Ministry of Transport towards using cost-benefit techniques to determine the future of loss-making railway services.

Back to Competition and Private Ownership?

That the nationalized industries should act as semi-commercial organizations, except where the Government rules to the contrary on welfare grounds, will probably meet with general agreement. It has been urged that the industries which are now in public ownership should become fully commercial in the sense of striving, like private firms, to maximize their profits. The obvious objection to this is that some of the nationalized industries such as electricity and gas possess considerable monopoly power. Under these circumstances profit maximization is likely to lead to the earning of monopoly profits and the misallocation of resources.[105] This is, of course, recognized by the advocates of full commercial behaviour who go on, logically enough, to suggest that the nationalized industries should not only be deprived of all protection but also that they should be broken up so as to produce internal competition. 'At the least,' declares Professor Wiseman, 'they should be broken into smaller and competitive units, subjected to outside competition, and required to act as commercial undertakings. If possible they should be returned to private ownership.'[106]

Professor Wiseman never stops to inquire whether, for instance, there is any case on welfare grounds for the protection of the coal industry, although it is a strong one.[107] He simply refers to cheap oil imports having 'produced successful pressure for heavier taxes on fuel oil'.[108] Still worse, Professor Wiseman gives scant attention to the effect which the break-up and denationalization of the industries now in public ownership would have on their operating efficiency. He ignores the disruption and disorganization which the liquidation of the industries' administrative structure would inevitably cause. He disregards the likelihood that in most industries denationalization would remain incomplete.[109] In practice what would happen, as it did when BRS was partly sold up, was that the rump of the undertaking would remain in public ownership under a demoralized management which would have to cope with the difficult task of slimming down its now unnecessarily large body of administrative staff.[110]

Some public undertakings such as the railways would almost certainly prove completely unsaleable and the advocates of denationalization would have to content themselves with decentralization. Yet any weakening of the industries' managerial structure and central control might well turn out to be a disaster, just as it did in the case of the regionalization of the railways.[111] If the history of the nationalized industries has one lesson to teach, it is the damage which ideologically inspired administrative changes can have on their working. Again Professor Wiseman passes hastily over the great strides in efficiency which the nationalized industries have been making and ignores the absence of any positive arguments for believing that their performance would be improved by their return to a private sector whose record has been less satisfactory.

Finally he shows himself to be ignorant both of the enormous expense of creating any meaningful competition in those of the nationalized industries which are octopoid and provide their own distribution systems, and of the economies of unified ownership which most of the industries have been able to secure. 'It is open to question,' he writes, 'whether there are many nationalized industries in which technical conditions of production make monopoly inevitable. Electricity supply is a possible case: but even there it is *only* the national grid that creates a problem.'[112] Professor Wiseman would seem to have forgotten about local distribution – or does he really imagine that it would be worth laying two electric cables (or gas pipes) down every street? Moreover, even in those industries where internal competition is technically possible it would be foolish to overlook the benefits which they have derived from unified ownership. As we have seen the progress which has been made in the field of productivity bargaining has been partly due to the fact that the undertakings possess their own negotiating structure. Again the Coal Board's success in finding jobs for displaced miners has not been due to good luck but to careful central planning.[113]

Although such views do not yet hold sway among economists they are increasingly heard. For instance, Professor A. R. Prest has recently advocated, although on somewhat different grounds, that the nationalized industries should be disposed of.[114] The constant harping by those economists who are associated with the Institute of Economic Affairs on the supposed advantages of competition and private ownership is creating a climate of opinion favourable to outright or partial denationalization. This is shown by the proposal by the Edwards Committee on Air Transport that the air corporations should relinquish some of their routes in the interests of private aviation; by the decision of the present Government that such a handover should take place; and by the way in which it has embraced the policy of hiving off the ancillary activities which the nationalized industries now run. That such decisions and declarations derive almost entirely from an ideological commitment to private ownership and from its equation with competition, is shown by the fact that no attempt has been made to justify them in detail or to explain how competition will be increased. In a report of 267 pages the Edwards Committee did not find room to present a clear and argued case for the transfer of the air corporations' routes to its so-called 'second force' airline. The best that it could manage was one or two brief comments such as the statement that it was motivated by a sense of fair-play to those who had ventured their resources in building up private air services. It did not however occur to the Committee that it was inequitable that public property, in the form of routes which the air corporations had built up, should be handed over to private shareholders free of charge. Nor did the Committee's findings about the performance of the corporations or the possibility of providing healthy competition in aviation provide any justification for what it recommended. It had few criticisms but much praise for BEA and BOAC – while the handing over of their routes to

Q

a private operator does nothing, as a moment's reflection shows, to increase competition.[115] In so far as the air corporations possess a monopoly, and they are of course in competition with foreign operators, then this would simply be transferred to what the Committee persisted in describing as the second force.

Despite or perhaps because of its obvious bias against public enterprise the recommendations of the Edwards Committee are now in the process of being implemented by the Government. BOAC's West Africa routes on which it earns a profit of £1·3 million are to be transferred to Caledonian/BUA and it has been announced that the latter will 'be given preference over other operators in the licensing of new scheduled routes'.[116] Furthermore Mr John Davies, the Minister of Trade and Industry, told the Conservative Party Conference in October 1970 that the nationalized industries should withdraw from their ancillary activities.[117] What, if anything, will he hived off is not known at the time of writing but what is clear is that the process will do less than nothing to promote competition. When the subsidiary activities are sold they are likely to be bought up either by private firms in the industry, or by concerns in a different line of business which have decided to diversify. If they are purchased by their private rivals competition is reduced, while if they are bought by concerns from another industry it is in no way increased.

The only way in which hiving off might stimulate competition would be for the subsidiary activities to be broken up and sold off showroom by showroom and shipping route by shipping route. However, such a method would have grave disadvantages. Economies of scale would be lost and piecemeal denationalization would take years to complete and cause the maximum disruption. For this reason it seems most unlikely that it will be adopted and virtually certain that any subsidiary undertakings which are hived off will be sold *en bloc*, although even this would involve the loss of economies of scale where the boards co-operate among themselves to buy in bulk, as they do in gas and electricity when purchasing appliances.

Apart from the lack of any case on grounds of competition for stripping the nationalized industries of their ancillary undertakings, there are powerful arguments against doing so. The process would only cause demoralization and absorb time and energy which should be devoted to the real economic problems which the industries face. Moreover, as I have argued elsewhere, the ancillary undertakings are in most cases integral parts of the organizations to which they belong and have in general been well managed.[118] The number and strength of the objections to hiving off and its all too obvious ideological motivation mean that, except in the case of the air corporations, it may not be put into practice. However, this increases the possibility that the Government will press ahead with its other main policy for the nationalized industries – their partial return to private ownership by the creation and sale of a large block of voting shares.

This is an interesting and at first sight attractive proposal which does not have any of the obvious disadvantages of hiving off. One of the principal arguments which has been given in its favour is that the burden of public sector borrowing would be reduced. During the past few years the nationalized industries have financed about half of their capital requirements for themselves. Almost all of their remaining capital requirements have been met by the Government, although a not inconsiderable sum is now being raised by means of borrowing abroad. The Government in its turn borrows from the market or raises the money through taxation by running a budget surplus. It therefore appears that, in so far as the nationalized industries' borrowing requirements are met from the budget surplus, the Conservatives are right in claiming that taxation could be reduced if a BP solution were put into operation, and the industries were able to meet part of their needs direct from the market.

What, however, the denationalizers have to explain is why investors should be more willing to lend to the nationalized industries once they have been partly denationalized than they are to lend to the Government. It is no answer to say that after partial denationalization the industries will be more nearly self-financing and need to borrow less. For it is by no means obvious how this can be achieved without an increase in their prices, and public enterprise does not need to be returned to private ownership in order to charge more. The question thus remains how, when they have been transformed into mixed undertakings, the nationalized industries will be able to tap funds which are not available for Government borrowing.

This the denationalizers have failed to answer. It depends, states Professor Prest, 'on whether the rather gloomy view taken of such possibilities under the present set-up is based on the belief that sources of finance are not readily available or that the impetus to seek them out is not very great. If the latter is the case, then it can be maintained that the argument for denationalization is reinforced. But this is clearly speculative; the only way of finding out for certain is to put the idea to the test.'[119] This begs the question and is a flagrant piece of economic Micawberism – denationalize and hope that something will turn up.

Since the advocates of denationalization are unable or unwilling to answer the question of what new funds the industries could tap we must answer it for them. There is obviously no reason why denationalized industries should be able to raise money through fixed interest stock more readily than the Government, unless, of course, they offer very much more attractive terms than those offered by the latter at present. What Professor Prest and the other advocates of denationalization are hoping is that they will be able to raise money by issuing equity shares on which a variable dividend is paid. However, in view of the very limited amount which private firms raise in this way it seems highly unlikely that the industries would be able to attract any substantial amount of funds without offering a very high rate of profit. The reduction in taxation because of the lower amount which the nationalized industries would need to borrow from the Exchequer would, of course, lead to some increase in saving. But it seems likely that most of the money left in private pockets would, other things being equal, be devoted to extra consumption.

To attract funds by offering a very high rate of return would involve a large rise in the industries' prices. But if all the talk about tapping new sources of funds only boils down to a rise in prices, denationalization is totally irrelevant because it can take place while the industries remain in public ownership. The rise in prices and profits would in this case make the industries more nearly self-financing and obviate the need for them to raise extra finance from the market. Furthermore there is little doubt that the price increase would need to be less sharp under public ownership because of the difficulty, if the industries were partly denationalized, of convincing investors that the Government would not in some way interfere in their running and impair their profitability. Only if they were seen to be earning very large profits, which would require a very large price increase, would the market be reassured. Moreover, if prices are to be raised it is preferable on grounds of equity that the industries should not be denationalized. If they are the public will have to bear the burden of a heavy price increase the extra revenue from which will go to private shareholders; whereas if the industries stay nationalized the assets which are purchased with the revenue will be in public ownership.

A second argument for turning the nationalized industries into mixed undertakings is that this would put a stop to unwarranted Government interference in their management. If partial denationalization would simply mean an end to what Mr Davies describes as 'excessive public scrutiny', there could be no quarrel. What, however, it would almost certainly mean in practice would be an end to any effective Government supervision of the industries. The advocates of partial denationalization give the game away when they call their proposal 'the BP solution' and when they concede that it would probably be necessary to erect a system of public utility regulation on the American model.[120] As the BP experience shows, the Government has virtually no control over a company in which there is a large private stake. It may be replied that the Government can and should be prepared to play a more active part in the control of the nationalized industries even when they have been partly denationalized. But in practice it is highly unlikely that it would, because our society is still dominated by the ethic of private enterprise, the most important element of which is that the state should not interfere with management.

At first sight foreign experience with mixed undertakings appears to show that a large private stake is compatible with continued operation as a nationalized concern. In Italy, for instance, private investors own a substantial proportion of the equity of the companies owned and controlled by the great state holding companies, ENI and IRI. It is, however, significant that ENI and IRI are themselves in 100 per cent state ownership and that private participation is restricted to their subsidiaries. It must also be remembered that under Italian company law minority shareholders have virtually no rights. There is, therefore, no reason to believe that the so-called BP solution means anything other than the effective denationalization of public enterprise. However, as we have argued in this chapter, Government supervision and public accountability appear to have made an important contribution to the success of the industries which are in public ownership. To denationalize because ministerial control has its darker side would be to throw away the baby with the bath water.

Paradoxically if the left-wing view of the nationalized industries is correct then their transfer to private ownership would make little or no difference because their conduct is already virtually indistinguishable from that of large private firms. These firms, so the argument runs, act commercially and try to earn profits, but this to an increasing extent is what the nationalized industries try to do. Therefore, in practice, public enterprise has turned out to act in almost exactly the same way as private enterprise. However, like many other simple syllogisms this argument proves too much. For it follows that the only way in which the nationalized industries can distinguish themselves from private firms is not to act commercially and not to earn profits. To the left-winger therefore the nationalized industries are only behaving in a desirable manner when they are making losses and the test of whether a socialist policy is being pursued is whether a loss is being incurred. At this point the simple-minded socialist will no doubt try to wriggle out of the ridiculous position into which he has got himself. But there is no escape and no misrepresentation. That the earning of profits is a sinful activity is an article of faith to socialists of the simpler sort, from which it follows that only loss-making is honourable.

What is wrong with this argument is that it assumes that because in our society profits are often earned in anti-social ways it is illegitimate to make a profit at all. But this does not follow because not all profits are earned at the expense of society. The question which must therefore be asked about an undertaking or industry, whatever its ownership, is how its profits have been earned. It is this question which throughout this book we have in one form or another been asking about public enterprise, and trying to answer. That this is the right question about public enterprise has been cogently argued by Professor John Sheahan. In his examination of the performance of the French nationalized industries he observes that the consensus of the best studies is that they

> have acted very much as private enterprise might have done in the same markets. Their general conclusion that this is unfortunate is well expressed by the outcry of Bernard Chenot: 'What good does it do to nationalize a firm if it is to be directed in the exactly same way as a private enterprise?' The question posed by Chenot, and most of the investigations underlying it, have a built-in confusion. They imply that behavioural characteristics of all firms seeking profit are interchangeable. If this were so, government enterprise orientated towards the welfare of the firm itself would indeed do little good. But if it be recognized that in most markets there are many alternative ways of trying to earn profits, with varying implications for economic efficiency and social welfare, it becomes clear that there may be important scope for gain by introduction of new decision groups with different methods of promoting the welfare of their firms. Three main groups of reasons suggest that private markets may fall significantly short of possible levels of efficiency. The first is that managements may fail to search aggressively for improvements, for such reasons as reluctance to accept dilution of ownership to the degree necessary to reach optimal scale, high valuations on leisure or on present location leading to rejection of profitable changes, or simply the potent capacity of humans for repetition through habit and inertia. The second, often related to the first, is the possibility of agreements on pricing or other aspects of performance that lower community welfare even though they aid profits. The third is that lack of information beyond the horizon of separate firms may lead to inferior choices even by well-managed, competitive firms. All three of these factors may be affected by the introduction of government enterprise, even if the state firm does aim primarily at its own growth.[121]

Although this is by no means a full statement of the reasons why public enterprise can be expected to earn its profits in different and better ways than private enterprise, Professor Sheahan makes the point with admirable clarity.

That the nationalized industries have in fact earned their profits by what on balance have been superior means, in terms of the national welfare, to those employed by private industry has been the central thesis of this book. This was foreseen with great prescience by R. H. Tawney and we can do no better than to end this book as we began by quoting his words. The advantages of public ownership, he wrote in 1919 when arguing the case for the nationalization of the coal industry,

do not repose upon the assumption that any preternatural degree of intelligence will be displayed by the personnel of a nationalized system – an assumption which, since such a system will naturally employ many, if not most, of the existing officials, would clearly be illegitimate. They are of a kind which a public and representative body, of its very nature, possesses, and which private ownership (whatever its other merits) cannot pretend to cultivate. Such a body can handle the problem of organizing production and distribution as a whole, instead of piecemeal. It can wait, and need not snatch at an immediate profit at the cost of prejudicing the future of the industry. It can enlist on its side motives to which the private profit-maker (if he is aware of their existence) cannot appeal. It can put the welfare of human beings, worker and consumer, first.[122]

REFERENCES

THE annual reports of the main public undertakings (for which see Table 1) are referred to by the bodies' initials together with the year, except that EA is used for the British Electricity Authority to avoid confusion with BEA. Other annual reports are referred to by the name or initials of the body and the year. The Select Committee on Nationalized Industries is referred to by the initials SCNI followed by NCB for coal (1958); by AC for Air Corporations (1959); by BR for British Railways (1960); by GI for the Gas Industry (1961); by ES for Electricity Supply (1963); by BOAC for British Overseas Airways Corporation (1964); by LT for London Transport (1965); by BEA for British European Airways (1967); by MC for Ministerial Control (1968); by NSG for North Sea Gas (1968); and by CB for National Coal Board (1969). Where these or other reports have two or more parts these are indicated by the appropriate figure, e.g. BTC 1960.2 means the second volume of the British Transport Commission's Annual Report for 1960. Other abbreviations used for publications to which frequent reference is made are as follows:

AAS	*Annual Abstract of Statistics*
BRB/MTR	British Railways Board *Development of the Major Railway Trunk Routes*
BRB/RBR	British Railways Board *The Reshaping of British Railways*
BTC/MBR	British Transport Commission *Modernisation and Re-equipment of British Railways*
BTC/RM	British Transport Commission *Report on the Modernisation and Re-equipment of British Railways*
BTR	*British Transport Review*
H; H/WA	*Hansard*; *Hansard* Written Answers
MLG/EPG	*Ministry of Labour Gazette*; *Employment and Productivity Gazette*
MPSD	Ministry of Power *Statistical Digest*; *Digest of Energy Statistics*
NCB/ACO	National Coal Board *Report of the Advisory Committee on Organisation*
NCB/IIC	National Coal Board *Investing in Coal*
NCB/PFC	National Coal Board *Plan for Coal*
NCB/RPC	National Coal Board *Revised Plan for Coal*

475

NIE   *National Income and Expenditure*
UN/ECE/P   United Nations, Economic Commission for Europe
Productivity of Underground Coal Workings

In the notes which follow Command Papers are referred to by number only. For titles and dates of publication see the Key to Command Papers Cited on pages 514–15.

PART ONE: TECHNICAL EFFICIENCY

Chapter 1: *Introduction*

1. See pp 31, 32.
2. *The Radical Tradition* (1964) p 160.
3. *A Textbook of Economic Theory* (1953) p 88.
4. *Public Enterprise* (1968) edited R. Turvey pp 7, 8.
5. BTC 1948 p 31, 1949 pp 13, 14, 248, 1950 pp 13, 14, 1951 p 7.
6. THC 1964 p 37, 1968 p 19. (All references to the THC Reports are to the privately printed version.)
7. See pp 36–39.
8. Cmnd 4018 p 33.
9. Ministry of Transport *Passenger Transport in Great Britain* 1967 pp 4, 48.
10. SCNI/BR p 335; AAS 1967 p 199; Table 3; THC 1963 p 18.
11. See pp 59, 289 for the nationalized industries' share of investment and employment.
12. Cmnd 3437 p 4.
13. NIE 1969 pp 13, 15, 23, 39.
14. NIE 1968 p 25; BOAC 1962–3 p 21, 1963–4 p 10; BEA 1963–4 p 24, 1964–5 p 23; Information from BRS.
15. UN *Yearbook of National Accounts Statistics* 1967 pp 79, 297, 551, 753.
16. NIE 1969 pp 23, 39.
17. See Table 8.
18. H/WA 8 June 1967.

Chapter 2: *Productivity: The Early Years*

1. See pp 109–14.
2. These figures include those who work in the industries' subsidiary activities, which are not covered by the productivity calculations, but the same trend would be shown if they had been excluded.
3. AAS 1957 p 105, 1963 p 105.
4. EA 1947–8 p 89; NCB 1946 p 2; GC 1948–50 p 21; BTC 1952 p 93; the figures for electricity and gas would have been somewhat smaller if the subsidiaries of holding companies had been eliminated (EA 1947–9 p 306; Cmd 6699 pp 13, 14).
5. *BRS Magazine* December 1950 p 92; BTC 1952 p 93.
6. G. W. Quick Smith BTR 1952 p 199; see also C. Sharp *The Problem of Transport* (1965) pp 65, 66.
7. PEP *Report on the British Coal Industry* (1936) pp 42, 49, 53, 56, 51; there was

no great change in concentration between the mid-thirties and nationalization (PEP *The British Fuel and Power Industries* (1947) p 268).

8. PEP *Report on the Gas Industry* (1939) p 48.

9. Acton Society Trust *Patterns of Organization* p 27, Cmd 9672 p 36.

10. SCNI/GI p 10.

11. NCB/ACO pp 4, 35, 41, 49.

12. GC 1950–51 pp 48, 49; West Midlands Gas Board 1949–50 p 3; Wales Gas Board 1949–50 p 10; London Electricity Board 1948–9 p 2; North Western Electricity Board 1948–9 p 6; South Wales Electricity Board 1948–9 p 7.

13. East Midlands Gas Board 1949–50 p 2; GC 1952–3 p 57.

14. NCB 1947 pp 6, 7.

15. NCB/ACO pp 39, 46; W. W. Haynes *Nationalization in Practice* (1953) p 291.

16. *Oxford Economic Papers* 1953 p 99.

17. Acton Society Trust *Management under Nationalization* p 46; see also p 39.

18. BTC 1950 pp 142, 143.

19. Acton Society Trust *Management under Nationalization* pp 39, 40, 42, 43, 60; W. W. Haynes *op cit* p 307.

20. Ministry of Fuel and Power *Electricity Supply 1947–48 Return of Engineering and Financial Statistics* p xxii; Cmd 6699 p 13.

21. Acton Society Trust *op cit* pp 31–35; SCNI/GI p 10.

22. A. J. Pearson *The Railways and the Nation* (1964) pp 62, 64, 65, 68.

23. MPSD 1961 p 24.

24. OEEC *Industrial Statistics 1900–57* p 27.

25. W. W. Haynes *op cit* pp 363–4; but see pp 367, 368.

26. NCB 1948 pp 98, 99, 1949 p 106, 1951 p 84.

27. NCB/ACO p 24.

28. MPSD 1966 p 156; information from CSO.

29. MPSD 1967 p 174.

30. Information from GC.

31. GC 1952–3 p 19.

32. BTC 1948 p 100, 1951 p 47.

33. P. E. Hart *Journal of Industrial Economics* 1953–4 p 55 for the first part of the quotation, pp 56, 57 for the second part.

34. K. F. Glover & D. N. Miller *Journal of the Royal Statistical Society Series A* 1954 pp 298, 301, 308, 310; Ministry of Transport *The Transport of Goods by Road* 1958 pp 9, 14.

35. P. E. Hart *op cit* pp 51, 52.

36. *The Economist* 25 November 1950 p 899.

37. P. E. Hart *Journal of Industrial Economics* 1957–8 p 62; Gilbert Walker *Oxford Economic Papers* 1953 p 100.

38. *A Report on Traffic, Costs, and Changes of Freight Transport in Great Britain* (unpublished) p 190.

39. Gilbert Walker *Road and Rail* (1947 2nd ed) pp 103–6; *Oxford Economic Papers* 1953 p 105; G. W. Quick Smith BTR 1952 pp 200–6, *Large Scale Operations in Road Haulage*. A paper presented to the Scottish Section of the Institute of Transport in Edinburgh 22 January 1958 (unpublished) pp 7, 8.

40. C. Y. Hardie BTR 1953 pp 327–30; BTC 1956 p 47.

41. S. E. Finer *Anonymous Empire* (1958) pp 49, 71.

42. NCB/ACO p 2.

43. SCNI/GI p 10.

44. Cmd 9672 p 36; on BRS see also Gilbert Walker *Oxford Economic Papers* 1953 pp 99, 100.

45. See, for instance, Acton Society *Patterns of Organization* pp 23–26; *The Future of Nationalization* (1953) pp 170, 191–6.

46. *Patterns of Organization* pp 25, 26; *Management under Nationalization* pp. 9, 74.

47. *Management under Nationalization* p 8.

48. *Patterns of Organization* p 26.

49. *Management under Nationalization* pp 78, 79.

50. *Ibid* pp 23, 24; my italics.

51. *Ibid* pp 17, 18.

52. NCB/ACO p 64.

53. Acton Society *Management under Nationalization* p 36; for BRS see pp 43, 46, 47.

54. *Ibid* pp 21, 23.

55. *Ibid* pp 37, 48.

56. *Ibid* pp 28, 30, 31, 33.

Chapter 3: *Stagnation*

1. See pp 217, 218, 238–40, 243–8.

2. *Second Report of the Road Haulage Disposal Board* p 2; BTC 1954 and 1956.2 p 141.

3. BTC 1957 p 71; BRS 1957 p 1.

4. See BTC 1956 p 75.

5. Figures for the parcels service are not available before 1955. But if it is assumed that its mileage and employment were about the same in 1953 as in 1955 it appears that the number of capacity ton miles per worker declined by about 5 per cent in the rest of the undertaking between 1953 and 1956 (Information from BRS etc.).

6. S. E. Raymond BTR 1955 pp 566, 568.

7. Table 3; BTC 2 Statements VIII–3, X–14.

8. BTC 1950 pp 77, 78, 134–6, 205, 1952 p 18.

9. See pp 24, 28–30.

10. BTC 1952 pp 176, 177, 1953.2 pp 32, 33, 1954 p 73,.2 pp 32, 33.

11. Tables 21, 22; BTC 1956.2 p 85.

12. BTC 1955 p 80.

13. BTC 1953.2 pp 82–84, 1956 p 85,.2 pp 82–84.

14. BTC 1954.2 p 52; *BRS (Parcels) Limited Prospectus* para 10.

15. Major-General G. N. Russell BTR 1950 p 55; BTC 1952 p 93.

16. BTR 1956 p 113.

17. NCB 1957 p 25.

18. NCB 1958 pp 12, 19.

19. Cmd 6610 p 138.

20. NCB/ACO pp 23, 24, 38, 45, 64.

21. R. J. S. Baker *The Management of Capital Projects* (1962) pp 58–61, 65, 66; NCB 1956 p 20.

22. NCB/PFC p 63; NCB 1951 pp 23, 24, 1954 p 39, 1956 pp 51, 58, 1959 p 23, 1960 p 19; Ministry of Fuel and Power and British Intelligence Objectives Sub-Committee *Technical Report on the Ruhr Coalfield*. 3 Appendix 13 p 3.

23. NCB 1948 pp 15, 16; NCB/PFC pp 62, 63.

24. See p 67.

25. H. H. Wilson and R. B. Dunn *Minutes of Proceedings of the National Association of Colliery Managers* 1958 pp 14, 17; NCB 1955 pp 22–24, 1958 p 13.

26. *Lloyds Bank Review* January 1951 pp 42, 43; NCB 1955 pp 23, 24.

27. C. A. Roberts in *National Coal Board: The First Ten Years* (1956) edited G. Nott-Bower and R. H. Walkerdine, p 14; NCB/ACO pp 20–22, 57–71.

28. Cmd 7647 p 51; BTC 1949 p 19, 1951 p 1, 1952 p 3; information from CSO; P. Redfern *Journal of the Royal Statistical Society Series* A 1955 p 160.

29. BTC 1958.2 p 202.

30. BTC Statement V-8, 1954.2 p 140.

31. BTC Statement VII-1, 1949 p 84, 1952 p 88, 1953 p 37, 1954 p 36, 1956 p 36.

32. BTC 1949 p 83, 1950 p 113, 1952 p 87, 1954 p 35.

33. Board of Trade *Census of Production*. 3 Trade L 1951 Table 8, 1954 Table 5(A); BTC Statement VII-1; BTC/MBR pp 16, 18, 20; BTC/RM p 33.

34. E. S. Cox *British Railways Standard Steam Locomotives* (1966) pp 16, 30; Cmd 8647 pp 5–7; A. J. Pearson *Man of the Rail* (1967) p 111.

35. *Journal of the Institute of Transport* 1948–50 p 233; E. S. Cox *Locomotive Panorama* (1966). 2 pp 2, 28.

36. E. S. Cox *ibid.* 2 pp 2, 114, 117, 120.

37. *Ibid.* 2 pp 1, 2.

38. PEP *Locomotives : A Report on the Industry* (1951) pp 10, 11; A. J. Pearson *Man of the Rail* p 110–12, *The Railways and the Nation* (1964) pp 66, 67; G. F. Allen *British Railways Today and Tomorrow* (1959) p 25; SCNI/BR Q 1127.

39. Letter to Author; see also his remarks at Institute of Transport 21 November 1949.

40. Ministry of Transport *Transport Services in the Highlands and Islands* p 22, 23; R. Brady *Crisis in Britain* (1950) pp 264, 265.

41. H. C. Johnson BTR 1955 pp 289–92; see p 242.

42. BTC 1949 pp 344, 373, 1958.2 p 211.

43. BTC 1949 p 379, 1958.2 p 217; Stewart Joy *The Variability of Railway Track Costs and their Implications for Policy, with Special Reference to Great Britain* (unpublished University of London Thesis 1964) p 215.

44. Sir Cyril Hurcomb *Transactions of the Manchester Statistical Society* 29 March 1950 pp 14, 15.

45. BTC/MBR 21, 22; G. F. Allen *British Railways Today and Tomorrow* pp 105–7, *British Rail After Beeching* (1966) pp 242, 243.

46. C. D. Foster *The Transport Problem* (1963) pp 72–75; D. H. Aldcroft *British Railways in Transition* (1968) pp 61–67; BTC 1950 p 71, 1951 pp 71–75; SCNI/BR p 449.

47. BTC 1949 pp 62, 90, 373, 1950 pp 112, 1952 p 74, 1954.2 p 196, 1958.2 p 211; EA 1951–2 pp 41, 42; CEA 1956–7 p 42; S. E. Parkhouse *Journal of the Institute of Transport* 1951 pp 215, 216.

48. BTC 1951 p 9, 1956.2 p 149; SCNI/BR p 390.

49. BTC 1953 p 9.

50. *Transactions of the Manchester Statistical Society* 29 March 1950 pp 20, 23–25.

51. BTC *Integration of Freight Services by Road and Rail: A Statement of Policy* pp 5, 6.

52. BTC 1951 pp 4, 5, 1952 p 8.

53. *A Report on Traffic, Costs, and Charges of Freight Transport in Great Britain* pp 173, 229.

54. *Ibid* p 201.

55. *Ibid* pp 203, 204.

56. *Ibid* p 218.

57. *Ibid* p 215.

58. *Transactions of the Manchester Statistical Society* 29 March 1950 pp 14, 15.
59. J. R. Sargent *British Transport Policy* (1958) pp 49–58; BTC 1952 p 57.
60. BTC 1953 pp 8, 9, 1955 p 7, 1956 p 11; Sargent *op cit* pp 40–48, 59–61.
61. See pp 217, 218, 237–48.
62. Letter to author.
63. BTC 1953 p ix; A. J. Pearson *The Railways and the Nation* pp 74, 75.

Chapter 4: *1958–68 : The Productivity Decade*

1. See pp 36, 37.
2. See p 105.
3. AAS 1963 p 105, 1969 p 121.
4. GC *Investment in Natural Gas* p 11; SCNI/CB pp 68–70,.2 p 479; MPSD 1968–9 p. 41.
5. EC 1968–9 p 3.
6. See pp 81, 82.
7. Information from BEA and BOAC.
8. Cmnd 3470 p 26; information from BR and Freightliners Ltd.
9. See p 85.
10. Cmnd 2873 p 21.
11. Statistical information from NCB; E. H. Sealy *The Mining Engineer* January 1963 p 357.
12. BRB/RBR pp 52, 53; Table 5.
13. BRB/RBR pp 8, 9, 19; BRB 1963.2 pp 20, 53, 1967 p 2, 1968 p 109.
14. See pp 413–19.
15. International Civil Aviation Organization (henceforth ICAO) *Digest of Statistics* 99, 137, 142; BEA 1958–9 Appendix 8 and 14, 1968–9 Appendix 10; SCNI/BOAC.2 p 236; BOAC 1967–8 p 25; information from BOAC.
16. BTC 1958.2 p 169; the supporting workers comprised cleaners, coalmen, fire-droppers and steamraisers.
17. P. L. Cook *Railway Workshops : the Problems of Contraction* (1964) p 23.
18. EC 1958–9 p 32; CEGB *Statistical Year Book* 1969 Tables 6 and 8.
19. Sir Ronald Edwards *Lloyds Bank Review* July 1967 p 12; EC *Handbook of Electricity Supply Statistics* 1969 p 93; R. D. V. Roberts *British Journal of Industrial Relations* 1967 p 56.
20. Information from NCB; NCB 1967–8 p 10,.2 p 86.
21. *National Provincial Bank Review* August 1966 p 6.
22. ECSC *Eleventh General Report* p 523; NCB 1967–8 p 10,.2 p 91.
23. ICAO *Digest of Statistics* 99, 137, 142; BEA 1958–9 Appendix 14; SCNI/BOAC.2 p 236; information from BOAC.
24. BTC 1958.2 pp 158, 169; BRB 1967 p 101, 1968 p 112.
25. AAS 1967 p 203, 1969 p 218.
26. Cmd 6610 p 50; M. Heinemann *Britain's Coal* (1944) p 89; W. H. B. Court *Coal* (1951) pp 277–80; R. F. Lansdown and F. W. Wood in *National Coal Board: The First Ten Years* edited Sir Guy Nott-Bower and R. H. Walkerdine pp 42, 43; NCB 1948 p 16, 1949 pp 57, 58, 1955 pp 23, 24.
27. See p 41.
28. ECSC *11th General Report* p 247, *15th General Report* p 95; NCB 1966–7.2 p 115, 1968–9.2 p 84.

29. R. F. Lansdown and F. W. Wood *op cit* pp 39, 41; information from NCB.

30. NCB 1967–8 p 10; information from European Communities Information Service.

31. GC 1954–5 pp 7, 8, 1956–7 p 7, 1958–9 p 4; SCNI/GI.2 p 605; PEP *A Fuel Policy for Britain* (1966) p 71.

32. SCNI/GI pp 66, 67; PEP *A Fuel Policy for Britain* p 72.

33. GC *Gas Goes Ahead* pp 14, 15, *Catalytic Rich Gas Process* pp 1, 5; information from West Midlands Gas Board.

34. GC 1968–9 p 132.

35. G. F. Allen *British Rail After Beeching* (1966) pp 6–10; BTC/RM p 9; Cmd 9880 p 15.

36. German Federal Railway *Zahlen von der Deutchen Bundesbahn* 1969 p 10; French National Railways *Activité et Productivité de la SNCF en 1967* p 8; Swiss Federal Railways *The Swiss Federal Railways Move with the Times* p 5; BRB 1967 pp 41, 99, 1968 p 40; International Union of Railways *International Railway Statistics* 1967 Table 1–11.

37. G. F. Allen *British Rail After Beeching* p 45; BRB 1966 p 38, 1967 p 41; *Eastern Rail News* August 1966.

38. *International Railway Statistics* Table 2–111; BRB 1968 p 2.

39. See pp 183, 184, 316.

40. Cmd 9880 p 36; Cmnd 813 p 50; SCNI/BR Q 1129, 1130, 1565–71; G. F. Allen *op cit* pp 252, 253; BTC 1959 p 85, 1961 p 32, 1962.2 p 126; BRB 1968 pp 13, 108; *Rail News* October 1969.

41. BTC 1958.2 p 134; BRB 1968 p 108; *International Railway Statistics* 1967 Table 1–32, average for Germany, France and Italy.

42. Cmd 2600 pp 101–3; Cmd 3420 pp 7, 11; BTC 1948 p 318; S. E. Parkhouse *Journal of the Institute of Transport* 1951 pp 213–15; NCB 1952 pp 37, 38.

43. Cmd 9880 pp 35, 36; Cmd 3420 p 40; see pp 243–5.

44. BTC/MBR pp 24, 25; BR *Facts and Figures about British Rail* 1966 p 7; BRB 1967 p 40.

45. Information from BRB; DB *A World on Rails* p 42; *Modern Transport* December 1967 p 54.

46. Information from BRB; BTC/RBR pp 30, 34, 35; G. F. Allen *op cit* pp 263, 264; see pp 213, 219.

47. A. J. Pearson *Man of the Rail* p 185.

48. G. F. Allen *op cit* pp 282–4; National Economic Development Office *Through Transport to Europe* pp 58, 59.

49. G. F. Allen *op cit* pp 281, 284, 285; BRB/RBR p 148; Royal Commission on Trade Unions and Employers' Associations *Minutes of Evidence* Q 2518; BRB 1963 p 12, 1965 pp 5, 50, 1967 p 30, 1968 pp 13, 105: British Rail *Freightliner: A New Transport System for Modern Industry* p 4; information from Freightliners Ltd.

50. G. F. Allen *op cit* p 282; *Modern Railways* April 1968 p 180; SNCF *The Railways of France* pp 100, 101.

51. BRB 1966 p 9; Federal Power Commission 1964 p 48, *National Power Survey* p 59; *Rail News* October 1969.

52. See pp 148–55.

53. See pp 381–7.

54. Cmnd 4018 p 20.

55. *Financial Times* 8 November 1968; for the financial consequences of flying British see Chapter 12.

56. NCB 1956 p 56, 1960 p 15, 1963–4 p 17, 1967–8 p 13; H. E. Collins *Mechanization and Automation in the British Coal Industry* Paper 125 7th World Power Conference 1968 pp 4–6; information from NCB.
57. *Financial Times* 2 November 1968.

Chapter 5: *Productivity Bargaining and Labour Relations*

1. Cmnd 3627 pp 50, 80, 81.
2. SCNI/BR pp lxv, lxvi, Q 1503; BTC 1956 pp 14, 15, 1960 p 11, 1962 p 16; BRB 1963 p 40, 1964 p 40, 1965 p 44, 1967 p 38; Cmnd 2873 pp 11, 23.
3. BRB 1963 p 40, 1964 pp 40, 41.
4. George B. Baldwin *Beyond Nationalization* (1955) pp 174–6.
5. NCB 1967–8 pp 43, 44 etc.; for other benefits from the abolition of piece work see Cmnd 2919 p 14.
6. NCB 1956 p 60, 1957 p 20, 1959 p 19, 1960 p 16, 1963–4 p 16, 1967–8 p 12.
7. Royal Commission on Trade Unions and Employers' Associations *Research Papers* 4 p 22; SCNI/BOAC.2Q 589–91.
8. Cmnd 3924 pp 22–24; SCNI/GI.2 pp 498, 502, Q2139 but see also Q1982–4; W. R. Branson *Institution of Gas Engineers Publication 626* pp 4, 5.
9. Cmnd 3726 pp 2–7.
10. Cmnd 3848 pp 9, 10 and 3868 p 9.
11. Cmnd 3311 p 1.
12. BRS 1957 pp 1, 2; BTC 1960 p 17.
13. Cmnd 3311 pp 49, 50.
14. Cmnd 2695 pp 11, 12; Cmnd 3847 p 23.
15. Cmnd 2361 pp 32, 51.
16. Sir Ronald Edwards *An Experiment in Industrial Relations* (EC) pp 6, 9, 32–7.
17. BEA 1964–5 p 37; Royal Commission on Trade Unions and Employers' Associations *Research Paper 4* pp 16, 20. *British Journal of Industrial Relations* 1965 p 399.
18. ASLEF *Productivity Payments for Footplate Staff* p 15.
19. Cmnd 2779 pp 17, 22.
20. BRB 1966 and 1967 p 30; *British Journal of Industrial Relations* 1968 p 389; *Economist* 17 August 1968 pp 50, 51; *Financial Times* 15 and 16 August 1968.
21. Cmnd 3498 pp 52–53.
22. SCNI/LT.2 pp 351, 352.
23. *Financial Times* 16 and 22 July 1968.
24. Sir Ronald Edwards *op cit* pp 13, 14; R. D. V. Roberts *British Journal of Industrial Relations* 1967 p 56.
25. MPSD 1963 p 109, 1965 p 125, 1967 p 151; MLG/EPG.
26. Information from BRS; BRS 1957 p 1; THC 1967 pp 13, 15, 17, 19; MLG/EPG.
27. LTB 1965 p 62, 1968 p 74; Ministry of Transport *Passenger Transport in Great Britain* 1967 p 62; *Financial Times* 22 July 1968.
28. Cmnd 2873 p 41; BRB 1968 pp 100, 112; *Economist* 17 August 1968 p 52.
29. *Economist* 17 August 1968 p 52.
30. BRB 1966 p 30; *Financial Times* 16 August 1968.
31. Cmnd 3311 pp 19, 20, 61; but see Sir Ronald Edwards *An Experiment in Industrial Relations* p 16.
32. There is very little evidence of any type about the outcome of the airways'

bargains but for the failure of one minor productivity deal, if such it can be called, see SCNI/BEA pp li, lxiii, lxiv, Q1125.

33. Cmnd 3426 pp 15, 21, 22; Cmnd 2779 p 17; BRB 1965 p 39.

34. See Cmnd 3311 p 19 for the electricity industry's caution.

35. Cmnd 2873 p 21; BRB 1968 pp 13, 112.

36. *Source-Book on Restrictive Practices in Britain* edited Graham Hutton p 24.

37. R. D. V. Roberts *British Journal of Industrial Relations* 1967 pp 56, 57; Cmnd 3311 pp 59, 60.

38. MLG/EPG; Cmnd 3230 p 27; Royal Commission on Trade Unions and Employers' Associations *Minutes of Evidence* Q 1789.

39. Richard E. Caves and Associates *Britain's Economic Prospects* (1968) p 369.

40. Cmnd 3311 p 36; Royal Commission on Trade Unions and Employers' Associations *Research Papers 4* pp 30, 31.

41. See p 82.

42. BRS 1957 p 1.

43. C. Kerr and A. Siegel in *Industrial Conflict* edited A. Kornhauser, R. Dubin, A. M. Ross (1954) p 190.

44. L. J. Handy *British Journal of Industrial Relations* 1968 pp 49, 50.

45. NCB 1957 p 48, 1968–9 p 37.

46. A. I. Marsh and W. E. J. McCarthy Royal Commission on Trade Unions and Employers' Associations *Research Papers 2*, Part 2 p 82; G. Baldwin *op cit* pp 172–4.

47. E. Wigham *What's Wrong with the Unions?* (1961) pp 97–99; H. A. Turner, G. Clack, G. Roberts *Labour Relations in the Motor Industry* (1967) Chapter V, pp 331–5.

48. Cmnd 3623 pp 36, 262, 263.

49. H. A. Turner *The Trend of Strikes* (1963) pp 9, 10; E. H. Phelps Brown *The Economics of Labour* (1962) pp 169, 170.

50. Cmnd 3623 pp 338, 339; *Report of the Railway Pay Committee of Inquiry* p 18.

51. Cmnd 2873 p 9.

52. SCNI/BR p 435, 445.

53. MPSD 1968–9 p 39; information from NCB.

54. NCB 1962 p 27.

55. Ministry of Labour *Dismissal Procedures: Report of a Committee of the National Joint Advisory Council on Dismissal Procedures* pp 3, 6, 7, 10–13.

56. Ministry of Labour *Sick Pay Schemes: Report of a Committee of the National Joint Advisory Council* pp 5, 6; DEP *Labour Costs in Great Britain in 1964* p 20; information from DEP; the figure for the nationalized industries does not cover BRS or the buses; Gerald Rhodes *Public Sector Pensions* (1965) pp 260, 271, 286, 287; NIE 1969 p 15 for private sector employment less self employed from AAS 1967 p 109.

57. *The Lorry Driver* (1968) pp 118–35, 212–13, 237, 239.

58. *British Journal of Industrial Relations* 1967 p 62.

59. *Industrial Relations* 1966–7 pp 100, 110.

60. Cmnd 3924 p 24.

61. *An Experiment in Industrial Relations* p 11.

62. BRB 1968 p 44; *Financial Times* 16 August 1968; information from Mr Neal.

Chapter 6: *Productivity in Perspective*

1. See pp 60–62.

2. W. E. G. Salter *Productivity and Technical Change* (1966 edition) p 206.

3. Calculated from H/WA 8 June 1967.

4. W. E. G. Salter *op cit* pp 201–05.

5. W. Beckerman in *Economic Growth in Britain* edited P. D. Henderson (1966) pp 70, 71.

6. Henceforth all calculations exclude coal.

7. *Economic Journal* 1960 p 29.

8. *Transactions of the Manchester Statistical Society* November 1964 pp 19, 20.

9. A. W. Stonier and D. C. Hague *A Textbook of Economic Theory* chap. 11.

10. But see pp 190–9.

11. *Economic Journal* 1960 pp 20, 21.

12. Coal wages, salaries, national insurance contributions and concessionary coal from MPSD 1960 pp 33, 35 and other staff expenses from NCB 1958.2 p 30; electricity wages and salaries from MPSD 1960 p 85 and other staff expenses from EC 1958–9 p 75; gas wages and salaries from *Census of Production* 1958 and other staff expenses from GC 1958–9 p 159; information on British Rail from BRB and net output calculations for London Transport Railways; air corporations from BEA 1958–9 Statement B and BOAC 1957–8 p 31–36, 1958–9 pp 47–53; manufacturing from NIE 1969 pp 21, 23.

13. For gas holders and most production plant the annual capacity figures (MPSD 1968–9 p 106) were multiplied by the cost per unit of capacity in 1958 (SCNI/GI.2 p 601). For oil-based plant expenditure was converted to 1958 prices and accumulated. For mains Dr Feinstein's estimate of the gross capital stock in 1938 was converted to 1958 prices (*Domestic Capital Formation in the United Kingdom 1920–1938* (1965) p 94; P. Redfern *Journal of the Royal Statistical Society* Series A 1955 p 171). Investment in mains at 1958 prices was added year by year and an estimate mains scrapped was deducted. Similarly Feinstein's estimate for the railways' permanent way and buildings was converted to 1958 prices (C. H. Feinstein *op cit* p 150; Redfern *op cit* p 171); new investment at 1958 prices was added (BTC Statement V–10; NIE 1962 p 58); and the estimated value of lines closed was subtracted. The latter was obtained by multiplying the mileage (BRB Statement 5–D) by an estimate of the replacement cost per mile based on the original cost of branch lines closed in 1958 (SCNI/BR p 388; P. Redfern *op cit* p 170). For rolling stock the railways publish the original cost of the assets in use (BTC Statement V–8; BRB Statement 3–A). As this is the cumulative total of past investment the age structure of their assets was calculated from statistics of rail investment (B. R. Mitchell *The Journal of Economic History* (1964) p 336; C. H. Feinstein *op cit* p 150) and was then converted to 1958 prices (P. Redfern *op cit* pp 170, 171). *Note:* This is only a summary description of the way in which the calculations were made.

14. Manufacturing profits and stocks from NIE 1969 pp 21, 39, 78; net fixed assets and depreciation from CSO.

15. AAS 1969 Tables 136, 144, 242, etc.; MLG/EPG for hours.

16. Information from British Electric Traction; BTC 1958.2 pp 160, 161, 1962.2 p 205; THC 1967 p 81.

17. *Census of Production* 1935 Part 4, Section 4 pp 5, 6.

18. Pre-war rail productivity was calculated from R. Stone and D. A. Rowe *The Measurement of Consumers' Expenditure and Behaviour in the United Kingdom 1920– 1938.*2 pp 63, 64, 71; Ministry of Transport *Railway Returns* and *Return of Staff Employed by the Railway Companies.* A production index with 1935 revenue weights and comprising six indicators was constructed.

19. MPSD 1956 p 22, 1968–9 p 41.

20. W. E. G. Salter *Productivity and Technical Change* p 183.

21. MPSD 1965 pp 115, 139, 148; *Census of Production* 1935 Part 4, Section 4 p 6.

22. C. H. Feinstein *Domestic Capital Formation in the United Kingdom 1920–1938* (1965) pp 83, 90, 91, 95, 103, 134, 151; for wages, salaries and employers' contributions see A. Chapman *Wages and Salaries in the United Kingdom 1920–1938* (1953) pp 67, 68, 72, 100–03, 143, 144, 242. The production series were the same as those used for the labour productivity calculations except that manufacturing output was taken from K. S. Lomax *Journal of the Royal Statistical Society Series A* 1959 p 192.

23. These figures differ from those given in Table 9 because coal output has been measured, as for pre-war, by its tonnage and because no deduction has been made from the capital stock in respect of colliery closures because Feinstein did not make one.

24. C. H. Feinstein *London and Cambridge Economic Bulletin* December 1963 Table 3; the figures for 1948–68 are higher than those in Table 7 because they were calculated by dividing manufacturing output by man hours rather than by the method described on p 20.

25. *Transactions of the Manchester Statistical Society* November 1964 p 14.

26. See pp 363–5.

27. Cmd 6610 especially pp 13, 14, 32, 33, 67–69, 76–79, 96.

28. L. Lister *Europe's Coal and Steel Community* (1960) p 453; MPSD 1957 p 20; Cmd 6610 p 141; Cmd 2600 pp 127, 128.

29. UN/ECE *Quarterly Bulletin of Coal Statistics for Europe* 1957.4 p 8; OEEC *Energy Statistics 1900–55* p 27.

30. See p 39.

31. Ministry of Transport *Report of the Committee on Main Line Railway Electrification* 1931 pp 17–23.

32. G. F. Allen *British Railways Today and Tomorrow* pp 20–24.

33. Cmd 2600 pp 97, 100, 101.

Chapter 7: *International Productivity Comparisons for Fuel and Power*

1. *The Future of Steel* Institute of Economic Affairs Occasional Paper 6 pp 16, 17.

2. UN/ECE *Concentration Indices in the European Coal Industry* 1968 pp 5, 6.

3. EEC *Energy Statistics Yearbook* 1966 p 68, *Energy Statistics* 1969.2 p 40; ECSC *Eleventh General Report* 1962–3 p 255.

4. UN/ECE *Economic Bulletin for Europe*.3 1949 p 16; EEC *Energy Statistics Yearbook* 1966 p 68; ECSC *Thirteenth General Report* p 354; OEEC *Report on the Progress of Western European Recovery* 1949 p 23, *Industrial Statistics 1900–1955* p 31.

5. OEEC *Report on the Progress of Western European Recovery* p 23.

6. *Economic Bulletin for Europe*.3 1949, p 16.

7. UN/ECE *Quarterly Bulletin of Coal Statistics for Europe* 1952.4 p 8.

8. W. C. Baum also noted it in his *French Economy and the State* (1958) p 195.

9. Table 10; UN/ECE *Quarterly Bulletin of Coal Statistics for Europe* 1957.4 p 6, 1959.4 p 6.

10. UN/ECE *Capital Formation and Costs of Production in the European Coal Industry* 1962 Tables 7, 8; Baum *op cit* p 192; L. Lister *Europe's Coal and Steel Community* p 114.

11. A. Hellemans *Minutes of Proceedings of the National Association of Colliery Managers* 1954–5 pp 19, 20; *Staatsmijnen in Limburg* 1955 p 8; G. J. Bakker and H. Le Clercq *Mining Engineer* 1961–2 p 623; UN/ECE *Concentration Indices in the European Coal Industry* 1964 and 1968 Table 2.

12. OEEC *Coal and European Economic Expansion* p 48; Hellemans *op cit* pp 19, 20.

13. Cd 2353 p 4; information from NCB.

14. SCNI/NCB p 165; A. M. Wandless in *Economic Aspects of Fuel and Power in British Industry* papers presented at a conference organized by the Manchester Joint Research Council 1958 p 57; information from NCB.

15. Ministry of Fuel and Power and British Intelligence Objectives Sub-Committee *Technical Report on the Ruhr Coalfield.*3 Appendix 8 p 2; Dr H. R. Sander *Mining Engineer* January 1965 p 243; the 1963 figures include the coalfields of Aachen and Lower Saxony but they are so small that this can have made little difference.

16. *Technical Report on the Ruhr Coalfield.*3 Appendix 8 p 2; UN/ECE/P p 34.

17. *Concentration Indices in the European Coal Industry* 1964 and 1968 Table 2; UN/ECE/P p 7; UN/ECE *Economic Survey of Europe in 1951* p 161.

18. Cmd 6610 pp 16, 17, 20, 24, 26; M. Farrell and R. Jolly *Journal of Industrial Economics* July 1963 p 205; H. R. Sander *Mining Engineer* 1964–5 p 243; H. M. Watkins *Coal and Men* (1935) pp 112–19; L. L. Van Praag *Minutes of Proceedings of the National Association of Colliery Managers* 1952 p 110; interview with D. N. Simpson of the NCB.

19. Henceforth all figures are for OMS underground unless otherwise stated.

20. Information from NCB.

21. Information from Dr H. R. Sander.

22. G. Armstrong and A. M. Clarke 'Exploration and Exploitation in British Coal-fields' in *Compte Rendu de Congrès 6e de Stratigraphie et de Geologie du Carbonifère* 1969.2; information from NCB.

23. Armstrong and Clarke *op cit*; information from NCB; A. Hellemans *Minutes of Proceedings of National Association of Colliery Managers* 1954–5 pp 19, 20.

24. Cmd 6610 p 30; W. W. Haynes *Nationalization in Practice* p 12.

25. UN/ECE/P pp 7, 14, 125; UN/ECE *Economic Survey of Europe in 1951* p 161; ECSC *Fourteenth General Report* p 120.

26. UN/ECE/P pp 14, 40; information from Mr A. M. Clarke and Mr D. N. Simpson of the NCB; see also D. H. A. Matthews *Mining Engineer* 1960–61 p 509.

27. UN/ECE/P pp 7, 20, 34, 46; information from NCB.

28. UN/ECE/P pp 17, 42; G. J. Bakker and H. Le Clercq *Mining Engineer* 1961–2 p 623.

29. Information from NCB; H. R. Sander *Mining Engineer* 1964–5 p 243; G. J. Bakker and H. Le Clercq *Mining Engineer* 1961–2 p 623; UN/ECE/P pp 7, 61, 71, 75.

30. UN/ECE/P pp 7, 19, 34, 40, 44, 94.

31. Cmd 6610 p 20; NCB *Training Schemes for Dutch Mineworkers* 1956 pp 2, 3.

32. UN/ECE/P p 17.

33. UN/ECE *Concentration Indices in the European Coal Industry* 1968 Table 2.

34. Cmd 6610 pp 16, 17.

35. H. R. Sander *Mining Engineer* 1964–5 p 243.

36. Ministry of Fuel and Power and British Intelligence Objectives Sub-Committee *Technical Report on the Ruhr Coalfield.*3 part 1 p 1.

37. *Concentration Indices in the European Coal Industry* 1968 Table 2.

38. Cmd. 6610 p 24.

39. *Coal Mining in Poland* Report by the Technical Mission of the National Coal Board 1958 pp 4, 5.

40. A. Zauberman *Industrial Progress in Poland, Czechoslovakia, and East Germany 1937–1962* (1964) p 132.

41. *Coal Mining in Czechoslovakia* Report by the National Coal Board Technical Delegation 1959 p 4.

References

487

42. UN/ECE/P pp 36–39; W. W. Haynes *Nationalization in Practice* p 5.

43. H. R. Sander *Mining Engineer* 1964–5 p 243.

44. MPSD 1967 p 81.

45. L. L. Van Praag *Minutes of Proceedings of the National Association of Colliery Managers* 1952 p 110.

46. Information from NCB and Dr H. R. Sander; NCB *International Coal Statistics* October 1969; EEC *Energy Statistics*; UN/ECE *Quarterly Bulletin of Coal Statistics for Europe*.4 1965 p 97; *Concentration Indices in the European Coal Industry* 1968 pp 4, 5. The German figure allows for the fact that a seven-hour shift is worked at hot faces. The published figures for the Campine and Czechoslovakia have been adjusted to an eight-hour shift. The Polish figure has been increased by the percentage by which the ECE's standardized figure for 1962 was above the published figure for that year.

47. *Journal of the Statistical Society* 1884 p 622.

48. *Times Business News* 20 June 1967.

49. *Investor's League Bulletin* (Special) June 1962 p 10.

50. Federal Power Commission *Statistics of Privately Owned Electric Utilities in the United States* 1966 p xvi.

51. Edison Electric Institute *Statistical Year Book* 1968 pp 31, 49; US Department of Labour *Monthly Labour Review* Table C I; MPSD 1967 pp 135, 153; MLG/EPG for British hours.

52. Anglo-American Council on Productivity *Electricity Supply* pp 55, 56, 59; Edison Electric Institute *Statistical Year Book* 1968 p 49; information from EC.

53. EC 1966–7 pp 142–5, 159.

54. Federal Power Commission *Statistics of Privately Owned Electric Utilities in the United States* 1966 Section IV; MPSD 1967 p 141; EC 1966–7 pp 142–5.

55. Federal Power Commission *Statistics of Privately Owned Electric Utilities in the United States* 1966 Sections IV and V for the basic figures for employees (18,175) and sales (26,264 million kWh); Mr F. R. Forte of the Electric Council of New England for the breakdown of the wage and salary bill which showed that 20·7 per cent was on construction and other accounts; EC 1966–7 pp 142–3 for sales by the selected Area Boards (65,446 million kWh including a small allowance for CEGB direct sales), pp 158, 159 for their employment (58,020), and their share by sales of CEGB employment (36,331), p 13 for the proportion (29 per cent) of the national wage and salary bill which was on capital, contracting, and retailing etc.

56. *Electric Utilities – Costs and Performance* (1961) pp 155–9, 164–6, 175–80; *Statistics of Privately Owned Electric Utilities in the United States* 1966 Section IV.

57. *Statistisches Jahrbuch für die Bundesrepublik Deutschland* 1969 p 229; MPSD 1968 –9 pp 114, 115; MLG/EPG for British hours; it was assumed that, excluding holidays, British workers worked for 48½ weeks per year.

58. *Electricity Supply in Western Germany* p 23.

59. Information from EC.

60. EDF 1967 pp 22, 67; *Statistiques Sociales* April 1969 Supplement p 87; MLG/EPG; SCNI/ES.3 p 252; information from EC.

61. *Financial Times* 16 July 1968; *Times Business News*, 7 July 1969; MPSD 1968–9 pp 114, 125 etc.

62. UNIPEDE *Economie Electrique*.3 1968; *Times Business News* 7 July 1969; MPSD 1968–9 p 125.

63. See pp 81, 82.

Chapter 8: *International Productivity Comparisons for Transport*

1. See D. L. Munby. *Bulletin of the Oxford University Institute of Statistics* 1962 p 139; *Activité et Productivité de la SNCF en 1967* p 30; Cmnd 3656 p 28.
2. Svenska Handelsbanken *Sweden's Economy 1960–4* p 33 or 34.
3. UN/ECE *Economic Survey of Europe in 1956* Chapter VI p 12, 13.
4. UN/ECE *Annual Bulletin of Transport Statistics for Europe* 1958 p 82, 1967 p 63; information from BR.
5. See p 71.
6. BTC 1959.2 p 261, 1960.2 p 269; BRB 1963.2 p 49, 1964.2 p 37, 1968 p 105; International Union of Railways *International Railway Statistics* Table 3–2.
7. G. F. Ray and R. E. Crum in National Institute *Economic Review* May 1963 p 33.
8. *Report of the Committee on Carriers' Licensing* p 34.
9. *Ibid* p 35; B. T. Baylis *European Transport* (1965) p 119; BRB 1968 p 105.
10. *Bulletin of the Oxford University Institute of Statistics* 1962 pp 138, 139.
11. The distribution of continental traffic by distance was calculated from information from SNCF and UN/ECE *Annual Bulletin of Transport Statistics for Europe* 1966 Table 11.
12. *Annual Bulletin of Transport Statistics for Europe* 1966 px; German Federal Railway *DB – A World on Rails* p 28.
13. *International Railway Statistics* 1966 Table 2–3; *DB–A World on Rails* p 62.
14. BRB/RBR p 23; BRB/MTR p 29; Ministry of Transport *Transport for Industry : Summary Report* p 53 and BRB 1966.2 p 39; information from British Rail. A revenue weight of £17·2 per ton was finally adopted on the assumption that in 1966 BR carried 4¼ million tons of part-load traffic.
15. BRB 1966.2 p 39; Cmnd 3470 p 25; information from BR; *DB–A World on Rails* p 28; *Activité et Productivité de la SNCF en 1967* p 29; *International Railway Statistics* 1966 Table 2–3.
16. BR's expenditure on freight vehicles and containers (BRB 1966.2 p 30) and an estimate of the running costs of freight trains, derived from their proportion of freight traction hours (pp 30, 40), was knocked off the total direct costs of freight transport (Cmnd 3439 p 63) to obtain terminal costs as a residual. The revenue which the continental railways forgo because of the traffic which they do not load or unload was then calculated from its tonnage and BR's average terminal costs per ton (*International Railway Statistics* 1966 Table 2–3).
17. *International Railway Statistics* 1960 p 159; information from German Federal Railway.
18. Employment for continental railways as shown in *International Railway Statistics* 1966 Table 1–4 cols 20, 23, 28 plus 4,300 for Italy (see 1966 p 138); plus 30,000 for France (see 1964 Table 1 – 4 col 29); plus, say, 10,000 for Germany (see 1960 p 159). Employment for BR is the average of the beginning and the end of 1966 i.e. 352,000 (BRB 1966.2 p 45); less motor drivers at 9,500 (BRB 1966.2 p 45) and for comparison with Germany and Italy an estimate of workers engaged on new rolling stock i.e. 7,000 (see H/WA 8 June 1967; BRB 1965 p 58, 1966 p 44).
19. BRB 1967 pp 86, 101.
20. *International Railway Statistics* 1967 Tables 1–31, 1–32, 2–2; rail output calculations for wagon-load traffic.
21. SCNI/BR pp 475, 481, 483; UN *Monthly Bulletin of Statistics* July 1965, July

1966, July 1967, Table 54; *Monthly Digest of Statistics* July 1965, July 1966, July 1967.

22. *International Railway Statistics* 1967 Tables 1–31, 1–32; G. F. Allen *British Rail after Beeching* p 366; see pp 72, 73.

23. See pp 243–5.

24. *National Provincial Bank Review* August 1968 p 5; BRB 1968 p 108; SCNI/MC.3 p 205.

25. BRB 1968 p 111; Table 14; *International Railway Statistics* 1967 Table 2–111.

26. *International Railway Statistics* 1967 Table 2–2; BRB 1968 p 104; BRB/RBR pp 8, 21; BRB/MTR p 36.

27. BRB 1967 pp 96, 99; *Annual Bulletin of Transport Statistics for Europe* 1967 Table 21; *International Railway Statistics* 1967 Table 2–111.

28. G. F. Allen *British Rail after Beeching* pp 165, 166, 170; *International Railway Statistics* 1967 Table 2–2.

29. *Activité et Productivité de la SNCF en 1967* pp 27, 33; SCNI/BR p 474.

30. Rail output calculations; *International Railway Statistics* 1967 Table 2–111; BRB/MTR p 36; BRB 1966 p 18, 1967 p 11; Stewart Joy *The Variability of Railway Track Costs and their implications for Policy with special reference to Great Britain* p 215.

31. See pp 47, 49.

32. BRB 1964 p 17, 1965 p 25, 1966 p 18, 1967 p 11, 1968 p 13 Statement 5B; *British Railways Yearbook* 1965 pp 32, 35; Stewart Joy *op cit* pp 240–47.

33. See pp 220, 221.

34. BRB 1968 p 111; Stewart Joy *Journal of Industrial Economics* 1964–5 pp 74–84, *The Variability of Railway Track Costs and their implications for Policy with special reference to Great Britain*.

35. Table 14; *Annual Bulletin of Transport Statistics for Europe* 1967 Table 21.

36. *International Railway Statistics* 1967 Tables 1–11 and 2–111; BRB 1967 p 96.

37. See pp 228–30.

38. See p 263–5.

39. See p 107.

40. *A Study of the Domestic Passenger Air Fare Structure* pp 37, 38, 97, 99.

41. ICAO *Digest of Statistics* 142.

42. ICAO *Digest of Statistics* 137 and 142.

43. Cmnd 4018 pp 24, 25.

44. OECD *Labour force statistics* 1957–68, *Industrial Production Historical Statistics* 1957–66, *Industrial Production Quarterly Supplement to Main Economic Indicators* 1969.4; UN *The Growth of World Industry* 1967.

45. Production and employment from EEC *Energy Statistics*; hours worked based on shifts worked per underground worker from UN/ECE *Quarterly Bulletin of Coal Statistics for Europe* and *Annual Bulletin of Coal Statistics for Europe*, allowing for changes in shift length from UN/ECE *Concentration Indices in the European Coal Industry* 1968 pp 5, 6.

46. See p 107.

47. Iron and Steel Institute *The Iron and Steel Industry of Japan* (1964) p 122; Erik Ruist in *Labour Productivity* edited J. T. Dunlop and V. P. Diatchenko (1963) p 172; A. Silberston and C. F. Pratten *Bulletin of the Oxford University Institute of Economics and Statistics* 1967 pp 378, 379.

48. Netherlands Central Bureau of Statistics *Statistical Studies No. 18, January 1966, Comparisons of Labour Productivity in the United Kingdom and the Netherlands* 1958 Table 5.

49. A. Maddison, Royal Commission on Trade Unions and Employers' Associations *Selected Written Evidence* p 644.

50. L. Rostas *Comparative Productivity in British and American Industry* (1948) p 59; M. Frankel *British and American Manufacturing Productivity* (1957) pp 64–69.

51. Source as for Table 17.

PART TWO: FINANCES

Chapter 9: *Prices, Wages and Profits*

1. eg MLG/EPG March 1970 p 267; *Monthly Digest of Statistics* March 1970 p 139.

2. The necessary revenue figures were mainly taken from Annual Reports and the MPSD e.g. MPSD 1968–9 pp 157, 160, 163; BRB 1968 p 79; LTB 1968 pp 62, 63; THC 1968 pp 73, 83. Index for all goods and services estimated from NIE 1968 Tables 11, 12, 14, 15 etc.

3. See p 209.

4. *Report on Nationalization* 1958 p 17.

5. MLG September 1958 for electricity, gas and airways and also for coal earnings. Adult male workers in coal calculated from NCB 1958.2 pp 129, 136, 137. Rail figures from BTC *Annual Census of Staff* 1958.

6. Cmnd 827 p 219.

7. H/WA 17 June 1964 cols 193–8.

8. Conservative and Unionist Central Office *The Campaign Guide 1964* p 77.

9. P. E. Hart *Journal of Industrial Economics* 1953–4 pp 55, 56.

10. Henceforth the nationalized industries' surpluses before interest will be referred to as their profits.

11. BOAC 1968–9 p 3.

12. BOAC 1957–8 p 12, 1958–9 p 13, 1959–60 p 11, 1961–2 pp 28, 113, 1963–4 p 65, 1964–5 p 79; SCNI/BOAC.2 p 302.

13. BOAC statement B 2 (i) etc.

14. NCB 1947 pp 10, 11, 122–4.

15. See p 37.

16. BTC 1958 p 78; SCNI/LT.2 pp 382, 384.

17. BRB 1968 pp 71, 79.

18. G. F. Fiennes *I Tried to Run a Railway* (1967) p 110; information from Mr Fiennes.

19. Information from Mr Fiennes; SCNI/BR pp xiv, xv, 490, Q305.

20. Interview with Lord Beeching (who stresses electrification) 12 March 1969; BTC/MTR p 74; G. F. Fiennes *op cit* pp 93, 94, 104, 105, 110, 130, 131; Stewart Joy *The Variability of Railway Track Costs and their Implications for Policy with Special Reference to Great Britain* pp 111–20, 125, 126.

21. BRB 1967 p 96.

22. Cmnd 3439 p 63; BRB/RBR pp 20, 37, 87.

23. Cmnd 3439 p 63; BRB/RBR p 20.

24. GC 1948–50 p 61; NCB 1967–8.2 p 28; EC 1966–7 p 59.

25. BTC 1950 pp 240, 244, 245; H 30 April 1951 col. 860; NCB 1948 p 142; see pp 192, 193.

26. Cmnd 1337 p 5.

27. Federation of British Industries *Report on Nationalization* pp 15, 16; F. Cassell

and J. Hughes in *Nationalization* edited A. H. Hanson (1963) pp 221, 269, 270; NIE 1969 pp 73, 102.

28. R. Maurice *National Accounts Statistics: Sources and Methods* (1968) p 383.

29. SCNI/ES.3 p 192.

30. Cmd 9672 p 88; EA 1954–5 pp 123, 131; information from EC in response to a Parliamentary question.

31. SCNI/ES.3 p 28; see pp 195, 384.

32. SCNI/GI.2 p 555.

33. Cmnd 2862 p 4; GC 1961–2 pp 125, 127, 1962–3 pp 109, 111, 113, 115, 117, 129; SCNI/MC.3 p 58.

34. Cmnd 3924 p 64.

35. Information from BEA and BOAC.

36. NIE 1969 p 67.

37. See p 249; BRB 1968 p 108; SCNI/MC. 3 p 205; *Modern Railways* 1969 p 285.

38. Depreciation charges were calculated from the Report's estimate (p 43) of expenditure on depots, road and rail vehicles and containers with BRB 1963.2 p 14. These were converted to 1967 prices with the official price index for fixed assets (NIE 1968 p 20) and divided by the Reports' middle estimate of freightliner traffic in 1973. Actual depreciation on freight trains included that on road and rail freight vehicles, containers, marshalling yards and half of the figure for locomotives (BRB 1967 pp 77, 79, 96).

39. Cmnd 2919 p 9; NBC 1969 p 11.

40. Monopolies Commission *Colour Film* pp 134, 135.

41. *Ibid* pp 63, 65; Monopolies Commission *Report on the Supply of Chemical Fertilizers* pp 149, 150, 154; *Report on the Supply of Certain Industrial and Medical Gases* pp 60, 61.

42. W. B. Reddaway *Effects of UK Direct Investment Overseas: An Interim Report* (1967) pp 53, 54.

43. Cmnd 3437 p 18 H/WA 17 March 1970 col 84.

44. SCNI/ES.3 p 337; Cmnd 3437 p 18; H/WA 8 June 1967.

45. *Sunday Times* 10 May 1970.

46. *Economic Journal* 1965 pp 66–80.

47. See, however, A. J. Merrett and A. Sykes *The Banker* April 1962 p 230.

48. Cmnd 1337 p 15.

49. C. H. Feinstein *Domestic Capital Formation in the United Kingdom 1920–1938* p 81; NCB 1954 p 93, 1956.2 p 45.

50. C. H. Feinstein *op cit* p 82; information from CSO.

51. NCB 1968–9.2 p 26.

52. BTC.2 Statements V–4, VI–4; THC 1967 pp 64, 71 etc.

53. BTC.2 Statements V–4, VI–3; THC 1967 pp 64, 68 etc.

54. See column 9.

55. EC 1958–9 p 6.

56. Federal Power Commission *Electric Utility Depreciation Practices* 1961 pp 1, 2, 4; EC 1961–2 p 93; SCNI/ES 3 pp 190, 191, 193, 194.

57. *Investors' League Bulletin* (Special) June 1962 p 11.

58. Capital expenditure, where necessary allowing for Scotland and excluding scrap and other capital receipts, from C. H. Feinstein *Domestic Capital Formation in the United Kingdom 1920–1938* p 90; EA *Power and Prosperity* p 120; EA 1947–9 Statement A16 and corresponding statements in later electricity reports; MPSD 1948–9 p 125 etc. for generation investment in the South of Scotland; EC 1966–7 p 6 etc. and information from EC on capital work in progress.

59. These extra profits relate solely to England and Wales, the Scottish Electricity Boards' figures being taken at their face value.

60. NIE e.g. 1969 pp 78, 79; quoted manufacturing companies' share of the increase in the book value of total manufacturing stocks was calculated and they were allocated this proportion of manufacturing stock appreciation. Manufacturing profits and net assets are from *Economic Trends* April 1962 pp xv–xvii; *Statistics on Incomes, Prices, Employment and Production* Part C; *Financial Statistics* February 1969 Tables 69–71, March 1970 Tables 76–78.

61. NIE 1969 p 81.

62. THC pp 65, 66; information from Board of Inland Revenue.

63. Cmnd 4018 pp 30, 33.

64. H/WA 3 December 1965, 28 April 1969; Cmnd 4018 pp 18, 30, 33; information from BOAC.

65. EC 1968–9 p 17; Federal Power Commission *Statistics of Privately Owned Electric Utilities in the United States 1966* Tables 8 and 11.

66. International Union of Railways *International Railway Statistics* 1967 Tables 3–3 and 3–5; no allowance has been made for special pension contributions.

67. *Modern Railways* 1968 pp 178, 179, 520; *Bulletin of International Union of Railways* 1968 pp 319, 320; *International Railway Statistics* 1967 Tables 3–3, 3–5, p 143. For Italy it was arbitrarily assumed that half the state reimbursement of 88·5 million lira represented revenue for traffic carried free of charge.

68. *Bulletin of International Union of Railways* July-August 1969 p 251; *International Railway Statistics* 1967 Table 3–5.

Chapter 10: *British Rail's Loss of Traffic*

1. BTC 1955 p 11; SCNI/LT.2 pp 382–7.

2. BTC 1948 p 198, 1954 p 51; AAS 1957 p 205.

3. Table 3, K. F. Glover *Journal of the Royal Statistical Society Series A* 1960 p 122.

4. Cmd 9880 p 12; BTC 1962 pp 196, 197; this figure is slightly higher than the one given in the Table 21 because British Rail's subsidiary activities made a small profit.

5. Cmd 9880 p 5; SCNI/BR Q 197 p 300; NUR *Planning Transport for You* p 42.

6. BTC/RM, p 43.

7. Cmd 9880 pp 26, 29, 43.

8. BTC 1957 p 1.

9. These figures were obtained from those given in Table 3 by knocking off London Transport – see *Economic Trends* August 1960 p xi and February 1966 p vi for London Transport's weight.

10. SCNI/BR p 470; Cmnd 3439 p 63.

11. BRB 1968 pp 79, 96–98, 112; Table 19.

12. See pp 252, 253.

13. See pp 151, 152.

14. H/WA 3 December 1965; AAS 1969 pp 209, 217; in 1957 the ton mileage of road freight was fractionally lower than it had been in 1956 due, presumably, to the Suez fuel restrictions.

15. *Report of the Committee on Carriers' Licensing* p 28.

16. AAS 1967 p 202, 1969 p 217; BRB/RBR p 93.

17. AAS 1963 p 190; BRB Statement 5B.

18. Information from CEGB; CEA 1957–8 p 48; CEGB 1968–9 p 12; BTC 1957.2 p 196; BRB 1968 p 105.

19. H/WA 3 December 1965; BRB 1964–8 Statement 5B.

20. *A Report on Traffic, Costs, and Charges of Freight Transport in Great Britain* pp 215, 218.

21. BTR 1956 p 244.

22. A. A. Walters and C. Sharp *A Report on Traffic, Costs and Charges of Freight Transport in Great Britain* pp 169, 183, 215.

23. G. W. Quick Smith *Journal of the Institute of Transport* 1955 p 72; Sir Cyril Hurcomb *Transactions of the Manchester Statistical Society* 29 March 1950 pp 14, 15.

24. A. A. Walters and C. Sharp *A Report on Traffic, Costs, and Charges of Freight Transport in Great Britain* p 216.

25. *Ibid* pp 174–7, 184.

26. See pp 55, 56.

27. Cmd 9880 p 24.

28. See pp 53, 54.

29. Cmnd 3656 pp 16, 20; in fact the Board's figures show that in 1967 revenue per ton mile for iron and steel was lower than in 1963, though higher than in 1964 and 1965 (p 6).

30. BTC.2 1958–61 Statement IX–7, 1962.2 Statement IX–2; BRB 1963–8 Statement 5B. Allowance was made in both estimates for statistical breaks in 1959 (the inclusion of dock railway receipts) and 1963 (the exclusion of free-hauled traffic). The estimate for general goods traffic includes finished steel between 1957 and 1962 (i.e. 4·3 + 0·9 billion ton miles in 1962) but excludes steel materials and other so-called minerals. For 1962–8 iron and steel products and materials are excluded but other minerals (at 1·8 billion ton miles) are included. It was assumed that between 1962 and 1963 the average haul for general goods traffic increased by the same percentage as the haul for all non-coal traffic.

31. Information from BRB.

32. Information from Freightliners Ltd; BRB 1968 p 105.

33. B. Deakin and T. Seward *Productivity in Transport* (1969) p 63.

34. Cmnd 2695 pp 17, 19; information from RHA.

35. Table 19.

36. *Op cit* pp 46, 60, 61; information from Mr Deakin.

37. B. Deakin and T. Seward *Productivity in Transport* p 70; Deakin and Seward say 29 commodities because they also obtained information about coal.

38. BRB/RBR p 82; information from Mr Deakin.

39. Information on liner train tariffs from Freightliners Ltd.

40. Private information.

41. *The Allocation of Freight Traffic – A Survey* Report to the Ministry of Transport by Clifford Sharp, Leicester University pp 33, 35, 36.

42. BTC 1957.2 pp 206, 215, 1962.2 pp 170, 173; BRB 1968 p 106.

43. BRB 1966 pp 4, 5, 10, 1968 p 11.

44. Information from Fords at Halewood etc.

45. *Transport Age* December 1964 p 3.

46. See pp 73, 74 for their history.

47. Information from Freightliners Ltd.

48. B. T. Bayliss and S. L. Edwards *Transport for Industry: Summary Report* p 44.

49. BRB/RBR pp 25, 47.

50. Stewart Joy *The Variability of Railway Track Costs and their Implications for Policy with Special Reference to Great Britain* p 253.

51. Information from British Rail, these figures include coal traffic.

52. Central Transport Consultative Committee 1957 p 11.

53. BTC 1962.2 pp 72, 75; H/WA 24 July 1964; THC 1963 p 56.

54. W. R. Cook *Journal of Transport Economics and Policy* September 1967 p 337.

55. BTC 1957 p 70, 1960 p 84; London Midland Region *Freight Handbook 1967* pp 11, 17, 46.

56. Central Transport Consultative Committee 1957 p 11; Cmnd 1824 p 99; BTC 1959 p 84; Cmnd 585 p 9; *Journal of Transport Economics and Policy* September 1967 p 336.

57. G. F. Allen *British Rail after Beeching* p 280.

58. See above p 206.

59. BRB/RBR pp 44–6; G. F. Allen *op cit* p 300.

60. Information from National Carriers.

61. See pp 247, 248.

62. BTC 1961 p 20, 1962 pp 24, 25; BRB 1963 pp 5, 6, 8, 1964 p 7.

63. K. R. Sealy, J. A. H. Britton, P. M. O'Sullivan, D. N. M. Starkie *A Transport Study of the Ford Motor Company Plant at Dagenham* (unpublished) pp 23, 28–31; *Transport Age* December 1964 p 3.

64. *Journal of Transport Economics and Policy* September 1967 pp 336, 337.

65. *The Allocation of Freight Traffic – A Survey* Report to the Ministry of Transport by Clifford Sharp, Leicester University p 117; information from Mr Sharp.

66. G. F. Allen *op cit* p 54; BRB/RBR pp 90–92; BRB 1964 pp 8, 9, 1965 p 12, 1967 p 10.

67. BRB 1963 pp 11, 12, 1964 p 11, 1965 pp 14, 15, 1968 pp 12, 105; BRB/RBR p 35; MPSD 1968–69 p 80; Cmnd 3439 p 63; BRB *Facts and Figures about British Rail 1966* p 5; information from Freightliners Ltd.

68. BRB/RBR p 41.

69. BRB/RBR p 59.

70. BRB/RBR pp 41 (paragraph 6), 92 (paragraph 4).

71. BRB/RBR pp 91, 92.

72. BRB/RBR p 90.

73. BRB/RBR pp 91, 147.

74. BRB/RBR pp 143, 147, 148.

75. BRB 1965 p 26; information from Freightliners Ltd; see p 74.

76. BRB/RBR p 90.

77. See pp 29, 30, 53, 54, 205, 206.

78. A. A. Walters and C. Sharp *A Report on Traffic, Costs and Charges of Freight Transport in Great Britain* pp 181, 182.

79. *Ibid* pp 179, 180.

80. *The Allocation of Freight Traffic – A Survey* Report to the Ministry of Transport by Clifford Sharp, Leicester University p 27.

81. *Journal of Transport Economics and Policy* September 1967 p 332 and for the last sentence p 329.

82. *Transport for Industry: Summary Report* pp ii, iii, 39.

83. *Ibid* pp 5, 40.

84. *Bedford Transport Magazine* March 1964 p 262.

85. *Journal of Transport Economics and Policy* September 1967 p 333.

86. *Integration of Freight Transport: A Survey of Users' Attitudes* pp 16–18; my italics.

87. Mr Sharp's inquiries suggest that firms are adopting a more open-minded attitude to freightliners. However, in view of their manifest quality it would be very remarkable

if they were not, and therefore wrong to conclude that there is no prejudice against BR.

88. BTC 1957.2 pp 264, 265; AAS 1969 p 217; LTB 1967 p 39; BRB/RBR p 21; BTC 1961 p 57, 1962 p 50.

89. BRB/RBR p 8; BTC 1961.2 pp 176, 179; BRB 1967 pp 51, 94.

90. B. Hinchliffe *Railway Magazine* December 1963 p 78; Cmd 3751 p 37.

91. SCNI/BR Q 1178; Cmd 7344 p 30; Cmd 7647 p 51; BTC 1951 p 112, 1952 p 85.

92. B. Hinchliffe *Railway Magazine* October 1963 p 78; G. F. Allen *British Rail after Beeching* pp 167, 168.

93. B. Hinchliffe *Railway Magazine* August 1969 p 442.

94. *Ibid* p 442; SNCF *The Railways of France* p 72; *Modern Railways* 1969 p 423.

95. *The Year Book* 1967 p 80.

96. G. F. Allen *op cit* pp 165, 170; information from BR.

97. SCNI/BR p 472; Central Transport Consultative Committee 1960 p 7; H/WA 5 June 1967, 19 January 1970.

98. Information from German Federal Railway.

99. Information from BR; *Activité et Productivité de la SNCF en 1967* p 36.

100. G. F. Allen, *op cit* pp 165, 166.

101. BRB 1966 p 15, 1968 p 40; BRB/MTR p 7; Central Transport Consultative Committee 1962 p 11; C. J. Allen *The Year Book* 1969 p 52.

102. NIE 1968 Tables 27 and 28, 1969 Tables 24 and 25; National Institute *Economic Review* May 1963 p 31.

103. BTC 1961 p 59, 1962 p 52; SCNI/BR p 470; Cmnd 813 pp 23, 24.

104. *Economic Review* May 1963 pp 31, 32.

105. BRB 1968 p 104; LTB 1968 p 63; NIE 1969 p 30; *Passenger Transport in Great Britain* 1967 pp iv, 12; R. Maurice *National Accounts Statistics: Sources and Methods* p 173.

Chapter 11: *The Rail Deficit*

1. See pp 70, 71, 79, 83, 84.

2. BRB/RBR p 1.

3. SCNI/BR p xxxiii.

4. BRB/RBR p 8.

5. A. W. Tait BTR April 1953 p 291; E. R. Williams BTR April 1956 p 57; here and subsequently I have relied on information and impressions obtained through interviewing.

6. H. C. Johnson BTR 1955 pp 289–92; Cmd 9880 p 19; BRB/RBR pp 77–89.

7. BTC *Electrification of Railways* 1951 pp 9, 17.

8. SCNI/BR Q 1610, 1719.

9. SCNI/BR Q 1817, 1818.

10. See pp 294–8, 336, 337.

11. BTC/RM p 43; BTC 1953 pp 8, 9.

12. See p 45; E. S. Cox *Locomotive Panorama*.2 p 117; BTC 1952 p 6, 1953 p 35.

13. Central Transport Consultative Committee 1954 p 6.

14. BTC/MBR p 32.

15. Central Consultative Committee 1956 p 4.

16. SCNI/BR p 390; Central Transport Consultative Committee 1960 p 4, 1961 p 5.

17. BTC/MBR p 32; BRB/RBR p 8.

18. A. W. Tait BTR April 1953 p 291; SCNI/BR p liv.

19. BRB/RBR p 19.

20. E. S. Cox *op cit* pp 126, 127.

21. Cmd 9880 p 14; this passage specifically refers to the stopping services.

22. SCNI/BR pp 350–52.

23. Cmd 9880 p 16.

24. Loss in 1961 excluding interest and replacement cost depreciation estimated from BRB/RBR p 8; Cmnd 3439 p 63; BRB 1966 p 54.

25. Cmnd 813 p 8; BRB/RBR p 19.

26. Cmd 9880 p 19; BTC/MBR pp 25, 26; BTC/RM pp 26–28.

27. BTC. 1954.2 p 147, 1961.2 pp 148, 268, 269; BRB/RBR p 46.

28. SCNI/BR p xlvii.

29. BRB/RBR p 46; BRB Statements 5 B,C,D; BTC 1962.2 pp 204, 205.

30. A. P. Hunter BTR 1954 pp 199–201; E. W. Arkle BTR 1955 pp 417, 418; A. S. Kirby and D. A. F. Quekett BTR 1956 pp 43, 44; L. S. Sherwood BTR 1959 p 164.

31. G. F. Allen *British Rail after Beeching* pp 305, 306.

32. P. L. Cook *Railway Workshops : The Problems of Contraction* pp 5, 6, 19, 24.

33. G. F. Allen *op cit* pp 90–96; *British Railways Today and Tomorrow* pp 53, 54.

34. P. L. Cook *op cit* pp 22–24.

35. Cmd 9191 pp 7–9; SCNI/BR pp ix, 310.

36. *Some Thoughts on the Organization of Public Passenger Services in Cities* paper read on 27 January 1966 at Mullards Ltd, Blackburn, (unpublished) p 4.

37. SCNI/BR pp 302, 491, 492.

38. Cmd 9191 pp 6, 7; BTC 1958 p 16.

39. A. J. Pearson *The Railways and the Nation* p 78.

40. BTC 1961 p 20.

41. Cmd 9191 p 10.

42. Cmnd 3656 p 15; see pp 217, 218.

43. Cmd 9191 p 14.

44. *Sunday Times* 7 January 1968 p 22.

45. H 10 March 1960 col 643.

46. BRB/RBR p 1.

47. BRB/RBR pp 54, 55.

48. BRB/RBR pp 19, 54, 55.

49. BRB 1966.2 p 13, 1968 p 79.

50. BRB/RBR pp 48, 94, 95, 97, 140; BRB 1963–7 Table 5D, 1966 p 19.

51. BRB 1967 p 38.

52. Cmnd 2764.2 p 204; AAS 1969 pp 127, 136; these figures include London Transport railways.

53. BRB 1967 p 2.

54. See BRB 1965 p 4.

55. Cmnd 3439 pp 4, 5; BRB 1967 p 24.

56. See BRB 1965 p 1.

57. Cmnd 3439 pp 4, 5; BRB 1967 p 24.

58. BRB/RBR p 19, .2 Map 9; BRB 1963.2 p 53.

59. BRB/RBR pp 10, 64; BTC 1961.2 p 72.

60. BRB/RBR p 10; in the Report the revenue corresponding to the least used half of the route is estimated at £20 million, but this was based on the mistaken assumption

that the track over which the least freight passed was also the track over which the fewest passengers travelled.

61. BRB/RBR pp 9, 10, 64; BTC 1961.2 p 72.

62. BRB/RBR p 19.

63. Cmnd 3439 p 1; BRB 1966.2 p 43.

64. Sir Stanley Raymond *Sunday Times* 7 January 1968.

65. BRB/MTR pp 6, 7.

66. BRB/MTR pp 9, 45.

67. BRB/MTR pp 8, 45; Stewart Joy *Journal of Industrial Economics* 1964–5 pp 82, 83.

68. Stewart Joy *The Variability of Railway Track Costs and their Implications for Policy with Special Reference to Great Britain* pp 75, 76.

69. Cmnd 3439 p 49.

70. Cmnd 3439 pp 1, 20.

71. Cmnd 3439 p 20.

72. Sir Stanley Raymond *Sunday Times* 7 January 1968 p 21.

73. See pp 427–31.

74. Herbert Morrison *Socialization and Transport* (1933) p 88.

Chapter 12: *BOAC Losses*

1. BOAC 1951–2 p 3, 1948–9 p 4, 1947–8 p 14, 1950–51 p 7, 1951–2 pp 4, 5; BSAA 1946–7 p 4, 1947–8 p 4.

2. BEA 1947–8 pp 10, 12, 16, 1948–9 p 41, 1953–4 p 12.

3. Cmd 6712 p 7.

4. John Longhurst *Nationalization in Practice* (1950) pp 14, 152, 153.

5. Cmnd 2853 p 19.

6. Cmd 7307 pp 6, 10.

7. Sir Miles Thomas *Out on a Wing* (1964) p 295.

8. Cmd 7307, pp 23–26; Cmd 7478 pp 4, 5, 9–12, 15–17. BOAC was to a limited extent responsible for the fact that the aircraft was less economic than had been anticipated.

9. BOAC 1946–7 pp 13, 14.

10. Sir Miles Thomas *Out on a Wing* p 285; BOAC 1948–9 p 1.

11. BSAA 1946–7 p 6, 1947–8 pp 4, 6, 1948–9 pp 7, 10, 13; BOAC 1949–50 p 5.

12. BOAC 1946–7 pp 13, 39, 40, 1948–9 p 28, 1951–2 p 55.

13. BOAC 1946–7 p 15.

14. BOAC 1947–8 pp 14, 15.

15. Cmd 7647 p 55; BOAC 1947–8 p 10, 1948–9 p 5, 1950–51 p 18, 1954–5 p 8.

16. Cmd 6712 p 5; SCNI/BOAC.2 pp 233–5; BOAC 1946–7 p 6, 1949–50 p 50, 1950–51 p 46.

17. BEA 1950–51 p 33, 1952–3 pp 66, 67.

18. BEA 1950–51 Appendix 7; commissions and incidental revenue have been split in proportion to other revenue.

19. J. Longhurst *Nationalization in Practice* (1950) p 176.

20. *Ibid* Chapters ix and x.

21. BOAC 1947–8 pp 40, 55, 1948–9 pp 5, 26, 41, 1949–50 pp 11, 27, 43.

22. BOAC 1947–8 p 40, 1948–9 p 41.

23. *Op cit* p 140.

24. ICAO *Statistical Summary* 9 p 86; BOAC 1948–9 pp 26, 41.

25. Information from CAB; CAB *Handbook of Airline Statistics* 1965 pp 96, 239.

26. Sir Miles Thomas *Out on a Wing* pp 275–8.

27. BOAC 1946–7 pp 31, 32, 1951–2 p 48; allowance was made for the absorption of BSAA (BOAC 1948–9 pp 38, 40, 1949–50 p 48).

28. SCNI/AC p 332.

29. Ministry of Aviation *The Financial Problems of the British Overseas Airways Corporation* p 6; BOAC 1953–4 p 8; R. Miller and D. Sawers *The Technical Development of Modern Aviation* (1968) pp 43, 178–81.

30. *The Financial Problems of BOAC* p 7; but see BOAC 1954–5 p 2 and SCNI/AC Q 1817.

31. SCNI/AC pp xxxvii–xxxix.

32. SCNI/AC p xxxix, xl.

33. SCNI/AC Q 1707, 2275; BOAC 1957–8 p 10.

34. SCNI/AC Q 1520, 1522, 1707.

35. SCNI/BOAC p 76, .2 p 297.

36. SCNI/BOAC.2 p 295; H/WA 3 December 1965.

37. SCNI/BOAC.2 p 290.

38. *The Financial Problems of BOAC* p 10.

39. SCNI/BOAC.2 pp 231, 235; see p 260.

40. BOAC 1958–9 p 19, 1961–2 p 103, Appendix I, 1964–5 Appendix II; Table 21; *The Financial Problems of BOAC* p 10.

41. *Corbett Report* pp 30–32; SCNI/BOAC p 55, 56, .2 Q 665–7; BOAC 1961–2 p 77.

42. BOAC 1961–2 p 77; *Corbett Report* p 33.

43. *The Financial Problems of BOAC* p 11; see also *Corbett Report* pp 48, 49.

44. Sir Miles Thomas *Out on a Wing* p 327.

45. BOAC 1954–5 p 1, 1955–6 p 1, 1958–9 p 2, 1961–2 pp 9, 10; SCNI/BOAC p 27.

46. BOAC 1961–2 pp 9, 10, Appendix 1; SCNI/BOAC.2 p 287; the figure of £4¼ million disregards the extra depreciation which had later to be provided.

47. BOAC 1961–2 pp 3, 9, 10, 12, 1962–3 p 27, Appendix I; *The Financial Problems of BOAC* p 14.

48. BOAC 1961–2 pp 3, 4, 1962–3 p 55; the figure of £7·7 million is the loss in 1961–2 and 1962–3 before provision for extra depreciation.

49. *The Financial Problems of BOAC* p 14.

50. SCNI/BOAC.2 Q 1048; BOAC 1963–4 p 65.

51. SCNI/BOAC.2 p 286.

52. SCNI/BOAC pp 29, 30; BOAC 1962–3 p 8.

53. *The Financial Problems of BOAC* p 11.

54. BOAC 1961–2 p 91, 1963–4 pp 64, 65, Appendix II.

55. BOAC 1956–7 p 4; Ministry of Aviation *The Financial Problems of BOAC* p 6; D. Corbett *Politics and the Airlines* (1965) p 150.

56. SCNI/AC Q 1462, 1465, 1466.

57. BOAC 1957–8 pp 1, 2.

58. SCNI/AC p 313, Q 2138, 2146; H 22 July 1964 col 492.

59. BOAC 1954–5 p 21.

60. S. Wheatcroft *Air Transport Policy* (1964) p 115.

61. *Ibid* pp 93, 96, 97; BOAC 1961–2 p 33.

62. BOAC 1957–8 p 12, 1958–9 p 13, 1959–60 p 11, 1961–2 pp 23, 28, 1962–3 p 19, 1963–4 p 29, 1964–5 p 30, 1965–6 p 29; SCNI/BOAC pp 44, 49.

63. Sir Miles Thomas *Out on a Wing* pp 281, 334; SCNI/AC p 302; BOAC 1952–3 p 22, 1953–4 p 23, 1954–5 p 20.

64. *The Technical Development of Modern Aviation* p 190.
65. BOAC 1954–5 p 20; Corbett *op cit* pp 149, 150.
66. See p 281.
67. Cmnd 2853 pp 7, 8; SCNI/AC p 314.
68. SCNI/BOAC pp 16, 17.
69. SCNI/BOAC pp 17, 18, .2 Q 1594–6.
70. SCNI/BOAC p 19.
71. SCNI/BOAC p 17.
72. SCNI/BOAC pp 19, 20.
73. SCNI/BOAC p 19, .2 Q 1604, 1605; H 22 July 1964 col 498.
74. Cmnd 2853 p 19; SCNI/BOAC.2 Q 1565.
75. SCNI/BOAC p 21; Cmnd 2853 p 126.
76. SCNI/BOAC p 21; H 22 July 1964 col 498.
77. Estimates Committee *Transport Aircraft* 1963–4 Q 1543, 1544; H 22 July 1964 cols 498–501.
78. SCNI/BOAC.2 Q 1173, 1186.
79. SCNI/BOAC p 22.
80. SCNI/BOAC p 23, Q 1749, .2 p 227; BOAC 1968–9 p 46.
81. SCNI/BOAC p 22, .2 p 295; H 22 July 1964 col 501, 502.
82. BOAC 1965–6 p 60.
83. H/WA 28 March 1969.
84. Cmnd 4108 p 91, 92; Air Transport Licensing Board 1964 p 17.
85. ICAO *Digest of Statistics* 142.
86. *Corbett Report* pp 7–21; but see pp 22–24.
87. SCNI/BOAC p 101.
88. Julian Amery H 22 July 1964 col 496.
89. BEA 1953–4 and 1954–5 Appendix 7, 1961–2 pp 31, 32, 1962–3 p 26.
90. SCNI/BEA pp xxii–xxv, Q 370, 373, 388, 403, 416–19; R. Miller and D. Sawers *The Technical Development of Modern Aviation* pp 202, 203; Cmnd 4018 pp 197, 198; S. Wheatcroft *Air Transport Policy* p 94.
91. Cmnd 2853 pp 18, 19, 125; SCNI/BEA Q 1479.
92. Cmnd 2853 pp 7–9, 74.
93. BEA 1950–51 p 65, 1951–2 pp 11, 12, 40; 1955–6 p 42, 1960–61 p 28; SCNI/BEA Q 370; see pp 257, 258, 268, 269.
94. Cmnd 2853 pp 11, 12.
95. Sir Miles Thomas *Out on a Wing* p 284.
96. See p 263.
97. R. Miller and D. Sawers *op cit* pp 177–84.
98. R. Miller and D. Sawers *op cit* p 195; Sir Miles Thomas, *op cit* p 328; Estimates Committee *Transport Aircraft* 1963–4 Q 487.
99. Merton Peck in *Britain's Economic Prospects* edited R. E. Caves pp 475, 476.

Chapter 13: *Investment and Demand*

1. Tables 2 and 23; BRB 1967 p 90.
2. See pp 39, 42.
3. Cmnd 4578 pp 25–30.
4. SCNI/MC.3 p 230.
5. NIE 1969 Tables 1, 37, 52 etc; Cmnd 3995 p 17.
6. NCB/PFC pp 20–24, 33.

R

7. NCB/PFC pp 26–33; NCB 1949 pp 52, 53; Cmd 8647 pp 3, 8; MPSD 1950 p 93.

8. MPSD 1967 p 99.

9. Cmd 8647 pp 8, 13.

10. Cmd 8647 pp 210, 211, 217.

11. *The Price of Fuel* (1953) pp 18, 16.

12. C. A. R. Crosland *Britain's Economic Problem* (1953) pp 112–13, 215.

13. NCB/PFC p 21.

14. NCB/IIC p 13.

15. NCB 1954 pp 26, 27; NCB/IIC p 14.

16. Louis Lister *Europe's Coal and Steel Community* p 113.

17. OEEC *Europe's Growing Needs of Energy : How can they be met?* pp 27, 55.

18. NCB/RPC p 8.

19. AAS 1967 p 140.

20. See M. Posner *Annals of Collective Economy* 1962 pp 353–5.

21. Cmnd 2805 pp 3, 4.

22. OEEC *Towards a New Energy Pattern in Europe* pp 40, 41, 60.

23. NEDC *Growth of the United Kingdom Economy to 1966* p 7.

24. W. Beckerman and Associates *The British Economy in 1975* (1965) p 302.

25. NEDC *Growth of the United Kingdom Economy to 1966* pp 1, 73, 74; MPSD 1966, p 175.

26. NCB/CB.2 Q 2071, 2072, 2074.

27. BTC/MBR p 34.

28. BTC/RM pp 10, 11; BTC 1954.2 p 70.

29. BTC/RM pp 8, 9.

30. BTC/RM pp 7, 8.

31. AAS 1957 p 203; K. F. Glover *Journal of the Royal Statistical Society Series A* 1960 p 122; BTC/MBR p 8; BTC/RM p 9.

32. British Iron and Steel Federation *Steel – the Facts* p 16; AAS 1969 p 161.

33. C. Foster *The Transport Problem* p 105; BTC/RM p 8.

34. Cmnd 813 pp 20–22, 29; AAS 1963 p 191.

35. Cmnd 813 p 24; AAS 1963 p 191.

36. H/WA 3 December 1965.

37. Cmnd 2764.2 p 204.

38. BRB/MTR pp 48, 50; AAS 1967 p 202.

39. Cmnd 813 p 22; AAS 1967 p 202; BRB 1963.2 p 49.

40. AAS 1969 p 217.

41. SCNI/ES pp 31–33, .2 p 13.

42. T. W. Berrie in *Public Enterprise* edited R. Turvey p 180; calculated from the figures for six winters ahead.

43. SCNI/ES .2 Q 1230.

44. SCNI/ES.3 p 334; information from EC.

45. SCNI/ES.3 pp 207, 334.

46. EC 1961–2 p 15, 1965–6 p 9; Cmnd 3575 p 8; NEDC *Growth of the United Kingdom Economy to 1966* p 77.

47. Cmnd 3575 p 8; information from EC.

48. SCNI/ES pp 37, 38, 42.

49. SCNI/ES p 194.

50. SCNI/ES p 35.

51. SCNI/ES pp 37, 95.

52. Federal Power Commission *National Power Survey* pp 194, 195; T. W. Berrie in *Public Enterprise* edited R. Turvey p 180.

53. See pp 311, 312.

Chapter 14: *Capital and Yield*

1. SCNI/NCB pp xii, xxiv.
2. A. Beacham in *The Structure of British Industry* (1958) edited Duncan Burn pp 125, 143.
3. NCB/IIC pp 12, 14, 16, 17; E. F. Schumacher in *National Coal Board: The First Ten Years* edited Sir Guy Nott-Bower and R. H. Walkerdine pp 61, 62.
4. See SCNI/NCB Q 605.
5. See p 40.
6. E. F. Schumacher *op cit* p 62.
7. NCB/RPC pp 15, 23; NCB.2 Schedule 2; CSO price index for coal investment.
8. AAS 1967 p 140; NCB 1963–4 p 4; NEDC *Growth of the United Kingdom Economy to 1966* p 71.
9. Information from NCB.
10. BTC/MBR pp 5, 7; the £1,240 million includes a small amount of port investment; Cmnd 813 pp 1, 2, 14; BTC/MBR p 18.
11. Calculated using official price indices for railway vehicles and for building and works; Cmnd 813 pp 1, 2.
12. Cmnd 813 p 2; BTC/RM p 21.
13. BTC/MBR pp 18, 21, 26.
14. BTC/MBR p 26; BTC.2 Statement VII–1; BRB Statement 5D.
15. BTC/MBR pp 15–17, 26; BTC/RM pp 33, 34; BTC.2 Statements VII–I, VII–2; BRB Statement 5D, 1966 p 37.
16. BTC.2 Statement V–8; BRB Statement 3A.
17. BTC/MBR pp 15, 16; BTC/RM p 16; BRB 1968 p 108.
18. BTC/RM p 16; BTC/MBR pp 15, 16; BTC Statement VII–1; BRB Statement 5D.
19. BTC/MBR p 21, 32; BRB 1968 pp 106, 108.
20. BTC/MBR p 21; BTC.2 Statement VII–1; BRB Statement 5D; BTC/RM p 34; BRB 1965 p 28.
21. See p 71.
22. BTC/MBR p 18; SCNI/BR p 397.
23. G. F. Allen *British Rail after Beeching* p 127; SCNI/MC.2 Q 1498; SCNI/BR p 397.
24. SCNI/BR p 397; BTC/MBR pp 10, 11.
25. See pp 315, 316.
26. H/WA 18 November 1968.
27. CEB 1947 p 8.
28. The early estimates made by the North of Scotland Hydro-Electric Board were extremely inaccurate but by the early fifties its forecasts seem to have become satisfactory (SCNI Scottish Electricity Boards p 197; SCNI Reports of Former Select Committees p 40).
29. SCNI/ES.3 pp 32, 33; information from CEGB.
30. Cmnd 3960 pp 7, 10, 12.
31. Cmnd 3960 p 10 for the first part of the quotation and p 35 for the second.
32. See pp 299–301.

33. NEDC *Growth of the United Kingdom Economy to 1966* p 79.

34. NCB/PFC pp 10, 12, 30; NCB/IIC p 16; NCB 1950 pp 207, 215; MPSD 1968-9 p 41.

35. R. J. S. Baker *The Management of Capital Projects* pp 44-7, 56, 57; NCB/ACO p 64; see pp 40-42.

36. SCNI/MC.3 p 50.

37. BTC/RM pp 24, 29, 30.

38. S. E. Parkhouse *Journal of the Institute of Transport* September 1951 pp 211-18, 242.

39. See p 45.

40. E. S. Cox *Locomotive Panorama*.2 p 117.

41. A. J. Pearson *The Railways and the Nation* pp 82, 87.

42. SCNI/BR Q 1065.

43. A. J. Pearson *Man of the Rail* p 172; private information.

44. See pp 336, 337.

45. Information from BRB; BRB 1968 p 100.

46. For the Commission's policy towards the stopping services see pp 237-42.

47. Cmnd 813, p 12.

48. See pp 327-29.

49. See p 332.

50. Cmd 9389 pp 5, 6; SCNI/ES.3 p 187; Sir Christopher Hinton *Three Banks Review* December 1961 p 4.

51. Cmd 9389 p 5; Hinton *op cit* p 4; M. G. Webb, *Scottish Journal of Political Economy* 1968 p 27.

52. SCNI/ES.3 p 187.

53. SCNI/ES.3 p 186; Hinton *op cit* pp 9, 11; H 9 July 1954 cols 2507-9; see pp 356-58.

54. D. P. Sayers, J. S. Forrest, F. J. Lane *The Proceedings of the Institution of Electrical Engineers* 1952.2 pp 585-90; E. S. Booth, D. Clark, J. L. Egginton, J. S. Forrest *ibid* 1962 Part A pp 496-501.

55. F. H. S. Brown and R. S. Edwards *Economica* 1961 pp 298-301. This is only an outline and not a full description of the CEGB's method.

56. SCNI/MC.3 pp 90, 103; R. W. Bates *The Determinants of Investment in the Nationalized Electricity Supply Industry in Great Britain* (unpublished Sheffield thesis) p 179.

57. SCNI/MC.3 pp 89, 90.

58. SCNI/MC.3 p 106.

59. See SCNI/ES.2 Q 1301; SCNI/MC.3 pp 100, 101.

60. See p 341; SCNI/GI.2 p 566; SCNI/MC.3 p 57.

61. Information from THC; BTC 1961 p 38; SCNI/MC.3 pp 137-8.

62. National Institute *Economic Review* November 1964 pp 38, 40.

63. T. Barna *Investment and Growth Policies in British Industrial Firms* (1962) pp vii, 4, 5, 33.

64. B. Williams and W. P. Scott *Investment Proposals and Decision* (1965) pp 9, 10, 54.

65. E. Lundberg *Economic Journal* 1959 pp 665, 669.

Chapter 15: *The Evaluation of Investment*

1. D. F. Istvan *Capital-Expenditure Decisions* (1961) p 96.

2. F. H. S. Brown and R. S. Edwards *Economica* 1961 pp 299-301; see p 331.

3. SCNI/NCB p 153.
4. *Oxford Economic Papers* 1959 pp 265, 267.
5. SCNI/NCB pp 153, 158, 159.
6. SCNI *Reports of Former Select Committees* pp 47, 50.
7. SCNI/NCB pp 152, 154.
8. *The Transport Problem* p 97.
9. *The Transport Problem* p 96; BTC/MBR p 7.
10. BTC/MBR p 31, 32.
11. See pp 324, 325.
12. SCNI/BR pp 398–406.
13. BTC 1961 p 6, 1962 p 7; SCNI/MC.3 p 182.
14. SCNI/MC.3 p 184.
15. SCNI/GI.2 pp 564, 565; SCNI/MC.3 pp 57, 58, 65.
16. See pp 341, 342.
17. G. Lawson *The Accountants Journal* 1964 pp 226, 267, 268.
18. D. F. Istvan *Capital-Expenditure Decisions* pp 60, 61.
19. For a full discussion of dcf see A. J. Merrett and A. Sykes *The Finance and Analysis of Capital Projects* or H. Bierman and S. Smidt *The Capital Budgeting Decision*.
20. F. H. S. Brown and R. S. Edwards *Economica* 1961 p 301.
21. SCNI/MC p 95,.3 p 186.
22. See pp 343, 344; SCNI/MC.2 p 249.
23. SCNI/MC.2 Q 669, 980,.3 p 138.
24. SCNI/MC pp 98, 99,.2 Q 1977,.3 pp 197–9.
25. H/WA 22 November 1968.
26. SCNI/MC.2 Q 485, 486; SCNI/CB pp 40, 41,.2 Q 650, 651, 1426–9.
27. Professor Maurice Peston *The Times* 14 November 1967 p 25.
28. *Accountants Journal* 1964 p 276; National Institute *Economic Review* November 1964 p 41.
29. *The Director* November 1970 p 336.
30. *Trade and Industry* 23 December 1970 p 523.
31. See pp 202, 207–9.
32. Henceforth all references to changes in price refer to changes in relative prices.
33. NCB/PFC pp 3, 34, 36.
34. SCNI/MC.3 p 52.
35. This was pointed out at the time in an extremely perceptive article in the *Economist* 18 November 1953 p 824.
36. SCNI/MC.3 pp 50, 51.
37. BTC/MBR pp 31–35; private information.
38. Cmnd 813 pp 27, 29; BTC 1960 pp 13, 14; private information.
39. See p 250.
40. See F. H. S. Brown and R. S. Edwards *Economica* 1961 pp 300, 302.
41. SCNI/MC.3 p 185.
42. Cmnd 3439 pp 17, 62, 63.
43. SCNI/MC.3 pp 91, 95.
44. See p 342; Cmnd 2919 p 8.
45. R. W. Bates, *The Determinants of Investment in the Nationalized Electricity Supply Industry in Great Britain* pp 181, 182.
46. R. E. Baxter and R. Rees *Economic Journal* 1968 pp 279–96.
47. See pp 368, 369.
48. WMGB 1961–2 p ix; T. C. B. Watson *The Influence of Raw Materials and*

Markets on the Pattern of Gas Production paper delivered to an International Symposium on European Energy at Grenoble University in May 1965, Map C; SCNI/GI.2 p 597.

49. SCNI/GI pp 97, 98, .2 p 448, 449.

50. See p 369.

51. Here and in the rest of this Chapter I have relied on information I gathered when studying the WMGB.

52. WMGB 1962-3 p 3.

53. See p 329.

Chapter 16: *Target Rates of Return*

1. NEDC *Investment Appraisal* p 12.

2. UN *Yearbook of National Accounts Statistics* 1967 Part D Table 2.

3. Cmnd 2300 pp 77, 78.

4. D. C. Corner and A. Williams *Economica* 1965 p 46.

5. W. Beckerman and Associates *The British Economy in 1975* pp 47, 48.

6. There is a further reason why the rise in private investment is unlikely to be as large as the fall in public investment: private investment has a very substantial import content whereas the nationalized industries rely almost exclusively on British plant and machinery.

7. Cmnd 3437 pp 5, 6; see p 331 for discounting and dcf.

8. SCNI/MC.3 pp 27, 28.

9. E.g. W. G. Shepherd *Economic Performance Under Public Ownership* (1965) pp 75-7.

10. A. J. Merrett and A. Sykes *District Bank Review* June 1966 p 31.

11. A. M. Alfred *District Bank Review* June 1968 p 24.

12. *Ibid* p 25.

13. See pp 318-20 for the Board's methods.

14. F. H. S. Brown and R. S. Edwards *Economica* 1961 pp 299, 301; SCNI/MC.3 p 94.

15. R. Meek *District Bank Review* March 1965 pp 51-55.

16. SCNI/MC.3 p 94.

17. For the switch over to dcf see pp 331, 332.

18. SCNI/MC.2 Q 669, 871, 981,.3 p 185; Cmnd 3924 p 11.

19. *District Bank Review* June 1968 pp 25-28.

20. Cmnd 3924 p 11.

21. SCNI/MC.3 p 164; see also .2Q 1960.

22. H/WA 19 January 1970; see p 332.

23. See pp 317, 318.

24. SCNI/ES.3 p 20.

25. Cmnd 1083 pp 3, 4.

26. SCNI/ES.2 Q 1032; but see .3 p 344.

27. C. Hinton *Three Banks Review* December 1961 p 10.

28. SCNI/ES.2 Q 96.

29. See p 318.

30. H/WA 31 March 1965.

31. See pp 325, 326 for coal's methods.

32. SCNI/MC.3 p 58; SCNI/GI.2 p 564.

33. SCNI/MC.3 pp 60-63.

34. See pp 341–45.
35. SCNI/ES p 52.
36. SCNI/MC.3 pp 49–55; SCNI/CB .2 Q 650.
37. NCB/PFC pp 3, 4, 35, 36; *Economist* 18 November 1950 p 824; MPSD 1967 p 64.
38. See Table 19 and pp 335, 336.
39. BTC/MBR pp 8, 35.
40. BTC/RM p 43.
41. BTC/MBR p 32.
42. See pp 327–29.

Chapter 17: *Economies of Scale in Gas and Electricity*

1. Cmd 6699 pp 18, 19, 39–41, 43, 44.
2. B. H. Wormsley, *Some Technological and Economic Problems of the Gas Industry* (unpublished University of London thesis 1954) pp 26–31, 112.
3. GC 1958–9 p 86.
4. T. C. B. Watson *The Influence of Raw Materials and Markets on the Pattern of Gas Production* p 8; J. Burns *Institute of Gas Engineers Transactions* 1957–8 p 699.
5. Cmd 6699 pp 18, 19.
6. B. H. Wormsley *op cit* p 164, 165; T. C. B. Watson *op cit* p 8, map B.
7. Cmd 6699 p 6.
8. PEP *Report on the Gas Industry* p 125; H. Finer *Municipal Trading* (1941) p 256.
9. H. Finer *op cit* p 254; Cmd 6699 p 15.
10. B. H. Wormsley *op cit* pp 8, 9, 11; Cmd 6699 pp 11, 13.
11. GC 1948–50 p 111; Eastern Gas Board 1949–50 p 3.
12. B. H. Wormsley *op cit* pp 112, 113, Table 5.1 (B); GC 1950–51 p 121.
13. B. H. Wormsley pp 130, 131.
14. B. H. Wormsley *op cit* p 152; E. A. G. Robinson *The Structure of Competitive Industry* (1958) pp 22, 23.
15. *Op cit* pp 161, 166, Table 6.1.
16. B. H. Wormsley *op cit* p 24, Table 2.5; GC 1948–50 p 73, 1950–51 p 88; SCNI/GI.2 Q 1415.
17. B. H. Wormsley *op cit* pp 166–8, 170–75.
18. Cmd 6699 pp 17, 37; T. K. Gribbin *Oxford Economic Papers* 1953 p 194.
19. GC 1951–2 p 3; 1952–3 p 5, 6; 1953–4 p 93.
20. *The Influence of Raw Materials and Markets on the Pattern of Gas Production* p 13, Maps B and C.
21. SCNI/GI.2 p 597; GC 1958–9 p 86, 1959–60 p 169.
22. GC 1953–4 p 33; see also pp 25, 26 and GC 1948–50 pp 74, 75, 1952–3 pp 62, 63.
23. SCNI/GI. 2 Q 1116, pp 504, 505.
24. SCNI/GI.2 Q 2214, pp 479, 482; GC 1955–6 p 169.
25. GC 1958–9 p 87; MPSD 1959 p 120; pre-war efficiency calculated from MPSD 1966 pp 146, 147.
26. GC 1952–3 p 58 etc.
27. SCNI/GI.2 Q 1415 2347.
28. MPSD 1966 p 156; information from CSO.
29. B. H. Wormsley *op cit* pp 29, 31; GC 1958–9 p 86.
30. MPSD 1959 pp 111, 119.
31. Table 4.

32. Cmnd 2862 p 24.

33. SCNI/GI.2 Q 641, 1341, 1342, p 443.

34. SCNI/GI.2 p 443 etc.

35. SCNI/GI.2 Q 897, 1135; NWGB 1960–61 Appendix 2.

36. *Economic Performance under Public Ownership* pp 101, 102, 119, but see SCNI/GI. 2 Q 543.

37. SCNI/GI.2 Q 2358.

38. N. V. Steenstrup *Institution of Gas Engineers Communication 731*, pp 3, 4, 10.

39. See SCNI/GI p 11.

40. See pp 68, 69.

41. *Financial Times* 22 May 1968.

42. *Report of the Committee Appointed to Review the National Problem of the Supply of Electrical Energy* 1926 p 9.

43. CEB 1938 pp 14, 15.

44. CEB 1938 pp 18, 19. I have introduced a few words in place of references to charts.

45. See *Report of the Committee on Electricity Distribution* 1936 pp 13, 20, 21, 68.

46. Cmd 9672 p 39.

47. CEA 1957 p 38; EA 1953–4 p 35.

48. *Report of the Committee on Electricity Distribution* p 25.

49. L. Gordon *The Public Corporation in Great Britain* (1938) p 154; PEP *The British Fuel and Power Industries* pp 311–19.

50. Cmd 9672 pp 12, 27.

51. Electricity Supply Act 1926 Sections 5 and 6; and 1919 Section 26. As a wartime measure the need for Parliamentary approval was temporarily waived by the Central Electricity Board (Provision of Generating Stations) Order, 1940.

52. See L. Gordon *The Public Corporation in Great Britain* pp 106, 107, 152.

53. Cmd 9672 pp 12, 27.

54. PEP *op cit* p 159; EA 1949–50 p 26.

55. EA 1949–50 p 26; but see CEB 1947 pp 4, 5.

56. Cmd. 9672 pp 28, 49.

57. EC *Handbook of Electricity Supply Statistics* 1969 p 32.

58. EA 1949–50 pp 37, 38.

59. Cmd 9672 p 27.

60. Cmd 9672 p 49.

61. *Report of the Committee of Enquiry into Economy in the Construction of Power Stations* p 8 and Schedule A.

62. *Ibid* pp 8–13; UN/ECE *Problems in the Design and Operation of Thermal Power Stations* I 1964 p 82.

63. British Productivity Council *Electricity Supply in Western Germany* pp 3, 4.

64. *Ibid* pp 5, 7.

65. *Ibid* pp 4, 25.

66. Federal Power Commission *National Power Survey* 1964 p 5.

67. Edison Electric Institute *1968 Year-End Summary of the Electric Power Situation in the United States* pp 27–32.

68. *National Power Survey* pp 14, 200.

69. *Op cit* pp 3, 196, 286; Federal Power Commission 1969 p 10; Jeremy Main *Fortune* November 1969 pp 116, 118, 119, 194.

70. *Economic Review* May 1966 pp 31, 32.

71. *Ibid* p 36.

72. *Ibid* p 41.

73. *Ibid* pp 36, 37, 40; Cmd 9672 pp 28, 29.

74. OEEC and OECD *Survey of Electric Power Equipment 1957, Eleventh-Eighteenth Survey of Electric Power Equipment.*

75. OECD *Nineteenth–Twenty-Second Survey of Electric Power Equipment*; UN/ECE *The Situation and Future Prospects of Europe's Electric Power Supply Industry in 1961–62* p 38, *The Electric Power Situation in Europe in 1963–1964 and its Future Prospects* p 3.

76. Edison Electric Institute 1964–8 *Year-End Summary of the Electric Power Situation in the United States, Interim Electric Power Survey* July 1969.

77. SCNI/ES.3 p 28.

78. Information from CEGB.

79. G. P. Palo, G. O. Wessenauer, J. R. Parrish, E. F. Thomas *TVA's Experience with Thermal Units with Capacity from 500 to 1150 Megawatts* VII World Power Conference, Paper 146 p 19.

80. F. H. S. Brown *The Duty and Development of Modern Power Station Plant* 27th Parsons Memorial Lecture, Institution of Mechanical Engineers p 7.

81. Federal Power Commission *National Power Survey* 1964.2 p 53.

82. G. P. Palo, G. O. Wessenauer, J. R. Parrish, E. F. Thomas *op cit* p 20.

83. Federal Power Commission *National Power Survey*.2 p 57.

84. Information from CEGB.

85. Federal Power Commission *Steam-Electric Plant Construction Cost and Annual Production Expenses* 1960, 1961 1966–8; OECD *Fourteenth Survey of Electric Power Equipment,* etc.

86. National Institute *Economic Review* May 1966 p 37; OECD *Twenty-Second Survey of Electric Power Equipment.*

87. *National Power Survey*.2 p 52.

88. *Economic Review* May 1966 p 37; OECD *Twenty-Second Survey of Electric Power Equipment.*

89. F. H. S. Brown *op cit* pp 9, 10; *The Engineer* 19 April 1968 p 618.

90. Cmd 6610 pp 99, 105, 137, 138.

91. NCB/PFC pp 3, 64, 68.

92. Cmnd 4018 pp 68–70, 77.

93. See pp 29, 30; A. J. Harrison *Oxford Economic Papers* 1963 p 305; G. W. Quick Smith BTR 1952 pp 200, 201, 204; T. G. Gibb *Institute of Transport Journal* 1963 p 121.

94. See pp 72, 73, 152, 252–54.

95. *Manpower in the Chemical Industry* pp 5, 13, 46, 54.

96. G. Maxcy and A. Silberston *The Motor Industry* (1959) pp 77–93; *Administered Prices Automobiles* Report of the Subcommittee on Anti-Trust and Monopoly of the Committee on the Judiciary United States Senate 85th Congress pp 14, 15; A. Silberston *Bulletin of the Oxford University Institute of Economics and Statistics* 1965 p 269.

97. *The Nationalized Industries* p 22.

98. H/WA 2 April 1965; Iron and Steel Board *Development in the Iron and Steel Industry* 1964 p 136 and information from Board; D. Burn *The Steel Industry 1939–1959* (1961) pp 258, 552.

99. R. Pryke *Why Steel* (Fabian Society) pp 14, 15, 29; British Iron and Stee Federation *The Steel Industry: The Stage 1 Report of the Development Co-ordinating Committee* pp 37–45.

Chapter 18: *Misallocation in Theory*

1. See H. Liebenstein *American Economic Review* 1966 pp 392–413; A. C. Harberger *American Economic Review, Papers and Proceedings* 1954 pp 77–87.

2. BRB 1968 p 79.

3. Information from Mr Lecomber.

4. This analysis rests upon a number of questionable assumptions. In particular it has been taken for granted that the railways' unit costs do not vary with the level of output and that BR has a homogeneous output. In reality it obviously provides a large number of different services; and, it seems likely that even where capacity has been adjusted to the level of output, BR's unit costs would decrease over at least part of the system if its traffic were to increase. This is because the cost of providing track and manning stations does not increase in line with traffic (see pp 252, 253). If the railways are operating under conditions of declining long-run marginal costs, it is under certain circumstances desirable on welfare grounds that loss-making routes should be subsidized. In particular this is economically legitimate where the loss is smaller than the consumer surplus and there is a net welfare gain through keeping the line open. On some loss-making routes such a gain is probably secured, and to this extent our estimate of the welfare loss which the rail deficit involves is an overstatement. But it must be remembered that BR provides a large number of different services and that some of these are profitable while others are highly unprofitable. As a result it is unrealistic to assume, as we have done, that the railways' unit costs exceed their unit revenue by a uniform 20 per cent. In some places the loss is far greater and our estimate of the welfare loss, which ignores the fact that some parts of the system are profitable, is an understatement (see pp. 183–5). Nevertheless it seems doubtful whether, on balance, the estimate is on the low side if only because of yet another debateable assumption. It has been tacitly assumed that consumers are rational and that the railways' demand curve reflects the advantage to be obtained from using the railways at different levels of price. There is reason to believe that this is not the case because firms tend to have an irrational bias against the railways and often fail to count the cost of running their own lorries (see pp 222–6). If so, the provision of rail freight services at a loss may well result in the level of demand being nearer the correct economic level than it would otherwise be, and in the transport costs of the nation being less than they would otherwise, even allowing for the fact that rail transport may not be a perfect substitute for road cartage.

5. See p 428.

6. Conservative and Unionist Central Office *The Campaign Guide 1964* pp 33, 34; Cmnd 4555 pp 92, 94.

7. Cmnd 3438 p 38.

8. AAS 1969 p 357; *Board of Trade Journal* April 1970 p 1107; Iron and Steel Board 1962 p 20.

9. K. Wigley *The Demand for Fuel 1948–75* (Department of Applied Economics, Cambridge, Programme of Growth directed R. Stone) pp 30–39.

10. *Ibid* p 115; Cmnd 3438 p 38; Cmnd 4555 p 94; NCB 1967–8.2 p 52.

11. Institute of Economic Affairs *Rebirth of Britain* (1964) p 89.

12. Information from NCB; NCB 1967–8.2 p 17.

13. Tables 21 and 22; *Rural Bus Services: Report of the Committee* pp 26, 42.

14. SCNI/LT.2 p 388.

15. In other words it was assumed that the industry's marginal costs increased in a straight line from a point where they were equal to the industry's overall average cost to a point where they were about 28 per cent above. The latter point corresponded to the industry's total production while the former corresponded to 64 per cent of total production because about 36 per cent of output was produced at a loss. NCB 1967–8.2 Table 2; information from NCB; K. Wigley *op cit* pp 30–39.

16. Cmnd 4018 p 33.

17. SCNI/LT.2 p 388; *Rural Bus Services, Report of the Committee*, pp 25, 42; Central Transport Consultative Committee 1956 p 11; BTC 1955.2 p 236; LTB 1964 p 46; THC 1964 p 75.

18. Mr Lecomber's long-term elasticity estimate turned out paradoxically to be only 0·6.

19. *Transactions of the Manchester Statistical Society* 11 February 1959 pp 16, 24.

20. See pp 335–37.

21. R. E. Baxter and R. Rees *Economic Journal* 1968 pp 282, 295; 1·3 per cent is the unweighted average.

22. *Ibid* p 295.

23. *The Demand for Fuel 1948–75* p 64.

24. MPSD 1968–9 pp 102, 125.

25. See pp 344, 345, 347–50.

26. See pp 354, 358, 359; SCNI/ES p 52.

27. See p 198.

28. SCNI/MC.3 p 107; EC *Handbook of Electricity Supply Statistics* 1969 p 46; EC 1962–3 p 35, 1968–9 p 148, 1969–70 p 151; MPSD 1968–9 pp 115, 125; Cmnd 2862 p 4; GC 1964–5 p 93, 1965–6 p 87, 1966–7 p 77, 1969–70 pp 124, 125, 128.

Chapter 19: *Misallocation in Practice*

1. *Financial Times* and *Guardian* 13 January 1965; Cmnd 2805 p 4; Cmnd 2798 pp 14, 15; MPSD 1967 p 64.

2. NCB 1957.2 pp 110, 111; 1964–5.2 pp 106, 107.

3. Information from NCB.

4. Information from NCB; NCB 1959 p 33, 1960 p 29, 1961 p 28, 1962 p 27, 1963–4 p 31, 1964 pp 32, 33.

5. NCB 1957.2 pp 124, 125, 1962 p 26; MPSD 1968–9 pp 48, 49.

6. NCB 1963–4.2 pp 120, 121.

7. NCB 1955 p 34, 1956 p 64, 1955–7.2 Table 17, 1964–5, 1965–6, 1966–7.2 Table 35.

8. NCB 1955, 1956 and 1957.2 Tables 18 and 19; 1965–6 and 1966–7.2 Tables 33 and 35.

9. NCB 1957.2 p 137, 1968–9.2 p 93.

10. *British Journal of Industrial Relations* 1968 pp 44, 45.

11. D. Ezra *Financial Times Annual Review* 3 July 1967 p 31 and information from Mr Ezra.

12. See p 401.

13. SCNI/ES.2 Q 837–46.

14. Cmnd 3438 p 26.

15. Monopolies Commission *Petrol* pp 172, 173.

16. See Cmnd 2764.2 p 58.

17. Cmnd 3438 p 25.

18. Information from Mr R. Lecomber.

19. See pp 413, 414.
20. Information from NCB in reply to Parliamentary Question.
21. NCB 1964–5.2 p 123.
22. J. W. House and E. M. Knight *Pit Closure and the Community* University of Newcastle upon Tyne Report to the Ministry of Labour p 35.
23. *Ibid* p 43.
24. SCNI *Gas, Electricity and Coal Industries* Q 216–20.
25. House and Knight p 44.
26. *Ibid* pp 42, 44, 45.
27. *Ibid* pp 40, 48.
28. Figure for all adult male workers in October 1968 and estimate for coal in 1968–9 from NCB 1968–9.2 p 98; UN/ECE *Concentration Indices in the European Coal Industry* p 4; UN/ECE/P p 158; MPSD 1968–9 p 41, 42.
29. House and Knight 28, 36, 38, 61.
30. *Ibid* pp 40, 41, 63, 64.
31. Department of Employment and Productivity *Family Expenditure Survey : Report for 1967* Table 2.
32. See p 396.
33. BRB/MTR p 48; BRB 1966.2 p 43; Cmnd 3439 p 63.
34. G. Clayton and J. H. Rees *The Economic Problems of Rural Transport in Wales* (1967) pp 9, 15–18, 27.
35. Cmnd 3439 p 63.
36. Central Transport Consultative Committee 1967 pp 12, 13.
37. *Ibid* p 13.
38. G. Clayton and J. H. Rees *op cit* p 18.

Chapter 20: *Conclusions: The Irrelevance of Ownership?*

1. See pp 395–400.
2. See pp 104, 105.
3. See pp 39, 42, 105.
4. See pp 115, 118.
5. See p 161.
6. See pp 113, 114, 116, 117.
7. See pp 108, 109.
8. See p 165.
9. See pp 62, 63.
10. See pp 99, 413–19.
11. See pp 163–5.
12. See pp 66–76.
13. See Chapter 17.
14. See pp 78–88, 249, 250, 263, 264, 368, 369.
15. See Chapters 14 and 15.
16. See pp 81–86, 88, 89, 148–54.
17. See pp 165–70.
18. See pp 60–62, 288.
19. See pp 178–83.
20. See pp 186–89.
21. See pp 190–97.
22. See pp 198, 199.

23. See pp 402–5.
24. See pp 413–19.
25. See pp 358–60.
26. See pp 234, 235, 240, 327–29.
27. See pp 325–27.
28. See pp 290–93.
29. See pp 292, 294.
30. See pp 294–98.
31. See Chapter 14.
32. See Chapter 15.
33. See pp 331–33.
34. See pp 351–56.
35. See pp 287–89.
36. See pp 347–50.
37. See pp 422–6.
38. See pp 419–22, 427.
39. See pp 427–32.
40. See pp 395–401.
41. See pp 401–4.
42. C. A. R. Crosland *The Future of Socialism* (1956) pp 479, 480; C. Foster *The Transport Problem* p 31.
43. C. A. R. Crosland *op cit* pp 470, 479; see Chapter 2 and pp 236–48.
44. See Tables 4, 6, 19 and pp 39–49, 70, 227, 228, 243.
45. See pp 39–44, 67–69, 368–73.
46. See pp 58, 68, 74, 80–84, 96, 331, 332; EC 1968–9 p 25; BRB 1968 pp 16, 17.
47. M. Deaglio *Private Enterprise and Public Emulation* p 35.
48. M. V. Posner and S. J. Woolf *Italian Public Enterprise* (1967) pp 26–28; M. Einaudi, M. Byé, E. Rossi *Nationalization in France and Italy* (1955) pp 209, 210; see p 166.
49. C. P. Kindleberger in *National Economic Planning* (1967) edited M. F. Millikan p 285 and in *France: Change and Tradition* (1963) edited S. Hoffman p 122, 131.
50. John Sheahan *Promotion and Control of Industry in Postwar France* (1963) pp 193, 196, 197, 199.
51. See p 382.
52. See pp 31–35.
53. See pp 20, 84.
54. See pp 12, 13; J. Hibbs *The History of British Bus Services* (1968) pp 211–13, 216, 220, 223, 227, 228.
55. See pp 44–46, 237–9; 246.
56. See pp 364–5.
57. See pp 89–91.
58. See pp 97–99.
59. See p 99.
60. See pp 413–19.
61. See p 200; SCNI/NCB pp xvii, 134, 135; Cmnd 3567 pp 5, 6; BRB 1968 p 17.
62. See pp 66–86.
63. Cmd 6610, 6699; *Report of the Committee Appointed to Review the National Problem of the Supply of Electric Energy 1925; Report of the Committee on Electricity Distribution 1936.*

64. Reports 5, 7, 8, 12, 21, 29, 36, 42, 48, 50, 56, 57, 59, 72, 79, 86, 88, 90, 99, 102, 112, 124, 129, 137, 138, 153, 155, 159, 162.

65. Cmd 9672; Cmnd 4018; NCB/ACO; Cmnd 3960; Cmnd 2361. The others were Cmd 8154, 8232, 9372; Cmnd 105, 262, 446, 605, 608, 695, 1859; *Report of The Committee of Enquiry into Economy in the Construction of Power Stations; Report of The Committee of Inquiry into London Transport; Report on Shortages of Gas Supplies in the West Midlands during the Winter of 1965–6*; the unpublished Swash and Corbett reports on BOAC.

66. See pp 467, 468.

67. NCB/ACO pp 64, 65; *Report of the Committee of Inquiry into London Transport* p 101; SCNI/AC pp xxxvii–xli, xlvii; SCNI/BR pp lxxxiv, lxxxvii, lxxxviii; Cmnd 2919 p 18; Cmnd 3656 p 23.

68. SCNI/LT p 104; Cmd 9672 p 145.

69. See pp 40, 41; SCNI/LT pp 51, 52.

70. BOAC 1966–7 p 60; SCNI/BOAC p 56; see also pp 263, 264.

71. See pp 243, 329.

72. See p 80; BRB 1968 pp 16, 17.

73. BRB 1968 pp 16, 17.

74. NCB 1955 p 25, 26; see p 40.

75. SCNI/NCB pp 155, 156; SCNI/ES.3 pp 305–32; SCNI/LT pp 50–52, 104,.2 440–50; SCNI *Reports of Former Select Committees*; SCNI/BOAC pp 44–62; SCNI/BEA pp lxiii; lxiv, D. Coombes *The Member of Parliament and the Administration* (1966) pp 169, 170; SCNI/MC.2 pp 485, 486.

76. See pp 42, 356–8; Cmnd 2805 pp 3, 4; W. G. Shepherd *Economic Performance under Public Ownership* pp 130–33.

77. SCNI/BR pp xxxiii, xl, xli, lii, liii, Q 1863, 1906–9; D. H. Alcroft *British Railways in Transition* (1968) p 156.

78. See pp 251–4, 272–6, 312.

79. See pp 463, 464.

80. SCNI/MC p 95,.3 p 25.

81. SCNI/MC p 95,.3 pp 57, 58, 65, 70.

82. See pp 341–5.

83. SCNI/MC.3 pp 67, 68, 84, 174.

84. See pp 338, 351; SCNI/BOAC Chapter VIII.

85. SCNI/MC p 190.

86. SCNI/MC p 116.

87. SCNI/MC p 124.

88. SCNI/MC p 121.

89. SCNI/MC.2 Q 597.

90. SCNI/MC.2 Q 686.

91. SCNI/MC.2 Q 819, 901, 903.

92. See SCNI/MC.2 Q 514, 520–21, 524, 525, 1313.

93. SCNI/MC.2 Q 991–3, 1013, 1015–19, 1025, 1026; THC 1968 Chapter 8.

94. *The Public and Private Sectors: Similarities and Contrasts* unpublished paper to LSE Seminar on Problems in Industrial Administration 21 February 1967 pp 2, 6.

95. See pp 317, 318, 358.

96. See pp 299, 312.

97. See pp 260, 265, 266.

98. See Chapter 12.

99. SCNI/MC.2 Q 358.

100. SCNI/MC p 154; NCB 1965–6 p 1, 1967–8 p 41; LTB 1965 p 6; BEA 1968–9 p 10.
101. BOAC 1961–2 pp 24, 25; SCNI/BOAC.2 p 255; see Chapter 12.
102. See p 276; BOAC 1964–5 pp 5, 6.
103. THC 1968 Chapter 8.
104. See pp 251–54.
105. The welfare loss as a result of monopoly pricing is analogous to the loss through indirect taxation (see p 400).
106. J. Wiseman in Institute of Economic Affairs *Rebirth of Britain* p 94.
107. See pp 419–27.
108. J. Wiseman, *op cit* p 97.
109. See *ibid* pp 95–98; SCNI/MC.2 p 603.
110. See pp 36–39.
111. See pp 236–48.
112. SCNI/MC.2 p 603; my italics.
113. See pp 89–91, 99.
114. *Public Sector Borrowing – The Problems Ahead* pp 20, 21.
115. Cmnd 4018 pp 259, 260.
116. *Times Business News* 17 December 1970; *Board of Trade Journal* 12 August 1970 p 322.
117. Verbatim Report, 88th Conservative Conference, Blackpool, 1970.
118. R. Pryke and M. Barratt Brown *Stop Messing Them About* (Public Enterprise Group).
119. *Public Sector Borrowing – The Problems Ahead* p 21.
120. Sir Keith Joseph *Financial Times* 17 March 1970.
121. *Promotion and Control of Industry in Postwar France* pp 190, 191.
122. *The Radical Tradition* p 127.

KEY TO COMMAND PAPERS CITED

Cd 2353 *Final Report of the Royal Commission on Coal Supplies* 1905

Cmd 2600 *Report of the Royal Commission on the Coal Industry* 1925

Cmd 3420 Ministry of Transport & Mines Department, Standing Committee on Mineral Transport *First Report* 1929

Cmd 3751 Royal Commission on Transport *Final Report: The Co-ordination & Development of Transport* 1931

Cmd 6610 *Coal Mining : Report of the Technical Advisory Committee* 1945

Cmd 6699 *The Gas Industry : Report of the Committee of Enquiry* 1945

Cmd 6712 Ministry of Civil Aviation *British Air Services* 1945

Cmd 7307 *Interim Report of the Committee of Enquiry into the Tudor Aircraft* 1948

Cmd 7344 Chancellor of the Exchequer *Economic Survey for 1948*

Cmd 7478 *Final Report of the Committee of Enquiry into the Tudor Aircraft* 1948

Cmd 7647 Chancellor of the Exchequer *Economic Survey for 1949*

Cmd 8647 *Report of the Committee on National Policy for the use of Fuel and Power Resources* 1952

Cmd 9191 Minister of Transport and Civil Aviation *Railways Reorganisation Scheme* 1954

Cmd 9389 Lord President of the Council & Minister of Fuel & Power *A Programme of Nuclear Power* 1955

Cmd 9672 *Report of the Committee of Inquiry into the Electricity Supply Industry* 1956

Cmd 9880 The British Transport Commission *Proposals for the Railways* 1956

Cmnd 585 *An Exchange of Correspondence between the Minister of Transport & Civil Aviation & the Chairman of the British Transport Commission* 1958

Cmnd 813 The British Transport Commission *Re-appraisal of the Plan for the Modernization & Re-equipment of British Railways* 1959

Cmnd 827 Committee on the Working of the Monetary System *Report* 1959

Cmnd 1083 Ministry of Power *The Nuclear Power Programme* 1960

Cmnd 1337 Chancellor of the Exchequer *The Financial & Economic Obligations of the Nationalized Industries* 1961

Cmnd 1824 *Report of the Committee of Inquiry into the Major Ports of Great Britain* 1962

Cmnd 2300 *Report of the Committee on Turnover Taxation* 1964

Cmnd 2361 *Report of a Court of Inquiry into the Causes & Circumstances of a dispute between the parties represented on the National Joint Industrial Council for the Electricity Supply Industry* 1964

Cmnd 2695 National Board for Prices & Incomes *Report No. 1 (Interim) Road Haulage Rates* 1965

Cmnd 2764 Secretary of State for Economic Affairs *The National Plan* 1965

Cmnd 2779 *Report of a Court of Inquiry under Mr A. J. Scamp into the issues arising in negotiations between the British Railways Board, the Associated Society of Locomotive Engineers & Firemen and the National Union of Railwaymen* 1965

Cmnd 2798 Ministry of Power *Fuel Policy* 1965

Cmnd 2805 Ministry of Power *The Finances of the Coal Industry* 1965

Cmnd 2853 *Report of the Committee of Inquiry into the Aircraft Industry appointed by the Minister of Aviation under the Chairmanship of Lord Plowden 1964–65*

Cmnd 2862 National Board for Prices & Incomes *Report No. 7 Electricity & Gas Tariffs* 1965

Cmnd 2873 National Board for Prices & Incomes *Report No. 8 Pay & Conditions of Service of British Railways Staff* 1966

Cmnd 2919 National Board for Prices & Incomes *Report No. 12 Coal Prices* 1966

Cmnd 3230 National Board for Prices & Incomes *Report No. 29 The Pay & Conditions of Manual Workers in Local Authorities, the National Health Service, Gas & Water Supply* 1967

Cmnd 3311 National Board for Prices & Incomes *Report No. 36 Productivity Agreements* 1967

Cmnd 3426 *Report of a Court of Inquiry under Professor D. J. Robertson into a Dispute between the British Railways Board & the National Union of Railwaymen concerning Guards and Shunters* 1967

Cmnd 3437 Chancellor of the Exchequer *Nationalized Industries : A Review of Economic and Financial Objectives* 1967

Cmnd 3438 Ministry of Power *Fuel Policy* 1967

Cmnd 3439 Ministry of Transport *Railway Policy* 1967

Cmnd 3470 Ministry of Transport *The Transport of Freight* 1967

Cmnd 3498 National Board for Prices & Incomes *Report No. 50 Productivity Agreements in the Bus Industry* 1967

Cmnd 3567 National Board for Prices and Incomes *Report No. 57 Gas Prices (First Report)* 1968

Cmnd 3575 National Board for Prices & Incomes *Report No. 59 The Bulk Supply Tariff of the Central Electricity Generating Board* 1968

Cmnd 3623 Royal Commission on Trade Unions & Employers' Associations 1965–1968 *Report*

Cmnd 3627 National Board for Prices & Incomes *Report No. 65 Payment by Results Systems* 1968

Cmnd 3656 National Board for Prices & Incomes *Report No. 72 Proposed Increases by British Railways Board in Certain Country-wide Fares and Charges* 1968

Cmnd 3726 National Board for Prices & Incomes *Report No. 79 Electricity Supply Industry National Guidelines Covering Productivity Payments* 1968

Cmnd 3848 National Board for Prices & Incomes *Report No. 90 Pay of Vehicle Maintenance Workers in British Road Services* 1968

Cmnd 3868 National Board for Prices & Incomes *Report No. 9. Pay of Maintenance Workers Employed in Bus Companies*

Cmnd 3924 National Board for Prices & Incomes *Report No. 102 Gas Prices (Second Report)* 1969

Cmnd 3960 *Report of the Committee of Enquiry into Delays in Commissioning CEGB Power Stations* 1969

Cmnd 3995 Chief Secretary to the Treasury *Loans from the National Loans Fund 1969–70* 1969

Cmnd 4018 *British Air Transport in the Seventies : Report of the Committee of Inquiry into Civil Air Transport* 1969

Cmnd 4555 *61st Report of the Commissioners of Her Majesty's Customs & Excise for the year ended 31st March 1970* 1971

Cmnd 4578 Chancellor of the Exchequer *Public Expenditure 1969–70 to 1974–75* 1971

Index

Kuwait Airways, 265-6

labour force:
of European railways, 143, 147
of European coal mines, 122
of nationalized industries, 21-2, 59
as percentage of all civil employment, 21, 59
see also individual industries
labour relations, 91-102, 447
labour-saving investment, 112, 407-
8
Lawson, G., 330, 333
Lecomber, Richard, 231, 396, 405,
409
Leach, C. H., 339-40
limestone, company trains for, 213
Little, Ian, 291
London Airport, 259
London Passenger Transport Board,
10
London Transport, 10, 12
Government control of fares of,
185
one-man buses of, 62, 84-5, 90,
452
output of, 15
productivity bargaining in, 83-5,
90
profits and losses of, 182-3, 403,
437, 448
workshops of, 451-2
see also buses nationalized
Longhurst, John, 260-2
Lorraine, coal pits in, 121-2, 128
Lufthansa (German airlines):
output of, 157, 159
productivity growth in, 156-7, 162
productivity level in, 159-60, 167
rate of return on capital in, 198,
277
Lurgi gas plant, 339-42, 344

McGowan Committee, on electricity
distribution, 376
Maddison, Angus, 166, 168
mail subsidy, to airlines in USA, 262
managers for nationalized industries,
21, 25, 442-3, 446-8
morale of, 31-5
motivation of, 445-6, 461-2
see also individual industries
manufacturing/private industry:
cost of capital to, 353, 355
depreciation provisions by, 188-9,
438

economies of scale in, 390-2
investment by, 323-4, 330, 333,
347-9, 351, 455
knowledge of transport costs, 222-
6
labour relations and strikes in, 91-
100
output of, 14-16; index numbers,
17, 106
prices charged by, index numbers,
175
productivity growth in, 103-5,
434; compared with other countries, 161-2; index numbers, 20,
106; pre-war, 117; in relation to
productivity growth, 108, 435
productivity level in, 167, 169-70
rate of return on capital in, 190-1,
196-9, 438
residual productivity of, 111-12,
117, 434
wages in, index numbers, 177
work study in, 79-80
Matthews, R. C. O., 109
Meco-Moore cutter-loader for coal,
67
Meek, Ronald, 354
Merrett, A. J., 353
merry-go-round working of coal
trains, 50, 70, 75, 188
method study, 79-81; *see also* work
study
Middle East Airlines, 265-6
Miller, R., 271, 282
Milward, Sir Anthony, 459
Ministry of Power, 299, 314, 317-18,
320, 331, 339, 343-5, 354, 356,
358-9, 455
Ministry of Transport, 36, 55-6,
234, 236, 246, 251-4, 356, 431,
455, 457-8
misallocation of resources:
in practice, 413-32, 440-2
in theory, 395-412
Missenden, Sir Eustace, 45
monopolies:
of electricity and gas industries,
465-7
potential welfare loss from, 395-6
Monopolies Commission, 188-9
Morrison, Herbert, 255
motor car industry:
economies of scale in, 390-1
productivity of, Britain and Japan,
166
strikes in, 96-7, 100

dirty money

dirty money

RICHARD STARK

Quercus

First published in Great Britain in 2009 by

Quercus
21 Bloomsbury Square
London
WC1A 2NS

A CIP catalogue record for this book is available
from the British Library

ISBN (HB) 978 1 84724 711 7
ISBN (TPB) 978 1 84724 773 5

10 9 8 7 6 5 4 3 2 1

Typeset in Swift by Ellipsis Books Limited, Glasgow
Printed and bound in Great Britain
by Clays Ltd, St Ives Plc.

This is for Dr Quirke,
and his creator – two lovely gents

dirty money

ONE

1

When the silver Toyota Avalon bumped down the dirt road out of the woods and across the railroad tracks, Parker put the Infiniti into low and stepped out onto the gravel. The Infiniti jerked forward toward the river as the Toyota slewed around behind it to a stop. Parker picked up the full duffel bag from where he'd tossed it on the ground, and behind him, the Infiniti rolled down the slope into the river, all its windows open; it slid into the gray dawn water like a bear into a trout stream.

Parker carried the duffel in his arms and Claire got out of the Toyota to open its rear door and say, 'Do you want to drive?'

'No. I've been driving.' He heaved the duffel onto the backseat, then got around to take the passenger side in front.

Before getting behind the wheel, she stood looking toward the river, a tall slender ash-blonde in black slacks and a bulky dark red sweater against the October chill. 'It's gone,' she said.

'Good.'

She slid into the Toyota then and kissed him and held his face in her slim hands. 'It's been a while.'

'It didn't come out the way it was supposed to.'

'But you got back,' she said, and steered the Toyota across the tracks and up the dirt road through scrub woods. 'Was one of the men with you named Dalesia?'

'Nick. They nabbed him.'

'He escaped,' she said, paused at the blacktop state road and turned right, southward.

'Nick escaped?'

'I had the news on, driving up. It happened a couple of hours ago, in Boston. They were transferring him from the state police to the federal, going to take him somewhere south to question him. He killed a marshal, escaped with the gun.'

Parker looked at her profile. They were almost alone on the road, not yet seven a.m., she driving fast. He said, 'They grabbed him yesterday. They didn't question him yet?'

'That's what they said.' She shrugged, eyes on the road. 'They didn't say so, but it sounded to me like a turf war, the local police and the FBI. The FBI won, but then they lost him.'

Parker looked out at this hilly country road, heading south. Soon they'd be coming into New Jersey. 'If nobody questioned Nick yet, then they don't know where the money is.'

With a head gesture toward the duffel bag behind them, she said, 'That isn't it?'

'No, that's something else.'

She laughed, mostly in surprise. 'You don't have that money, so you picked up some other money on the way back?'

'There was too much heat around the robbery,' he told her. 'We could stash it, but we couldn't carry it. We each took a little, and Nick tried to spend some of his, but they had the serial numbers.'

'Oh. That's why they caught him. Do *you* have some?'

'Not any more.'

'Good.'

They rode in silence for a while, he stretching his legs, rolling his shoulders, a big ropy man who looked squeezed into the Toyota. He'd driven through the night, called Claire an hour ago from a diner to make the meet and get rid of the Infiniti, which was too hot and too speckled with fingerprints. Now they passed a slow-moving oil delivery truck and he said, 'I need some sleep, but after that I'll want you to drive me to Long Island. All my identification got wasted in the mess in Massachusetts. I'd better not drive until I get new papers.'

'You're just going to talk to somebody?'

'That's all.'

'Then I can drive you.'

'Good.'

She watched the road; no traffic now. She said, 'This is still something about the robbery?'

'The third guy with us,' he said. 'He'll know what it means, too, that Nick's on the loose.'

'That the police don't know where the money is.'

'But Nick knows where we are, or could point in a direction. Are we all still partners?' He shook his head. 'You

5

kill a lawman,' he said, 'you're in another zone. McWhitney and I are gonna have to work this out.'

'But not on the phone.'

Parker yawned. 'Nothing on the phone ever,' he said. 'Except pizza.'

2

Once or twice, Claire had gotten too close to Parker's other world, or that world had gotten too close to her, and she hadn't liked it, so he did his best to keep her separate from that kind of thing. But this business was all right; everything had already happened, this was just a little tidying up.

She drove them eastward across New Jersey late that afternoon, and he told her the situation: 'There was a meeting that didn't pan out. A guy there named Harbin was a problem a lot of different ways. He was wearing a wire—'

'A police wire?'

'Which got him killed. Then it turned out there was federal reward money out on him, and it attracted a bounty hunter named Keenan.'

She said, 'This didn't have anything to do with you in Massachusetts.'

'Nothing. This was just an annoyance, Keenan trying to find everybody at the meeting, so somebody could lead him to Harbin, which nobody was going to do. He got hold of some phone records, Nick Dalesia made two calls to our place here, that brought him around.'

She glanced at him, then looked out at Interstate 80, pretty heavy traffic in both directions, a lot of big trucks, the kind of traffic where you didn't change lanes a lot. 'You mean,' she said, 'the law might come around now, using those same records.'

'I don't think so,' he said. 'Keenan was looking for connections. The law's looking for Nick, and they'll know he's too smart to go hole up with somebody he knows. They won't be spending time looking at phone bills.'

'Well, where are we going now?'

Parker was rested, most of the day asleep, but this car still felt too small. Maybe it was because he wasn't at the wheel. He stretched in place and said, 'Keenan's partner, a woman named Sandra Loscalzo, caught up with us in Massachusetts just before the job. McWhitney convinced her to go away, and when he got back to Long Island he'd lead her to Harbin.'

'Who's already dead.'

'Yes.'

'And McWhitney lives on Long Island?'

'He's got a bar there, and lives behind it.'

'And that's where we're going.'

'And when we get there, the next part is up to you.'

She frowned out at the traffic and the eastern sky darkening ahead of them. 'Is this something I won't like?'

'I don't think so. When we get there, I can go in and talk to McWhitney and you can wait in the car, or you come in, we have a drink, it's a social occasion.'

'There isn't going to be any trouble.'

8

'None. We've got to decide what to do about Loscalzo, and we've got to decide what to do about the money. There's too much heat up in that area right now—'

'Because of what you people did.'

'They're looking close at strangers,' Parker said, and shrugged. 'So we'll have to leave the cash where it is for a while, but if we leave it too long either they find Nick again and he trades the money for a better sentence, or he gets to it himself and cleans it out because he's desperate. Being on the run the way he is uses up a lot of cash.'

'You said they have the serial numbers,' she said, 'so he can't use it, can he?'

'He'll leave a wide backtrail, but he won't care.'

'But *you* won't be able to use it.'

'Offshore,' he said. 'We can sell it for a percentage to people who'll take it to Africa or Asia, it'll never get into the banking system again.'

'There are so many ways to do things,' she said.

'There have to be.'

She said, 'Before, you said you have to decide what to do about what's-her-name? The bounty hunter's partner.'

'Sandra Loscalzo.'

'Why don't you have to decide what to do about the man? Keenan.'

'He's dead, too.'

'Oh.'

He looked out at the traffic, which was thickening as they got closer to the city. They were both silent a while, and then he was surprised when she said, 'I'll come in with you.'

9

3

'We can't go there yet, you know,' McWhitney said, by way of greeting.

Standing at the bar, Parker said, 'Nelson McWhitney, this is my friend Claire.'

'Hello, friend,' McWhitney said, and dealt two coasters onto the bar, saying, 'Grab a stool. What can the house buy you?'

'I would take a scotch and soda,' Claire said, as she and Parker took the two nearest stools.

'A ladies' drink,' McWhitney commented. 'Good. Parker?'

'Beer.'

McWhitney's bar, in Bay Shore on Long Island's south shore, was deep and narrow, its dark wood walls and floors illuminated mostly by beer-sign neon. At eight-thirty on a Monday night in October it was nearly empty, two solitary men finishing whiskey along the bar and a yellow-haired woman hunched inside a black coat at the last dark table along the other side.

McWhitney himself didn't look much livelier, maybe because he too had had a rough weekend. Red-bearded and red-faced, he was a hard bulky man with a soft middle, a defensive lineman gone out of shape. He made their drinks, brought them over, and leaned close to say, 'Those two will be outa here in a couple minutes, and then I'll close up.'

Parker said, 'What do you hear from Sandra?'

Raising an eyebrow toward Claire, McWhitney said, 'Your friend's up to speed on you and me?'

'Always.'

'That's nice.' Nodding his head toward the rear of the bar, McWhitney said, 'Sandra's not quite that good a friend, but there she is, back there, waiting on a phone call.' He raised his voice: 'Sandra! Look who dropped by.'

When Sandra Loscalzo rose to come join them, she was tall and slender, in heels and jeans and the black coat over a dark blue sweater. She walked in a purposeful way, taking charge of her territory. She wasn't carrying a glass. At the bar, she said to Parker, 'The last time I saw you, you were driving a phony police car.'

Parker said, 'The police car was real. I was the phony. You were there?'

'Fifty-yard line.' She sounded admiring, but also amused. 'You boys are cute, in a destructive kind of way.' Looking at Claire, she said, 'Is he destructive at home?'

'Of course not,' Claire said, and smiled. 'I'm Claire. You're Sandra?'

'G'night, Nels,' called one of the customers, rising from his seat, waving a hand over his shoulder as he left.

'See you, Norm.'

Parker said to Sandra, 'You're waiting for a phone call.'

Sandra made a disgusted headshake and gestured at

McWhitney. 'This fellow and Harbin,' she said. 'Where's he stash him? In Ohio. *I'm* not going to Ohio, eyeball the fellow, that means, what I've got to do, I call my guy in DC, I pass along my tip, and I'm not even sure Nelson here isn't pulling my chain. What if Harbin *isn't* there? I don't keep a reputation with dud tips.'

McWhitney said, 'I don't give you dud tips. What's in it for me? He's right exactly where I told you.'

'Have a good one, Nels.'

'You too, Jack.' McWhitney waved, then said to Parker, 'About halfway between Cincinnati and Dayton, Interstate 75, they're putting in a new restaurant, rest area. There's a spot they're gonna blacktop for the parking lot very soon now but not yet, not till the structure's a little further along. A month ago, it was just messed-up fill in there, bulldozed a little, a lot of wide tire tracks. A few more weeks, they gotta lay that blacktop before winter freezes the ground, but not yet.'

'I hate it when somebody's plausible,' Sandra said. 'Everything fits together like Lego. Life doesn't do that.'

'Every once in a while,' McWhitney told her, 'the plausible guy has the goods.'

Parker said, 'So McWhitney gave you the tip, and you gave it to somebody you know in DC—'

'In the US marshals' office.'

'And they're sending somebody to check it out. If the body's there, you get your reward money. They're calling you here?'

'Not on the *bar's* phone,' she said. 'On my cell.'

'All right.'

'Pretty soon, they'll call,' Sandra said. She did all her

talking with her right hand in her coat pocket. 'If they say Harbin's there, fine. If they say Mr Harbin's still among the missing, I'm gonna feel very embarrassed.'

'He's there,' McWhitney said.

'But I'll get over my embarrassment,' she told them, 'because I'll still have a little something to give them, make up for the inconvenience. Originally, I just had Nelson here.' She smiled around at them all. 'But now,' she said, 'I got a twofer.'

4

McWhitney said, 'I'd better lock up.'

He had to walk down to the end of the bar and open the flap there to come out, then walk back past the others on this side. Sandra stepped back against the line of booths so he wouldn't pass behind her, then said to Parker, 'Funny you should happen by.'

'Is it?'

'You find yourself in the neighborhood, just the same day Dalesia slips his bonds.'

Returning to the others, staying now on this side of the bar, McWhitney said, 'Sandra, don't excite yourself. We aren't helping Nick. He isn't gonna let us know where he is.'

Skeptical, Sandra said, 'Why? Because you'd turn him in?'

'That's the last thing we'd do,' McWhitney said, 'and he knows it. Unless it was turn him in like you're turning in Harbin.'

She shook her head. 'You were a team.'

'Not any more.'

14

Parker said, 'If they take him again, all he has for bargaining chips is the money and us.'

'Well, it's me more than you,' McWhitney said. 'He knows this place here.'

'I think,' Claire said carefully, 'he knows our phone number.'

Sandra looked at her with a little smile. 'You mean, he *knows* your phone number. He's used your phone number. Roy Keenan and me, we looked at that number. Nick Dalesia never did have a wide range of telephone pals. Ms Willis stood out.'

Claire shrugged. 'I never actually met the man,' she said. 'I have no real link with him at all. I was looking for somebody to blacktop my driveway. I forget who said they'd have Mr Dalesia call me. I talked to him twice, but I thought he sounded unreliable.'

'That's nice,' Sandra said. 'As long as Nick isn't there to say it didn't happen that way.'

'That's what we're saying,' McWhitney told her. He had taken the stool next to Parker, with Claire beyond, the three facing Sandra with her right hand in her pocket and her back braced against the booth's tall coatrack.

'All right,' Sandra said. 'But while we're waiting here, it might be we could do some other business together. I mean, if this Harbin thing turns out to be on the up-and-up.'

McWhitney said, 'What kind of business?'

'You people took a lot of money up there in New England,' Sandra said, 'but then you had to leave it. That's only three days ago, too soon for you to dare to go back.' To Parker, she said, 'But Dalesia might go for it, that's why you came here to see McWhitney. How to keep the money safe from your friend without exposing yourselves to the law.'

Parker said, 'I think Nick's pretty busy right about now.'

'I think your Nick needs money bad right about now,' Sandra said.

McWhitney said, 'You aren't, I hope, gonna say we should tell you where it is, so you can go get it and bring it back to us.'

Sandra's free left hand made a shrugging gesture. 'Why not? One woman could get in there and out, and then you've got something instead of nothing.'

'If you come back,' McWhitney said.

Parker said, 'We'll take our chances. If you *don't* get in and out, if they grab you with the money, they're gonna ask you who told you where it was. What reason would you have not to tell them?'

Sandra thought about that, then nodded. 'I see how it could look,' she said. 'All right, it was just an offer.'

McWhitney said, 'I can't give you people meals in this place. How much longer you think we're gonna wait?'

'Until they call me,' she said.

Parker said, 'Call them.'

Sandra didn't like that. 'What for? They'll do what they're doing, and then they'll call me.'

'You call them,' Parker said. 'You tell them, speed it up, your tipster's getting anxious, he's afraid there's a double-cross coming along.'

'It won't do any good to push—' she said, and a small, flat, almost toneless brief ring sounded. 'At last,' she said, looking suddenly relieved, showing an anxiety of her own

16

she'd been covering till now. Her right hand stayed in the coat pocket while her left dipped into the other pocket and came out with the cell phone. Her thumb clipped into the second ring and she said, 'Keenan. Sure it's me, it's Roy's business phone. What have you got?'

Parker watched McWhitney. Was the man tensing? Had he given the bounty hunter the truth?

Suddenly Sandra beamed, the last of the tension gone, and her right hand came empty out of the pocket. 'That's great. I thought my source was reliable, but you can never be sure. I'll come into the New York office tomorrow for the check? Fine, Wednesday. Oh, Roy's around here somewhere.'

McWhitney looked very alert, but then relaxed again as Sandra said into the phone, 'My best to Linda. Thanks, she's fine. Talk to you later.' She broke the connection, pocketed the phone, and said to McWhitney, 'It worked out. He's who he is, he's where you said.'

'Like I said.' Now that it was over, McWhitney suddenly looked tired. 'Let me throw you people out of here now.'

As they walked down the bar toward the door, Sandra said, 'You got any more goods like that stashed around, you know what I mean, goods with some value on them, give me a call.'

'What I should have done,' McWhitney said, as he unlocked the door to let them out, 'I should have held out for a finder's fee.'

Sandra laughed and walked away toward her car, and McWhitney shut the door. They could hear the click of the lock.

5

Claire's place was on a lake in north-central New Jersey, surrounded mostly by seasonal houses, only a fifth or so occupied year-round. In several of these houses were hollow walls, crawl spaces, unused attic stubs, where Parker kept his stashes.

Two days after the overnight trip to Long Island, he finally stashed the duffel bag he'd brought from upstate New York, then drove to put gas in Claire's Toyota, paying with cash from the duffel, money on which nobody had a record of the numbers. Heading back, he was about to turn in at Claire's driveway when he saw through the trees another car parked down in there, black or dark gray. Instead, then, he went on to the next driveway and steered in there, stopping at a house boarded up for the winter.

He probably knew this house better than the owners did, including the whereabouts of the key that most of the seasonal people hid near their front doors where workmen or anybody else could find them. He didn't need the key this time. He walked around the side of the house opposite Claire's place and on the lake side came to a wide porch that in summer was screened. Now the screens were stored in the space beneath the porch.

Parker moved past the porch and across a cleared lane between the buildings kept open for utility workers and on to the blindest corner of Claire's house. Moving along the lake side, not stepping up on the porch, he could see across and through a window at the interior. Claire was seated on the sofa in there, talking with two men seated in chairs angled toward her. He couldn't see the men clearly, but there was no tension in the room. Claire was speaking casually, gesturing, smiling.

Parker turned away and went back to the next-door house, where he stepped up onto the porch, took a seat in a wooden Adirondack armchair there, and waited.

Five minutes. Two men in dark topcoats and snap-brim hats came out of Claire's front door, and Claire stood in the doorway to speak to them. The men moved together, as though from habit rather than intention. With the hats, they looked like FBI agents from fifties movies, except that in the fifties movies one of them would not have been black.

The two men each touched a finger to the brim of his hat. Claire said something else, easy and unconcerned, and shut the door as the men got into their anonymous pool car, the white driving, and went away.

Parker went back around this house to the Toyota, drove to Claire's place, and thumbed the visor control that opened the garage. When he stepped from the garage to the kitchen Claire was in there, making coffee. 'Want some?'

'Yes. FBI?'

'Yes. I told them my blacktop story, and said I'd try to remember who gave me Mr Dalesia's name, but it had been a while.'

He sat at the kitchen table. 'They bought it?'

'They bought the house, the lake, the attractive woman, the sunlight.'

'They gave you their card, and that was it?'

'Probably,' she said. 'They said they might call me if they thought of anything else to ask, and I said I thought I might be going on an early-winter vacation soon, I wasn't sure.' Bringing Parker's coffee to the table, she said, 'Should I?'

'Yes. We'll go together.'

Surprised, she sat across from him and said, 'You have a place in mind?'

'When I was in Massachusetts last week,' he said, 'they were talking about something called leaf peeping.'

Even more surprised, she said, 'Leaf peeping? Oh, that's because the fall colors change on the trees.'

'That's it.'

'People go to New England just to see the colors on the trees.' She considered. 'They call them leaf peepers?'

'That's what I heard.'

She looked out the kitchen window toward the lake. Most of the trees around here were evergreens, but there were some that changed color in the fall; down here, that wouldn't be for another month, and not as showy as New England. 'It makes them sound silly,' she said. 'Leaf peepers. You make a whole trip to look at leaves. I guess it is silly, really.'

Richard Stark

'We wouldn't be the only ones there.'

She looked at him. 'What you really want to do,' she said, 'is be near the money.'

'I want to know what's happening there. You have to drive and pay for the place we stay, because I don't have ID. And if I'm a leaf peeper, I'm not a bank robber.'

'You're a leaf peeper if you're with me.'

'That's right.'

'On your own, nobody would buy you for a leaf peeper,' she said, and smiled, and then stopped smiling.

Sensing a dark memory rising up inside her, he said, 'Everything's all finished up there. It's done. Nothing's going to happen except we look at leaves and we look at a church.'

'A church,' she echoed.

Rising, he said, 'Let me get a map, I'll show you the area we want. Then you can find a place up there—'

'A bed-and-breakfast.'

'Right. We'll stay for a week.' Nodding at the phone on the wall, he said, 'Then you can make your answering machine message be that you're on vacation for a week, and you can give the place you're gonna be.'

'Because,' she said, 'what's going to happen up there already happened.'

'That's right,' he said.

6

'You folks here for the robbery?'

The place was called Bosky Rounds, and the pictures on the website had made it look like somewhere that Hansel and Gretel might have stopped off. Deep eaves, creamy stucco walls, broad dark green wooden shutters flanking the old-fashioned multipaned windows, and a sun god knocker on the front door. The Bosky Rounds gimmick, though they wouldn't have used the word, was that they offered maps of nearby hiking trails through the forest, for those leaf peepers who would like to be surrounded by their subject. It was the most rustic and innocent accommodation Claire could find, and Parker had agreed it was perfect for their purposes.

And the first thing Mrs Bartlett, the owner, the nice motherly lady in the frilled apron and the faint aroma of apple pie, said to them was, 'You folks here for the robbery?'

'Robbery?' Claire managed to look both astonished and worried. 'What robbery? You were robbed?'

'Oh, not *me*, dear,' and Mrs Bartlett offered a throaty

chuckle and said, 'It was all over the television. Not five miles from here, last week, a week ago tomorrow, a whole *gang* attacked the bank's armored cars with *bazookas*.'

'Bazookas!' Claire put her hand to her throat, then leaned forward as though she suspected this nice old lady was pulling her leg. 'Wouldn't that burn up all the money?'

'Don't ask me, dear, I just know they blew up everything, my cousin told me it was like a war movie.'

'Was he *there*?'

'No, he rushed over as soon as he heard it on his radios.' To Parker she said, 'He has all these different kinds of radios, you know.' Back to Claire she said, 'You really haven't heard about it?'

'Oh, us New Yorkers,' Claire said, with a laugh and a shrug. 'We really are parochial, you know. If it doesn't happen in Central Park, we don't know a thing about it.' Handing over her credit card, she said, 'I tell you what. Let us check in and unpack, and then you'll tell us all about it.'

'I'd be delighted,' said Mrs Bartlett. 'And you're the Willises,' she said, looking at the credit card.

'Claire and Henry,' Claire said.

Mrs Bartlett put the card in her apron pocket. 'I put you in room three upstairs,' she said. 'It really is the nicest room in the house.'

'Lovely.'

'I'll give you back your card when you come down.' She turned to say to Parker, 'And you'll have tea?'

'Sure. Thanks.'

*

It was a large room, with two large bright many-paned windows, frills on every piece of furniture, and a ragged old Oriental carpet. They unpacked into the old tall dresser and the armoire, there being no closet, and Parker went over to look out the window toward the rear of the house. The trees began right there, red and yellow and orange and green. 'I'll have to look on the map,' he said. 'See where this is.'

'You mean, from the robbery site,' Claire said, and laughed. 'Don't worry, Mrs Bartlett will tell you, in detail. Will you mind sitting through that?'

'It's a good idea,' Parker said, 'for me to know what the locals think happened.'

'Fine. But one thing.'

He looked at her. 'Yeah?'

'If she gets a part wrong,' Claire said, 'don't correct her.'

Over tea and butter cookies in the communal parlor downstairs, Mrs Bartlett gave them an exhaustive and mostly accurate description of what had gone on up in those woods last Friday night. It turned out, she said, that two of the local banks were going to combine, so all of the money from one was going to the other. It was all very hush-hush and top secret and nobody was supposed to know anything about it, but it turned out *somebody* knew what was going on, because, just at this intersection here – she showed them on the county map – where these two small roads meet, nobody knows how many gangsters suddenly appeared with bazookas, and smashed up all the armored cars – there were four armored cars, with all the bank's papers and everything in addition to the money – and drove off with the one armored car with the money in it, and when the police found the armored car later all the money was gone.

Parker said, 'How did the gangsters know which armored car had the money in it?'

'Well, *that*,' Mrs Bartlett told them, leaning close to confide a secret, 'that was where the scandal came in. The wife of the bank owner, Mrs Langen, she was in cahoots with the robbers!'

Claire said, 'In cahoots? The banker's wife? Oh, Mrs Bartlett.'

'No, it's true,' Mrs Bartlett promised them. 'It seems she'd taken up with a disgraced ex-guard in her husband's bank. He went to jail for stealing something or other, and when he came back they started right up again where they left off, and the first thing you know they robbed her own husband's bank!'

'But the law got them,' Parker suggested.

'Oh, yes, of course, the police immediately captured *them*,' Mrs Bartlett said. 'They'll pay for their crimes, don't you worry. But not the robbers, no, not the people who actually took the money.'

'The people with the bazookas,' Parker said, because the Carl-Gustaf antitank weapons from Sweden had not been bazookas.

'Those people,' Mrs Bartlett agreed. 'And the money, too, of course. There've been police and state troopers and FBI men and I don't know what all around here all week. I even had three state police investigators staying here until Tuesday.'

'I'm sorry we missed them,' Claire murmured.

'Oh, they were just like anybody,' Mrs Bartlett said. 'You wouldn't know anything to look at them.'

'I suppose,' Claire said, turning to Parker, 'we ought to go see where this robbery took place.'

'It's *still* traffic jams over there,' Mrs Bartlett said. 'People going, and stopping, and taking pictures, though I have no idea what they think they're taking pictures of. Just some burned trees, that's all.'

'It's the excitement,' Claire suggested. 'People want to be around the excitement.'

'Well, if you're going over there,' Mrs Bartlett said, 'the best time is in the morning. Before nine o'clock.' She leaned forward again for another confidence. 'Tourists, generally, are very slugabed,' she told them.

'Well,' Claire said, 'they are on vacation.'

Parker said, 'So, when we go out to dinner, we shouldn't go in that direction.'

'Oh, no. There are some lovely places . . . Let me show you.'

There was a specific route Parker wanted, but he needed Mrs Bartlett to suggest it. He found reasons not to be enthusiastic about her first three dinner suggestions, but the fourth would be on a route that would take them right past the church. 'New England seafood,' he said. 'That sounds fine. You want to give Claire the directions?'

'I'd be very happy to.'

7

It was still a couple of hours before sunset, and Claire wanted to walk outside a while, to work off the stiffness of the long car ride. They stepped out the front door, and a young guy was just bouncing up onto the porch. 'Hi,' he said, and they nodded and would have passed him but he stopped, frowned, pointed at them, and said, 'I didn't talk with you folks, did I?'

'No,' Claire said.

'Well, let me—' He was patting himself all over, frisking himself for something, while he talked, a kind of distracted smile on his face. He looked to be in his early twenties, with thick windblown brown hair, a round expectant face, and large black-framed glasses that made him look like an owl. A friendly owl. He wore a dark gray car coat with a cell phone dangling in front of it from a black leather strap around his neck, and jeans and boots, and it was the car coat he searched as he said, 'I'm not a nut or anything, I wanna show you my bona fides, I've got my card here somewh— Oh, here it is.' And from an interior pocket he plucked a business card, which he handed to Claire.

The card was pale yellow, with maroon letters centered, reading

TERRY MULCANY
Journalist

laureled with phone, fax and cell phone numbers, plus an e-mail address. There was no terrestrial address.

Claire said, 'It doesn't say who you're a journalist for.'

'I'm freelance,' Mulcany said, smiling nervously, apparently not sure they'd be impressed by his status. 'I specialize in true crime. No, keep it,' he said, as Claire was about to hand the card back. 'I've got boxes of them.' The grin semaphored and he said, 'I lose them all the time, and then I find them.'

'That's nice,' Claire said. 'Excuse me, we were just—'

'Oh, no, I don't want to take up your time,' Mulcany said. 'I just— You heard about the robbery, here last week.'

'Mrs Bartlett just told us all about it.'

'Oh, is that her name, the lady here?'

Claire bent to him. 'You aren't staying here?'

'Oh, no, I can't afford this place,' and the smile flickered some more. 'Not until my advance comes in. I've got a deal with Spotlight to do a book on the robbery, so I'm just here getting the background, taking some pictures.'

'Well, I'm sorry, we can't help,' Claire told him. 'We just heard about the robbery ourselves half an hour ago.'

'That's fine, I don't expect—' Mulcany interrupted himself a lot, now saying, 'You're here for the foliage, aren't you?'

Claire nodded. 'Of course.'

'So you'll be out, driving around, walking around,' Mulcany said. 'If you see anything, anything at all, anything that seems a little weird, out of the ordinary, let me know. Call me on my cell,' he said, holding it up for them to look at. 'If you find me something and I use it,' he said, grinning in full, letting the cell phone drop to his coat front again, 'I'll give you the credit, and I'll put you in the index!'

'Well, I don't know what we might see,' Claire told him, 'but that's a tempting offer. I'll keep your card.'

'Great.' He was suddenly in a hurry to move on. 'And I gotta check a couple details with – What was her name again?'

'Mrs Bartlett. Like the pear.'

'Oh, great,' Mulcany said. 'That I can remember. Thanks a lot!' And he hurried into Bosky Rounds.

Claire laughed as she and Parker started away from the B and B and down the town road with its wide dirt strip instead of a sidewalk. 'Isn't that nice?' she said. 'You lost money on that expedition, but he's going to make some. So it's working out for somebody, after all.'

'I don't like him being here,' Parker said.

'Oh, he's harmless,' she said.

Parker shook his head. 'On some wall,' he said, 'that guy's got those wanted posters tacked up. This time, he looked at you. Next time, maybe he looks at me.'

8

As they drove toward their New England seafood dinner, Parker said, 'Nick's the one found the church. It's abandoned for years, off on a side road. The original idea was, we'd spend the first night there, split up the cash, head out in the morning. But the law presence was so intense we couldn't move, and we couldn't take the cash with us. So we left it there.'

'In the church.'

'We'll be going by it in a few minutes.'

'I won't see much in the dark.'

'I don't want you to even slow down,' Parker told her. 'The story the law is giving out is that Nick escaped before he could tell them anything, but they don't always tell the truth, you know.'

'You think they might know the money's there, in the church?'

'And they might have it staked out, waiting for us to come back. So we'll just drive by. In daylight, I'll try to get a better look at it.'

They kept driving, on dark, small, thinly populated roads, until he said, 'It's on the right.'

A small white church crouched in darkness, with parking around it. Claire looked at it as she drove by and said, 'I don't see anybody.'

'You wouldn't.'

They passed the church again on their way back from the not-bad seafood dinner, and still didn't see any sign of anybody in or near the place. But then they walked into Bosky Rounds and there in the communal parlor they did see somebody they knew: Susan Loscalzo.

She got to her feet with a big smile when they walked in, tossing *Yankee* magazine back onto the coffee table as she said, 'Well, hello, you two. Fancy running into you guys here.'

9

There were five guest rooms at Bosky Rounds, and with Sandra's arrival late this afternoon all five were occupied. Now, in another corner of the communal parlor, two couples murmured together, planning their itinerary for tomorrow. Glancing toward them, ignoring the fact that Parker and Claire hadn't said anything to her greeting, Sandra said, 'I saw a bar on the way here looking like it had possibilities. Want to check it out?'

'Sure,' Parker said, and to Claire he said, 'You want to come along?'

'Absolutely.'

Nodding, with a little smile at Claire, Sandra said, 'One car or two?'

'We'll follow you,' Parker said.

As they turned toward the front door, Sandra looked around and said, 'Where's Mrs Muskrat?'

Claire said, 'I think we're on our own till morning.'

'It's the kind of place,' Sandra said, 'I feel I oughta check in with the proctor before I do anything.'

Her car, in the gravel lot beside the building, was a

small black Honda Accord that would have been anonymous if it weren't for the two whip antennas arcing high over its top, making it look like some outsized tropical insect in the wrong weather zone. Sandra got behind the wheel with a wave, and Claire started the Toyota to follow.

Driving down the dark road with that humped black insect in front of her, Claire said, 'Tell me about Sandra. Does she have a guy?'

'She isn't straight,' Parker said. 'She lives with a woman on Cape Cod, and the woman has a child. Sandra supports the child. She thought she was the brains behind Roy Keenan and maybe she was. We got linked to her because she wanted the Harbin reward money and we led her to it. What she wants now I don't know.'

'The bank money?'

'Maybe.' Parker shook his head, not liking it. 'It's not in her line,' he said. 'I'd think she'd be out looking for another Roy Keenan now. I don't know what she's doing.'

'Was Roy Keenan straight?'

'Oh, yeah. That was just a business arrangement. She'd be out of sight with the handgun while Keenan asked the questions.'

Claire said, 'I don't mean to be a matchmaker, but why wouldn't McWhitney be a good new Roy?'

'Because he's too hotheaded and she's too hard,' Parker said. 'One of them would kill the other in a month, I don't know which. This looks like the place.'

It was. The Honda, antennae waving, turned in at an old-fashioned sprawling roadhouse with a fairly full parking lot to one side. The main building, two stories high, was flanked by wide enclosed porches, brightly lit, while the second floor was completely dark. A large floodlit sign out by the road, at right angles to the parking lot, told drivers from both directions WAYWARD INN.

They parked the cars next to one another and met on the gravel. 'I didn't go inside the place before,' Sandra said. 'It seemed to me, big enough for some privacy, dining rooms on both sides, bar in the middle.'

'Bar,' Claire said.

'You're my kind of girl,' Sandra told her, and led the way as Claire lifted an eyebrow at Parker.

The entrance was a wide doorway centered in the front of the building, at the end of a slate path from the parking area. Sandra pushed in first, the others following, and inside was a wide dark-carpeted hall with a maître d's lectern prominent. To left and right, wide doorways showed the bright dining rooms in the enclosed porches, the customers now thinning out toward the end of the day. Behind the lectern a broad dark staircase led upward, and next to that a dimly lit hall extended back to what could be seen was a low-lit bar. Atop the lectern a cardboard sign read PLEASE SEAT YOURSELF.

'That's us,' Sandra said, and led the way past the lectern and down the hall to the bar, which was more full at this hour than the dining rooms, but also quieter, with lower lighting. The room was broad, with the bar along the rear, high-backed booths on both sides, and black Formica-top tables filling the center.

Sandra pointed toward a booth on the left: 'That looks pretty alone.'

'Good,' Parker said.

They went over there, Sandra sitting to face the front entrance, Claire opposite her, Parker beside Claire. From where he sat, the bar's mirrored back wall gave him a good view of the hall down toward the entrance.

A young waitress in black appeared almost immediately, hugging tall black menus to her breast. 'Supper menu?'

'We ate,' Claire said. 'Just drinks.'

'I might as well look at it,' Sandra said.

Claire and Parker both ordered scotch on the rocks while Sandra decided on the popcorn shrimp and a glass of red wine. When the waitress went away, Sandra explained, 'I didn't really have dinner, I just drove up.'

'You were in a hurry,' Parker told her.

Sandra gave him a frank look. 'I wasn't out to make trouble for you boys last time,' she said, 'and I'm not now. But now the situation is different than it was.'

'Keenan's dead,' Parker suggested.

'And my government,' Sandra said, 'is jerking me around.'

Parker said, 'They want your source?'

'Absolutely not. That isn't the way it works.' To Claire she said, 'Sometimes the government needs information. The deal is, if you've got that information and you're a legitimate licensed investigator, and you give them that information, or you sell it to them, they don't turn around and use it against *you*. It's kind of immunity plus a paycheck.'

'Not bad,' Claire said.

Parker said, 'So what went wrong?'

'Harbin was too popular,' Sandra said, and the waitress

arrived with their orders. 'I gotta eat just a minute,' Sandra said.

She was hungry. She scarfed down a couple large mouthfuls of popcorn shrimp, with a swig of red wine as though it were beer, and Parker looked at the other customers in this room.

Tourists. Nobody that looked like a local, only visitors not ready for this day to end. Conversations were low and easy, but here and there punctuated by a yawn. Nobody looked like law.

Sandra waved at the waitress, then called to her, 'Same again,' and said to Parker, 'Three different agencies had money out on Harbin, and a fourth had a leash on him, and none of them knew anything about any of the others. So right now they gotta sort that out so they can decide, when they pay *me*, which agency budget does it come out of. Right now, they're fighting about it.'

'They're fighting about which of them has to pay you.'

'That's about it.' Sandra shrugged, and now she sipped a little wine. 'In the meantime, you know I've got expenses.'

'I know,' Parker said.

'Roy took too long on the Harbin thing,' Sandra said. 'That's why he got careless at the end there. He figured, no penny-ante punk could *really* just disappear like that. So we were pretty much running on empty when I finally got my answer to the question, and the bitch of it is, I'm *still* running on empty until they get their official heads out of their official asses.'

'That's too bad,' Parker said.

'Meaning,' Sandra said, 'why should you give a shit. The only other two places for cash money I know of right now, to tide me over, is your bank score and Mr Nicholas Dalesia.'

Parker said, 'Dalesia?'

'You don't think there's reward money out on him, right now?' Sandra asked. 'And only one agency, no waiting.'

'I don't know where he is,' Parker said. 'I told you that.'

'You did, and I believe you, and I believe if you found out where he was he wouldn't live long because he's a lot more dangerous to you than I am or anybody else.'

'Maybe.'

The waitress brought Sandra's seconds and she ate a while more, then said, 'You know Dalesia isn't ten miles from here right this minute.'

'Probably.'

'He's got no money, no ID, no transportation. Does he have anybody around here he can go to?'

'Not that I know of.'

Sandra considered. 'Maybe a shut-in, take over a house for a few days.'

Parker said, 'Even shut-ins get visitors, phone calls. Medicine delivered.'

'Well, he's a bad penny, he'll show up.' Sandra used the paper napkin on her lips and said, 'The point is, you see where I am.'

'In my face,' Parker said.

'Sorry about that,' Sandra said. 'I need cash, and this is where it is, or where it's gonna be. You know I've got dossiers on you and your partners.'

'That your lady friend is holding, out there on Cape Cod.'

'Well, she's gone visiting,' Sandra said.

Parker nodded. 'Is that right.'

'Maybe with family, maybe with friends. Maybe here, maybe there. She's hoping she'll hear from me pretty soon.'

Claire said, 'Sandra, you seem like a smart person.'

'Thank you,' Sandra said, and gave Claire a cool look with not much question in it.

'Which means,' Claire said, 'you already know what you want out of this talk here.'

'Sure,' Sandra said, and shrugged. 'A partnership.' She switched the cool look to Parker. 'Think of me as the successor firm to Nick Dalesia,' she said.

Parker said, 'You want his share?'

'I don't deserve his share,' Sandra said, 'because I wasn't around for the first part. But I deserve half of his share, and you and McWhitney split the other half.' Waving toward the waitress again, giving her the check-signing signal, she said, 'We're just doing a little business here, so I'll pick up the tab. You don't have to agree or say anything. I'm in, that's all. It's not your fault, and it's not mine, and we'll learn to live with it. And you'll find I have my uses. In the meantime, we'll all be cosy together, over at – What do they call that place?'

'The waiting room,' Claire said.

10

Following Sandra out the front door of Wayward Inn, Parker said quietly, 'Let her go first.'

'All right.'

They said good night, said they'd see one another tomorrow, and got into the cars. It took Claire a while to decide the best place to put her handbag, and by then Sandra had backed out, spun around, and headed for the exit.

As they followed, Parker said, 'Hang back. She won't let you disappear out of her mirrors, but she'll let you hang back.'

'You aren't going to do anything to her, are you?'

'I can't. When she and her partner Keenan were first looking for Harbin, they made dossiers of what they could find out about the people at that meeting where he disappeared. Nelson's bar, Nick phoning you. If something happens to Sandra, her friend on Cape Cod gives that stuff to the law.'

'They already know my phone number.'

'Getting it again, from a second direction, means they'll take a closer look. You don't want that.'

Claire shook her head, eyes on the taillights out in front of her. 'If I have to give up my house, I will,' she said. 'Be Claire somebody else, I will. But I won't want to.'

'We're trying to make it not happen,' Parker said. 'Right now, Sandra's on guard, something could kick her off. Her friend I don't know anything about. But so far, we can deal with it. The worst would be if McWhitney found out she was here.'

'Why?'

'He'd kill her, right away, first, worry about dossiers later. Then everybody has to move.'

Claire brooded about that. 'Do you think he'll come up?'

'Not now, not over the weekend, he's still got that bar to run. Early next week, he might. Up ahead there, at the intersection, you're gonna turn left. There's a deli on the right, parking lot beyond it. Make the turn, go in there, shut everything down.'

Claire nodded and said, 'I thought maybe we weren't going straight back.'

The intersection ahead was topped by a yellow blinker signal. Sandra's Honda drove under it and through. Claire, without a signal, made the left, made a right U-turn into the deli's parking lot, tucked the Toyota in next to a Dumpster back there, and switched everything off. They waited, and then a black car went by out there, from left to right, accelerating.

Parker said, 'Give her a minute, then go back out and go straight through the intersection.'

'All right,' she said. 'Where are we going?'

'To visit the money,' Parker said. 'Start now,' and she did. As they jounced out onto the road, he said, 'We don't wanna do all this dance and the money's long gone.'

'Stop at the road up there on the right. Then just drive around a while. Give me half an hour.'

'All right,' she said, and when she stopped at the corner, the two visible houses both dark for the night, she said, 'Will you bring some out?'

'No,' he said. 'We don't want samples. We just want to know it's there. And alone.'

He got out of the Toyota and walked down the dark side road. There was partial cloud cover above, but some starlight got through, enough to see the difference between the blacktop and the shoulder.

It was not quite midnight now, a Thursday in October, nothing happening on this secondary road at all, no lights in the occasional dwelling he walked past. Soon, ahead of him on the right, he could make out the white hulk of the church. It was a small white clapboard structure with a wooden steeple. Across the road, difficult to see at night, was a narrow two-story white clapboard house that must have been connected to the church. Both buildings had been empty a long time.

Parker started with the house first. If there were a law presence here, watching the place, this would be the most comfortable spot to wait in.

But the house was empty, and when he crossed the road, so was the church. There was no sign that anybody had been in it since he and Dalesia and McWhitney had quit it a week ago.

41

Finally, he went up to the choir loft to check on the money. The bank had been transporting its cash in standard white rectangular packing boxes, and the church had stored its missals and hymnals up in the choir loft in the same way; not identical boxes, but similar. Parker and McWhitney and Dalesia had mixed the bank's boxes in with the church's boxes and left them there, arranging them so that, if anybody came upstairs and started looking in these boxes, the first three would contain books.

They still did. And the ones behind and beneath them still contained the close-packed stacks of green. Nothing had changed. The money still waited for them.

When they got back to Bosky Rounds, someone was seated in the dark on the porch, in a rocking chair. Rocking forward into the light, Sandra said, 'Visiting our money?'

'Your part is still there,' Parker told her.

11

Breakfast at Bosky Rounds was in a room smaller than the communal parlor, an oblong crammed with square tables for two, at the right front corner of the building, with a view mostly of the road out front. Friday morning, Parker and Claire ate a late breakfast, each with a different part of the *New York Times*, Parker facing the doorway through which the entrance foyer and Mrs Bartlett's desk could be seen.

The small bell over the entrance tinkled and a woman appeared, stopping in front of Mrs Bartlett's desk, her profile to Parker. She was a good-looking blonde in her twenties, tall, slim in a tan deerskin coat over chocolate-colored slacks and black boots, with a heavy black shoulder bag hanging to her left hip. Parker knew her, and she would know him, too. Her name was Detective Second Grade Gwen Reversa.

Quietly, Parker said, 'Lift your paper. Read it that way.'

She did so, her expressionless face and the room behind her disappearing behind the newsprint. Out there, Mrs Bartlett and Detective Reversa talked, pals, greeting one another, discussing something. Parker couldn't quite hear what they were saying, and then the bell tinkled again, and when he said, 'All right,' and Claire lowered the paper, only Mrs Bartlett was there.

Claire said, 'Can I look?'

'She's gone.'

Claire looked anyway, then said, 'She's a cop.'

'State, plainclothes. You could hear what they were saying.'

Claire shrugged. 'She was just checking in. Wanted to know if Mrs Bartlett had seen anything interesting since last time they talked.' Without irony she said, 'The answer was no.'

'Good.'

'But she'd recognize you?'

'She made a traffic stop on me, before the job. She's the reason you had to report the Lexus stolen and get this rental.'

'I liked the Lexus,' Claire said.

'You wouldn't have.'

'Oh, I know.' Claire looked around again at the space where the detective had been. 'But she was *here*.'

'She's part of the search,' Parker said. 'She was on that heist from the beginning. She and a bunch more are still around because they know Nick's got to be somewhere around here and the money's got to be somewhere around here.'

'You can't stay here,' Claire said. 'Not if she knows what you look like.'

'I know,' he said. 'We've got to get this over with.'

*

There was a low flower-pattern settee in the corner of Mrs Bartlett's office, and Sandra Loscalzo was seated on it, looking at local maps and brochures from a display rack mounted on the wall. Mrs Bartlett was at her desk doing puzzles in a crossword book, and Parker stopped to say to her, 'We wondered if you could give us some advice.'

'If I can,' she said, putting down her pencil.

'We thought,' he said, 'we'd like to look at the country-side from a height somewhere that we could get a sense of the whole area.'

'Oh, I know just the place,' Mrs Bartlett said, and took one of the maps from the display rack near Sandra, who did not look up from her own researches. 'It was a Revolutionary War battle site. Just wonderful views. Rutledge Ridge.'

With a red pen, she drew the route on the map, naming off the roads as she went. They thanked her and took the map out to the Toyota.

Sandra drove up to the lookout five minutes after they arrived. Seemingly unbroken forest fell away on three sides in clumps and clusters of bright color, rising only in the north. A few other tourists were up here, but the parking and observation area was large enough for everybody to have as much privacy as they wanted.

Sandra got out of the Honda and came over to the low stone wall that girdled the view, Claire seated on the wall, Parker standing next to her. 'You know that cop,' she said, as a greeting.

'She knows me,' Parker said.

'I get that.' To Claire, Sandra said, 'Very smooth, with the newspaper.'

'*You* noticed.'

'Well, I take an interest.' To Parker, she said, 'You looked the place over last night. Can we go and get it? How much longer do we wait?'

'I don't want to wait at all, with that detective around,' Parker told her. 'But if she's still here, that means we've still got a lot of law to deal with. The law is looking for a lot of heavy boxes of cash. You rent a truck around here right now, somebody's gonna stop you just to see who you are.'

'What about three or four cars? You, me, Claire, and McWhitney.'

'Four strangers, all going off the tourist trails, getting together, making a little convoy.'

Sandra frowned out at the view, not seeming to see it. 'If I knew where this goddamn stash was—'

'In a church,' he said.

She looked at him, wanting to be sure he was serious. 'A church?'

Nick Dalesia found it. Long time abandoned. Water and electricity switched off but still there. The idea was to just hole up overnight, but the heat was too intense, we had to leave the cash behind.'

'In boxes.'

'Up in the choir loft. Already church boxes up there, hymns and things.'

'That's nice.' Sandra paced, rubbing the knuckles of her right hand into her left palm. 'I know you don't want to tell me where this church is, not yet, but that's okay. The time comes, we'll go there together.'

'That's right,' Parker said.

'Unless,' Claire said, 'you just can't stay here any more.'

'Well, he can't stay here any more,' Sandra said.

'If I go away and come back when the law is gone,' Parker said, 'a lot of things can happen.'

Sandra paced, rubbing those knuckles, then stopped to say, 'I tell you what. You and me, we drive down to Long Island, six, seven hours, we talk it over with McWhitney.'

Parker looked at her. 'You want to see McWhitney?'

Sandra shrugged. 'Don't worry, I'm no Roy Keenan, I won't turn my back on him. But we'll tell him, you and me, we got an understanding, right?'

'Half of Nick.'

'We'll go now,' Sandra said. 'Get there in daylight. Claire can hold the fort, let Mrs Muskrat know we're coming back. Right?'

'Sure,' Claire said. 'But why do you want to do the driving?'

'Because you are,' Sandra told her. 'And you are because he isn't sure his license would play nice with cop computers. Me, I'm so clean they give me a gold medal every time they see me.' She cocked a brow at Parker. 'Ready?'

Parker looked at his watch. Nearly ten. He said to Claire, 'I'll be back late tonight.'

She nodded. 'I'll be here.'

12

Sandra was not so much a speeder as permanently aggressive, taking what small openings the road and the traffic gave her. It wasn't yet three-thirty in the afternoon when she parked diagonally across the street from McWhitney's bar, named in neon in the front window McW. 'Surprise,' she said, and gave Parker a twisted smile.

'Not too many surprises,' Parker said.

Three-thirty on a Friday afternoon McW was a lot livelier than last time, about half full but with the clear sense that a greater crowd was on its way. McWhitney had a second bartender working, though he didn't really need him quite yet. McWhitney was busy, eyes and hands in constant motion, but he saw Parker and Sandra come in and immediately turned away, saying something to his assistant. Stripping off his apron, walking away, he pointed leftward at an empty booth and came down around the bar to join them at it.

'The lion lies down with the lamb,' he said, not smiling.

Sandra grinned at him. 'Which is which?'

'You got your Harbin,' McWhitney told her, not hiding his dislike. 'We got no more specials.'

Sandra turned to Parker. 'Tell him.'

'She's in on the church with us,' Parker said. 'For half of Nick.'

'In on the *church*?' McWhitney was offended. 'She's *been* there?'

'Don't know where it is,' Sandra said. 'He won't tell me. But I think I can help you get the money out.'

McWhitney frowned at Parker. 'I don't like this.'

'It isn't what any of us had in mind,' Parker agreed. 'But that neighborhood up there is still a hornet's nest, and the hornets are still out.'

'There's a cop up there can make him,' Sandra said, 'And almost did.'

McWhitney looked at Parker. 'The woman cop?'

'Her.'

McWhitney leaned back as his assistant bartender brought three beers, then left without a word. Taking a short sip, McWhitney said, 'So we all just gotta go away for a while.'

'Until what?' Parker asked him. 'Until they get Nick again? Until Nick gets in there on his own and cleans it out? Until some kids fool around in there one night and find it?'

McWhitney nodded, but pointed a thumb at Sandra. 'So what's she doing in it? She just happens to be this place, that place, and every time we see her we give her money? Half of Nick? What if Nick shows up?'

'You'll kill him,' Sandra said.

McWhitney shook his head. 'I still don't see what you're doing in here.'

'I'll help dig,' Sandra said, and nodded at the floor. 'Probably in that basement of yours.'

'Never mind my basement.'

'Also,' Sandra said, 'I have a way to get your money.'

Parker said, 'You didn't say that before.'

'I wanted to see how this meeting was gonna go, do I want to go through the trouble, or just screw you people and score it on my own.'

'Listen to this,' McWhitney said.

Parker said, 'You've figured out a way to get the money out.'

'I think so.' To McWhitney she said, 'You pretty well know the business operations around this neighborhood.'

'Pretty well.'

'Do you know a used-car lot, maybe kind of grungy, no cream puffs?'

McWhitney grinned for the first time since he'd laid eyes on Sandra. 'I know a dozen of them,' he said. 'Whadayou need?'

'A truck. A small beat-up old truck, delivery van, something like that. Black would be best, just so it isn't too shiny.'

'A truck.' McWhitney sounded disgusted. 'To move the stash.'

'That's right.'

'What makes this truck wonderful? It's invisible?'

'Pretty much so,' she said. 'Whatever color it is, and I really would like black, we use the same color to paint out whatever name might already be on it. Then, on both doors, in white, we paint Holy Redeemer Choir.'

'Holy shit,' McWhitney said.

'We're the redeemers,' Sandra told him. 'It's okay if the name on the doors is a little amateurish, but we should try to do our best with it.'

McWhitney slowly nodded. 'The choir's coming to get their hymnals.'

'And we'll *get* some, too,' Sandra said, 'in case anybody wants to look in back.'

'Jesus, you always gotta insult me,' McWhitney said. 'Here I was thinking you weren't so bad.'

'I was used to dealing with Roy,' she said, and shrugged.

Now McWhitney laughed out loud. 'You should thank me for breaking up the partnership.'

Parker said, 'Can you get this truck? Fix it up about the name?'

'It's gotta be me, doesn't it,' McWhitney said. He didn't sound happy.

'You've got the legal front,' Sandra said, and gestured at the bar around them. 'This needs to be a truck with clean title, because you *will* be stopped, once you get up in that area.'

Parker said, 'Can you do all that this afternoon, or do we have to wait till Monday?'

'If I start now and find it in the next hour,' McWhitney said, 'the dealer can still deal with Motor Vehicles today, and I can come up there tomorrow. Maybe with dealer plates, but all the paperwork.'

Taking out a business card, Sandra wrote the Bosky Rounds name and phone number on the back. As she pushed it across the table, she said, 'Call us when you get there, we'll go out to the place together. I'm looking forward to see this truck you get.'

'What you're looking forward to,' McWhitney told her, 'is what's in that church.'

Sandra smiled. 'Answered prayers,' she said.

13

Parker drove the first half of the trip back, because his ID wasn't likely to be an issue before they got to the search zone. They stopped for dinner midway, at a chain restaurant along the road, where no locals would look at them and remember them. While they waited for their food, Parker said, 'This whole thing is the wrong side of the street for you.'

Sandra grimaced. 'I don't think of it like that,' she said. 'What I think, there's no sides to the street because there is no street.'

'What is there?'

She studied him, trying to decide how much to tell him, moving her fork back and forth on the table with her left hand. Then she shrugged, and left the fork alone, and said, 'I figured it out when I was a little girl, what my idea of the world is.'

'What's that?'

'A frozen lake,' she said. 'Bigger than you can see the end of. Every day, I get up, I gotta move a little more along the lake. I gotta be very careful and very wary, because I don't know where the ice is too thin. I gotta listen and watch.'

'I've seen you do it.'

She grinned and nodded, as though more pleased with him than with herself. 'Yeah, you have.'

They were both silent a minute, and then their food came. The waitress went away and Sandra picked up her fork, but then she paused to say, 'You go see a war movie, the guy gets hurt, he yells "Medic!", they come take him away, fix him up. Out here, you get hurt, you yell "Medic!", you know what happens?'

'Yeah, I do.'

'There's no sides,' she said. 'No street. We just do what we've got to do to get across the lake.'

14

They got back to Bosky Rounds a little before nine that night. As Sandra pulled into a parking space beside the building, Claire came down off the porch, shaking her hand at them not to get out of the car. They waited, saying nothing, and she came over to slide into the backseat and say, 'We have to leave.'

He twisted half around in the seat to look at her, shadowed back there, far from the light on the porch. 'Why?'

'That woman detective was here again,' Claire said. 'I heard her talking to Mrs Bartlett. Because they haven't found Nick Dalesia, they're convinced all three of the robbers came back here, to get their money.'

Parker said, 'Why would they have an idea like that?'

'Because,' Claire said, 'they don't believe Nick could hide this long without help, and who else would there be to help him?'

Sandra said, 'I'd figure it that way, too.'

'Nick's running a string of luck,' Parker said. 'For him. Not good for the rest of us.'

'She brought wanted posters,' Claire said. 'Pictures of Nick, but drawings of the other two.'

'I've seen them,' Parker said. 'They're not close enough.'

'Not if you're just walking by,' Claire told him. 'But if you're sitting in that place having breakfast, and out in the office on the wall there's a drawing of you, people will make the connection.'

Parker said, 'She put posters on the wall?'

'They're papering the whole area, every public space.' Claire leaned forward to put her elbow on the seatback and say, 'I packed all of our things. Everything's in the car. I've just been waiting here for you to get back and then we can leave.'

'No,' he said.

'You can't stay,' she insisted.

'But not that way,' Parker said. 'They've got your name, they've got your address, they've got your credit cards. You stay here tonight, tomorrow morning you check out. If you leave here tonight, you're just pointing an arrow at yourself.'

Claire didn't like that. 'What are *you* going to do?'

'McWhitney's coming up tomorrow with a truck, we're gonna take that cash out of there. You've got my stuff in the car?'

'Yes.'

'We'll move it over to this car. You go back to the room until tomorrow. I'll show Sandra where the church is and I'll stay there tonight.' To Sandra he said, 'When McWhitney gets here, you can lead him to the church.'

Sandra said, 'That probably won't be until tomorrow afternoon.'

'When you come to the church,' Parker told her, 'bring me a coffee and Danish.'

Claire said, 'Then how will you get home?'

'I'll find a way,' he said.

15

'There won't be any twenty-four-hour delis around here,'
Sandra said.

'That's all right,' Parker said. 'I won't starve to death
between now and tomorrow afternoon. Take the right at
that yellow blinker up there.'

'The right,' she said, with some sort of edge, and looked
sidelong at him. 'That's where you lost me last night.'

'Thought I lost you.'

Now she laughed and made the right, and said,
'McWhitney's sore because McWhitney's a sorehead. You
know better.'

'We'll see how it plays out.'

'Don't fool around,' she said. 'We've got a deal.'

'I know that.'

'It's better for you. It's better for you and McWhitney
both.'

'You mean,' Parker said, 'we get our own pieces, and
part of Nick.'

'You get more than you were going to get,' she said,

'and now you're partners with somebody who can help you get it.'

'Don't sell me any more,' Parker said. 'I get the idea.'

'Sorry,' she said.

He said, 'I know, you were used to Keenan.'

'I'm getting over it.'

Till now there'd been no other traffic along this road, but a wavering oncoming light turned out to be a pickup truck, moving slowly and unsteadily, tacking rather than driving, with a driver fighting sleep. Sandra pulled far to the right to let him by, then looked in the rearview mirror and said, 'The funny thing is, most fools get away with being fools.'

'Until they count on it,' Parker said. 'There's a left turn coming up. Do you have a blanket or something in the trunk?'

'I keep a mover's pad back there,' she said. 'It's quilted, so I guess it's warm, but it's kind of stiff.'

'Doesn't matter. We're coming up on the church now. I don't want you to stop. Church on the right, house on the left, both white. See?'

'Very remote,' she said, as they drove on by.

'One of Nick's better ideas,' Parker said. 'Will you be able to find it tomorrow?'

'Oh, sure.' She laughed. 'I can usually find money.'

'Up ahead here,' he said, 'there's a little bridge over a stream. The road curves down to the right to the bridge, and just before it there's a parking area on the right.'

'For fishermen,' she suggested.

'Probably. Stop there, and I'll get out and take the blanket and walk back. And do you have a bottle of water?'

'Right under your elbow there.'

The road curved down and to the right, and ahead the old iron latticework of the bridge drew pale lines against the black. Sandra stopped the Honda. 'See you sometime tomorrow.'

'Right.' Carrying the bottled water, he got out of the car and opened the trunk to pull the stiff pad out. He shut the trunk, rapped his knuckles on it once, and she drove away, over the bridge, taking all the light with her.

It would take a minute to adjust his eyes to the night. While waiting, he did his best to fold the blanket-size quilted pad into something he could carry. Finally, the simplest way was over his shoulders, like a cloak, which made him look more like a Plains Indian than anything else. But it was warm and not awkward, and easy to walk with.

Twice on the way back he saw headlights at a distance and stepped off the road till they went by, once into some woods and the other time along a one-lane dirt road meandering uphill.

And then, there ahead of him, were the two small pale buildings in the dark. Both were empty, but the house might be warmer and just a bit more comfortable, without the church's high ceilings. He went there and let himself in and decided on the smaller of the bedrooms upstairs.

It had been a long day; he spread the moving pad on the floor, rolled himself in it, and was soon asleep, and when he woke muddy daylight seeped through the room's one window. He was stiff, and not really rested, but he got up and drank some of the water, then went outside to relieve himself. While he was out there, he went over to look at the church again, and nothing had changed.

It was a long empty day. For part of it he walked, indoors or out, and other parts he sat against a wall in the empty house or curled into the moving pad again and slept. He woke from one of those with the long diagonals of late afternoon light coming in the window and Nick Dalesia seated cross-legged on the floor against the opposite wall. The revolver in his right hand, not exactly pointing anywhere, would belong to the dead marshal.

Parker sat up. 'So there you are,' he said.

16

'Where's your car?' Nick sounded strained, jumpy, a man without time for conversation.

That's the reason I'm alive, Parker thought. He came across me here, he would have killed me, but he needs wheels and he couldn't find the ones that brought me here. 'Don't have one,' he said.

Nick was all exposed nerve endings. Any answer might make him start shooting, just to do something. Twisting his lips, he said, 'What did you do, walk? How'd you get here?'

'Somebody dropped me off.'

'Who?'

'You don't know her.'

'Her? Don't know her?'

'It was just somebody gave me a ride,' Parker said. 'What difference does it make?'

'I need a car,' Nick said, low and fervent, as though giving away a secret. Leaning forward, his whole body tense, he said, 'I've got to get *away* from here. North, I can get into Canada, I can stop running for a while, figure out what to do next.'

There was only one way Nick would stop running, but Parker didn't say so. Nodding at the gun, he said, 'You've got that. That should help.'

Nick looked at the gun with dislike. 'I paid a lot for this, Parker,' he said.

'I know that.'

Nick made an angry shrug. 'Some people,' he said, 'would rather be a hero than alive.'

'That's not us.'

'No.' Nick stared at Parker, as though something about him were both mysterious and infuriating. Then, abruptly, he punched the gun butt onto the floor next to his leg, with a hollow *thud* that made him blink. 'What are you *doing* here?' he demanded, as though it mattered.

'I wanted to look at the money.'

'You wanted to *take* the money.'

'Too soon for that,' Parker said. If he kept showing Nick this bland face, reasonable, no arguments, maybe Nick would calm down a little, just enough to listen to sense. But probably not.

So, how to get to him from across the room? Five feet of wooden floor between them, with a gun at the far end.

Still calm, still with the same even voice, Parker said, 'The law put it out that you got away from them before they could ask you anything. I didn't know if that was true or not. I figured, if the money's still here, it's true.'

'It might have helped me with those people before,' Nick said. 'But not now.'

'No, not now.'

Nick shook his head, moving from anger to disgust. 'You know how they got me.'

'It was almost me,' Parker told him. 'If I hadn't heard about you, I would have been passing that stuff myself.'

'I'd rather it was you,' Nick told him, too caught up in his problems to pretend. 'And I was the one that said, uh-oh, better throw that cash away.'

'Just what I did.'

'And came back *here*.' Nick's confusion and exasperation and need were so intense he was forgetting the revolver, letting it point this way and that way as he gestured, trying to explain the situation to himself. 'That's what I don't get,' he said, staring hard at Parker. 'That was over a *week* ago. You were out, you were free and clear, and you came *back*.' Suddenly suspicious, he threw a quick wary look toward the door and said, 'Is Nelson here?'

'No, Nick.'

'Did *he* drive you? He's off getting some food, is that it?'

'I don't travel with McWhitney,' Parker said. 'You know that.'

'I know you got a ride here,' Nick said. 'You got a ride here, and you're gonna stay a while, you're gonna sleep— Somebody's got to bring you food. Somebody with a car. Why don't *you* have a car?'

'I'm not gonna drive around this part of the world, Nick. I'm not gonna draw attention. I don't have good ID.'

'You wouldn't even *be*—' Nick stopped and frowned, then said, as though suddenly seeing the answer to some riddle, 'You're *waiting*.'

'That's right,' Parker said, and flipped the mat off his legs.

64

Nick clenched, the gun now pointing at Parker's eyes, trembling only a little. 'Don't move!'

'I'm not moving, Nick. I got stiff, that's all, sleeping here.'

'You could get stiffer.'

'I know that, Nick.' He's getting ready to shoot, Parker told himself. There's nothing more he's going to get from talking and he knows it. And he doesn't dare let me live.

'Parker . . .' Nick said, and trailed off, sounding almost regretful.

'We could help each other, Nick,' Parker said. 'Better for both of us. And I got water,' he said, holding the bottle up in his left hand. 'To keep me going till my ride gets here. It's just water. Check it out for yourself,' he said, and slowly lobbed the bottle underhand, in an arc toward Nick's lap.

Nick looked at the bottle rising and falling through the air and Parker's right hand grabbed up a corner of the mat. He snapped the mat around at Nick's head, and his body lunged after it.

The bullet first went through the quilted mat.

TWO

1

One week earlier, just two days after the big armored-car robbery, Dr Myron Madchen's week of horror began in earnest, and just when he'd thought his near-connection to the affair was buried and gone as though it had never been.

In a way, it *had* never been. He had not after all provided an alibi for one of the robbers, and he had not shared in the proceeds of the robbery. In fact, when the time finally came, he had had nothing to do with the matter. Everything had resolved itself with no action from him, and he was home free. Or so he'd thought.

That Sunday evening, two days after the robbery, he and Isabelle shared a fine dinner in a roadside restaurant called the Wayward Inn, where they cemented their plans for the future. A little patience was all they'd need. After all, the doctor was now a recent and unexpected widower, and it would be unseemly if he and Isabelle were publicly to make much of one another so soon.

So they'd driven to the Wayward Inn in separate cars, dined together, laughed together, gazed into each other's eyes, and parted with a chaste kiss in the parking lot. All the way home the doctor, a heavyset man in his fifties with thick iron-gray hair combed straight back and large eyeglasses, sang at the wheel, loud and off-key, a thing he'd never done before.

His house when he entered it seemed larger than before, and warmer. Also, it was empty, since he'd given Estrella a week off, with pay, feeling he'd rather be unobserved until he became more familiar with the new situation.

He'd forgotten to turn lights on when he'd gone out this evening. It hadn't been dark yet, and he wasn't used to the house being empty in his absence. Now he wanted light, all the light there was, and he went through the large house room by room, switching on lamps and track lighting and wall sconces and chandeliers everywhere, until he reached the small room off his bedroom, laughably known as his office – he'd be moving now to a larger space – and when he pushed the button for the ceiling light the voice in the corner said, 'Turn that off.'

He very nearly fainted. He clutched to the doorjamb so he wouldn't fall over, and stared at the robber.

One of the robbers, the one who'd been caught and then escaped, one of the two who'd threatened him last week when they were afraid he'd let something slip about their plans for the robbery. Which he was never going to do, never; it was important to him, too, or it had seemed vitally important before Ellen . . . had her heart attack.

'*Off.*'

'Oh! Yes!'

He'd been staring at the man, not even listening to what he'd said, but now he hit the button again and the room went back to semidarkness. The light from the bedroom behind him still showed his desk and chair, his filing cabinet, his framed degrees and awards, and in the darkest corner that hunched man in Dr Madchen's black leather reading chair, just watching him.

'What—' He shook his head, and started again: 'You can't be here.'

'I can't be anywhere else,' the man said. Dalesia; the television news had said his name was Dalesia.

'You can't be *here*.'

'Well, let's look at that, Doctor,' Dalesia said. He was tense but in control, a hard and capable man. He said, 'Why don't you go over and sit at your desk there, swivel the chair around to face me. Go ahead, do it.'

So the doctor did it, and then, in a low and trembling voice, said, 'I can't let anybody even know I know you.'

'If I leave here, Doctor,' Dalesia said, 'I'm gonna be sore. I'm gonna be sore at *you*. And then, in a couple hours, a couple days, when the cops get me again, guess who I'm gonna talk about.'

The doctor felt as though invisible straps were clamping every part of his body. He sat tilted forward, feet together and heels lifted, knees together, hands folded into his lap as though he were trying to hide a baseball. Slowly blinking at Dalesia, he said, 'Talk about me? What could you say about me? I didn't do anything.'

'You killed your wife.'

The doctor's mouth popped open, but at first all he did was expel a little puff of air. But then, needing to have that accusation unsaid, never said, he protested, 'That's— Nobody's even suggested such a thing.'

'I will.'

The doctor shook his head, still feeling those invisible bonds. 'Why would anybody believe you?'

'They didn't do an autopsy, did they?'

'Of course not. No need.'

'I'll give them the need.' Dalesia was much more comfortable in this room than the doctor was. 'If I stay here until the heat dies down,' he said, 'your wife had a heart attack. If I leave, you stuck her with a hypodermic needle.'

'They *won't* believe you,' the doctor insisted. 'There's no reason to believe you.'

'Doctor,' Dalesia said, 'we had our very first meeting about the robbery in your office. Your nurse and your receptionist saw me. You told us the money you'd get from us was your last chance, you were desperate, you had serious trouble.' He shrugged. 'Wife trouble, I guess.'

'I was going to run away.'

'Now you don't have to.'

The doctor's mind filled with regrets, that he had ever involved himself with these people, but then regrets for the past were overwhelmed by horror of the present. What could he *do*? He couldn't force the man to leave, Dalesia really would take his revenge. Let him stay, and somehow find a way to stick *him* with a hypodermic needle? But Dalesia was tough and hard, he'd never give Dr Madchen the opportunity. So what could he do?

Dalesia said, 'There's a little bedroom downstairs, by the kitchen. Whose is that?'

'What? Oh, Estrella.'

'Who's that, your daughter?'

'No, the maid, she's our maid.'

'Where is she?'

'With her family in New Jersey. I gave her the week off.'

'Well, that's good, then,' Dalesia said. 'I'll stay down there. I'll take off before this Estrella gets back, take your car, and that's the end of it.'

'Oh, no,' the doctor said. 'You can't take my car!'

'I gotta have wheels.'

'But you can't take my car.'

'Why not? You report it stolen.'

'But that would be the same thing,' the doctor told him. 'I'm safe because nobody's looking at me, that's what you said. I just had the one patient who was in the robbery with you, that's all. But if you tell them about me, they'll look at me.' Dr Madchen leaned earnestly forward. 'Mr Dalesia,' he said, 'this has all been an emotional nightmare for me. I'll let you stay, but when you go, steal someone else's car.'

Dalesia nodded at him. 'I could just kill you, you know.'

Humbly, the doctor said, 'I know you could.'

Dalesia shook his head, as though angry with himself. 'I'm not a nutcase,' he said. 'I'm not gonna hurt you unless I don't have any choice.'

'I know that,' the doctor said. 'You can stay. Use Estrella's room. But please don't take my car.'

'We'll see,' Dalesia said.

The next week was harrowing, Dr Madchen lived his normal life by day, doing his office hours in downtown Rutherford, seeing his patients, but always aware of that lurking demon waiting for him at home. If only he could just stay all night in the office, sleep on an examination table, eat at the luncheonette up at the corner.

But he didn't dare do anything outside his normal routine. Get up in the morning, eat breakfast with Estrella's closed door seeming to shimmer with what lay behind it, then go off to his office and return as late as possible at the end of the day.

He took Isabelle out to dinner twice that week, but the strain of this new secret was just too much for him. He couldn't possibly tell her what had happened. All he could do was wait for this horror to end.

At least the man Dalesia didn't intrude too much into the doctor's life. Estrella had her own television set and Dalesia seemed to spend most of his time in there watching it. From the sound, it was mostly the news channels. The doctor bought bread and cold cuts and cans of soup, and steadily they were consumed, but not in his presence.

The few times he did see Dalesia that week were unsettling, because it soon became clear that Dalesia was becoming more and more disturbed by the fix he was in. He'd gotten this far, to this temporary safety, but it couldn't last, and where could he go next? He had killed a US marshal, and every policeman in the Northeast was looking for him. The doctor began to fear that the man would eventually snap under the strain, that he would do something irrational that would destroy them both.

But it never quite happened, and on Friday evening, when Dr Madchen got home and knocked on Estrella's door, Dalesia appeared in the doorway more haggard than tense, as though now the strain were robbing him of strength. 'Estrella's coming back tomorrow,' the doctor said. 'I'm picking her up at the bus depot at three. You've been here almost a week. You really have to go.'

'I know,' Dalesia said, and half turned as though to look at the television set still running in the room behind him. 'They're not letting up,' he said.

'I've been stopped at roadblocks three times this week,' the doctor told him.

Dalesia rubbed a weary hand over his face. 'I gotta get away from here.'

'Please don't take my car. It won't do you any good, and it can only—'

'I know, I know.' Dalesia's anger was also tired. 'I need a car, but I can't use one all the cops are looking for.'

'That's right.'

'Okay,' Dalesia said. 'Tomorrow, when you go get this Estrella, you're gonna drive me somewhere.'

'Where?'

'I'll show you tomorrow,' Dalesia said, and went back into Estrella's room, and closed the door.

2

Captain Robert Modale of the New York State Police was a calm man and a patient man, but he knew a whopping waste of time when it was dumped in his lap, and he'd been given a doozy this time. Irritation, which is what Captain Modale had to admit to himself he was feeling right now, had the effect of making him even quieter and more self-contained than ever. As a result, he had ridden in the passenger seat of the unmarked state pool car, next to Trooper Oskott at the wheel, all the way across half of New York State and probably a third of Massachusetts with barely a word out of his mouth.

Trooper Oskott, looking awkward and uncomfortable in civvies instead of his usual snappy gray fitted uniform, had tried to make conversation a few times, but the responses were so minimal that he soon gave up, and the interstates merely rolled silently by outside the vehicle's glass while Captain Modale contemplated this whopping waste of time he had to deal with.

Which was going to be a two-day waste of time, at that. The captain had to travel these hundreds of miles on a

Friday, but he would reach Rutherford too late to meet with his Massachusetts counterparts until Saturday morning. In the meantime, the plan was that he and Trooper Oskott would bunk in a motel somewhere.

At first, though, it had looked as though no accommodation would be available, since it was the height of the fall foliage season over there in New England, and most inns of any kind were full. Captain Modale had been counting on that, the whopping waste of time called off for lack of housing, but then somebody made an early departure from a bed and breakfast with the disgusting name of Bosky Rounds, so the trip was on after all.

Bosky Rounds was not as repulsive as its name, though it was still not at all to the captain's taste. Nevertheless, the proprietor, Mrs Bartlett, did maintain a neat and cozy atmosphere, steered the captain and the trooper to a fine New England seafood dinner on Friday night, and furnished such mountains of breakfast Saturday morning that the captain, indulging himself far beyond his normal pattern, decided not to mention the breakfast to his wife.

Mrs Bartlett, in a side desk drawer in her neat office, seemed to keep an unlimited supply of local maps, on one of which she drew a narrow red pen line from where they were to the temporary unified police headquarters in the Rutherford Combined Bank building, that being the rightful owner of the money stolen last week.

When they went out to the car, they were preceded by another guest here, a brassy-looking blonde in black, who got into a black Honda Accord festooned with antennas. With just a quick glimpse of her profile, the captain found himself wondering, have I seen her before? Possibly in here last night, or at the restaurant. Or it could be she's just a kind of type of tough-looking blonde, striking enough to make you notice her, but also with a little warning sign in view.

Whatever the case, she was none of the captain's concern. He got into the pool car, and Trooper Oskott drove him over to the meeting.

What was normally a loan officer's space, a fairly roomy office with neutral gray carpet and furniture and walls, had been turned into the combined police headquarters, crammed with electronic equipment, extra tables and chairs, and easels mounted with photos, chain-of-command charts, progress reports, and particularly irritating examples of press coverage.

While Trooper Oskott waited at an easy parade rest out in the main banking area, still shut down since the robbery with all necessary bank transactions handled at another branch twenty-some miles away, Captain Modale went into the HQ room to be met by several of his opposite numbers, brought here at this hour specifically to meet with him.

What the captain read from those solemn faces and strong handshakes was a frustration even deeper than his own, and he decided to give up his bad temper at having his time wasted like this, because he knew these men and women were clutching at straws.

Three strangers had come into their territory, armed with antitank weapons illegal to be imported into the United States, and they'd made off with just about an entire bank's cash assets. One day later, the law had managed to lay its hands on one of the felons, but the very next day they lost him again, and lost one of their own as well. Now, in the nearly a week since, there had been no progress, no breaks, no further clues as to where any of the three men had gone.

One of the brass here to greet him, a Chief Inspector Davies, said, 'I'll be honest with you, Captain, this reflects on every one of us.'

'I don't see that, Inspector.'

'Yes, it does,' Davies insisted. 'The one man we got, and I'm afraid lost—'

'*We* lost him,' said the tight-lipped FBI agent Ramey that the captain had been introduced to. 'We'll be changing some procedures after this.'

'The point is,' Davies said, 'we know who he is. Nicholas Leonard Dalesia. He's not from the Northeast at all. He has no friends here, no associates, no allies. He hasn't stolen a car. He's been loose for almost a week in the middle of the biggest manhunt *we* can muster, and not a sign of him.'

'He's gone to ground,' said the captain.

'Agreed. But how? The feeling is, around here,' the inspector told him, 'the feeling is, the other two are with him.'

'I don't follow that,' the captain said.

'We know they had to leave the money behind, hide it somewhere,' the inspector told him. 'Are they with it now? One of them, the one you met, went over to New York State to engage almost immediately in another robbery. Did he do it for cash to tide the gang over while they're hiding out?'

'You're suggesting,' the captain said, 'the one that came to us managed to escape your manhunt, did that second robbery, and went right back *into* the search area.'

'You don't buy it,' Inspector Davies said.

'I know *I* wouldn't do it,' the captain said. 'If I got my hands on some different money, I'd just grab it and keep going.'

'Then where's Nicholas Leonard Dalesia? It just doesn't— Oh, Gwen, there you are. Come over here.'

A very attractive young woman in tans and russets had just entered the HQ room, and before the captain could show his bafflement – what was somebody like *that* doing here? – Inspector Davies all unknowing rescued him by saying, 'Detective Second Grade Gwen Reversa, this is New York State Police Captain Robert Modale. You're the two law officers who've actually seen and talked to that second man.'

After a handshake and greeting, Detective Reversa said, 'John B. Allen, that's who he was when I met him.'

'He called himself Ed Smith in my neighborhood.'

She smiled. 'He doesn't go in for colorful names, does he?'

'There's not much colorful about him at all.'

'Tell me,' Detective Reversa said, 'what do you think of the drawing?'

'Of Mr Smith?' The captain shook his head, 'It works in the wrong direction,' he said. 'Once you know it's supposed to be him, you can see the similarities. But I had a conversation with the man *after* I saw those posters, and I didn't make the connection.'

Inspector Davies said, 'While you're here, Captain, I'd

like you and Gwen to sit down with our artist and see if you can improve that picture.'

'Because you think he's come back.'

Detective Reversa said, 'But you don't.'

'I think,' the captain said carefully, not wanting to hurt anybody's feelings, 'the third man could very well still be here, helping Dalesia hide out. But the fellow I talked to? What do you think?'

'He's a cautious man,' she said, 'and not loud. No colorful names. I think he'd be like a cat and not go anywhere he wasn't sure of.'

Inspector Davies said, 'So the two of you could improve that drawing.'

The captain bowed in acquiescence. 'Whatever I can do to be of help.'

The artist was a small irritable woman who worked in charcoal, smearing much of it on herself. 'I think,' Gwen Reversa told her, 'the main thing wrong with the picture now is, it makes him look threatening.'

'That's right,' Captain Modale said.

The artist, who wasn't the one who'd done the original drawing, frowned at it. 'Yes, it is threatening,' she agreed. 'What should it be instead?'

'Watchful,' Gwen Reversa said.

'This man,' the captain said, gesturing at the picture, 'is aggressive, he's about to make some sort of move. The real man doesn't move first. He watches you, he waits to see what *you're* going to do.'

'But then,' Gwen Reversa said, 'I suspect he's very fast.'

'Absolutely.'

The artist pursed her lips. 'I'm not going to get all *that* into the picture. Even a photograph wouldn't get all that in. Are the eyes all right?'

'Maybe,' Gwen Reversa said, 'not so defined.'

'He's not staring,' the captain said. 'He's just looking.'

The artist sighed. 'Very well,' she said, and opened her large sketch pad on the bank officer's desk in this small side office next to the main HQ room. 'Let's begin.'

The three had been working together for little more than an hour when Inspector Davies came to the doorway and said, 'You two come listen to this. See what you think.'

The larger outer room now contained, in addition to everything else, a quick eager young guy with windblown hair and large black-framed glasses like a raccoon's mask. He mostly gave the impression of somebody here to sell magazine subscriptions.

The inspector made introductions: 'Captain Modale, Detective Reversa, this is Terry Mulcany, a book writer.'

'Mostly fact crime,' Mulcany said. He looked nervous but self-confident at the same time.

'That must keep you busy,' the captain commented.

Mulcany flashed a very happy smile. 'Yes, sir, it does.'

The inspector said, 'Mr Mulcany believes he might have seen your man.'

Surprised, dubious, the captain said, 'Around here?'

'Yes, sir,' Mulcany said. 'If it was him.'

The captain said, 'Why do you think it was him?'

'I'm just not sure, sir.' Mulcany shrugged in frustration. 'I've been talking to so many people in this neighborhood this past week, unless I make notes or tape somebody it all runs together.'

Gwen Reversa said, 'But you think you saw one of the robbers.'

'With a woman. Yesterday, the day before, I'm not really positive.' Shaking his head, he said, 'I didn't notice it at the time, that's the problem. But this morning, I was looking at those wanted posters again, just to remind myself, and I thought, wait a minute, I saw that guy, I talked to him. Standing ... outdoors somewhere, with a woman, good-looking woman. Talking to them just for a minute, just to introduce myself, like I've been doing all week.'

'And he looked like the poster,' the inspector suggested.

'Not exactly,' Mulcany said. 'It could have been, or maybe not. But it was close enough, I thought I should report it.'

Gwen said, 'Mr Mulcany, would you come over here?'

Curious, Mulcany and the others followed her into the side office, where the artist was still touching up the new drawing. Stepping to one side, Gwen gestured at the picture. The artist looked up, saw all the attention, and cleared out of the way.

Mulcany crossed to the desk, looked down at the drawing, and said, 'Oh!'

Gwen said, 'Oh?'

'That's him!' Delighted, Mulcany stared around at the others. '*That's* what he looks like!'

3

Nelson McWhitney liked his bar so much that, if the damn thing would only turn some kind of profit, he might just stay there all the time and retire from his activities in that other life. His customers in the bar were more settled, less sudden, than the people he worked with in that other sphere. His apartment behind the place was small but comfortable, and the neighborhood was working-class and safe, the kind of people who didn't have much of anything but just naturally watched one another's backs. About the only way anybody could get hurt really badly around here was by winning the lottery, which occasionally happened to some poor bastard, who was usually, a year later, either dead or in jail or rehab or exile. McWhitney did not play the lottery.

McWhitney did, however, sometimes play an even more dangerous game, and he was planning a round of it just now. When he got out of bed Saturday morning, he had two appointments ahead of him, both connected to that game. The second one, at eleven this morning, was a three-block walk from here to pick up the truck he'd bought yesterday, which would have the Holy Redeemer Choir name painted on the doors by then, and be ready for the drive north. And the first, at ten, was with a fellow he knew from that other world, named Oscar Sidd.

Because of the meeting with Oscar Sidd, McWhitney had only one beer with the eggs and fried potatoes he made in his little kitchen at the rear of the apartment before going out front to the bar, where he put a few small bills in the cash register to start the day.

He had the *Daily News* delivered, every morning pushed through the large letter slot in the bar's front door, so he sat at the bar and read a while, digesting his breakfast. He had some tricky moments coming, but he was calm about it.

Oscar Sidd was a frugal man; at exactly ten o'clock, wasting no time, he gave two hard raps to the glass of the front door, wasting no energy. A dark green shade was lowered over that glass, but this would be Oscar.

It was. A bony man a few inches over six feet, he wore narrow clothing that tended to be just a little too short for him. He came in now wearing a black topcoat that stopped above his knees with sleeves that stopped above the sleeves of his dark brown sport coat, which stopped above his bony wrists, and black pants that stopped far enough above his black shoes to show dark blue socks.

'Good morning, Nels,' he said, and stepped to the side so McWhitney could shut the door.

'You okay, Oscar?'

'I'm fine, thank you.'

'You want a beer?'

'I think not,' Oscar said. 'You go ahead, I'll join you with a seltzer.'

'I'll join us both with a seltzer,' McWhitney said, and gestured at the nearest booth. 'Sit down, I'll get them.' He wouldn't be introducing Oscar Sidd to his private quarters in back.

Oscar slid into the booth, facing the closed front door, opening his topcoat as McWhitney went behind the bar to fill two glasses with seltzer and ice and bring them around the end of the bar on a tray. He dealt the glasses, put the tray back on the bar, sat across from Oscar, and said, 'How goes it?'

'Colder this morning,' Oscar said. He didn't touch his glass, but watched McWhitney solemnly.

'You keep up with the news, Oscar,' McWhitney suggested.

'If it's interesting.'

'That big bank robbery up in Massachusetts last week.'

'Armored car, you mean.'

McWhitney grinned. 'You're right, I do. You noticed that.'

'It was interesting,' Oscar said. 'One of them got picked up, I believe.'

'And then lost again.'

Oscar's smile, when he showed it, was thin. 'Hard to get reliable help,' he said.

McWhitney said, 'Did you notice how it was they got onto him?'

'The bank's money is poisoned, I believe,' Oscar said. 'Traceable. It can't be used.'

'Well, not in this country,' McWhitney agreed.

Oscar gave him a keen look. 'I begin to see why we're talking.'

McWhitney, having nothing to say, sipped his seltzer.

Oscar said, 'You are suggesting you might have access to that poisoned cash.'

'And I know,' McWhitney said, 'you do some dealings with money overseas.'

'Money for weapons,' Oscar said, and shrugged. 'I am a . . . junior partner in a business trading weaponry.'

'What I'm interested in,' McWhitney said, 'is money for money. If I could get that poisoned cash out of the States, what percentage do you think I could sell it for?'

'Oh, not much,' Oscar said. 'I'm not sure it would be worth it, all that trouble.'

'Well, what percent do you think? Ten?'

'I doubt it.' Oscar shrugged. 'Most of the profit would go in tips,' he said. 'To import officials, shipping company employees, warehousemen. You start playing with those people, Nels, many many hands are out.'

'It's an awful lot of money, Oscar,' McWhitney said.

'It would very quickly shrink,' Oscar said, and shrugged. 'But since it's there,' he went on, 'and since you do have access to it, and since we are old friends' – which was not strictly speaking true – 'it is possible we could work something out.'

'I'm glad to hear it.'

Oscar looked around at the dark wood bar. 'Do you have this money with you now?'

'No, I'm on my way to get it.'

'The police theory,' Oscar said, 'according to the

television news, is that the thieves hid their loot some-where near the site of the robbery.'

'The police theory,' McWhitney said, 'is, you might say, on the money.'

'But you believe,' Oscar said, 'you could now go to this area and retrieve the cash and bring it safely home.'

'That's the idea,' McWhitney said.

'And are you alone in this endeavor?'

'Well,' McWhitney said, 'that's the complication. There's other people involved.'

'Other people,' Oscar agreed, 'do tend to be a compli-cation. In fact, Nels, if I may offer you some advice . . .'

'Go ahead.'

'Leave the money there,' Oscar said. 'The little profit you'd realize from an offshore trade becomes ridiculous if you have to share it with others.'

'I may not have to share it,' McWhitney said.

Oscar's thin face looked both amused and disapproving. 'Oh, Nels,' he said. 'And do you suppose your partners have similar thoughts?'

McWhitney shook his head, frowning for a stressful instant at the scarred wood tabletop. 'I don't think so,' he said slowly. 'Could be. I don't know.'

'A dangerous arena to walk into.'

'I know that much.' McWhitney gave Oscar an impas-sioned look. 'I'm not talking about *killing* anybody, Oscar. I'm not talking about a double-cross.'

'No.'

'You said it: a dangerous arena. If I have to defend myself I will.'

'Of course.'

'There's three of us.'

'Yes.'

'Maybe three of us come out with the money, maybe one of us comes out, maybe nobody comes out.'

'You're determined to know which.'

'Oh, I am,' McWhitney said. 'And so are the others. If at the end— If at the end, I'm clear of it, and I've got the money, and it's just me, I want to be able to think you'll be there for the export part.'

'You won't be mentioning me to the others.'

'No.'

Oscar considered. 'Well, it's possible,' he said. 'However, one caveat.'

'Yeah?'

'If you come out trailed by ex-partners,' Oscar told him, 'I do not know you, and I have never known you.'

'That's one thing I can tell you for sure,' McWhitney promised. 'I won't be trailed by any ex-partners.'

4

Terry Mulcany couldn't believe his good luck. He'd been in the right place at the right time, that's all, and now look. Here he was in the exact center of the manhunt, hobnobbing with the major headhunters. Well, not exactly hobnobbing, but still.

Mulcany knew he didn't belong here. He wasn't at this level. A young freelancer from Concord, New Hampshire, he had two trade paperback true-crime books to his credit, both to very minor houses and both milking, to be honest, very minor crimes. A few magazine sales, a whole drawerful of rejections, and that was his career so far.

But not any more. This is where it all would change, and he could feel it in the air. He was an insider now, and he was going to stay inside.

If only he could remember where exactly he'd run into that robber and his moll. Outside some B and B around here, that's all he could bring to mind. A white-railed porch, greenery all around; hell, that described half the buildings in the county.

But even if he could never finally pinpoint where he and the robber had met, what he *did* remember was enough. He had come to this temporary police HQ just in time to end a disagreement between two of the top brass, and since it was the *top* top brass his evidence supported, he was in.

Apparently, it had been the local honcho, Chief Inspector William Davies, who believed one of the men they were looking for had left this area, pulled another robbery in New York State, and then come back here with the cash to finance the gang while they were hiding out. The other honcho, Captain Robert Modale from upstate New York, had insisted the robber, having safely gotten away from this area, would never dare come back into it. It was Mulcany's positive identification of the man that proved the chief inspector right.

Fortunately, Captain Modale didn't get sore about it, but just accepted the new reality. And accepted Terry Mulcany along with it. As did all of them.

The woman artist had left now, to have many copies made of the new wanted poster, and the others had moved into that office. Chief Inspector Davies sat at the desk where the artist had done her drawing, while Captain Modale and Detective Gwen Reversa – *there's* a picture for the book jacket! – pulled up chairs to face him, and Terry Mulcany, with no objection from the others, stood to one side, leaning back into the angle between the wall and the filing cabinet. The fly on the wall.

At first, the three law officers discussed the meaning of the robber's return, and the meaning of the woman who'd been seen with him, and the possibility the man was actually bold enough to be staying at one of the B and Bs nearby.

But what the sighting of the robber mostly did was put new emphasis on the whereabouts of the stolen money. 'We probably should have done this before,' Inspector Davies said, 'but we're sure going to do it now. We'll mobilize every police force in the area, and we will search every empty house, every empty barn, every empty garage and shed and chicken coop in a one-hundred-mile radius. We will *find* that money.'

'And with it, with any luck,' Captain Modale said, 'the thieves.'

'God willing.'

'Inspector,' Mulcany said from his corner, 'excuse me, not to second-guess, but why wasn't that kind of search done before now?' He asked the question with deference and apparent self-confidence, but inside he was quaking, afraid that by drawing attention to himself he was merely reminding them that he didn't really belong here, and they would rise up as one man (and woman) and cast him into outer darkness.

But that didn't happen. Treating it as a legitimate question from an acceptable questioner, the inspector said, 'We were concentrating on the men. We were working on the assumption that, if we found the men, they'd lead us to the money. Now we realize the money will lead us to the men.'

'Thank you, sir.'

Detective Reversa said, 'Captain, I don't understand what happened last weekend over in your territory. What was he doing there? Did he have confederates?'

Captain Modale took a long breath, a man severely tested but carrying on, 'It really looks,' he said, 'as though the fella did the whole thing by the seat of his pants. If he ever had any previous connection with Tom Lindahl, we have not been able to find it. Of course, we can't find Tom Lindahl either, and unfortunately he's the only one who would know most of the answers we need.'

Detective Reversa asked, 'Tom Lindahl? Who's he?'

'A loner,' Modale said, 'just about a hermit, living by himself in a little town over there. For years he was a manager in charge of upkeep, buildings, all that, at a racetrack near there. He got fired for some reason, had some kind of grudge. When this fellow Ed Smith came along, I guess it was Tom's opportunity at last to get revenge. They robbed the track together.'

Detective Reversa said, 'But they're not still together. You don't think Lindahl came over here.'

'To tell you the truth,' Modale said, 'I thought we'd pick up Lindahl within just two or three days. He has no criminal record, no history of this sort of thing, you'd expect him to make nothing but mistakes.'

'Maybe,' Detective Reversa said, 'our robber gave him a few good tips for hiding out. Unless, of course, he killed Lindahl once the robbery was done.'

'It doesn't look that way,' Modale said. 'They went in late last Sunday night, overpowered the guards, and made off with nearly two hundred thousand dollars in cash. None of it traceable, I'm sorry to say.'

Inspector Davies said, 'One hundred thousand dollars would be a good motive for the pro to kill this Lindahl.'

'Except,' Modale said, 'his car was found Tuesday night

in Lexington, Kentucky, two blocks from the bus depot there. People who travel by bus use more cash and fewer credit cards than most people, so he won't stand out. If he's traveling by bus and staying in cheap hotels in cities, spending only cash, he can pretty well stay out of sight.'

Detective Reversa said, 'How long can he go on like that?'

'I'd say,' Modale told her, 'he's already got where he wants to go. Anywhere from Texas to Oregon. Settle down, get a small job, rent a little place to stay, he can gradually build up a new identity, good enough to get along with. As long as he never commits another crime, never attracts the law's attention, I don't see why he can't live the rest of his life completely undisturbed.'

'With one hundred thousand cash dollars,' Inspector Davies said, sounding disgusted. 'Not bad.'

Oh, Terry Mulcany thought, if only *that* could be my story. Tom Lindahl and the perfect crime. But where is he? Where are the interviews? Where are the pictures of him in his new life? Where is the ultimate triumph of the law at the very end of the day?

No, Tom Lindahl was safe from Terry Mulcany as well. He would stay with the true crime he had, the armored car robbery, with bazookas and unusable cash and three professional desperados, one of them now an escaped cop killer. Not so bad, really.

THE LAND PIRATES; working title.

5

Oscar Sidd's car was so anonymous you forgot it while you were looking at it. A small and unremarkable four-door sedan, it was the color of the liquid in a jar of pitted black olives; dark but weak, bruised but undramatic.

Oscar sat in this car up the block from McW after his meeting with Nelson McWhitney. Some time today the man would set out on his journey to get the Massachusetts money. Oscar would trail him in this invisible car, and McWhitney would never know it. Out from beside the bar would come McWhitney's red pickup truck, and Oscar would slide in right behind.

Except it wasn't the pickup that emerged, it was McWhitney himself, from his bar's front door. He paused in the open doorway to call one last instruction to his bartender inside, then set off on foot, down the sidewalk away from Oscar Sidd.

That was all right. Oscar could still follow. He put the forgettable car in gear, waited till McWhitney was a full block ahead, then slowly eased forward.

McWhitney walked three blocks, hands in pockets,

shoulders bunched, as though daring anyone or anything to try to slow him down. Then, taking his hands out of his pockets, he turned right and crossed the tarmac to a corner gas station that was also a body repair and detailing shop. He went into the office there, so Oscar stopped at the pumps and filled the tank, using a credit card. He expected to make a long drive today.

McWhitney was still in the office. When he came out, surely, he would be getting into one of the vehicles parked around the periphery here; but then which way would he travel?

The Belt Parkway was down that way, several blocks to the south; Oscar was going to guess that's where McWhitney would head, if his final goal was Massachusetts. Therefore, when Oscar left the station, he drove half a block north and made a U-turn into a no-parking spot beside a fire hydrant. He sat there and tuned his radio to a classical music station: Schumann.

Oscar Sidd was not as important in the international world of finance as he liked to suggest, but the reputation itself sometimes brought useful opportunities his way. This cash of McWhitney's now; that could be useful. In fact, he did have ways to launder hot money overseas, mostly in Russia, though the people you had to do business with were among the worst in the world. You were lucky to come away from them without losing everything you possessed, including your life. Still, McWhitney's money might be worth the risk. Oscar would trail along and see what opportunities might arise.

It was nearly ten minutes before McWhitney emerged, and then Oscar nearly missed him, it was so unexpected.

A small battered old Ford Econoline van, a very dark green, with HOLY REDEEMER CHOIR in fairly rough white block letters on the door, came easing out of the gas station and paused before joining the moderate traffic flow.

It took Oscar a few seconds to realize the driver of the van, hunched forward to look both ways, was McWhitney, then the van bumped out to the roadway and turned right, just as Oscar had expected. He let one other car go by, to intervene between himself and the van, then followed.

The van up there was old, its bumper and the lower parts of its body pockmarked with rust, but the New York State license plate it sported was new, shiny, and undented. That name he'd seen on the door, Holy Redeemer Choir, that was also new, and must be the reason McWhitney had left the van at that shop.

Why would McWhitney use a name like that? What would it mean?

He wasn't surprised, several blocks later, when the van signaled for a right and took the on-ramp to the Belt Parkway, heading east and then north. We're going to New England, he thought, pleased, and the radio switched to Prokofiev.

6

The police meeting in the bank building was breaking up, and Gwen walked out to the main bank lobby with Captain Modale from New York State, saying, 'I want you to know, Bob, I'm glad you made the trip over here.'

'Somewhat to my surprise,' the captain told her, with a little grin, 'I am as well. All the way over here yesterday, I'll have to tell you the truth, I was in quite a sour mood.'

They'd stopped in the lobby to continue their conversation as the others left. Gwen said, 'You thought it was going to be a big waste of time.'

'I did. Mostly, because I was convinced my Ed Smith was likely to be anywhere on earth except this neighborhood right here.'

'I'm almost as surprised as you are,' Gwen told him. 'When I talked with my John B. Allen, he just didn't seem like somebody who'd take unnecessary risks.'

'I imagine,' the captain said, 'two million dollars could be quite a temptation.'

'Enough for him to make a mistake.'

'We can only hope.'

'But now we've got a better likeness,' Gwen said, 'we

maybe have more than hope. Which is the main reason *I'm* so glad you came over. We'll have the new poster up this afternoon, and if he's still in this general area we'll definitely scoop him in.'

'I almost wish I could stay for it,' the captain said. 'But I'm sure you'll let us know.'

'You'll be the *first* to know,' Gwen promised him, and laughed. 'I'll e-mail you his mug shot.'

'Do.' The captain stuck his hand out. 'Nice to meet you, Gwen.'

'And you, Bob,' she said, as they shook hands. 'Safe trip back.'

'Thank you.' The captain turned. 'Trooper Oskott?'

The trooper had been seated at a loan officer's desk, reading a hunting magazine, but he now stood, pocketed the magazine, and said, 'Yes, sir.'

The two men left, and Gwen paused to get out her cell phone and call her current boyfriend, Barry Ridgely, a defense lawyer who spent his weekdays in court and his Saturdays on the golf course. When he answered now, in an outdoor setting from the sound of it, she said, 'How many more holes?'

'I can do lunch in forty minutes, if that's what you want to know.'

'It is. You pick the place.'

'How about Steuber's?' he said, naming a country place that had originally been very Germanic but was now much more ordinary, the Wiener schnitzel and saurbraten long departed.

'Done. See you there.'

*

Leaving the bank building, putting her cell phone away, Gwen turned toward her pool car when someone called, 'Detective Reversa?'

She turned and it was Terry Mulcany, and it seemed to her he'd been waiting on the sidewalk specifically for her to come out. 'Yes?'

'I've been waiting for you to come out,' he said. 'I have two questions, if you don't mind.'

'Not at all. Go ahead.'

'Well, the first is,' he said, 'I know my publisher, when the book comes out they're going to want pictures, and particularly the detectives who worked on the case. So what I was wondering is, if you've got a picture of yourself you especially like.'

And have you, she wondered, asked the same question of the other detectives on the case? Of course not. Smiling, she said, 'When the time comes, your editor can call me or someone else at my barracks. I'm sure there won't be any problem.'

'That's fine,' he said, with a hint of disappointment. What had he been hoping for? That she would suddenly hand him her *Playboy* playmate photo?

Wanting to get to Steuber's, she said, 'Was there something else?'

'Yes. The other thing,' he said, 'is, I've been trying to remember where I saw that guy.'

'My John B. Allen.'

'Yeah.' He twisted his face into a Kabuki mask, to demonstrate the effort he was putting in. 'I don't know why,' he said, 'but there's something about a pear it reminds me of. The place where I saw them.'

She did her own Kabuki mask. 'A pear?'

'You know this area,' he said, 'a lot better than I do. Is there someplace around here called like the Pear Orchard, or Pear House, or something like that?'

'Not that I've ever heard of.'

'Oh, well,' he said, and elaborately shrugged. 'If I figure it out, I'll give you a call.'

'You do that,' she said.

Barry's current client was a veterinarian who either had or had not strangled his wife. A jury would answer that question very soon now, probably early next week, and at lunch Barry was full of the problems besetting a poor defense counsel merely trying to put his client in the best possible light. 'The judge just isn't gonna let me show the video in my summation,' he complained, crumbling a roll in vexation. His client, in happier times, had won a humanitarian award from some veterinarian's association, and Barry insisted that no one who watched the video of the man's acceptance speech would ever be able to convict him of anything more nefarious than littering. 'He's not even gonna let me show a *photo* of it.'

'Well,' Gwen said, being gentle, 'that is kind of far from the subject at hand.'

'Which of course is what the judge insists. But if I were to just *mention* it, the award, that could be even worse than—'

'Bartlett,' Gwen said.

Barry frowned at her. 'What?'

'Bartlett pear,' Gwen said, 'Mrs Bartlett. Bosky Rounds.'

101

'Gwen,' he said, 'is this supposed to be making sense?'

Beaming at him, Gwen said, 'All at once, it does.'

7

When Trooper Louise Rawburton signed in at the Deer Hill barracks at three fifty-two that afternoon, she was one of sixteen troopers, eleven male and five female, assigned to the four-to-midnight shift, two troopers per patrol car, doing this three-month segment with Trooper Danny Oleski, who did most of the driving, which was okay because it left her more freedom to talk. Danny didn't mind her yakking away, so it made for a happy patrol car, and if it wasn't for the system of rotation she knew she and Danny would have been happy as a team on their tours of duty forever.

However, the system of rotation was, everybody agreed, all in all a good idea. Put two straight men who get along with each other into the confines of a patrol car for several hours a day and they'll swap old stories, tell jokes, recommend movies and generally make the time go by. Make it one straight man and one straight woman and they'll do all the same things, but after a while they'll start to smile on each other a little differently, they'll start to touch, start to kiss, and down that road lies marital unhappiness

103

and inefficient policing. A three-month rotation is usually short enough to keep that sort of thing from happening, to almost everybody's relief.

When Louise joined Danny and the other fourteen troopers in the shape-up room for the day's assignments from Sgt. Jackson, she expected today's tour to be more of the same: roadblocks. For over a week now, most of their on-duty time had been spent mounting roadblocks, the only variant being that the roadblocks were shifted to slightly different locations every day.

No one would say that the roadblocks had been completely unsuccessful. A number of expired licenses had been found, lack of insurance, faulty lights, the occasional drunk. But as to the *purpose* of the roadblocks, to nab the three men who'd destroyed three armored cars and made off with the fourth, full of cash, over a week ago, not a glimmer, The one man who'd been captured, and subsequently lost, was the result of a tip from a deli clerk who'd been passed one of the known stolen bills. Still, the powers that be felt better if they could mess up the whole world's schedules by littering the highways and byways with roadblocks, thus assuring the whole world that *something was being done*, so that's what Louise and Danny and the rest had been up to and would continue to do.

Except not. 'This afternoon,' Sgt. Jackson told them, pacing back and forth in front of where they stood on the black linoleum floor in the big square empty room with tables and chairs stacked along the rear, 'our orders are a little different.'

An anticipatory sigh of relief rose from the sixteen, and

Sgt. Jackson gave a little shrug and said, 'We'll see. Ladies and gentlemen, our mission has changed. We're not going to stand around any longer and wait for those fugitives to come to us. We are going to actively search for them by trying to find that stolen money.'

One of the troopers said, 'How we supposed to do that, Sarge? Hang out in delis?'

'Those three did not manage to transport their loot away from this part of the world,' Jackson told him. 'That's the belief we're operating from. Now, it's a big untidy pile, that money, and the idea is, if we look for it, we'll find it, and if we find it, the fugitives won't be too far away from it.'

There was general agreement in the room on that point, and then Jackson said, 'What our job is today, you are each getting a sector, and you are to physically eyeball every empty or abandoned building in that sector. Empty houses, barns, everything. On the table by the door there's a packet for each patrol, with your sector laid out in it, and by the way, a new suspect sketch on one of the fugitives. This is supposed to be closer to the real man.'

'What'll they think of next?' asked a wit.

Riding shotgun, Louise ran an eye down the printout of the roads and intersections in their sector, then unfolded the new suspect sketch and studied it. 'Oh, that one,' she said.

Danny, driving, glanced once and away. 'That one,' he agreed.

'He doesn't look as mean this time,' she decided.

'He was always a good boy,' Danny said.

'Did somebody ever say that in a movie?' Louise wanted to know. 'You hear it all the time.'

'Beats me.'

Putting away the sketch, Louise went back to the printout, studied it some more, and said, 'We should start from Hurley.'

'Real backwoods stuff.'

'That's what they gave us. Oh!' she said, surprised and delighted, 'St Dympna!'

'Say what?'

'That's where I went to church, when I was a little girl. St Dympna.'

'Never heard of it,' he said. 'What kind of name is that?'

'She was supposed to be Irish. Most churches with saints' names are Roman Catholic, but we weren't. We were United Reformed.' Louise laughed and said, 'The funny thing is, when they founded the church, they just wanted some unusual name to attract attention, so they picked St Dympna, and then, too late, they found out she's actually the patron saint of insanity.'

Danny looked at her. 'You're putting me on.'

'I am not. Turned out, there's a mental hospital named for her in Belgium. When I was a kid, that was the coolest thing, our church was named for the patron saint of crazy people.'

'Is it still going?'

'The church? Oh, no, it got shut down, must be more than ten years ago.'

'Ran out of crazy people,' Danny suggested.

'Very funny. No, it's really way out in the sticks. There weren't so many small farms after a while, and people

106

moved closer to town, until there was almost nobody left to go there, and nobody could afford to keep it up. It shut down when I was in high school. There was some hope an antiques shop would buy it, but it never happened.'

'So that's got to be one of the places on our list.'

'It sure is.' Louise smiled in nostalgia, and looked at the road ahead. 'I'm looking forward to seeing it again.'

8

Mrs Bartlett was sorry to see Captain Robert Modale and Trooper Oskott leave Bosky Rounds. Not that the room would go begging; this time of year, she always had a waiting list, and would surely fill that room again no later than Monday. But she'd liked the captain, found him quiet and restful, and a happy surprise after the unexpected departure of Mr and Mrs Willis.

The Willises had also been quiet and restful, not like some. Her in particular. Claire Willis. Mrs Bartlett never did get a good reading on her husband, some sort of humorless businessman who clearly didn't really care about anything but his business and was taking this vacation solely to make his wife happy; which was of course a mark in his favor.

But the rest was all her. She did all the driving and all the talking, and even made the apologies when they unexpectedly had to depart because of some crisis back home with his business.

Mrs Willis had been so apologetic and so understanding, even offering to pay the unused portion of their stay, that

Mrs Bartlett couldn't even get irritated. Of course she refused the extra payment, and assured Mrs Willis she'd fill the room in no time, and then, the Willises barely gone and before she'd even had time to turn to her waiting list, here came the call from the New York State Police, needing a room for just the one night.

It was a sign, Mrs Bartlett felt. She and Mrs Willis had behaved decently toward each other, and this was Mrs Bartlett's reward. She certainly hoped Mrs Willis was rewarded, perhaps with something other than that cold-fish husband of hers.

Barely half an hour after the departure of Captain Modale, here came Gwen Reversa, looking as fresh and stylish as ever, though Mrs Bartlett could never quite get over her feeling that an attractive young woman like Gwen was never supposed to be a policeman. Still, here she was, carrying yet another of those wanted posters. Mrs Bartlett frankly didn't like the look of those things, and felt they did nothing for the decor and atmosphere of Bosky Rounds, but there was apparently to be no choice in the matter. Her front room was a public space, and the public spaces must willy-nilly be filled up with these dreadful-looking gangsters.

Still, she couldn't help saying, '*Another* one, Gwen? I'm not going to have much wall left.'

'No, it's a replacement,' Gwen told her, going over to where the two drawings and one photograph were already tacked to the wall. 'You know that Captain Modale who was here.'

'A charming man.'

'Well, he and I both encountered the same one of the

suspects. This one,' she said, taking the latest poster from its manila folder and holding it up for Mrs Bartlett to see. 'We worked together with the artist,' she said, 'and we think this picture is much closer to the real man. See it?'

Mrs Bartlett didn't want to see it. Squinting, nodding, she said, 'Yes, I see it. It takes the place of one of the others, does it?'

'Yes, this one. Here, I'll take the old one with me.' While she was tacking the new poster in the old one's place, she said, 'Did a reporter named Terry Mulcany talk to you?'

'Oh, the true-crime person.' she said. 'Yes, he was all right. He seemed awfully rushed, though.'

Gwen turned away from the wall, folding the old poster and putting it into her coat pocket as she said, 'He thought he possibly saw that man somewhere around this house.'

'In *this* house? Gwen!'

'Not in the house, near it. Outside. With a woman.'

'Gwen,' Mrs Bartlett said, and pointed toward the row of posters, 'not one of those people has ever set foot in Bosky Rounds. Can you imagine? What on earth would they ever do *here*?'

'Well, they have to sleep somewhere.'

Frosty, Mrs Bartlett said, '*Those* are not my customers, Gwen.'

Laughing, Gwen said, 'No, I suppose not. Still, if you see anybody who looks like that,' and pointed again at the new poster, 'be sure to call me.'

'Of course. Of course I will.'

Gwen left, and Mrs Bartlett spent the next few minutes sending out e-mails to her waiting list, telling them an unexpected five-day vacancy had just come up. As she was finishing that, Ms Loscalzo, from number two upstairs at the back, came through, heading out, carrying her usual big ungraceful black leather shoulder bag. 'Off for more scenery,' she said, as though it were a joke, or a difficult chore of some kind.

'Enjoy the day, dear,' Mrs Bartlett said.

'That's a good idea,' Ms Loscalzo said, waved, and marched off.

Mrs Bartlett couldn't help but wonder about Sandra Loscalzo. Most tourists this time of year were couples or groups, almost never singles. You'd go to the movies or a museum by yourself, but you wouldn't drive around the countryside looking at the changing leaves all on your own in your car. Anyway, most people wouldn't.

Also, Ms Loscalzo seemed a little coarser, a little more – Mrs Bartlett was almost ashamed of herself, thinking such a thing – working-class than most of the leaf peepers she'd seen over the years. And she didn't wear a wedding ring, though that didn't necessarily mean anything. It could be she was recovering from having been recently divorced, and needed a change to get her just for a little while out of her regular life. That might be it.

As she thought about Sandra Loscalzo, Mrs Bartlett found herself unwillingly gazing at the posters of the wanted robbers, diagonally across the room from her desk, and especially that new one, nearest her along the wall.

Oh, my goodness. She stared at the poster, then rose and walked over to frown at it from a foot away.

It couldn't be. Could it? Could that nice Claire Willis be married to *that*? It was impossible.

But it was true. The more she stared at that cold face, the more she saw him standing there, just behind his wife, saying little, showing almost no emotion, certainly no enthusiasm for looking at leaves.

But why would Claire Willis be married to a bank robber? It was ridiculous. Mrs Bartlett would be more willing to believe Sandra Loscalzo was married to such a man; not Claire Willis.

There had to be an explanation. Maybe the police had their eye on the wrong man all along, or maybe this was just as inaccurate a sketch as the first one. They got it wrong before, maybe they got it wrong again.

Should she phone Gwen, let the police detective sort it out? Mrs Bartlett had the uneasy feeling that was exactly what she should do now, but she didn't want to. It wasn't Henry Willis she was thinking of, it was Claire. She didn't want Gwen glaring down her nose at Claire Willis. Whatever was in the woman's life, Mrs Bartlett certainly didn't want to be the one who made things worse. She couldn't call Gwen because she couldn't make trouble for that nice Claire Willis.

And there was a second reason as well, even stronger than that, though she barely acknowledged it to herself. But the fact is, she had been very remiss. Oh, yes, she'd assured Gwen, over and over, she had studied those posters, she was ready to do her civic duty if any of those robbers happened to wander into Bosky Rounds.

But had she studied? Had she paid attention? The man had been right *here*, in this house, in this room, and she had never noticed. How could she possibly make that phone call now and say, 'Oh, Gwen, I just happened to notice ...'

No. She couldn't do it. She couldn't phone Gwen, not now, not ever, and the reason was, she was just too embarrassed.

9

Sandra drove south and east out of town, headed for the Mass Pike. When McWhitney had phoned her this morning from Long Island he'd told her their new truck was an Econoline van, dark green, not black, and he expected to get to her around five. She hadn't told him she'd bird-dog him the last part of the trip, but that's what she intended to do. Always err on the side of caution, that was her belief.

She'd expected two or three roadblock stops along the way, but yesterday's heavy police presence had suddenly evaporated. Where had they gone? Had they caught Nick again? If so, she and McWhitney were going to have to rethink their approach to the money in the church, and Parker might already be in trouble over there. She turned on the car radio, looking for all-news stations, but heard about no developments in the search for the robbers.

So where were all the cops? Sandra didn't like questions without answers. She had half a mind to just keep driving south, and let this whole business alone.

Well, she could still bird-dog McWhitney. If something

seemed weird with him, or if he got nabbed by the cops, she'd be long gone.

There were two gas stations near the turnpike exit he'd be taking. She chose the one in the direction he would go, parked among a few other cars along the side perimeter, and used her hands-free cell to call him in the truck.

'Yeah?'

Of course he wouldn't say hello like everybody else. Sandra said, 'Just wondering how you're coming along.'

'Fine.'

That was helpful. 'About how long, do you figure?'

'You're impatient for that green, huh?'

'I don't wanna be doing my hair when you get here.'

That made him laugh, and loosen up a little. 'Do your hair tomorrow. I'll be there in less than an hour.'

'Where are you now?'

'On the Pike, be getting off in five, ten minutes.'

'I'll be here,' she promised, and broke the connection, and spent the next seven minutes watching traffic come down the ramp and peel away.

If Roy Keenan were still alive, and still her partner, he'd be waiting north of here right now for Sandra to tell him when the van came off the turnpike and what it looked like. Then he'd follow from in front, keeping the van visible in his rearview mirror, so that Sandra could hang well back, ignoring the van as she watched for other inter-ested parties. But Roy was gone and hadn't as yet been replaced, so she'd do it this way.

Sandra had gotten her private investigator's license a year after leaving college, and had worked for the first few years mostly on unimportant white-collar criminal matters for a large agency with many business clients. She investigated inside-job thefts at department stores, trade-secret-selling employees, minor frauds, and slippery accounting.

The work, which had at first been interesting, soon became a bore, but she couldn't find an acceptable alternative until, at a fingerprinting refresher course given by the FBI, she'd met Roy, whose previous woman partner had just left him to get married. 'Well, that won't happen to me,' Sandra assured him.

They became a very good partnership. She kept her private life to herself, and Roy was fine with that. Sometimes they were flush and other times money was tight, but they'd never been scraping the bottom of the barrel until this protracted, expensive, frustrating search for Michael Maurice Harbin, a search that *still* hadn't paid off, and the reason she was now waiting for an extremely dangerous felon in a Ford Econoline van.

There. Very good, good choice, a dark green beat-up little van. Holy Redeemer Choir.

She started the Honda, gave the van a chance to roll farther down the road to the north, then started to ease out after him, but abruptly stopped.

She'd almost missed him, dammit, she must be more distracted than she'd thought. Because there he was, in a little nondescript no-color car, just easing into McWhitney's wake.

What he'd done, this guy, he'd come down the ramp and stopped at the yield sign at the bottom, even though there wasn't any traffic to yield to. He stayed there almost ten seconds, a long time, until a car did come along the secondary road going in his direction. Then he pulled in behind that car. Sandra knew that maneuver, she'd done it herself a hundred times.

Now she accelerated across the gas station tarmac to the road, so she could get a close-up of the tail as he drove by. Cadaverous guy in black, hunched forward, very intense, very focused.

Sandra did the same thing he'd done, waited for another car to intervene, then joined the cavalcade. Out here there were towns to go through, every one of them with one traffic light. The first time they were all stopped at a light she took a hurried look at her Massachusetts map, then when they started moving again she called McWhitney and said, 'You've got a tin can on you, you know about that?'

'What? Where are you?'

'Listen to me, Nelson. He's in a nothing little car, two behind you.'

'Jesus Christ!'

'Tall bony guy in black, looks like he's never had a good meal in his life.'

'That son of a bitch.'

'You know him, I take it. Pal of yours?'

'Not any more.'

'Okay.'

'Don't worry, Sandra, I'll get rid of him.'

'Not in that truck,' Sandra told him. 'We don't want any problems with that truck. I'll deal with it.'

'The dirty bastard.'

'Up ahead, you got Route 518.'

'Yeah?'

'Take the left on 518, the right on 26A, right on 47, it'll take you back to this road, then just head on up, same as before.'

'And you'll be up there.'

'I'll do the cutout, catch up with you later. Here comes 518.'

The traffic light up ahead was green. The van's turn signal went on, and then the follower. They went off to the left, and Sandra continued north, saying to McWhitney, 'You wanna tell me about him?'

'His name is Oscar Sidd, he's supposed to know about moving money out of the country.'

'You told him what we've got.'

'So we'd have some place to take it after.'

'And you just happened to forget to mention your friend Oscar to me.'

'Come on, Sandra. I never thought he'd pull something like *this*. What does he want, something to fall off the back of the truck?'

'If he forgot to mention to you, Nelson, that he was gonna take a drive up here today, he wants more than a skim, doesn't he?'

'The bastard. He's out of his league, if that's what he's thinking.'

'He is and it is. If you see me, a little later, don't slow down.'

'There you go insulting me again.'

'Have a nice ride, Nelson,' she said, and broke the connection.

A few minutes later she was stopped at the red light

for the intersection with Route 47. When it turned green, she drove more slowly, looking for a place to roost, and found it at a small wooden town hall on the edge of town, up a rise higher than the road. Saturday afternoon, it was deserted, no cars in the parking lot beside the building. She pulled in there, up the steep driveway to the parking lot beside the town hall, then swung around to face south, opened the passenger window, and waited.

Not quite ten minutes, and here came the van. Well behind it, but with no intervening vehicle this time, came Oscar Sidd in his no-brand jalopy. Sandra popped the glove compartment and took out her licensed Taurus Tracker revolver, chambered for the .17HMR, a punchier cartridge than the .22, in a very accurate handgun.

As the van went by, Sandra leaned over to the right window, curled her left hand onto the bottom of the frame, the side of her right hand holding the Tracker on the back of her left, and popped a bullet into Oscar Sidd's right front tire.

Very good. The car jerked hard to the right, ran off the shoulder, and slammed into the rise, jolting to a stop. The windshield suddenly starred on the left side, so Mr Sidd's head must have met it.

Sandra started the Honda, closed the right window, put the Tracker away, and drove back down to the road. When she went past the other car, its hood was crumpled and steaming, and Mr Sidd was motionless against the steering wheel.

Redial. 'Nelson?'

'What's happening?'

'That's me behind you now. See me?'

'Oh, yeah, the black waterbug.'

'Thank you. Can you find that church from here?' Because she wasn't sure she'd be able to.

'Sure.'

'Then I'll stay back here,' she said, 'keep an eye out, see are there any more friends of yours coming along.'

She did recognize the road the church was on, when McWhitney turned into it, and hung back even farther than before. There had still been no roadblocks, though she had seen the occasional police car, moving as though with a purpose, not just idly on patrol.

What had changed in the world? She'd considered talking it over with McWhitney and decided it was better not. If everything was okay at the church, fine. If it turned out there was some sort of trouble there, let McWhitney walk into it, at which point Sandra would just drive on by, nothing to do with that van, and head for Long Island.

There it was, church on the right, white house on the left. McWhitney turned in at the house, because that's where Parker would be, and Sandra lagged back so far that McWhitney was already out of the van, looking impatient, before she pulled in beside him. She opened her door, McWhitney said, 'You wanna take a lotta time here?' and a gunshot sounded from the house.

10

It had been the worst week in Nick Dalesia's life, but it never quite went entirely all to hell. Every time things looked hopeless there'd be one more little ray of possibility, just enough to get him moving again. He was beginning to think that hopelessness was the better option. More restful, anyway.

Public transportation had seemed like the best way to get clear of the search area right after the robbery. Who knew that all he had to do to get himself scooped up like a marlin in a net was buy a sandwich to eat on the bus to St Louis, paying for it with a twenty from the bank?

He was certain he was done for then, with all those lawmen's hands on his elbows, and he spent the first night in the solitary holding cell at some state police building in western Massachusetts trying to figure out what he could trade for a better deal.

The money certainly. McWhitney: he could point a finger right directly at that bar of his. And Parker, he could give them leads on him, too. And the story of the killing of Harbin for wearing the federal wire, and the names of the other people present at that meeting. There was a lot he could give them, when he added it all up. He was still going to do serious time, and he knew it, but he'd be a little more cushioned than if he'd walked in empty-handed.

But then, early next morning, they didn't question him at all, so he didn't get to tell them which top lawyer they should call, who happened to be a guy Nick didn't know but had read about in the newspapers, and who would be perfect for Nick's defense, and who would be bound to take the job because this was a high-profile case and that was a lawyer who liked high-profile cases.

But then none of that happened, and then, early in the morning, he was rousted out and put into a small office with a cup of coffee and a donut. It was the US marshals who had their hands on him, and they didn't care to question him about anything, they were just there to conduct him to someplace else.

One marshal in the room, an automatic sidearm in a holstered belt strapped over his coat, his partner gone off to see about transportation. The coffee was too hot to drink, so Nick threw it in the marshal's face, grabbed the automatic, whammed the guy across the forehead with it, and headed for the door.

Locked. The marshal must have a key. Nick turned back and the guy was conscious, coming up to a sprawled seated position, groping in a dazed way inside his coat, coming out with something.

The son of a bitch had another gun! Nick lunged across the space between them, shoved the automatic barrel into the guy's chest to muffle the sound, and shot him once.

All the guy had needed to do was lie there till Nick was out of the room, then yell like an opera singer, but no. Nick found the keys, and got moving.

Getting through and out of that state police building had been very tough. It was a maze, and the alarm was already out. He eventually went out a window to a fire escape and down to where he could jump onto the roof of a garage, and then get to the ground and gone.

He kept the automatic. He'd paid for it, he'd paid a lot, and he was gonna keep it.

He carjacked an early-morning commuter drinking his cardboard container of coffee at a red light, but he couldn't keep that vehicle long; just enough time to get to some other town. And while he drove, he tried to think where to go next.

Forget transportation, public or otherwise. Any traveling he did would get him picked up right away. What he had to do was go to ground and stay there, maybe a week, maybe even longer.

But where? Who did he know in this part of the world? Where would he find a safe place to hunker down?

He was just about to abandon his carjacked wheels when he remembered Dr Madchen. Not a criminal, not somebody the police would have any reason to look at. But Nick did have a handle on his back, because the doctor had some kind of connection with the local guy in the setup of the robbery, and the doctor would provide him an alibi.

When, just before the robbery, it had looked as though the doctor was calling attention to himself, being coy, being stupid, Nick and Parker had gone to his home to have a word with him. That was all it took, and in any case the robbery went wrong so quickly there was no alibi in the world that would help the local guy and so, after all, the doctor did nothing. Which meant he was clean; but if Nick asked him to help, he would help.

The week at the doctor's house was grueling. Nick had a terrific sense of urgency, a need to take action, but there was never anything to do. All week the television news told him the heat was still on, and he knew he was the reason why. If it was just the bank's money, they'd ease off after a while, but he'd killed one of their own, and they weren't about to let up.

He kept trying to make plans, come to decisions, but there was simply not a single move he could make. If he left Dr Madchen's house, how long would it take them to catch up with him? No time at all. But how could he stay here, like this, as though his feet were nailed to the floor?

He had never thought before that he might some day go crazy, but now he did. The jangling electric need to *do* something, *do* something, when there was nothing to be done; there was nothing worse.

He thought sometimes he'd kill the doctor, take his car and whatever valuables he had in the house, and head north. But then he'd remember the roadblocks, and he knew it couldn't happen. He didn't have safe ID. They had his *picture*. What was he going to do?

By Friday evening, when the doctor told him the maid would be coming back tomorrow and Nick couldn't stay at the house any longer, Nick was ready to go, it hardly mattered where. He'd been more beaten down by the week of inaction than if he'd spent a month in a war zone. When the doctor gave him the ultimatum – too timid for an ultimatum, but that's still what it was – he actually welcomed it, as a change, any change from being in this paralysis, and he knew immediately what he was going to do.

'Tomorrow,' he told the doctor, 'when you go get this Estrella, you're gonna drive me somewhere,' and the next day he had the doctor drive him past the church, but without stopping or pointing it out or making it seem as though the church had anything to do with his plans. But then, a little farther on, where the road curved and dipped down to a bridge over a narrow stream, Nick said, 'Stop here, I'll get out and you drive on.'

The doctor stopped, beside the road just before the bridge, and Nick got out, then stooped to look back into the car and say, 'We never met each other, Doctor. If you make no trouble for me, I'll make no trouble for you.'

'I won't make any trouble.'

Nick believed him; the doctor's face looked as whipped as his own. 'Thanks,' he said, and shut the car door, and the doctor's Alero wobbled away over the bridge and out of sight.

Nick saw no other cars as he walked back to the church. Would it all be the same? He was counting on it. His idea, if it could even be called an idea, was to grab as much of the money as he could, steal a car from somewhere around here, then drive it strictly on back roads, keeping away from the roadblocks.

Canada was still the best hope he had, if he had any

125

hope at all. He'd head north, up through the winding little roads in the mountains. He'd sleep in the car and only use the bad money in places where he would immediately be moving on, paying only for food and gas.

Somewhere up near the border he'd have to leave that car and walk, however far it was until he reached some town on the Canadian side. There, he could do a burglary or two to get some safe Canadian money, steal another car, and make his way to Toronto or Ottawa. There he could come to at least a temporary stop, and try to figure out the rest of his life from there. It wasn't much of a plan, but what else did he have?

The church looked the same. When they'd first holed up in here, McWhitney had kicked open the locked side door so they could carry the boxes of money in, then they'd kicked it shut again so that it looked all right unless you really examined it. Had anything been done to change that? Not that Nick could see. He leaned on the door and it fell open in front of him.

The money was still there, up in the choir loft, untouched. Nick filled his pockets, then went downstairs and outside, this time not bothering to pull the door shut.

He was going to keep walking down the road, looking for a vehicle parked outside somebody's house or a passing driver to carjack, when he glanced at the house across the road and decided it wouldn't hurt to see what might be inside there that could be of use. He expected the place to be empty, but was quiet as a matter of habit, and when he walked into one of the upstairs bedrooms somebody was asleep in there, on the floor, covered with a rough-looking quilt.

A bum? Nick edged closer, and was astonished to see it was Parker.

What was Parker doing here? He had come for the money, no other reason.

So where was his car? Nick had been on both sides of the road and he hadn't seen any car. Was it hidden somewhere? Where?

He hunkered against the wall, across the room from Parker, trying to decide what to do, whether he should go look for the car, or wake Parker up to ask him where it was, or just kill him and keep moving, when Parker came awake. Nick saw that Parker from the first instant was not surprised, not worried, not even to wake up and find somebody in the room with a gun in his hand.

We used to be partners, Nick thought, with a kind of dull disbelief. Could we be partners again? Could we get out of this mess together?

We're not partners, he thought, as Parker looked at him with that lack of surprise and said, 'So there you are.' I don't have partners any more, Nick thought. I only have enemies now.

'Where's your car?' he asked.

Parker bullshitted him. He danced around without moving, without trying to get up from the floor, just saying things, dancing around. He doesn't have a car. But why doesn't he have a car? Somebody dropped him off, some woman dropped him off, some woman Nick doesn't know dropped him off.

Bullshit! Where did this woman come from, all of a

sudden? Why is Parker asleep *here*? Now angry, angry at Parker, at the marshal, at the world, Nick pounded the pistol butt on the floor and demanded, 'What are you *doing* here?'

'I wanted to look at the money.'

'You wanted to *take* the money.'

No, Parker told him, no, too early for that. And more bullshit, more bullshit, while Nick tried to figure out what Parker was up to.

'You were out, you were free and clear, and you came *back*.' With sudden tense suspicion, with a quick shiver up the middle of his back, he said, 'Is Nelson here?'

But Parker said no, he didn't travel with McWhitney, and Nick could believe that. But what was he *doing* here? With sudden conviction, Nick said, 'You're waiting.'

'That's right,' Parker said, and as though it didn't matter he flipped that rough quilt off his legs.

Nick didn't like that movement. He didn't like any move-ment right now. Aiming the automatic at Parker's face, on the brink of using it, only holding back because he needed to know what was going on here, who was Parker waiting for, where was there a *car* in this for Nick, he aimed the automatic at Parker's face and yelled, 'Don't move!'

'I'm not moving, Nick. I got stiff, that's all, sleeping here.'

'You could get stiffer,' Nick said, and as he said it he knew he couldn't wait any more. He didn't care about Parker any more, didn't need the answers to any ques-tions, didn't have any questions left.

But Parker was still talking, moving his hands now,

saying they could help each other, saying, 'And I got water,' holding up a clear bottle in his left hand.

Water? What did Nick care about water? But he looked at the bottle.

'It's just water. Check it out for yourself,' Parker offered, and slowly lobbed the bottle toward him underhand, in a high arc, toward the ceiling, toward his lap.

Nick's eyes followed the movement of the bottle for just a second, for one second too long, and something like a great dark wing slashed across the room at him, Parker lost and hidden behind it, the quilt twisting toward him through the air. He fired, with nothing to aim at, and a hard hand chopped down on the gun wrist. The automatic skittered away across the wood floor and Parker's other hand clawed for his throat. Nick screamed, kicked his heels to the floor to jolt himself away, flopped over to his right, found his elbows and knees beneath himself, and lunged out and away, up off the floor and through the closed window.

THREE

1

Parker reached for that fleeing body, but the hours spent asleep on the floor had left him too stiff, his movements less coordinated than he was used to. He missed Nick entirely, and watched him crash through the window, the force of his impact taking out the wooden crosspieces and mullions, shattering the glass, leaving a jagged hole with fresh wind blowing in.

Cursing the stiffness, Parker turned the other way and grabbed the automatic off the floor. Then he used the wall to help him to his feet, and hobbled to the gaping window.

Nick was out of sight. He'd landed on weedy lawn back here, twelve feet down, with the woods half a dozen fast paces away.

Fresh blood hadn't yet darkened on the zigzag edges of glass. Nick was hurt out there. How badly?

A sound on the stairs, behind him. Had Nick come *in*? Without his gun?

Parker moved to the corner farthest from the doorway

and waited. He heard the heavy steps coming up the stairs, and then silence. He waited.

'Parker?'

Parker leaned against the wall behind him. 'Nelson,' he said.

McWhitney appeared in the doorway, his own gun loosely in his hand, but reacted when he saw what Parker was carrying: 'Whoa! What's this?'

'Nick's gun,' Parker pointed at the slashed window. 'That was Nick.'

'He was *here*?'

'In and out.'

'We heard the crash. Sandra went around back.' Crossing to the wrecked window, he said, 'How come he didn't do you?'

'He wanted to know where my car was.'

McWhitney laughed, first surprised and then amused. 'The greedy bastard. Where's he been keeping himself the last week?'

'He didn't say.'

McWhitney leaned forward to look out the window and down, and call, 'What do you see?'

'Broken glass,' Sandra called back. 'Broken wood. What happened up there?'

'Nick went out the window.'

'*Nick*?'

'We'll come down,' McWhitney told her.

They went downstairs and around to the back, to find Sandra standing where Nick must have landed, frowning away to the woods behind and to the right of the house. Turning to them, she said, 'What happened here?'

'I was asleep,' Parker said, 'and then Nick came in. He wanted a car.'

'You don't have a car,' Sandra told him.

Parker shrugged. 'We discussed it. Then I got his gun, and he went out the window.'

'You didn't push him out.'

'I didn't want him out. I wanted him in there.'

McWhitney said, 'We gotta find him now, Parker.'

'I know.'

'Wait a second,' Sandra said. 'We're here, we've got the van. Let's pick up the money and get *out* of here.'

'Sandra,' McWhitney said, 'Nick has run out his string. Wherever he was holed up, he isn't there any more. He's on foot, he's cut up from that window, he's a dead duck. If the cops get their hands on him, he puts me right out of business. The bar, everything. I'm on the run the rest of my life.' To Parker he said, 'You, too.'

'Not so much.'

'Enough. Enough to give your friend Claire some nervous moments.'

'That's true.'

Sandra said, 'What are you gonna do, run around in the woods? You're not gonna find him in there. Maybe he's bleeding to death.'

'We can't take the chance,' McWhitney said.

Sandra thought about it, and realized she had to bend on this. 'Five minutes.'

Parker said, 'Sandra, we'll give it what it takes.'

'I'll be with the cars,' she told them. She was disgusted.

'With your piece in your lap,' McWhitney advised.

'Now you're insulting *me*.'

She headed off around the house and Parker walked over to where dry fallen leaves had been recently scuffed, showing streaks of wetter leaves beneath. The streaks pointed at an angle away from the right rear corner of the house.

Parker and McWhitney, both with guns in their hands, followed the streak line's direction, away from the house. They kept parallel to each other, but a few paces apart. Away from the house, the narrow tall scrubby second-growth trees were like an army of lancers, all upright, with daylight in vertical strips between. The ground was rocky and uneven, but trended upward, with clusters of thorny shrubs intermixed with nearly bare areas of grass and weed.

They walked along the scrub ground for two or three minutes, watching in every direction, and then McWhitney stopped and said, 'I'm not seeing anything.'

'Neither am I.'

Parker looked back and the house was almost completely hidden back there, just a few hints of white. 'We don't have him,' he said.

Complaining, McWhitney said, 'I'm not a tracker, I'm a bartender. This isn't where I do my best work.'

They turned around, headed back to the house, and Parker said, 'When you get home, just in case, you gotta start building an alibi.'

'Oh, I know. What's that?'

Ahead and to their left, a piece of dark gray cloth flapped, its corner stuck to the thorny lower branch of a wide-spread multiflora rose. They went over to look at it, and Parker said, 'That's the pants he was wearing.'

'The road's right over there.'

'I know it. There's blood on these thorns here.'

'The son of a bitch is hurt,' McWhitney said, 'but he won't stop. Can we get to the road this way?'

'If we want to bleed like Nick. Easier back around by the house.'

They retraced their steps to the house, and when they came around the side of it Sandra got out of her Honda and said, 'Give me some good news for once.'

'We're alive,' McWhitney told her.

'Try again.'

Parker looked at the van with holy redeemer choir on the doors. 'Looks good.'

Sandra said, 'So why don't we use it?'

Parker told her, 'You drive your car and the van over to the church, we'll take one look along the road for Nick.'

She heaved a sigh, to show how patient she was. 'Done,' she said.

They walked along the road while she shuttled the vehicles behind them. A red pickup went by, with two guys in hunting caps in it, neither of them Nick; everybody waved.

In a ditch there was a space of tangled smears where somebody or something had slid down out of the roadside scrub, maybe fallen here, then moved on. Impossible to say which direction he had taken.

McWhitney said, 'I could take Sandra's car, follow down this road. Or she could, while we move the boxes.'

'Waste of time,' Parker said. 'You can't find a man on foot with a car. We just get the cash, and clear out of here.'

137

As they walked back toward the church McWhitney, sounding irritated but resigned, said. 'Alibi. Parker, I'm gonna have to call in every marker I got out. And just hope it turns out enough people owe me something.'

2

Sandra had everything ready. The van, its rear doors open, was backed against the concrete landing and steps that led to the side door McWhitney had kicked in more than a week ago. She'd moved her Honda farther forward along that side wall of the church, facing out, tucked in close enough to the church to block from the road much of the view of what would be going on between doorway and van.

McWhitney approved: 'Good work.'

'You boys do the heavy lifting,' she said. 'I'll sit in my car and watch. If I see something I don't like, I'll honk twice. And then probably drive like hell.'

Parker said, 'If they're that close, you shouldn't run away. You should draw on us and make a citizen's arrest.'

'That's right, Sandra,' McWhitney said. 'You're the upright citizen. You've got licenses and everything.'

'Just what I always wanted,' she said. 'Caught in the cross fire. Start: let's get out of here.'

They started. They had a lot of weight to carry, boxes of money and boxes of hymnals, out of the choir loft, down the stairs and into the van. To their right, Sandra sat in her Honda with the engine on, the radio playing soft rock as she read a *Forbes* magazine.

The money boxes and hymnal boxes were different brands of the same kind of mover's carton, white, rectangular, with deep-sided lids fitting over them, like the boxes seen carrying evidence into federal courtrooms. Since the hymnals had been on top upstairs, for camouflage, most of them had to be moved first and set aside so the money boxes could be loaded into the van. They developed a two-man bucket brigade system, so they wouldn't get in each other's way on the stairs, and within half an hour the van was two-thirds full, with more money boxes still upstairs.

'We'll have to leave those,' Parker said. 'We need space for the other boxes in front and on top, to show at the roadblocks.'

'I hate to leave any of it,' McWhitney said, 'but you're right.'

There were four money boxes still upstairs. They restacked hymnal boxes on top of them, then went down to finish loading the van and, as they did, Parker saw a streak of mud on the floor that hadn't been there before. It was near the closed door to the basement, a place they'd holed up in after the robbery, a one-time community room from which all the appliances had been removed.

They each carried a carton of hymnals out to the van and Parker said, 'You keep working, I got something to do.'

McWhitney was curious, but kept working, as Parker

moved forward to Sandra in the Honda and said, 'I need a flashlight.'

'Sure,' she said, and took one from a small metal box of supplies she kept bolted to the floor in front of the seat, to the right of the accelerator. 'What for?'

'Tell you when I get back.'

The basement, as he remembered it, would be pitch-black, because it had plywood panels that slid across in front of the windows, for when they used to show movies down there. That meant he wouldn't be able to open the door at the head of those stairs without Nick, down below, knowing he was coming down.

Why would Nick come back *here*, of all the places in the world? Maybe he still thought there was some chance he could find an edge for himself. Or maybe he just didn't have any place else to go any more. Maybe his life was a maze, and this was the far end of it, and he didn't have any other choices.

Parker opened the door, slid through, shut the door behind himself. As dark as he remembered. He silently went down two steps, then sat on that step and waited. Nick wouldn't have another gun, but he might have something.

No light down there, no sound. Parker waited, then abruptly there was a sound, and an instant later light; gray daylight. Nick was sliding back one of the plywood panels, baring a window. Maybe he thought that would level the playing field somehow.

Parker put the unnecessary flashlight on the step behind him, stood, and took the marshal's automatic from his pocket.

Nick said, 'Hold it, Parker. You want to see this. Take a look out there. I mean it, take a look.'

'At what?'

Nick backed away from the window, gesturing for Parker to help himself. 'Do yourself a favor,' he said.

Parker went down the rest of the stairs, crossed to the head-high window, and looked out at a state police patrol car, stopped in front of Sandra's Honda, just blocking it. Two uniforms were getting out of the patrol car, shrugging their gunbelts at their waists as they moved toward Sandra, one of them a man, the other a woman, both white.

Looking at the automatic in Parker's hand, Nick said, 'You don't want to make any loud noises. Not now.'

3

Had Sandra honked twice, when she saw the patrol car, as she'd said she would? If so, Parker hadn't heard it down here. Concrete-block walls, room mostly underground, plywood over the windows. But a shot would be something else. Cops would hear a gunshot.

'We don't want them looking in that window,' he said, and slid the plywood closed with his right hand as his left hand reached for Nick.

'Hey!'

Nick had backpedaled, but his shout told Parker which way he was moving. And then his ragged breath gave him the spot, and then Parker had his hands on him.

This had to be fast, and then he had to find that window and slide the plywood open just far enough so he could find his way back to the stairs and collect the flashlight. Bring it back, shut out the daylight again, switch on the flash, shine it quickly around.

There. Across the rear end of the room had been a kitchen. The appliances were long removed, making broad blank insets in the Formica counter that ran all across the back, but the sink was still there, set into the counter, with closed cabinet doors beneath. They opened outward to the left and right, with no vertical post between them.

Parker opened the cabinet doors and saw that the pipes for the sink were under there, but nothing else. Plenty of room.

He dragged Nick across the linoleum floor, bent him into the space under the sink, and shut the doors. Then he went back upstairs and outside, where the male cop was giving McWhitney back his license and registration and the female cop was looking at one of the hymnals from a carton in the van.

'Hello,' Parker said, and they all looked at him. He nodded at Sandra and said, 'There's nothing down there.'

'Good,' she said, and explained to the cops, 'This is Desmond. He's the other volunteer.'

'I'm in recovery,' Parker said.

The male cop said, 'You were in the basement?' Nobody interrogates somebody in recovery.

'We wanted to know if there was anything useful down there,' Parker said. 'But it's been cleaned out.' To Sandra he said, 'The refrigerator's gone, dishwasher, everything.'

The female cop pointed at the flashlight Parker carried. 'No electricity in there?'

'No water, nothing.' He looked over his shoulder at the building. 'Empty forever.'

'Not forever,' she said, and surprisingly smiled. 'I went to this church when I was a little girl.'

Sandra, delighted by the news, said, 'You did? What was it like?'

They all had to discuss that for a while. Parker saw that Sandra had toned herself down, made herself look softer, and that both cops had bought into the idea that she was connected to some sort of religious mission on Long Island, and that he and McWhitney were rehabilitated rough-neck volunteers.

After the reminiscence about the old days at the church wound down, the male cop said, 'Louise, do we have to toss this place? These people have been all through it.'

'Maybe I'll just peek in,' Louise said. 'See what it looks like now.'

'It looks sad,' Sandra told her. 'Been empty a long time.'

Louise frowned, then shook her head at her partner. 'Maybe I don't wanna go in.'

'I think you're right,' he said, and told the others, 'We'll let you people finish up here.'

Louise said, 'I'm glad the hymn books are going to a good home anyway.'

Sandra said, 'Would you want one? You know, as a reminder.'

Louise was delighted. 'Really?'

'Sure, why not?' Sandra grinned at her. 'One hymn book more or less, you know?'

Louise hesitated, but then the male cop said, 'Go ahead, Louise, take it. You can sing to me while I drive.'

Louise laughed, and Sandra handed her a hymnal, saying, 'It couldn't go to a better person.'

McWhitney said, 'Could I ask you two a favor?'

'Sure,' said the male cop. His partner hugged the hymnal to her breast.

'We're driving a little truck,' McWhitney pointed out.

'Just what everybody's looking for. If we're gonna get stopped by all these roadblocks, we're not gonna get back to Long Island until Tuesday. If you could get the word—'

'Oh, don't worry about that,' Louise told him. 'The roadblocks are stopped.'

'They are?'

'That's why we're out here,' Louise said. 'We're searching every empty building in this entire area.'

'Not for the fugitives,' the male cop said. 'For the money.'

'It has to still be somewhere around here,' Louise explained. 'So this is a change of policy. The idea is, if we find the money, we'll find the men.'

'That makes sense,' Sandra said. 'Good luck with it.'

'Thanks.'

The cops moved off, Louise holding her hymnal. They got into their patrol car, waved, and drove off. McWhitney watched them go, then said, 'Good thing they didn't start that new policy yesterday.' Looking at Parker he said, 'We can throw those prayerbooks out of the van now. We get to take the rest of the money after all.'

4

'No, you don't,' Sandra said.

McWhitney glowered at her. 'How come?'

'You're still two guys in a truck,' she told him. 'They don't have to have roadblocks to see you drive by and wonder what you've got in there.'

'Sandra's right,' Parker said. 'And we've got to move. Those two are going into the house across the way.'

They watched as, across the road, the two cops left the patrol car, went up on the porch, tried the door, and stepped inside.

Sandra said, 'What do they find in there?'

Parker said, 'A broken window, and your mat.'

'I can live without the mat.'

McWhitney said, 'What if Parker drives your car? Then we're a man and a woman in a truck.'

'I'll drive my car,' Sandra told him.

Parker said, 'I'll ride with Sandra. We'll follow you, and we've got to go *now*. They're gonna find blood on the broken window. New blood.'

McWhitney was fast when he had to be. He nodded,

slammed the van doors, and headed for the cab of the truck. Parker and Sandra passed him on their way to the Honda, and Parker said, 'Head east.'

'Right.'

Sandra got behind the wheel, Parker in on the other side. She started the engine, but then waited for McWhitney to drive around her and turn right, toward the bridge over the little stream. As she followed, Parker looked back at the white house. The two cops were still inside.

'They'll call in reinforcements,' he said. 'But they won't come from this direction.'

'I wondered why you wanted to go east.'

Up ahead, McWhitney jounced over the bridge, the van wallowing from all the weight it carried. The Honda took the bridge more easily, and Sandra said, 'Did Nelson tell you about the guy who followed him?'

'Guy? No.'

'Oscar Sidd.'

'Never heard of him.'

'Nelson says he's somebody knows about moving money overseas. Nelson talked to him about our money, but he didn't expect Oscar to follow him.'

'Oscar thought he'd cut himself in.'

'That was the idea.'

'And Nels's idea, talking to him in the first place was, cut us out.'

'I noticed that, too.'

'What happened to Oscar?'

'I popped a tire, left him in a ditch.'

'Alive?'

'I don't kill people, Parker,' she said. 'All I shot was his tire. He maybe got a concussion from the windshield, but that's all.'

'So he's out of the picture. Fine.'

Sandra said, 'How long do we go east?'

'You can talk to Nels, can't you?'

'On our cells, sure.'

'Tell him, we'll be coming to a bigger road soon. He should turn right and look for a diner or someplace where we can stop and talk.'

It was a bar, a sprawling old wooden place with mostly pickup trucks out front, a pretty good Saturday afternoon crowd at the bar, and an active bumper pool table in the open area to the bar's left. On the other side were some booths. Pointing to them, McWhitney said, 'Grab a place. I'll buy.'

Parker and Sandra picked a booth, and she said, 'You want to drive the whole way tonight?'

'Away from here, anyway. Let's see what Nels thinks.'

'The thing is,' Sandra said, 'my stuff is still in my room at Mrs Chipmunk's. But if I go there, that leaves you being two men in a truck again.'

McWhitney came back, his big hands enclosing three beer glasses. Putting them on the table, he bent low and said, 'Drink up and we'll get outa here.' Then he sat, next to Parker.

Parker said, 'Something?'

'You see behind the bar,' McWhitney said, 'those posters. It's you and me and Nick again.'

'They've been around all week.'

'They got a new one of you over there,' McWhitney said. 'I hate to tell you this, but it's a lot closer.'

Sandra said, 'How'd they do that? It better not be Mrs Chipmunk. I don't want to walk into a lot of questions about who do I associate with.'

'You'll talk your way out of that,' Parker told her. 'But we've got to decide.' To McWhitney he said, 'Sandra has to go back to the place where she's staying, her stuff is there.'

'So you and me travel together, you mean.' McWhitney shook his head. 'Back to matching the profile.'

'If that new picture's that good,' Parker said, 'I can't chance a traffic stop. Sandra, you've got to drive me some more. Once we're south of the Mass Pike, we're out of the search area, we'll be okay. Drive me down there, then come back up. I'll go on with Nels, and you'll catch up with us at his place later.'

'Another two hours in the car,' she said. 'That's just great.'

5

They were still north of the Mass Pike, in hilly forested country with darkness beginning to spread, when a northbound state police car did a kind of stutter as it passed them, and Parker said, 'He's coming back.'

Sandra looked in her mirror. 'Yep. His Christmas tree went on. I guess I should do the talking.'

'No,' Parker said. 'He doesn't want us, he wants the van. Don't volunteer. If we stop, he'll throw a light on me.'

Sandra eased to the shoulder to let the cop go by, saying, 'I don't like to leave McWhitney alone.'

'With the money, you mean. But that's okay. He won't run out on us, he's too tied to that bar of his.'

'Then what was he gonna do with Oscar?'

Up ahead, McWhitney pulled off the road, the cop sliding in behind him. Parker said, 'He was gonna kill us with Oscar, if he could. Or else just let it play out and see what happens. If it falls that way, he can suddenly say, "Oh, here's a guy can help."'

'You have nice friends,' Sandra said.

'He's not my friend.'

Sandra drove over the hilltop and down the other side, and far ahead of them, downslope, the Mass Pike made a pale band of footlights between the darkening ground and the still-bright southern sky.

'I'm gonna stop there,' Sandra said, and nodded ahead toward an old grange hall converted to an antiques shop. An OPEN flag in red, white, and blue hung from a short pole slanting upward above the entrance. Two cars were parked in the small gravel lot at the side. She drove in, parked closer to the road than to the other cars, and watched the rearview mirror. After five minutes she said, 'It shouldn't take this long.'

'Maybe Nels doesn't look right for the part.'

'I'm going back.'

She U-turned out of the lot and drove back over the hill.

There had been two troopers in the patrol car, both now out. One stood beside McWhitney's open window, holding his license and registration, talking to him. The other had the rear doors of the van open. Two of the hymnal boxes were on the ground behind the van, their tops at a tilt. The trooper was leaning forward into the van, moving boxes, trying to see if there was anything else inside there. McWhitney's face, when they drove by, was bunched like a fist with his effort to stay calm and impassive.

'They didn't like his looks,' Parker said.

'All that trooper has to do,' Sandra said, 'is see there's two kinds of boxes in there.'

Parker looked ahead along the road, but in this direction there were no antiques shops, no buildings at all, just the bright-leaved trees on both sides, reflecting the last of the daylight. 'Just pull off on the shoulder,' he said, 'If it looks like they're calling for backup, we're getting out of here.'

'You know it.'

She angled them onto the shoulder and stopped, lights off and engine running, then watched the scene behind them in her mirror, while Parker adjusted the outside mirror on his side so he could also see what was going on.

There wasn't a lot of traffic at the moment on this two-lane road, and the few cars that did pass in either direction just went on by the stopped van and patrol car with its flashing lights. They were used to seeing troopers stop other drivers.

Finally the troopers decided to give up. The one handed McWhitney his papers, while the other stood and waited at the rear of the van, hands on his hips. Then the two walked back to their patrol car, with the lights still flashing on its roof. They left the two boxes of hymnals on the ground behind the open rear doors of the van.

'They're not neat,' Sandra said.

'They're punishing him for making them not like him,' Parker said, 'and then for not giving them a reason to pull him in.'

The troopers got into their car, its flashing lights went off, and they steered out past the van and away. Once they were out of sight, McWhitney, furious, came thumping out of the van to put the boxes back.

Parker said, 'Drive over there.'

Sandra made the U-turn, and they pulled in to a stop

behind the van. Just as McWhitney finished stowing the boxes and shutting the doors, Parker opened his window and called, 'We'll stop at a motel down by the Pike. This is enough for today.'

'More than enough,' McWhitney said, and stomped away to get behind the wheel.

Sandra didn't wait for him. She pulled out onto the road and ran them south again, saying, 'I'll drop you at the motel, but then I'm done.'

'I know.'

'I'll stay in touch with McWhitney, find out what's happening with the money.'

'You can tell your friend to come back from her vacation now.'

Sandra laughed. 'I already did.'

6

It was a chain motel with an attached restaurant and bar. Before dinner, Parker and McWhitney met for a drink in the bar, where Parker gave him cash to cover his room, since McWhitney had put the whole thing on his credit card. 'It's getting harder to operate without plastic,' McWhitney commented.

'I'm getting new when we're done with this.'

The bar was mostly empty, a dim low-ceilinged place with square black tables and heavy chairs on dark carpet. A young waitress in a short black skirt brought them their drinks, and McWhitney signed the bill. When she left, Parker said, 'I think I may know somebody who could take care of the money.'

'Somebody to take it off our hands?'

'He probably could,' Parker said. 'But he might not want to. We had a disagreement the last time around. But he's a businessman, he might go along with it.'

'Who and what is he?'

'A guy named Frank Meany. He works for a liquor import outfit in Jersey called Cosmopolitan Beverages. They're

155

mobbed up and they do a lot of under-the-counter stuff. Some of it is with Russia.'

'That sounds good. How come you didn't say anything about him before?'

'We didn't have the money before. Until I've got something to trade, I've got nothing to say.'

McWhitney nodded. 'What was the disagreement?'

'They involved themselves in somebody else's argument, somebody thought he had a beef with me.' Parker shrugged. 'I convinced them to get uninvolved.'

McWhitney laughed. 'Stuck their nose in somebody else's business, and you gave it a little bop.'

'Something like that. I'll try calling him tomorrow. If he tells me to go to hell, fine, I can't blame him. If he says, sounds good, let's meet, it could either mean it sounds good and he wants a meet, or he's holding a grudge and wants another crack at me.'

'But you figure this is a better bet than Oscar Sidd.'

'Maybe. Worth a try anyway.'

'And I bet you want me along, if the guy says okay, no hard feelings, let's meet.'

'That's right.' Parker gestured over his shoulder. 'Without the money.'

7

Around eleven Monday morning, Parker took Claire's car, still the rental Toyota, to the gas station not far from her house where he usually made his phone calls, to avoid leaving records on Claire's line. It was a process that required nothing more than patience and a lot of change. It was an exterior pay phone on a stick at the edge of the gas station property, unlikely to be observed or tapped. In this rural setting, there was little to draw anybody's attention.

'Cosmopolitan Beverages, how may I direct your call?'

'Frank Meany.'

'Who shall I say is calling?'

'Parker.'

There was a little pause. 'Is that all?'

'He'll know,' Parker said.

The operator was gone a long time, and when she came back she said, 'Mr Meany's in confer—'

'Tell him we both know all about that.'

'Sir?'

157

'Tell him we talk now, or we don't talk. I won't call back.'

'Sir, I can't—'

'Tell him.'

It was a shorter wait this time, and then the remembered voice of Frank Meany came on the line, a hard, fast, tough-guy voice. 'I thought we were done with one another.'

'You mean the little trouble. That's all over. Everything's fine now.'

'But here you are on the phone.'

'With a business deal.'

There was a little shocked silence, and then: 'A *what*?'

'I need expertise and a particular kind of access,' Parker said, 'and I think you're the guy has it.'

'Which expertise would that be?'

'Frank, do you really like long conversations on the phone?'

'I don't like long conversations with *you*.'

'Up to you.'

Parker waited while Meany tried to work it out. Meany was a hard-nosed businessman in that gray area where the legal part of what he did, importing hard and soft drinks from various parts of the world, spread a protective blanket over the illegal part. He wasn't his own boss, but worked for a man named Joseph Albert whom Parker had talked to on the phone that last time but had never met face-to-face. The conversation with Albert had been about how much of Albert's business he was willing to lose before backing away from his confrontation with Parker. The first asset Parker had been offering to remove was Meany. Happily for everybody, Albert had seen there was no reason to be a romantic; cut your losses, and go.

Would Meany still resent that? Of course. Would he be ruled by his resentment? Parker was betting he was too realistic for that.

Finally Meany said, 'You wanna come *here* again? I'm not sure I want you here.' *Here* being the corporate offices and warehouse of Cosmopolitan, in a bleak industrial area of the Jersey flats just south of where the New Jersey Turnpike Extension, a steel and concrete slab miles long, rose high and blunt over the industrial scree to the Holland Tunnel.

Parker said, 'No, I don't need to go there. Up in the northern part of the state, you know, off the Garden State Parkway, there's a state park. They got a picnic area there, right in front of the park police building. When people have lunch there, they feel very safe.'

'I bet they do,' Meany said. He sounded sour.

'I bet you and me, just you and me, I bet we could both get there today by two o'clock.'

'From here? Sure. What's in it for me?'

'That's what we're gonna talk about.'

Meany considered that, and then said, 'A little picnic lunch with you, in front of the park police.'

'But out of earshot.'

'Yeah, I got that. All right, No First Name. I'll see you at two o'clock.'

'Brown-bag it,' Parker said.

His second call was to McWhitney's cell phone. 'He's on. Two o'clock.'

'I'll be in red.'

159

8

Parker was the first to arrive. Leaving his car in the parking area, carrying a deli-bought Reuben-on-rye sandwich and a bottle of water in a brown paper bag, he chose a picnic bench midway between the facade of the low brick park police building and the narrow access road around to the parking area. He sat with the building to his right, access road to his left, parking area ahead.

It was a bright day, but a little too cool for lunch in the open air, and most of the dozen other picnic tables were empty. Parker put the paper bag on the rough wood table, leaned forward on his elbows, and waited.

The red Dodge Ram pickup was next, nosing in and around the access road to park so the driver was in profile to the picnic area. Then he opened a *Daily News* and sat in the cab, reading the sports pages at the back. Parker would have preferred him to move to a table, as being less conspicuous, but it wasn't a problem.

The next arrival might be. A Daimler town car, black, it had a driver wearing a chauffeur's cap, and it stopped on the access road itself. The driver got out to open the rear door, and Frank Meany stepped out, looking every-where at once. He was not carrying a brown bag.

Meany said a word to the driver, then came on, as the driver got back behind the wheel and put the Daimler just beyond the red pickup. A tall and bulky man with a round head of close-cropped hair, Meany was a thug with a good tailor, dressed today in pearl-gray topcoat over charcoal-gray slacks, dark blue jacket, pale blue shirt and pale blue tie. Still, the real man shone through the wardrobe, with his thick-jawed small-eyed face, and the two heavy rings on each hand, meant not for show but for attack.

Meany approached Parker with a steady heavy tread, stopped on the other side of the picnic table, but did not sit down. 'So here we are,' he said.

'Sit,' Parker suggested.

Meany did so, saying, 'You're not gonna object to the driver?'

'He gets out of the car,' Parker said, 'I'll do something.'

'Deal. Same thing for your friend in the pickup.'

'Same thing. You didn't bring a sandwich.'

'I ate lunch.'

Parker shook his head, irritated. As he took his sand-wich out of the bag and ripped the bag in half to make two paper plates, he said, 'People who ride around in cars like that one there forget how to take care of themselves. If I'm looking at you out of one of those windows over there, and you're not here for lunch, what are you here for?'

'An innocent conversation,' Meany said, and shrugged.

'In New Jersey?' Parker pushed a half sandwich on a half bag to Meany, then took a bite of the remaining half.

Meany lifted a corner of bread, 'Reuben,' he decided. 'Good choice.' Lifting his half of the sandwich, he said, 'While I eat, you talk.'

'A couple weeks ago, up in Massachusetts, there was an armored car robbery. The news said two point two million.'

'I remember that,' Meany said. 'It made a splash.'

Parker liked it that Meany didn't want to rehash their last meeting, because neither did he. He said, 'They caught one of the guys right away, because it turned out they had all the money's serial numbers.'

'Tough,' Meany said. His small eyes watched Parker as intently as if Parker were a tennis match.

'The people who have the money can't spend it,' Parker said.

Meany put what was left of his sandwich down onto the paper bag. 'You're saying you have it.'

'No, I'm saying you have business overseas.'

Meany thought about that, and slowly nodded. 'So the way you're thinking about it, I could take this money and make it meld into the international flow and just be anonymous again.'

'That's right.'

Meany thought about that, looking off toward the Palisades. 'It might be possible,' he said.

'Good.'

'And then we'd share whatever I got out of it.'

'No,' Parker said, 'it wouldn't work like that. You'd buy it from us and we'd go away.'

Watchful, Meany said, 'What price are you thinking about?'

'Ten cents on the dollar. In front.'

'And the take on this robbery was over two mil?'

'There was some slippage. Call it two even.'

'Two hundred grand.' Meany said, and shook his head. 'I couldn't give you all that in front.'

'I can't get it any other way.'

Meany said, 'Yeah, but what are you gonna do if I just say no?'

Parker said, 'You fly to Europe sometimes. You go business class, right?'

'So?'

'Anybody else in the plane?'

Laughing, Meany said, 'I get it. There's gotta be other customers out there. Where's this money now?'

'Long Island.'

'So you got it out of Massachusetts.'

'That's right.'

'And now you're ready to trade. This was north of two mil? How can I be sure?'

'Read the news reports. Look, Meany, I'm saying ten percent on the dollar. You can't get a steeper discount than that. If the final number's a little off, one way or the other, who's gonna complain?'

Meany thought about it. 'And you're gonna want cash.'

'Real, unmarked, and unstolen.'

Meany laughed, 'That's what we usually deal in. I'm gonna have to consult.'

'With Mr Albert.'

Meany didn't like the reminder. 'That's right, you had that phone call with Mr Albert. He didn't like it I let you get that close to him.'

'No choice.'

Meany nodded, 'Well, Mr Albert's a sensible man,' he said, 'He understood I didn't have any other choice either.'

'Good. So he might like this.'

'He might, I might not mention the vendor's you.'

'That's all right with me.'

'I thought it would be,' Meany said. 'So where do I get in touch with you?'

Parker looked at him. 'I like the way you never give up,' he said. 'When should I call you?'

Meany grinned. He was liking the conversation more than he'd thought he would. He said, 'You got any time problems on your hands?'

'No. Where it is it's safe for as long as we want.'

'Too bad. I'd rather you were under the gun.'

'I know that.'

Meany thought it over. 'Call me Thursday,' he decided. 'Three in the afternoon.'

'Good.'

Meany waved a hand over the sandwich remnants. 'We don't have to do lunch,' he said.

Massachusetts

Two and a half weeks after the big armored car robbery, and still neither the robbers nor the money had been found. No one would admit it, but law enforcement was no longer completely committed to the hunt. The track was cold, and so was the case.

On that Monday afternoon, troopers Louise Rawburton and Danny Oleski were nearing the end of an eight-a.m.-to-four-p.m. tour, when they passed St Dympna United Reformed Church. Louise happened to be driving at that moment, Danny every once in a while insisting she take a turn, so she braked when she saw the church and said, 'There it is again.'

Danny looked at it. 'So?'

'I wanna see it,' she said, and pulled off the road to stop beside the church. 'I'm sorry we didn't go in there last time.'

'Well, we were kind of busy last time. And we had to report that broken window across the road.'

'Well, we're not busy now. Come on, Danny.'

So Danny shrugged and they both got out of their

165

cruiser, adjusted their belts, and went up to the broken side door. It was early twilight here at this time of year, still plenty of light, but it would be dark inside the church, so they both carried their flashlights. They pulled the door open and stepped in, their light beams shining across the rows of pews and, near the doorway, three of the hymnal boxes squatted on the floor.

'Looks like,' Danny said, 'they couldn't fit them all.'

'Suppose we should take these? Donate them to somebody.'

'We can take them back to the barracks anyway,' Danny said.

'Good idea.'

Aiming the flashlight this way and that, he said, 'It's a real shame. This building's still in good shape.'

Louise bent to one of the boxes and tugged. 'These things are heavy,' she said.

'Well, yeah, they would be. Books.'

'Maybe we should just take some of them now,' she said. 'Be sure there's anybody wants them.'

'Just take one book,' Danny said. 'They're not going anywhere.'

Louise lifted the top off the box she'd been trying to lift, and they both looked in at the rows of greenbacks. The two flashlight beams trembled slightly, converging on all that money.

'Oh, my God,' Danny whispered.

'Oh, Danny,' Louise wailed, 'Oh, no, Danny, it was *them*.'

'We talked with them,' Danny said. He was wide-eyed with shock. 'We stood out there and we talked with them.'

'That goddamn woman gave me a *hymnbook*.'

Danny's flashlight suddenly spun around, to fix on the basement door. 'Why was he down *there*?' he asked. 'What was he doing down *there*?'

Bitterly, Louise imitated the guy who'd come up out of the basement. 'Oh, there's nothing down there. Appliances all gone, everything gone.'

'Louise,' Danny said, 'what was he *doing* down there?'

She had no answer. He walked over to that door and pulled it open and shone the flashlight down the stairs. Then he uselessly clicked the light switch a few times. Then his nose wrinkled and he said, 'Jesus Christ. What's that smell?'

Detective Gwen Reversa knew there were times she received an assignment only because she was a woman, and was thought therefore to be of a more sympathetic nature than the average male cop. She didn't disagree with the assessment, but it irritated her anyway. She would have preferred gender-blind assignments, but when the woman's touch was wanted, she knew she was always going to be that woman.

In her current case, for instance, she was clearly the only one in the office even considered to take the squeal. It was a wrongful death emerging out of a long-term case of simple slavery. The perps were a middle-aged Chinese couple named Cho, early beneficiaries of the Chinese economic miracle. The Chos designed toys, which were made in their mainland factories and sold worldwide. So successful were they that five years ago they'd bought an estate in rural Massachusetts, less than three hundred miles from either Boston or New York, and now split their time between China and the United States.

Their staff in the Massachusetts house was five Chinese nationals with no English, illegally brought in, mistreated, and paid nothing. The finale came when the Chos' cook died of a burst appendix. The Chos, unwilling to risk exposure by seeking medical assistance, had preferred to believe the cook was malingering and could be cured with a few extra beatings. When they'd tried to bribe a local mortician to keep the death quiet, he instead went to the police.

So now Gwen was here in this stately New England country house filled with bright-colored Oriental decorations, sitting with a woman named Franny from Immigration and a translator named Koh Chi from a nearby community college. The four remaining staff/slaves, frightened out of their wits, were haltingly telling their stories in Mandarin, while Koh Chi translated and a tape recorder stood witness. The Chos themselves were at the moment in state holding cells, and would be questioned when their attorney arrived from Boston tomorrow.

This particular job was slow and tedious, but also heartbreaking, and Gwen wasn't entirely displeased when the cell phone in her shoulder bag vibrated. Seeing it was her office, she murmured to Franny, 'I have to take this,' and went out to the hall to answer.

It was Chief Inspector Davies. 'Are you very tied up there?'

'Pretty much, sir.'

'They found some of the money,' he said.

It had been too long. She said, 'Money, sir?'

'From the armored car.'

'Oh, my gosh! They *found* it?'

'Some of it. Also a body. We're working on ID now.'

'I'll be right there,' she said, and went back to explain to Franny and to make her promise to send a tape after the interviews.

It was the conference room at the state police barracks this time. In addition to Chief Davies at the head of the table, there were a pair of state troopers sitting along one side, a man and a woman, who introduced themselves as Danny Oleski and Louise Rawburton. Both looked very sheepish. It wasn't a usual thing to see a state trooper look sheepish, so Gwen wondered, as she took a chair across from them, what was going on.

Introductions over, Inspector Davies said, 'Let the troopers tell you their story.' He himself was looking grim; 'hanging judge' was the phrase that came to Gwen's mind.

The troopers glanced at each other, and then the woman, Rawburton, said, 'I'll tell it,' and turned to Gwen. 'Out on Putnam Road,' she said, 'there's a church called St Dympna that was shut down some years ago. My family went there when I was a little girl. The week before last, when we were told to forget the roadblocks and concentrate on empty buildings instead, St Dympna was in our area.'

'When we got there,' the male trooper, Oleski, said, 'two men and a woman were unloading boxes of hymnals from the church into an old Econoline van. It had the name Holy Redeemer Choir on the doors.'

'We looked in a couple of the boxes,' Rawburton said, 'and they were hymnals. When I said I used to go to that church the woman even gave me one of them.'

Oleski said, 'The minister's house was across the road. Also empty. Upstairs, we found a back window broken out, looked as though it could have been recent. When we went back to our car to report the broken window, the van was gone.'

Gwen said, 'I think I know where this story is going. You went back to the church. Why was that?'

'We happened to go by it,' Rawburton said, 'and we didn't go inside last time, and I realized I just wanted to see what it looked like.'

Gwen said, 'You didn't go in last time?'

Oleski said, 'The three people were very open. I looked at license and registration, all fine. One of the men was in the basement when we got there, and he came up and said everything was stripped out down there, appliances and all of that.'

'They were happy to have us search,' Rawburton said. 'They *seemed* happy. There just didn't seem to be any point.'

Gwen said to Oleski, 'You looked at his license. Remember the name?'

Oleski twisted his face into agonized thought. 'I've been going nuts,' he said. 'It was Irish or Scottish. Mac Something. I just can't remember.'

'I Googled Holy Redeemer Choir in Long Island, just now,' Rawburton said. 'There is no such thing.'

'When you went in there today,' Gwen said, 'what did you find?'

'Three boxes of hymnals on the floor,' Oleski said. 'But

when we opened them, it was all money. And when I opened the basement door, the smell came up.'

'It was Dalesia,' Davies said. 'We've got a positive ID now.'

'I keep thinking,' Rawburton said, 'we should have done more, but *what* more? We checked the driver's ID, the car registration, looked in boxes.'

'That you opened?' Gwen asked. 'Or that they opened?'

Oleski said, 'One I opened, two they opened, the second one when the woman gave Louise the hymnbook.'

'That's a nice touch, isn't it?' said Davies, the hanging judge.

Gwen said, 'And the two men? Any idea who they were?'

Rawburton, looking and sounding more sheepish than ever, said, 'They're the two from the posters.'

'But that new one, of the guy that was in the basement,' Oleski said, 'we didn't get to see that until after we'd met them. And it was a lot closer than the first one.'

Gwen shook her head and said to Davies, 'Nine days ago. They were here, just the way you said, and so was the money, and nine days ago it all left.'

'There's no trail,' Davies said.

'When I think how many times,' Gwen said, 'they just slid right through.' The idea she never would be calling Bob Modale over in New York to describe the arrest of John B. Allen and Mac Somebody grated on her, but she'd get over it. 'Inspector,' she said, 'I should get back to my Chinese slaves. At least there, I think I can deliver a happy ending.'

FOUR

1

Tuesday afternoon, Parker tried calling the phone number in Corpus Christi that had once belonged to Julius Norte, the ID expert, now dead. Had his business been taken over by somebody else?

No; it was a Chinese restaurant now. And when he looked for Norte's legitimate front business, a print shop called Poco Repro, through information, there was no listing.

So he'd have to start again. The guy who'd given him Norte's name in the first place was an old partner named Ed Mackey, who didn't have a direct number but did have cutouts, where messages could be left. Parker used the name Willis, which Mackey would know, left the gas station phone booth number, and said he could be called there Wednesday morning at eleven.

He was seated in position in the car at that time, when the phone rang, and got to it before it could ring again. 'Yes.'

'Mr Willis.' It was Mackey's voice. 'I guess you're doing fine.'

'I'm all right. How's Brenda?'

'Better than all right. She doesn't want me to take any trips for a while.'

'This isn't about that. Remember Julius Norte?'

'Down in Texas? That was a sad story.'

'Yeah, it was. I wondered if anybody else you know was in that business?'

'Time for a new wardrobe, huh?' Mackey chuckled. 'I wish I could say yes, but I've been making do with the old duds myself.'

'Well, that's okay.'

'No, wait. Let me ask around, there might be somebody. Why don't I do that, ask some people I know, call you tomorrow afternoon if I've got anything?'

'That would be good.'

'If I don't get anything, I won't call.'

'No, I know.'

'Three o'clock all right?'

'I got another phone thing at three tomorrow. Make it two forty-five.'

Again Mackey chuckled, saying, 'All at once, you sound like a lawyer. I hope I have reason to call you tomorrow.'

'Thanks.'

On Thursday afternoon, he was parked beside the phone-on-a-stick a few minutes early. At quarter to three the phone did ring and it was Mackey. 'I got a maybe,' he said.

'Good.'

'It's a friend-of-a-friend kind of thing, so there's no guarantees.'

'I got it.'

'He's outside Baltimore, the story is he's a portrait painter.'

'Okay.'

'You call him, it's because you want a picture of yourself or the missus or the dog or the parakeet.'

'Uh-huh. What name do I use?'

'Oh, with him? Forbes recommended him, Paul Forbes.'

'Okay.'

'Here's his cell.' Mackey gave him a phone number. 'His name, he says his name, is Kazimierz Robbins. Two Bs.'

'Kazimierz Robbins.'

'I don't know him,' Mackey warned. 'I only heard he's been around a few years, people seem to trust him.'

'Maybe I will, too,' Parker said.

'Hell-lo.' It was an old man's voice, speaking with a heavy accent, as though he were talking and clearing his throat at the same time.

'Kazimierz Robbins?'

'That's me.'

'A friend of mine told me you do portraits.'

'From time to time, that's what I do, although I am to some extent retired. Which friend told you about me?'

'Paul Forbes.'

'Ah. You want a special portrait.'

'Very special.'

'Special portraits, you know, are special expensive. Is this a portrait of yourself, or of your wife, or of someone close to you?'

'Me.'

'I would have to look at you, you see.'

'I know that.'

'Are you in Baltimore?'

'No, I'm north of you, but I can get there. You give me an address and a time.'

'You understand, my studio is not in my home.'

'Okay.'

'I use the daylight hours to do my work. Artificial light is no good for realistic painting.'

'Okay.'

'These clumpers and streakers, they don't care what the color is. But I care.'

'That's good.'

'So my consultations are at night, not to interfere with my work. I return to my studio to discuss the client's needs. Could you come here tonight?'

'Tomorrow night.'

'That is also good. Would nine o'clock be all right for you?'

'Yes.'

'Excellent. And when you come here, sir, what is your name?'

'Willis.'

'Willis.' There was a hint of 'v' in the name. 'We will see you then, Mr Willis,' he said, and gave the address.

Five minutes later, Parker called Cosmopolitan Beverages and was put through to Meany, who said, 'Mr Albert said, if I want to deal with a son of a bitch like you, it's okay with him.'

'Good.'

'The price is acceptable, and we'll work out delivery.'

'Good.'

'One step first.'

'What's that?'

'We have to see what we're getting. We need a sample.'

'Fine. It's still ten for one.'

Meany sounded doubtful. 'Meaning?'

'We give you ten K, you give us one K.'

Meany laughed. 'I love how we trust each other,' he said.

'Or,' Parker said, 'you could just give me your cash, and hope for the best.'

'No, we'll do it your way. How do you want to work this?'

'I'm busy the next couple of days,' Parker told him. 'A guy I know will call and set up the switch.'

'I've probably seen this guy.'

'Maybe.'

'In a red pickup?'

Parker waited.

'Okay,' Meany said. 'This guy will call me. What's his name?'

Parker thought. 'Red,' he said.

'Red. I like that. You're easier to deal with,' Meany said, 'when you're not trying to prove a point.'

'Red will call you.'

Hanging up, Parker dialed McWhitney's bar, got him, and said, 'I'm on a pay phone,' and read off the number. Then he hung up.

It was five minutes before the phone here rang. Parker picked up and immediately reeled off Meany's name and phone number, then said, 'Ten grand for one. They need a sample, I'm busy, so you work out the switch. Your name is Red.' When he hung up, McWhitney hadn't said a word.

2

Before the Massachusetts armored car job went sour, Parker had had clean documents under a couple of names, papers that were good enough to pass through any usual level of inspection. In getting out from under that job, he'd burned through all of his useful identification, and made it very tough to move around. He had to deal with that right now, make it possible to operate in the world.

How much of a problem this lack of identification meant was shown by the fact that Claire had to drive him to Maryland Friday afternoon. With no driver's license and no credit cards, he couldn't rent a car, and if he borrowed hers and drove it himself and something went wrong, it would kill her identity as well.

Early in the evening of Friday they checked into a motel north of Baltimore and had an early dinner, and then she drove him to Robbins' address on Front Street in a very small town called Vista, near Gunpowder Falls State Park. They'd driven several uphill miles of winding road, but if there was a vista it was too dark to see.

The town, when they got there, wasn't much: one

crossroads, a church and firehouse, and half a dozen stores, a couple of them out of business. Robbins' building in this commercial row, two stories high and narrow, with large plate-glass windows flanking a glass front door, still bore a wooden sign above the windows reading vista hardware. Inside, through the front windows, the interior was brightly lit, but had not been a hardware store for a long time.

Parker said, 'You want to come in or wait?'

'Easier if I wait.'

She had parked at the curb in front of the place, the only car stopped along here. Getting out to the old uneven slate sidewalk, Parker saw that the interior of the building was now a kind of gallery, a high-ceilinged room with large paintings on both white-painted side walls. In the middle of the room stood a large easel with a good-size canvas on it, in profile to the windows so that the subject couldn't be seen. In front of the canvas, stooped toward it, brush in right hand, was what had to be Robbins, a tall narrow figure dressed in black, head thrust up and forward as he peered at his work. What he most looked like, the thin angular dark figure in the brightly lit room, was a praying mantis.

Parker rapped a knuckle on the glass of the front door. The painter looked this way, tapped his forehead with the handle end of his brush in salute, put the brush down on the tray beneath the canvas, and walked over to unlock and open the door. His walk looked painful, a little crabbed and distorted, but it must have been that way a long time, because he didn't seem to notice.

He pulled the door open, his leathery face welcoming but wary, and said, 'Mr Willis?'

'For now.'

He smiled. 'Ah, very good. Come in.' Then, looking past Parker, he said, 'Your companion does not wish to join us?'

'No, she doesn't want to be a distraction.'

'Very astute. I find all beautiful women a distraction.' Closing the door, he said, 'I think you would prefer to call me Robbins. Kazimierz is not easy for an American to pronounce.' He gestured toward the rear of the long room, where a couple of easy chairs and small tables made a kind of living room; or a living room set.

As they walked down the long room, on an old floor of wide pine planks, Parker said, 'Why didn't you change the first name?'

'Ego,' Robbins said, and motioned for Parker to sit. 'Many are Robbins, or my original name, Rudzik, but from earliest childhood Kazimierz has been me.' Also sitting, he leaned forward onto his knees, peered at Parker, and said, 'Tell me what you can.'

'I no longer have an identity,' Parker said, 'that's safe from the police.'

'Fingerprints?'

'If we're at the point of fingerprints,' Parker said, 'it's already too late. I need papers to keep me from getting that far.'

'And how secure must these be?' He gave a little finger wave and said, 'What I mean is, you want more than a simple forged driver's license.'

'I want to survive a police computer,' Parker said. 'I don't have a passport; I want one.'

'A legitimate passport.'

'Everything legitimate.'

Robbins leaned back. 'Nothing is impossible,' he said. 'But everything is expensive.'

'I know that.'

'We are speaking of approximately two hundred thousand dollars.'

'I thought it might be around there.'

Robbins cocked an eyebrow, watching him. 'This number does not bother you.'

'No. If you do the job, it's worth it.'

'I would need half ahead of time. In cash, of course. All in cash. How soon could you collect it?'

'I brought it with me in the car.'

Robbins gave a surprised laugh. 'You *are* serious!'

'I'm always serious,' Parker told him. 'Now you tell me how you're gonna do it.'

'Of course.' Robbins thought a minute, looking out over his studio. The paintings on the walls, mounted three or four high, were all portraits, some of well-known faces ranging from John Kennedy to Julia Roberts, some of unknown but interesting faces. All were slightly tinged with a kind of darkness, as though some sort of gloom were being hidden within the paint.

Finally, Robbins nodded to himself and said, 'You know I come from the East.'

'Yes.'

'I did this kind of work for the authorities back there,' he said. 'For many years. False identities, false papers. There was much work of that kind to be done in those days.'

'Sure.'

'I imagine there is work of that kind to be done in this country as well,' Robbins said, and spread his hands in fatalistic acceptance. 'But I am a foreigner, and not that much to be trusted. And I am certain there are Americans who can do the same work.'

'Sure.'

'I still retain many contacts with my former associates, and in fact travel east two or three times a year. When a change as complete as you need is called for, my old friends are often of assistance.'

'Good.'

'Yes.' Robbins leaned forward, 'When my part of the world was the proletarian paradise,' he said, 'unfortunately, the infant mortality rate was higher than one would prefer. Many children, born around the same time as yourself, are memorialized by nothing more than a birth certificate and a small grave.'

'I get that.'

'We start with such a birth certificate,' Robbins told him. 'To explain your lack of accent, we add documentation that your family emigrated, I think to Canada, when you would have been no more than thirteen years of age. Do you know people in Canada?'

'No.'

'Unfortunate.' Robbins shook his head at the difficulty. 'What we must do,' he said, 'is bring you to this country very recently, so you will be applying for a Social Security card only now.'

Parker considered that. 'I was the Canadian representative of an American company,' he decided.

'You can do that?'

'Yes. I'll have to phone the guy to tell him about it, that's all.'

'Good. Do you have an attorney you can trust?'

'I can find one.'

'I think,' Robbins said, 'you changed your name many years ago, when you were first in Canada. Because of your schoolmates, you see. But never officially. So now that you are in the US, you will first go to the court to have your name legally changed from whatever is on that birth certificate to whomever you would rather be than Mr Willis.'

'Go through the court,' Parker said.

'If we are going to legitimize you,' Robbins said, 'we must use as many legitimate means as possible. What state do you live in?'

'New Jersey.'

'They process many name changes there,' Robbins assured him. 'It will not be a problem. So with your birth certificate and your court order for the name change, you will apply for and receive your Social Security card. After that, there is no question. You are who you say you are.'

'You make it sound pretty easy,' Parker told him.

'And yet, it is not.' Robbins' smile, when he showed it, was wintery. Reaching for a yellow legal pad and a ball-point pen on the table beside himself, he said, 'Your employer while you lived in Canada?'

'Cosmopolitan Beverages. They're based in Bayonne, New Jersey.'

'And the man there I would talk to? To get some employment documents, you see.'

'Frank Meany.'

186

'You have his e-mail address?'

'No, I have his phone number.'

'Ah, well, that will do.'

Parker gave him the number and, as he wrote it down, Robbins said, 'E-mail has the advantage, you see, that it has no accent. The only three things left for right now are the money, and I must take a photograph of you, and you must tell me your choice of a name.'

'I'll bring the money in,' Parker said, and went outside, where Claire lowered the passenger window so he could lean in and say, 'It's gonna be all right. We're still happy with the name?'

'I am. You want the money from the trunk?'

'Yes.'

Opening the trunk, he brought out the duffel bag he'd brought down with him from upstate New York and carried it into Vista Hardware, where Robbins had moved to stand beside a refectory table along the right wall, beneath portraits of Kofi Annan and Clint Eastwood. In all the pictures, the eyes were as wary as Robbins' own.

He seemed amused by the duffel bag. 'Usually,' he said, 'people who traffic in large quantities of cash carry briefcases.'

'The money's just as good in this.'

'Oh, I'm sure it is.'

Robbins picked up from the floor under the table a cardboard carton that had originally contained a New Zealand white wine. 'It will be just as good in this as well,' he said.

Parker started lifting stacks of currency from the duffel bag. They were both silent as they counted.

3

Driving east across New Jersey on Interstate 80 Monday afternoon, Parker passed a car with the bumper sticker DRIVE IT LIKE YOU STOLE IT, which was exactly what he was doing. On long hauls like last weekend's trip down to Maryland, it would be too risky for him to drive, but for the sixty-mile run across the state from Claire's place to Bayonne there shouldn't be a problem. He held himself at two miles above the speed limit, let most of the other traffic hurry by – including DRIVE IT LIKE YOU STOLE IT – and stayed literally under the radar.

To get to Cosmopolitan Beverages, he had to drop south of the interstates just before the Holland Tunnel, and drive down into what was still called the Port of New York, even though years ago, with the changeover from longshoremen to containers, just about all the port's activity had moved over to the Jersey side of the bay: Newark, Elizabeth, Jersey City, and Bayonne.

Bayonne, being at the southeast edge of northern New Jersey, with Staten Island so close to its southern shore there was a bridge across, was protected from the worst of the Atlantic weather and out of the way of the heaviest of the shipping lanes. This was the home of the legitimate part of Cosmopolitan Beverages, in an area totally industrial, surrounded by piers, warehouses, gasoline storage towers, freight tracks, chain-link fences, and guard shacks. Most of the traffic here was big semi trailers, and most of those were towing the large metal containers that had made this port possible.

In the middle of all this, standing alone on an island of frost-heaved concrete spottily patched with asphalt, stood a broad three-story brick building long ago painted a dull gray. On its roof, in gaudy contrast, a gleaming red-and-gold neon sign proclaimed COSMOPOLITAN in flowing script and, beneath that, BEVERAGES in smaller red block letters.

A chain-link fence stretched across the concrete-and-asphalt area in front of the building, extending back on both sides toward the piers and Upper New York Bay. Gates in both front corners of the fence stood open and unguarded, the one on the left leading to a mostly full parking lot beside the building, the one on the right opening to a smaller space with only two cars in it at the moment, and with a sign on the fence near the gate reading VISITOR PARKING.

Parker turned in there, left the Toyota with the other visiting cars, and followed a concrete walk across the front of the building to the revolving-door entrance. Inside was a broad empty reception area, containing nothing but a wide low black desk on a shiny black floor. Mobbed-up businesses do try to look like normal businesses, but not very hard. It hadn't occurred to anybody there to put visitor seating in the reception area because they really didn't care.

The wall behind the desk was curved and silver, giving a spaceship effect. Mounted on that wall were bottles of the different liquors the company imported, each in its own clear plastic box, with that brand's Christmas gift box next to it.

The man seated at the desk was different from the last time Parker'd been here, a few years ago, but from the same mold; thirties, indolent, uninvolved. The only thing professional about him was his company blazer, maroon with CB in ornate gold letters on the pocket. He was reading a *Maxim* magazine, and he didn't look up when Parker walked over to the desk.

Parker waited, looking down at him, then rapped a knuckle on the shiny black surface of the desk. The guy slowly looked up, as though from sleep. 'Yeah?'

'Frank Meany. Tell him Parker's here.'

'He isn't in today,' the guy said, and looked back at his magazine.

Parker plucked *Maxim* from the guy's hands and tossed it behind him over his shoulder. 'Tell him Parker's here.'

The guy's first instinct was to jump up and start a fight, but his second instinct, more useful, was to be cautious. He didn't know this jerk who'd just come in and flipped his magazine out of his hands, so he didn't know where in the pecking order he was positioned. The deskman knew he himself was only a peon in the grand scheme of things, somebody's nephew holding down a 'job' until his parole was done. So maybe his best move was not to take offense, but to rise above it.

Assuming a bored air, the deskman said, 'You can bring back my magazine while I'm calling.'

'Sure.'

The deskman turned away to his phone console and made a low-voiced call, while Parker watched him. When he hung up, he was sullen, because now he knew Parker was somewhere above him in importance. 'You were gonna get my magazine,' he said.

'I forgot.'

Sorely tried, the deskman got to his feet to retrieve the magazine himself, as a silver door at the far right end of the silver wall opened and another guy in a company blazer came out. This one was older and heavier, with a little more business veneer on him. Holding the doorknob, he said, 'Mr Parker?'

'Right.'

Parker followed him through the silver door into another world. Beyond the reception area, the building was strictly a warehouse, long and broad, concrete-floored, with pallets of liquor cartons stacked almost all the way up to the glaring fluorescents just under the ten-foot ceiling. There was so much clatter of machinery, forklifts, cranes, that normal conversation would have been impossible.

Parker followed his guide through this to Meany's office, off to the right, a roomy space but not showy. The guide held the door for Parker, then closed it after him, as Meany got up from his desk and said, 'I didn't know you were coming. Sit down over there.'

It was a black leather armchair to the right of the desk. Parker went to it and Meany sat again in his own desk chair. Neither offered to shake hands.

191

Meany said, 'What can I do you for today?'

'You liked the sample.'

'It's very nice money,' Meany said, 'Too bad it's radio-active.'

'Do you still want to buy the rest of it?'

'If we can work out delivery,' Meany said. 'I got no more reason to trust you than you got to trust me.'

'You could give us reason to trust each other,' Parker said.

Meany gave him a sharp look. 'Is this something new?'

'Yes. How that money came to me, things went wrong.'

Meany's smile was thin, but honestly amused. 'I got that idea,' he said.

'At the end of it,' Parker told him, 'my ID was just as radioactive as that money.'

'That's too bad,' Meany said, not sounding sympathetic. 'So you're a guy now can't face a routine traffic stop, is that it?'

'I can't do anything,' Parker told him. 'I've got to build a whole new deck.'

'I don't get why you're telling me all this.'

'For years now,' Parker told him, 'I've been working for your office in Canada.'

Meany sat back, ready to enjoy the show. 'Oh, yeah? That was you?'

'A guy named Robbins is gonna call you, ask for some employment records. I know you do this kind of thing, you've got zips, you've got different kinds of people your payroll office doesn't know a thing about.'

'People come into the country, people go back out of the country,' Meany said, and shrugged. 'It's a service we perform. They gotta have a good-looking story.'

'So do I.'

Meany shook his head. 'Parker,' he said, 'why in hell would I do *you* a favor?'

'Ten dollars for one.'

Meany looked offended. 'That's a deal we got.'

'And this is the finder's fee,' Parker said, 'for bringing you the deal.'

Sitting back in his chair, Meany laced his fingers over his chest. 'And if I tell you to go fuck yourself?'

'Tell me,' Parker said, 'you think there's anybody else in this neighborhood does export?'

'You'd walk away from the deal, in other words.'

'There's no such thing as a deal,' Parker told him. 'There never was, anywhere. A deal is what people say is gonna happen. It isn't always what happens.'

'You mean we didn't shake hands on it. We didn't do a paper on it.'

'No, I mean, so far it didn't happen. If it happens, fine. If it doesn't, I'll make a deal with somebody else, and it'll be the same story. It happens, or it doesn't happen.'

'Jesus, Parker,' Meany said, shaking his head. 'I never thought I'd say this, but you're easier to put up with when you have a gun in your hand.'

'A gun is just something that helps make things happen.'

'What I don't get,' Meany said, 'is how this finder's fee that you call it is gonna give us reason to trust each other. That's what you said, right?'

'You're gonna know my new straight name,' Parker pointed out. 'And how I got it. So then we've both been useful to each other, so we have a little more trust for each other. And I know, if sometime you decide you don't like me, you could wreck me.'

'I *don't* like you.'

'We'll try to live with that,' Parker said.

Meany gave an angry shake of the head, then reached for notepad and pen. 'The guy that's gonna call me, he's named Robbins?'

'Kazimierz Robbins.'

Meany looked at the notepad and pen. 'Robbins will do,' he decided.

As Meany wrote, Parker said, 'The other thing is the money switch.'

Meany put down the pen. 'You wouldn't just like to drop it off here.'

'No. Tomorrow, at one p.m., one of your guys in the maroon coats drives onto the ferry at Orient Point out on Long Island that goes over the Sound to New London in Connecticut. He's got our money in boxes or bags or what-ever you want. On the ferry, he gets out of the car and one of us gets into it. If that doesn't happen, he drives off, turns around, takes the next ferry back. At some point, we'll take the car. He stays on the ferry while it goes back and forth, and after a while the car comes back with the money for you in it, and he takes it and goes.'

Meany said, 'And what if the car doesn't come back? You've got our money, but we don't have yours.'

'Then how do you help me get my new ID? See?' Parker spread his hands. 'It's how we build trust,' he said.

4

On the way back to Claire's place, Parker stopped at the usual gas station, phoned McWhitney's bar, and when the man came on said, 'I'm in a phone booth.' When McWhitney called back five minutes later Parker said, 'It's worked out with Meany.'

'The ferry switch? No snags?'

'Nothing to talk about. I'll have Claire drive me to the city tomorrow morning, and then I'll take the train out to your place.'

'Doesn't that get old?'

'Yes. I'm working on that problem, too. I told Meany we'd do the switch around one. You call Sandra.'

'Why do we want to bring her in?'

'Because Meany doesn't know her. If they try something after all, she can be useful.'

'All right. I suppose it makes sense.'

'She can earn her half of Nick. She can come to Orient Point and take the same ferry as us and not know us.'

'I'll see you in the morning,' McWhitney said, and hung up.

*

When he got to Colliver's Pond, the body of water Claire's house was on, he drove past her place and a further mile on around the lake to another seasonal house where he had a stash. More than half of the money in the duffel bag from upstate New York had been spent.

With a green Hefty bag on the seat beside him, he drove back to Claire's house, and as he came down the driveway she stepped out the front door and signaled him not to put the car in the garage. He rolled his window down and she said, 'I've been needing the car, I've got some shopping to do.'

'We won't have this crap much longer,' he said, getting out of the Toyota.

'I know. Don't worry about it.'

He carried the Hefty bag through the house into the garage, then didn't feel like being indoors, so went out around the back to the water. There were two Adirondack chairs there, on the concrete jetty beside the boathouse. He sat there and looked out over the lake and didn't see any other people. Three months ago this whole area had been alive with vacationers, but now only the few year-rounders were left, and they were all in their houses.

The strong breeze that ruffled the lake and blew past him had hints of frost in it. It was past five on an early November day, and the light was fading fast. Once these two problems were taken care of, the money and the new identification, it would be time for them to head somewhere south.

He didn't hear the car coming back, but he heard the garage door lift open, and got up to go inside, help her unpack the groceries, and then go sit in the living room while she went to her office to listen to her messages. They'd eat out tonight; when she came back, they'd decide where.

But when she walked into the living room, there was a troubled look on her face. 'One's for you.'

It was McWhitney. 'Evening, Mr Willis. I hope I'm not interrupting anything. This is Nelson, the bartender from McW, and I'm sorry to have to tell you you left your brief-case here. Your friend Sid found it and turned it over to me. He doesn't want a reward or anything, but he and a few of his pals are waiting around outside to be sure everything's okay. I hope to hear from you soon. I hope there wasn't anything valuable in there.'

5

Parker had had enough. But he knew this was exactly the kind of situation that makes an angry man impatient, an impatient man careless, and a careless man a convict. He was angry, but he would control it.

'I'm sorry,' he said, 'but I got to ask you to drive me to the city.'

She gave him a curious look. 'But that's the place we went to, isn't it? Where I met Sandra.'

'Right.'

'But that's out on Long Island.'

'I'll take a train.'

'You will not,' she said. 'Come on, let's go.'

'One minute,' he said, and went through to the pantry, where he took down from a shelf an unopened box of Bisquick. He turned it over and the bottom had been opened and reclosed. He popped it open and shook out, wrapped in a chamois, a Beretta Bobcat in the seven-shot .22, a twelve-ounce pocket automatic, which he put in his right pants pocket, then returned the chamois to the box and the box to the shelf.

Claire had her coat on, standing by the door between kitchen and garage. Parker chose a loose dark car coat with several roomy pockets, and transferred the Bobcat to one of them. 'Ready.'

As they went out to the car, she said, 'You can tell me what this is along the way.'

'I will.'

He waited till they were away from the house, then said, 'This is about doing something with that money.'

'Overseas. You told me.'

'That's right. On his own, Nels talked to a guy he knew that could maybe do that, but Nels didn't know him as well as he thought.'

'Is this Sid?'

'You mean Nels's message just now. The guy's name is Oscar Sidd. I've never seen him, but he's been described to me. It turned out, when Nels went up to New England to get the money, Oscar Sidd followed him.'

'To see if he could get it all for himself.'

'That's right. Sandra saw what he was up to, and cut him out of the play.'

'But now he's back,' Claire said.

'He has to know the money's somewhere around Nels. So what Nels was saying is, Oscar Sidd's outside the bar with some friends of his, or some muscle he bought. To keep things quiet, he's waiting out there until the other customers leave. Then they'll go in and ask Nels where the money is. They'll have plenty of time to ask.'

Claire nodded, watching the road. Full night was here now, oncoming traffic dimming its lights. 'When will the customers leave?'

199

'On a Monday night in November? No later than nine o'clock.'

She looked at the dashboard clock, 'It's five-thirty.'

'We'll get there.'

'Not if you take a train.'

'Nels will hold them off for a while. It won't be that sudden.'

'That's why I'll drive you there.'

'You don't want to be at that bar, not tonight. Or anywhere near it. Let me off a block away.'

'Fine. I can do that.'

'And don't wait for me, Nels and I were going to make the money transfer tomorrow anyway. So you just let me off and go back.'

'I might stay in the city. Have dinner and go to a late show.'

'Good idea.'

'And if anything comes up, call me on my cell.' She looked at him and away, 'All right?'

'Sure,' he said.

6

At eight thirty-five on this Monday night McW was the only establishment showing lights along this secondary commercial street in Bay Shore. Parker walked down the block toward the place, seeing a half dozen cars parked along both sidewalks, including, across the way and a little beyond McW, a black Chevy Tahoe parked some distance from the two nearest streetlights. There were some people sitting in the Tahoe, impossible to say how many.

The simplest thing for the problem at hand – and for the anger – would be to go over there and put the Bobcat to work, starting with the driver. But it was better to wait, to take it slow.

To begin with, the people in the Tahoe wouldn't be likely to let somebody just come walking across the street toward them with his hand in his pocket. And he didn't know what the situation was right now inside the bar. So he barely looked over at the Tahoe, but instead walked steadily on, both hands in his pockets, then turned in at McW.

Other than McWhitney, there were four men in the bar. On two stools toward the rear were a pair of fortyish guys in baseball caps, unzippered vinyl jackets, baggy jeans with streaks of plaster dust, and paint-streaked work boots; construction men extending the after-work beer a little too long, by the slow-motion way they talked and lifted their glasses and nodded their heads.

Closer along the bar was an older man in a snap-brim hat and light gray topcoat over a dark suit, with a small pepper-and-salt dog curled up asleep under the stool beneath him as he nursed a bronze-colored mixed drink in a short squat glass and slowly read the *New York Sun*; a dog walker with an evening to kill.

And on the other side, at a booth near the front, facing the door, sat a bulky guy in a black raincoat over a tweed sports jacket and blue turtleneck sweater, a tall glass of clear liquid and ice cubes on the table in front of him. This last one looked at Parker when he walked in, and then didn't look at him, or at anything else.

'I'll take a beer, Nels,' Parker called, and angled over to sit at the club-soda-drinker's table, facing him. 'Whadaya say?'

'What?' The guy was offended. 'Who the hell are you?'

'Another friend of Oscar.'

The guy stiffened, but then shook his head. 'I don't know Oscar, and I don't know you.'

Parker took the Bobcat from his pocket and put it on the table, then left it there with his hands resting on the tabletop to both sides, not too close, 'That's who I am,' he said. 'You Oscar's brother?'

The guy stared at the gun, not afraid of it, but as though

waiting to see it move. 'No,' he said, not looking up. 'I got no brothers named Oscar.'

'Well, how important is Oscar to you, then? Important enough to die for?'

Now the guy did meet Parker's eyes, and his own were scornful. 'The only thing you're gonna shoot off in here is your mouth,' he said. 'You don't want a lotta noise to wake the dog.'

Parker picked up the Bobcat and pushed its barrel into the guy's sternum, just below the rib cage. 'In my experience,' he said, 'with a little gun like this, a body like yours makes a pretty good silencer.'

The guy had tried to shrink back when the Bobcat lunged at him, but was held by the wooden back of the booth. His hands shot up and to the sides, afraid to come closer to the gun. He stared at Parker, disbelieving and believing both at once.

McWhitney arrived, with a draft beer he put on the table out of the way of them both as he said, calmly, 'How we doing, gents?'

'Barman,' Parker said, keeping his eyes on the guy's face and the Bobcat in his sternum, 'reach inside my pal there and take out his piece.'

'You cocksucker,' the guy said, 'you got no idea what's gonna hit you.' He glowered at Parker as McWhitney reached inside his coat and drew out a Glock 31 automatic in .357 caliber, a more serious machine than the Bobcat.

'Put it on the table,' Parker said. 'And your towel,' meaning the thin white towel McWhitney carried looped into his apron string.

McWhitney draped the towel on top of the Glock. 'What now?'

'Our friend,' Parker said, 'is gonna move to the last booth, and sit facing the other way. He does anything else, I kill him. And you bring him a real drink.'

'I will.'

Parker brought the Bobcat back and put it in his pocket, his other hand on the towel on the Glock. To the guy he said, 'Up,' and when the guy, enraged but silent, got to his feet, Parker said, 'You got anything on your ankles?'

'No.' The guy lifted his pants legs, showing no ankle holsters. Bitterly, he said, 'I wish I did.'

'No, you don't. Go.'

The guy walked heavily away down the bar, working his shoulder muscles as though in preparation for a fist-fight.

Parker said to McWhitney, 'Time to close the place.'

'Right.'

McWhitney went away behind the bar again and Parker put the Glock and the towel in another of his pockets. He closed a hand around his beer glass but didn't drink, and McWhitney called, 'Listen, guys, time to drink up. I gotta close the joint now.'

The customers were good about it. The two construction guys expressed great surprise at how late it was, and comic worry about how their wives would take it. Livelier and more awake once they were on their feet, each assured the other they would certainly tell the wife it was the other guy's fault.

The newspaper reader simply folded his paper and

stuffed it into a pocket, got to his feet, picked up his dog's leash, and said, 'Night, Nels. Thank you.'

'Any time, Bill. Night, guys.'

Down at the rear, the bulky guy's back was to the room, as he'd been instructed. Quietly the newspaper reader and more loudly the construction men left the place, Parker trailing after. All called good night again through the open door.

The other three all went off to the left, the dog walker more briskly, his dog trotting along beside him, the construction men joking as they went, weaving a little. Parker angled rightward across the street, then down that sidewalk past the Tahoe, hands in his pockets.

When he was a few paces beyond the Tahoe, he heard its doors begin to open. He turned, taking the Glock and the towel from his pocket, and three men were coming out of the Tahoe, both sides in front and the sidewalk right side in back. All were concentrating on what was in front of them, not what was behind them.

The guy from the front passenger seat was tall and skinny, to match the description of Oscar Sidd. He shut his door and took one pace forward toward the front of the car when Parker shot him, holding the Glock straight-armed inside the towel.

Sidd dropped and the other two spun around, astonished. Parker held the Glock in the towel at waist height, pointed away to the right, and called, 'Anybody else?'

The two stared at him, then across the Tahoe roof at each other. The guy on the street side couldn't see Oscar. The other one looked down at the body, looked at his partner, and shook his head.

The driver jumped behind the wheel and the other one into the backseat. The engine roared and the lights flashed on, showing the Tahoe had dealer plates. The driver at first accelerated too hard, so that the wheels spun and smoked, but then he got under control and the Tahoe hurried away from there.

Parker carried the Glock and the towel back into the bar. The bulky guy was still in position in the rear booth. Parker called to him, 'Come here,' and the guy, sullen-faced, came down along the bar to stand in front of him, look at the Glock, and say, 'Yeah?'

'I hope you got your own car here.'

The guy frowned at the front door. 'Where are they?'

'Gone. Except for Oscar. He's dead out there. He was shot with this gun of yours.' Putting it on the bar, Parker said, 'Hold on to it, Nels.'

'Will do.'

Parker looked at the guy. 'Did somebody hear me fire one shot? I don't know. Did somebody call the cops? I don't know. Will Oscar be there when they get here? That's up to you.'

'Jesus Christ,' the guy said, and it was equal parts curse and prayer. He hurried out the door and Parker said to McWhitney, 'Let me use your phone.'

'Sure.'

Parker called Claire's cell phone. 'Are you still on the Island?'

'Yes. Are you finished already?'

'Come back, we'll get dinner around here somewhere together—'

'I'll tell you where,' McWhitney said.

'—and spend the night down here, and then you go home tomorrow and I'll come back to Nels.'

'What happened?' she said.

'I'm not angry any more,' he said.

7

The sign in the window of the door at McW read CLOSED at nine-thirty the next morning, and the green shade was pulled down over the glass, but the door was unlocked. Parker went in and McWhitney was seated at the first booth on the left, drinking a cup of coffee and reading the *Daily News*. He looked up when Parker walked in and said, 'Claire get off?'

Parker sat on a stool with his back against the wood of the bar. 'Yes.'

McWhitney nodded at the wall above the backbar, where a television set on a shelf was switched on with the sound turned off. 'There's news on the news.'

'For us?'

'They found Nick's body.'

Parker shrugged. 'Well, that's all right.'

'You want coffee, by the way?'

'No, Claire and I ate.'

'Well, maybe the Nick thing is all right and maybe it isn't.' McWhitney waggled his palm over the newspaper, to indicate the question.

Parker said, 'Why wouldn't it be all right? We're done up there.'

'The hymnbooks,' McWhitney said. 'I was gonna drop them off at a church around here. Just to get rid of them, but now I don't know. Can they be traced back to the church up there? I don't want anything anywhere around me that hooks to anything in Massachusetts.'

'We'll dump them somewhere else,' Parker said.

McWhitney shook his head, 'I never thought I'd sit around,' he said, 'and try to figure out what to do to get rid of a load of hot hymnbooks.'

'The money's mostly what we have to deal with,' Parker said. 'Make the load lighter. Hefty bags are good for that.'

'Maybe three of them. It's a lot of cash.'

'Where's the truck?'

'In an open parking lot a couple blocks from here. I figured,' McWhitney said, 'a piece of crap like that little truck, if we give it a lotta security, it'll look like something might be inside there.'

'Hymnbooks.'

'Right.' McWhitney yawned and pushed the *News* away from himself, 'I talked on the phone with Sandra this morning,' he said. 'She checked the ferry on the Web. The one we want's at one o'clock. Takes an hour and twenty minutes, we come back on the three.'

'Fine,' Parker said. 'But now I'm thinking about another complication from Nick.'

McWhitney laughed. 'That Nick,' he said. 'He's one complication after another, isn't he? What now?'

'The troopers that stopped by when we were unloading the boxes out of the church,' Parker said.

'Sure. The woman went to that church when she was a little kid.'

'And now they found Nick,' Parker said. 'Do they start to wonder about that truck?'

'Well, shit,' McWhitney said.

'They didn't write anything down,' Parker said. 'They looked at your license but they didn't do anything about it.'

'No, that's right.'

'But they're going to remember those words on the door. Holy Redeemer Choir.'

'And they'll look here, and they'll look there, and they won't *find* any Holy Redeemer Choir.'

'At least, not the same one.'

McWhitney looked bleak. 'And we're gonna take that same truck on a ferry to New England.'

'That place where you had the name painted on,' Parker said, 'is he around here?'

'Yeah, walking distance. In fact, I walked it.'

'Could he paint the name out again?'

Getting up from the booth, McWhitney said, 'Let me call him, I mean, why not?'

'We should have just time before we have to go get the ferry. And if not, we'll get the next ferry.'

Walking around the end of the bar to the phone, McWhitney said, 'When this is over, I'm gonna be nothing but a bartender for a long long time to come.'

8

On the phone the car painter told McWhitney he could do a quick spray job of the body color over the names on the doors in five minutes, so he and Parker walked to the parking lot where McWhitney had left the truck. Along the way, Parker said, 'The only thing we've got to do today is the money switch, get that stuff out of our hands. The hymnbooks is something for later.'

'I don't like it,' McWhitney said, 'but I know you're right.'

'Where's your pickup?'

'Behind my place. If there was room, I'd have put the truck back there, too, but it's too tight.'

'We'll switch the boxes of books to the pickup,' Parker said, 'then take care of the money.'

'Okay, fine.'

Along their walk they came to a deli, where Parker bought a box of ten large Hefty bags. Then they went on to reclaim the van and drive it the four blocks to the body shop and auto paint place, a sprawling low dark-brick building taking up most of this industrial block. The closed garage door in the middle of the otherwise blank wall had a big sign, red letters on white, HONK, so McWhitney honked, and in a minute a smaller door that was part of the garage door opened and a guy in coveralls looked out.

McWhitney called, 'Tell George it's Nelson,' and the guy nodded and went back inside, shutting the door.

They waited another two or three minutes, and then the full garage door lifted and another guy in coveralls came out, this one also wearing a baseball cap, black-framed eyeglasses, and a thick black moustache. He came over to McWhitney at the wheel of the van, grinned at him, grinned at the name on the door, and said, 'Well, it looks like you got religion and then you lost it again.'

'That's about it.'

'It's a quick job, but I need to do it inside, I need the compressor.'

'Sure.'

George leaned closer to McWhitney's window, 'The job may be quick,' he said, with a friendly smile, 'but it isn't cheap.'

McWhitney slid a hundred-dollar bill from his shirt pocket, and extended it, palm down, toward George, saying, 'A quick job like this, it doesn't even have to show up in the cash register.'

'That's very true,' George said, and made the hundred disappear. 'You can both stay in the car,' he said. 'Follow me.' And he turned away, walking back into the building, McWhitney following.

Inside, the building was mostly one broad open space, concrete-floored, full of racket. Auto-body parts were being pounded or painted, other parts were being moved on metal-wheeled dollies over the concrete floor, and at least two portable radios were playing different ideas about music. A couple of dozen men were working in here, all of them in coveralls, most of them either shouting or singing.

There was no way to have a conversation in here, not once you got half a dozen feet in from the door. George directed them with hand gestures. While the first guy shut the door behind them, George guided them on a path through automobiles, automobile parts, and machinery to a large oblong cleared area with a big rectangular metal grid suspended above it. From the grid, large shiny metal ductwork extended up to the ceiling.

George had McWhitney park directly beneath the grid, then went away and the loud whine of an air compressor joined the mix of noise. George came up the left side of the van from behind, carrying a spray gun attached to a black rubber hose, and hunkered down beside McWhitney's door. The whining went to a higher pitch, then lower again, and George walked his spray gun and hose back down the left side and up the right side to do the same to the other door. He stepped back, looked at his work, nodded to himself, and carried the spray gun away again.

When he next came into view, he motioned to them to follow him, and McWhitney steered the van along more lanes through the work to a different garage door that opened onto the side street. They drove out and stopped on the sidewalk, so both Parker and McWhitney could get out and look at the doors.

The words were gone, without a trace. The fresh paint

was darker and shinier than the rest, but nevertheless the same color.

George, standing beside McWhitney to look at his work, said, 'It'll dry pretty fast, and then it'll be the same color as the body.'

'Good.'

'Being out here and not in the shop, it'll get some dust and dirt on it, so it won't be as perfect as it might be. You'll get some little roughness.'

'George,' McWhitney said, 'that really doesn't matter. This is fine.'

'I thought so,' George said. He was still happy. 'Any time we can be of service,' he said, 'just give us a call.'

9

The alley beside McW led to a small bare area behind the building, paved long ago with irregular slabs of slate. The area was confined by the rear of McWhitney's building, the flank of the building next door across the alley, and by two eight-foot-high brick walls on the other two sides. The local building code required two exits from any commercial establishment, and in McW's case the second exit was through the door that led to this area from the bedroom of McWhitney's apartment behind the bar. The space was large enough for McWhitney to park his pickup back there and K-turn himself out again, but not much more.

Now McWhitney backed the van down the narrow alley until he was past his building, with the pickup in the clear area to the left. He and Parker got out of the van, McWhitney backed the pickup closer to the van's rear doors, and they started emptying the van.

The first boxes out were filled with hymnals, heavy but not awkward to move. Then there were the money boxes.

The money inside the boxes was all banded into stacks

of fifty bills, always of the same denomination. The bands, two-inch-wide strips of pale yellow paper, were marked DEER HILL BANK, DEER HILL, MA. The stacks made a tight fit inside the boxes.

It turned out to be easiest to dump a box over, empty the money onto the floor of the van, and then stuff it all into the Hefty bags. The emptied box, with its cover restored, would be stacked with the others in the bed of the pickup.

As they worked, McWhitney said, 'It's a pity about this stuff. Look how beautiful it is.'

'It'll tempt you,' Parker said. 'But it's got a disease.'

'Oh, I know.'

When they were finished, the pickup, sagging a bit, was crammed with boxes, empty and full, and three roundly stuffed Hefty bags squatted in the back of the van. McWhitney looked at his watch. 'My barman'll be here in fifteen minutes,' he said, 'and then we can take off. Come on inside.'

To obey the fire code, the door at the back of his building had to be openable from inside at all times during business hours, but from outside it took a key to get in. McWhitney unlocked the door and they went through his small but neat living quarters to the bar, where McWhitney said, 'You want a beer for the road?'

'Later.'

'I don't trust later, I'll take mine now. You want to call Sandra?'

'Sure. Give me the phone.'

McWhitney slid the phone across the bar to Parker, drew himself a draft, and watched the conversation.

'Keenan.'

'Hello, Sandra.'

'I'm on my way,' she said. 'I think I should be there ahead of everybody so I can see if anybody has extra company.'

'Good idea. We'll be in the same van, but it doesn't have any words on it any more.'

'Oh, you got the news. If that cop didn't have her girlish memories of that church, she wouldn't have any reason to remember us *or* the van.'

'Well, it doesn't matter any more. See you later.'

Parker hung up, and McWhitney said, 'What doesn't matter any more?'

'The cops at the church.'

'I don't intend to drive through their territory for quite a while,' McWhitney said, and opened the drawer in the backbar beneath the cash register. 'This piece we took from the fella last night,' he said. 'I don't feel like I want it in my joint any more, and on the other hand, where we're going, what we're doing, it might not be a bad idea to bring along an extra gun.'

'Sure. Bring it.'

McWhitney tried to stuff it into the inside pocket of his jacket, but it was too large and too heavy. 'I'll carry it in the glove compartment,' he decided. 'Then drop it off the ferry. If things are going well.'

10

From where they were in Bay Shore on the south shore of Long Island, it was about seventy miles to the Orient Point ferry farther east and up on the north shore. Half of that trip was on highway, starting with the Sagtikos Parkway north, and then the Long Island Expressway east, but at Riverhead the Expressway, which had been getting thinner and thinner of traffic, ran out and from there they were on smaller roads on this less populated end of the island, with the ferry terminal still thirty-five miles ahead.

They'd been driving beyond the Expressway for about five minutes, first on Edwards Avenue north almost to Long Island Sound, and then east on Sound Avenue, when McWhitney, looking alert, said, 'Yeah?' He cocked his head, listening, and Parker knew Sandra was calling him on his hands-free phone. Around them now was mostly sand and scruffy wasteland, with a mix of small homes and businesses, some of them already shut for the season.

'Sure,' McWhitney told the space in front of him, and took his foot off the accelerator. The van dropped about

ten miles an hour in speed, and then he tapped the accelerator again, maintaining that new speed, for two or three
minutes.

Parker watched and waited, not wanting to interrupt
if Sandra had anything else to say, and then McWhitney
said, 'Okay, got it. Let me know if they do anything else.'

Parker said, 'Somebody following us?'

'A black Chevy Suburban with dealer plates,' McWhitney
said. 'Whatever speed I like, he likes.' Gradually he was
accelerating back up to his previous speed.

'The car Sidd and the others had last night,' Parker
said, 'was also a Chevy with dealer plates. This is Sidd's
pals.'

McWhitney grinned. 'They got a friend in the car business.'

'They came along after us,' Parker said, 'because they
wanted to know where we were going.'

'Then they've pretty well got it figured out by now,'
McWhitney said. 'Once you get out here past Riverhead,
there's only three things you can do. Take the ferry,
swim, or turn around.'

'The question is,' Parker said, 'do we take them out, or
do we ignore them?'

'It's a public highway in the middle of the day,'
McWhitney said. 'Not a lot of traffic, but there's *some*. It
just makes more trouble to try to deal with them. And
they're not gonna want to try to mess with us either, not
while we're moving out here in the daylight.'

'What about on the ferry?'

'No privacy.' McWhitney shrugged, 'I'll stay with the
van. There's other people gonna stay in their cars, not

go upstairs. They read their paper, do some work, I won't be alone. You go find the blazer and get his keys.'

'A time is gonna come,' Parker said, 'when we'll have to deal with those people.'

'That's the time,' McWhitney said, 'they'll be delivered into our hands. What?'

That last wasn't directed to Parker, but to the voice in his ear, because after listening McWhitney laughed and said, 'That's very nice. You just make it up as you go along.'

Parker said, 'She's gonna move on them?' He didn't like that idea. It would be better if they didn't know about Sandra until and unless she was really needed.

But McWhitney said, 'No. She wanted me to slow down again because she's gonna accelerate out ahead of them to be in front when they board.'

Parker nodded. 'That's good.'

'Then,' McWhitney said, 'we'll see what trouble she can make.' Again he laughed. 'I bet she can make a little,' he said.

11

At the ferry terminal, a large flat open space at the end of the North Fork of Long Island, facing south though the ferry would travel north, the drivers first paid their fares, and then the cars were lined up in rows on a large parking area with lanes painted on it. There they would wait for the southbound ferry to come in and unload its group of cars and foot passengers, before they'd be boarded in the order in which they'd arrived.

The van's position was halfway down the third occupied lane. That lane filled up pretty fast, and then more cars came down on the right beside them, filling in the next lane. Out in the water, the large white-and-blue ferry could be seen slowly maneuvering itself toward the dock.

Into a silence, in the van, McWhitney suddenly said, 'What?' Then, to Parker, he said, 'She says to look over our shoulder.'

Parker tried to look back through the van's rear window, but there was nothing to see except the front of the car tucked in close behind them. So he bent to the side until he could look in his outside mirror, and there, two cars behind them, was Sandra's black Honda with its whip antennas. Behind it he could just see a black Chevy Suburban.

'She's back there and so are they,' he said.

'I hate to be followed,' McWhitney said. 'It makes me antsy.'

'We'll tell them,' Parker said.

It was about fifteen minutes more before the ferry was loaded for the trip to Connecticut. Once everybody was aboard and the ferry was moving out of its slip into Gardiner's Bay, Parker said, 'I'll find the guy now.'

'I'm keeping the doors locked,' McWhitney said. 'No point being *too* carefree.'

Parker got out of the van and McWhitney clicked the door locked behind him. He made his way up the metal stairs to the upper deck, where there were lines at the refreshment stand. Big windows looked out onto the view of sea and sky, and there was bench seating both inside and out.

Parker didn't see the bulky guy from last night, and he didn't see Sandra, but looking through a side window he saw a maroon blazer out there, the guy strolling along the rail. When he stepped out, it was the same guy who'd led him back to Meany's office at Cosmopolitan Beverages last week.

Parker said, 'So here we are.'

'Here we are,' the guy agreed. Out here, he was smiling, relaxed. 'I want to thank you,' he said. 'You got me a day off and a nice jaunt on the ocean.'

'That's fine,' Parker said, and looked around. He still didn't see anybody else he knew.

The guy picked up on his tension. 'Everything okay? Is it all right to give you the keys?'

'Yeah. Do it now.'

The guy pulled keys from his pocket and handed them to Parker, saying, 'About the middle, on the left. It's a Subaru Forester, green. Anything I should know about?'

'No. A couple of people are trying to deal themselves in. We'll take care of it.'

'Frank would like his car back,' the guy said, and grinned again, this grin a little less relaxed. 'And the other, too, of course.'

'It's taken care of,' Parker said. 'I gotta go. If they see me talking to you, they say, who's that?'

The guy's grin this time was self-confident. 'They don't wanna know.'

'Hold the thought,' Parker said, and went back inside.

Now he saw the bulky guy from last night, on line at the refreshment stand. Parker skirted the line without being seen, went on down to the cars, found the Forester, and unlocked his way in. On the backseat were two liquor cartons. He didn't bother to look in them.

From here, the Chevy Suburban was almost parallel to him, two cars over, with Sandra's Honda in front of it, and McWhitney in the van closer to the front of the ship. Parker put the key in the ignition, and waited.

There was a glitch in unloading the ferry in New London. The first cars got off all right, including McWhitney in the van, but then Sandra couldn't seem to start the Honda.

She ground the starter, and people behind her began to honk and shout and get out of their vehicles. Other lines of cars moved, but that one was stuck. When Parker drove off, the bulky guy and one other from the Suburban were pushing the Honda.

McWhitney had waited beside the road. He was laughing when Parker went by, and rolled in to follow him. They drove into town, found a supermarket, and Parker went to the rear of its parking lot. McWhitney stopped next to him, still laughing, and got out of the van to say, 'She got them to help. You believe the balls on that woman?'

'Let's do this fast,' Parker said. 'We've got half an hour before the ferry goes back.'

As they started the transfer of the three Hefty bags and the two liquor cartons, McWhitney said, 'I've been thinking about this. We're still gonna have money in this van. Not the dirty two mil, the clean two hundred K.'

'That's right,' Parker said.

'So they'll still have something to go after,' McWhitney said. 'So what I think, I don't take the ferry back. You do and Sandra does, you give the beverage guy this Subaru and you travel with Sandra, come back together to my place.'

'It'll take you five hours to come around,' Parker said, 'Almost all the way back to the city, and then out onto the Island.'

'But they know this van,' McWhitney said, 'And we rubbed their noses in it pretty good last night, so now they got an extra motivation. You know I'm not gonna skip out on you because I'm not gonna skip out on my bar. You'll be there by five-thirty, I'll be there by eight. And Sandra can keep in touch with me.'

'All right,' Parker said. 'I'll see you there.'

12

It was a shorter wait this time for Parker to board the ferry, driving the Forester up the ramp, following the hand signals of the ferry crew, coming to a stop very near the front of the boat. The three large Hefty bags filled most of the space behind him, one on the rear seat and two squeezed into the cargo area.

Once again he waited for the ferry to move away from the land and make its turn before he got out of the Forester, locked it, and headed for the stairs. He didn't look for Sandra's Honda yet, but would find it when he needed it.

Frank Meany's man was promenading on the same side deck as last time. He looked relaxed enough to retire. Seeing Parker, he smiled and said, 'Everything all right, your end?'

Handing him the car keys, Parker said, 'About all you're going to see in your rearview mirror is Hefty bags.'

'Frank loves Hefty bags,' the guy said. 'Nice to see you again.'

Parker went back inside, and saw Sandra coming up the stairs. He went over to her and said, 'I'm traveling with you.'

'Not yet,' she said. 'I'm here for the ladies'. I'll be right back.'

She went on to the restrooms, and Parker waited near a window in a spot where people coming up the stairs would face the other way. But none of the trio from the Suburban came up, and a few minutes later Sandra returned, waved to Parker, and the two of them went down the stairs to the cars, he saying, 'Nelson didn't like bringing the good money back on the boat with those other guys around, so he's gonna drive.'

'That'll take him forever.'

'He figures to get to his place by eight. We'll wait for him there.'

'Okay, good,' she said, and pointed. 'I'm over this way.'

'I'm not seeing the Suburban,' he said.

'What?' She looked around. 'Oh, for Christ's sake. They've gotta be here.'

'You go that way, I'll go this way, but I don't think so.'

They moved among the cars and met at the Honda. Looking across it at him, she said, 'What are we gonna do?'

'First we get in the car.'

She unlocked them in, and when both doors were shut he said, 'Call Nelson.'

'I can't,' she said. 'With the steel hull on this thing, I get no reception.'

'Go out on a deck.'

'It's still no good.'

Parker looked at her. 'You can't call Nels till we get to Long Island?'

'I hate it as bad as you do,' she said.

He shook his head. 'Over an hour before we can call him.'

'He'll be all right,' she said. 'He's a big boy.'

'Yeah, he is,' Parker said. 'And they're three big boys.'

At Orient Point, once they were off the ferry, Sandra pulled onto the verge of the road, out of the flow of debarking cars, and called McWhitney. Parker watched her face, and saw that McWhitney wasn't picking up.

Then she said, 'I'm getting his voice mail. What the fuck, I might as well leave a message. Nelson, call me.' She broke the connection and said, 'Shit. I needed that money.'

'They're still out there,' Parker said. 'They haven't gone to ground anywhere, not yet. They've got to come back to the Island. If nothing else, they've got to give the car back.' Looking out the windshield, he said, 'If we knew what the dealer was, we could be waiting for them.'

'Oh, well, I can do *that* part,' she said.

'You can?'

She gestured to the notepad she kept mounted on the top of the dashboard. 'Any car I'm following, or I'm interested in, every time, I write down their plate number.'

Parker looked at it. 'And you can get the dealer from that?'

'Sure, Keenan and I always cultivated cash-only friendships at the DMV. Hold on.'

From her bulky purse she drew a slender black book,

opened it, and dialed a number. 'Hi. Is Matt Devereaux there? Thanks.'

She waited. Beside them, the last of the cars from the ferry were trickling by.

'Hello? Hey, Matt, it's Sandra Loscalzo, how you doing? Well, I've got a cute one here, if you could help me. It's a dealer's plate, so I'm not talking about the car this time, I'm talking about the dealer. Sure.' She reeled off the number, then also gave him her cell number, and hung up.

'He'll call back in five minutes,' she said, and put the Honda in gear. 'We might as well start. Wherever the dealer is, he isn't gonna be this far out on the Island.'

Matt did call her back in five minutes, while they were still in the cluster of traffic from that ferry, everybody westbound on Route 25. 'Keenan. Hey, Matt. That's terrific. Say again.'

She nudged Parker and pointed at the pad on the dashboard. He picked up the small magnetized pen she kept there, and she said, 'DiRienzo Chevrolet, Long Island Avenue, Deer Park.' She spelled 'DiRienzo,' then said, 'Thanks, Matt. I'll catch up with you later. Roy? I haven't seen him for a while.' Breaking the connection, she said, 'Well, that's true. Deer Park's just a little beyond Bay Shore. Any point going there now?'

'Every point,' Parker said, 'but not yet. We'll go to that neighborhood, find a diner, get something to eat, get in position before eight.'

'What if they don't bring it back till tomorrow?'

'They don't want it any more,' Parker said, 'and their

229

friend at the dealer's gonna get nervous if it stays out overnight.'

Sandra frowned out at the slow-moving traffic all around them. They wouldn't get clear of this herd from the ferry for another half hour or more, when they reached the beginning of the Expressway. 'You're a strange guy to partner with,' she said.

'So are you.'

'Do me a favor. Don't kill anybody.'

'We'll see,' he said.

13

Half a dozen car dealers were clustered along both sides of the wide road in this neighborhood, all of them proclaiming, either by banner or by neon sign, OPEN TIL 9! All the dealerships were lit up like football stadiums, and in that glare the sheets of glass and chrome they featured all sparkled like treasure chests. This was the heart of car country, servicing the after-work automotive needs of the bedroom communities.

At seven thirty-five, when Sandra drove down the road to see DiRIENZO writ large in neon on their side, she said, 'What do you want to do?'

'Pull in. We'll look at cars.'

There were three separate areas for cars at the DiRienzo lot: new, used, and the customers'. Sandra followed the signs and put the Honda in with the customer cars, then said, 'Now I'm shopping with you. I need this to come to an end.'

He shook his head and got out, and she followed suit, and immediately a short clean young fellow in suit and tie appeared, smiled a greeting, and said, 'You folks looking for a family sedan?'

Sandra's smile was sweeter than his. 'We're just looking around.'

'Go right ahead,' he said, with a sweeping arm gesture that offered them the whole place.

'Thank you.'

'I'm Tim, I work here.' He produced a business card, which he handed to Sandra, who took it. 'Take your time. If I can help you with anything, I'm right here.'

'Thank you.'

They walked away from him, and Sandra said, 'Do we want a new family sedan or a used family sedan?'

'We want to get over near the building. I need to see how they're going to come in, what they'll do.'

The building was broad, one tall story high, the front mostly wide expanses of plate glass, the rest a neutral gray concrete. A few of the most special cars were given their own spaces on the gleaming floor of the inside showroom, with desks and cubicles and closed-off offices behind. On the right side of the building, farther back than the plate glass, the gray concrete wall continued, with three large overhead doors spaced along the way, all of them at the moment shut.

Parker and Sandra saw that, then moved on past the front of the building, Parker saying, 'They'll bring it in there, by the doors. Their own car will be back with the customer parking. We'll see what happens when they make the transfer.'

'We've got at least half an hour to wait,' she said. 'What do we do in the meantime?'

'Look at cars.'

*

It was more like fifty minutes, and twice in that time they could see the fellow who'd first greeted them look over in their direction, frowning. But he never quite made the move to find out what they were up to.

Sandra said, 'Is that it?'

It was. They were walking among the new cars, and the Suburban had to circle around that area to get to the side entrances. They angled to move toward where it would finish up, and as it drove by them Sandra said, 'That's weird.'

Parker had been looking the other way, not wanting the bulky guy from last night to see and recognize him, but now he turned back, watched the Suburban move slowly among the cars and customers, and said, 'What's weird?'

'Only the driver in front, three others in back. What would they do that for?'

Ahead, the Suburban made the turn to go around the corner of the building, putting itself into profile, and Parker could see the middle man of the three in back. 'It's Nelson,' he said.

'My God,' she said, staring, 'it is! Did he go over to them?'

'No.'

'Well, why lug him around?'

The Suburban stopped in front of the middle overhead door as another suited salesman, a little older, smiling broadly and making gestures of greeting, came around toward it from the front entrance. The driver stepped out to the macadam. The three in the backseat stayed in the car.

'I'll tell you why,' Parker said. 'Oscar Sidd told them it

233

was going to be two million dollars of poisoned money. They opened the boxes and they only found two hundred thousand. They think it's the same money, and they want to know where the rest of it is.'

Sandra stared toward McWhitney. 'He's their prisoner in there.'

'And that's why he's alive.'

Across the way, the driver and the salesman had shaken hands, and now the driver was explaining something. The salesman looked toward the Suburban's backseat, then bowed his head and seriously listened. The driver, finished, patted his arm and walked away toward the customer parking area. The salesman stood waiting, hands clasped in front of himself, like an usher at a wedding.

Parker, watching the Suburban, said, 'Go get your car, bring it here.'

'I'm better as a spectator,' she said, 'than a participant.'

'Not this time. Do it.'

She went away and the salesman conferred with a guy in work clothes, who'd come out a side door and who now bent down to start removing the front license plate.

Now a white Buick Terrazza came out of customer parking and angled over to stop beside the Suburban. Parker moved in closer as the two in back, one of them the bulky guy from last night, hustled McWhitney out of the backseat of the Suburban, wanting to move him quickly and smoothly across to the backseat of the Terrazza.

It didn't happen. Because there were so many other people around, and so much bright light was shining down, they couldn't grasp him as they might have liked.

In that instant when all three men were between cars, the two on the outside crowding McWhitney but not quite touching him, he suddenly swept his bent left arm up and back, the elbow smashing into the cheek of the guy on that side, who staggered back into the side of the Suburban and slid sideways to the ground, unmoving.

While the bulky guy on the right was still figuring out a reaction, McWhitney used the same cocked left arm to drive a straight hook into his face, while his right hand lunged inside the guy's jacket.

Parker trotted forward, the Bobcat in his hand inside his pocket. The driver, with his Terrazza between him and the action, drew a pistol and yelled at McWhitney, 'Hold it! Hold it!' He fired the pistol, not to hit anybody but to attract attention, which he did, from everywhere on the lot.

'Not the model!' yelled the salesman. 'Not the model!' Behind him the workman stood, bewildered, the front license plate and a screwdriver in his hands. People everywhere on the lot were craning their necks, trying to see what was going on.

McWhitney was having trouble with the bulky guy. The two of them were struggling over the gun, still half in the guy's jacket pocket.

Parker knew he was too far away with this little gun, but he aimed and fired the Bobcat, then hurried forward again. He almost missed completely, but he saw it sting the bulky guy's left ear, making him first lose his concentration on McWhitney and then lose the gun.

It was the same one Parker had taken from him last

night, which McWhitney had put in the glove compartment of the van. Now McWhitney clubbed the guy with it and, as he fell, stooped and fired one shot through both backseat windows of the Terrazza and into the driver, who dropped backward, his own gun skittering away.

'NOT THE MODEL!'

McWhitney shoved the salesman back into the workman, and both fell down, as he jumped behind the wheel of the Suburban. He had to back around the Terrazza to get away from the building, as Sandra in the Honda stopped beside Parker, who slid aboard. The two men McWhitney had clubbed were both moving; the one he'd shot was not.

With people all around yelling and waving their arms and jumping out of the way, McWhitney slashed through the lot and bumped out to the roadway, forcing a place for himself in among the traffic already there. Demurely, Sandra and the Honda trailed after.

14

Traffic on this commercial road, headed straight south across the Island, was fairly heavy, which meant no one could get much of an edge. Parker could see the black Suburban most of a long block ahead of them, seven or eight cars between, with no way to close the gap. Then the Suburban went through a yellow light, the traffic behind it stopped, and Parker watched the Suburban roll on out of sight.

Was there any pursuit? He twisted around to look out the Honda's rear window just in time to see the Terrazza make the left at the intersection behind them, the lack of glass in its back side window obvious even at this distance. 'They're up,' he said.

Sandra looked in her mirror, but too late. 'Who's up?'

'Somebody in the Buick. One or both of those guys are still in play.'

'But they turned off?'

'They know this part of the Island, and they know where McWhitney's headed. They'll get there first.'

'And we're too far back to let him know.'
'We'll just go to his place and see what happens,'

McW and its entire block were dark, though there were lights on in some of the apartments above the stores. There was no traffic and no pedestrians in this part of Bay Shore at nine o'clock on a Tuesday night. But a black Suburban with a missing front license plate was parked in front of the bar. The white Buick Terrazza was nowhere in sight, but if they'd gotten here before McWhitney they would have tucked it away somewhere.

Parker and Sandra left the Honda and went over to McW. The green shade was pulled down over the glass of the entrance door and the CLOSED sign was in place. Deeper in the bar, the faint nightlights were lit, but that was all.

Parker listened at the door, but heard nothing. They had to be inside there, but somewhere toward the back.

He turned to her. 'You got lockpicking tools?'

'It would take a while,' Sandra said, looking at the door. 'And what if somebody comes along?'

'Not for here, for the back,' Parker nodded at the alley beside the building. 'And we'll need a flashlight.'

'Can do.'

They went back to her car, and from the toolbox next to the accelerator she removed a black felt bag of locksmith's tools, plus a narrow black flashlight.

Parker said, 'You know how to use those?'

'I took a course,' she said. 'It's standard training in my business. Show me the door.'

Parker led the way down the alley and around to the back, where the pickup truck could barely be made out in the thick darkness. Faint illumination from the sky merely made masses of lighter or darker black.

'I'll hold the light,' he said. 'The door's over here.'

He held the flashlight with fingers folded over its glass, switched on the light, then separated his fingers just enough to let them see what they needed to see. Sandra went down to one knee and studied the lock, then grunted in satisfaction, and opened the felt bag on the stone at her feet. Then she looked up. 'What's the other side of this?'

'His bedroom. They're most likely farther to the front, the living room. More comfortable.'

'Not for Nelson,' she said, and went to work with the picks from the felt bag.

It took her nearly four minutes, and at one point she stopped, sat back on her heels, and said, 'I am rusty, I must admit. I took that course a while ago.'

'Can you get it?'

'Oh, sure. I'm just not as fast as I used to be.'

She bent to the lock again, Parker keeping the narrow band of light on her tools, and at last, with a slight click, the door popped a quarter inch toward her. That was the other part of the fire code: exit doors had to open outward.

While she put her tools away, Parker pulled the door a little farther open, pocketed the flashlight, put the Bobcat in his hand, and eased through. Sandra rose, put the felt bag in her pocket, brushed the knees of her slacks, and followed. Now her own pistol was in her hand.

Voices sounded, and then a strained and painful grunt. The bedroom door, opposite them, was partly open, showing one side of the kitchen, the room illuminated only by the lights and clocks on the appliances. The sounds came from beyond that, the living room.

Parker went first, silently crossing the room toward the kitchen doorway. Sandra followed, just behind him and to his right, so that she and her pistol had a clear view in front.

They stepped through into the kitchen. The sounds came from the living room, lit up beyond the next doorway, but only one vacant corner of it visible from here. Parker skirted the table in the middle of the room, and made for that doorway.

'You cocksucker, you make us mad, we *won't* split with you.' It was the bulky guy's voice.

'Yeah.' A second man, probably the other one in the Buick.

More sounds of beating, and then the bulky guy, exasperated, said, 'We're trying to be decent, you son of a bitch. You're *gonna* tell us, and what if we're mad at you then?'

There was no talk for a few seconds, only the other sounds, and then the bulky guy said, 'Now what?'

'He passed out.'

'Get some water from the kitchen, throw it on him.'

Parker gestured for Sandra to stay back, and stood beside the doorway. The Bobcat was too small to hold by the barrel and use the butt as a club, so he simply raised it above his head with the butt extending just a little way below his fingers. When the other one came through the doorway, Parker clubbed straight down at his head, meaning to next step into the doorway and shoot the bulky guy.

But it didn't work. The Bobcat was an inefficient club, and his own fingers cushioned the blow. Instead of dropping down and away, leaving the doorway cleared for Parker, he lurched and fell leftward, toward Parker, who had to push him away with his left hand and club again with his right, this time backhanded, scraping the butt across the bridge of his nose.

The guy crashed to the floor, at last out of the way, but when Parker took a quick look into the living room the moment was gone. McWhitney was slumped in a chair from the kitchen, tied to the chair with what looked like extension cords. The bulky guy was out of sight. Was he in some part of the living room Parker couldn't see, or farther away, in the bar?

The guy on the floor was dazed, but moving. 'Mike!' he called. 'Mike!'

'Who the hell is it?' The question came from the corner of the living room down to the right of the doorway.

The one on his back on the floor skittered away until his head hit the stove, while he called, 'It's the guy killed Oscar!'

'And who else?'

'Some woman.'

Parker moved along the kitchen wall toward the spot where Mike would be just on the other side.

'Mike! He's gonna shoot through the wall!'

Parker looked at him. 'I don't need you alive,' he said.

The guy on the floor lifted his hands, offering a deal. 'We can all share,' he said. 'That's what we were trying to tell your pal there.'

Sandra said, 'Make him come over here.'

Parker nodded. 'You heard her.'

'No,' the guy said.

'You go over there, you live,' Parker told him. 'You stay where you are, you die.'

The guy started to roll over.

'No,' Parker said. 'You can move on your back. You can get there.' Over his shoulder to Sandra, he said, 'This is taking too long.'

She said, 'Don't kill anybody unless you have to.'

'I think I have to,' Parker said.

'Mike!' cried the guy on the floor. 'Mike! What the hell are you doing?'

That was a good question. Parker went to the doorway, flashed a quick look through, then had to duck back again when Mike fired a fast shot at him, very loud in this enclosed space, the bullet smacking into the opposite wall. But in that second what he saw was that Mike had pulled the extension cords off McWhitney, and had the groggy McWhitney sagging on his feet with Mike's left arm around him to hold him as a shield.

Parker looked again and Mike was dragging McWhitney backward toward the door to the bar. He didn't waste a shot in Parker's direction this time, but called, 'You come through this door, you're dead,' then backed through the doorway, shoved McWhitney onto the floor on this side of it, and slammed the door shut.

Parker turned on the one on the floor. 'The money?'

Now that Mike had quit him, the guy was trying to figure out how to change sides, 'In the bar,' he said. 'He carried the boxes in before we jumped him.'

Parker turned to Sandra. 'You let this thing move,' he told her, 'I'll kill *you.*'

242

'I'll kneecap him twice,' Sandra offered.

But Parker was already on his way, back through the bedroom and out the door to the darkness. He found his way down the alley to the street, turned toward the bar, and its door was propped open, Mike just carrying the first carton of money out, in both arms.

Parker stepped forward and pushed the barrel of the Bobcat into Mike's breadbasket. He fired once, and there was very little noise. 'It works,' he said, and Mike, eyes and mouth open, darkness closing in, fell down, and back into the bar. Parker kicked his legs out of the way, pulled the liquor carton full of money back inside, and shut and relocked the door.

Going through the bar to the apartment, he stopped in the living room to pick up the extension cords Mike had used to truss McWhitney and brought them to the bedroom, where nothing had changed. Tossing the extension cords onto the floor next to the guy, Parker said to Sandra, 'Tie him up. Let's get this over with.'

Sandra put her pistol away. 'On your stomach. Hands behind your back.' As he did so, and she went to one knee beside him, she said to Parker, 'What about the other one?'

'He wasn't so lucky.'

'Jeeziz,' said the guy on the floor.

'Stay lucky,' Sandra advised him. When she was satisfied he wasn't going anywhere, she stood and said, 'What now?'

'Let's see what Nels looks like.'

He didn't look good, but he looked alive, and even groggily awake. The two guys working him over had been eager but not professional, which meant they could bruise

him and make him hurt, but couldn't do more permanent damage unless they accidentally killed him. For
instance, he still had all his fingernails.

Parker lifted him to his feet, saying, 'Can you walk?'

'Uuhh. Where . . .'

With Parker's help, McWhitney walked slowly toward
the bedroom, as Parker told him, 'One of them's dead in
the bar, the other one's alive right there. Tomorrow, you
can deal with them both. Right now, you lie down. Sandra
and me'll split the money and get out of here.'

He helped McWhitney to lie back on the bed, then said
to Sandra, 'If we do this right, you can get me to Claire's
place by two in the morning.'

'What a good person I am,' she said.

'If you leave me here,' the guy on the floor said, 'he'll
kill me tomorrow morning.'

Parker looked at him. 'So you've still got tonight,' he
said.